A Practical Approach to Evidence

Peter Murphy MA LLB

First published in Great Britain 1980 by Financial Training Publications Limited
Avenue House, 131 Holland Park Avenue, London W11 4UT

© Financial Training Publications Limited, 1980
Reprinted 1982
Reprinted 1984

ISBN: 0 906322 05 7

Printed in Great Britain by Livesey Limited, Shrewsbury

Contents

A: Fundamentals of evidence 1.1 What evidence is 1.2 The varieties of evidence 1.3 Facts which may be proved 1.4 Admissibility and weight 1.5 Tribunals of law and fact: judicial discretion 1.6 Evidence illegally or unfairly obtained 1.7 The best-evidence rule B: Proof without evidence 1.8 When evidence may not be required 1.9 Formal admissions 1.10 Judicial notice 1.11 Presumptions

A: Brief for the prosecution Instructions to Counsel Indictment Depositions Previous convictions of defendants and witness Notice of alibi B: Brief for the defence Instructions to Counsel on behalf of the defendant Coke Proof of evidence of Coke Instructions to Counsel on behalf of the defendant Littleton Proof of evidence of Littleton Proof of evidence of Mrs Littleton

A: The burden of proof 3.1 Introduction 3.2 The legal or persuasive burden 3.3 The evidential burden 3.4 Where the legal burden lies 3.5 Where the evidential burden lies B: The standard of proof 3.6 Introduction 3.7 Criminal cases 3.8 Civil cases 3.9 Matrimonial causes 3.10 Questions for counsel

Table of Cases

Table of Statutes

Table of rules of court

Preface

The law of evidence underlies the whole practice of law in every field capable of leading to litigation. Not only a thorough understanding of the rules of admissibility, but also a mature feel for the weight and tactical significance of evidence should be a part of the foundation of every practice. Cases are probably won and lost more often for reasons of evidential acumen, or the lack of it, than for reasons of any other sort. At the same time, evidential problems have a habit of arising, to quote a celebrated rule to be found in Chapter 14 of this book, *'ex improviso,* which no human ingenuity could foresee'. Law and practice can almost always be made the subject of prior research; as often as not, evidence presents problems without warning calling for immediate reaction. Failure to object at the right time, or the making of an unfounded objection may in some cases have serious consequences for the fate of the piece of evidence concerned, or the case as a whole. One's opponent's objections, whether well or ill founded must be dealt with. A colleague at the Bar once said to the author that there was, in his opinion, only one rule of evidence, namely a reaction of instinct on hearing any words spoken in court, which said either, 'Yes, that's all right,' or 'No, we can't have that.' That sort of instinct exists and very often works even before the witness speaks at all; it takes time to develop; time, and a thorough knowledge of the rules; but it is of incalculable importance.

Given all this, it is somewhat surprising to survey the textbooks on the subject and to find that they are prone to two distinct tendencies. There are those which treat the subject in a highly academic way, divorced from the realities of practice. There are those which treat the subject as a mass of apparently unrelated minutiae, divorced from any discernible theme. There is also, happily, the matchless but demanding work of Professor Cross, comparisons of which are vain. The present work is intended simply to meet the long-felt need of students from the Bar examinations, now joined by students for the Law Society's examinations, and those on degree courses, for a book soundly based around the considerations of practice in the courts. It is hoped that those concerned professionally with the law of evidence may also find it useful. There are, no doubt, many matters of great interest in academic terms which will not be found here; but equally, the important, recurring issues are dealt with in the context of their practical operation, and of the rules of practice which apply to them.

The book is constructed around the facts of a fictitious, but not unrealistic case. All the characters and events in it are fictitious, and any resemblance to persons living or dead entirely coincidental. But the issues which it raises will be familiar to every criminal practitioner. The papers in the case occupy the whole of Chapter 2. It should not be thought that civil evidence is neglected. It is impossible, without an unacceptable sacrifice of realism, to incorporate into one case every important rule of evidence. But in every chapter subsequent to Chapter 2, the reader will find references back to the case of *The Queen* v *Coke and Littleton,* and the reader should familiarise himself with the papers at the outset and return to them time and time again to gain some insight into the practical implications of the rules dealt with in the text. At the end of each chapter, there are questions which counsel acting might have to solve, and these also should be considered. One of the peculiar problems of evidence is that evidential questions rarely come in ones. Cases like *R* v *Christie* [1914] AC 545 sometimes seem to be authority for almost everything that matters. It will be found that throughout the book, reference to rules outside the scope of the chapter under consideration will be made, simply because rules of evidence can rarely be dealt with in isolation from each other. The reader might do very much worse than to read the book from cover to cover, quite quickly and superficially, before beginning serious study.

An attempt has been made to state the laws as at 30 June 1980. Evidence is a subject prone to fashion, and at present, after the recent popularity of evidence illegially and unfairly obtained, public policy and confidentiality are in vogue. At the time of writing, the House of Lords has not yet given its reasons for its decision in *British Steel Corporation* v *Granada Television Ltd* (see 11.5) and whether some new twist will emerge remains to be seen.

My thanks are due to my publishers, who have displayed a quite remarkable cheerfulness and tolerance, to Mr Derek French for preparing the indexes of cases and statutes; without their professional skills, this book would never have seen the light of day. It is also a pleasure to thank Miss Diana Bailey MSc and Mr Brian Parkin MSc, MPhil, MI Biol (the former an old forensic friend and adversary) for their help with the forensic evidence in Coke and Littleton; my colleagues and students at the Inns of Court School of Law for their inspiration over the last two years; and above all my wife, Hilary Pearson MA (Oxon), LLB (Lond), Barrister-at-Law, who brought to bear upon the project of writing this book not only her greater experience in the teaching of evidence, but also the considerable volume of love and understanding necessary to sustain me through its darkest hours.

Islington
1 July 1980

Preface to Reprinted First Edition

No branch of the law remains static for long. In the short period since first publication, a number of developments have occurred which are noted here so as to bring *A Practical Approach to Evidence* up to date as at 1 August 1982.

In the statutory field, all references to the Magistrates' Courts Act 1952, should be read so as to substitute the corresponding reference to the Magistrates' Courts Act 1980. This Act, which came into force on 6 July 1981, supersedes the 1952 Act and re-enacts its provisions though with few differences of evidential significance. The 1980 Act also re-enacts important sections of the Criminal Justice Act 1967.

The Magistrates' Courts Rules 1981, which came into operation on 6 July 1981, have superseded the Magistrates' Courts Rules 1968, and the various subsequent amendments thereto.

On the subject of privilege (Chapter 11), The Supreme Court Act 1981, s.72, abrogates the privilege against self-incrimination in certain intellectual property cases. The observation in 11.8, note 105, concerning privilege and patent agents should be read in the light of the Patent Act 1977, ss.103, 104, which were inadvertently omitted from the original first edition. An important concession to confidentiality of sources of information contained in publications has been made by the Contempt of Court Act 1981, s.10.

The reader also should refer to the following cases decided since first publication, which are noted with reference to the chapters to which they are relevant:

Chapter 1
R v *Trump* (1979) 70 Cr App R 300 (evidence illegally or unfairly obtained).
Morris v *Beardmore* (1980) 71 Cr App R 265 (evidence illegally or unfairly obtained).

Chapter 4
R v *McGee* (1980) 70 Cr App R 247 (Criminal Evidence Act 1898, s.1(f)(ii)).
R v *Redgrave* (defendant's good character: *R* v *Rowton*).
R v *Varley* [1982] 2 All ER 519 (Criminal Evidence Act 1898, s.1(f)(iii)).
R v *Stubbs* [1982] 1 All ER 424 (cross-examination relevant to credit).

Chapter 5
R v *Barrington* [1981] 1 WLR 419 (similar fact evidence: criminal cases).
Maile v *Lenton, The Times,* 9 February 1982 (similar fact evidence: civil cases).

Chapter 6
R v *Nembhard* [1982] 1 All ER 183 (dying declarations).
R v *Kelsey* (1981) 74 Cr App R 213 (hearsay: identification).

Chapter 7
R v *Evans* (1981) Crim LR 699 (admissions by agents).
R v *McCarthy* (1980) 70 Cr App R 270 (voire dire).
Greaves v *D and P* (1980) 71 Cr App R 232 (Judges' Rules, Rule II).
R v *Hudson* (1981) 72 Cr App R 163 (confessions: oppression).
Prasad v *R* (1981) 72 Cr App R 218 (confessions).
R v *Duncan* (1981) 73 Cr App R 359 (exculpatory statements).
R v *Brophy* [1981] 3 WLR 103 (voire dire).
R v *Rennie* [1982] 1 All ER 385 (confessions).

Chapter 8
R v *Cook* (1980) 71 Cr App R 205 (Criminal Evidence Act 1965).
R v *Patel* [1981] 3 All ER 94 (Criminal Evidence Act 1965).

Chapter 9
Moses v *Winder* (1980) Crim LR 232 (automatism: expert evidence).

Chapter 10
Hunter v *Chief Constable of West Midlands* [1981] 3 WLR 906 (issue estoppel).

Chapter 11
British Steel Corporation v *Granada Television Ltd.* [1980] 3 WLR 774 (confidentiality).
Khan v *Khan* [1982] 2 All ER 60 (self-incrimination).

Chapter 12
R v *Exton, The Times*, 7 July 1981 (unsworn statements from dock).
R v *Khan* (1981) Crim LR 330 (competence: children of tender years).
R v *Yacoob* (1981) 72 Cr App R 313 (competence and compellability: burden of proof).
R v *Governor, Pentonville Prison, ex parte Schneider and another* (1981) 73 Cr App R 200 (competence for prosecution).

Chapter 13
R v *Weeder* (1980) 71 Cr App R 228 (treatment of evidence of identification).
R v *Fenlon* (1980) 71 Cr App R 307 (refreshing memory).
R v *Kelsey* (1981) 74 Cr App R 213 (refreshing memory: verification of document).
McShane v *Northumbria County Council* (1981) 72 Cr App R 208 (treatment of evidence of identification).
R v *Horsham JJ ex parte Bukhari* (1981) 74 Cr App R 291 (evidence of identification)

Chapter 14
R v *Fenlon* (1980) 71 Cr App R 307 (cross-examination: Sexual Offences Amendment Act 1976, s.2).

Chapter 15
R v *Jenkins* (1981) 72 Cr App R 354 (corroboration of accomplice).
R v *Chauhan* (1981) 73 Cr App R 232 (distress as corroboration).
R v *Lucas* [1981] QB 720 (lies as corroboration).
R v *Beck* [1982] 1 All ER 807 (corroboration of accomplice).

Chapter 16
R v *Marlborough Street Magistrate, ex parte Simpson and others* (1981) 73 Cr App R
291 (Bankers' Books Evidence Act 1879).
R v *Grossman* (1981) 73 Cr App R 302 (Bankers' Books Evidence Act 1879).

San Francisco
1 August 1982
                                                        Peter Murphy

Part 1 Proving the Case

1 Evidence: The Science of Proof

A: FUNDAMENTALS OF EVIDENCE

1.1 What evidence is

The story is told of an irascible county court judge who was constantly interrupting a litigant in person as the latter tried, evidently commanding an insufficient degree of credibility, to give his evidence in the case in which he was concerned. At length, the exasperated litigant exclaimed: 'Your Honour, I'm telling the truth!' only to receive the reply: 'That may very well be so, but I don't believe you.' Whether or not this story is, as it well may be, apocryphal, it neatly illustrates the selfsame truth as does the following exchange between Bench and Bar, witnessed by the present author: counsel having objected to the tendering by his opponent of a piece of documentary evidence, which appeared to be relevant to the case but inadmissible in law, the judge asked: 'Am I not to hear the truth?', an enquiry which sounds reasonable enough, but which attracted the somewhat startling answer: 'No, Your Lordship is to hear the evidence.'

The moral of these stories is that in any form of litigation, whatever the actual truth or merits of the case (if indeed, these can ever be ascertained) they are worthless unless they can be demonstrated in such a way that the court or tribunal seized of the litigation is prepared to accept and act on them. In any litigation, criminal or civil, one party or the other sets out to demonstrate to the court that his assertions are true (or, at least, probably true) and that accordingly he is entitled to succeed. The plaintiff in a civil case, the prosecutor in a criminal case, each sets out to prove the essential elements of the claim or charge, as ascertained from the relevant rules of the substantive law and reflected in the pleadings or indictment. It must be demonstrated to the court that those rules of substantive law, so reflected, apply to the facts of the case which has been brought, and consequently the plaintiff or prosecutor must find some way of first establishing to the court's satisfaction what the facts actually are (1). If the defendant disputes those facts, or even if he is not prepared to concede them to be as the plaintiff or prosecutor asserts them to be, then the latter must demonstrate them to the court as being either true or sufficiently probable for the court to act on them, in the sense of marrying them up with the elements of the claim or charge, so that the court can find that the plaintiff or prosecutor has made out his case and is entitled to succeed.

This basic analysis of the process of litigation expresses the need for, and offers some definition of, 'evidence'. Evidence may be defined as any material which tends to

---

1 What facts a particular party must prove, and the standard to which he must prove them in any given case, are in themselves often difficult questions and are considered under the head of Burden and Standard of Proof in Chapter 3, post.

persuade the court of the truth or probability of some fact asserted before it. The word 'tends' in this definition is used to emphasise the unhappy truth, brought home so cogently to the litigant in the county court described above, that evidence will persuade a court of the truth or probability of the facts asserted only if it is regarded as truthful, reliable and sufficiently cogent. The definition is necessarily silent about the quality of the material offered. Any material that, if accepted as truthful, reliable and sufficiently cogent, would be capable of persuading the court as desired, may properly be described as evidence.

The innocent, or naive, might reasonably assume from this that once it is shown that material is available which, if accepted in this way, would be capable of having the desired persuasive effect, and which may therefore be described as evidence, it is only necessary to consider the mechanics by which such material may be placed before the court. Indeed, an important part of the law of evidence does concern the ways in which the material is to be presented, and Part 4 of this book is concerned with that very topic. But the critical areas of the law of evidence concern the large number of different rules which exclude from consideration by a court, or which limit the power of a court to consider, material of certain kinds, even though that material undoubtedly satisfies our definition of evidence. In other words, evidence is subject to various exclusionary rules, often resembling in their operation some forensic game of chess, by which it is ordained that litigants shall prove the facts necessary to their case. It must be emphasised that the exclusionary rules are by no means necessarily based upon the persuasive value which the material might enjoy if placed before the court. Much evidence is excluded which is clearly capable of impressing as truthful, reliable and cogent, although with the exception of material which is excluded on the simple ground of some overriding policy of the law, some reason, however historical and however tenuous, can usually be found to provide some measure of justification for the rule.

Given that it must be desirable for a court to decide a case on the basis of the fullest information available, it is at first sight strange that English law has what has been termed an 'exclusionary' attitude towards evidence, that is to say that the law requires a party who seeks to tender evidence to be prepared to show, if called upon to do so, that the evidence does not offend against any of the exclusionary rules. It might be thought that a more satisfactory approach would be a generally inclusionary rule that evidence should be put before the court unless some real and obvious injustice or prejudice might be caused to an opponent out of all proportion to the probative value of the evidence in question. Nothing in such a rule would imply any element of quality in the evidence so admitted, but would leave the court free to make the most informed judgment possible on the evidence as a whole given in the case. There is some sign in recent legislative measures concerned with the law of evidence that the possibilities of the inclusionary approach are beginning to be realised. In particular, the Civil Evidence Acts 1968 and 1972 have sought, in civil proceedings, to draw the emphasis of the rules of law away from the possibilities of exclusion, and towards the idea of a norm of inclusion, combined with a vigilant scrutiny of the true value of evidence and its potential, if any, for prejudice. But the greater part of the law of evidence has not yet been viewed in this light.

Historically, it is possible to identify a number of major factors in the development of the law (dating from the late eighteenth century, which saw the beginning of the modern rules) which have influenced the present state of the rules of evidence. It is important to notice these factors now, because, as Maitland said of the forms of action, though dead, they rule us from their graves, and they crop up time and time again in the examination of the rules of admissibility which occupy Parts 2 and 3, and to some extent Part 4, of this book. Without some understanding of the background, certains parts of the law of evidence are virtually incomprehensible.

The prevalence of trial by jury. The common law was closely bound up with the peculiar exigencies of jury trial, and because any evidence admitted had to be considered by a body of laymen, the law took a protectionist stand against permitting anything which might influence a jury to give effect to an unsound approach to the case, or which might impose on them the need for unreasonable analytical skills. Thus, it was feared that to require juries to weigh up the value of hearsay evidence, or evidence of character, would be to impose too great a burden, and a burden which, if not faithfully borne, might result in an irretrievable prejudice to a party against whom such evidence was tendered. There is, of course, a risk that a jury may, despite careful direction, act upon the wrong principles and it is no doubt necessary to regulate to some extent the material placed before juries. But whether the rules which have developed to keep certain types of evidence from them really operate to prevent them acting misguidedly is open to question. It will become apparent, from the rules discussed in Part 2 of this book, that juries are habitually called upon to perform considerable feats of analysis, not to say of mental gymnastics. Nonetheless, no major rule of evidence has developed without unmistakable signs of tailoring to the supposed needs of juries, and without doubt it is the comparative rarity of jury trial in civil cases, in modern practice, which has prompted the willingness to experiment with the inclusionary approach in such cases. The Civil Evidence Acts 1968 and 1972 have effectively reversed some two centuries of painstaking jurisprudence concerning the circumstances in which hearsay evidence may be adduced, and this has been almost entirely because it has been felt so much safer to trust the trained mind of the judge sitting alone with the task of weighing and sifting such evidence, than it ever was to entrust the same task to a jury. The conduct of criminal cases is still regulated, with comparatively minor statutory modifications, by that same painstaking jurisprudence of the common law.

The dread of manufactured evidence. The common law lived in constant fear of perjury, fabrication and attempts to abuse or pervert the course of justice. The fear had far-reaching consequences, not only in the rejection of specific kinds of evidence which were thought to be particularly prone to abuse (hearsay, again, was a principal offender) but also in the wholesale rejection as witnesses of interested parties or their spouses, in any circumstances. The rule that the parties and their spouses were incompetent to give evidence began to be relaxed in civil cases as late as 1851, and it was not until the Criminal Evidence Act 1898 that the accused in a criminal case became competent to give evidence in his own defence. As a result, provision had often to be made for the proof of facts without recourse to the evidence of those most easily able to deal with them. The rule was also responsible for many quirks of what is now the law of privilege, not to mention the curious procedure of making an unsworn statement from the dock. And the modern law of competence and compellability has yet to recover from some of the complications deriving from its history. One subsidiary factor, closely bound up with the fear of fabrication, which has also left its mark, is the oath. The solemnity and sanctity of sworn evidence, and the rule that at common law, evidence might not be given except on oath, has invested the law of competence (including the process of being sworn, which has been updated at last by the Oaths Act 1978) with a number of curious features, in particular with respect to the evidence of children of tender years.

The harshness of the criminal law in the late eighteenth and nineteenth centuries. Most of the major common-law rules of evidence owe much of their force to judicial attempts, during the formative years of the modern law of evidence, to mitigate some of the harshness of criminal law and procedure towards the accused. Faced with a system in which death was the sentence prescribed for many (at some periods all) felonies, but which denied to the accused the right of representation by counsel in such cases until 1836 (2), and the right to give evidence in his defence until 1898, the judges took seriously their role as the defendant's guardian, and developed many exclusionary rules with a view to redressing the balance. The general exclusion of character evidence, the stringent conditions of admissibility of confessions, the preservation of the defendant's right to remain silent without risk of an adverse inference being drawn against him, the right in every case to make an unsworn statement from the dock, the very burden and standard of proof in criminal cases, all owe much to that period of legal development and have, to a very large extent, retained the characteristics which they then took on; indeed, such characteristics have in most cases remained virtually unchanged, despite the radical changes in criminal process which have since taken place.

'Evidence' must, therefore, be seen not only in the context of the mechanics by which it is to be presented, but first and foremost, in the context of what evidence the law allows to be presented. 'Judicial evidence', as evidence to be presented to a court is sometimes rather unnecessarily called, must not only tend to persuade the court of the truth or probability of the fact in support of which it is tendered, but must also comply with the rules on admissibility; if it does not, the adversary system of litigation dictates that a party shall not be permitted to adduce it. Much of the remainder of this book is concerned with the application of those rules in particular cases. To return to the stories with which this chapter began, it may be pertinent to observe that no case, however compelling in law, can be any stronger than the legally admissible evidence available to prove it to a court. It is not the truth that counts in any piece of controverted litigation, but the evidence, and on that cynical note, we must pass to consider evidence in a little more detail.

1.2 The varieties of evidence

No subject has suffered more from a hopeless diversity and inconsistency of terminology than evidence. It is impossible to reconcile the various usages, judicial and extra-judicial, which have been made of the terms employed to identify and separate different kinds of evidence. Attempts to make some scientific categorisation of evidence have occasioned endless academic wrangling, and have all failed to at least some extent, simply because evidence has not developed in a scientific way. It is the most pragmatic of subjects, having been constrained during its growth, not by any desire to create a scientific or consistent code, but by the necessities of practice from which the rules have sprung. Evidence underlies the whole practice of law in every field of litigation. It does not lend itself easily to academic classifications. In this book, the use of technical terms will be avoided, or at least simplified, wherever this can be done. But some form of sign convention is needed, and this will be achieved by adopting the following use of terminology. For convenience, we shall look first at the varieties judged by their substantive content and then at the varieties judged by their physical form.

2   The accused was allowed counsel in cases of treason as early as 1695, and appears to have enjoyed the right in the case of misdemeanours from early times.

1.2.1 *Substantive definitions*

Substantively, evidence knows only one major division, and that is between 'direct' and 'hearsay' evidence. A statement by a witness (sometimes called 'testimony') of what he himself perceived or did, or the production of a document or object in order to demonstrate its existence and nature, is direct evidence. Hearsay evidence is given when a witness recounts a statement made (orally, or in a document or in any other way) by another (or by himself) and asserts that the statement was true.

Direct evidence has the overriding merit that it consists of the personal knowledge and recollection of the witness (or of the self-evident character of the document or thing) and is accordingly readily open to assessment and challenge. Hearsay evidence, on the other hand, not only carries a built-in risk of inaccuracy through repetition and lack of personal knowledge, but is difficult to assess or challenge in many instances. For this reason, the common law permitted hearsay evidence to be given only in rare, exceptional cases (3).

In proving the contents of a document as direct evidence, resort may be had, according to the nature of the case, to either 'primary' or 'secondary' evidence. Primary evidence consists of producing the original, or admitting what its contents are. A copy of a document or an oral description of its contents is secondary evidence. Primary evidence is in general required as a matter of law, but in certain exceptional instances, the contents of a document may be proved by secondary evidence (4).

In some cases, a distinction must be made 'conclusive' and 'presumptive' (or prima facie) evidence. Conclusive evidence is rare (5). The term means simply, that where evidence of a particular kind is given, the law deems it to conclude the issue on which it is given, and does not allow the court to question that issue further, or any other party to give evidence to contradict it.

1.2.2 *Definitions of form*

Evidence which falls into any of the above categories in its substance or contents must, of course, have or be put into a form in which it can be presented to the court. Evidence is received by a court in the following forms:

(a)   Oral evidence: evidence consisting of what is said by any witness in the course of testifying in the instant proceedings. Oral evidence must, with very few exceptions, be given on oath or affirmation (6) and in court, though if a witness is unable to attend court, his evidence may in some cases be taken out of court on commission or, in criminal cases, by a justice of the peace. There are also in some important instances provisions for evidence to be given on affidavit (7) and, in criminal cases, by written statement in a prescribed form (8). These instances, where they occur, may be regarded as the equivalent of oral evidence and indeed, evidence so given has in law the same effect as oral evidence given in court.

(b)   Documentary evidence: evidence afforded by any document produced for the inspection of the court, whether as direct or hearsay evidence of its contents. A

---

3   The subject of the admissibility of hearsay evidence is a large and complicated one, occupying the whole of Chapters 6, 7 and 8, post.

4   In the case of documents requiring enrolment, there is a further kind of primary evidence. See generally, 16.2, post. Where a document is permitted to be proved as hearsay evidence of its contents, the strict rules are relaxed, to some extent. See, for example, Civil Evidence Act 1968, s. 6(1).

5   For a statutory example, see Civil Evidence Act 1968, s. 13(1).

6   See Chapter 12, Section B, post.

7   An affidavit is a written statement of the evidence of the deponent, made on oath or affirmation. See generally RSC, Ord.38, r. 2; Ord.41.

8   See, e.g., Criminal Justice Act 1967 s, 2(1), s. 9(1).

document may also be produced as a piece of real evidence as defined in (c) below. The normal sense of the word 'document' is of some writing or other inscription by which information may be communicated, but modern technology has opened up new possibilities in the form of tape, film and the like, so that the range of materials which may be so described has expanded somewhat the more traditional understanding of the word (9).

(c)   Real evidence: a term employed for convenience only to denote any material from which the court may draw conclusions or inferences by using its own senses. The genus includes material objects produced to the court for its inspection, the presentation of the physical characteristics of any person or animal, the demeanour of witnesses (which may or may not be offered or presented to the court by design), views of the *locus in quo* or of any object incapable of being brought to court without undue difficulty and such items as tapes, films and photographs which may be significant over and above the sum total of their contents as such. These are all considered in Chapter 16, Section B, post. What is of importance in each case is the visual, aural or other sensory impression which the evidence, by its own characteristics, produces on the court, and on which the court may act to find the truth or probability of any fact which seems to follow from it.

1.3   Facts which may be proved

The purpose of evidence being to demonstrate to the court the truth or probability of the facts upon which the success of a party's case depends in law, it follows that evidence must be confined to the proof of facts which are required for that purpose. The proof of supernumerary or unrelated facts will not assist the court, and may in certain cases prejudice the court against a party, while having no probative value on the issues actually before it. It is by no means always easy to determine what facts are required and what are supernumerary, especially in relation to matters said to form part of the 'res gestae', or to be relevant to the facts in issue. These are considered in their proper place, together with the problems which may arise. The facts which a party is permitted to prove are: (a) facts in issue in the case; (b) facts constituting part of, or accompanying and explaining a fact in issue, described as part of the 'res gestae'; (c) facts relevant to a fact in issue; and (d), where appropriate, standards of comparison.

1.3.1   Facts in issue

The facts in issue in a case are the facts which a party to litigation (including the prosecution in a criminal case) must prove in order to succeed in his claim or defence and to show his entitlement to relief (or to obtain a conviction). What these facts may be are not really the concern of the law of evidence, but may be derived from the substantive law applicable to the cause of action, charge or defence in each case. In procedural terms, they are to be found in the pleadings, indictment or charge, as the case may be.

In a civil case, any fact is in issue if, having regard to the pleadings and the substantive law, it is a fact necessary to the success of any claim or defence disclosed on the pleadings. In respect of the facts that a party must prove in order to establish his claim or defence, the party is said to bear the legal burden of proof (10). There are also facts in

---

9   The meaning of the term is considered further in 16.1 post. For certain purposes, the word has been given particular connotations by statute: see, e.g., Criminal Evidence Act 1965, s. 1(4); Civil Evidence Act 1968, s. 10(1).

10   This should be read with Chapter 3, where the legal and evidential burdens of proof are discussed. A fact will be in issue if any party must or should, to avoid the risk of failure, assert it as part of his case.

issue, which are the subject of an evidential burden of proof, in the sense that at any particular stage of the proceedings, the state of evidence is such that a party will run the risk of failure if he does not establish, at least prima facie, certain facts contradicting the case of his opponent.

The number of facts in issue will depend entirely on the nature of the case. In a typical action for negligence, the facts in issue will be those which, if proved, will establish that the defendant owed a duty of care to the plaintiff, that the defendant was in breach of that duty of care and that such breach caused to the plaintiff loss and damage for which he is entitled in law to recover; together with any further facts dictated by the nature of the defence, if it goes beyond a mere denial of those pleaded by the plaintiff (11), for example such facts as may establish contributory negligence, volenti non fit injuria or act of God.

In a typical action for breach of contract, the facts in issue will be those which, if proved, would establish a binding and enforceable contract between the plaintiff and the defendant, the due performance of any conditions precedent, a breach by the defendant of the contract and that such breach caused loss to the plaintiff for which he is entitled in law to recover; together with any further facts dictated by the nature of the defence, if it goes beyond a mere denial of the plaintiff's case, such as fraud, illegality, infancy or accord and satisfaction.

The pleadings in a civil action are of cardinal importance, in that their object is precisely that the court should be informed what the issues are. By RSC, Ord.18, r. 7(1):

. . . every pleading must contain, and contain only, a statement in a summary form of the material facts on which the party pleading relies for his claim or defence, as the case may be, but not the evidence by which those facts are to be proved, and the statement must be as brief as the nature of the case admits.

Although RSC Ord.20, provides for various rights and powers to amend pleadings, when the case comes to trial, the court will adjudicate on the pleaded issues only and will require the evidence to be directed to the facts in issue as ascertained from the pleadings (12). The court will not (at least without giving leave to amend, on such terms as may be just) adjudicate on other issues or allow evidence directed to other issues.

In criminal cases, the facts in issue are ascertained by reference to the essential elements of the offence as charged in the indictment or summons. The position here is rendered somewhat simpler by the fact that a plea of not guilty puts in issue all the facts necessary to establish the commission by the defendant of the offence charged, and the prosecution bear the legal burden of proving every such element of the offence (13). There are, however, exceptional cases where the defendant bears the burden of proving some element of his defence, for example insanity within the M'Naghten Rules. In yet other cases the defendant has an evidential burden of raising certain issues which go beyond a mere denial of his guilt as alleged by the prosecution, for example provocation, before the prosecution are required to rebut them in the discharge of their overall burden of proving his guilt (14). In such cases, the issues raised by the defence are just as much proper subjects of evidence, as being facts in issue, as those raised by the prosecution. But the evidence must be confined to the matters raised by the indictment

11 See RSC, Ord.18, r. 8(1).
12 See *Esso Petroleum Co. Ltd* v *Southport Corporation* (HL) [1956] AC 218.
13 *Woolmington* v *DPP* (HL) [1935] AC 462; *R* v *Sims* (CCA) [1946] KB 531, per Lord Goddard CJ at 539.
14 As to these cases, see 3.4.2 and 3.5.2, post.

or charge. The indictment is subject to amendment (15), but the evidence must be directed towards the essential elements of the offence charged in the indictment, as amended if at all. And despite the rule that in summary trial no point can be taken on formal defects of the process or any variance of the evidence from the actual wording of a summons (16), the evidence in a summary trial too must be directed only to the elements of the offence charged. The facts in issue in a criminal case will be the commission by the defendant of the actus reus, the presence of any necessary general or specific intent, and any defence, going beyond a mere denial of the prosecution case, which the defence must or may raise.

Also treated as facts in issue in any case, are facts which affect either the credibility of a witness, or the admissibility of any evidence. Such facts are known as 'secondary' or 'collateral' facts in issue. Evidence may be called, for example, tending to show that a witness for the other side is biased or partial, or suffers from some medical condition which renders his evidence unworthy of belief; or to show that a confession is admissible inasmuch as it was made voluntarily, or that secondary evidence of the contents of a document may be adduced because the original cannot be found after due search. These are facts which go to the admissibility or weight of evidence called in support of or to prove the 'primary' facts in issue.

1.3.2   Facts forming part of the res gestae

It is not always obvious where a fact begins and ends. To state a fact or event in isolation, without reference to its antecedents in time, place or surrounding circumstances, may render the fact, so stated, difficult or even impossible to comprehend. Other facts or circumstances may be so closely connected with the fact in issue as to be, in reality, part and parcel of the same transaction (17). Such ancillary facts are described, rather unhappily, as forming part of the res gestae of the fact in issue, and may be proved. The witness is permitted to state facts, not in meaningless isolation, but with such reasonable fullness and in such reasonable context as will make them comprehensible and useful. The rule is not confined by any strict limits of time or place. In the Australian case of *O'Leary* v *R* (18), a number of men employed at a timber camp went on a drunken orgy lasting several hours, during which a number of serious assaults were committed, and after which one of their number was found dying, having himself been savagely assaulted. On the prosecution of another of them for his murder, it was held that the episode should be looked at as a whole, including the occurrence of the previous assaults. Dixon J said:

> The evidence disclosed that, under the influence of the beer and wine he had drunk and continued to drink, he engaged in repeated acts of violence which might be regarded as amounting to a connected course of conduct. Without evidence of what, during that time, was done by those men who took any significant part in the matter and especially evidence of the behaviour of the prisoner, the transaction of which the alleged murder formed an integral part could not be truly understood and isolated from it, could only be presented as an unreal and not very intelligible event. The

15 Indictments Act 1915, s. 5.
16 Magistrates' Courts Act 1952, s. 100.
17 This way of describing evidence admissible under the res gestae principle has been held not to be the most accurate when the evidence is hearsay, but remains, it is submitted, a sound statement of the rule for general purposes: *Ratten* v *R* (PC, Victoria) [1972] AC 378 at 389, per Lord Wilberforce.
18 (1946) 73 CLR 566.

prisoner's generally violent and hostile conduct might well serve to explain his mind and attitude and, therefore, to implicate him in the resulting homicide.

And in *R* v *Nye and Loan* (19), the Court of Appeal held that a statement made to a police officer by the victim of an assault identifying his assailant, some minutes after the assault, and after the victim had been sitting in his car recovering from the combined effects of the assault and the road traffic accident which preceded it, was admissible under the rule as accompanying and explaining the fact in issue, namely whether the assailant had assaulted the victim.

This rather flexible principle habitually involves admitting evidence, at least in criminal cases, as an exception to the rule against hearsay, since it is likely to consist (as in *Nye and Loan*) of statements made by those involved in or witnessing a fact or event, which are tendered with a view to showing that the facts stated by them are true (20). Almost all the crucial decisions are of this kind, rather than of the kind in *O'Leary,* and the subject is accordingly dealt with fully in the context of common-law exceptions to the rule against hearsay in 6.6, post. In all probability, the reason why there are fewer decisions where no element of hearsay is involved is simply that the rule causes no real difficulty unless the extension into surrounding circumstances is as marked as it was in *O'Leary*. In almost all cases, some matter is admitted as part of the res gestae: be it the manner in which a blow was struck, the appearance of the victim afterwards, the tone of voice in which words were spoken, or many other circumstances of obvious probative value which are immediately connected with a fact in issue.

1.3.3   Facts relevant to facts in issue
In *DPP* v *Kilbourne* (21) Lord Simon of Glaisdale said:

Evidence is relevant if it is logically probative or disprobative of some matter which requires proof. It is sufficient to say, even at the risk of etymological tautology, that relevant (i.e., logically probative or disprobative) evidence is evidence which makes the matter which requires proof more or less probable.

This is, perhaps, a simpler and more satisfactory, if less comprehensive definition of relevance, than the classic formulation in Stephen's *Digest,* according to which the word signified that (22):

any two facts to which it is applied are so related to each other that according to the common course of events one either taken by itself or in connection with other facts proves or renders probable the past, present or future existence or non-existence of the other.

The need for the proof of facts relevant (within the terms of these or similar definitions) to facts in issue is an obvious one. In some cases, the fact in issue can be proved by the direct evidence of someone who perceived it, as where the witness saw the defendant shoot the deceased. But in very many cases, no such evidence is available, or such direct

19   (CA) (1977) 66 Cr App R 252.
20   In civil cases, such evidence would now be admissible, if hearsay, under s. 2 of the Civil Evidence Act 1968.
21   (HL) [1973] AC 729 at 756.
22   *Digest of the Law of Evidence,* 12th ed., art. 1. The definition was somewhat different in earlier editions, but this seems to be the author's mature view.

evidence as there is may be of little weight. Clearly, any facts related to the commission of an offence by the relationship of relevance are to be provable so as to demonstrate the truth or probability of the fact in issue (that the defendant murdered the deceased). Thus, if the defendant was later found in possession of some article of the deceased's property which would ordinarily have been about his person at the time of the shooting, these facts are relevant to the fact in issue because they make it more probable (if accepted) that the fact in issue is true. Equally, if the shooting took place in London, proof of the fact that, at the time of the shooting, the defendant was in Manchester would be relevant as disprobative of the fact in issue. Each of these pieces of evidence involves the drawing of an inference, in order to reach the conclusion that the fact in issue is true or untrue, more probable or less probable. For this reason, evidence which goes to prove relevant facts is often spoken of as 'circumstantial' (23), by way of contrast with direct evidence of the fact in issue itself.

Relevant facts are easier to identify than to describe in the abstract (24). Provided that the relationship between the allegedly relevant fact and the fact in issue is probative or disprobative, the former may be proved in support of or in contradiction of the latter. *Joy* v *Phillips, Mills & Co. Ltd* (25) was an action concerning the death of a stable-boy, who had been kicked by a horse, and evidence was admitted to prove that the boy had previously been in the habit of teasing horses, and that, when found, he was holding a halter which he had no occasion to be using at the time. In this case, the relevant fact was proved by evidence of acts earlier in time than the fact in issue, but it is equally permissible to call evidence proving relevant facts which were contemporaneous with, or subsequent to the fact in issue. In *Woolf* v *Woolf* (26), it was held that proof of the fact that a couple, who were not married to each other, occupied the same bedroom was clearly probative of an allegation that they had committed adultery, and of the existence at that time of an adulterous relationship. In *R* v *Dalloz* (27), the fact that a driver was proved to have been speeding at a given point was held to be relevant to prove that he had been speeding some short time and distance before.

Some facts may be relevant to more than one issue, and of these no more need be said. But irrelevant and insufficiently relevant evidence will, at the other extreme, be rejected. Like relevance, irrelevance and insufficient relevance are matters of degree, and easier to identify than to describe. It has been held irrelevant to an allegation of negligence that after an accident allegedly caused by such negligence, the defendants altered their practice (28). The fact was perfectly consistent with an intention, in the light of fresh information, to improve an existing practice, whereas negligence is to be judged in the light of existing knowledge. And where a brewer brought an action against a publican for breach of covenant to buy beer from the brewer, the brewer was not permitted to prove, in reply to a defence that the beer previously supplied by him was bad, that he had supplied good beer to other publicans (29). It is obvious from these illustrations that insufficiently relevant, or irrelevant, evidence, in addition to its lack of probative value on the facts in issue, carries with it the risk of prejudice against the party affected by it, and paves the way for the opening up of numerous collateral inquiries which can have no value to the proper decision of the case.

23 The word 'circumstantial' has sometimes been accorded a derogatory sense, as if such evidence could have little weight. But, as the illustrations in the text may show, it is often more cogent than indifferent direct evidence, such as a hesitant or uncertain identification.
24 An invaluable analysis of the cases is given in Cross, *Evidence*, 5th ed. p. 38 et seq.
25 (CA) [1916] 1 KB 849.   26 (CA) [1931] P 134.   27 (CCA) (1908) 1 Cr App R 258.
28 *Hart* v *Lancashire & Yorkshire Railway Co.* (1869) 21 LT 261.
29 *Holcombe* v *Hewson* (NP) (1810) 2 Camp 391.

It sometimes happens that the relevance of a particular fact is not immediately clear upon its being proved in evidence. This is usually because of the simple truth that evidence must be called in order and by one witness at a time. The trial judge is entitled to insist that the relevance of a fact be demonstrated to him, before permitting evidence of that fact to be given. But the practice is to allow proof of the fact 'de bene esse', at least where counsel undertakes to demonstrate the relevance of the point in due course. If it does not appear, later, that its relevance has been established, the jury must be directed to ignore it, although in some cases, it may be necessary to discharge them if the fact is highly prejudicial. An illustration is where counsel seeks to put in a document in cross-examination, strict proof of which and the relevance of which to the defence must await the presentation of the defence case. Other facts, described as 'conditionally relevant', whose actual relevance may stand or fall by reference to other evidence, include statements made in the presence of the accused, which must be proved, but whose relevance may depend on later evidence of the accused's reaction to them (30).

1.3.4 Standards of comparison
Wherever it is necessary to judge the conduct of a party against an objective standard, it may be proved what such objective standard is, or was at the material time and in the material circumstances. Negligence is a common example. The standard of the reasonable man demands that evidence may be given to show how others might reasonably have behaved in similar circumstances, and this fact, if established, is relevant to the necessary assessment of how the party accused in fact behaved. Where the objective standard is one which involves conduct in a situation outside the everyday experience of the court, the standard may be proved by expert evidence of the conduct in such circumstances, for example of a reasonable member of a trade or a profession (31), or of the accepted practice of commercial men (32). In a common situation of everyday life, it may be a matter of which the judge could take judicial notice, or find proved by the direct evidence of the witnesses.

1.4 Admissibility and weight

1.4.1 Admissibility
Evidence is said to be admissible, or receivable, if it may be given for the purpose of proving facts before the court, when judged by the law of evidence. Although, as we have seen, evidence must be sufficiently relevant in order to be admissible, the converse proposition is not valid: not all relevant evidence is admissible. Much hearsay evidence, strictly excluded at common law, is highly relevant within the definitions discussed in 1.3, but because a rule of evidence precludes its use, it is inadmissible (33). Similarly, evidence which is excluded by reason of some rule of public policy, or which is the

30   See Chapter 7, Section C, post.
31   *Chapman* v *Walton* (1833) 10 Bing 57. The evidence must show what the generally accepted conduct would be, not merely what the witness himself would have done, and as to the limitations on the province of expert evidence, see generally 9.3.2, post. Such evidence is very common in, e.g., medical and legal negligence cases.
32   *Noble* v *Kennoway* (1780) 2 Doug KB 510; *Fleet* v *Murton* (1871) LR 7 QB 126.
33   With regard to evidence of character, there is some controversy (making no practical difference whatever) whether such evidence is generally inadmissible because it is irrelevant, or is generally inadmissible, despite its relevance, for other reasons of fairness. The view adopted in Chapters 4 and 5 of this book is the former. The latter appears to depend upon a failure to appreciate the fact that relevance in law is not necessarily coextensive with relevance as the word is commonly used. If a man is of bad character, such fact tends to show that he is likely to commit offences, but not, it is submitted, that he committed a particular offence charged. There are cases (discussed in Chapter 5) where for particular reasons, such evidence may be so relevant, and it is then admissible. Similar arguments may be raised over evidence of opinion, previous judgments and doubtless other cases.

subject of privilege, though often highly relevant, is inadmissible in law. It is this that gives to the law of evidence its exclusionary aspect to which reference was made earlier in this chapter. Inadmissible evidence cannot be entertained by the court, whatever its relevance, and indeed however cogent it might have been.

The question of admissibility is one of law, and is determined by the lex fori, that is the law of England, even when the question is one of the admissibility of evidence originating abroad, or where the facts in issue arose abroad or have some foreign aspect.

The rules of admissibility are considered in Parts 2 and 3 of this book.

1.4.2 Weight

The weight of evidence is a qualitative assessment of the probative value which admissible evidence has in relation to the facts in issue. To say that evidence is relevant and admissible concludes the issue of law, that a party is entitled to bring that evidence before a court. Such evidence then has the potential to persuade the court of the truth or probability of the facts towards which it is directed. But its actual persuasive value in relation to those facts depends upon the view taken by the court, as a matter of fact, of the truthfulness, reliability and cogency of the evidence. Depending upon such a view, evidence may be of virtually no weight at all, or may rest on one of an infinite number of points on the upwards sliding scale, ending with evidence which is so weighty as almost to conclude the case in itself (34). Although the weight of evidence is a question of fact, and strictly cannot arise until the evidence is first shown to be relevant and admissible, it is not always possible to segregate these qualities of law and fact altogether. The relevance of evidence is closely bound up with its weight and to say that evidence is insufficiently relevant to be admitted, necessarily involves, to that extent, some judgment on its weight. And where the judge has a discretion whether to admit or exclude evidence (as to which see 1.5, post) it is both usual and legitimate for him to take into account the likely weight of the evidence, if admitted, and to compare this with its likely prejudicial effect.

The assessment of weight depends upon a multiplicity of factors, which would be almost impossible to define, but which may certainly include matters extraneous to the evidence itself, for example other evidence given in the case, or the demeanour of the witness who gives the evidence. In cases where hearsay evidence is admissible by virtue of the provisions of the Criminal Evidence Act 1965 or part 1 of the Civil Evidence Act 1968, Parliament has provided a statement of the matters to be considered in assessing the weight of evidence so admitted (35). The various factors so enumerated would appear to be those which any reasonable tribunal would in any event take into account, and it is submitted that the exercise is not really very beneficial and is probably unnecessary.

To say that evidence lacks weight does not mean that such evidence is perjured or dishonestly motivated, or even exaggerated. It is true that evidence having these characteristics will lack weight, but equally, so will evidence which is unreliable because the witness's recollection has failed him, or because he had no adequate opportunity to perceive the facts of which he speaks, or because his knowledge of the facts is insufficient, or, in the case of an expert witness, because his expertise or experience or opportunity to investigate is too limited. So, too, will any evidence which is for any reason unable to afford the court the assistance it needs in relation to the facts in issue.

34 The use of the word 'conclude' to express very weighty evidence should not be confused with its use to describe evidence which as a matter of law may not be contradicted, and so 'concludes' an issue: see 1.2.1, ante.
35 Criminal Evidence Act 1965, s. 1(3); Civil Evidence Act 1968, s. 6(3).

1.5 Tribunals of law and fact: judicial discretion

1.5.1 Tribunals of law and fact

Any process of trial of litigation must provide for the determination of both issues of law and issues of fact. Broadly speaking, in any case tried by a judge sitting with a jury, questions of law arising in the case fall to be determined by the judge and questions of fact by the jury. Jury trial is now rare in civil cases (36), and the functions of the jury will be considered principally in relation to criminal trials on indictment, in which they are always employed. Where a judge sits alone to consider a civil case, he is himself the tribunal of law and fact and determines all issues of both kinds. In the case of magistrates' courts and tribunals, the court or tribunal is entitled to decide all matters of law and fact canvassed before it, but on matters of law should seek and accept the advice of their clerk or legally qualified chairman (37).

Questions of law comprise matters relating to the substantive law governing the claim or charge, the admissibility of evidence, any rules of law or practice governing the production or effect of evidence and the question whether there is sufficient evidence to warrant consideration by the tribunal of fact at all. The judicial function also includes the determination of necessary questions ancillary to the trial itself, such as whether cause has been shown in the challenge of a juror, whether the jury, or a particular member of the jury should be discharged, and matters concerning the administration of the trial, for example bail.

Questions of fact comprise the decision of all matters concerning the truth or probability of all facts in issue as derived from the substantive law, pleadings, indictment or charge (seen in the light of the burden and standard of proof applicable to the issues) and the weight of any evidence admitted for the purpose of proving or disproving the facts in issue. In a criminal trial, a jury also decide, if necessary, whether the defendant stands mute of malice or by visitation of God, and the question of fitness to plead; but if the defendant is found fit to plead, another jury must be empanelled to try him.

Many issues involve in part a question of law and in part (if the question of law be answered in a way which does not preclude it) a question of fact. Thus, in defamation actions, it is a question of law whether the words complained of are capable of bearing defamatory meaning, and a question of fact whether they are defamatory of the plaintiff. Where corroboration is required as a matter of law, or is to be looked for as a matter of practice, it is a question of law what evidence given, if any, is capable of constituting corroboration, and a question of fact whether such evidence does afford corroboration of the evidence requiring it. There are very many similar matters which consist of mixed issues of law and fact, and in a jury trial, the judge must decide the issue of law, direct the jury accordingly, and then leave the jury to consider any issue of fact permitted or called for by his ruling.

There are cases in which the distinction between matters of law and fact is not entirely clear, and in case of doubt, reference must be made to the appropriate substantive law to establish what matters are to be determined by the judge, and what by the jury. To take just one example, in an action for malicious prosecution, it is a question of fact for the jury to determine what steps the defendant took to inform himself of the truth of the

---

36   Juries are employed in civil cases to try actions for defamation, malicious prosecution, false imprisonment and cases in which fraud is alleged. But their use is not mandatory in such cases, and is not excluded in other cases. See RSC, Ord.33, r. 5.

37   Stipendiary magistrates are in theory in the same position as lay justices, but the clerk's advice may be less crucial in practice. At courts martial, the tribunal must accept the advice of their judge-advocate on matters of law.

charge, and whether the defendant honestly believed in the truth of the charge; it is for the judge to rule as a matter of law whether the defendant had, in the light of the facts found, any reasonable and probable cause. But in other cases, what is reasonable is a question of fact, for example, whether allegedly provocative words or conduct would have led a reasonable man to react as the defendant did. Moreover, some questions of substantive fact, for instance the proper interpretation of foreign law, are decided by the judge (38).

The functions of the trial judge in relation to matters involving the law of evidence are concerned with the questions of admissibility of and the rules governing the production and effect of evidence. A judge sitting alone in a civil case must direct his mind to questions of weight also, but the critical area concerns the functions of the judge and jury in a criminal trial, and the necessary demarcation between those functions.

1.5.1.1 Admissibility.

Questions of the admissibility of evidence are matters of law for the judge, with which the jury are not concerned. Because of the impossibility of conducting such an argument without the jury hearing what may be held to be inadmissible evidence, the practice is for the jury to retire during the argument. Counsel should inform each other of any questions of admissibility which are to be referred to the judge, and the controverted evidence should not be opened to or referred to in the presence of the jury, unless and until it is ruled to be admissible. Questions of admissibility are properly decided at the stage when they naturally arise in the course of the case, but where the prosecution (or in some cases the defence) cannot coherently open or begin to present their case without reference to the controverted evidence, the judge should be invited to rule on it as a preliminary issue. Such a case would be where the only evidence against a defendant is a confession, the admissibility of which is disputed. The jury should, however, be present when the judge rules on the question of competence to give evidence of a child of tender years, or a person subject to some disability of mind (39), because the matter is one which must affect their view of the weight of any such evidence given and will not involve their exposure to the substance of the evidence. There are as many questions of admissibility which may arise as there are rules of evidence, and to multiply examples would be pointless.

It should, however, be noted that the determination of questions of admissibility, while a matter of law, may involve the hearing of evidence tendered to prove secondary facts in issue (see 1.3.1, ante) or facts relevant to secondary facts in issue. This evidence is heard on the 'voire dire', in what is termed a 'trial within a trial', in the absence of the jury, and the judge must decide the secondary facts in issue before he can rule on admissibility. The practice in relation to the voire dire is considered in detail elsewhere (40). In other cases, the question may not involve any issue of fact, but require legal argument only. Instances of each are: where it is sought to prove that a confession is admissible, the prosecution must prove that it was made voluntarily, and if disputed, evidence must be heard from those to whom the confession was made, and may be heard from the defendant and his witnesses, if any; where, however, it is submitted that a witness may not be required to answer a particular question because of the incidence of privilege, or that evidence of similar facts is sufficiently probative to be admissible to prove the offence charged, such questions are usually (though not invariably) matters for legal argument on the basis of agreed or assumed facts.

38 Questions of foreign law are questions of fact, and should be proved by expert evidence: see 9.6.5, post.
39 See *R* v *Reynolds* (CCA) [1950] 1 KB 606.   40   See 3.5.3 and 7.9, post.

1.5.1.2 Production and effect. The judge must direct the jury with regard to all matters which arise concerning the production, significance and effect of the evidence given, and the use which they are entitled to make of that evidence. This duty includes the explanation of the burden and standard of proof, the operation of any presumptions, the nature of, and any requirement for, corroboration and where, it at all, it may be found, the rules regarding the evidential value of confessions, the significance of any character evidence, the position of the defendant as a witness in his own defence, and any other such matters which may arise.

The judge is entitled to comment on the weight or credibility of any evidence given, provided that he impresses upon the jury that they are the judges of the facts, and it is their view which counts. In some cases, stronger comment is permissible than in others (41), and in certain cases, some observation on the weight of evidence may be essential if the jury are to be properly informed about their task (42).

1.5.1.3 Leaving the case to the jury. It is the judge's duty to consider whether there is sufficient evidence to warrant leaving the case to the jury at all. This is a matter of law, usually decided at the close of the prosecution case. But it may be decided at any time thereafter, and whether or not any submission is made to the judge to withdraw the case. The judge should withdraw the case from the jury if there is no or insufficient evidence on which the jury, properly directed, would be entitled to find that the charge has been made out, or where, although there is some evidence on which they could do so, it is so slight or unsatisfactory that it would not be safe to leave it to them on such a basis (43). The jury are entitled, purely from their consideration of the facts, to stop the case in favour of the defendant at any time after the close of the prosecution case, but may only return a verdict of guilty after the completion of the summing-up. Submissions of no case to answer are also possible in civil cases, whether or not tried with a jury, though in such cases, complex rules come into play which are outside the scope of the present work, and for which reference should be made to the *Supreme Court Practice*.

1.5.2 Judicial discretion

The categorisation of evidence as either admissible or inadmissible is one well suited to the adversary system of litigation, in the sense that the parties should be free to approach the presentation of their case in the confidence that the rules will be consistently observed. But the question also arises whether the judge, in addition to deciding questions of admissibility, may by virtue of his function of conducting the trial fairly in the interests of all the parties, superimpose upon the questions of admissibility some discretionary decision, either to admit evidence which is technically inadmissible (inclusionary discretion) or to exclude evidence which is technically admissible (exclusionary discretion) so as to meet the justice of any particular case. It must be said that in general, the common law has not accorded any substantial degree of discretion, perhaps rightly in the interests of certainty, and the only discretion which can safely be regarded as established is a limited area of exclusionary discretion relating to evidence tendered for the prosecution in criminal cases.

---

41   The cases are carefully and fully analysed in Archbold, *Criminal Pleading, Evidence and Practice*, 40th ed., para. 599 et seq.
42   For example, in identification cases: see *R v Turnbull* (CA) [1977] QB 224, and generally 13.3.3.2 post.
43   See *R v Young* (CCA) [1964] 1 WLR 717: Practice Direction [1962] 1 All ER 448 but; the judge must not usurp the function of the jury — weak cases, like strong ones, are proper to be considered by the jury: see *R v Barker* (CA) (1975) 65 Cr App R 287 n.

1.5.2.1 Inclusionary discretion.   At common law, there is no discretion to admit inadmissible evidence, either in civil or criminal cases. In *Sparks* v *R* (44) it was argued that it was 'manifestly unjust' for the jury to be left in ignorance of the fact that a girl aged under four, whom the defendant was charged with indecently assaulting, but who was not called to give evidence (doubtless because of her age), had told her mother that her attacker was coloured, the defendant being white. The evidence was hearsay and, in a criminal case, inadmissible because it fell under no recognised exception to the rule against hearsay. Clearly, the interests of justice might be thought to call for the exercise of some discretion to admit the evidence, if any such discretion existed. But the Privy Council dealt with the question solely on the footing of admissibility, and rejected the contention that the evidence could have been admitted. Lord Morris of Borth-y-Gest said (45):

> It was said that it was, 'manifestly unjust for the jury to be left throughout the whole trial with the impression that the child could not give any clue to the identity of her assailant'. The cause of justice is, however, best served by adherence to rules which have long been recognised and settled.

If any discretion had existed, it would undoubtedly have been considered in that case, and no other authority supports the existence of an inclusionary discretion at common law.

There are, however, some statutory powers to override formal defects or to admit evidence notwithstanding failure to observe applicable procedural requirements, such as that conferred by s. 8(3)(a) of the Civil Evidence Act 1968 (effected by RSC, Ord.38, r. 29) to permit the admission of hearsay statements technically admissible under ss. 2, 4 or 5 of that Act, notwithstanding the failure of a party to comply with the mandatory rules of court governing their admission.

1.5.2.2 Exclusionary discretion: civil cases.   No well defined exclusionary discretion can be demonstrated which applies to civil cases, although it may be that by some process akin to that of discovering a new planet, some discretion must be taken to exist because of the provision of s. 18(5) of the Civil Evidence Act 1968 (echoed in s. 5(3) of the Civil Evidence Act 1972, except that the latter refers to 'civil proceedings' instead of 'legal proceedings') that:

> Nothing in this Act shall prejudice —
> (a)   any power of a court in any legal proceedings, to exclude evidence (whether by preventing questions from being put or otherwise) at its discretion.

There are undoubtedly certain cases where the assessment of relevance or the balancing of competing interests bears a superficial resemblance to the process of the exercise of discretion (46). But these are, in reality, a function of the decision of the question of admissibility, and the separate question of an exclusionary discretion cannot be inferred solely from this particular judicial exercise. The existence of such a discretion appears never to have been canvassed except in the context of the cases dealing with

44   (PC, Bermuda) [1964] AC 964   45   Ibid at 978. The appeal was allowed for other reasons.
46   As Professor Cross points out in relation to his treatment of inclusionary discretion: *Evidence*, 5th ed. p. 37.

confidential information. It is quite clear as a matter of law that confidentiality is, in itself, no ground for preventing the asking of questions or the operation of discovery designed to elicit information imparted to a witness 'in confidence', or the contents of any 'confidential' document (47). But it has been suggested that the court may, none-theless, exercise some discretion to prevent the compelling of disclosure, where the confidence is serious and one which in the public interest generally ought to be respected, and where the relevance and weight of the information in terms of the proceedings as a whole would be relatively small (48). But in *D* v *NSPCC* (49) Lord Simon of Glaisdale appears to have regarded the matter as one based on no foundation more secure than that of the comity between Bench and Bar and the professional judgment of advocates. One might perhaps add to that the obvious forensic reluctance to insist upon pressing a matter to the extent of alienating the tribunal, unless that matter is one which can hardly be avoided. Lord Simon's view was that 'if it comes to the forensic crunch . . . it must be law, not discretion, which is in command', and that the particular question of confidence was one more suited to review by Parliament as a matter of law. In summary, therefore, it would seem that the existence of any exclusionary discretion capable of standing in the way of forensic intransigence cannot be established, though the point is by no means beyond argument.

1.5.2.3 Exclusionary discretion: criminal cases In criminal cases, it is now estab-lished that there is one area of exclusionary discretion that is applicable generally to evidence tendered on behalf of the prosecution. In comparatively recent times its operation has been expressed by Roskill J in the following terms (50):

> A trial judge always has an overriding duty in every case to secure a fair trial, and if in any particular case he comes to the conclusion that, even though certain evidence is strictly admissible, yet its prejudicial effect once admitted is such as to make it virtually impossible for a dispassionate view of the crucial facts of the case to be thereafter taken by the jury, then the trial judge, in my judgment, should exclude that evidence.

The discretion is, then, to be exercised in the light of a process of balance between the probative value of the admissible evidence and its capability to influence the jury against the defendant in a 'prejudicial' way, that is to say in a way which has no actual probative value in relation to the facts in issue, but draws the attention of the jury to material adverse to the defendant in a general sense. In earlier times, there had been considerable judicial reluctance to allow any discretion to interfere with the rules of law, even for the purpose of the overriding duty to secure a fair trial, and this reluctance survived as far as a faint cry of dissent in *R* v *Christie* (51). But since that time, it has never been doubted, and the balancing process was clearly described by Lord du Parcq in delivering the advice of the Privy Council in *Noor Mohamed* v *R* (52):

> . . . in all such cases the judge ought to consider whether the evidence is sufficiently

---

47 Such matter is admissible in law, unless it must be excluded for some reason of public policy, or is also the subject of a specific private privilege: see Chapter 11, post.
48 See, e.g., *Attorney-General* v *Mulholland; Attorney-General* v *Foster* (CA) [1963] 2 QB 477, per Donovan LJ at 492.
49 (HL) [1978] AC 171 at 239.
50 *R* v *List* [1966] 1 WLR 9, at 12.
51 (HL) [1914] AC 545, per Lord Halsbury reported only at 10 Cr App R 141 at 149.
52 (PC, British Guiana) [1949] AC 182 at 192. See also *R* v *Christie* (HL) [1914] AC 545, per Lord Moulton at 559.

substantial, having regard to the purpose to which it is professedly directed, to make it desirable in the interest of justice that it should be admitted. If, so far as that purpose is concerned, it can in the circumstances have only trifling weight, the judge will be right to exclude it. To say this is not to confuse weight with admissibility. The distinction is plain, but cases must occur in which it would be unjust to admit evidence of a character gravely prejudicial to the accused even though there may be some tenuous ground for holding it technically admissible. The decision must then be left to the discretion and sense of fairness of the judge.

The modern application of the discretion is probably somewhat broader than that suggested by Lord du Parcq's words, in the sense that the extremes of the balance, 'trifling weight' and 'gravely prejudicial', would probably now not be insisted upon strictly, so long as the prejudicial value can be shown to outweigh any realistic probative value. In *R* v *Sang* (53) Lord Diplock, having considered the authorities, summed up the position by saying:

> So I would hold that there has now developed a general rule of practice whereby in a trial by jury the judge has a discretion to exclude evidence which, though technically admissible, would probably have a prejudicial influence on the minds of the jury, which would be out of proportion to its true evidential value.

Viscount Dilhorne (54) employed the same phrase. Lords Salmon and Fraser of Tully-belton (55) held that the discretion lay to exclude evidence, where to do so is necessary to ensure a fair trial. Lord Scarman (56) adopting the words of Lord Reid in *Myers* v *DPP* held that the discretion lay to exclude, 'if justice so requires', adding that it was not confined to cases in which the prejudicial effect outweighs the probative value, but was confined to cases in which there can be said to be an 'unfair use of evidence'. It is doubtful whether these slightly different statements of the rule, culled from a consider-able body of case-law, create any real doubt concerning the court's task, which is to weigh the probative value to the prosecution against the prejudicial effect on the defendant, as far as both can be gauged, and to take the course which seems calculated to produce a fair trial.

The House of Lords in *R* v *Sang* were unanimous in holding that there is only one discretion, in the terms stated above, albeit that such discretion may operate in a number of different situations and upon quite diverse pieces of evidence. Before turning to the most commonly recurring of these particular applications, however, it is pertinent to note that, as Lord Salmon said (57):

> I recognise that there may have been no categories of cases, other than those to which I have referred, in which technically admissible evidence proffered by the Crown has been rejected by the court on the ground that it would make the trial unfair. I cannot, however, accept that a judge's undoubted duty to ensure that the accused has a fair trial is confined to such cases. In my opinion the category of such cases is not and never can be closed except by statute.

The most common applications of the discretion in criminal practice are as follows.

53   (HL) [1979] 3 WLR 263 at 269.   54   Ibid at 273.
55   Ibid, Lord Salmon at 279, Lord Fraser at 284,   56 Ibid at 286.
57   Ibid at 279; and cf Lord Scarman at 286–7.

Each is dealt with in somewhat more detail in its proper place in this book, but it is convenient to state them as the major examples of Lord Salmon's open category.

(a)   Evidence admissible under the similar-fact principle, while having a high level of probative value in order to be admissible in the first place, is often capable of having a very serious prejudicial effect because of its exposure of a highly specific aspect of the defendant's character. Clearly, the judge should consider the exercise of discretion in any such case (58).

(b)   Where the prosecution propose, on a charge of handling stolen goods, to tender evidence of other occasions on which the defendant has been instrumental in the handling of stolen goods, or has previously been convicted of theft or handling stolen goods, with a view to proving that he knew or believed the goods to be stolen, as permitted by s. 27(3) of the Theft Act 1968. Here, the probative value may not be very great but there is a substantial possibility of prejudice to the defendant, who may be made to look like a general villain (59).

(c)   Where the defendant has become liable to be cross-examined as to his character, by virtue of s. 1(*e*) or (*f*) of the Criminal Evidence Act 1898, for similar reasons, the judge may exercise his discretion to exclude such cross-examination altogether, or to confine it to those aspects of the defendant's character which appear to be likely to assist the jury in their assessment of the case or of the defendant's credibility (60).

(d)   Where a confession has been obtained in breach of the Judges' Rules (which are rules of practice for the guidance of police officers conducting investigations and interrogations) the judge may exclude such confession, if, by reason of the breach, weighed with the other circumstances of the case, it would be unfair to the defendant to admit it (61).

As Lord Fraser of Tullybelton recognised in *Sang* (62) the exercise of the discretion is a subjective matter, and much will turn on the facts of each individual case. As has been said of the concept of 'unfairness to the accused' in another context (63), it may be an amalgam of many relevant factors, and not least will be the extent to which the evidence would assist the jury in their task of deciding the facts in issue. In one sense, all relevant evidence is 'prejudicial' to the defendant, quite legitimately, the more so if its probative value is high. But evidence may be admissible as a matter of law, if it is relevant to the charge, even though coincidentally it may introduce material which could 'prejudice' him (in the unfair sense) in the eyes of the jury, and evidence is often admitted on that basis. It is when that balance is upset to a real degree in favour of prejudice (in the unfair sense) that discretion may be exercised. It does not follow that discretion must be exercised in any particular case — such is not the nature of discretion, and it is difficult to construct grounds of appeal on the basis of a refusal to exercise an exclusionary discretion, because the trial judge is usually far better placed to assess the matter than an appellate court. Although the appellate courts will sometimes intervene in a case of obvious prejudice arising, for example from the admission of probatively weak similar-

---

58   *Noor Mohamed* v *R* (PC, British Guiana) [1949] AC 182. See also 5.1 and 5.2, post.
59   *R* v *Herron* (CCA) [1967] 1 QB 107, decided under the corresponding provisions of the Larceny Act 1916; see also *R* v *Knott* (CA) [1973] Crim LR 36, and 4.5, post.
60   *Selvey* v *DPP* (HL) [1970] AC 304. See also 4.14.3.3, post.
61   *R* v *May* (CCA) (1952) 36 Cr App R 91. See also 7.7, post.
62   *R* v *Sang* (HL) [1979] 3 WLR 263 at 284.
63   In *King* v *R* (PC, Jamaica) [1969] 1 AC 304 at 318–19, per Lord Hodson delivering the advice of the Privy Council.

fact evidence, interference must usually be based on some argument against admissibility in law. In *Selvey* v *DPP* (64) the House of Lords counselled that, while there was a discretion to prevent cross-examination concerning character, in a case where the defendant had made imputations against the character of a witness for the prosecution, within the meaning of s. 1(*f*)(ii) of the Criminal Evidence Act 1898, that discretion would not always be exercised in favour of the defendant merely because the making of such imputations was a necessary part of his defence. Many cases are to be found where admissible evidence has been 'admitted as probative of the offence charged, even though, coincidentally, such evidence exposes to the jury some damaging aspect of the defendant's character (65). It is, therefore, of no avail to seek to lay down further definitive guidelines. The question is essentially one of fact, bearing in mind the extent of the discretion as defined by the cases we have considered: the overriding duty of the judge being to ensure that there is a fair trial.

It should be emphasised that the discretion to exclude refers only to evidence tendered by the prosecution. There is no discretion to exclude, at the instance of one defendant, evidence sought to be called by another. Thus, although the prosecution may be restrained from cross-examination concerning character where such a course is technically justified under s. 1(*f*)(ii) of the Criminal Evidence Act 1898, there is no power to prevent a co-defendant from cross-examining to the same effect when he is entitled to do so by virtue of s. 1(*f*)(iii) of the Act (66). Clearly, the requirement of a fair trial of persons jointly accused demands that each defendant be free to present his case within the limits of relevance and admissibility.

1.6 Evidence illegally or unfairly obtained

Whether the courts should refuse to entertain evidence because it has been obtained by the party tendering it in an illegal or improper manner is a question principally of policy, to which no answer is to be found in the law of evidence as such. Given that the evidence is relevant and does not offend against any of the substantive rules of admissibility, the question resolves itself into whether the courts should admit the evidence as admissible to prove the offence charged, or the claim, and leave the party aggrieved to his civil remedy in respect of any actionable wrong indulged in to obtain it, or whether the courts should act as 'watchdogs' and should decline to allow a party guilty of such wrongdoing to profit by it. A secondary issue is whether, if the evidence so obtained is admissible in law as being relevant and not contrary to the substantive rules, the judge may exclude it in the exercise of some discretion. It is not proposed here to delve into the merits of this controversy, save to record the present author's feeling that the state of the present law, while having the merit of unassailable logic, probably does scant credit to the law's reputation as a public guardian.

1.6.1 Admissibility
The courts have, from an early stage, rejected the concept that evidence should be held to be inadmissible merely on the ground of the manner in which it is obtained. In *Jones* v

64   [1970] AC 304.
65   See, e.g., *R* v *Chitson* (CCA) [1909] 2 KB 945; *R* v *Kurasch* (CCA) [1915] 2 KB 749. See generally 4.11 and Chapter 5, post, and, on a similar point, *Turner* v *Underwood* (DC) [1948] 2 KB 284, which should, however, be seen in the context of the point made in 7.10.2, post.
66   *Murdoch* v *Taylor* (HL) [1965] AC 574. See generally 4.14.3.3, post.

Owens (67) where a constable, in the course of an unlawful search of the defendant, found a quantity of young salmon, which became the subject of a charge, Mellor J said that if such evidence could not be used against him, it would be 'a dangerous obstacle to the administration of justice'. And in *R* v *Leatham* (68) referring to a letter which had been found only because of inadmissible confessions made by the defendant, Crompton J went so far as to say that 'if you steal it even, it would be admissible.' In more recent times, the rule has been restated in the leading case of *Kuruma son of Kaniu* v *R* (69), in which the defendant was charged with the unlawful possession of ammunition during a period of emergency in Kenya. The ammunition was found during an unlawful search, and it was contended on appeal to the Privy Council that the evidence of the finding was inadmissible because of the manner in which it had been obtained. In delivering the advice of the Privy Council, Lord Goddard CJ rejected the argument decisively, saying:

> In their Lordships' opinion the test to be applied in considering whether the evidence is admissible is whether it is relevant to the matters in issue. If it is, it is admissible and the court is not concerned with how the evidence was obtained. While this proposition may not have been stated in so many words in any English case there are decisions which support it, and in their Lordships' opinion it is plainly right in principle.

The rule has been reaffirmed on several occasions since then , and in *Jeffrey* v *Black* (70), the Divisional Court had no doubt that the decision should be accepted, the facts being that, the defendant having been arrested for the theft of a sandwich from a public house, police officers quite improperly searched his home and found quantities of cannabis and cannabis resin. It is relevant to note, for future reference, that this principle of admissibility applies even to cases of 'entrapment' and where evidence is obtained as a result of the activities of an *'agent provocateur'*. Both terms refer to cases in which the defendant is lured into or encouraged in the commission of an offence, for which he is subsequently prosecuted. Two distinct situations may be identified: the first where the *agent provocateur* infiltrates himself into the performance of an offence already under way, for example by posing as a receiver of stolen goods; the second where the agent himself initiates the commission of the offence, and where but for such initiation the offence might not have been committed. It has been held that the distinction may be relevant for the purpose of deciding with what offence the defendant should be charged (71) and for the purpose of mitigation of sentence in certain cases (72). But entrapment is not a defence in English law, and accordingly it has been held that evidence obtained through the agency of an *agent provocateur,* or during entrapment, is not inadmissible, even though the courts have sometimes deprecated the use of such methods, especially those falling within the second kind of situation referred to above. However, in *R* v *Mealy and Sheridan* (73) the Court of Appeal rejected the very argument that evidence had been obtained in any way unfairly, saying that it was the commission of the offence, and not the evidence, which had been so obtained. This extraordinary view is granted by the learned editors of Archbold (74) the accolade that: 'once stated this point is

---

67   (1870) 34 JP 759.   68   (1861) 8 Cox CC 498.
69   (PC, Eastern Africa) [1955] AC 197 at 203.   70   (DC) [1978] QB 490.
71   See *R* v *Macro* (CA) [1969] Crim LR 205.   72   *R* v *Birtles* (CA) [1969] 1 WLR 1047.
73   (1974) 60 Cr App R 59. In *R* v *McEvilly; R* v *Lee* (1973) 60 Cr App R 150, a differently constituted Court of Appeal appears to have assumed (obiter) that if the commission of an offence had been induced, which offence would not otherwise have been committed, the evidence should be rejected as unfairly obtained. This can no longer be regarded as sound.
74   40th ed., para. 1409.

self-evident', and is much stressed in the argument in that work. But since in any event, the evidence would be admissible, whether obtained unfairly or not, it seems pointless to pursue it here.

1.6.2 Discretion

The door having been firmly closed in terms of admissibility, the argument must be switched to discretion. Until recently, it was not possible to be certain, from the pronouncements of the courts, whether any discretion to exclude illegally or unfairly obtained evidence existed, and if so, within what guidelines it operated. There was certainly authority capable of supporting a general discretion. In *Kuruma* Lord Goddard CJ had said (75):

> No doubt in a criminal case the judge always has a discretion to disallow evidence if the strict rules of admissibility would operate unfairly against an accused. This was emphasised in the case before this Board of *Noor Mohamed* v *R*, and in the recent case in the House of Lords, *Harris* v *DPP* [(76)]. If, for instance, some admission of some piece of evidence, e.g., a document, had been obtained from a defendant by a trick, no doubt the judge might properly rule it out.

Following this pronouncement, the existence of such a discretion was reaffirmed by many courts, almost always while declining to accept that it should be, or have been, applied on the facts before them. In *Callis* v *Gunn* (77), Lord Parker CJ dealing with the question of the admissibility of fingerprint evidence, said:

> In my judgment fingerprint evidence taken in these circumstances is admissible in law subject to this overriding discretion. That discretion, as I understand it, would certainly be exercised by excluding the evidence if there was any suggestion of it having been obtained oppressively, by false representations, by a trick, by threats, by bribes, anything of that sort.

In *R* v *Murphy* (78) in a powerfully reasoned judgment, the Courts Martial Appeal Court for Northern Ireland went so far as to analyse the matters which should be taken into account in the exercise of discretion in such cases. The court was dealing with an extremely grave case, in which a serving soldier was charged with disclosing information which might be useful to an enemy. In relation to methods of obtaining evidence, the court said: 'A trick is a method as old as the constable in plain clothes . . . and the day has not come when it would be safe to say that the law could be enforced without resort to it.'

The court went on to hold that the proper test for the exercise of the discretion was one of balancing the gravity of the charge, the position of the defendant, and the methods used. In words subsequently adopted by the Privy Council (79), Lord McDermott said that unfairness to an accused was not susceptible of close definition, but:

> . . . must be judged of in the light of all the material facts and findings and all the surrounding circumstances. The position of the accused, the nature of the investigation, and the gravity or otherwise of the suspected offence may all be relevant. That is

75 (PC, Eastern Africa) [1955] AC 197 at 204.
76 [1952] AC 694.   77   (DC) [1964] 1 QB 495, at 502.
78 [1965] NI 138.   79   In *King* v *R* [1969] 1 AC 304 at 319.

not to say that the standard of fairness must bear some sort of inverse proportion to the extent to which the public interest may be involved, but different offences may pose different problems for the police and justify different methods.

The Divisional Court in *Jeffrey* v *Black,* a case in which the gravity of the offence and the problems posed thereby to the police bear an amusing contrast to those in *Murphy,* also asserted the existence of the discretion, for the purpose of holding that magistrates had been wrong in exercising it in favour of the defendant. Lord Widgery CJ stressed that the exercise of discretion should be comparatively rare, and added (80):

> But if the case is exceptional, if the case is such that not only have the police officers entered without authority, but they have been guilty of trickery or they have misled someone, or they have been oppressive or they have been unfair, or in other respects they have behaved in a manner which is morally reprehensible, then it is open to the justices to apply their discretion and decline to allow the particular evidence to be let in as part of the trial.

Lord Widgery pointed out that the discretion was not confined to any particular case, or to any particular court, but was '. . . a discretion which every judge has all the time in respect of all the evidence which is tendered by the prosecution.'

In *R* v *Payne* (81), the Court of Criminal Appeal held that discretion should have been exercised in favour of the defendant, in circumstances where he had been examined by a doctor at a police station, having been assured that it would be no part of the doctor's duty to examine him to assess his unfitness to drive. The doctor was subsequently called for that purpose. The precise reasoning behind the court's decision is not stated in terms of general principle, but it is quite clear that the judgment of Lord Parker CJ is based upon the unfairness to the defendant implicit in the way in which the evidence was obtained. In the later case of *R* v *Ameer and Lucas* (82) Judge Gillis sitting at the Central Criminal Court, following a lengthy trial within a trial, gave a reasoned judgment to support his exercise of the discretion for excluding evidence tendered by the prosecution in an entrapment case, taking into account the nature of the case as a whole, and of the evidence tendered which appeared to him to be highly unsatisfactory.

In the light of *R* v *Sang* (83), much of this weight of authority seems to be of no more than historical interest, but it remains important for the purpose of understanding the speeches of the House of Lords in that case. The defendant was charged with conspiracy to utter counterfeit United States banknotes. He alleged by counsel that he had been induced by an informer, acting on the instructions of the police, to commit an offence which, but for such persuasion, he would not have committed. As it was by then clear that this was no ground in law for seeking to exclude the evidence, counsel sought to investigate the matter in a trial within a trial, with a view to persuading the judge to exercise his discretion to exclude it. The trial judge, taking the view that he had no such discretion, and having heard argument on the basis that what the defendant alleged was true, ruled accordingly (84). The Court of Appeal dismissed an appeal against convic-

---

80   [1978]QB 490 at 498.   81   [1963] 1 WLR 637.
82   (CA) [1977] Crim LR 104; a judgment which is entitled to rather more respect than has been accorded to it by the appellate courts.
83   (HL) [1979] 3 WLR 263
84   The judge's view was supported by some authority, for example the decision of the Court of Appeal in *R* v *Willis* [1976] Crim LR 127.

tion, and the defendant appealed to the House of Lords. The House of Lords held:

(a)   That the judge had a general discretion to refuse to admit evidence tendered by the prosecution on the ground that its probative value was outweighed by its prejudicial effect. (This part of the decision was considered in 1.5.2.3, ante.)

(b)   That with the exception of evidence consisting of admissions and confessions and other evidence obtained from the accused after the commission of the offence (for example, documentary evidence) (85), the judge had no discretion to exclude evidence obtained by improper or unfair means, the court being concerned with the relevance of the evidence and not its source.

The essence of the decision is that, although there is always a discretion of the kind described in 1.5, ante, to exclude evidence because to admit that evidence at the trial would be unfair (and there may be cases where evidence illegally or unfairly obtained may fall into this category), there is no discretion to exclude because the method by which the evidence was obtained was unfair. The use, not the source, of the evidence is the court's concern. The result is that the law relating to evidence illegally or unfairly obtained is, in this respect, the same as that pertaining to any other evidence, except confessions and other evidence obtained from the defendant (86).

The House of Lords acknowledged, as they were bound to acknowledge, the weight of existing authority. Faced with this, Lord Diplock and Viscount Dilhorne attacked the tree at the root. Of Lord Goddard's words in *Kuruma,* Lord Diplock said (87):

That statement was not, in my view, ever intended to acknowledge the existence of any wider discretion than to exclude (1) admissible evidence which would probably have a prejudicial influence upon the minds of the jury that would be out of proportion to its true evidential value; and (2) evidence tantamount to a self-incriminatory admission which was obtained from the defendant, after the offence had been committed, by means which would justify a judge in excluding an actual confession which had the like self-incriminating effect. As a matter of language, although not as a matter of application, the subsequent dicta go much further than this; but in so far as they do so they have never yet been considered by this House.

Viscount Dilhorne said, dealing with the observations in *Callis* v *Gunn* and *Jeffrey* v *Black* (88):

With great respect I do not think that these observations were correct. I have not been able to find any authority for the general principle enunciated by Lord Parker or for these statements by him and by Lord Widgery. If there is any authority for it, it conflicts with Lord Goddard's statement in *Kuruma* v *R* that the court is not concerned with how evidence is obtained.

---

85   The admissibility of confessions and the exercise of discretion in such cases is subject to separate and well established rules, which are not affected by *Sang*. See Chapter 7, post. The reference to 'other evidence obtained from the accused' is to incriminating documents or material of any other kind obtained by search or inquiry.
86   Because of the requirements relating to confessions (Chapter 7, Section A, post) a confession obtained even by an innocent misrepresentation may have to be excluded, and such a course was taken by Melford Stevenson J in *R* v *Kwabena Poku* [1978] Crim LR 488, apparently as a matter of law, rather than discretion.
87   [1979] 3 WLR 263 at 270–1. And see per Viscount Dilhorne at 274.
88   Ibid at 275.

It is submitted with respect that neither of these passages is tenable in the light of the authorities to which they refer, and in particular both seem to overlook the clear tenor of Lord Goddard's remarks with regard to discretion in *Kuruma*. Nonetheless, there is certainly no doubt that the House of Lords was entitled to depart from the view taken in the earlier cases, which had not received unambiguous support from the House of Lords. Lord Fraser (89) found that 'it is not easy to see how evidence obtained from other sources [than the defendant], even if the means for obtaining it were improper, could lead to the accused being denied a fair trial.' Doubtless in many cases this will be so, and even if it were not, the general discretion remains to ensure that a fair trial is had. But it should be appreciated that *Sang* is a far-reaching decision, which does not, with respect, justify the opening words of Lord Salmon's speech (90). It has the effect of laying down for the first time that confessions, and other incriminating material obtained from the accused after commission of the offence, are now the only kinds of evidence known to English law that may be excluded, even as a matter of discretion, because of the manner in which they have been obtained.

1.7 The best-evidence rule

The 'best-evidence' rule is one of the ghosts of the law of evidence. It has never enjoyed any really certain existence, having originated, so far as can be ascertained, at some time during the eighteenth century and having since made ephemeral appearances, somewhat after the manner of a comet, usually when least expected. The rule itself is a relatively straightforward one, which was stated by Lord Hardwicke LC in *Omychund v Barker* (91) to be that: 'The judges and sages of the law have laid it down that there is but one general rule of evidence, the best that the nature of the case will admit.'

The rule is in any case a sound one in terms of weight, but the main problem presented is its effect on admissibility. Lord Hardwicke's dictum was given in the context of allowing to be admitted the evidence of a witness who, under the previous rules of common law, was incompetent to take the oath and so to give evidence. But apart from cases of necessity, such as those where a material witness was dead, or the original of a document lost, the rule was never employed to justify the admission of evidence on the ground that a party need do no more than produce the best evidence available in the circumstances of the case. And even the cases of necessity were developed by the courts simply as exceptions to the rule against hearsay, or the rule requiring strict proof of the contents of documents, without reference to a general best-evidence rule. What is more significant is that, had the rule been one of general application, it might have justified the admission of a good deal of hearsay evidence which could be fairly described as the best evidence available, but which was in fact never allowed to be admitted at common law, even in the absence of other evidence.

The history of the rule therefore suggests that evidence has always been held admissible or inadmissible by reference to specific rules of law, and not in accordance with any general theory that the best available evidence must be accepted, whatever form it may take. But the rule was used during the eighteenth and nineteenth centuries to justify the exclusion of evidence tendered of a fact, when 'better' evidence might have been called. Thus, oral evidence of the condition of material objects was rejected on the ground that

89   Ibid at 283–4.
90   'My Lords, this is a strange appeal which plainly has no hope of succeeding', Ibid at 276. Later, at 279, Lord Salmon said that he did 'not propose to comment upon the obiter dicta in *Callis v Gunn* or in *Jeffrey v Black*'.
91   (1745) 1 Atk 21 at 49.

such objects might have been produced (92), and circumstantial evidence of an event on the ground that direct evidence might have been called (93). But the exclusion was never absolute, and was gradually repudiated. Today, its appearance is rare, although it arose intriguingly in *R* v *Quinn; R* v *Bloom* (94) in which the Court of Criminal Appeal rejected an argument that the trial judge ought to have permitted the showing to the jury of a film depicting strip-tease acts, the nature of which was said to render the defendants guilty of keeping a disorderly house. The film had been made by the defence as a reconstruction of the acts, some three months after the events complained of, and was supported by evidence that it accurately depicted the acts in question. Ashworth J, giving the judgment of the court, pointed out that a forensic demonstration was not to be given in the form of a reconstruction made privately for use at trial, and added:

> Indeed, in this case, it was admitted that some of the movements in the film (for instance, that of a snake used in one scene) could not be said with any certainty to be the same movements as were made at the material time. In our judgment, this objection goes not only to weight, as was argued, but to admissibility: it is not the best evidence.

It can be said with some certainty today that the rule, such as it was, is virtually extinct and that evidence which satisfies the specific rules of admissibility will be admitted. The rule has, however, one echo in the requirement that primary evidence (usually the original) be adduced to prove the contents of a document relied upon as direct evidence, secondary evidence (copies or oral evidence) of the contents being inadmissible, except, in certain circumstances. The detail of this requirement is considered in 16.2, post.

Before parting with the best-evidence rule, it is also worth noting that, quite apart from any question of admissibility, it is clearly desirable that the best evidence be produced which is available, from the point of view of weight, and that the absence of more satisfactory evidence be accounted for, if possible. It is a legitimate matter for comment that more persuasive evidence, or more reliable evidence of a fact, has been ignored in favour of evidence which is demonstrably less so.

B: PROOF WITHOUT EVIDENCE

1.8   When evidence may not be required

In view of the remarks made at the beginning of section A about the importance of evidence in the establishment of any claim or charge, the title of this section may occasion some surprise. But there are some circumstances in which the court will accept, as established, facts in issue, or relevant facts, without requiring proof or complete proof by means of evidence. The cases to be considered under this head are all self-explanatory, and operate to give effect to what may be thought (with the exception of presumptions, perhaps) to be fairly sensible ways of saving time and costs. The cases are (a) where the fact is formally admitted for the purposes of the proceedings, (b) where a notorious or readily demonstrable fact is 'judicially noticed' and (c) where a fact is presumed to be true in favour of the party seeking to prove it.

92   *Chenie* v *Watson* (NP) (1797) Peake Add Cas 123.   93   *Williams* v *East India Co.* (1802) 3 East 192.
94   [1962] 2 QB 245. It is interesting to speculate what the best evidence would have been.

1.9 Formal admissions

Proof may be dispensed with altogether where a fact is formally admitted for the purposes of the proceedings, and so ceases to be in dispute between the parties. Before the coming into force of s. 10 of the Criminal Justice Act 1967 formal admissions were possible only in civil cases, but now may be made also in criminal cases.

1.9.1 Civil cases

In civil cases, formal admissions may be made in various ways. If a fact is in issue, it may be admitted on the pleadings, and if so admitted, the fact is almost invariably deemed to be conclusively established against the admitting party unless the admission is deleted by amendment (95). Formal admissions may also be made in response to a notice to admit or to interrogatories, or at any stage by agreement between the parties before or at trial. In the latter event, the admissions should be in written form and signed by or on behalf of each party concerned.

The effect of the admission is such that a party may rely on any fact admitted, which is in his favour, for any purpose (including the signing of judgment, if the admission extends to all the facts in issue). Evidence concerning a fact admitted is neither needed nor admissible. Care must be taken not to rely solely on admissions, where some further inference falls to be drawn from the facts admitted before judgment can follow; the court will act upon admitted facts, but will require evidence on any further facts necessary for success in the case. When a formal admission is made in civil proceedings it is binding only for the purpose of those proceedings, but in such proceedings is conclusive of the facts admitted.

1.9.2 Criminal cases

By s. 10 of the Criminal Justice Act 1967:

(1) Subject to the provisions of this section, any fact of which oral evidence may be given in any criminal proceedings may be admitted for the purpose of those proceedings by or on behalf of the prosecutor or defendant, and the admission by any party of any such fact under this section shall as against that party be conclusive evidence in those proceedings of the fact admitted.

(2) An admission under this section —

(a) may be made before or at the proceedings;

(b) if made otherwise than in court, shall be in writing;

(c) if made in writing by an individual, shall purport to be signed by the person making it . . .;

(d) if made on behalf of a defendant who is an individual, shall be made by his counsel or solicitor;

(e) if made at any stage before the trial by a defendant who is an individual, must be approved by his counsel or solicitor (whether at the time it was made or subsequently) before or at the proceedings in question.

(3) An admission under this section for the purpose of proceedings relating to any matter shall be treated as an admission for the purpose of any subsequent

---

95 An admission may also be made by default of pleading, or by failing in certain cases to traverse a fact by a pleading: see RSC, Ord.27, r. 1; Ord.18, r. 13 and r. 14. For the practice in the county court see CCR, Ord.9 rr. 1–3; Ord.20. An admission in a pleading which is amended to delete it may sometimes be relied upon as an informal admission: see 7.1, post.

criminal proceedings relating to that matter (including any appeal or retrial).

(4)   An admission under this section may with the leave of the court be withdrawn in
        the proceedings for the purpose of which it is made or any subsequent criminal
        proceedings relating to the same matter.

The section provides a self-contained code for formal admissions in criminal cases, which had previously not been possible. The major differences between criminal procedure and the common-law practice in civil cases are the requirements in s. 10(2) concerning form and approval in certain circumstances and the possibility of withdrawal of the admission with leave of the court under s. 10(4). Unless withdrawn, however, the admission is similarly conclusive and presumably leave should be granted only where there is a real and appreciable risk that an admission has been made inadvisedly, or is for any reason suspect. There is no objection of principle to a formal admission by the defence of all the facts alleged by the prosecution, where these are not in dispute and the defence turns on other matters but care must be taken to ensure that the jury appreciate the significance of what is being done, and can distinguish the facts as admitted from any argument addressed to them (96). The admissions should, and sometimes must be, in writing, but if they are not, should at least be in a form capable of being accurately recorded in the shorthand note (97).

Two general matters merit observation, with respect to both civil and criminal proceedings. The first is that formal admissions must be distinguished carefully from the informal admissions and confessions dealt with in Chapter 7, Sections A and B, post. The latter are merely pieces of evidence tendered among others as constituting evidence against a party supplied by his own acts and words, and may be rejected by the court as inadmissible or of negligible weight, or be made the subject of evidence to contradict or discredit them; they are in no sense formal admissions and are most certainly not conclusive. The second is that in both civil and criminal cases, it is the duty of legal advisers to consider what formal admissions, if any, can and should properly be made on behalf of their clients for the purposes of any proceedings in which they are engaged. Of course, care must be taken not to make unjustified admissions, but failure to admit facts which are not really disputed wastes time and costs, and the latter may be visited on the client.

1.10   Judicial notice

By a rule applicable both to civil and criminal cases generally, no evidence is required of a fact of which the court will take judicial notice, that is to say a fact of which the court will acknowledge the truth without the necessity for proof. Facts which will be judicially noticed are those which are notorious, or which are readily demonstrable by reference to proper sources. If the fact is not one which will be judicially noticed, it must be proved by evidence. There are obviously very many facts which will be judicially noticed, and the process is capable of saving a great deal of time which would otherwise be spent in calling the substantial volumes of evidence often curiously necessary to prove the most self-evident facts. As Professor Cross has demonstrated (98), the process of judicial notice is carried on habitually in almost every case which comes before the courts, often without being recognised as such, because of numerous tacit assumptions; the relevance of

96   *R* v *Lewis* (CA) [1971] Crim LR 414.   97   *R* v *Lennard* (CA) [1973] 1 WLR 483.
98   *Evidence*, 5th ed., p. 161–2.

the defendant's possession of a jemmy to a charge of burglary against him is based on an assumption of fact that a jemmy is frequently employed for the purposes of burglary. We must look, however, principally at judicial notice in the sense of conscious application of the judicial mind to the facts concerned. This in turn involves consideration of (a) notice of notorious facts, (b) notice after reference to sources. In addition there are some cases where judicial notice is to be taken by statute, generally of seals and their authenticating or official devices; these need not be considered specifically here.

1.10.1 *Notorious facts*

Matters of common knowledge, which are too notorious to be capable of serious dispute or debate will be judicially noticed without reference to any source. There are so many instances in the decided cases, and so many more potential subjects of such notice that any attempt at compilation would be pointless, but it would seem that Professor Cross's category of tacit notice would probably fall under this head. The flavour of the subject will be sufficiently apparent by reference to a few examples, and those most beloved of textbook writers include the facts that a fortnight is too short a period for human gestation (99), that cats are normally kept for domestic purposes (100), that criminals have unhappy lives (101) and that the advancement of learning is among the purposes for which the University of Oxford exists (102). The imagination will readily supply a fund of similarly notorious facts in circumstances of all kinds, but those given also serve to suggest the difficulties of proof by evidence which are surmounted by judicial notice in relation to apparently obvious facts.

1.10.2 *Notice after reference*

This type of notice, while undoubtedly well established, creates one or two problems of a kind which are by no means purely theoretical, in that it explores very keenly the dividing line between the taking of judicial notice and the reception of evidence. The actual differences between the two processes are clear. Judicial notice involves a finding of fact by the judge, after which the jury (if there is one) should be directed on the basis that the fact is established. It involves the proposition that no evidence should be admissible to contradict directly the fact judicially noticed. Judicial notice creates a precedent in law, at any rate coterminous with the demonstrability of the truth of the fact noticed: judicial notice that camels are domestic animals may be taken as a universal truth affecting camels generally (103), whereas the status of a particular foreign sovereign may be noticeable only until the next *coup d'état,* and must be established anew by reference in each case. But the taking of evidence has none of these characteristics. Matters sought to be established by evidence are questions of fact for the jury. Save in the rare case of legally conclusive evidence, evidence may always be contradicted and explained by contrary evidence. Evidence has effect for the purposes of the instant proceedings only, and (save for the very limited possibility of estoppel) has no effect to prove facts in any other proceedings. Despite these distinctions, however, the two processes come very close where the judge makes reference to a source for the purpose of informing himself, and thereafter taking judicial notice.

---

99   *R* v *Luffe* (1807) 8 East 193. But not curiously, that 360 days is too long: see *Preston-Jones* v *Preston-Jones* (HL) [1951] AC 391.
100   *Nye* v *Niblett and Others* (DC) [1918] 1 KB 23.   101   *Burns* v *Edman* [1970] 2 QB 541.
102   *Oxford Poor Rate Case* (1857) 8 E & B 184; at the present author's university, this decision was generally regarded as a common-law exception based on the obvious difficulty of proving such a proposition by evidence.
103   *McQuaker* v *Goddard* (CA) [1940] 1 KB 687.

It seems clear that the judge should take judicial notice, whether or not he refers to any source, only of facts which appear to him, in the light of his information, to be either sufficiently notorious or to be readily demonstrable. In *Brune* v *Thompson* (104), it was held that judicial notice could not be taken that part of the Tower of London lay within the City of London, it being equally notorious that part of it lay in the county of Middlesex. It is for the party inviting judicial notice to provide any necessary source of reference, and the judge may refuse to notice any fact for which a proper reference is not provided, a course adopted by Lord Ellenborough in *Van Omeron* v *Dowick* (105), when declining to notice a royal proclamation in the absence of the official *Gazette* containing it. It is obviously desirable that all those facts which in reality require evidence should be left to be proved by evidence, and not short-circuited by the taking of judicial notice.

Judicial notice after reference is taken of the following matters, which are shortly stated here (106):

(a)   Of the existence and contents of statutes and of the law of England (including, now, the law of the European Communities); of the procedure and privileges of both Houses of Parliament; and of the jurisdiction and rules of each division of the High Court.

(b)   Of customs which have been settled by judicial decision, or certified to and recorded in any division of the High Court, such as those of the City of London certified by the Recorder of London. Recent customs must have been recognised more than once by judicial decision, but there is no other requirement concerning frequency of recognition, and the courts incline against requiring proof by evidence over and over of apparently well established customs (107).

(c)   Of professional practice, for example that of the Ordnance Survey (108) or of conveyancers (109) in interpreting references on maps or conveyancing documents.

(d)   Of political matters and affairs of state, or the view of the government on such matters. The practice in such cases is to obtain and act upon the certificate of the Secretary of State, which is for this purpose a source from which the facts contained in it are readily demonstrable, and authoritatively stated (110).

(e)   Readily demonstrable public facts, for example of historical or geographical fact, or the meaning of words in common usage. For these purposes, reference may be made to apparently objective and authoritative public works, such as histories, maps and dictionaries.

The matters referred to in (d) and (e) above pose a problem of demarcation as between evidence and judicial notice, inasmuch as facts of public concern, stated in public documents, may be proved by evidence of the contents of those documents. The rule is one of common law, but in civil cases, now enjoys the statutory authority of s. 9 of the Civil Evidence Act 1968 in the cases there referred to (111). So far as the matters in

104   (1842) 2 QB 789.   105   (NP) (1809) 2 Camp 42.
106   The detail of these matters is comprehensively set out, together with the relevant authorities, in Phipson, *Evidence*, 12th ed. paras 49 et seq.
107   *Brandao* v *Barnett* (HL) (1846) 12 Cl & F 787; *George* v *Davies* (DC) [1911] 2 KB 445.
108   *Davey* v *Harrow Corporation* (CA) [1958] 1 QB 60 at 69.   109   *Re Rosher* (1884) 26 ChD 801.
110   The court regards itself incompetent to judge such matters, and will defer to the view of the responsible minister on behalf of the government: *Duff Development Co. Ltd* v *Government of Kelantan* (HL) [1924] AC 797; *The Parlement Belge* (CA) (1880) 5 PD 197; *Mighell* v *Sultan of Johore* (CA) [1894] 1 QB 149.
111   See generally 6.8 post.

(e) are concerned, it may be that the use of such works before taking judicial notice must be confined to what Phipson (112) calls 'refreshing the memory of the judge', in the sense that only notorious or readily demonstrable facts so ascertained may be noticed, any others being a proper subject for evidence. The matters in (d) are in practice more easily disposed of. In practice a certificate of the Secretary of State is invariably regarded as conclusive evidence of the truth of any statement it makes concerning foreign affairs, the status of foreign sovereigns and governments, relations with or between foreign powers and so on. Whether its contents are regarded as matters of conclusive evidence or of judicial notice makes little real difference of practice, despite the varying pronouncements on the subject (113).

There is no such easy solution, however, to two far more formidable and practically significant problems. These arise: (a) where the court takes judicial notice after receiving evidence on the fact noticed; and (b) where the process of judicial notice is bound up with personal knowledge on the part of the judge.

1.10.2.1 Judicial notice after evidence. There seems to be no doubt that a judge may inform himself by hearing evidence, as well as by reference to works, on matters which he is invited to notice judicially. The *locus classicus* is *McQuaker* v *Goddard* (114). Branson J, faced with the problem of deciding whether a camel was a wild or domestic animal for the purpose of the common-law rules governing liability for animals, not only heard a great deal of conflicting expert evidence about the behaviour of camels, but himself consulted books on the subject. Having done so, the learned judge took judicial notice of the fact that the camel was a domestic animal. Both the trial judge, and Clauson LJ in the Court of Appeal, which upheld the decision, made it clear that the process was one of judicial notice, and that the evidence was directed only at assisting the judge to come to his view. Although it may be conducive to the peace of mind of camels and their owners to have a view of them embedded in precedent, it is by no means easy to see how a fact could properly be described as either 'notorious' or 'readily demonstrable', while attracting such a difference of expert opinion, and if the same process could be applied to any such case, the function of a tribunal of fact in assessing evidence might be seriously eroded. The fact that a judge (or jury) forms a view of evidence given in one case cannot generally assist another tribunal of fact in a subsequent case. But it is submitted that this use of judicial notice is proper, provided that it is restricted to the notice of constant facts (such as the nature of camels) which are not dependent upon the facts of any given case.

1.10.2.2 Personal knowledge. The question to what extent a judge may make use of any personal knowledge which he may have of the facts canvassed before him, is an unresolved one. It seems clear that any person involved in a case as a member of a tribunal of fact may not act on his personal knowledge of the particular facts of a case, in the sense of supplementing the evidence from fortuitous personal knowledge (115). But in a more general sense, it has been held that, 'properly and within reasonable limits', a judge may apply such general knowledge as he may have of the subject-matter to the

---

112 *Evidence*, 12th ed. para 60.
113 In *Duff Development Co. Ltd* v *Government of Kelantan* (HL) [1924] AC 797, Lords Finlay and Sumner seem to contradict each other on the point, see at 813 and 824.
114 [1940] 1 KB 687.
115 If a member of the tribunal of fact has such particular knowledge then he should be sworn and give evidence but play no further part judicially in the case: *R (Giant's Causeway etc. Tramway Co.)* v *Antrim Justices* [1895] 2 IR 603; cf *R* v *Antrim Justices* [1901] 2 IR 133.

process of understanding and evaluating the evidence (116). Outside such limits, a judge should exclude from his mind such personal knowledge as he has, and it would seem wrong for him either to act evidentially on such knowledge, or to use that knowledge in the process of judicial notice. Justices and jurors have been held to be entitled to make use of such local or general knowledge as they may have. In *Ingram* v *Percival* (117), it was held that justices had acted properly in making use of their local knowledge of tidal conditions. But in *Wetherall* v *Harrison* (118), while holding that the Bench had been entitled to take into account the professional knowledge of one of their number in evaluating medical evidence called for the prosecution, and to draw on their own wartime experience of inoculations, the Divisional Court stressed that such knowledge might be drawn on only to evaluate evidence given, and not used as evidence in itself. So far as justices (and jurors) are concerned, the court accepted that they must be free to draw on such knowledge, if only because they are not trained judicially to exclude extraneous matters from their minds, but the rule is anyway one of common sense given that one has local benches and juries.

In a sense, the use of such knowledge may be said to be a form of subjective judicial notice, but it is obvious from the above observations that it is qualitatively very different from true judicial notice, and it is probably best regarded as one means open to the judge of testing the weight of the evidence before him. Certainly the preponderance of authority would not extend the taking of judicial notice to facts within the personal knowledge of a judge or magistrate, simply because personal knowledge does not make a fact either notorious or readily demonstrable; only common or readily ascertainable knowledge would appear to have that effect. This is not to say that a court should sit with its mind switched off, merely that there must be a judicial exercise of the mind to keep the available information in its proper place (119).

1.11 Presumptions

Where a presumption operates in favour of a party who seeks to prove a fact, the court is entitled to find established and to act on that fact, notwithstanding that no evidence is called to prove it, or that the evidence to prove it may be insufficient. Thus, where a fact is presumed in favour of a party, the burden of disproving that fact (rebutting the presumption) lies upon his opponent, and unless the opponent succeeds in discharging that burden, the court will find against him on that fact. A presumption is a device for fixing the burden of proof in relation to certain facts, notwithstanding the incidence of the burden of proof in relation to the case generally. It would be comforting to suppose that presumed facts had in common some feature which made it reasonable, in the absence of some unusual factor which required to be demonstrated in order to displace the normal order of things, which justified their occupying this privileged position, but no such feature is discernible. Indeed, presumptions have defied most attempts to classify them coherently. In this book, classification will be kept to a minimum, and we shall concentrate on understanding how presumptions work, with the aid of reference to the most common and important of them.

116 *Reynolds* v *Llanelly Associated Tinplate Co. Ltd* (CA) [1948] 1 All ER 140 (trial judge wrong to make use of personal knowledge in evaluating prospects of a workman with certain skills and of certain age).
117 (DC) [1969] 1 QB 548.   118 (DC) [1976] QB 773.
119 Where a tribunal sits as a specialist body, for example an industrial tribunal, it may make much freer use of its expertise, and act on its own view: *Dugdale* v *Kraft Foods Ltd* [1976] (EAT) 1 WLR 1288; but the rule appears to extend only to such specialist bodies carrying out a specialist statutory function.

In its true sense, a presumption requires two things: (a) that certain facts shall be proved (the 'primary facts'); and (b) that those facts being proved, some other fact (the 'presumed fact') shall be taken by the court to be true in the absence of evidence to the contrary. Instances of this are the presumption of a valid marriage, on proof that the parties have been through a ceremony of marriage, and the presumption of legitimacy on proof that the child was born during lawful wedlock or within the normal period of gestation after the termination of such lawful wedlock. The textbooks tend to describe such cases as 'rebuttable presumptions of law', but the phrase is necessary only if it is accepted that the term 'presumption' can properly be applied to certain quite different cases, which will now be distinguished:

(a)   Rules of law which provide that some fact shall be taken in all cases to be true,. without proof of any primary fact, until the contrary is proved. Into this category fall the 'presumptions' of innocence and sanity. These are really no more than expressions of the incidence of the burden of proof in such cases. In one sense, any fact may be said to be true unless somebody proves the contrary, but in reality, such facts fall to be proved in accordance with the normal rules of evidence, including the burden of proof: this is dealt with in Chapter 3, post.

(b)   Rules of law which preclude the assertion of some necessary fact, without which cases of a certain sort cannot be maintained. Such are the rules that a child under the age of ten cannot be guilty of a criminal offence, and that a boy under fourteen cannot be guilty of rape. It is now almost universally agreed that such rules are rules of substantive law, and have nothing to do with the rules of evidence. Though sometimes termed 'irrebuttable' or 'conclusive' presumptions, they are clearly not presumptions at all. An irrebuttable presumption is a contradiction in terms.

(c)   Inferences of common sense, which a tribunal of fact may (purely as a question of fact), but need not, draw, having regard to the recurrence or common incidence of certain items of circumstantial evidence, are sometimes known as 'presumptions of fact'. The phrase fully justifies Phipson's stricture that (120), 'in reality it is no more than a slightly grandiose term for the ordinary processes of judicial reasoning about facts.' The phrase expresses the relationship between pieces of circumstantial evidence, and facts in issue or relevant facts in the case. Where a defendant is found in possession of recently stolen goods, or is caught in the act of destroying some item of evidence, then obviously it is open to a jury to draw the inference and find proved that he knew or believed the goods to be stolen, or that the evidence was unfavourable to him, as the case may be. To speak of a presumption is unnecessary and misleading, because the jury are not in any circumstances bound to draw that inference, even if no evidence is called for the defence. Much of the difficulty arises because of inexact usage, both judicial and extra-judicial. The high-water mark of the inexactitude led the House of Lords in *DPP* v *Smith* (121) to seek to elevate into a principle of law, effectively into a true presumption, the fairly obvious proposition of common sense that a man apparently in normal control of his faculties should be taken to have intended the natural and probable consequences of his act. In the course of his speech, with which the other Lords agreed, Viscount Kilmuir went so far as to say that it did not matter whether one called it a presumption of law or of fact. By s. 8 of the Criminal Justice Act 1967, Parliament put the matter back where it

---

120   *Evidence*, 12th ed. para 2116.
121   [1961] AC 290.

belonged — in the area of fact for the jury. The section is worth citing in full, because it expresses very well how such inferences operate:

A court or jury, in determining whether a person has committed an offence, —
(a)   shall not be bound in law to infer that he intended or foresaw a result of his actions by reason only of its being a natural and probable consequence of those actions; but
(b)   shall decide whether he did intend or foresee that result by reference to all the evidence, drawing such inferences from the evidence as appear proper in the circumstances.

Thus reduced into real terms, the misuse of the word 'presumption', lacking as it does any legal force in this context, is exposed. None of this makes it any less likely that a jury will act on such evidence in appropriate cases.

The three misuses of the word 'presumption' described above will not be further considered, and we shall now turn to the most important true presumptions, rebuttable presumptions of law, in relation to which on proof of some primary fact or facts, the court will find proved a presumed fact, in the absence of evidence to the contrary. It is not proposed to consider the presumptions arising from possession of or title to land, or the maxim *res ipsa loquitur,* for which reference should be made elsewhere in works dealing with the substantive law. The law relating to the statutory presumptions arising under s. 11 and s. 12 of the Civil Evidence Act 1968 is dealt with in 10.10, and that relating to certain presumptions about the due execution of documents in 16.3.3, post.

1.11.1   Presumption of legitimacy
It will be presumed that a child is the legitimate child of a husband and wife, and accordingly that access took place between them resulting in conception of the child, on proof of the following primary facts: (a) that the child was born to the wife; (b) that it was born during lawful wedlock or within the normal period of gestation after wedlock has ended; and (c) that the husband was alive at the date of conception.

The history of this presumption is hedged about with historical considerations, principally the concern of the common law not to permit proceedings to bastardise children and so subject them to the then considerable stigma of illegitimacy. The presumption itself remains useful, although its force has been somewhat weakened by the provision now embodied in s. 43(1) of the Matrimonial Causes Act 1973 that the evidence of a husband or wife is admissible in any proceedings to prove that intercourse did or did not take place between them during any period, and that in s. 16(4) of the Civil Evidence Act 1968 that either spouse is compellable to give evidence of such matters in civil proceedings, though not in criminal.

Proof of the primary facts must be properly made. But conversely the mere fact of voluntary separation during the marriage (122) or the mere fact that divorce proceedings have been commenced or a decree nisi granted (123), or even that at the time of the birth the mother has remarried following decree absolute (124) will not affect the operation of the presumption, if they are so proved. However, where the separation is by virtue of a

---

122   *Ettenfield* v *Ettenfield* (CA) [1940] P 96.   123   *Knowles* v *Knowles* [1962] P 161.
124   *Maturin* v *Attorney-General* [1938] 2 All ER 214; *Re Overbury, Sheppard* v *Matthews and Others* [1955] Ch 122.

court order, be it a non-cohabitation clause in an order of magistrates or a decree of judicial separation, the presumption will be effective against the contrary presumption that the order of the court was obeyed (125). Where the child is born more than nine months after such an order is made, it will be presumed to be illegitimate (126).

At common law, there was originally a rule of law precluding proceedings to bastardise a child if, at the time of conception, the husband was 'within the four seas', so that lawful access could have taken place. Although this rule of law was abrogated, it left in its wake much uncertainty about what evidence was needed to rebut the newer presumption of legitimacy. The decisions of the House of Lords in *Preston-Jones* v *Preston-Jones* (127) and *Blyth* v *Blyth* (128) failed to resolve the position clearly, and eventually it was provided for by s. 26 of the Family Law Reform Act 1969 by which:

Any presumption of law as to the legitimacy or illegitimacy of any person may in any civil proceedings be rebutted by evidence which shows that it is more probable than not that that person is illegitimate or legitimate, as the case may be, and it shall not be necessary to prove that fact beyond reasonable doubt in order to rebut the presumption.

The presumption is, of course, comparatively unlikely to be of significance in criminal proceedings, and despite the tacit suggestion in the section that the higher standard might apply to such proceedings, it is submitted that it would depend entirely on whether the prosecution or the defence sought to rebut the presumption. It is most improbable that the defence would be subjected to such a standard in view of the general rule affecting the standard of proof in criminal cases (as to which see Chapter 3, post). In civil cases, the section seems to have rendered it unnecessary to consider the older authorities on whether certain kinds of evidence were capable of rebutting the presumption; evidence of intercourse by the wife with other men, or of the husband's impotence or frequent absence, or evidence derived from blood tests, or any other admissible evidence may be brought to rebut it. But the provision shows clearly how the presumption works: the party alleging legitimacy may rely upon it unless and until evidence is brought to the contrary to the required standard of proof; he need not himself offer evidence to support it once he proves the primary facts.

1.11.2 Presumptions of marriage

It will be presumed that a man and woman are validly married on proof of either of the alternative primary facts: (a) that they went through a ceremony of marriage; or (b) that they have cohabited together. The presumption extends to include the necessary presumption of formal capacity to marry.

In *Piers and Another* v *Piers* (129) where the marriage had been celebrated in a private house and there was no evidence that the necessary special licence had been obtained, the presumption was held nevertheless to apply. And where cohabitation is shown, the presumption is not rebutted merely where it is shown that such cohabitation preceded any ceremony between the parties (130) or even by evidence that the marriage, if celebrated, took place under a system of law which required registration of it, and that no entry appeared in the relevant register (131).

---

125 *Hetherington* v *Hetherington* (1887) 12 PD 112.   126 Ibid.
127 [1951] AC 391.   128 [1966] AC 643.
129 (HL) (1849) 2 HL Cas 331.   130 *Hill* v *Hill* (PC, Barbados) [1959] 1 WLR 127.
131 *Re Taplin, Watson* v *Tate* [1937] 3 All ER 105.

The effect is that the presumption is a strong one, although its importance has naturally declined somewhat with the advent of modern records, which are admissible in evidence. The presumption may not be employed to prove the validity of an alleged existing marriage in prosecutions for bigamy; in such a case, the existing valid marriage must be proved by direct evidence that the defendant was a party to a ceremony which resulted in a valid marriage, though apart from the identity of the defendant, this may be proved by production of a certified copy of the entry in the relevant register (132).

It is clear that strong evidence is needed to rebut the presumption, where it applies. In *Piers and Another* v *Piers* Lord Cottenham LC, citing with approval words from older authority said (133): 'The presumption of law is not lightly to be repelled. It is not to be broken in upon or shaken by a mere balance of probability. The evidence for the purpose of repelling it must be strong, distinct, satisfactory and conclusive.' The word 'conclusive' has been rightly criticised as begging the issue, but it is apparent that strong evidence is necessary. In *Mahadervan* v *Mahadervan* (134), the Divisional Court held that the presumption might be rebutted only by evidence which satisfied the court beyond any reasonable doubt that the marriage was not a valid one, though today it might well be held that the ordinary civil standard of proof applies (see 3.9, post). The evidence must nonetheless be cogent. Evidence of incapacity (135) or of a valid prior marriage (136) will suffice, but not where the prior marriage is of doubtful validity (137).

In *Mahadervan* v *Mahadervan*, it was argued that the presumption did not apply in favour of a foreign marriage, at least where such marriage, if proved, would invalidate an English one celebrated subsequently. Of this argument, Sir Jocelyn Simon P said (138):

To accept it would give expression to a legal chauvinism that has no place in any rational system of private international law. Our courts in my view apply exactly the same weight of presumption in favour of a foreign marriage as of an English one, and the nationality of any later marriage brought into question is quite immaterial.

1.11.3   Presumption of death

A person will be presumed to have died on proof of the following primary facts: (a) that there is no acceptable evidence that the subject has been alive at some time during a continuous period of seven years or more; (b) that there are persons likely to have heard from him, had he been alive, who have not heard of him during that period; and (c) that all due inquiries have been made with a view to locating the subject, without success (139).

The existence of a person likely to have heard of the subject appears to be a necessary requirement, and was so treated by Sachs J in his judgment in the leading modern case of *Chard* v *Chard* (139). The learned judge refused to presume a wife to be dead, even though there was no evidence that she had been alive since 1918; the issue was whether she was alive in 1933 (when she would have been aged 43) in which year the husband had gone through a ceremony of marriage with the petitioner, who now sought a decree of

---

132   *R* v *Kay* (1887) 16 Cox CC 292; in *R* v *Shaw* (1943) 60 TLR 344, where evidence was given of a ceremony and the defendant did not give evidence, the Court of Criminal Appeal held the evidence to be sufficient. The prior marriage may sometimes be proved by admission by the defendant; but see 7.3, post.
133   2 HL Cas 331 at 362, citing *Morris (otherwise Williams)* v *Davies and Another* (1837) (HL) 5 Cl & F 163 at 265, per Lord Lyndhurst.
134   [1964] P 233.   135   *Tweney* v *Tweney* [1946] P 180
136   *Gatty and Gatty* v *Attorney-General* [1951] P 444   137   *Taylor* v *Taylor* [1967] P 25
138   (DC) [1964] P 233 at 247.
139   *Chard* v *Chard* [1956] P 259, per Sachs J at 272.

nullity based on its bigamous character. The husband had spent most of the intervening period in prison, and there was no reason to suppose that he was likely to have heard of his first wife between 1918 and 1933. Sachs J inferred on the facts that the wife was alive in 1933 and granted the decree, rejecting the operation of the presumption of death. There is some ground for saying that the absence of a person likely to have heard may be remedied by the making of all reasonable inquiries (140), but the better view seems to be that the two primary facts are separate, and that each is necessary. What amounts to the making of reasonable inquiries, and what amounts to the absence of acceptable evidence that the subject is alive during the period, are questions of fact in every case.

The presumption is only that the subject died at some time during the period; his death on any particular day will not be presumed, and must be proved by evidence if in issue. In *Re Phené's Trusts* (141), the court, while prepared to presume that a nephew of the testator was dead in 1868, he having last been heard of as a deserter from the United States Navy in 1860, it would not presume that he survived the testator, who had died in January 1861. Indeed, strictly, the presumption is only that the subject is dead at the date of trial, although in a number of decisions it appears to have been applied retrospectively, in the sense that it has been assumed that the presumption might have applied at some earlier time. In *Chipchase* v *Chipchase* (142), the wife married H1 in 1915, and having heard nothing of him after 1916, went through a ceremony of marriage with H2 in 1928. When the wife applied for a maintenance order against H2 in 1939, it was successfully objected that the 1928 marriage was not shown to be valid, there being no evidence that H1 was dead in that year. The Divisional Court remitted the case to the magistrates to consider whether there was any evidence to rebut the presumption of death, although strictly the presumption should have had effect only as from the date of trial in 1939, and not 1928. More significantly, the same more liberal view has been taken in cases of succession (143), so as to permit the distribution of property along the lines dictated by a presumption that the testator died within a period before trial, and it may be said with some caution that this view is likely to be adopted in future.

The period of seven years is, however, strictly insisted upon, and it is often pointed out that, though the rule is to some extent illogical, a period of six years and 364 days is not enough. Nor is there any presumption that the subject died from any particular cause, died childless or died celibate, though these matters may be capable of inference on the evidence, as a question of fact (144). It should be remembered that it is always open to the court to infer death (or that someone is alive) as a matter of fact, on the evidence, as it is to make any other proper inferences from the evidence (145). No question of the presumption arises in such a case; it is a matter of circumstantial evidence and what is sometimes called the 'presumption of continuance' — an instance of which is that if a person is shown to be alive at a certain time, his continuing life may be inferred — is no more than an example of such an inference, and will yield to the presumption of death where the latter applies.

The following statutory provisions should be noted in connection with presumptions of death:

140   *Doe* d *France* v *Andrews* (1850) 15 QB 756, per Alderson B.
141   (1870) 5 Ch App·139.   142   [1939] P 391.
143   *Re Aldersey, Gibson* v *Hall* [1905] 2 Ch 181; though a contrary view was taken in other cases, e.g. *Re Rhodes, Rhodes* v *Rhodes* (1887) 36 ChD 586.
144   *Re Jackson, Jackson* v *Ward* [1907] 2 Ch 354.
145   As in *Re Watkins, Watkins* v *Watkins* [1953] 1 WLR 1323, where despite the absence of inquiries, which precluded reliance on the presumption, the court inferred death from the circumstantial evidence, including a very long absence.

(a)   By s. 184 of the Law of Property Act 1925, if commorientes die after 1925, and it is to be decided who died first, it shall be presumed that they died in order of seniority, and consequently that the younger was the survivor (146). This rule does not apply to cases where A is proved to have died at a certain time, and B has not been heard of for seven years or more prior to A's death, when the presumption is that A survived B.

(b)   By s. 19(3) of the Matrimonial Causes Act 1973, on a petition for presumption of death and dissolution of marriage:

> In any proceedings under this section the fact that for a period of seven years or more the other party to the marriage has been continually absent from the petitioner and the petitioner has no reason to believe that the other party has been living within that time shall be evidence that the other party is dead until the contrary is proved.

For the purpose of assessing whether or not the petitioner has had reason to believe that the other party has been living, only events during the period of seven years are relevant (147).

(c)   By the proviso to s. 57 of the Offences against the Person Act 1861 (which defines the offence of bigamy):

> Provided, that nothing in this section contained shall extend to . . . any person marrying a second time whose husband or wife shall have been continually absent from such person for the space of seven years then last past, and shall not have been known by such person to be living within that time.

Despite sometimes inconsistent authority, it seems that the defendant bears an evidential burden of raising by evidence the issue of absence for seven years, whereupon the prosecution must prove beyond reasonable doubt (as part of the legal burden of proof on them) that he did know the spouse to be living during that period of time (148).

1.11.4   Presumption of regularity

The 'presumption of regularity', often expressed in the Latin tag, *omnia praesumuntur rite et solemniter esse acta,* really embodies three separate presumptions, which may be described as follows:

(a)   On proof of the primary fact that some official or public act has been peformed, or that a person acted in an official or public capacity, it is presumed that the act done complied with any necessary formalities, or that the person so acting was properly appointed for the purpose, as the case may be. This presumption applies to judicial acts in the sense that it is presumed that a person presiding over an inferior court or a tribunal, was validly appointed to do so (149). It applies to a great variety of other official acts, such as those performed by constables or justices of the peace (150), and even to

---

146   The rule does not apply to all cases. See, in respect of spouses, one of whom dies intestate, the modification introduced by the Intestates' Estates Act 1952, s. 1(4). See also the Cestui que Vie Act 1666.
147   *Thompson* v *Thompson* [1956] P 414, per Sachs J at 425.
148   *R* v *Curgerwen* (CCR) (1865) LR 1 CCR 1.
149   *R* v *Roberts* (CCR) (1878) 14 Cox CC 101. But there is no presumption that the court or tribunal had jurisdiction in any particular matter: *Christopher Brown Ltd* v *Genossenschaft Oesterreichischer Waldbesitzer Holzwirtschaftsbetriebe Registrierte Genossenschaft mbH* [1954] 1 QB 8, per Devlin J at 13.
150   *Berryman* v *Wise* (1791) 4 TR 366.

acts of divine service performed in a building, which were presumed to have been performed after due consecration (151).

It is sometimes said that this presumption cannot be relied on to establish an ingredient of a criminal offence, if the substance of the act or appointment is disputed at the trial (152). But there is authority that such dispute must be made by way of challenge by evidence, which if correct, weakens the authority of the rule (153). It may be that the presumption ought to apply, even in such cases, because it may be rebutted by very slight evidence of irregularity, and saves much specious dispute.

(b)   On proof of the primary fact that a mechanical instrument is usually in order and working correctly, it will be presumed that it was so working and in order when used on a relevant occasion. Automatic traffic signals are a good example (154) and numerous other devices, for example the speedometer of a police vehicle proved to have been recently checked for accuracy, are treated in the same way.

(c)   On proof that necessary business transactions have been carried out, which require to be effected in a certain order, it will be presumed that they were effected in that order (155).

1.11.5   Conflicting presumptions
Where two presumptions apply to the same facts, and produce conflicting results, they are cancelled out, and the burden of proof operates as if neither presumption applied. Thus, in *R* v *Willshire* (156), on a prosecution for bigamy, a presumption in favour of the validity of one of the defendant's four marriages conflicted directly with the absence of the conditions necessary for the presumption of death in relation to a former wife, who therefore had to be taken as alive at the date of the marriage in question. The issue whether the prosecution had proved beyond reasonable doubt that she was alive at the date of the subsequent marriage in question was left to the jury, unencumbered by any presumption.

151   *R* v *Cresswell* (CCR) (1873) 1 QBD 446.
152   *Scott* v *Baker* DC [1969] 1 QB 659.
153   *Campbell* v *Wallsend Slipway & Engineering Co. Ltd* (DC) [1978] ICR 1015.
154   *Tingle Jacobs & Co.* v *Kennedy* (CA) [1964] 1 WLR 638n.
155   *Eaglehill Ltd* v *J Needham (Builders) Ltd* (HL) [1973] AC 992.
156   (CCR) (1881) 6 QBD 366.

2   The Queen v Coke and Littleton

A: BRIEF FOR THE PROSECUTION

Instructions to Counsel

Counsel is instructed in the prosecution of these two defendants, who are due to stand
trial at the Oxbridge Crown Court upon the indictment sent with these papers. Counsel
also has the statements of witnesses tendered in the committal proceedings on behalf of
the prosecution, and a letter from solicitors representing the defendant Littleton, giving
notice of alibi as required by s. 11 of the Criminal Justice Act 1967.

There are a number of matters of evidence which Counsel will no doubt wish to
consider. Both complainants are under the age of eighteen. The elder sister, Margaret,
has been in trouble for shoplifting. On the other hand, the defendant Coke has a
previous conviction for rape, said to have been committed under very similar circumstances. In the case of Littleton, the evidence of identification will be of crucial importance, especially in view of his defence of alibi.

The fact of sexual intercourse between Coke and Margaret Blackstone seems to be
undisputed, but is in any event supported by the forensic evidence suggesting that the girl
had had recent sexual intercourse. There is also the fact which appears to be strongly
disputed, that the same defendant was probably the author of the questioned written
exhibit, which may assist in the question of his state of mind at the relevant time. Counsel
will no doubt wish to consider the state of the expert evidence.

Certain issues arise from the evidence of the police officers, in respect of the search of
Coke's flat, apparently without a search warrant, and from the circumstances in which
Coke subsequently made his incriminating statement under caution. Counsel's attention
is also drawn to the admission of guilt said to be contained in the tape-recorded
conversation at the police station between Littleton and his wife. Questions arise
concerning the use of the tape and the possibility of privilege in relation to the
conversation.

Counsel is instructed to consider and advise on these and any other points of evidence
which may arise.

Indictment

IN THE CROWN COURT AT OXBRIDGE

THE QUEEN v HENRY EDWARD COKE and
MARTIN STEPHEN LITTLETON

Charged as follows:

COUNT 1

Statement of Offence

Rape contrary to section 1(1) of the Sexual Offences Act 1956.

Particulars of Offence

Henry Edward Coke on the 8th day of July 1979 raped Margaret Ann Blackstone.

COUNT 2

Statement of Offence

Indecent Assault contrary to section 14(1) of the Sexual Offences Act 1956.

Particulars of Offence

Martin Stephen Littleton on the 8th day of July 1979 indecently assaulted Angela Hazel Blackstone.

W. RUSSELL COX

Officer of the Court

Depositions

STATEMENT OF WITNESS

(Criminal Justice Act 1967, s. 2, s. 9; Magistrates' Courts Rules 1968, r.58)

Statement of: Margaret Ann Blackstone

Age of Witness   17 (born 3 May 1962)

Occupation of Witness   Schoolgirl

Address of Witness   4 The Hyde, Oxbridge.

This statement, consisting of 2 pages, each signed by me, is true to the best of my knowledge and belief, and I make it knowing that if it is tendered in evidence, I shall be liable to prosecution if I have wilfully stated in it anything which I know to be false or do not believe to be true.

Dated the 12th day of July 1979.

Signed: M.A. Blackstone

Witnessed: Dennis Bracton D/S

Helen Blackstone (mother)

I am a schoolgirl aged seventeen and live with my parents and my sister Angela at the above address. I have known Henry Coke for quite a long time, because he goes to a youth club which my friends and I go to at weekends. I think he lives in Plowden Drive in Oxbridge. From time to time he has approached me at the club and asked me to go to bed with him, but I have always refused.

On Sunday, 8 July, I was walking after lunch in the park with Angela, when I saw Henry Coke coming towards us with another man who looked rather older, whom I did not know. We all started talking, and Henry said he had a new álbum by a band we liked and invited us to his flat to listen to it. I did not really want to go, but Angela was very excited about the idea and so we did. When we got there, Henry put the record on and made us all some coffee. I was sitting on the divan and Henry came and sat next to me. Angela was sitting on the window-ledge next to a large armchair where the other man was sitting.

After a while, Henry started making suggestions to me that we should have sexual intercourse. I told him to stop and that I did not want him even saying such things while my sister was around. At first he seemed to accept this, but then he got very persistent and started trying to hold my hand and put his arm round my shoulder. I pushed him away. All of a sudden, he pushed me backwards very hard, so that I fell on my back on the divan. I was so taken by surprise that I did not try to get up straight away, and then Henry put his hand up my skirt and pulled my pants down to my ankles. I was very frightened and just lay there. It was only when I saw that he was unzipping his trousers that I started to scream and fight. I was expecting the other man to stop him, but he did nothing. Henry was far too strong for me and he had sexual intercourse with me. I understand what this means, and that is what happened. I did not consent to it, and did nothing to lead Henry to think that I might consent.

When it was over, I got up quickly. I was terribly distressed. To my horror, I saw that Angela was sitting on the other man's lap and that he had his hand up her skirt. I shouted at her to come with me, and we both ran out of the flat and home. Neither of them made any effort to stop us.

When we got home, I could not bring myself to say anything to my mother, and ran straight upstairs, but Angela said something, and shortly afterwards, my mother came up and asked me what had happened. I didn't want to say anything, but after some time my mother more or less dragged the truth out of me, and then called the police. I then went to bed until a bit later, when a lady doctor came and examined me.

I didn't see what was happening to Angela while Henry was having intercourse with me. It was only afterwards that I noticed that she was sitting with the other man. I think I would recognise the other man if I saw him again.

<u>Signed</u>:   M. A. Blackstone   <u>Witnessed</u>:   Dennis Bracton D/S
                                                         Helen Blackstone (mother)

STATEMENT OF WITNESS

(Criminal Justice Act 1967, s. 2, s. 9; Magistrates' Courts Rules 1968, r. 58)

Statement of: Angela Hazel Blackstone

Age of Witness   13 (born 4 June 1966)

Occupation of Witness   Schoolgirl

Address of Witness   4 The Hyde, Oxbridge.

This statement, consisting of 2 pages, each signed by me, is true to the best of my knowledge and belief, and I make it knowing that if it is tendered in evidence, I shall be liable to prosecution if I have, wilfully stated in it anything which I know to be false or do not believe to be true.

Dated the 12th day of July 1979.

> Signed: Angela H. Blackstone
>
> Witnessed: Dennis Bracton D/S
>   Helen Blackstone (mother)

I am a schoolgirl aged thirteen and I live with my parents and my sister Margaret at 4 The Hyde, Oxbridge. On Sunday after lunch, Margaret and I went for a walk in the park. We quite often do that. While we were walking, we met two men who I didn't know. One was a bit older than Margaret, and the other was even older, about the same as my uncle Paul, who is about thirty, I think. The older man didn't say much, but the younger one said he had the Least's new album and said we could listen to it. So we went home with him, and the older man came as well.

When we got there, I sat on the window ledge drinking some coffee and listening to the record, which was great. The younger man was sitting next to Margaret on the sofa. They were talking and messing about. Then they seemed to be having an argument and I saw Margaret fall backwards and the man fall on top of her. Margaret was shouting to the man to stop. I didn't understand what was going on, and I was frightened. The older man was sitting in an armchair by the window told me not to worry, they were only playing. He lifted me off the window-ledge and sat me on his lap. He didn't want me to watch Margaret, and asked me if I liked boys. I wanted to listen to the music, which was very good. Then he put his hand up my skirt and asked me if I liked it. I said I didn't, but he still kept on, and he was rubbing his leg against me.

After one or two minutes, Margaret got up off the sofa. She was crying a lot and shouted to me to come home with her, which I did. Margaret was crying all the way home but she wouldn't tell me what was the matter, and she went straight to her room when we got home. I thought I had better tell mummy in case anything was the matter with Margaret, so I told her everything that had happened.

Later on Sunday afternoon, a policeman came round with a lady police officer and I told them what had happened. Then we went out in the police car, and drove round the streets near the park. While we were doing this, I saw the older man walking along. I am sure it was the same man. We got out and went up with the police to the man, and I pointed at him and said it was the same man who had been sitting in the armchair. Then mummy took me back home while the police spoke to the man. Later on, a lady doctor came and examined me.

<u>Signed:</u>   Angela H. Blackstone   <u>Witnessed:</u>   Dennis Bracton D/S
                                                          Helen Blackstone (mother)

STATEMENT OF WITNESS

(Criminal Justice Act 1967, s. 2, s. 9; Magistrates' Courts Rules 1968, r. 58)

Statement of: Helen Blackstone

Age of Witness   Over 21

Occupation of Witness   Housewife

Address of Witness   4 The Hyde, Oxbridge.

This statement, consisting of 1 page, signed by me, is true to the best of my knowledge and belief, and I make it known that if it is tendered in evidence, I shall be liable to prosecution if I have, wilfully stated in it anything which I know to be false or do not believe to be true.

Dated the 12th day of July 1979.

Signed: Helen Blackstone

Witnessed: Dennis Bracton D/S

I live with my husband and two children, Margaret Ann (aged seventeen, born on 3 May 1962) and Angela Hazel (aged thirteen, born on 4 June 1966) at the above address. I now produce copies of the certificates of birth of both my children, marked 'HB1' and 'HB2' respectively.

On Sunday, 8 July, the children went for a walk together after lunch round the park, as they quite often do. They left the house at about 2 o'clock. They are usually back by 3 o'clock to half past, and on this occasion, I noticed that it was a little after 4 o'clock. I heard Margaret running upstairs, and Angela went into the kitchen very quietly, which is unusual. I went into the kitchen and asked Angela if everything was all right. She told me that she and Margaret had been with two men at a flat, and that one of the men had done something to Margaret which upset her. They seemed to be fighting. Angela also said that the other man had sat her on his lap and put his hand up her skirt and kept rubbing his leg against her. She said she didn't like it.

I was very alarmed by all this, and I went up to Margaret's bedroom, where I found her on the bed sobbing violently. She did not want to talk about it, but being sure by now that something terrible had just happened, I shouted at her and slapped her. She then told me that she had been raped by Henry Coke at his flat. I at once went and called the police, and when they came some time later, they talked to both children. They said that Margaret should go to bed until a doctor came to look at her. Angela and I were asked to go out in the police car with them to have a look around.

As we were driving in Plowden Drive, which is not far from the park, Angela suddenly pointed to a man walking towards the police car, and said that it was the man who had touched her while they were sitting in the chair. The car stopped, and the officers and I and Angela approached the man. Angela pointed to the man and said: 'That's him.' The man said he didn't know what she was talking about, or words to that effect, and the officers told me to take Angela home, which I did.

Shortly after we got back home, a doctor arrived from the police and examined both children in my presence.

Signed: Helen Blackstone   Witnessed: Dennis Bracton D/S

STATEMENT OF WITNESS

(Criminal Justice Act 1967, s. 2, s. 9; Magistrates' Courts Rules 1968, r. 58)

Statement of: Dr Susan Geraldine Vesey

Age of Witness   Over 21

Occupation of Witness   Medical Practitioner

Address of Witness   27 Random Cuttings, Oxbridge.

This statement, consisting of 1 page, signed by me, is true to the best of my knowledge and belief, and I make it knowing that if it is tendered in evidence, I shall be liable to prosecution if I have, wilfully stated in it anything which I know to be false or do not believe to be true.

Dated the 16th day of July 1979.

Signed: Susan Vesey

Witnessed: Dennis Bracton D/S

I am a medical practitioner in general practice at the above address. I also act as one of the surgeons to the Oxbridge Constabulary. On Sunday 8 July 1979, I was on call as duty police surgeon when as a result of a call from D/I Glanvil, I went to 4 The Hyde, Oxbridge, where I examined Margaret Ann Blackstone (D.O.B. 3 May 1962) and Angela Hazel Blackstone (D.O.B. 4 June 1966) who were identified to me by their mother, Mrs Helen Blackstone.

RESULTS OF EXAMINATION

Margaret Ann Blackstone

This girl was evidently distressed and crying at the time of my visit, though not hysterical. She was generally in excellent health. Examination of the genital area showed signs of recent sexual intercourse. There were traces of what appeared to be semen, and some reddening of the vaginal region. There was no bruising of or damage to the genitals. I took a vaginal swab which I placed in a sealed polythene bag and labelled 'SGV1'. I later handed this to D/S Bracton.

Angela Hazel Blackstone

This girl was composed and able to tell me what had happened to her. She was in excellent general health and examination revealed nothing of relevance to the inquiry.

Signed: Susan Vesey   Witnessed: Dennis Bracton D/S

STATEMENT OF WITNESS

(Criminal Justice Act 1967, s. 2, s. 9; Magistrates' Courts Rules 1968, r. 58)

Statement of: Geoffrey Glanvil

Age of Witness   Over 21

Occupation of Witness   Detective Inspector

Address of Witness   Oxbridge Police Station.

This statement, consisting of 2 pages, each signed by me, is true to the best of my knowledge and belief, and I make it knowing that if it is tendered in evidence, I shall be liable to prosecution if I have, wilfully stated in it anything which I know to be false or do not believe to be true.

Dated the 16th day of July 1979.

Signed: Geoffrey Glanvil D/I

Witnessed: Dennis Bracton D/S

On Sunday 8 July 1979, at about 4.15 p.m., I was on duty in plain clothes when as a result of information received, I went in an unmarked police car with D/S Bracton and WPC Raymond to 4 The Hyde, Oxbridge. I there saw a Mrs Helen Blackstone and her two daughters, Miss Margaret Ann Blackstone aged seventeen and Miss Angela Hazel Blackstone aged thirteen. As a result of what they told me, I advised Margaret Blackstone to go to bed at once and I called for the duty police surgeon to attend. WPC Raymond remained with Margaret at my request.

Together with D/S Bracton, Mrs Blackstone and Angela I then drove the police car slowly through a number of streets around the public park near The Hyde. As we were driving along Plowden Drive, I noticed a man walking towards us, tall, slightly built, about thirty to thirty-five, dark hair, wearing a light shirt and blue jeans. Angela pointed out this man at once as the man who had assaulted her. I stopped the car, and with the other occupants got out and approached the man. Angela looked at him, pointed at him and said: 'That's him.' The man replied: 'What on earth is she talking about?' I then asked Mrs Blackstone to take Angela home.

I said to the man: 'What is your name?' He said: 'Martin Littleton. Why?' I said: 'We are police officers. It is alleged that earlier this afternoon you assaulted that girl indecently.' He said: 'Rubbish. I've never seen her before in my life.' I said: 'Have you been at Henry Coke's flat today?' Littleton said: 'I know Henry Coke, but I haven't been there today. I've been at home on my own. In fact, I've only just got up. This must be some sort of mistake.' I said: 'Where do you live?' Littleton said: 'Eldon Villas, number 17.' I then arrested Littleton for indecent assault and cautioned him, and he replied: 'You've got the wrong man, I tell you.' We then conveyed him to Oxbridge police station where he was detained.

At about 5.30 p.m. the same afternoon with D/S Bracton, I went to a first floor flat at 52 Plowden Drive, where the door was opened by a youth of about eighteen years of age, medium build, fair hair and casually dressed. I said: 'Henry Edward Coke?' He said: 'Yes.' I said: 'We are police officers. You are under arrest for raping Margaret Blackstone earlier this afternoon,' and cautioned Coke, who replied: 'Yes, all right, I was expecting you.' While D/S Bracton sat with Coke, I then searched the flat. In a drawer of the bedside cabinet I found several sheets of notepaper upon which were written in ink references to Margaret Blackstone. I took possession of these sheets, which I now produce marked 'GG1'. We then conveyed Coke to Oxbridge Police Station, where he too was detained.

Later, at 7 p.m. the same day, with D/S Bracton, I interviewed Littleton at the police station in the CID office. I reminded him of the caution, and said: 'Now, what about it, Mr Littleton?' Littleton said: 'I'm not answering any questions. I want to see my solicitor.' I said: 'You can see a solicitor at a time convenient to me. I am investigating a serious offence.' Littleton said: 'Nothing to say.' I said: 'Very well, you will be detained over night and I will see you in the morning.' Littleton said: 'No. Please give me bail. My wife will be so worried.' I said: 'Bail is not on at the moment, but I will make sure your wife knows where you are.'

At 7.20 p.m. the same day, with D/S Bracton, I interviewed Henry Coke in the CID office. I said: 'You are still under caution. Do you want to tell me about it?' Coke said: 'Yes, I may as well. With form for the same thing, I reckon I'm going down for a while. Will you write a statement for me?' I said: 'Certainly.' I then wrote at Coke's dictation a statement under caution, between 7.30 and 8 p.m. without any break. I now produce this statement marked 'GG2'. After completing this statement, I said to Coke: 'You have not mentioned the sheets of paper referring to Margaret which I found in your room.' Coke said: 'No. Actually, those are not mine. Lots of my mates fancy Margaret.' I said: 'How do they come to be in your room on this particular day when you rape her?' Coke said: 'They may have been there for months.' I said: 'Will you supply me with specimens of your handwriting so that I can have a scientific comparison made?' He said: 'Yes, all right.' Coke then wrote at my dictation on a piece of paper which I now produce marked 'GG3'. I then handed exhibits 'GG1' and 'GG3' to D/S Bracton for transmission to the forensic science laboratory.

At about 8.45 p.m. the same day, Mrs Davina Littleton arrived at the police station, and was allowed to see her husband in a cell. I positioned myself nearby, so that I could hear clearly what was said, and recorded the conversation using a pocket cassette recorder. After some general conversation, Mrs Littleton asked: 'Martin, tell me the truth. Is there any truth in what the police say?' Littleton replied: 'Yes, I'm afraid so. I don't know what came over me. I just felt her up. I couldn't help myself. I can't explain it.' I now produce the cassette as exhibit 'GG4'.

The next morning at about 9 a.m. I formally charged Coke with rape and Littleton with indecent assault. They were cautioned and neither made any reply.

<u>Signed</u>:   Geoffrey Glanvil D/I   <u>Witnessed</u>:   Dennis Bracton D/S

STATEMENT UNDER CAUTION

GG2   Oxbridge Police Station

                                                       Date: 8 July 1979

                                                       Time: 7.30 p.m.

Statement of: Henry Edward Coke

Address: 52 Plowden Drive, Oxbridge

Age: 18

Occupation: Apprentice Tailor.

I, Henry Edward Coke, wish to make a statement. I want someone to write down what I say. I have been told that I need not say anything unless I wish to do so and that whatever I say may be given in evidence.

Signed: H.E. Coke

Witnessed: Geoffrey Glanvil D/I

It's difficult to know where to start really. I've known Margaret for years from the club and seeing her around. I've always fancied her. She's really lovely. I saw her down the club last night wearing one of those see-through blouses. I went home and thought about it a lot, and decided to do something about it. My mate Martin Littleton came round this morning and he had a couple of drinks with me at lunchtime. I told him that Margaret and her sister always went for a stroll in the park after lunch and I was telling him how much I fancied Margaret. We agreed we would meet them if we could and find some reason to take them back to my place. I was really only going to chat Margaret up a bit. Martin said he would look after the little girl for me. So we went up the park, and it went all right. They said they would come back with us to listen to a new record which is very popular down the club at the moment. I put the record on and started chatting Margaret up, while Martin talked to the little girl. Margaret didn't want to know. She was giving me no joy at all. I suddenly came over all funny. I felt I had to have her at all costs. It wasn't difficult. She was sitting next to me on my divan bed. I pushed her backwards on to the bed. She looked rather surprised more than anything else. She had taken her shoes off and she wasn't wearing tights, so I had her pants off quite easily. It was only then she started struggling. It was no trouble. I had it off with her. Then she started crying, which was a bit silly, because she would have enjoyed it if she'd thought about it. She called over to her sister and dragged her off. She was carrying her shoes. I don't think she remembered her pants. I threw them out afterwards.

After she went I was worried. Obviously, I knew you would probably come for me, but actually, I was more worried about Martin. It was only when I had finished with Margaret that I saw what he was up to with the little girl. He was touching her up and fondling her. I know I was a bit forceful with Margaret, but at least she is old enough. Doing that to a kiddy is really sick. No way was I involved with that. I want to make that clear. That is down to Martin on his own. Once I discovered what was going on, I gave Martin a mouthful. We had quite an argument and I threw him out. I don't know what happened to him after that.

I would like to say I'm sorry for what happened. I really like Margaret and I didn't want to hurt her. It's all very silly. Why can't girls say yes sometimes and just enjoy it?

Signed: H.E. Coke

Witnessed: Geoffrey Glanvil D/I

I have read the above statement and I have been told that I can correct, alter or add anything I wish. This statement is true. I have made it of my own free will.

<u>Signed:</u>   H.E. Coke

<u>Witnessed:</u>   Geoffrey Glanvil D/I

Statement taken by me Geoffrey Glanvil between 7.30 p.m. and 8 p.m. No breaks for refreshments.

<u>Signed:</u>   Geoffrey Glanvil D/I

STATEMENT OF WITNESS

(Criminal Justice Act 1967, s. 2, s. 9; Magistrates' Courts Rules 1968, r. 58)

<u>Statement of:</u>   Dennis Bracton

<u>Age of Witness:</u>   Over 21

<u>Occupation of Witness</u>   Detective Sergeant

<u>Address of Witness</u>   Oxbridge Police Station.

This statement, consisting of 2 pages, each signed by me, is true to the best of my knowledge and belief, and I make it knowing that if it is tendered in evidence, I shall be liable to prosecution if I have, wilfully stated in it anything which I know to be false or do not believe to be true.

<u>Dated</u> the 16th day of July 1979.

<u>Signed:</u>   Dennis Bracton D/S

<u>Witnessed:</u>   Geoffrey Glanvil D/I

On Sunday 8 July 1979 at about 4.15 p.m. I was on duty in plain clothes when as a result of information received, I went in an unmarked police car with D/I Glanvil and WPC Raymond to 4 The Hyde, Oxbridge. I there saw a Mrs Helen Blackstone and her two daughters, Miss Margaret Blackstone aged seventeen and Miss Angela Blackstone aged thirteen. As a result of what they said, D/I Glanvil advised Margaret Blackstone to go to bed and await the arrival of a doctor. D/I Glanvil then called for the duty police surgeon, Dr Vesey, to attend. WPC Raymond remained at the house with Margaret.

Together with D/I Glanvil, Mrs Blackstone and Angela, I then drove in the police car slowly around various streets near the park just by The Hyde. As we were driving along Plowden Drive, I saw Angela point to a man walking towards us, tall, slightly built, about thirty to thirty-five, dark hair, wearing a light shirt and blue jeans. D/I Glanvil stopped the car, and we all got out and approached the man. Angela looked at him, pointed to him and said: 'That's him.' The man replied: 'What on earth is she talking about?' D/I Glanvil then asked Mrs Blackstone to take Angela home.

D/I Glanvil said to the man: 'What is your name?' He said: 'Martin Littleton. Why?' D/I Glanvil said: 'We are police officers. It is alleged that earlier this afternoon you assaulted that girl indecently.' He said: 'Rubbish. I've never seen her before in my life.' D/I Glanvil said: 'Have you been at Henry Coke's flat today?' Littleton said: 'I know Henry Coke, but I haven't been there today. I've been at home on my own. In fact, I've only just got up. This must be some sort of mistake.' D/I Glanvil said: 'Where do you live?' Littleton said: 'Eldon Villas. Number 17.' D/I Glanvil then arrested Littleton for indecent assault and cautioned him, and Littleton replied: 'You've got the wrong man, I tell you.' We then conveyed Littleton to Oxbridge police station where he was detained.

At about 5.30 p.m. the same day, with D/I Glanvil, I went to a first-floor flat at 52 Plowden Drive, where the door was opened by a youth of about eighteen years, medium build, fair hair and casually dressed. D/I Glanvil said: 'Henry Edward Coke?' He said: 'Yes'. D/I Glanvil said: 'We are police officers. You are under arrest for raping Margaret Blackstone earlier this afternoon' and cautioned Coke, who said: 'Yes, all right, I was expecting you.' I then sat with Coke while D/I Glanvil searched the flat. In a drawer in a bedside cabinet I saw D/I Glanvil find a number of sheets of notepaper, of which he took possession. Coke was then detained at Oxbridge police station.

Later the same day at 7 p.m. with D/I Glanvil I interviewed Littleton in the CID office at Oxbridge police station. D/I Glanvil reminded Littleton of the caution and said:

'Now, what about it, Mr Littleton?' Littleton said: 'I'm not answering any questions. I want to see my solicitor.' D/I Glanvil said: 'You can see a solicitor at a time convenient to me. I am investigating a serious offence.' Littleton said: 'Nothing to say.' D/I Glanvil said: 'Very well, you will be detained overnight and I will see you in the morning.' Littleton said: 'No. Please give me bail. My wife will be so worried.' D/I Glanvil said: 'Bail is not on at the moment, but I will make sure your wife knows where you are.'

At 7.20 p.m. the same day, with D/I Glanvil I interviewed Henry Coke in the CID office. D/I Glanvil said: 'You are still under caution. Do you want to tell me about it?' Coke said: 'Yes, I may as well. With form for the same thing, I reckon I'm going down for a while. Will you write a statement for me?' D/I Glanvil said: 'Certainly.' D/I Glanvil then took a statement under caution from Coke, and while this was being done, I left the room to attend to other matters.

The next morning at about 9 a.m. I was present when D/I Glanvil formally charged Coke and Littleton with rape and indecent assault respectively. They were cautioned and made no reply.

During the evening of 8 July, I had taken possession from D/I Glanvil of exhibits GG1 and GG3. After the defendants had been charged, I took these exhibits from the police station to the surgery of Dr Susan Vesey at 27 Random Cuttings, Oxbridge. I there collected from the doctor a swab contained in a polythene bag marked 'SGV1'. I then conveyed these exhibits personally to the appropriate departments of the Oxbridge forensic science laboratory.

Signed: Dennis Bracton D/S   **Witnessed:** Geoffrey Glanvil D/I

STATEMENT OF WITNESS

(Criminal Justice Act 1967, s. 2, s. 9; Magistrates' Courts Rules 1968, r. 58)

<u>Statement of:</u>   Lorraine Raymond

<u>Age of Witness</u>   Over 21

<u>Occupation of Witness</u>   Police Constable 24

<u>Address of Witness</u>   Oxbridge Police Station.

This statement, consisting of 1 page, signed by me, is true to the best of my knowledge and belief, and I make it knowing that if it is tendered in evidence, I shall be liable to prosecution if I have, wilfully stated in it anything which I know to be false or do not believe to be true.

<u>Dated</u> the 16th day of July 1979.

<u>Signed:</u>   Lorraine Raymond WPC 24

<u>Witnessed:</u>   Dennis Bracton D/S

On Sunday 8 July 1979, at about 4.15 p.m. I was on duty in uniform at Oxbridge Police Station, when as a result of information received, I went with D/I Glanvil and D/S Bracton, to 4 The Hyde, Oxbridge, where I saw a Mrs Helen Blackstone and her two daughters, Miss Margaret Blackstone aged seventeen and Miss Angela Blackstone aged thirteen. As a result of what they said, D/I Glanvil advised Margaret Blackstone to go to bed and await the arrival of the police surgeon. At D/I Glanvil's request, I remained in the bedroom with Margaret while the other officers went out in the police car with Mrs Blackstone and Angela.

While we were together, Margaret was initially upset but recovered her composure rapidly. I asked her various questions, in reply to which she gave me an account of her having been raped by a young man known to her called Henry Coke.

At about 4.50 p.m. just after Mrs Blackstone and Angela had returned to the house, the duty police surgeon, Dr Susan Vesey, arrived and I then left and returned to the police station.

<u>Signed:</u>   Lorraine Raymond WPC 24   <u>Witnessed:</u>   Dennis Bracton D/S

STATEMENT OF WITNESS
(Criminal Justice Act 1967, s. 2, s. 9; Magistrates' Courts Rules 1968, r. 58)

<u>Statement of:</u>   Philip Hale BSc

<u>Age of Witness</u>   Over 21

<u>Occupation of Witness</u>   Higher Scientific Officer

<u>Address of Witness</u>   Forensic Science Laboratory, Portland Road, Oxbridge.

This statement, consisting of 1 page, signed by me, is true to the best of my knowledge and belief, and I make it knowing that if it is tendered in evidence, I shall be liable to prosecution if I have, wilfully stated in it anything which I know to be false or do not believe to be true.

<u>Dated</u> the 20th day of July 1979.

<u>Signed:</u>   Philip Hale

<u>Witnessed:</u>   Dennis Bracton D/S

I have specialised for the last seven years in the scientific examination of documents and comparison of handwriting. On Monday, 9 July 1979, I received from D/S Bracton exhibits GG1 and GG3 which were identified by means of labels.

Exhibit GG1

This was a bundle of four sheets of lined white notepaper containing various short passages in cursive handwriting in blue ball-point ink. The passages contained references in a sexual context to someone called Margaret Blackstone. I took this to be questioned writing.

Exhibit GG3

This was a single sheet of plain notepaper containing the following words in cursive handwriting in blue ball-point ink: 'Margaret. Margaret Blackstone. I want you. I need you. I must have you. I think about Margaret all the time.'

I took this to be the known handwriting of Henry Edward Coke.

I examined and compared these exhibits.

Results of examination

I found a high probability that the writer of exhibit GG3 also wrote the text of exhibit GG1. I cannot wholly exclude the possibility that the writer of GG1 was a different person from the writer of GG3 but in my opinion this is unlikely.

After examination, I returned the exhibits to Oxbridge police station where I handed them to D/S Bracton.

I have prepared a chart of comparison of the two exhibits which I can use to illustrate my conclusions if necessary.

<u>Signed:</u>   Philip Hale   <u>Witnessed:</u>   Dennis Bracton D/S

STATEMENT OF WITNESS

(Criminal Justice Act 1967, s. 2, s. 9; Magistrates' Courts Rules 1968, r. 58)

<u>Statement of:</u>   Ernest Espinasse MSc, PhD

<u>Age of Witness</u>   Over 21

<u>Occupation of Witness</u>   Higher Scientific Officer

<u>Address of Witness</u>   Forensic Science Laboratory, Portland Road, Oxbridge.

   This statement, consisting of 1 page, signed by me, is true to the best of my knowledge and belief, and I make it knowing that if it is tendered in evidence, I shall be liable to prosecution if I have, wilfully stated in it anything which I know to be false or do not believe to be true.

   Dated the 16th day of July 1979.

<u>Signed</u>:   Ernest Espinasse

<u>Witnessed</u>:   Dennis Bracton D/S

On Monday 9 July 1979, I received from D/S Bracton a polythene bag bearing an identifying label marked 'SGV1' and containing a sterilised cotton swab.

   I specialise in the detection and identification of traces of blood, semen and other biological matter and in the scientific examination of specimens and exhibits within these fields. I examined exhibit SGV1.

Results of examination

This exhibit yielded positive and readily detectable evidence of human spermatozoa, seminal acid phosphatase and seminal blood-group antigens. From the presence of these factors and the high level at which they were detected, I am able to say that the subject of the swab had had sexual intercourse within a recent time of the taking of the swab. I can say that such intercourse definitely occurred within forty-eight hours of the taking of the swab, and in all probability, within a very much shorter time. I can illustrate and support my conclusions if necessary.

   After examination, I resealed the exhibit in sterile material and placed it in a safe place in the laboratory.

<u>Signed</u>:   Ernest Espinasse   <u>Witnessed</u>:   Dennis Bracton D/S

Previous convictions of defendants and witness

CONVICTIONS RECORDED AGAINST: Henry Edward Coke
CONVICTED IN NAME OF: (As above)
C.R.O. No: HEC 3421   D.O.B.: 4/3/61

DATE	COURT	OFFENCE	SENTENCE
16/4/76	Oxbridge Crown	Rape (M/O Induced girl to visit him to listen to records and raped her)	Borstal training (released on 14/10/77)

CONVICTIONS RECORDED AGAINST: Martin Stephen Littleton
CONVICTED IN NAME OF:
C.R.O. No: D.O.B.: 11/2/46

DATE	COURT	OFFENCE	SENTENCE
		NONE RECORDED	

CONVICTIONS RECORDED AGAINST: Margaret Ann Blackstone
CONVICTED IN NAME OF: (As above)
C.R.O. No: D.O.B.: 3/5/62

DATE	COURT	OFFENCE	SENTENCE
27/11/78	Oxbridge Juvenile	Theft (shoplifting)	Conditional discharge 2 years

Notice of alibi

THOMAS, WATSON & CO.

Solicitors and	19 College Row	A. Hughes-Thompson
Commissioners for	Oxbridge	R. Sims LLB
Oaths	Oxshire XX5 3BR	
	Tel: Oxbridge 7541	

Our Ref: RS/MSL
Your Ref:

The Prosecuting Solicitor
Oxbridge Constabulary
Police Headquarters
Oxbridge

23 July 1979

Dear Sir

The Queen v Coke and Littleton

We act in the above matter for the defendant Martin Stephen Littleton, who is charged with indecent assault.

We are instructed by our client to supply you now, at the first practicable opportunity, with details of our client's alibi, which will be his defence at trial.

On 8 July 1979, a Sunday, our client was asleep in bed until about 2 o'clock that afternoon, having retired to bed after a heavy day's work on the Saturday, shortly before midnight. He got up between about 2.30 and 3 p.m., had something to eat, and feeling slightly unwell, went out for a walk at about 4.15 p.m. or a little after. This was the first time our client had left his house at 17 Eldon Villas, Oxbridge, on that day. It was in the course of that walk that he was stopped by police and arrested.

There are no witnesses in support of the alibi. Our client was alone at home at all material times.

Yours faithfully

Thomas, Watson & Co

B: BRIEF FOR THE DEFENCE

Instructions to Counsel on behalf of the defendant Coke

Counsel is instructed on behalf of the defendant Coke, who is charged with rape, as appears from the indictment and statements of the prosecution witnesses sent herewith. The defendant wishes to plead not guilty to this charge, and Counsel will see from his proof of evidence which follows, that he does not deny having sexual intercourse with Margaret Blackstone on the relevant occasion, but says that such intercourse took place with her consent. Counsel will please consider the implications of this defence, and of the fact that according to Coke, the girl is somewhat promiscuous, in the light of the defendant's previous conviction for rape.

The defendant Littleton is of course separately represented, because of the clear conflict of interest between the two, and it is not known what he may say about Coke. It is believed that he may be putting forward a defence of alibi, which would result in a direct conflict of evidence between the defendants. Littleton is apparently a man of previous good character.

Counsel will see that Coke has some serious challenges to the police evidence, both with regard to the search of his flat and his arrest, and his subsequent treatment at the police station. It may be that these matters will affect the admissibility of Coke's alleged oral and written admissions to the police, which on the face of it are very damaging to his case. There is also concern about the written notes found by the police. Coke is adamant that he did not write these, and Counsel will no doubt wish to consider carefully the evidence of the handwriting expert.

Counsel will please consider these matters and the evidence in general.

Proof of evidence of Coke

HENRY EDWARD COKE of 52 Plowden Drive, Oxbridge, will state as follows:

I have been charged with raping a girl called Margaret Blackstone at my flat on 8 July 1979. To this charge I wish to plead not guilty. I admit that I had sexual intercourse with her, but it was with her consent. What happened was as follows.

I have known Margaret for quite a long time, because we both go to the same youth club at weekends. Margaret is a really good-looking girl, and all my mates fancy her as well. I have never made any secret of that fact that I do. I have tried chatting her up at the club on various occasions, and although she was usually with someone else, she gave me the impression that I would be all right if I played my cards right. I decided to try my luck. By this, I mean that I was going to try to have sexual intercourse with her, but not by force or against her will. I saw Margaret the night before the alleged rape, Saturday the 7th at the club, and I made up my mind to meet her 'accidentally' the next afternoon when she was walking with her sister in the park, as she usually does.

In fact, the next morning, my mate Martin Littleton came round. He is a fair bit older than my crowd, and is married, but he helps out at the pub I use as my local and we get on very well. I told him about what I had in mind while we were having a drink at lunchtime. Martin agreed to talk to the little girl while I made my number with Margaret, if we could persuade them to come back to my place with us. We went round the park, and there they were, so we asked them back to listen to a new album from the Least, which all the kids like at the moment, and they came. Margaret seemed quite happy about it. She came and sat next to me on the divan bed and we drank coffee while we listened to the album. She took her shoes off. We were getting on really well. Martin was laughing and talking to the little girl the other side of the room near the window.

Margaret and I then lay down on the sofa, and she made it clear that she wanted to have sexual intercourse with me. She took off her pants, and we had intercourse. This was entirely with her consent. The story she has told to her mother and the police is quite untrue. I think she has made this up because she is embarrassed about doing it with her sister there, and because obviously she was going to be asked how her younger sister came to be interfered with while Margaret was with her. Also, Margaret was not a virgin at the time. Several of my mates have had it off with her. She will do it with anyone. Apparently she threatened to complain that my mate Kevin had raped her last year, when he hadn't at all. She was convicted of shoplifting last year, and it seems she is rather dishonest.

I want to make it clear that I had nothing to do with Martin interfering with the little girl. All I saw was that he was touching her up, when Margaret and I had finished. Margaret must have seen that as well, because she dragged the little girl off pretty quickly. She didn't even wait to put on her shoes, which she carried, and she left her pants behind. I threw them away later on. I was disgusted with Martin. We had a big row, and I threw him out.

I thought then that the police would be round, but there was nothing I could do. Mr Glanvil and Mr Bracton came round at about 5.30 that afternoon. They did not say anything to me, as they say. They rushed in without a word, and started searching the room. I knew who they were. I did say: 'I was expecting you,' which was true, but this was while they were searching the room. I also asked them if they had a search warrant, and was told to shut up. Glanvil found some pieces of paper with a few bawdy remarks about Margaret on them. I think they had been there for ages. My mates used to come round and we would talk about girls and so on, and I think one of them must have written it for a laugh. I certainly did not. I did give the police specimens of my handwriting later, and I am surprised at the conclusions reached by the expert. I definitely did not write those remarks, and I note that he cannot say for certain that I did.

After they had finished the search, Glanvil just said: 'Right, come on.' They took me to the police station. I was not told I was being arrested, and I was not cautioned. Later that day, the officers came to see me in an office and questioned me. It is true that I signed a statement under caution, but this was only because the officers shouted at me and threatened me that if I did not admit raping Margaret, they would do me for interfering with the little girl as well, and Glanvil said they would 'lock me up and throw away the key' for that. I believed this, because I was really horrified by the idea of touching up children, and I could see that they could make it look bad for me. So I made up the statement and dictated it to them. Some of it was of course true, but not the bit about how the intercourse came about. I did not say before making the statement: 'Yes, I may as well. With form for the same thing, I reckon I'm going down for a while.' I just agreed at the end of a session of threats to make one.

It is true that, unfortunately, I have been convicted of rape before. This was in April 1976. I was sent to Borstal, and was there until October 1977. On this occasion, I was guilty and pleaded guilty. I did intend to persuade the girl to make love but I went too far. However, I learned my lesson from this, and I would not have done this again. I have never been in trouble apart from this, and am now apprentice to a tailor. I started this after a course we had in Borstal, and I want to get on with it and lead a useful life.

Instructions to Counsel on behalf of the defendant Littleton

Counsel is instructed on behalf of the defendant Littleton, a man of good character who has been charged with indecently assaulting a girl of thirteen, as appears from the indictment and statements of the witnesses for the prosecution. Littleton wishes to plead not guilty to this charge, and sets out his defence in the proof of evidence which follows. A proof of evidence from Mrs Littleton is also available, which supports what the defendant has to say in certain important respects.

Counsel will appreciate that in view of the defence of alibi, the issue of identification is crucial to the case. The admissibility and quality of the evidence for the prosecution must be questionable in this respect. Unfortunately, no witness is available to support the alibi itself. It will be particularly important to ensure that the jury hear the whole of the tape of the conversation between the defendant and his wife if it is used in evidence at all, but Counsel will no doubt be anxious to exclude it if this can be done.

Unfortunately, it is believed that the defendant Coke will say that Littleton was at his flat on the day in question and may say that Littleton did in some way assault the girl. In this connection, it is worth observing that Coke has a previous conviction for rape, and it may be that he is protecting the man who was actually there.

Counsel will please consider the matters of evidence which arise in this case.

Proof of evidence of Littleton

MARTIN STEPHEN LITTLETON of 17 Eldon Villas, Oxbridge, will state as follows:

I have been charged with indecently assaulting a girl of thirteen called Angela Blackstone. I wish to plead not guilty. I am a man of thirty-three years of age, married, and I am of good character.

I have a number of part-time occupations, one of which is helping out at a public house called the Turk's Head in Oxbridge. I have come across a youth called Henry Coke there, and I have been to his place in Plowden Drive once or twice. On Sunday, 8 July 1979, the day of the alleged assault, I got up late, about 2.30 or 3 o'clock, as far as I can remember. My wife had been at her sister's over the previous night. I had a bite to eat. Then, because I felt a bit headachy, I went out for a walk in the direction of the park.

I started walking down Plowden Drive in the course of my walk, as this road is on the way from my house to the park. I noticed that there was a car coming towards me rather slowly, but I thought nothing of it until it stopped, and a small girl whom I have never seen before in my life got out with a woman and two men, and came up to me. The girl said something like: 'That's him' and pointed at me. I had no idea what was going on. The police officers then told me what was alleged, and they have correctly recorded my answers, which were to the effect that there had been a mistake over the identity of the attacker. I am sure the girl is genuinely convinced that I assaulted her, but I was not at Coke's flat that day and have no idea what happened. The police did not believe me, and I was arrested and taken to the police station.

Later on, the officers wanted to ask me some more questions, but I refused to answer until I had seen my solicitor, and I was not allowed to see him. Because of this, I was kept in overnight, which really upset me. My wife was due back that afternoon and would have been worried. In fact, the police contacted her, and she arrived at the station to see me later that evening. It now appears that the police recorded what we said to each other during the few minutes we were allowed in my cell. It is true that we had the conversation to which D/I Glanvil refers in his statement, but as should appear from the cassette, my wife's question was asked under the great stress which she felt at what had happened. I very foolishly lost my temper and answered in an ironical vein, intended to convey nothing more than anger that she should even have asked the question. I had in fact told her the truth already, exactly as it appears in this statement, and I hope this is also recorded on the cassette. I was not making any sort of admission that I had committed the offence.

I see that Henry Coke has told the police that I was at his flat and somehow helped him in his plan to rape Margaret Blackstone, and then myself molested her sister. This is quite untrue. I cannot think why he should have said this, as I have never offended him as far as I know, except that he is obviously trying to shield whoever was there, to cover up his own guilt. Coke has been in trouble of this sort before. He has been to Borstal for some offence involving a different girl, although I do not know the details of this.

Proof of evidence of Mrs Littleton

DAVINA MARY LITTLETON of 17 Eldon Villas, Oxbridge, will state as follows:

I am the wife of Martin Stephen Littleton and live with him at the above address.

On Saturday, 7 July 1979, I went for the day to my sister who lives at Winchelham, because it was her little boy's birthday. Martin was working all day on that Saturday, so he remained at home, and I arranged to stay the night and return the next day.

On the Sunday, 8 July, I arrived home at about 6 o'clock in the evening to find the house empty. This was rather unusual, as Martin usually stays in if he is not working. By 8 o'clock, I was getting worried. Just about then, I had a telephone call from the Oxbridge police saying that Martin had been arrested. They wouldn't tell me why over the phone. I was frantic. I got to the police station as quickly as I could and I saw Inspector Glanvil, who told me what they said had happened. I told him it was absurd, and said I wanted to see my husband. After some discussion, I was granted permission to do this, and after some delay, I was shown into a cell, where he was.

It appears that our conversation was recorded by the police, and I have done my best to recall it. Unfortunately, I was in such a state that only two things stand out clearly. Firstly, Martin told me that there must have been a mistake because he had been at home when the offence was supposed to have been committed. Then, a bit later, I very foolishly begged him to tell me whether there was any truth in what was said about him. I only did this because of the state I was in. It caused Martin to lose his temper, and he did reply in the words recorded by the police. However, it was quite clear that he was speaking in a bitter, sarcastic tone, and he did not mean that he was really guilty. If he had meant that, I think I would have had complete hysteria on the spot, and it would have shown in the recording. I would have been very angry and distressed.

From my knowledge of Martin, which goes back about nine years, six of them as his wife, the suggestion that he would interfere with children sexually is ludicrous. I have often seen him with children of friends and relatives, and his attitude towards them has always been quite normal. He is very popular with everyone who knows him, and has a good reputation for honesty and helpfulness.

3 The Burden and Standard of Proof

A: THE BURDEN OF PROOF

3.1 Introduction

The term 'burden of proof' refers to the general rule that in any legal proceedings, a party who asserts any fact for the purpose of establishing his case or defence bears the burden of proving that fact to the required degree of proof. It is incumbent on the party making an assertion against his opponent to justify that which he asserts. The reasons for the existence of such a burden are reasons of practical good sense in regulating the conduct of litigation, and it has been said judicially that the principle is 'an ancient rule founded on considerations of good sense and it should not be departed from without strong reasons' (1).

Even the simplest litigation usually consists of a number of different issues, proof of which is vital to the success of a party's case. Equally, within those various issues are numbers of individual facts which may have to be proved in order to establish the issues themselves. Accordingly, the term 'burden of proof' is ambiguous, standing alone. It may mean the obligation to prove an issue vital to the success of the case; it may mean the obligation to prove individual facts which in turn go to prove the issue. It is therefore generally accepted that there are two burdens of proof, corresponding to those two obligations which may lie upon a party (2). These burdens may be defined as follows.

3.2 The legal or persuasive burden

This is the burden which lies upon every party under the general rule to convince the tribunal of fact (3) of the truth or probability of some fact that is in issue in the case and is vital to the success of his case. It follows that failure to discharge this burden to the required standard of proof is fatal to the case. Whether this has been achieved is a matter for the tribunal of fact to consider on the whole of the evidence given in the case.

3.3 The evidential burden

This is the burden of adducing sufficient evidence to justify a favourable finding on a given fact. Obviously, failure to present evidence on any relevant fact involves the risk of

---

1 *Joseph Constantine Steamship Line* v *Imperial Smelting Corporation Ltd* (HL) [1942] AC 154 per Viscount Maugham at 174.
2   Some writers point out that there may be more than two burdens, but such analysis is of purely theoretical interest, and does not appear to affect the practical working of the law.
3   See 1.5.1, ante.

an adverse finding. It is no more than a risk, since the e...
may not be accepted, but the risk is there. An adverse...
the importance of the fact in the case, lead to failure i...
lead to failure in the case, as would happen if there was ...
burden assessed on the whole of the evidence. Successful ...
burden therefore means no more than presenting evidence that ...
finding of fact possible, though not inevitable. It creates a sim...
opponent to adduce evidence in reply or to risk a finding adverse to him. ...
that the evidential burden in relation to a given fact may lie on different p...
case progresses.

We must now consider in a little more detail where the two burdens of proof lie...
question of where a burden lies may be of importance in various situations, for example:

(a) Where the right to begin (i.e., to open the case and call evidence first) is disputed or unclear.

(b) Where a defendant submits, at the close of the case for the prosecution, or the case for the plaintiff, that there is no case to answer.

(c) Where the tribunal of fact is left in doubt on the whole of the evidence.

(d) Where an appellate court is called upon to consider the correctness of a summing-up or judgment dealing with the burden of proof.

3.4 Where the legal burden lies

3.4.1 Civil cases

The burden of proving any vital issue in a case lies on the party who asserts the issue and who must establish the issue in order to succeed. The question of what is a vital issue depends upon the nature of the case, and is a question of law. The question is: what must the plaintiff prove to make out a case, for example, of negligence or breach of contract? The answer lies in showing what the constituent elements of the action are. Any element without which the case would be insufficient in law is a vital issue, the proof of which lies on the plaintiff. If the plaintiff fails to prove any one such issue, the defendant will successfully submit that there is no case to answer. The same is true of a defence raised on the other side. Where the defendant relies upon a specific defence in order to defeat the claim, the burden of proving such defence lies on him. This will apply to any defence going beyond a mere denial of the plaintiff's case, or beyond merely putting the plaintiff to proof of that which he asserts.

It is a sound rule, therefore, that every party must prove each necessary element of his case. There are cases, however, where it is not easy to determine to whose case an issue is essential, and who should be held to fail if the issue is not proved. In such cases, the courts have inclined to require proof of the party to whom the least difficulty or embarrassment will be caused by the burden, and in deciding this, a sound rule of thumb is to require proof of a positive rather than a negative proposition. Thus, in *Joseph Constantine Steamship Line* v *Imperial Smelting Corporation Ltd* (4) charterers claimed damages from the shipowners for breach of charterparty. The defendants claimed that the contract had been frustrated by the destruction of the ship by explosion, the cause of which was unclear. Such frustration would have concluded the case in favour of the defendants in the absence of any fault on their part. In view of the unsatisfactory state of

4 [1942] AC 154.

...nce, the question of who bore the burden of proving or disproving fault was of ...mportance. The House of Lords held that to require the defendants to prove a ...ve (the absence of fault) would be unduly onerous. The reality was that the ...iffs asserted the existence of fault and should be required to prove it. Similarly, in ...*son and Another* v *Patent Steam Carpet Cleaning Ltd* (5) the defendants were guilty ...the unexplained loss of the plaintiffs Chinese carpet, which had been delivered to ...em for cleaning. A clause in the contract signed by the plaintiffs would have exempted the defendants from liability for negligence, but not for any fundamental breach. It was necessary to determine where the burden of proof on the latter issue lay. The Court of Appeal held that the defendants would find the burden far less onerous, the circumstances being within their competence, and accordingly they bore the burden of proof. This is in accord with the rule in cases of bailment that it is for the defendant to show that the loss or damage was not caused by want of reasonable care on his part.

Any question of which party relies on an issue as an essential part of his case, or of who asserts a positive proposition can in most cases be resolved by reference to the pleadings. The pleadings usually make clear in what way the case or defence is put, and fix the legal burden accordingly. The art of pleading enables any assertion to be made in more than one way, and care must be taken to look at the reality and not the language of the pleading. The mere use of negative language should not be allowed to obscure the fact that a positive claim or defence is being asserted, and the substance not the form of the pleading is the true guide. Thus, an assertion that a tenant has failed to repair premises pursuant to his covenant is an affirmative allegation, the proof of which lies on the asserting landlord, even though couched in language in negative form (6).

The above rules will suffice to pin-point the incidence of the legal burden in civil cases. The specific examples which follow, taken from common kinds of action, follow from the legal requirements of establishing the cause of action or defence and would be reflected in the pleadings. They are intended as illustrations, and are in no way exceptional.

(a) *Contract*. The plaintiff bears the burden of proving the contract, the due performance of conditions precedent, breach of contract by the defendant and consequent loss to the plaintiff; the defendant of proving any special facts upon which his defence is founded, such as infancy, fraud, or accord and satisfaction. A party relying on an exceptive clause in the contract will usually bear the burden of proving that he falls within its ambit. Thus, where the plaintiff alleged failure to deliver goods, the defendant bore the burden of proving that he fell within an exceptive clause exempting him where the ship and goods were lost by the perils of the sea. The plaintiff would then have to prove any negligence on the part of the defendant disentitling the defendant to the protection of the clause (7).

(b) *Negligence*. The plaintiff bears the burden of proving the duty of care, breach by the defendant of such duty and consequential loss to the plaintiff; the defendant of proving any special facts upon which his defence is founded, such as Act of God, *volenti non fit injuria*, or contributory negligence.

(c) *Malicious prosecution*. The plaintiff bears the burden of proving not only the unsuccessful prosecution of him by the defendant, but also the absence of any reasonable

---

5   [1978] QB 69.
6   *Soward* v *Leggatt* (1836) 7 C & P 613; see also *Osborn and Another* v *Thompson* (NP) (1839) 9 C & P 337 (assertion that horse unsound, contrary to warranty).
7   *The Glendarroch* (CA) [1894] P 226.

and probable cause for the prosecution, this being an essential element of the plaintiff's case, even though expressed as a negative (8). By way of contrast, in an action for false imprisonment, where the plaintiff proves the fact of restraint, restraint being prima facie tortious, it is for the defendant to prove lawful justification for his act (9).

(d) *Bailment.* Once the plaintiff proves the fact of the bailment, the burden lies on the defendant to show that the loss of or damage to the goods was not caused by any want of reasonable care on his part (10).

The incidence of the legal burden may in civil cases be varied by agreement between the parties (11). It may also be provided for expressly by some rule of law, for example the provision that in cases of unfair dismissal, the fact of dismissal being proved, the respondent employer bears the burden of showing that it was fair, notwithstanding that the applicant relies on the contrary assertion for his cause of action (12).

3.4.2 Criminal cases

In criminal cases, the guidelines offered by pleadings are of little assistance. Coke and Littleton face the assertions made against them as they are particularised with the brevity dictated by the Indictment Rules 1971 in the indictment, albeit their possession of the depositions (committal statements) ensures that they should know the case they have to meet. Except for the notice of alibi furnished by Littleton, their answer to the charges will be confined to an oral plea of not guilty to the general issue (i.e., their guilt or innocence). In view of the fact that their defences do in a sense involve affirmative assertions (in Littleton's case, his alibi; in Coke's case, that Margaret Blackstone consented to sexual intercourse) it is not easy to apply the civil rule to determine where the burden lies in each case.

In fact, it has long been recognised that criminal cases are subject to a wide, general rule which overrides the pleadings test in identifying the affirmative assertion. The rule is that in criminal cases, the legal burden of proving every element of the offence charged, and therefore the guilt of the defendant, lies from first to last on the prosecution. Although now subject to important exceptions, and although the evidential burden does not always coincide with the legal, this principle is undoubtedly of general application. In *Woolmington* v *DPP* (13) the defendant was charged with the murder of his wife. His defence was that the gun had gone off accidentally. The jury were directed that once the prosecution proved that the deceased was killed by the defendant, it was for the defendant to show that the killing was not murder. This was held by the House of Lords to be a misdirection. Viscount Sankey LC expressed the rule in striking words which have become justly celebrated (14):

> Throughout the web of the English criminal law one golden thread is always to be seen, that it is the duty of the prosecution to prove the prisoner's guilt. . . . If, at the end of and on the whole of the case, there is a reasonable doubt, created by the evidence given by either the prosecution or the prisoner, as to whether the prisoner killed the deceased with a malicious intention, the prosecution has not made out the

8   *Abrath* v *North Eastern Railway Co.* (CA) (1883) 11 QBD 440; affirmed (HL) (1886) 11 App cas 247.
9   *Hicks* v *Faulkner* (DC) (1881) 8 QBD 167.
10   *Brook's Wharf & Bull Wharf Ltd* v *Goodman Brothers* (CA) [1937] 1 KB 534: *Port Swettenham Authority* v *T.W. Wu & Co. (M) Sdn Bhd* (PC, Malaysia) [1979] AC 580.
11   See, e.g., *Levy* v *Assicurazioni Generali* (PC, Palestine) [1940] AC 791.
12   Employment Protection (Consolidation) Act 1978, s. 57(1).
13   [1935] AC 462.   14   Ibid. at 481–2.

case and the prisoner is entitled to an acquittal. No matter what the charge or where the trial, the principle that the prosecution must prove the guilt of the prisoner is part of the common law of England and no attempt to whittle it down can be entertained.

The rule applies in general even where part of the case for the prosecution involves a negative, e.g. that Coke had sexual intercourse with Margaret Blackstone without her consent. Lack of consent is an integral part of the prosecution's case on a charge of rape, and the burden of proving that element of the offence lies consequently on the prosecution. The converse also applies, so that the defendant does not bear any legal burden of proving even affirmative facts in support of his defence. Thus, Littleton need not prove that he was at home when he is alleged to have been indecently assaulting Angela Blackstone, any more than Coke need prove that his sexual intercourse with Margaret Blackstone was consensual. Of course, these statements only concern the incidence of the legal burden; the situation is not necessarily so simple when one considers the evidential burden and tactical matters.

The rule with regard to the legal burden in criminal cases is subject to three important classes of exception:

(a)   Where the burden is put on the defendant by statute.

(b)   Where the defendant has to prove that he is authorised to do something that is generally proscribed.

(c)   Where the defendant pleads insanity.

3.4.2.1   Statutory exceptions.   There are a number of instances where statute expressly lays a legal burden of proving some issue in a criminal case upon the defendant. It should be noted that the burden relates only to the issue dealt with by the statute, and that subject to the issue so dealt with, the prosecution must still prove the guilt of the defendant. Three examples of some importance will suffice:

(a)   *Diminished responsibility.* 'On a charge of murder, it shall be for the defence to prove that the person charged is by virtue of this section not liable to be convicted of murder' (Homicide Act 1957, s. 2(2)). See also *R* v *Dunbar* (15).

(b)   *Offensive weapons.* 'Any person who without lawful authority or reasonable excuse, the proof whereof shall lie on him, has with him in any public place any offensive weapon shall be guilty of an offence . . .' (Prevention of Crime Act 1953, s. 1(1)).

(c)   *Corruption.* 'Where in any proceedings against a person for an offence under the Prevention of Corruption Act 1906 or the Public Bodies Corrupt Practices Act 1889 it is proved that any money, gift or other consideration has been paid or given to or received by [certain specified persons] the money, gift, or consideration shall be deemed to have been paid or given and received corruptly as such inducement or reward as is mentioned in such Act unless the contrary is proved.' (Prevention of Corruption Act 1916, s. 2.) See also *R* v *Carr-Briant* (16).

3.4.2.2   Statutory offences made subject to exceptions etc.   It was said above in relation to civil cases that it is a sound rule that the burden of proof should fall upon the party

---

15   (CCA) [1958] 1 QB 1. The law in cases where the prosecution seek to establish diminished responsibility is considered under the heading of insanity (3.4.2.3, post).
16   [1943] KB 607.

asserting the affirmative proposition. Although this rule i.
criminal cases, it is now settled that in one type of case, the
burden of proving an affirmative. This is in cases where the o.
the enactment creating it to be subject to limited exceptions, pe
proscribed when committed by persons of a certain class, posses.
tions or holding certain licences. Clearly it is a light burden to a defe.
he falls within the excepted class, compared to that which would have t.
prosecution in proving that the defendant is not such a person, particu.
members of the class are numerous or difficult to trace.

Curiously, the position was for a long time clearer in relation to offe.
summarily in the magistrates' courts than in relation to more serious offences
indictment. In a summary trial, the matter is governed by s. 81 of the Magistrates' .
Act 1952 which provides that:

> Where the defendant to an information or complaint relies for his defence on any
> exception, exemption, proviso, excuse or qualification, whether or not it accompanies
> the description of the offence or matter of complaint in the enactment creating the
> offence or on which the complaint is founded, the burden of proving the exception,
> exemption, proviso, excuse or qualification shall be on him; and this notwithstanding
> that the information or complaint contains an allegation negativing the exception,
> exemption, proviso, excuse or qualification.

This section applies to a very large number of common summary offences, of which
driving a motor vehicle on a road without being the holder of a current driving licence
may be cited as an example (17).

A more general approach was worked out in *R* v *Edwards* (18). The defendant was
charged on indictment with selling liquor without a licence. The sale of liquor was
proved, but the prosecution did not call evidence to show that the defendant was not the
holder of a licence. It was argued on his behalf that the prosecution had failed to
discharge the legal burden of proof on them in this respect. For the prosecution, it was
contended that even though in this instance, it was comparatively simple to consult the
records of the licensing justices to establish the status of the defendant, the burden of
proving that he was the holder of a licence lay on the defendant; that s. 81 was a statutory
enactment of a general rule of the common law; and that it was undesirable that the
burden of proof on such an issue should be held to vary according to the procedural
factor of mode of trial (19). The Court of Appeal accepted the arguments put forward for
the prosecution. The prosecution need not make out a prima facie case that the
defendant falls within the exception, whether the exception is expressed as such or as a
proviso or in any other language having the same effect, and this applies whether or not
the facts in issue are for any reason within the peculiar knowledge of the defendant
(hence irrespective of the difficulty or ease with which the prosecution could have proved
the negative) (20). The legal burden on the issue lies upon the defendant in such a case.

17   For examples of the working of the section, see *John* v *Humphreys* (DC) [1955] 1 WLR 325; *R* v *Ewens*
(CCA) [1967] 1 QB 322.
18   [1975] QB 27.
19   This argument is supported by the fact that in drafting an indictment, the prosecution are not required to
negative an exception, proviso, excuse or qualification: Indictment Rules 1971, r. 6(c).
20   At common law, a distinction, now obsolete, was to be found between provisos and exceptions, see *R* v
Jarvis (1756) 1 East 643n. In wider terms, it was thought that a party who asserted the affirmative of a matter
peculiarly within his own knowledge bore the burden of proof on the matter, see *R* v *Turner* (1816), 5 M & S 206 at
211 per Bayley J.

Insanity. The defence of insanity has lost much of its former significance since
olition of the death penalty, and its formulation has been much criticised both on
and medical grounds. Nonetheless, it remains the subject of an exception to the
on burden of proof. The position is set out clearly in the answers given by the judges
e House of Lords in consequence of *Daniel M'Naghten's Case* (21) as the following
ract will show, and the rule has been recognised and followed in subsequent cases
2).

Question 2: 'What are the proper questions to be submitted to the jury, where a
person alleged to be afflicted with insane delusion respecting one or more particular
subjects or persons, is charged with the commission of a crime (murder, for example),
and insanity is set up as a defence?'
Question 3: 'In what terms ought the question to be left to the jury as to the prisoner's
state of mind at the time when the act was committed?'
Answers (to the second and third questions): 'That the jurors ought to be told in all
cases that every man is to be presumed to be sane, and to possess a sufficient degree of
reason to be responsible for his crimes, until the contrary be proved to their satisfaction; and that to establish a defence on the ground of insanity, it must be clearly
proved that, at the time of the committing of the act, the party accused was labouring
under such a defect of reason, from disease of the mind, as not to know the nature and
quality of the act he was doing; or, if he did know it, that he did not know he was doing
what was wrong.'

It will be observed that question 2 postulates the setting up of insanity as a defence;
that is to say, the issue of insanity is raised by the defence for the purpose of obtaining a
verdict of not guilty by reason of insanity. It should not be forgotten that, by virtue of s. 6
of the Criminal Procedure (Inasnity) Act 1964, where the defendant in a trial for murder
contends either that he is insane or that he is suffering from diminished responsibility,
the court shall allow the prosecution to adduce or elicit evidence tending to prove the
other of those contentions. In this event, the prosecution bear the burden of proving the
contention which they make (23). The burden of proving either defence is therefore
borne by the defence in so far as they raise the issue, by way of defence, and the
prosecution bear no burden unless and until they go beyond mere denial of the defence
and affirmatively assert that the defendant was suffering from the 'other' disability i.e.
that which the defendant himself has not raised by way of defence.
   The general rule in cases of insanity is undoubtedly capable of causing difficulties for
juries in cases where the defence is put forward as an alternative to some other defence,
for example non-insane automatism, where the prosecution bear the legal burden in all
respects and must therefore rebut the defence raised. The jury must then be directed to
consider two quite separate burdens of proof in relation to these aspects of the case,
when on the facts the defences may be closely interrelated (24).
   In all the exceptional cases in which the defence bear some legal burden, the burden is

21   (1843) 10 Cl & F 200 at 209–10.
22   *R v Smith* (CCA) (1910) 6 Cr App R 19 and see *R v Carr-Briant* (CCA) [1943] KB 607 for useful general
observations on defence burdens.
23   And in contrast to the position where the defence bear the burden, it seems that the prosecution must prove
the contention beyond reasonable doubt: see *R v Grant* [1960] Crim LR 424 and Section B, post. The burden and
standard of proof on an issue of fitness to plead depend similarly on the question of who raises it: *R v Podola*
(CCA) [1960] 1 QB 325; *R v Robertson* (CA) [1968] 1 WLR 1767.
24   See, e.g., *Bratty v Attorney-General for N. Ireland* (HL) [1963] AC 386.

confined to that of proving the issue to which it specifically relates. In all other respects, the prosecution bear the overall burden of proving the guilt of the defendant, according to the general rule of *Woolmington's* case. Thus, where insanity or diminished responsibility is raised, the prosecution must first prove that the defendant committed the actus reus of the offence; failing this, the defendant would have no case to answer, and no question of his raising a defence would arise. Equally, in a case of conduct proscribed subject to an exception, the prosecution must first prove that the defendant behaved in the way proscribed, or no question of proof of any exception can arise. In other words, the burden on the defence relates to a specific issue only; in no other respect is the defendant called upon to prove his innocence.

3.5   Where the evidential burden lies

3.5.1   Generally
The burden of adducing sufficient evidence to justify a favourable finding on a given fact may lie upon different parties at different stages of a trial. For this reason, the evidential burden is sometimes said to 'shift' during a case, although this is not strictly accurate, because in reality the successful discharge of such a burden by one party creates for his opponent the risk of failure on that fact, and therefore gives rise to a new evidential burden lying on the opponent. The simplest way in which to detect the evidential burden of proof is to ask: If no evidence, or no further evidence were given about this fact, which party would now run the risk of failure? The party running the risk bears the evidential burden at that point. Again, it should be emphasised that failure is only a risk, because the evidence given on the other side may be insufficient or may be rejected. At the outset of the case, therefore, the evidential burden will lie upon the party asserting the affirmative of the fact to be proved. For this reason, it usually coincides at that stage with the incidence of the legal burden. However, once evidence is given by the asserter which renders possible a finding in his favour on the fact, the opponent incurs an evidential burden while the legal burden remains on the asserter throughout the case.

These principles may conveniently be illustrated by the possible course of Coke and Littleton. The prosecution can only discharge their legal burden of proof by proving to the required standard (beyond reasonable doubt) that Coke had sexual intercourse with Margaret Blackstone without her consent, and that Littleton assaulted Angela Blackstone in an indecent fashion. This is a matter for the jury to consider on the whole of the evidence called for both sides. However, the evidential burden of proving the necessary facts in support of those propositions may be discharged by the prosecution's adducing evidence to show a prima facie case. This means evidence on which a jury, properly directed, could but need not convict. This burden having been discharged, the prosecution have prevented the case from being withdrawn from the jury on a submission of no case to answer; but have done no more.

At this stage, since this is not one of the exceptional cases in which Coke or Littleton bears any legal burden of proof, neither is under any obligation to give or call evidence in his defence. If they take this course, the jury must decide the case on the prosecution's evidence alone and assess whether the prosecution's legal burden has been discharged. In taking this course, however, Coke and Littleton run the clear risk that the evidence for the prosecution will be believed and that the jury will accordingly make adverse findings of fact which may be serious enough to result in conviction. It follows, therefore, that even though they bear no legal burden, the making out by the prosecution of a prima facie case gives rise to an evidential burden on the defendants. The evidential burden began by coinciding with the legal burden, but after sufficient evidence had been given, the evidential burden was discharged and a new one incurred by the defendants or, if you prefer, the evidential burden shifted to the defendants while the legal burden remained on the prosecution.

Precisely the same considerations prevail where the prosecution prove facts which would entitle, but do not oblige, the jury to infer some guilty state of mind which is necessary to proof of the offence charged. Instances are where the prosecution prove recent possession of stolen goods, or lead evidence of a previous conviction for theft or handling stolen goods in the circumstances permitted by s. 27(3) of the Theft Act 1968. The evidence led for the prosecution creates an evidential burden on the defendant, in the sense that in the absence of some explanation consistent with innocence which the jury accept, the jury may infer guilty knowledge. The legal burden of proving guilty knowledge nonetheless remains on the prosecution.

3.5.2   Defences involving new issues

Neither the legal nor the evidential burden resting on the prosecution obliges them to anticipate defences which may or may not be raised, or explanations consistent with innocence which may or may not be proffered by the defence. As Hale CJ put it aptly, this would be 'like leaping before one come to the stile' (25). Thus, while the prosecution must of course rebut the defendant's denial of guilt by his plea and any challenges to their evidence, no burden lies on them to deal with any further issues unless these are expressly raised by the defence. If, therefore, the defendant wishes to rely on some defence or explanation which goes beyond a mere denial of or challenge to the prosecution's evidence, he bears an evidential burden of raising the issue by evidence sufficient to justify a finding in his favour on the issue involved (26).

The burden on the defendant has been variously described in the cases, and it is frequently said that he must 'lay a proper foundation' for the issue. It is submitted that this must mean only that he bears no more than an evidential burden. Once he discharges this burden by adducing sufficient evidence to make the issue a proper one for the jury to consider, it follows from the incidence of the legal burden that the prosecution must then rebut his case beyond reasonable doubt in order to prove guilt. If, however, the defendant fails to discharge the evidential burden, the issue will not be left to the jury and the prosecution need not deal with it.

It is of vital importance to distinguish cases where the defence bear this evidential burden of raising the issue from the exceptional cases discussed previously in which the legal burden of proving some issue is cast on the defence. Indeed, in the cases where the evidential burden only is involved, for example provocation or self-defence, the use of the word 'defence' has been rightly criticised as tending to suggest a legal burden of proof which the defence do not bear; it would be preferable to refer to them as 'explanations involving new issues', so as to stress that like any other explanation offered, the prosecution must rebut them in order to prove guilt; nonetheless, they are almost always referred to as defences.

The cases which arise most commonly where the defence must raise an issue before the prosecution need rebut the explanation are as follows — (the list is not intended to be

25   *Sir Ralph Bovy's Case* (1684) 1 Vent 217.
26   The issue must be raised by evidence, not e.g. by a mere assertion by defence counsel: *Parker* v *Smith* (DC) [1974] RTR 500. But whether the evidence is elicited by cross-examination of the prosecution witnesses or is called by the defence is immaterial: *Bullard* v *R* (PC, Trinidad & Tobago) [1957] AC 635.

exhaustive): non-insane automatism (27); provocation (28); self-defence or prevention of crime (29); drunkenness (30); duress (31); mechanical defect (32); reasonable excuse for failing to supply a specimen for a laboratory test in excess-alcohol cases (33); impossibility of carrying out conspiracy at common law (34).

3.5.3 Secondary facts

An evidential burden lies also upon the asserter of a secondary fact, that is to say, a fact which affects the admissibility of evidence or the construction of a document, and consistently with the general rule, the burden so imposed lies on the party who asserts the affirmative proposition.

Thus, a party who asserts that a witness is incompetent, or that secondary evidence is admissible of a lost document, or that the deceased was under a settled, hopeless expectation of death so as to render admissable a statement as a dying declaration, or that the relationship between his opponent and a witness is such as to give rise to bias in the witness's evidence, bears in each case the burden of adducing evidence to support the assertion (35). The same applies to a party who wishes to adduce parol evidence to complete a written contract, or who asserts a certain interpretation of an ambiguous document (36).

As to secondary facts, two distinct situations may arise. The first relates to evidence as to which the judge need do no more than satisfy himself that there is a prima facie case that the evidence tendered is genuine and original, its value and weight being a matter for the jury. Here it is not the admissibility of the evidence as such which is in issue, but merely whether the piece of evidence tendered appears to the judge to be what it purports to be and is tendered as being. As an instance of the first, among the questions which may have to be considered in the case of Coke and Littleton is that of the admissibility or otherwise of the tape-recording said to contain incriminating conversation between Littleton and his wife. If the prosecution seek to adduce the tape in evidence, they must adduce some preliminary evidence to show that it is the original, and that it has not been edited or interfered with. Should this matter be disputed in itself, it would in due course be a matter for the jury, so that the judge need be satisfied only that there is evidence fit to be left to the jury on the issue (37). In the second situation, however, the question of admissibility is a preliminary issue of law quite unrelated to the qualitative question which the jury may later have to decide about the evidence if it is admitted. Into this category might fall the admissibility of Littleton's actual words as a confession. In this case, the judge will decide and rule on the question, having heard evidence from both sides in the absence of the jury, and the asserter must then prove his case on this point to the required standard. Further issues of admissibility may arise if Littleton asserts some privilege for the conversation. He would then bear the burden of adducing evidence tending to show that such evidence was inadmissible.

27   *Hill* v *Baxter* (DC) [1958] 1 QB 277; *Bratty* v *Attorney-General for N. Ireland* (HL) [1963] AC 386.
28   *Bullard* v *R* (PC, Trinidad & Tobago) [1957] AC 635; *R* v *McPherson* (CCA) (1957) 41 Cr App R 213.
29   Criminal Law Act 1967, s. 3, now governs the law. See also on the question of the burden *R* v *Lobell* (CCA) [1957] 1 QB 547; *R* v *Abraham* (CA) [1973] 1 WLR 1270.
30   *Kennedy* v *HM Advocate* 1944 JC 171.
31   *R* v *Gill* (CCA) [1963] 1 WLR 841.   32   *R* v *Spurge* (CCA) [1961] 2 QB 205.
33   *R* v *Clarke* (CA) [1969] 1 WLR 1109.   34   *R* v *Bennett and Others*, *The Times* 11 August 1978.
35   E.g., *R* v *Thompson* (CCR) [1893] 2 QB 12 (confession); *R* v *Jenkins* (CCR) (1869) LR 1 CCR 187 (dying declaration).
36   *Tucker* v *Bennett* (CA) (1887) 38 ChD 1 (parol evidence); *Falck* v *Williams* (PC, New South Wales) [1900] AC 176 (construction).
37   *R* v *Robson; R* v *Harris* [1972] 1 WLR 651; *R* v *Stevenson and Others* [1971] 1 WLR 1.

Similarly, the judge may receive evidence with regard to the admissibility of Coke's previous conviction as similar-fact evidence and whether Coke's alleged oral and written confessions were made voluntarily, and the burden lies on the prosecution who seek to have the evidence admitted. The admissibility of confessions is, as we shall see, governed by special considerations (Chapter 7, post).

Again, it will be observed that although the form of an assertion may be positive (arguing for admissibility) or negative (arguing for inadmissibility) the burden lies upon the party who in effect asserts the affirmative of the issue, with a view to establishing that part of his case. More detailed rules of evidence relating to individual questions of admissibility will be dealt with elsewhere as they occur.

Although most of the examples given of the working of the evidential burden have been drawn from criminal cases, the position is the same in civil cases. Thus, if the plaintiff in an action for possession for unauthorised sub-letting makes out a prima facie case by showing that a person other than the lessee is in possession, apparently as a tenant, an evidential burden lies upon the defendant to prove that the occupier is there in some other capacity (38). Where a landlord shows a prima facie case of title by proving payment of rent by the tenant, the evidential burden lies on the tenant to prove mistake or ignorance of the facts (39). And where it was proved that statutory precautions had not been observed in relation to a mine, the owner of the mine bore the evidential burden of proving that an explosion, which might have occurred because of the lack of such precautions, had not been caused by his lack of care for the safety of those working at the mine (40).

B: THE STANDARD OF PROOF

3.6 Introduction

The term 'standard of proof' refers to the extent or degree to which the burden of proof must be discharged. It is the measurement of the degree of certainty or probability which the evidence must generate in the mind of the tribunal of fact; the level at which the tribunal of fact must be convinced by the evidence before the party bearing the burden of proof becomes entitled to succeed in the case, or to have a favourable finding of fact on some issue which he has set out to prove. It is a measurement therefore of the quality and cogency required of evidence tendered with a view to discharging the burden of proof. The standard of proof demanded varies according to the nature of the case, and sometimes according to the nature of the issue to be proved, but the fundamental divergence is that between criminal and civil cases.

3.7 Criminal cases

3.7.1 Prosecution
The standard of proof required of the prosecution in the discharge of the legal burden of proving the guilt of the defendant is a high one. There are two classic formulations of the standard required.

(a) 'Beyond reasonable doubt'. This formulation has been approved on more than

38 *Doe* d *Hindly* v *Rickarby* (1980) 5 Esp 4.
39 *Hindle and Another* v *Hick Brothers Manufacturing Co. Ltd* (CA) [1947] 2 All ER 825.
40 *Britannic Merthyr Coal Co. Ltd* v *David* (HL) [1910] AC 74.

one occasion by the House of Lords (41) and has become a part of the English language. In *Miller* v *Minister of Pensions* (42), Denning J elaborated on the nature of proof beyond reasonable doubt in these terms:

> It need not reach certainty, but it must carry a high degree of probability. Proof beyond reasonable doubt does not mean proof beyond the shadow of a doubt. The law would fail to protect the community if it admitted fanciful possibilities to deflect the course of justice. If the evidence is so strong against a man as to leave only a remote possibility in his favour which can be dismissed with the sentence 'of course it is possible, but not in the least probable,' the case is proved beyond reasonable doubt, but nothing short of that will suffice.

This formulation fell for a time into some disfavour because of supposed difficulties in explaining to juries the nature of reasonable doubt, if they experienced problems of understanding. Expressions intended to be helpful, but of questionable value, such as, 'a reasonable doubt is one for which you could give reasons if asked' found disfavour in the higher courts and led to some successful appeals against conviction. As a result, the second formulation gained wide favour.

(b) 'Satisfied so that they feel sure' (or more simply 'sure of guilt'). This formulation was advocated by Lord Goddard CJ in *R* v *Summers* (43), when he said:

> If a jury is told that it is their duty to regard the evidence and see that it satisfies them so that they can feel sure when they return a verdict of guilty, that is much better than using the expression 'reasonable doubt' and I hope in future that that will be done.

It is apparent that the only real objection advanced to 'beyond reasonable doubt' is that further attempts to elucidate the phrase might be unhelpful or misleading. In modern practice, much more emphasis is placed on the substance of the direction to the jury as a whole than on the adoption of any particular formula. As long as the judge successfully conveys the high degree of probability required, the direction will be proper. In *R* v *Hepworth and Fearnley* (44) Lord Goddard himself observed that a judge would be 'on safe ground' if he directed a jury that 'You must be satisfied beyond reasonable doubt', and added: 'and one could also say: "You must feel sure of the prisoner's guilt." ' The matter was cogently expressed by Lord Diplock in *Walters* v *R* (45) when he pointed out that the judge has the opportunity of assessing the jury during a trial, and can select whatever formula he feels will best assist that jury, avoiding all gloss upon the formula which he uses, as far as possible.

Against this background, the question is simply whether the judge has succeeded overall in stressing the high standard for which the jury should look. In *Ferguson* v *R* (46) the composite formulation 'satisfied beyond reasonable doubt so that you feel sure of the defendant's guilt' was upheld as 'generally safe and sufficient', the Privy Council stressing that there is no set form of words and the test is one of successful communication of the standard in whatever words may be employed. In the ordinary case, of course, use of a

---

41   *Woolmington* v *DPP* (HL) [1935] AC 462 at 481; *Mancini* v *DPP* (HL) [1942] AC 1 at 11.
42   [1947] 2 All ER 372 at 373.
43   (CCA) [1952] 1 All ER 1059. The passage quoted is taken from the report in 36 Cr App R 14 at 15. The All ER report reads a little differently, albeit to the same effect.
44   (CCA) [1955] 2 QB 600.   45   (PC, Jamaica) [1969] 2 AC 26 at 30.
46   (PC, Grenada) [1979] 1 WLR 94. See also *R* v *Kritz* (CCA) [1950] 1 KB 82 per Lord Goddard CJ at 89.

time-honoured phrase is wise and above criticism. By way of contrast, the appellate courts have found wanting a number of lesser expressions which do not adequately convey the standard. Into such a category fall: 'satisfied' (standing alone) (47); 'pretty certain' (48); 'reasonably sure' (49).

In cases where the formula 'beyond reasonable doubt' is used, the use of further comment by way of elucidation is still far from clear. It is submitted that the use of such phrases and analogies should be resorted to only when the jury seem in danger of failing to understand what is required of them, and that the judge must exercise his discretion in this respect. In *R* v *Ching* (50), the Court of Appeal said: 'We point out and emphasise that if judges stopped trying to define that which is almost impossible to define there would be fewer appeals.' The court nonetheless recognised that exceptional cases would remain where some further assistance to the jury would be called for. While endorsing earlier criticisms of efforts to define a reasonable doubt as one for which a reason could be given (51), the court upheld the direction given by the trial judge that a reasonable doubt was: 'something to which you can assign a reason. The sort of matter which might influence you if you were to consider some business matter . . . a matter for example, concerning a mortgage of your house.' The reference to matters related to the personal affairs of the jurors was also approved in *Walters,* but subject to the qualification that the comparison must be with affairs of importance in their lives; and in *R* v *Gray* (52) it was held by the Court of Appeal to be a misdirection to compare the standard of proof with the degree of care which the jury might exercise in their 'everyday affairs'.

There may of course be problems in the use of any formula, and the strongest safeguard still seems to be that of judicial flexibility to meet the needs of individual juries. Nonetheless, it is submitted that the traditional formula 'beyond reasonable doubt' is to be preferred to that of 'feeling sure of guilt'. The latter may in many cases actually suggest too high a standard, and will sometimes tend to confuse legal with scientific certainty (53). On the other hand, experience has shown that the phrase 'beyond reasonable doubt' has passed into the language by dint of long usage, is understood by juries and can if necessary be elaborated on without confusion.

3.7.2   Defence

In the exceptional cases where the defence bear some legal burden of proof on an issue affecting guilt (see 3.4 ante) it is not necessary for the issue to be proved beyond reasonable doubt. The standard of proof required of the defence has been defined as 'not higher than the burden which rests upon a plaintiff or a defendant in civil proceedings' (54). The standard required in such cases is always the same, regardless of the issue to be proved. The civil standard of proof is that on the balance of probabilities (see post, 3.8).

3.7.3   Secondary facts

It has already been noted in 3.5.3 that there are two distinct situations. Where the judge has to decide a question of admissibility of evidence as a matter of law, the issue is unrelated to any consideration of the weight which such evidence may or may not have with the jury, if admitted. It is accordingly a matter which the judge decides once and for

---

47   *R* v *Hepworth and Fearnley* (CCA) [1955] 2 QB 600.   48   *R* v *Law* (CA) [1961] Crim LR 52.
49   *R* v *Head and Warrener* (CCA) (1961) 45 Cr App R 225.   50   (1976) 63 Cr App R 7 at 11.
51   See, e.g., *R* v *Stafford; R* v *Luvaglio* [1968] 3 All ER 752n.
52   (1973) 58 Cr App R 177.
53   See for example *R* v *Bracewell* (CA) (1978) 68 Cr App R 44.
54   *R* v *Carr-Briant* (CCA) [1943] KB 607 at 610.

all, and with which the jury are not concerned. The rule in such cases is that the same standard is required on the secondary issue as is required for the discharge of the legal burden in the main issue, and therefore that where the prosecution contend for the admissibility of any evidence and such question depends on the proving of certain secondary facts, the prosecution are required to prove such secondary facts beyond reasonable doubt (55).

Although this rule is not easy to justify logically, because the burden on the prosecution is no more than evidential, it has the salutary effect of subjecting often highly damaging evidence to close scrutiny before it reaches the jury. The prosecution will therefore bear the burden of proving the voluntariness of Coke's confessions beyond reasonable doubt by calling evidence in the absence of the jury about how they came to be made.

On the other hand, certain questions which fall to be decided by the judge affecting admission of evidence, require him to do no more than satisfy himself in a preliminary inquiry that there is some evidence fit to be left to the jury of the very fact which the jury have to decide. In other words, the judge need only satisfy himself that the issue in question should not be withdrawn from the jury; he decides whether there is a prima facie case upon which the jury could reach a conclusion and he is therefore considering the same issue as they must later consider. Such a case is the Littleton tape-recording. Given that the contents of the tape are not objectionable in themselves, the prosecution are entitled to put the tape before the jury, provided only that the judge is satisfied that the tape is prima facie original and has not been interfered with (56). The standard in such a case is therefore certainly no higher than the balance of probabilities. In *R v Angeli* (57) the Court of Appeal held that the trial judge had been right to apply that standard to the question whether it was 'proved to his satisfaction' as required by s. 8 of the Criminal Procedure Act 1865 that samples of handwriting said to be that of the defendant were genuine, so as to permit their submission to the jury and their comparison by expert evidence to disputed writings. Again, this question, i.e. whether the various samples were written by the defendant, was ultimately one which the jury would have to decide, and the judge had only the limited function of making the preliminary inquiry stipulated by the Act.

3.8 Civil cases

The standard of proof required of any party to civil proceedings for the discharge of the legal burden of proof is proof on the balance of probabilities. This means no more than that the tribunal of fact must be able to say, on the whole of the evidence, that the case for the asserting party has been shown to be more probable than not. If the probabilities are equal, i.e. the tribunal of fact is wholly undecided, the party bearing the burden of proof will fail (58).

That this standard is clearly lower than that required of the prosecution in a criminal case has given rise to the difficult problem of defining the proper standard where allegations are made in a civil case which amount to conduct by the opponent of a criminal or quasi-criminal nature. The proof of matrimonial offences, which at one time

---

55 See, e.g., *DPP v Ping Lin* (HL) [1976] AC 574. Presumably, if the defence make the contention, the standard is the balance of probabilities.
56 See *R v Robson; R v Harris* [1972] 1 WLR 651; *R v Stevenson and Others* [1971] 1 WLR 1.
57 [1979] 1 WLR 26.   58   *Miller v Minister of Pensions* [1947] 2 All ER 372.

bore a quasi-criminal stigma, has also caused formidable problems which are considered in 3.9, post.

It now seems clear that the standard of proof where criminal or quasi-criminal conduct is alleged in a civil suit is the normal balance of probabilities. Unfortunately, however, the issue has been clouded more than somewhat by the tendency of judges to stress that the more grave the allegation, the clearer should be the evidence adduced to prove it. There are dicta which suggest (wrongly, it is submitted) that there is some sort of sliding scale of standards of proof between the ordinary balance of probabilities, used in cases where no criminal or quasi-criminal stigma attaches to the allegations made, and some higher degree of proof (though falling short of the criminal standard) used in the cases now being considered.

In *Bater* v *Bater* (59) the issue before the Court of Appeal was the proper standard of proof of a matrimonial cause, but in the course of his judgment, Denning LJ said in more general terms:

As Best CJ and many other great judges have said, 'in proportion as the crime is enormous, so ought the proof to be clear'. So also in civil cases, the case may be proved by a preponderance of probability, but there may be degrees of probability within that standard. The degree depends on the subject-matter. A civil court, when considering a charge of fraud, will naturally require for itself a higher degree of probability than that which it would require when asking if negligence is established. It does not adopt so high a degree as a criminal court, even when it is considering a charge of a criminal nature; but still it does require a degree of probability which is commensurate with the occasion.

This passage was considered by the Court of Appeal (of which Denning LJ was a member) in *Hornal* v *Neuberger Products Ltd* (60), an action for damages for breach of warranty and fraudulent misrepresentation. Hodson LJ pointed out that no responsible counsel or judge would make or consider any serious allegation without admitting that cogent evidence was called for to prove it. There is a necessary distinction between the balance of probabilities and the quantity and cogency of the evidence needed to tilt the balance in favour of the allegation; the latter may legitimately be held to vary with the subject-matter, while the former remains constant. In most cases, the result will be the same, whatever the mental processes involved, and as Denning LJ said in *Bater,* the difference of opinion about standard of proof may be no more than a matter of words. Nonetheless, problems can be avoided by precision of words, and it is submitted that the language of Morris LJ in *Hornal* correctly represents the position:

But in truth no real mischief results from an acceptance of the fact that there is some difference of approach in civil actions. Particularly is this so if the words which are used to define that approach are the servants but not the masters of meaning. Though no court and no jury would give less careful attention to issues lacking gravity than to those marked by it, the very elements of gravity become a part of the whole range of circumstances which have to be weighed in the scale when deciding as to the balance of probabilities (61).

The law was stated with equal clarity by Ungoed-Thomas J in *Re Dellow's Will Trusts*

59 [1951] P 35 at 37.   60 [1957] 1 QB 247.   61 Ibid. at 266.

(62) where a wife was the general legatee under the will of her husband. They had died on the same occasion, the wife being deemed the survivor under s. 184 of the Law of Property Act 1925. The question arose whether the wife had feloniously killed the husband. The learned judge, observing that 'there can hardly be a more grave issue than that' went on to hold that he was satisfied that the allegation was proved. He said referring to the passage cited above from the judgment of Morris LJ in *Hornal*:

> It seems to me that in civil cases it is not so much that a different standard of proof is required in different circumstances varying according to the gravity of the issue, but, as Morris LJ says, the gravity of the issue becomes part of the circumstances which the court has to take into consideration in deciding whether or not the burden of proof has been discharged. The more serious the allegation the more cogent is the evidence required to overcome the unlikelihood of what is alleged and thus to prove it.

3.9 Matrimonial causes

In modern practice, there seems to be little reason to differentiate between matrimonial causes and civil cases in general, and for most purposes of evidence, any distinctions are unimportant. However, in relation to the standard of proof, the position is far from clear. As Professor Cross has said, 'it would be rash to essay a general statement with regard to the standard of proof in matrimonial causes' (63). And in *Bastable* v *Bastable and Sanders* Willmer LJ was driven to observe: 'If I may say so with all possible respect, sitting in this court I do not find it altogether easy to follow the directions contained in various statements made by members of the House of Lords' (64).

The source of the trouble is that until the wholesale change in the philosophy of matrimonial law embodied in the stream of reforming legislation beginning with the Divorce Reform Act 1969 (now replaced by the Matrimonial Causes Act 1973) and continuing at the time of writing to the Domestic Proceedings and Magistrates' Courts Act 1978, the law was governed by the concept inherited from the ecclesiastical courts that the 'matrimonial offence' was a grave charge having quasi-criminal character, a concept reinforced by the stigma which proof of such an offence commonly involved. This led naturally to the view that a high standard of proof was required for the proof of such an offence. In *Bater* v *Bater* (65) the question arose in relation to a petition on the ground of cruelty whether the trial judge had directed himself correctly that such an offence had to be proved beyond reasonable doubt. The Court of Appeal unanimously held that he had been correct. The decision corresponded to that in *Ginesi* v *Ginesi* (66) in which the same standard was held to be applicable to allegations of adultery, and the proposition was assumed in *Preston-Jones* v *Preston-Jones* (67), where the issue was whether the standard of proof should be higher rather than lower than beyond reasonable doubt, in a case where the only evidence of adultery was that the husband proved continuous non-access to the wife during the period of 186 to 360 days before the birth of the wife's child.

Some encroachment on the rule was made in *Blyth* v *Blyth* (68), in which Lord Denning, in a passage with which Lord Pearce concurred, suggested that the grounds for divorce, like any other allegation made in a civil case, might be proved by a prepon-

62 [1964] 1 WLR 451 at 454–5. And see *Post Office* v *Estuary Radio Ltd* (CA) [1968] 2 QB 740.
63 Cross, *Evidence*, 4th ed. p. 103.   64 (CA) [1968] 1 WLR 1684 at 1685.
65 [1951] P 35.   66 (CA) [1948] P 179.   67 (HL) [1951] AC 391.   68 (HL) [1966] AC 643.

derance of probability (69). The issue in *Blyth*, however, was limited to the standard of proof required on the question whether the petitioner had condoned his wife's adultery and, in so far as wider propositions were concerned, any assertions must have been obiter. Nonetheless, they left the way clear for further consideration, and in *Bastable* the Court of Appeal seized the opportunity to apply to an allegation of adultery the standard which Denning LJ had laid down in *Hornal* v *Neuberger Products Ltd* (70) for civil cases in general, namely proof on the balance of probabilities subject to the requirement of evidence of cogency proportionate to the nature of the charge.

The divergence of authority has never been resolved. It is submitted, however, that the appropriate standard is that applicable to any other civil litigation. The concept of the matrimonial offence has now disappeared (71) and the sole ground for divorce is that the marriage has broken down irretrievably. It cannot now be argued that the consequences of divorce demand any higher standard of proof, as once they did. It is perhaps unfortunate that Parliament did not take the opportunity of making the matter clear once and for all, but some indication of its intention may be gleaned from the provision in s. 26 of the Family Law Reform Act 1969 that: 'Any presumption of law as to the legitimacy or illegitimacy of any person may in any civil proceedings be rebutted by evidence which shows that it is more probable than not that that person is illegitimate or legitimate, as the case may be, and it shall not be necessary to prove that fact beyond reasonable doubt in order to rebut the presumption.' The presumption of legitimacy weighed heavily in many adultery cases in former times, and it is difficult to suppose that a higher standard would now be required to prove adultery as such, or indeed any other fact material to matrimonial causes (72). Indeed, it may be confidently asserted that the imposition of any higher standard of proof would be contrary to the spirit of the new matrimonial law, and to the policy of the courts, expressed by procedural and substantive emphasis, of diverting the mainstream of litigation away from detailed investigations of the causes of the breakdown and into the fields of proper provision for the affected members of the family.

3.10 Questions for counsel

1   Where does the burden of proving the guilt or innocence of Coke and Littleton lie?
2   What standard of proof is required?
3   Does either defendant bear any legal burden of proof on any issue in the case?
4   Does either defendant bear any evidential burden of raising any issue before the jury need consider it?
5   What will the position be as to burden of proof if the prosecution succeed in establishing a prima facie case at the close of their case?

---

69   Subject to the observation made by Lord Denning on other occasions that the degree of proof should be commensurate with the gravity of the charge.
70   (CA) [1957] 1 QB 247.   71   See, e.g., *Wachtel* v *Wachtel* [1973] Fam 72.
72   This suggestion is intended to encompass not only the facts available to prove irretrievable breakdown, but also the wide variety of other issues which may arise, e.g. the presumption of a valid marriage following a ceremony and cohabitation, see *Mahadervan* v *Mahadervan* [1964] P 233.

Part 2   The Great Questions of Admissibility

4   Evidence of Character

4.1   Uses of the word 'character'

The word 'character' bears at least three distinct meanings in the context of the law of evidence. Firstly, it may refer to the reputation in which a person is held in his neighbourhood, among those by whom he is known; secondly, it may refer to the disposition of a person to behave in a certain way; thirdly, it may refer to specific incidents in the personal history of the subject, for example previous convictions for criminal offences.

At common law, in the rare instances when the admission of character evidence was considered at all, only the first of the three meanings referred to above, that of general reputation in the neighbourhood, achieved any real recognition, and the scope of character evidence was accordingly very narrow and generally unhelpful. But in modern law, the restrictive rules of the common law have been, or more accurately are being, eroded by a wider approach, which would permit consideration of character in all its aspects. There is still a resistance, probably diminishing, to the wide view, but the rules laid down by the Criminal Evidence Act 1898 on which all the most important questions of the admissibility of character evidence now turn, seem to demand, and have consistently been construed as demanding, terms of reference broad enough to look at character as a whole. Although the common-law position has never been expressly abrogated, it would seem undesirable that the construction of the word should be held to differ in two contexts which are so closely linked in practice, and many authorities now consider the wider construction to have been firmly adopted for all purposes.

4.2   Possible uses of character evidence

Evidence of character must be considered in relation to two possible uses: (a) for the purpose of establishing or attacking the credit of a party to a case or a witness; and (b) for the purpose of having some probative value in relation to the facts in issue in the case.

4.2.1   To attack credit
As a broad principle, the credit of any party or witness is open to attack, with a view to showing that because of some aspect of character, usually but not exclusively the disposition of the subject to behave in a certain way, that party or witness is unworthy of belief, or is unlikely to give reliable evidence. The attack is commonly launched in cross-examination, and usually ends there because of the rule that a cross-examiner cannot introduce further evidence to contradict a witness's answers to questions concerning credit, although the rule has important exceptions which are considered in detail in 14.7, post. The position of the defendant in a criminal case was specially provided for by the Criminal Evidence Act 1898, which, for the first time, made a defendant a

competent witness in his own defence. The liability of a defendant to attack in this way is exclusively governed by statute, and is considered in section C of this chapter.

4.2.2   To prove a fact in issue

As a matter of evidence, the fact that a person has in the past been guilty of discreditable acts has no relevance to proving that he was guilty of a particular discreditable act now alleged against him. Of course it may be argued that someone who has offended in the past is likely to do so again, but the law has never favoured proof by evidence of past disposition. The law will not 'give a dog a bad name and hang him'. If guilt depended on a past record the law would have ceased to try cases on their facts, and the defence of an innocent man of bad character would have become difficult and in some cases practically impossible. For the same reason, if the dog happens to have a good name, the law will not, for that reason, acquit him.

The common law therefore developed a general, though not absolute, rule that evidence of the character of a party is inadmissible to prove or disprove facts in issue in a case. Although the rule generally applies to evidence of bad and good character alike, there are some differences in the way it is applied to the two types of evidence. There is a highly specialised category of evidence of bad character, called 'similar-fact evidence' (see Chapter 5), which is held to be probative of misconduct because it identifies a particular offender with a specific type of misconduct, which can be shown to be his individual 'hallmark'. It is possible in criminal cases for a defendant to tender evidence of his good character on the issue of his guilt or innocence (see section B of this chapter). Finally, there are a limited number of cases, described in section A of this chapter, where character is itself to be proved as a fact in issue in the case, or as a relevant fact.

A: CHARACTER IN ISSUE

4.3   Introduction

Only in relatively few cases is the character of a party directly in issue as being itself the subject-matter of the litigation, or as being directly relevant to the determination of the facts in issue in the proceedings. Even in such cases, it does not by any means follow that every aspect of a party's character is in issue, so that while one particular aspect of it may be the subject-matter of the proceedings, a party's character in general terms may not even be relevant to the facts in issue. In other cases, a party's entire character may be in issue in the case. In any event, to the extent that character is itself in issue or is directly relevant to the facts in issue, it may be proved by evidence like any other fact in issue or relevant fact.

4.4   Civil cases

The obvious example in civil cases is that of actions for defamation. On the issue of liability, the character of the plaintiff (which is, at the outset, presumed rebuttably to be good) will not necessarily be in issue, as where the defence is one of privilege or fair comment on a matter of public interest; but if the defence is one of justification, at least some aspect of the plaintiff's character, to an extent determinable from the pleadings, will be the subject-matter of the case (1). The pleaded particulars may be broad enough to put in issue the plaintiff's character in every sense, so as to comprise his general reputation, his disposition to behave in certain ways or specific incidents of his conduct; or they may be limited to one or more aspects of character only.

In a more limited context, character will always be directly relevant to the measure of damages, assuming that the issue of liability is determined in favour of the plaintiff. What is relevant here, however, is the reputation which the plaintiff may be taken as having enjoyed before publication of the defamatory matter, and the extent to which his reputation has been affected adversely by the defamation. Thus, evidence of character for this purpose is limited to evidence of reputation. Evidence of specific conduct would be excluded as irrelevant because it would tend to show only what the plaintiff's reputation ought to have been, and not what it in fact was (2).

4.5 Criminal cases

In criminal cases, the obvious prejudice to a defendant likely to result from any exposition of his character has led to a considerable reluctance to entertain offences which make a man's bad character part of the case against him. However, there are cases, limited in number as are their civil counterparts, where character is itself in issue. In criminal cases, this is almost always because some aspect of character is an essential element of the offence (hence, in issue in the case) and so may be proved by evidence like any other fact in issue. These cases are various, and little useful purpose would be served by an attempt at classification, but the following examples will illustrate the genus.

In certain cases, the offence may be committed only by persons who have been sentenced on a previous occasion. By virtue of the Firearms Act 1968, s. 21, it is an offence for a person who has been sentenced to imprisonment for a term of three years or more to have a firearm or ammunition in his possession at any time. The jury must be sure, before they can convict, of each element of the offence; one of the elements is that the defendant is a person who has, on a previous occasion, been sentenced to such a term of imprisonment. No other aspect of his character is relevant to guilt, and the jury must be directed to ignore the implications of the evidence for the defendant's character generally, in considering that issue. At a somewhat lower level, the offence of driving a motor vehicle on a road while disqualified for holding or obtaining a driving licence, contrary to s. 99 of the Road Traffic Act 1972, involves proof that the defendant was, on the material date, a person so disqualified. The fact of disqualification alone is in issue, the defendant's character otherwise being irrelevant to guilt. These cases do, nonetheless, provide a stark instance of the risk of prejudice, against which the tribunal of fact must warn itself.

At a summary level, the jungle of minor statutory provisions governing numerous forms of public behaviour contains some fairly Draconian incursions into an even wider element of character. Thus, the offence of loitering or soliciting for the purpose of prostitution, contrary to s. 1 of the Street Offences Act 1959 can be committed only by a

---

1   See generally *Gatley on Libel and Slander,* 7th ed., paras 351, 1235, 1243, 1313; *Fountain v Boodle* (1842) 3 QB 5. The principle is by no means confined to defamation cases. See *Hurst v Evans* [1917] 1 KB 352, where the defence to an action against an insurance company was that the loss was sustained by the dishonesty of the plaintiff's servant; it was admissible to prove that the servant was a known associate of burglars and had entered the plaintiff's service on a forged reference: (general and specific character).
2   See *Plato Films Ltd v Speidel* (HL) [1961] AC 1090. Lord Radcliffe suggested that specific acts might be relevant as part of the picture of general reputation, provided that they were sufficiently notorious. Ibid at 1131. See also *Scott v Sampson* (DC) (1882) 8 QBD 491 per Cave J at 503.

'common prostitute', a fact which may be proved by previous convictions or other evidence of the defendant's way of life generally, and is frequently proved by the assertion of the arresting officer in evidence, unless expressly disputed. And on an even more nebulous basis, the notorious offence of frequenting or loitering with intent to commit an arrestable offence, contrary to s. 4 of the Vagrancy Act 1824 as amended, is committed by a 'suspected person or reputed thief', a fact often proved by the officer's observation immediately prior to the arrest of the defendant. Furthermore, the required intent may be proved by the 'known character' of the defendant, in conjunction with the circumstances of the case (Prevention of Crimes Act 1871, s. 15).

In other instances, limited evidence of character is expressly made admissible by statute, not as being itself in issue, but as being directly relevant to one element of the offence, that of the state of mind of the defendant. The Theft Act 1968, s. 27(3) provides:

Where a person is being proceeded against for handling stolen goods (but not for any offence other than handling stolen goods), then at any stage of the proceedings, if evidence has been given of his having or arranging to have in his possession the goods the subject of the charge, or of his undertaking or assisting in, or arranging to undertake or assist in, their retention, removal, disposal or realisation, the following evidence shall be admissible for the purpose of proving that he knew or believed the goods to be stolen goods:—

(a)   evidence that he has had in his possession, or has undertaken or assisted in the retention, removal, disposal or realisation of, stolen goods from any theft taking place not earlier than twelve months before the offence charged; and

(b)   . . . evidence that he has within the five years preceding the date of the offence charged been convicted of theft or of handling stolen goods (3).

B: CHARACTER NOT IN ISSUE

4.6   Introduction

In the cases described in the previous section, which must be regarded as exceptional, evidence of the character of a party is to a greater or lesser extent admissible, not because it is evidence of probative value in relation to some other fact in issue, but because character is itself in issue in the case. In the great majority of cases, both civil and criminal, character is not itself in issue and must therefore be judged solely according to its probative value, if any, in relation to the facts in issue. In general, judged by such a test of relevance, it fails, and is accordingly inadmissible to prove or disprove facts in issue in the case.

4.7   Civil cases

In civil cases where the character of a party is not in issue, it is inadmissible for the purpose of proving or disproving any fact in issue in the case, because of its evidential irrelevance. The rule applies to bad and good character alike. Thus, the defendant to a

---

3   The judge apparently has a discretion to exclude evidence admissible under this provision where its prejudicial value greatly outweighs its value as evidence: *R* v *Herron* (CCA) [1967] 1 QB 107 (decided under the corresponding provision of the Larceny Act 1916); *R* v *Knott* (CA) [1973] Crim LR 36. The extent of the evidence admitted must be carefully confined to that permitted by the section: *R* v *Bradley* (CA) [1980] Crim LR 173. See also the Prevention of Crimes Act 1871, s. 15; Official Secrets Act 1911, s. 1(2).

civil action for keeping false weights (4) or for the impeachment of a will for fraud (5) will not be allowed to assert his good character, for the purpose of disproving the claim. Nor may a husband seek to prove his 'general humanity' in answer to his wife's specific charges of cruelty (6).

4.8 Criminal cases

4.8.1 Evidence of bad character

It is a fundamental rule of English law that the prosecution may not, for the purpose of proving his guilt, adduce evidence of the character of the defendant, whether in terms of his general reputation, of his disposition to behave in a certain way or of his previous criminal convictions or other specific acts of misconduct (6a). So jealously does the law exclude such matters, because of their irrelevance to the issue of guilt and because of the risk of prejudice to the defendant, that even an inadvertent reference to the character of the defendant in the course of evidence will usually result in the discharge of the jury and a new trial (7). These observations apply with equal force to prevent a defendant from adducing evidence of the bad character of a co-defendant for the purpose of proving the guilt of the co-defendant.

4.8.2 Evidence of good character

4.8.2.1 Admissibility. Out of a conspicuous concern at common law to offer as much latitude as possible to a defendant, in view of the procedural and evidential incapacities from which he suffered before the gradual reforms of the nineteenth century, was born a rule peculiar to criminal trials, which ran contrary to the logic of the treatment of character evidence. This was that the defendant might in every case prove his general good character. Before the Criminal Evidence Act 1898 rendered the defendant a competent witness in his own defence, this could be achieved only by cross-examination of witnesses for the prosecution, or by calling character witnesses for the defence, and, as will be discussed in 4.12, post, s. 1(*f*)(ii) of the Act had to make provision for the giving of such evidence by the defendant himself.

There was much discussion at common law about the kind of evidence which was permitted by the rule. In the end, it seemed to be settled that it was confined to evidence of general reputation. In *R* v *Rowton* (8) the defendant was charged with indecent assault on a boy of fourteen. The defendant was a schoolmaster. The question arose of the limits of admissible evidence of character offered by a witness, and it was held that the evidence was confined to that of the general reputation of the defendant in the neighbourhood, and therefore excluded both evidence of specific (creditable) acts on other occasions, and the witness's own opinion of the defendant. *Rowton* itself was the subject of powerful dissent, and the ink was scarcely dry on the judgments before it was doubted. Although the case has never been specifically reversed, the practice in modern

---

4 *Attorney-General* v *Bowman* (1791) 2 Bos & P 532n.
5 *Goodright*, ex dem *Faro* v *Hicks* (1789) Bull NP 296.
6 *Narracott* v *Narracott and Hesketh* (Court for Divorce & Matrimonial Causes) (1864) 3 Sw & Tr 408.
6a The rules of admissibility of similar-fact evidence (see Chapter 5) are distinct from this general proposition, and depend on the specific probative value of such evidence. See *Makin and Makin* v *Attorney-General for New South Wales* (PC, New South Wales) [1894] AC 57 per Lord Herschell at 65, a classic statement of the distinction. Evidence of character, including previous findings of guilt, is admissible also for the purpose of rebutting the presumption of *doli incapax* in the case of a child offender between the ages of ten and fourteen: *R* v *B*; *R* v *A* (CA) [1979] 1 WLR 1185.
7 This is, however, a matter within the discretion of the judge, who must take into account a number of factors, which are discussed in 4.16, post. See generally *R* v *Lemsatef* (CA) [1977] 1 WLR 812.
8 (CCR) (1865) Le & Ca 520.

times is to allow the defendant to state his character as widely as he wishes, with the exception that he may not relate specific creditable acts of his on other occasions. This more lenient view may be justified on several grounds: that reputation in a neighbourhood is an ephemeral and largely meaningless concept in days of widespread social mobility, and may well give a positively misleading appraisal of the defendant's true character; that in any case reputation is often undeserved; and that the consistent interpretation of the Criminal Evidence Act 1898 has been favourable to a wider view (9) and it is surely undesirable that two such different meanings should be assigned to the word 'character'.

A further justification for the modern view is that the evidence called by the defence is open to challenge by the prosecution, albeit at common law, the challenge, like the evidence itself, was confined to matters of general reputation. In *R* v *Rowton,* the consequence of this was that the evidence of the rebutting witness, who was plainly ignorant of the defendant's reputation in the neighbourhood but stated his own opinion of the defendant, was held to have been wrongly admitted. But there is no doubt that the prosecution may attack any evidence of good character, both by way of cross-examination and by themselves calling evidence in rebuttal, and the prosecution surely are not limited as to rebuttal where the defence are not limited in their evidence. A defendant who gives evidence of his good character, or elicits his good character in cross-examination of the witnesses for the prosecution, may be cross-examined about his character, both general and specific, under the provisions of the Criminal Evidence Act 1898 s. 1(*f*)(ii) (see 4.12, post). Any witnesses called on behalf of the defendant to speak about his character may be cross-examined on that topic and, like any other witness, may themselves be attacked in terms of their credit. Furthermore, the prosecution are entitled to call evidence in rebuttal of the evidence called for the defence (10), and this includes, in modern law, the right to prove the previous convictions of the defendant, if they are not admitted (11). The outer limits of the rule are perhaps drawn by cases such as *R* v *Wood and Parker* (12) where it was held that it was permissible to cross-examine character witnesses to show that the defendant was rumoured to have participated in offences other than that charged. The rule makes perfect sense, to the extent that general reputation must take account of rumour as well as other intangibles, of which it is largely composed. Nonetheless, it is submitted that the decision would be unlikely to be followed today unless a defendant rested his evidence specifically upon general reputation within the meaning of the common-law rule.

It must also be stressed that, for the purposes under consideration, character is indivisible; the defendant cannot assert part of his character, which he believes to be good and therefore favourable to him, without opening up to scrutiny his character as a whole (13). The rule is one of obvious justice, in so far as the court should not be misled. On the other hand, Professor Nokes has drawn attention to the fact that, if a man is charged with forgery, cross-examination about his conviction for cruelty to animals 'can have no purpose but prejudice' (14). In *R* v *Winfield* (15), the defendant was charged with indecent assault on a woman and produced a character witness who, in cross-examination, revealed the defendant's previous conviction for dishonesty. The Court of

9   *R* v *Dunkley* (CCA) [1927] 1 KB 323; *Stirland* v *DPP* (HL) [1944] AC 315 per Lord Simon LC at 325; *Jones* v *DPP* (HL) [1962] AC 635 per Lord Denning at 671; and see also the speech of Lord Devlin at 694 et seq.
10   The same is true where an assertion of good character is made in an unsworn statement from the dock: *R* v *Campbell; R* v *Lear; R* v *Nicholls* (CA) (1979) 69 Cr App R 221. But contrast the position as to rebuttal where the defendant does not raise his good character, but loses his shield in the other circumstances envisaged by s. 1(f)(ii): *R* v *Butterwasser* (CCA) [1948] 1 KB 1; 4.9, post.
11   *R* v *Redd* (CCA) [1923] 1 KB 104.   12   (1841) 5 Jur 225.
13   *Stirland* v *DPP* (HL) [1944] AC 315 per Lord Simon LC at 326.
14   *Introduction to Evidence,* 4th ed., 140.   15   [1939] 4 All ER 164.

Criminal Appeal accepted this as proper, though it is not apparent that the jury were really assisted by, or that they would have been misled in any material sense by being denied access to, that information. It may be that the answer lies in the power of the trial judge to limit cross-examination, even where permitted in law, in the interests of ensuring a fair trial, and there are instances of the opening up of character being limited for this reason (16). .

4.8.2.2   Evidential value.   There are in theory two possible views on the use which may be made by the jury of evidence of good character called by the defence. On one view, it might go only to the credit of the defendant as a witness. On the other, it might go further than that, and cast doubt on the case for the prosecution, by showing that the defendant is less likely, because of his character, to have committed the offence charged. Only in recent times does a clear judicial preference appear to have emerged for the latter view. There were earlier pronouncements in its favour (17) but these were taken as having been supplanted by the decision in *R* v *Falconer-Atlee* (18), in which the 'credit only' direction was strongly affirmed. The logical result of *Falconer-Atlee* was that if the defendant chose not to give evidence in his defence then evidence of good character elicited in cross-examination, or given by character witnesses, would not be relevant for any purpose, and the jury should be directed to disregard it. This consequence arose, and was squarely faced by the trial judge, in *R* v *Bryant*; *R* v *Oxley* (19). The Court of Appeal, while dismissing the appeal against conviction, held that the judge had been wrong to direct the jury that since the defendant's credit was not in issue, the evidence of his good character could have no value. This approach was said by the Court of Appeal to be 'too restrictive'. The court added (21):

> The possession of a good character is a matter which does go primarily to the issue of credibility. This has been made clear in a number of recent cases. But juries should be directed that it is capable of bearing a more general significance which is best illustrated by what was said by Williams J in *R* v *Stannard and Others* [(20)]: 'I have no doubt . . . that evidence to character must be considered as evidence in the cause. It is evidence, as my brother Patteson has said, to be submitted to the jury, to induce them to say whether they think it likely that a person with such a character would have committed the offence.'

The result of these rules, in the case of Coke and Littleton, may be summarised as follows. The offences charged do not involve, as an essential element, any aspect of the character of the defendants. Nor is there any statutory provision which would entitle the prosecution to prove character as being in some way relevant to an element of the offence. In the case of Coke, therefore, the prosecution would not be permitted to prove the conviction of rape on the previous occasion, which is irrelevant (evidentially) to the issue of his guilt as now charged (22). In the case of Littleton, he may assert his good character, by way of defence, in any of the following ways: (a) by cross-examination of a witness for the prosecution (in this case, D/I Glanvil as the officer in charge of the case would be preferable) to show that he has not previously been convicted of any offence

16   See, e.g., *Selvey* v *DPP* (HL) [1970] AC 304, where the trial judge seems to have limited the exploration of character to sexual matters.
17   *R* v *Stannard and Others* (1837) 7 C & P 673; *R* v *Bellis* (CCA) [1966] 1 WLR 234.
18   (CA) (1973) 58 Cr App R 348.   19   [1979] QB 108.
20   (1837) C & P 673 at 675.   21   [1979] QB 108 at 119.
22   This assumes that the previous matter is not admissible under the similar-fact principle: see Chapter 5, post.

and that nothing is known adverse to his character; (b) by himself giving evidence of his general character, lack of previous convictions and sexual disposition; (c) by calling character witnesses to any of these matters, for which purpose his wife would seem a likely choice in view of the matters in her proof of evidence concerning Littleton's disposition in sexual matters and towards children generally. The jury would be entitled to regard such evidence as relevant to the issue of his guilt or innocence, and on a charge of this sort, the evidence may well carry considerable weight, but it is subject to challenge by the prosecution in cross-examination and by rebutting evidence, if material presents itself for the purpose.

It is usually a safe principle that a defendant with bad character, conscious of the risk of prejudice, would wish always to keep the record from the jury, and this would certainly be sound here, where Coke's offence is liable to be particularly prejudicial, to the mind of the jury, because of its similarity to that charged. But in some cases, a defendant may take a different view, and assert his 'limited good character'. The idea is becoming more prevalent as it is recognised that juries are increasingly well informed, both by the administrative process under which they are summoned, and less formally, by realistic presentation by the media, and that they are increasingly disinclined to hold a man's past against him. There is a school of thought among many advocates that the jury should be trusted with the defendant's record as an alternative to taking the risk that silence on the subject will prompt speculation. Most jurors now serve in a number of cases during their term of service, and are not slow to appreciate why no reference to character is made in one case, when in the previous case, the defendant's good character was loudly proclaimed. In many cases, the jury will give credit to a defendant who is frank with them. The weapon is particularly useful where the defendant's previous record is for offences quite different in nature from that now charged, or where he states that in the past he has always recognised his guilt by pleading guilty, but is now contesting the case because he is innocent. If this line is taken, it is tactically essential to bring out the whole of the defendant's character in chief. If it is (and it will be) dragged out in cross-examination, after a partial revelation, all hope of credit for frankness will be lost, and the jury will be rightly suspicious. It must be stressed that, though the ploy is often valid, it would be dicing with death in a case such as Coke's, because of the nature of his previous conviction.

C: THE DEFENDANT IN CRIMINAL CASES — THE CRIMINAL EVIDENCE ACT 1898

4.9   Introduction

Before the Criminal Evidence Act 1898 came into effect, the defendant in a criminal case was not a competent witness in his own defence. S. 1 of the Act rendered him competent (though not compellable) as a witness for the defence at every stage of the proceedings (23). This would have meant, in the absence of further provision, that like any other witness, the defendant would be open to attacks on his credit by cross-examination concerning his character. Because of the risk of prejudice peculiarly associated with character in criminal cases, Parliament determined to afford the defendant a substantial,

23 The competence of the defendant is considered generally in Chapter 12, post. Until earlier in the nineteenth century, the parties to civil cases had likewise been incompetent on their own behalf, but their emancipation as witnesses was not accompanied by protection of the sort offered by the 1898 Act in criminal cases. Indeed, they also became compellable.

albeit not unlimited, protection against such attack, in the no doubt justified belief that the right to give evidence might otherwise be rarely exercised.

The protection was achieved by building into the Act a complete code regulating the cross-examination of a defendant who chooses to give evidence as permitted by the statute. The code, as enacted by s. 1 provisos (*e*) and (*f*), stands in full force today, subject only to one amendment to s. 1(*f*)(iii) by the Criminal Evidence Act 1979 designed to restore the original intention of Parliament. It is worth reading the code as a whole, before considering it in more detail.

Provided as follows:— . . .

(*e*) A person charged and being a witness in pursuance of this Act may be asked any question in cross-examination notwithstanding that it would tend to criminate him as to the offence charged:

(*f*) A person charged and called as a witness in pursuance of this Act shall not be asked, and if asked shall not be required to answer, any question tending to show that he has committed or been convicted of or been charged with any offence other than that wherewith he is then charged, or is of bad character, unless —

(i)   the proof that he has committed or been convicted of such other offence is admissible evidence to show that he is guilty of the offence wherewith he is then charged; or

(ii)   he has personally or by his advocate asked questions of the witnesses for the prosecution with a view to establish his own good character, or has given evidence of his own good character, or the nature or conduct of the defence is such as to involve imputations on the character of the prosecutor or the witnesses for the prosecution; or

(iii)   he has given evidence against any other person charged in the same proceedings.

The pattern of the code is that, although of course the cross-examination of the defendant may freely seek to convict him of the offence charged, he is invested with what is usually referred to as a 'shield' in respect of other offences and of his bad character. This shield may be 'lost' in any of the circumstances envisaged by s. 1(*f*) (i), (ii) or (iii), the consequence of which is that the defendant becomes liable to be cross-examined about the matters otherwise prohibited, and then stands in effect in the same position as witnesses generally. It is important to note that the Act is only dealing with cross-examination, which is obviously available only where the defendant chooses to give evidence. Thus, in *R* v *Butterwasser* (24) the nature or conduct of the defence involved imputations on the character of the witnesses for the prosecution, so that the defendant lost his shield, by virtue of s. 1(*f*)(ii). He declined to give evidence, and called no witnesses to his character. The prosecution were allowed to call evidence of the defendant's bad character. An appeal against conviction was allowed, because that evidence was wrongly admitted. The Act referred only to cross-examination, and gave no right to the prosecution to adduce evidence (25). The position is, as we have seen, different where the defendant by whatever means asserts his good character, in which

24   (CCA) [1948] 1 KB 1.
25   On the duty of counsel representing a defendant who does not give evidence, but who wishes allegations to be put to witnesses for the prosecution amounting to imputations on character, see 14.4.

case the prosecution are entitled at common law to rebut, in addition to cross-examining under s. 1(*f*)(ii).

Perhaps the most significant feature of the code, however, is one not so readily apparent on the face of it, namely that the effect of any evidence elicited by cross-examination under proviso (*e*) and (*f*)(i) is one of relevance to the offence charged (i.e. going to the issue in the case); whereas the effect of similar evidence elicited under proviso (*f*)(ii) and (iii) is to go only to the credit of the defendant as a witness. We therefore return to the two possible uses of character evidence, with which this chapter began. It will be convenient to consider the provisions under those headings, but before doing so, we must examine some general questions about the prohibition in s. 1(*f*).

4.10   S. 1(f): the prohibition

'A person charged and called as a witness in pursuance of this Act shall not be asked, and if asked shall not be required to answer, any question tending to show that he has committed or been convicted of or been charged with any offence other than that wherewith he is then charged, or is of bad character . . .'

4.10.1   'If asked shall not be required to answer'
The wording of the Act is clearly designed and intended to apply to cross-examination, and the reference to 'being required' shows that it is not intended to inhibit the evidence given by the defendant in chief, so he is at that stage free to deal with the matters referred to (26). Of course, if he does so, then his character is opened up to cross-examination.

4.10.2   'Any questions tending to show'
The words quoted mean 'tending to reveal to the jury'. In *Jones* v *DPP* (27) the defendant sought to explain his giving of an alibi, which he later admitted to be false, on the basis that he had 'been in trouble with the police before' and did not want to be in trouble again. After admitting the alibi to be false, the defendant had given a second alibi, which was so completely identical to one given by him in relation to another case, that the prosecution sought and obtained leave to cross-examine him with regard to what his alibi had been on 'another occasion'. No details of the nature of the previous 'trouble' were introduced. On appeal, it was argued that the cross-examination contravened the prohibition in s. 1(*f*). A majority of the House of Lords held that it was proper, in that the defendant, by the way in which his defence was conducted, had already told the jury that he had been involved in 'trouble', so that the questioning did not reveal to the jury anything which they did not already know, and did not, therefore, 'tend to show' any prohibited matter which the defence had not already introduced (28).

It is the effect of the questions put that must be considered. If a question in fact has the effect of revealing prohibited matter, if truthfully answered, it is improper — for example, a question which, if answered truthfully, would oblige the defendant to say that he had been in prison at a certain time (29). Often the effect of a line of cross-

---

26   *Jones* v *DPP* (HL) [1962] AC 635 per Lord Reid at 663. But questions by the judge or counsel for a co-defendant would be caught by the Act: *R* v *Ratcliffe* (CCA) (1919) 14 Cr App R 95; *R* v *Roberts* (CCA) [1936] 1 All ER 23.
27   [1962] AC 635.
28   The minority held the line of cross-examination to be proper for equally cogent reasons, Lord Denning because it was admissible under proviso (*e*) and Lord Devlin because it was relevant to an issue of fact raised by the defendant in evidence in chief, namely his identification as having been at the scene of the crime at a material time.
29   *R* v *Haslam* (CCA) (1916) 12 Cr App R 10.

examination must be looked at; the whole line may contravene the prohibition, even though individual questions may be perfectly proper in themselves. The prohibition is not limited to questions taken individually.

4.10.3 'Committed or been convicted of or been charged with'
The prohibition is not limited to actual convictions, and even questions tending to show the commission of an offence not charged must be disallowed, for example, questions tending to show acts of dishonesty concurrent with, but other than those charged (30).

The word 'charged' refers to a formal charge of an offence, not merely to suspicion, so that in *Stirland* v *DPP* (31), where the defendant, charged with forgery, gave evidence that he had never before been charged with any offence, it was improper to cross-examine him to the effect that he had previously been dismissed from his employment with a bank because of suspected forgery: the defendant's evidence was correct and not subject to the challenge offered to it — the only effect of the cross-examination was one of pure (and unwarranted) attack on character. The wording would be wide enough, however, to include previous offences with which the defendant had been charged, but of which he had been acquitted, though questions of relevance often arise in relation to previous acquittals.

4.10.4 'Any offence'
The absence of limitation shows that the prohibition extends to offences committed after, as well as those committed before, the offence charged (32). Where the shield is lost, it is therefore proper (subject to the judge's discretion) to cross-examine about such offences, and it has been held to be within the judge's discretion, in such a case, to allow cross-examination of a defendant, otherwise of good character, about offences committed some ten months after the offence charged (33).

4.10.5 'Or is of bad character'
There has been much speculation about the meaning which Parliament intended to give to the word 'character' when enacting the 1898 Act. It is variously argued that Parliament intended either to maintain the narrow definition, insisted upon in *R* v *Rowton* (34), of general reputation only, or, by the reference to previous specific incidents, to open up the subject of character to a more comprehensive definition. Whatever Parliament actually intended, it is now settled that the word has acquired a wide connotation, for the purposes of the Act, and that the disposition of a defendant is included in his 'character' for this purpose (35). Since previous convictions and offences, and sometimes previous charges, are added by the specific words, it follows that the Act is broad enough to incorporate each of the three possible meanings of the word 'character' set out in 4.1, ante. It is submitted that this is sensible and satisfactory for the practical working of the Act, and deserves more enthusiastic support than the grudging status of 'too late to argue the contrary' which has sometimes been accorded to it. Indeed, the facts of *R* v *Dunkley*, in which Lord Hewart CJ employed exactly that epithet (36), seem to show that much of the 'code' in particular the operation of the part of s. 1(*f*)(ii) dealing with 'imputations on the character of the prosecutor or the witnesses for the prosecution', would be meaning-

30 *R* v *Wilson* (CCA) (1915) 11 Cr App 251.
31 (HL) [1944] AC 315.   32 *R* v *Wood* (CCA) [1920] 2 KB 179.
33 *R* v *Coltress* (CA) (1978) 68 Cr App R 193.   34 (CCR) (1865) Le & Ca 520; see 4.8, ante.
35 See *R* v *Dunkley* (CCA) [1927] 1 KB 323 and the rather eccentric decision in *Malindi* v *R* (PC, Rhodesia & Nyasaland) [1967] 1 AC 439, which is surely questionable on the facts.
36 See [1927] 1 KB 323 at 329.

less on a *Rowton* view. It is difficult to see how there can be an 'imputation' on a general reputation; it may be that the section is intended to mean: 'If the nature or conduct of the defence is such as to involve an assertion that the prosecutor is or the witnesses for the prosecution are of bad general reputation', but this would be a question of fact (whether or not the subject had a certain reputation) whereas the actual line of defence envisaged by the section is that the subject is not entitled to his apparent reputation. It would only be in rare cases, and for few and unimportant purposes, that the Act would come into effect, if read in such a way (which the wording will not support). It surely cannot be argued that a defendant may not allege the fabrication of evidence against him by a prosecution witness, because to do so would attack, not the witness's actual reputation, but his entitlement to a good reputation? Equally artificial would seem any similar limitation on the extent of cross-examination of the defendant, where permitted by the section.

4.11   Cross-examination relevant to guilt as charged: s. 1(e) and s. 1(f)(i)

(*e*)   A person charged and being a witness in pursuance of this Act may be asked any question in cross-examination notwithstanding that it would tend to criminate him as to the offence charged:

(*f*)   A person charged and called as a witness in pursuance of this Act shall not be asked, and if asked shall not be required to answer, any question tending to show that he has committed or been convicted of or been charged with any offence other than that wherewith he is then charged, or is of bad character, unless —

(i)   the proof that he has committed or been convicted of such other offence is admissible evidence to show that he is guilty of the offence wherewith he is then charged; . . .

It seems that s. 1(*e*) and s. 1(*f*)(i) are alike concerned with cases where a line of cross-examination is designed to prove guilt as charged. S. 1(*e*) really does no more than preserve the obvious rule that any evidence relevant to guilt as charged is, prima facie, admissible to prove guilt as charged. On the assumption that s. 1(*e*) and s. 1(*f*)(i) are intended to be separate and mutually exclusive, it would therefore seem that it is to be no answer to the admission of evidence relevant to guilt as charged, that such evidence tends, incidentally, to expose some element of the character of the defendant. On this basis, s. 1(*f*)(i) will specifically apply to the limited cases where the matters generally prohibited by s. 1(*f*) are themselves relevant to guilt as charged: these cases will be those where (a) character evidence is itself in issue or is made directly relevant to some fact in issue (see 4.5, ante); or (b) the evidence is admissible by virtue of the similar-fact principle (see Chapter 5, post). It is worthy of note, that unlike exceptions (ii) and (iii), s. 1(*f*)(i) operates as a matter of law, because of the relevance and admissibility of the evidence, and requires no step to be taken by the defence to bring it into play.

In *R* v *Chitson* (37) the defendant was charged with unlawful sexual intercourse with a girl. The girl gave evidence that the defendant had boasted to her of his relationship with another girl. It was held proper to cross-examine the defendant about his relationship with the other girl, because it supported the case for the prosecution to show that one

---

37   (CCA) [1909] 2 KB 945. Curiously, the evidence did not prove a criminal offence on the previous occasion, because there was no evidence of the age of the girl on that occasion, but clearly, it was evidence which, incidentally to its relevance to guilt as charged, exposed some part of the defendant's character in the broad sense.

part of the victim's evidence was admitted by the defendant to be true. The test, therefore, was one of relevance to guilt as charged, and that criterion being satisfied, it was no answer to the cross-examination that the evidence also exposed some aspect of the defendant's character. And in *R* v *Kurasch* (38) the defendant's answer to a charge of conspiracy to defraud, by means of a mock auction, was that he was a mere servant of the proprietress of the auction rooms. He was rightly cross-examined to show that the proprietress was, in fact, his mistress.

But on the same reasoning, it follows from the test of relevance, that even if cross-examination is justifiable in terms of s. 1(*e*) or (*f*), it will be allowed only where relevant. For this purpose, it matters not whether it be relevant to guilt or credit or whether the cross-examination is justified under s. 1(*e*) or any of the three exceptions to s. 1(*f*). In *Maxwell* v *DPP* (39) a defendant charged with manslaughter gave evidence of his general good character, by asserting that he was of 'good, clean, moral character'. The allegation against the defendant being that he had performed an illegal abortion, which had resulted in death, he was then cross-examined to show that on a previous occasion, he had been charged with, but acquitted of, the same offence in similar circumstances. The questioning was held to be improper. Although he had given evidence of his good character, and although the fact that he had previously been charged was within the terms of the section, the evidence of the previous acquittal was simply not relevant, because it did not have the effect of contradicting the evidence of the defendant in chief. Stripped of that quality of relevance, it lacked any evidential value and was purely prejudicial. Although relevance is often a problem in cases of previous acquittals, it seems that what matters is the form of the assertion made by the defendant. Thus, in *R* v *Waldman* (40) where the defendant said that he had a 'good reputation for honesty', he was rightly cross-examined both as to a previous conviction and a previous acquittal for receiving stolen goods, both incidents being clearly relevant to his reputation.

Quite apart from the rule as to relevance, which applies alike to s. 1(*e*) and s. 1(*f*) in each of its exceptions, it must be noted that the wording of s. 1(*f*)(i) expressly excludes any reference to the defendant having previously been charged with an offence; only the fact of his having committed or been convicted of such offence is said to be admissible, and indeed, it is obvious that a previous charge, standing alone or with an acquittal, cannot have any relevance to guilt as charged, although it may be relevant to credit. Hence, under s. 1(*f*)(i), previous acquittals are not within the proper scope of cross-examination (41).

4.12 Cross-examination relevant to credit: s. 1(f)(ii)

. . . unless — . . .

(ii) he has personally or by his advocate asked questions of the witnesses for the prosecution with a view to establish his own good character, or has given evidence of his good character, or the nature or conduct of the defence is such as to involve imputations on the character of the prosecutor or the witnesses for the prosecution; . . .

Under this exception and under s. 1(*f*)(iii), where cross-examination is permitted by the section, it goes to the credit of the defendant only, and not to his guilt as charged.

38 (CCA) [1915] 2 KB 749. 39 (HL) [1935] AC 309.
40 (CCA) (1934) 24 Cr App R 204. See also *R* v *Meehan and Meehan* (CA) [1978] Crim LR 690.
41 *R* v *Cokar* (CCA) [1960] 2 QB 207.

This will be considered in more detail in 4.14, after the detailed working of the two exceptions has been described.

4.12.1 *'Good character'*

It is envisaged that the defendant may attempt to establish his good character by either of the two methods described in the section, or by both together; in any such case, the shield is lost. However, what amounts to an assertion of good character may not always be easy to determine. It may be assumed that the rule will cover any evidence adduced by the defence which is not otherwise relevant to the issue of guilt and which in fact has the effect of inviting the jury to infer that the defendant is a man less likely, from whatever considerations of character, to have committed the offence charged than would otherwise have appeared to them to be the case. The most obvious case is where the defendant asserts that he has no previous convictions, or that he is a man above suspicion or of good moral character, in whatever terms, or that the offence charged is contrary to his disposition. But the assertion may be less direct, as where the defendant asserts that he is married with a family and in regular employment (42), or that he is a religious person (43), or that he is a member of a generally respected profession, institution, society or club (44) or that he has other attributes which people in general would be likely to think creditable.

However, it is submitted that where any such attributes are of direct relevance to the defence, apart from any assertion of good character, the defendant would not be within the scope of the exception. Thus, if a defendant charged with going equipped for burglary or theft, sought to explain his possession of certain implements by reference to his trade as a builder, it is submitted that he would not thereby 'give evidence of his good character' for this purpose, though if he went on to say that he earned his living honestly by building and had no inclination to steal, he would have exceeded his necessary assertion of his defence and put his character in issue. On a not dissimilar point, it was held in *R* v *Thomson* (45) that where a defendant explained his running away from a police officer by saying that he had been fined, and thought that he would be arrested for non-payment of the fine, he did not assert his character, but merely accounted for an otherwise incriminating piece of evidence against him. He had not in any way misled the court, or sought to assert his character as such, and it was wrong of the trial judge to compel him to say for what offence he had been fined, and to allow cross-examination concerning his previous convictions.

4.12.2 *'The nature or conduct of the defence'*

Quite independently of the assertion of the defendant's good character, the shield will be lost if 'the nature or conduct of the defence is such as to involve imputations on the character of the prosecutor or the witnesses for the prosecution.' Such imputation may be made by cross-examination of the prosecutor or his witness or in evidence by the defendant. The use of the two words 'nature' and 'conduct' implies that the very assertion of certain lines of defence may in itself lead to the loss of the shield, as opposed

---

42   *R* v *Baker* (CCA) (1912) 7 Cr App R 252; *R* v *Coulman* (CCA) (1927) 20 Cr App R 106.
43   *R* v *Ferguson* (CCA) (1909) 2 Cr App R 250.
44   Presumably this may be impliedly asserted by appearance or dress, e.g., a school tie. It is a moot and interesting question how far a defendant may safely appear respectably or tidily dressed in court, without risking making an implied assertion of good character. Occasionally, the appellate courts have had to intervene to prevent absurd results, as in *R* v *Hamilton* (CA) [1969] Crim LR 486, where the trial judge wrongly ordered the defendant to remove his regimental blazer before giving evidence.
45   (CCA) [1966] 1 WLR 405.

to the deliberate presentation of the case in certain ways. Indeed, it has been held that even where the making of such imputations is an indispensable part of the defence, and is regretted, the shield will be lost. In *Selvey* v *DPP* (46), the defendant was charged with buggery with M. In addition to the allegation that no such act had ever occurred, it was suggested to M in cross-examination (inevitably, since it was the defence) that M had offered to commit buggery with the defendant in return for money, and had falsely accused the defendant when the offer was refused. It was held that the defendant had lost his shield. And in *R* v *Bishop* (47) where, on a charge of burglary, the defendant sought to explain his presence in a room where his fingerprints were found by alleging that he had had a homosexual relationship with the occupier, who was a witness for the prosecution, it was held that the shield was lost, even though the allegation was directed, not at discrediting the witness, but at refuting an essential element of the offence, namely that the defendant had been a trespasser in the room.

4.12.3 'Imputations on the character'

It seems that any charge of faults or vices, reputed or real, will amount to an imputation on character. The classic case is, of course, the stark attribution to the prosecutor or his witness of the actual offence charged (48), but precisely the same result will follow where the charge made involves some other offence, or, as in *R* v *Bishop,* behaviour which is not criminal, but might be thought morally discreditable, in the light of current public opinion. Consequently, the evaluation of 'imputations' should be expected to be fluid and not static. It is an open question whether, had the relationship in *R* v *Bishop* been a heterosexual one, the same result would have obtained, and whether it would have mattered whether the relationship was or was not adulterous. But where the charge is of a trivial or inconsequential nature, and involves nothing seriously discreditable, it is wrong to hold that the shield has been lost, so that the judge erred in permitting a defendant charged with assault to be cross-examined about a previous conviction for assault, merely because a prosecution witness, who admitted having been drunk on the relevant occasion, was asked in cross-examination whether he had also sworn (49).

It seems that an allegation, however expressed, which amounts to an accusation of malicious prosecution or fabrication of evidence, must constitute an imputation on character. Such charges are found in a variety of forms, such as allegations that a confession has been obtained by bribes or threats (50), or has been fabricated (51), or that unnecessary remands have been asked for to enable false evidence to be obtained (52). The judge will look at the actual effect of the defence, and the loss of the shield cannot be avoided by the phrasing of questions so as to make what is in reality a clear allegation of fabrication appear to be no more than a suggestion of some innocent error (53). It is suggested that where such serious allegations must be made in the course of the defence, the best course for counsel is to make them in unambiguous terms, and to put in the defendant's character in chief, thereby avoiding at least the unpleasant process of having it dragged out in cross-examination (54).

---

46   (HL) [1970] AC 304.   47   (CA) [1975] QB 274.
48   See e.g. *R* v *Hudson* (CCA) [1912] 2 KB 464.
49   *R* v *McLean* (CA) [1978] Crim LR 430. But what if the witness had been said to be, not drunk, but under the influence of drugs?
50   *R* v *Wright* (CCA) (1910) 5 Cr App R 131.   51   *R* v *Clark* (CCA) [1955] 2 QB 469.
52   *R* v *Jones* (CCA) (1923) 17 Cr App R 117.
53   *R* v *Tanner* (CA) (1977) 66 Cr App R 56. The test is whether it follows from the cross-examination that the evidence has been 'made up' rather than wrongly recorded.
54   For the duty of counsel where he is instructed to make imputations on character, see 14.4, post.

A distinction which is well established, is that the mere assertion by a defendant of his innocence of the offence charged will not amount to an imputation on the character of the prosecutor or his witnesses, whereas an assertion which goes beyond what is necessary for the denial of guilt is capable of being so regarded, if in other respects it appears to amount to one (55). If the rule were otherwise, then in many cases, the mere entering of a plea of not guilty would in itself amount to an imputation on character, because the very contesting of a charge is often of necessity an assertion, at least by implication, that the witnesses on the other side are prepared to, and do in due course, commit perjury, or that they have fabricated evidence against the defendant. The rule is, therefore, necessary to the proper administration of justice, to avoid defences being inhibited by the intrusion of character in many cases. And even if the denial is couched in strong terms, the shield will remain intact if that is all it is (56).

The rule is not always easy to apply, and there is a very fine line in some cases between denial and imputation on character. If Coke alleges that Margaret Blackstone consented to have sexual intercourse with him, that is an allegation which operates to deny an essential element of the offence charged, that is to say, that he had sexual intercourse with her without her consent. Nonetheless, on the principle of *Selvey* v *DPP* (56), it ought perhaps to be regarded as an imputation. For reasons which have never been consistently stated, an allegation of consent in rape cases has always been considered a denial of guilt, and no more (57), so that Coke may challenge this part of the case without losing his shield. Of course, quite a different position would emerge if Coke went beyond that, and with leave (58) cross-examined Margaret to the effect that she was promiscuous, or had 'had it off with several of his mates' or that she had threatened dishonestly to accuse his mate Kevin of raping her the previous year. These questions would not be of direct relevance to the question of consent on the material occasion, and would, in effect go only to credit. They would, therefore, bring s. 1(*f*)(ii) into play (59). Of course, Coke would also lose his shield by bringing out Margaret's conviction for shoplifting, which would be an obvious imputation on character. It would seem, in view of the nature of Coke's previous conviction, and the unlikelihood of Margaret's credibility being affected adversely on this matter solely by her conviction for shoplifting, that any cross-examination concerned with credit would have to be directed boldly to sexual matters. In particular, the false allegation about Kevin may justify the loss of the shield, if the jury might take a very different view of Margaret as a witness, but it must be emphasised that the choice facing a defence advocate in such a case is a difficult one calling for mature judgment.

An imputation may be made, not only by cross-examination of the prosecutor or his witness, but by the defendant himself in evidence. Normally, the defendant would, in order to lend credibility to his imputation, wish to go into the witness-box and support on oath the matters which have been put on his behalf in cross-examination. If he does not,

---

55   The rule is sometimes charmingly illustrated by comparing *R* v *Rouse* (CCR) [1904] 1 KB 184 ('liar' held to be merely an emphatic denial of guilt) with *R* v *Rappolt* (CCA) (1911) 6 Cr App R 156 ('such a horrible liar that his brother would not speak to him' held an imputation).

56   *Selvey* v *DPP* (HL) [1970] AC 304.

57   *R* v *Turner* (CCA) [1944] KB 463; *R* v *Cook* (CCA) [1959] 2 QB 340 in which Devlin J at 347 considered rape cases to be *sui generis*. The more usual view is that an allegation of consent is mere denial of guilt: *Selvey* v *DPP* (HL) [1970] AC 304.

58   Leave is required to cross-examine the complainant about her sexual experience with other men: Sexual Offences (Amendment) Act 1976, s. 2.

59   Like other cross-examination concerned with credit, Margaret's answers would be final, subject to the exceptions discussed in 14.7, post. It may be that her denial of a wrongful threat to Kevin could be contradicted. On the other hand, answers relevant to consent are not collateral, and may be contradicted by rebutting evidence: *R* v *Riley* (CCR) (1887) 18 QBD 481. They are relevant to guilt, not to credit, and this includes the complainant's voluntary sexual association with the defendant.

the judge is likely to comment in his summing-up, even though the prosecution may not do so in a closing speech; in any case, his absence from the box in such circumstances is unlikely to pass unnoticed by the jury. If Coke goes into the witness-box to support the allegations made against Margaret, he may be cross-examined about them. Even if no imputation were made on Margaret's character in cross-examination of her, or by Coke in chief, he may be drawn to make some imputation in the course of cross-examination by the prosecution. His answers in cross-examination are strictly part of the prosecution case, and not an aspect of the 'nature or conduct of the defence' (60) and it would seem to be wrong to hold that s. 1(*f*)(ii) is brought into play if he is drawn for the first time to make some involuntary remark amounting to an imputation. To that extent, Coke would be protected against remarks made by him in answer to hostile questioning. However, if in cross-examination, he merely reinforces imputations already made by him or on his behalf, and expressly repeats them, then his shield will be lost.

4.12.4 'The prosecutor or the witnesses for the prosecution'

Imputations, of whatever nature, do not fall within the terms of the section unless they relate to the character of the prosecutor or a witness for the prosecution. Thus, in *R* v *Lee* (61) the defence were entitled to cross-examine the witnesses for the prosecution with a view to showing that two men, not called as witnesses, might have been guilty of the offence charged, and did not thereby invoke s. 1(*f*)(ii). And in *R* v *Biggin* (62), a murder case, it was held that the deceased, against whom allegations of improper advances were made by the defendant with a view to establishing provocation, was not 'the prosecutor' within the meaning of the section. It is, of course, only in cases of these kinds that it is likely to be of interest to the defence to make allegations against persons not called as witnesses for the prosecution, but it seems that when they arise, the imputations may be made with impunity.

4.13 Cross-examination relevant to credit: s. 1(f)(iii)

> . . . unless — . . .
> (iii) he has given evidence against any other person charged in the same proceedings.

4.13.1 'Has given evidence against'

What has to be considered is the effect of the defendant's evidence on the case for the co-defendant. The expression 'given evidence against' does not connote any hostile intent by the defendant towards the co-defendant. As Lord Morris of Borth-y-Gest put it in *Murdoch* v *Taylor* (63) it is irrelevant whether the evidence is 'the product of pained reluctance or of malevolent eagerness'. It is, therefore, the impact of the evidence, not the motive with which it was given, which is material; an objective assessment must be made of the effect likely to be produced on the jury.

Lord Morris went on to say: 'If, while ignoring anything trivial or casual, the positive evidence given by the witness would rationally have to be included in any survey or summary of the evidence in the case which, if accepted, would warrant the conviction of the "other person charged . . ." then the witness would have given evidence against such other person.'

60   *R* v *Jones* (CCA) (1909) 3 Cr App R 67.   61   (CA) (1975) 62 Cr App R 33.
62   (CCA) [1920] KB 213.
63   (HL) [1965] AC 574 at 584. The likelihood of one defendant 'giving evidence against' another is not by itself a ground for ordering separate trials: *R* v *Hoggins* (CA) [1967] 1 WLR 1223.

It will, therefore, be sufficient if the evidence given materially undermines the defence of the co-defendant, or supports the prosecution case against him, and therefore makes more likely the conviction of the co-defendant. Accordingly, if evidence designed to assist the case of the witness also has the effect of supporting a material part of the prosecution's case against the co-defendant, which the co-defendant denies, and so does more to undermine the case for the co-defendant than that of the prosecution, s. 1(*f*)(iii) will be brought into play (64). But the wording has produced some curious, if strictly logical results. In *R* v *Bruce and Others* (65), Bruce, McGuiness and others were charged jointly with robbery, by surrounding and robbing the victim. They were convicted by the jury of theft. McGuiness's defence was that there had been a plan to rob, but that he had not been a party to it. Bruce's defence was that there had never been a plan to rob at all. The Court of Appeal held that Bruce had not 'given evidence against' McGuiness, within the meaning of the section. Although his evidence contradicted that of McGuiness, its effect, if believed, was to render it more likely that McGuiness would be acquitted, there having been no plan to commit the offence charged. It was a mere denial by Bruce of a part of the prosecution case, which McGuiness admitted.

4.13.2 'Any other person charged in the same proceedings'
The words 'in the same proceedings' were substituted by the Criminal Evidence Act 1979 for the original 'with the same offence', which had given rise to many problems and had, in the end, been interpreted very narrowly (66). The new wording restores the intention of the Act, and is wide enough to cover any case where the defendants are being tried before the same court on the same occasion, and not only where they are jointly charged, in the sense that a joint enterprise in respect of one offence is alleged against them.

It follows that if Coke gives evidence in his defence that he was with Littleton on 8 July 1979 and that Littleton was present in his flat during the afternoon, while he was having sexual intercourse with Margaret Blackstone, he would seriously undermine Littleton's defence of alibi and would 'give evidence against him' for the purposes of s. 1(*f*)(iii). This would entitle counsel for Littleton to cross-examine Coke about his character, under the exception.

4.14   S. 1(e) and (f): some general considerations

4.14.1   Evidential effect of cross-examination
It has already been observed that an important distinction must be made between answers elicited in cross-examination under s. 1(*e*) and s. 1(*f*)(i), which deal with matters relevant to guilt, and those elicited under s. 1(*f*)(ii) or (iii), which are relevant to credit only. When summing up evidence given under s. 1(*e*) and (*f*)(i), therefore, it is appropriate to direct the jury that they may regard the evidence as part of the case against the defendant, which may go to establish some element of the offence charged, or to corroborate other evidence against him. The same direction, given in respect of evidence elicited under s. 1(*f*)(ii) or (iii) would be a serious misdirection, resulting almost certainly in the conviction being quashed (67). The proper direction in such cases is that the evidence is relevant to the assessment of the likelihood of the defendant's evidence of good character, or of the likely truth or force of his imputations on character or his

64   *R* v *Hatton* (CA) (1976) 64 Cr App R 88.   65   [1975] 1 WLR 1252.
66   See, e.g., *Commissioner of Police of the Metropolis* v *Hills* [1978] 3 WLR 423; *R* v *Rockman* (CA) (1977) 67 Cr App R 171.
67   See, e.g., *R* v *Vickers* (CA) [1972] Crim LR 101.

evidence against the co-defendant (68). Where the jury reject evidence of good character, or find groundless some imputation on character, it is also probable and proper that they should draw some adverse inference about the defendant's general credit as a witness (69).

4.14.2   Scope of permitted cross-examination
In the light of the above principles, it would seem to follow that where the defendant is cross-examined about his previous convictions, under s. 1(*f*)(ii) or (iii), the cross-examination should be limited to the exposure of the character itself, and should not be permitted to extend to the detail of the previous offences, for example the manner in which such previous offences were committed. The detail would be irrelevant to character evidence *per se,* because what is material to credit is the fact that the defendant is a man with a criminal record for a certain type of offence, and no more. Detail would also be irrelevant where the fact of a previous conviction or sentence was relevant as an element of the offence now charged, but no further. On the other hand, evidence of the detail would be natural and essential in most cases under s. 1(*e*) and (*f*)(i), where the previous matters are relevant to guilt. Indeed, in 'similar fact' cases, this would be the whole purpose of the evidence.

In *R v France and France* (70), the defendants were charged with theft from a jeweller's shop, by the distinctive method of taking property while the shopkeeper's attention was distracted. The defence involved imputations on the character of the witnesses for the prosecution, so that the prosecution cross-examined a defendant about his previous convictions for dishonesty. The defendant was asked, despite objection, about the method of committing a previous offence which had also involved the deliberate distraction of attention in order to facilitate theft. The prosecution did not contend that the earlier theft was admissible as similar-fact evidence, so that the cross-examination could only be justified by reference to s. 1(*f*)(ii). The conviction was quashed by the Court of Appeal. While the issue of credit might demand some investigation of the scale of the defendant's previous offences, the admission of the detail went beyond the bounds of relevance to credit, and was obviously gravely prejudicial. The court did not attempt to lay down the boundaries of cross-examination for every case, and *France* was distinguished by a differently constituted Court of Appeal in *R v Duncalf and Others* (71). Five defendants visited a total of eleven shops in the course of under an hour, and were charged with conspiracy to steal. The defence involved imputations on character, and though the facts are not entirely clear, it is not suggested in the report that the cross-examination which resulted was based by the prosecution otherwise than on s. 1(*f*)(ii). It was held that the defendants had rightly been cross-examined to show, not only that they had previous convictions, but that those convictions were for offences of a very similar nature, apparently because whatever the position under s. 1(*f*)(ii), such cross-examination would have been justifiable under s. 1(*f*)(i). *France* was distinguished, in the words of Roskill LJ, on the basis that: 'The appellants in *R v France* had denied being present at all at the scene of the alleged theft. In the present case the appellants' presence was admitted and the sole issue was one of their intent. We do not see why this evidence was not admissible on this issue within proviso (*f*)(i) [(72)] to s. 1 of

---

68   *R v Cook* (CCA) [1959] 2 QB 340.
69   *R v Richardson; R v Longman* [1969] 1 QB 299.   70   [1979] Crim LR 48.   71   [1979] 1 WLR 918.
72   The passage cited appears at 924, and is evidently a revised text. The report in [1979] 2 All ER 1116 at 1122 contains a reference to justification of the questions under s. 1(*f*)(ii) which must have been wrong, if it was put in that way.

the Criminal Evidence Act 1898.' It is submitted that *Duncalf* might have set to rest the confusion of the various purposes for which cross-examination may be allowed if it had distinguished more clearly between s. 1(*f*)(i) and (ii); though the decision seems justified on the facts.

It appears to be the practice, where evidence is relevant to credit, to permit the defendant to be asked how he pleaded on a previous occasion on which he was convicted. It is submitted that although some objection in terms of theory can be made to the practice, in that it appears to admit, in the case of a plea of not guilty and subsequent conviction, some evidence of opinion short of general reputation, the question ought to be allowed as tending to show that the defendant's evidence must be seen, in terms of credit, as that of a man who on a previous occasion, has unsuccessfully denied his guilt and, perhaps, been disbelieved on his oath.

4.14.3   Role of judge
All matters concerning the admissibility of cross-examination under s. 1(*e*) and (*f*) are matters of law for the judge, who should be invited to give a ruling on the matter in the absence of the jury before such cross-examination proceeds. The following are questions and considerations within the province of the judge.

(a)   *Warning.* Where a defendant proceeds in such a way as to risk exposing his character under s. 1(*f*)(ii), it is desirable that the judge should warn the defendant in good time of the possible consequences of his defence or evidence. This applies even where the defendant is represented, when the warning should be addressed to counsel (73).

(b)   *Leave.* In all but the clearest cases, leave of the judge should be sought before proceeding to cross-examine under s. 1(*e*) or (*f*). Even if there is no dispute about the operation of the section, it is a matter of law for the judge whether an imputation on character has been made, or whether one defendant has given evidence against another. Of course, if the judge has already ruled previous offences admissible as similar fact, where previous matters are in issue in the case, or where the defendant has given evidence of his good character, then no leave need be asked, as there is then no question of law for the judge to determine.

(c)   *Discretion.* The judge has a discretion, in all cases where cross-examination is technically permissible under s. 1(*f*)(ii) to disallow it in a particular instance, where it 'may be fraught with results which immeasurably outweigh the result of the questions put by the defence and make a fair trial almost impossible' (74). This would occur where the prejudicial value of the cross-examination would be almost bound to damn the defendant in the minds of the jury, because of the nature of his character. It would also be right for the judge to take into account the gravity of any imputations made, when compared with the detail of the defendant's character likely to be revealed. And although it is no answer in law to the operation of s. 1(*f*)(ii) that an imputation is an essential part of the defence and directed only to rebutting some aspect of the prosecution case, it may be a matter which will weigh favourably in the question of discretion, contrasted with a case where an indiscriminate attack is launched on the general integrity of the witnesses for the prosecution. It is not, however, a decisive consideration (75).

The existence of the discretion makes it important that an application for leave be made in all cases where the exercise of the discretion may be relevant.

73   *R* v *Cook* (CCA) [1959] 2 QB 340, emphasised in *Selvey* v *DPP* (HL) [1970] AC 304. For the practice in magistrates' courts, see *R* v *Weston-super-Mare Justices, ex parte Townsend* (DC) [1968] 3 All ER 225n.
74   *R* v *Jenkins* (1945) (CCA) 31 Cr App R 1 per Singleton J at 15.   75   *Selvey* v *DPP* (HL) [1970] AC 304.

It was held by the House of Lords (Lord Pearce dissenting) in *Murdoch* v *Taylor* (76) that the judge has no discretion to restrain cross-examination on behalf of a co-defendant under s. 1(*f*)(iii), and in this case, the judge's function is confined to the decision whether the exception has, or has not, been brought into play. It is thought that as between co-defendants, the judge should not restrain the free conduct of the defence to the fullest permissible extent, whereas it is clearly desirable that the judge should retain some residual control over the conduct of the case by the prosecution.

4.14.4 Who may cross-examine

It has been assumed, thus far, that the prosecution has an interest in cross-examining under s. 1(*f*)(ii) and the co-defendant under s. 1(*f*)(iii), and this is almost invariably the case. However, nothing in the Act prevents cross-examination by the prosecution under s. 1(*f*)(iii) or by the co-defendant under s. 1(*f*)(ii), and it must be taken that these courses are possible in some cases (77). It was specifically envisaged in *Murdoch* v *Taylor* (78) that the former course might be taken and postulated that the prosecution would be subject to the judge's discretion. Presumably, this would arise where defendant A had for any reason neglected to avail himself of the Act and where the prosecution had an interest in contesting the evidence given against him by defendant B, as being contrary to their own case against defendant B, whom they seek to cross-examine. In the latter case, presumably defendant A would wish to cross-examine to dissociate himself forcibly from some attack made upon the prosecution witnesses by defendant B, but there are obvious dangers in doing that, and it seems that the court would have a discretion to prevent such cross-examination, in a case where defendant A could not have been adversely affected by the course taken by the defence of defendant B (79). Where defendant A gives evidence of his good character, it is submitted that he may be cross-examined on the subject on behalf of defendant B.

4.15 Introduction of character by co-defendant outside the Act

Although the defence must be given the fullest possible freedom to conduct the case as they see fit, the judge must hold the balance between defendants charged in the same proceedings. Evidence of character is, of course, in general irrelevant to prove guilt, and where this is so, it cannot acquire relevance to that issue merely because it is elicited for the co-defendant instead of the prosecution. It appears, therefore, that only where, exceptionally, the character of defendant A is relevant directly to the question of the guilt or innocence of defendant B is defendant B entitled to introduce it and then subject to the discretion of the judge. In *R* v *Miller and Others* (80) Devlin J allowed defendant B, who was jointly charged with defendant A with evading import duties on certain goods, to establish by cross-examination of a witness for the prosecution that defendant A had been in prison on certain dates, when the importations had come to an end. The relevance of this evidence was that it tended to show that defendant A had principally been responsible for the importations, and so strengthened the case of defendant B. This decision was approved in *R* v *Neale* (81) by the Court of Appeal. On the facts, the

76   [1965] AC 574.
77   See *R* v *Russell* (CA) [1971] 1 QB 151; *R* v *Lovett* (CA) [1973] 1 WLR 241. The present decisions must be read with care, as they often turn on the now replaced wording 'charged with the same offence' in s. 1(*f*)(iii) which inhibited much cross-examination which would now be permitted under that exception.
78   [1965] AC 574 per Lord Donovan at 593.   79   *R* v *Lovett* (CA) [1973] 1 WLR 241.
80   (1952) 36 Cr App R 169.   81   (1977) 65 Cr App R 304.

evidence sought to be elicited by defendant B concerning defendant A's known propensity to commit arson, was held to be irrelevant to defendant B's defence of alibi, on a joint charge of arson. Had the jury had to decide which of the two had committed arson, both being present, the result would, it seems, have been different (82).

In all cases where the character of one defendant is not relevant to the guilt of the co-defendant, the co-defendant is not at liberty to introduce it, any more than the prosecution, unless the case falls within the exceptions provided by s. 1 of the Criminal Evidence Act 1898.

4.16 Inadvertent references to character

It happens not infrequently that, because of some inadvertent reference in the witness-box, or the wrongful exposure to the jury of some document, part of the bad character of a defendant is unintentionally exposed to the jury, when it is not admissible for any purpose. In such a case, the judge has power to discharge the jury and order a new trial, if application is made to him on behalf of the defendant affected, or presumably of his own motion. The question of discharge of the jury is in all cases one within the discretion of the judge. It by no means follows that the jury must in every case be discharged. The judge must weight the gravity of the revelation to the case for the defence, and must take into account the prejudice and inconvenience which a retrial may cause to any co-defendants. If the slip is inconsequential, or occurs in the course of a long trial and is likely to be forgotten by the jury (83), or where the matter can be dealt with by a firm direction, it will be proper to continue. It would also be manifestly right to continue where the defendant, seeing the trial go against him, 'inadvertently' lets slip something of his past record. But in general, it is submitted that the interests of justice require the discharge of the jury, the appearance of a fair trial being as important as the reality. It is difficult wholly to exclude the possibility that the jury will be influenced wrongly against the defendant.

4.17 Spent convictions

The Rehabilitation of Offenders Act 1974 provides that in certain cases, convictions recorded against an offender shall become 'spent', and that the offender shall be treated in law as if he had not committed the offence: see s. 4(1). The section does not apply in various situations of which one is the use of previous convictions in the course of criminal proceedings. Where, therefore, it is permissible to introduce evidence of previous convictions, the fact that a conviction is spent does not prevent its being referred to, as a matter of law. However, unless clearly cogent as similar-fact evidence or of particular relevance to credit, convictions old enough to be spent will be unlikely to carry much wieght, and may often create in the mind of the jury a sense of unfairness to the defendant. Quite apart from this, it is obviously desirable that the spirit of the Act should be observed, and for this purpose, an important practice direction was issued by the Lord Chief Justice on 30 June 1975 (84). The most significant provisions for present purposes

---

82   Cf *Lowery* v *R* (PC, Victoria) [1974] AC 85.
83   As in *R* v *Coughlan and Young* (CA) (1976) 63 Cr App R 33, where the slip was 'sensibly' ignored by all concerned, and mentioned later to the judge. In the context of the trial as a whole, the error had no significance. It must always be right to approach the matter calmly, to allow a lapse of time before raising the matter, so that the significance to the jury will be minimised. It must be remembered that such questions loom larger in the minds of lawyers than of laymen and, if played down, the reference is often, in the long run, unimportant.
84   [1975] 1 WLR 1065.

are para. 4, which indicates that no reference should be made to a spent conviction. 'When such reference can be reasonably avoided', and para. 6, which provides: 'No one should refer in open court to a spent conviction without the authority of the judge, which authority should not be given unless the interests of justice so require.'

It is also of importance to observe the provisions of s. 16(2) of the Children and Young Persons Act 1963:

> In any proceedings for an offence committed or alleged to have been committed by a person of or over the age of twenty-one, any offence of which he was found guilty while under the age of fourteen shall be disregarded for the purposes of any evidence relating to his previous convictions; and he shall not be asked, and if asked shall not be required to answer, any question relating to such an offence, notwithstanding that the question would otherwise be admissible under section 1 of the Criminal Evidence Act 1898.

4.18 Questions for Counsel

1 May the prosecution make use of Coke's previous conviction for rape, in order to assist in proving his guilt on the charge of raping Margaret Blackstone?

2 May Littleton seek to establish his good character, by way of defence? If so:

(a) What matters may be canvassed, by way of 'character evidence' for this purpose?

(b) By what means may Littleton establish his good character?

(c) If Littleton were not of good character, what steps might the prosecution take to deal with a false or misleading assertion of good character by him?

(d) What will be the evidential value of Littleton's good character, if established?

3 What advice would you give to Coke about the voluntary exposure of his character to the jury, if it were contemplated?

4 Assuming that Coke gives evidence in his defence, what would be the effect of the following:

(a) Coke's counsel has cross-examined Margaret, seeking to show that she consented to have sexual intercourse with him on the occasion of the alleged rape?

(b) Coke's counsel has cross-examined Margaret seeking to show that (i) she is promiscuous; and (ii) that last year, she falsely accused Kevin of raping her?

(c) Coke's counsel has suggested to Margaret in cross-examination that she is dishonest, as evidenced by her conviction for shoplifting, and is given to telling lies?

(d) Coke has given evidence in chief that he went to a good school and is honest and hard-working?

5 What would be the effect of the matters raised in question 4 if Coke

(a) declined to give evidence? (Matters (a), (b) and (c) only.)

(b) declined to give evidence, but raised all four matters in an unsworn statement from the dock?

6 What would be the effect of Coke's giving evidence in chief that Littleton was with him throughout the relevant Sunday, and in particular while Margaret and Angela were at his flat?

5 Similar-fact Evidence

A: CRIMINAL CASES

5.1 · Introduction

One of the more unpleasant surprises awaiting counsel for Coke, when he receives his brief, is the revelation that in April 1976 his client was convicted of rape and sentenced to a term of Borstal training, from which he was released less than two years prior to the offence now charged. As shown in Chapter 4, evidence of character and disposition is in general inadmissible as such, and it is only in limited circumstances and for limited purposes that it is received.

However, there are circumstances in which such evidence is held to become relevant to an issue in the case and is admitted on such issue. In some circumstances character evidence may be relevant to the question of guilt itself and not a mere question of credit. The Criminal Evidence Act 1898, s. 1(*f*)(i) permits cross-examination of a defendant about another offence, where 'the proof that he has committed or been convicted of such other offence is admissible evidence to show that he is guilty of the offence wherewith he is then charged.' This covers the exceptional instances in which previous conviction is an essential element of the offence charged (see 4.5, ante) but is not limited to such cases.

While it is true that evidence of general disposition and character offers the jury no positive evidence of the defendant's guilt as charged, some specific fact or facts in that character or disposition may offer very clear evidence. This occurs where the prosecution can point to a previous offence which, because of its nature or method of commission or attendant circumstances, bears an unmistakable similarity to the offence charged; a similarity which goes beyond a matter merely of curiosity or coincidence, and drives the jury to say, 'This is the work of the same man.' The outstanding features of the direct evidence relating to the offence charged, when compared with those of the previous offence, reveal distinctly what is sometimes called the 'hallmark' of a particular offender. Such a stage is of course reached only when the features are very remarkable and the similarity very obvious.

The rule of admissibility of such evidence is not confined to the operation of s. 1(*f*)(i), which applies only when the defendant elects to give evidence and thereby renders himself liable to cross-examination. There is a general rule in favour of the reception of specific evidence of character or disposition which, because of its high degree of similarity to some aspect of the direct evidence, tends to identify the defendant as the author of the offence charged, or to rebut any defence of innocent association, mistake, coincidence and the like. Evidence, in other words, which goes beyond mere evidence of disposition or character and in itself offers positive indications not only that the present offence was committed, but that it was committed by the defendant. Any such rule would obviously create difficulties for the defence of Coke, both because evidence of the circumstances of the earlier rape would call into question his state of mind with regard to consent, and because the surrounding circumstances of the earlier rape (including the *modus operandi*) may be thought to bear a striking resemblance to those of the offence now charged. The evidence would certainly be likely to lead a jury to take a very different view of Coke's case than they would if confronted only with the Blackstone incident as now charged. The element and degree of similarity will be found on analysis to be the true origin of any probative value which the evidence may possess. It not only marks out the propensities of a particular individual to a degree far more specific than would mere general disposition, but also inevitably puts a new dimension on any explanation offered by the defence involving innocent conduct or state of mind on the single occasion of the offence charged. For this reason, evidence admitted as probative in this way is usually referred to as 'similar-fact evidence'.

In *Makin and Makin v Attorney-General for New South Wales* (1) the defendants were charged with the murder of a child, whose skeleton was found in their back garden and whom they had 'adopted' from its mother in return for a sum of money, inadequate for its maintenance. The facts were consistent with the allegation that the defendants had killed the child for the maintenance, but equally were consistent with natural death followed by an irregular burial. It was held that evidence of the finding of other remains of children similarly 'adopted' by the defendants, which had been buried in the garden of a previous residence of the defendants, was rightly admitted to show the nature of the defendants' practice and so to prove the fate of the child in question. The effect of the evidence was to render any suggestion of accident or coincidence incredible by any reasonable tribunal, and thus it went far beyond mere evidence of disposition to behave in a certain way. Viewed from a positive standpoint, the evidence went to prove a systematic course of conduct characteristic of those particular defendants, which supported the allegation of their conduct in relation to the offence charged. Lord Herschell LC expressed the rule of admissibility in clear and cogent terms which have never been surpassed, saying (2):

It is undoubtedly not competent for the prosecution to adduce evidence tending to show that the accused has been guilty of criminal acts other than those covered by the indictment, for the purpose of leading to the conclusion that the accused is a person likely from his criminal conduct or character to have committed the offence for which he is being tried. On the other hand, the mere fact that the evidence adduced tends to show the commission of other crimes does not render it inadmissible if it be relevant to an issue before the jury, and it may be so relevant if it bears upon the question whether the acts alleged to constitute the crime charged in the indictment were designed or accidental, or to rebut a defence which would otherwise be open to the accused.

5.2 Degree of probative value required

The test of admissibility of evidence of similar facts is one of probative value in relation to the offence charged. While such probative value is found in the element of 'striking similarity' often referred to in the cases, the latter phrase has been described as no more than a convenient label, which must not be allowed to obscure the true test (3). It

1 (PC, New South Wales) [1894] AC 57.   2 Ibid at 65.
3 *R v Scarrott* (CA) [1978] QB 1016 at 1021–2 per Scarman LJ. *R v Rance; R v Herron* (CA) (1975) 62 Cr App R 118.

remains true, nonetheless, that it is to the degree of similarity that reference must be made in order to determine the probative value of the evidence in question.

Thus, in the celebrated case of *R* v *Smith* (4) where the defendant was charged with the murder of a woman with whom he had gone through a ceremony of marriage, evidence of the deaths of two other women with whom the defendant had gone through a ceremony of marriage was held to have been rightly admitted. In each case, the deceased woman was found drowned in her bath; in each case, the door of the bathroom would not lock; in each case, the defendant had informed a medical practitioner that the woman suffered from epileptic fits; and in each case, the woman's life was insured for the benefit of the defendant. The devastating degree of similarity was clearly probative of the guilt of the defendant of the offence charged. Conversely, in *Noor Mohamed* v *R* (5) the Privy Council rejected an attempt to shore up an otherwise unpromising case by the introduction of tenuous evidence bearing only a superficial similarity to the circumstances of the offence charged. The defendant was charged with the murder of a woman with whom he lived by causing her to take cyanide — a substance which the defendant had in his possession lawfully in the course of his trade as a goldsmith. There was no direct evidence that the defendant caused the deceased to take the cyanide, and there was some evidence that she might have committed suicide. Weak evidence tending to suggest that the defendant had previously killed his wife by causing her to take cyanide on the pretence that it was a cure for toothache, was held to have been wrongly admitted.

The question of admissibility is one of law for the judge, who must rule on the relevance and probative value of the evidence. If the judge decides in law in favour of admitting the evidence, he may nonetheless refuse in his discretion to admit it, if, in his opinion, its prejudicial effect is likely to outweigh its probative value. Similar fact is necessarily prejudicial to the defendant, exposing as it does a sensitive aspect of his character or disposition, and in some cases, the risk of the jury being wrongly influenced by the sheer damning of the defendant's character cannot be justified by the degree of probative quality offered. If, however, the evidence is admitted, the jury must consider it in the light of the evidence as a whole (6). The authorities seem to suggest that the requisite degree of probative value can be found if the proposed similar-fact evidence: (a) goes to the offence itself and not merely to peripheral circumstances; and (b) exhibits strikingly similar features which are not so commonplace as to be evidentially insignificant.

5.2.1 Similarity going to the offence itself

The similarity must relate to the offence itself, and evidence which does no more than suggest similar behaviour in other or peripheral respects should not be admitted. Thus, in *R* v *Rodley* (7), the defendant was charged with housebreaking with intent to rape. It was proved that he had climbed down the chimney of a house, and was then surprised by the girl's father. His defence was that he intended only to court the girl with her consent. Evidence was held to have been wrongly admitted that an hour later, and some three miles away, he entered another house by the chimney and had sexual intercourse with a different girl with her consent. The evidence disclosed nothing of real probative value in

4 (CCA) (1915) 11 Cr App R 229. This extraordinary case may perhaps be best explained by misquoting Lady Bracknell (Wilde, *The Importance Of Being Ernest*). To lose one 'wife' under such circumstances may be regarded as a misfortune; to lose a second looks like carelessness; to lose a third looks like murder. It would be hard to think of better evidence of system than that offered by the facts of the case.
5 (PC, British Guiana) [1949] AC 182.
6 See *DPP* v *Boardman* (HL) [1975] AC 421 per Lord Salmon at 463.
7 (CCA) [1913] 3 KB 468.

relation to the offence charged and, in particular, nothing of relevance to the alleged intent, even though it drew attention to the defendant's somewhat individual approach to entering houses. The point was also made forcibly in the more recent decision in *R* v *Tricoglus* (8) in which the defendant was charged with the rape of A. A's evidence was that she had accepted a lift from a bearded man driving a Mini. Evidence was rightly admitted from G to the effect that, some twelve days before the rape of A, she (G) had been raped in the same cul-de-sac as A by a bearded man from whom she had accepted a lift. G identified the defendant's car when shown it, after some uncertainty about its make. On the other hand, evidence was wrongly admitted from M and C, who had been offered, but had refused lifts from a bearded man driving a Mini, even though there was a close connection in time and place and even though C had recorded, correctly save for one figure, the registration number of the defendant's car.

5.2.2   *Striking similarity in significant features*
A high degree of similarity, and a similarity in features which are themselves striking and not commonplace, are essential if any probative value is to be extracted from similar-fact evidence.

Even before any question of the degree of similarity arises, the question whether the facts themselves are striking or commonplace must be examined. If they are commonplace, their similarity will have little or no significance; similarity of commonplace matters is only to be expected and has no special evidential significance. In this respect, it is particularly important to bear in mind the warning given by Scarman LJ in *Scarrott* that it is probative value, and not mere similarity, which matters. In the same judgment, Scarman LJ went on to say (9):

> Positive probative value is what the law requires, if similar fact evidence is to be admissible. Such probative value is not provided by the mere repetition of similar facts; there has to be some feature or features in the evidence sought to be adduced which provides a link — an underlying link as it has been called in some of the cases. The existence of such a link is not to be inferred from mere similarity of facts which are themselves so commonplace that they can provide no sure ground for saying that they point to the commission by the accused of the offence under consideration.

It must also be self-evident that, unless the degree of similarity is striking, no inference can safely be drawn so as to connect the defendant with the offence charged. Anything less than striking similarity to the extent of the hallmark of a particular offender is evidence of mere disposition, and must be rejected.

5.3   Application of the rule

These principles are easy enough to state, but have caused some difficulty in practice in relation to sexual cases, which were for some long time viewed as being subject to special rules. Although the House of Lords has decisively rejected any special categorisation of these offences (10) it remains desirable to examine separately the application to them of the rule, and then to look at the more straightforward history of other offences.

8   (CA) (1976) 65 Cr App R 16.
9   (CA) [1978] QB 1016 at 1022.
10   In *DPP* v *Boardman* [1975] AC 421 at 430.

5.3.1 *Sexual cases*

Although now discredited, the 'special category' view was firmly held in many of the older cases, and has made one or two surprising reappearances in cases after *Boardman*.

The view can be traced back at least as far as *Thompson* v *R* (11), in which the defendant was charged with acts of gross indecency with boys on 16 March. The evidence was that the man who had committed the acts had made an appointment to meet the same boys at the same place and for the same purpose on 19 March. On the latter date, the defendant was arrested at the meeting-place, and said: 'You've got the wrong man.' The issue from the first to last was identification. The House of Lords upheld the admission of evidence of finding in the defendant's room photographs of naked boys, and finding on the defendant himself, when he was arrested, a powder-puff. Various grounds were advanced to justify the reception of this evidence. Lord Finlay LC thought that the defendant's possession of these articles showeed that he had the same 'abnormal propensities' as the man who had committed the acts on 16 March. Lord Atkinson and Lord Parker of Waddington both considered (the latter with 'some hesitation') that it was relevant to the issue of identification. But it was Lord Sumner who in the following words paved the way for an unfortunate segregation of sexual (specifically, it seems, homosexual) offences, so far as the reception of similar fact evidence is concerned (12):

> A thief, a cheat, a coiner, or a housebreaker is only a particular specimen of the genus rogue, and, though no doubt each tends to keep to his own line of business, they all alike possess the by no means extraordinary mental characteristic that they propose somehow to get their living dishonestly. So common a characteristic is not a recognisable mark of the individual. Persons, however, who commit the offences now under consideration seek the habitual gratification of a particular perverted lust, which not only takes them out of the class of ordinary men gone wrong, but stamps them with the hallmark of a specialised and extraordinary class as much as if they carried on their bodies some physical peculiarity.

Although Lord Sumner's observations may have been intended to apply to specific sexual offences having relatively unusual features, there is no doubt that they were interpreted to mean that sexual offences, at least if committed against children or if involving some form of homosexual behaviour, were in themselves so distinctive as to justify the admission of evidence which on strict analysis proved no more than a fairly general sexual propensity. This interpretation had two consequences. The first was that evidence that the defendant was a homosexual became admissible to show that he committed the homosexual offence charged. The second that evidence of homosexual behaviour on other occasions became admissible for the same purpose. Happily, both consequences have been eroded greatly, even if not entirely.

In *R* v *King* (13) the defendant was charged with various offences relating to gross indecency, attempted buggery and indecent assault. It was held that the answer 'Yes' given by the defendant in cross-examination to the question, 'Are you a homosexual?' was admissible, in a case where the defendant denied committing the acts alleged. The Court of Appeal held that the evidence came 'plainly within the principle' in *Thompson*. Lord Parker CJ said: 'It is no different putting to a man the question "Are you a homosexual?" from putting to him certain indecent photographs of a homosexual nature

11 [1918] AC 221.   12 Ibid at 235.   13 [1967] 2 QB 338.

found in his possession and saying to him: "Are these yours?" ' (14). The jury were, however, rightly directed that such evidence did not of itself mean that the defendant had committed any offence. In *R* v *Horwood* (15) some inroad was made on *King's* case. It was held that, assuming that the admission of homosexuality did not mean that the defendant had committed any offence, it was only in (16):

> . . . very exceptional circumstances that evidence of this nature can be admitted to rebut innocent association. *R* v *King* was an exceptional case; the admitted facts were such that the admission that the defendant was a homosexual could properly be said to be relevant to the issue before the jury. In our judgment that decision cannot be taken as authority for the proposition that in all cases where a man is charged with a homosexual offence he may be asked either by the police or in the witness-box the question: 'Are you a homosexual?'

In fact, it is submitted, assuming that the evidence does not mean that the defendant has committed the offence charged, it is difficult to see why the evidence should ever be admitted, unless the defendant denies being a homosexual or having ever committed homosexual acts and makes such denial a part of his defence. If this proposition be accepted, it must have been equally valid at the time of the decision in *Thompson,* because of the statement of principle enunciated by Lord Herschell LC in *Makin* (see 5.1).

The second consequence has proved somewhat more resilient. The cry of Lord Sumner was taken up in a number of subsequent cases, notably by Lord Goddard CJ in *R* v *Sims* (17). Sims was charged with offences of sodomy and gross indecency with four different men on different occasions. Application was made for the separate trial of these charges. The refusal of the application was upheld, on the ground that the evidence on each was probative of each other charge. The specific feature in such cases, it was said, lay in 'the abnormal and perverted propensity which stamps the individual as clearly as if marked by a physical deformity.' The Court of Criminal Appeal added, significantly (18): 'Sodomy is a crime in a special category. . . . On this account, in regard to this crime we think that the repetition of the acts is itself a specific feature connecting the accused with the crime.'

The court would have been prepared to extend the same rule to offences against children. In *R* v *Southern* (19) where the defendant was charged with one offence against a boy of thirteen and one offence some four months later against a girl of five, the Court of Criminal Appeal held that the two should have been tried separately because: . . . 'although they were offences of the same class, arising from filthy lust, they were not the same in law, nor were they in fact connected except by the circumstance that the same man was accused of both.' Of this decision the court in *Sims* said: 'If the court in *Southern's* case intended to go to the length of saying that because one count related to a little boy and another to a little girl separate trials should have been granted, we are not disposed to follow the decision' (20).

14 Ibid at 346.   15   (CA) [1970] 1 QB 133.
16   Ibid per O'Connor J at 139. It is not clear why the court regarded *King* as exceptional, as the principle in *Thompson* was never confined to cases where identity was in issue: see *R* v *Twiss* (CCA) [1918] 2 KB 853, and *DPP* v *Boardman* (HL) [1975] AC 421 per Lord Hailsham of St Marylebone at 452 and Lord Cross of Chelsea at 458. The answer given in *Horwood* was such as to be of no real evidential value in any event. It was: 'I used to be: I'm cured now. The doctor's given me some pills to take when the urge comes on. I go out with girls now like anyone else.'
17   [1946] KB 531.   18   Ibid at 540.   19   (1930) 22 Cr App R 6.   20   [1946] KB 531 at 543–4.

The state of the law in consequence of *Thompson* was reviewed in *DPP* v *Boardman* (21). The defendant, the headmaster of a boarding school, was charged with committing buggery with S, a boy of sixteen (as to which he was convicted of an attempt) and with inciting H, a boy of seventeen, to commit buggery with him. The similarity of these offences was said to lie in the facts that both boys were pupils at the school; that the defendant disturbed both in a dormitory; that he used similar words in order to induce their participation; and that he preferred to play the passive role in the act of buggery. While both Lords Wilberforce and Cross of Chelsea described the case as 'borderline', the House of Lords held that the evidence on each charge was probative of both that charge and the other, so that in considering each charge evidence relating to the other was admissible as similar fact (22). Counsel for the prosecution expressly disavowed any desire to argue that the mere fact of homosexuality in itself could ever be sufficient to justify the reception of similar fact, so that the House was in effect invited to consign the basis of *Thompson* and *Sims* to the past. The House took up the challenge, holding that homosexual cases were not to be placed in any special category. As Lord Wilberforce observed (23): 'In matters of experience it is for the judge to keep close to current mores. What is striking in one age is normal in another: the perversions of yesterday may be the routine or the fashions of tomorrow'. Lord Salmon said: 'It is plain . . . that the principles stated by Lord Herschell [in *Makin*] are of universal application and that homosexual offences are not exempt from them as at one time seems to have been supposed: see *Thompson* v *R* . . . and *R* v *Sims*' (24). Accordingly, the law is that in any criminal case, evidence of similar facts may be admitted as probative of the offence charged if such probative value can be demonstrated from the striking similarity of the facts to the offence charged. The point was also made by Lords Hailsham of St Marylebone and Cross of Chelsea that no logical distinction could be drawn between cases where the defendant advanced the defence of 'Innocent association' and cases of complete denial of the offence charged.

The emphasis on the features, rather than the nature of the offence charged was neatly expressed by Lord Hailsham as follows (25):

. . . whilst it would certainly not be enough to identify the culprit in a series of burglaries that he climbed in through a ground floor window, the fact that he left the same humorous limerick on the walls of the sitting room, or an esoteric symbol written in lipstick on the mirror, might well be enough. In a sex case, to adopt an example given in argument in the Court of Appeal, whilst a repeated homosexual act by itself might be quite insufficient to admit the evidence as confirmatory of identity or design, the fact that it was alleged to have been performed wearing the ceremonial head-dress of a Red Indian chief or other eccentric garb might well in appropriate circumstances suffice.

The application of these apparently clear principles since *Boardman* has, however, proved unexpectedly erratic; unexpectedly because of the promising start made by *R* v *Novac and Others* (26). One defendant had on various occasions met boys in places of

21 [1975] AC 421 at 430.
22 The effect of such a ruling is of course that the jury may regard the evidence on each charge as evidence in relation to both, as opposed to keeping the two separate, as in other cases of joint trial, and in the light of *DPP* v *Kilbourne* (HL) [1973] AC 729, the evidence may be mutually corroborative.
23 [1975] AC 421 at 444.
24 Ibid at 461.   25   Ibid at 454.
26 (1976) 65 Cr App R 107 (CA, Bridge, LJ, Wien and Kenneth Jones JJ).

amusement, had offered them money to play gambling machines and then shelter at his home. The defendant then committed acts of buggery and attempted buggery while sharing a bed with the boys. Of this evidence, Bridge LJ said (27):

> We cannot think that two or more alleged offences of buggery or attempted buggery committed in bed at the residence of the alleged offender with boys to whom he had offered shelter can be said to have been committed in a uniquely or strikingly similar manner. If a man is going to commit buggery with a boy he picks up, it must surely be a commonplace feature of such an encounter that he will take the boy home with him and commit the offence in bed. The fact that the boys may in each case have been picked up by [the defendant] in the first instance at amusement arcades may be a feature more nearly approximating to a 'unique or striking similarity' within the ambit of Lord Salmon's principle [in *Boardman*]. It is not, however, a similarity in the commission of the crime. It is a similarity in the surrounding circumstances and is not, in our judgment, sufficiently proximate to the commission of the crime itself to lead to the conclusion that the repetition of this feature would make the boys' stories inexplicable on the basis of coincidence.

The sex offender in the Red Indian head-dress was referred to by the trial judge in *Novac* in his summing-up, without disapproval by the Court of Appeal. Nonetheless, his war cry went unheeded in *R v Johannsen* (28) in which, although the facts were virtually indistinguishable from those of *Novac,* the decision in *Novac* appears not to have been cited to the court. The result was a regression the *Thompson/Sims* approach. The court dealt with the argument for the appellant that there was no striking similarity sufficient to admit similar fact, in these terms (29):

> We do not find it necessary to set out in much detail the sordid evidence given in this case. . . . The prosecution's case was that between May and December 1975 he made a practice of accosting boys in amusement arcades and similar places, offering them money or a meal or treating them to a game, taking them to his accommodation or on to the beach, and there committing the offences charged. His particular homosexual propensities were to handle the boys' penises and getting them to do the same with his, fellatio and buggery. . . . We have no hesitation in deciding that there were striking similarities about what happened to each of the boys — the accostings in the same kind of places, the enticements, the visits to his accommodation, his homosexual propensities and his ways of gratifying them.

Faced with this outright conflict of approach, yet another Court of Appeal in *R v Scarrott* (30) made it plain that each case must be looked at on its own facts, and that no general rule could be laid down so as to be given the status of a rule of law, except the need to find in any case, as a condition of admissibility, that the similar-fact evidence became, on the facts of the case considered as a whole, probative of the offence charged. Both *Novac* and *Johannsen* were cited to the court. Scarman LJ, referring to, 'I hestitate to say a striking similarity, but certainly a remarkable similarity between the salient facts' of the two, observed that 'it is very difficult to determine why or how the court reached

---

27 Ibid at 112.   28   (1977) 65 Cr App R 101 (CA, Lawton LJ, Nield and Boreham JJ).
29 Ibid at 103.
30 [1978] QB 1016 (CA, Roskill and Scarman LJJ and Wien J). Wien J had been a member of the court in *Novac*.

the decision that it did in these cases.' This difficulty arose not because of any error in either the decisions or the reports of them, but because each had been determined after a proper investigation of its own facts, and by the drawing of a line on the basis of those facts.

It is submitted that the Court of Appeal, differently constituted, has varied in its approach to the law, and while each case must indeed turn on its own facts, *Johannsen* is irreconcilable with the principles laid down in *Boardman* and should not be followed. There is some sign that the court will prefer the approach in *Novac*. In *R* v *Inder* (31) a conviction was quashed where the features said by the prosecution to display a 'uniquely or strikingly similar' quality, were in fact no more than the 'stock in trade of the seducer of small boys' and were such as 'appear in the vast majority of cases that come before the courts'. And in *R* v *Clarke* (32) the court held that three counts alleging attempted buggery and indecent assault on the defendant's stepson should have been severed from four counts of sexual offences against his stepdaughter, not because the sexes of the children differed, but because no sufficient similarity was shown by the evidence. It is submitted that the difference in sex must be one factor to be taken into account in applying the test, but clearly need not be the only nor even the dominant factor.

5.3.2 *Cases other than sexual cases*
Outside the sphere of sexual cases, the application of the rule has been rather less difficult to follow. The examples which follow are offered for the purpose of illustrating the application in certain specific types of case.

In *R* v *Straffen* (33) the defendant was charged with the murder of a girl, a murder committed during a fairly short period of time when he was an absconder from Broadmoor. Evidence was rightly admitted that the defendant had twice previously killed small girls by the same method (strangulation) and had left their bodies in a substantially similar condition, i.e. unconcealed and sexually unmolested. In *R* v *Morris* (34) indecent photographs taken of a girl by the defendant, who had pleaded guilty to the indecent assault of that girl, were admitted on a charge of the murder of a different girl, where the photographs bore a striking resemblance to the appearance of the dead body of the murdered girl on its discovery.

In *R* v *Mansfield* (35) the defendant was charged, *inter alia,* with three counts of arson. The fires were started within a period of three weeks, the first in an hotel where the defendant lived, the second and third in an hotel where he worked as a kitchen porter. In each case, the method of starting the fire was distinctive; in each the defendant had an opportunity to start the fire; in each case, he was seen nearby acting suspiciously, and lied to the police when questioned; and in the case of the third fire, a waste-paper bin from the defendant's room was found near the site of the fire. It was held that evidence of each fire was admissible in relation to each count, and accordingly that the trial judge had rightly refused to sever the indictment.

In *R* v *Rance; R* v *Herron* (36), Rance, the managing director of a building company, was convicted of corruptly procuring the payment of money to Herron, a local councillor (who was convicted of corruptly receiving the money). This payment had been procured by means including the signature by Rance of a false certificate describing Herron as a 'subcontractor'. Rance said that he must have been deceived into signing the certificate.

31 (CA) (1977) 67 Cr App R 143. 32 CA (1977) 67 Cr App R 398.
33 (CCA) [1952] 2 QB 911. See also *R* v *Evans* (CCA) [1950] 1 All ER 610.
34 (CA) (1969) 54 Cr App R 69. 35 (CA) [1978] 1 WLR 1102. 36 (1975) 62 Cr App R 118.

Evidence was rightly admitted of similar payments to other councillors supported by other false certificates. It is noteworthy that the Court of Appeal held that the mere existence of some dispute about the similar-fact evidence (in this case, the defendant said that he believed the other certificates to be genuine) did not prevent the evidence from being admitted. This factor does, of course, set one additional problem for the jury to solve. It would seem that even a dispute about the facts themselves, as opposed to the defendant's state of mind, would not prevent similar-fact evidence from being adduced. Naturally, if the jury did not find the similar facts proved, they would in any case be of no evidential value.

It may be seen from *R* v *Mustafa* (37) and from *R* v *Seaman* (38) that even in offences of a much more common type, such as theft, evidence of similar facts may be admissible to show system or identification, where the degree of distinctiveness is high. In a common-place offence, however, it seems that only a peculiarly distinctive *modus operandi* would suffice to distinguish the particular characteristics of the offence from the multitude of necessarily similar offences committed by others under the like circumstances. Although the facts of *Mustafa* seem compelling enough, it is unlikely that evidence of any lesser value could really suffice, unless the direct evidence in the case was in any event very strong. In a common offence, it must always be proportionately harder to argue for any hallmark of a particular individual offender, and the risk of prejudice is obviously very considerable (39).

5.4 Similar fact called for defence

Similar-fact evidence is admissible for the defence as it is for the prosecution, and subject to the same conditions, although its scope would not be as obvious in view of the incidence of the burden of proof in most instances. Most of the problems in this area have been raised by evidence which is designed to affect adversely the case for a co-defendant, or which has that effect.

The rule is that a defendant is not entitled, any more than is the prosecution, to adduce evidence which goes only to show disposition or character unless either he has become entitled to investigate the character of the co-defendant by the operation of the Criminal Evidence Act 1898, s. 1 (proviso *f*), or the evidence sought to be adduced has probative value in relation to the guilt of the co-defendant on the offence charged.

Thus, in *R* v *Nightingale* (40) where the defendant was charged with affray and wounding with intent, and said that he found the weapon used, a knife, on the ground during the fight and used it in self-defence, the trial judge was held to have erred in permitting a co-defendant to elicit evidence that the defendant had on two previous occasions been convicted of having an offensive weapon. In one of the previous cases, the offensive weapon was a knife, in the other a broken bottle. Presumably, evidence that the defendant habitually carried a knife might have been admitted in rebuttal of any evidence given by him that he had not been carrying a knife on this particular occasion, but it is clear that the evidence adduced bore no special features.

Some support for a more general attack on the disposition of the co-defendant is

---

37   (CA) (1976) 65 Cr App R 26.
38   (CA) (1978) 67 Cr App R 234.
39   One of the arguments on appeal in *Mustafa* related to prejudicial effect, it being undisputed that the evidence had probative value because of a high degree of similarity. The decision in *Seaman* must surely be open to grave question.
40.   (CA) [1977] Crim LR 744.

sometimes sought in the decision in *Lowery* v *R* (41). The facts of this case were, however, quite specific, in that one of the two defendants (and no one else) had undoubtedly murdered a girl in circumstances which revealed no motive beyond a sadistic pleasure in killing. Evidence adduced by one defendant from a psychologist that the other was more likely to have committed the offence, in that he was aggressive and had relatively little self-control, was held to have been rightly admitted, in that it went beyond mere criminal disposition. Although not a case of similar-fact evidence the terms of the judgment of the Privy Council are such as to be wide enough to admit such evidence in corresponding circumstances. However, it is clear that where the evidence goes only to credit, such as to the question whether the defendant should be believed in his evidence on the issue of provocation, and does not go directly to an issue in the case as it arguably did in *Lowery,* the evidence will be rejected (42). And where evidence of similar facts is irrelevant to the defence of the defendant who adduces it even though it may bear on the guilt of the co-defendant, it will also be rejected. In *R* v *Neale* (43) the defendants were charged with arson. The defence of one was that he was not present when the fire was started. It was held that the trial judge had rightly rejected evidence that the co-defendant had previously started fires in similar circumstances. Although such evidence might support the prosecution's case against the co-defendant, it could not be relevant to the defence of alibi.

B: CIVIL CASES

5.5 Application to civil cases

Although it has been said that in civil cases, even where similar-fact evidence is technically admissible, the court has a discretion, and should refuse to admit it unless it would not only 'afford a reasonable presumption as to the matter in dispute, but would be reasonably conclusive, and would not raise a difficult and doubtful controversy of precisely the same kind as that which the jury have to determine' (44). The rule in modern times is almost certainly the same as that in criminal cases. Now that jury trial is comparatively rare in civil cases, the judge has ample power to reject evidence which will not assist him in the determination of the pleaded issues, and can deal with the likelihood of prejudice in the same way.

The modern position was stated by the Court of Appeal in *Mood Music Publishing Co. Ltd* v *De Wolfe Ltd* (45). The plaintiffs were the owners of the copyright in a musical work called 'Sogno Nostalgico'. They alleged that the defendants had infringed such copyright by supplying for broadcasting a work entitled 'Girl in the Dark'. It was not disputed that the works were similar, but the defendants contended that the similarity was accidental, and denied copying even though 'Sogno Nostalgico' was composed prior to 'Girl in the Dark'. It was held that evidence was admissible to show that on other occasions the defendants had reproduced works subject to copyright; one of the three relevant occasions being a reproduction by the defendants as a result of an 'entrapment' set up by the plaintiffs for the express purpose of obtaining evidence against the defendants. Lord Denning MR said (46):

    41   (PC, Victoria) [1974] AC 85. See also *R* v *Bracewell* (CA) (1978) 68 Cr App R 44.
    42   *R* v *Turner* (CA) [1975] QB 834.   43   (CA) (1977) 65 Cr App R 304.
    44   *Managers of Metropolitan Asylum District* v *Hill and Others (Appeal No. 1)* (HL). (1882) 47 LT 29 at 35 per Lord Watson. See also *Attorney-General* v *Nottingham Corporation* [1904] 1 Ch 673.
    45   (CA) [1976] Ch 119.   46   Ibid at 127.

The criminal courts have been very careful not to admit such evidence unless its probative value is so strong that it should be received in the interests of justice: and its admission will not operate unfairly to the accused. In civil cases the courts have followed a similar line but have not been so chary of admitting it. In civil cases the courts will admit evidence of similar facts if it is logically probative, that is, if it is logically relevant in determining the matter which is in issue: provided that it is not oppressive or unfair to the other side: and also that the other side has fair notice of it and is able to deal with it.

No better contrast could be provided than that in a sequel to the *Mood Music* case, namely *E.G. Music v S.F. (Film) Distributors* (47), in which the third defendants had been the defendants in the *Mood Music* case. The plaintiffs sought discovery of all the infringements alleged in *Mood Music* with a view to their admission as similar-fact evidence in relation to the infringement alleged in the instant case. Whitford J rejected the application on the ground that such evidence was relevant only to the credit of the third defendants and was not relevant to any issue on the pleadings.

Other examples of the same principles are given below, the rule of admissibility being the same.

Where it is relevant to prove the behaviour of an animal, in addition to the conduct of the animal on the relevant occasion, its conduct of a similar nature on other occasions may be admitted, if it is such as to have probative value in relation to the matters alleged (48).

In cases of libel, prior libels of the plaintiff written by the defendant are admissible to prove actual malice or deliberate publication, as are the circumstances surrounding publication of such prior libels (49).

In *Sattin v National Union Bank* (50) a plaintiff who claimed in respect of the loss by the defendant bank of a diamond which he deposited with them as security for an overdraft, was held to be entitled to adduce evidence of another occasion when jewellery so deposited had been found to be missing. The Court of Appeal's decision was based on the entitlement of the plaintiff to rebut the defence that the defendants had used reasonable safeguards in securing the property deposited with them by customers.

C: GENERAL CONSIDERATIONS

5.6 Uses of similar-fact evidence

In the older cases, great importance was attached to the purpose for which similar-fact evidence was sought to be admitted, and in particular, it was held that it could be admitted only for the purpose of rebutting a defence actually raised by the defendant, such as mistaken identity, coincidence, innocent association and the like, which defences were clearly open to attack by evidence of strikingly similar behaviour on other occasions. As Lord Sumner said in *Thompson v R* (51): 'The mere theory that a plea of not guilty puts everything material in issue is not enough for this purpose. The prosecution cannot credit the accused with fancy defences in order to rebut them at the outset with some damning piece of prejudice.'

47 [1978] FSR 121.
48 *Osborne v Chocqueel* (DC) [1896] 2 QB 109 (a bulldog).
49 *Barrett v Long* (HL) (1856) 3 HL Cas 395.
50 (1978) 122 SJ 367.   51   (HL) [1918] AC at 232.

However, once it is accepted that the test of admissibility is one of relevance and probative value in relation to the offence charged, there can be no logical basis for the rejection of evidence unless and until some specific defence is raised. If the evidence is no more than 'prejudice' then it should not be admitted in any event. And in more recent authorities, a more consistent approach has been adopted which has now replaced the older rule. In *R* v *Sims* Lord Goddard CJ put the matter very clearly (52):

It has often been said that the admissibility of evidence of this kind depends on the nature of the defence raised by the accused. . . . If one starts with the assumption that all evidence tending to show a disposition towards a particular crime must be excluded unless justified, then the justification of evidence of this kind is that it tends to rebut a defence otherwise open to the accused; but if one starts with the general proposition that all evidence that is logically probative is admissible unless excluded, then evidence of this kind does not have to seek a justification but is admissible irrespective of the issues raised by the defence, and this we think is the correct view.

Although this statement met some criticism as going rather too far (53) it is undoubtedly the basis of the present law. The position was confirmed in the case of *Harris* v *DPP* (54), in which it was held that the words 'logically probative' do not open the door to unlimited evidence of disposition, but are apt to mean that the prosecution are not required to wait until the defendant has actually raised a specific defence (which in the absence of the evidence of similar facts, he may in some cases never be called upon to do because of lack of evidence against him) but are entitled to present as part of their case any evidence which is proper to prove the charge on the facts given, including any issue necessarily raised by the facts or which may properly be anticipated on the facts. To do so, observed Viscount Simon, involves no extension of the principle in *Makin,* and as was observed in *Noor Mohamed,* could hardly be described as 'crediting the accused with fancy defences' (55). Thus, once an issue is fairly before the court on a plea of not guilty, the evidence of similar facts, if admissible at all, is admissible at the outset and is generally probative of the offence charged. As long as this rule is understood, there can be little harm in cataloguing the issues to which similar-fact evidence can be said to go, but it would be a mistake to suppose that the catalogue can ever be a closed one.

One of the areas which has caused problems is that of the complete denial by the defendant that the act complained of ever took place at all. In *R* v *Chandor* (56) where the defendant was charged with offences against one boy in Croydon and against another in the Lake District, to which the defence was a complete denial, it was held that a succession of incidents was irrelevant to determine whether the incident had ever occurred, though such evidence might have been highly relevant on an issue of identity, intent or innocent association. The decision was followed in *R* v *Flack* (57) where the defendant was charged with three offences of incest with three different sisters, which he completely denied. It was held that the evidence on each charge was accordingly evidence on that charge only. These cases drew comment in *DPP* v *Boardman* both from Lord Hailsham of St Marylebone and Lord Cross of Chelsea. Lord Hailsham failed to see the logical distinction between cases of innocent association and complete denial,

52   (CCA) [1946] 1 KB 531 at 539.
53   See, e.g., *Noor Mohamed* v *R* (PC, British Guiana) [1949] AC 182 at 194, and by Lord Goddard CJ himself in *R* v *Hall* (CCA) [1952] 1 KB 302 at 306.
54   (HL) [1952] AC 694.   55   [1949] AC 182 at 191.   56   (CCA) [1959] 1 QB 545.
57   (CA) [1969] 2 All ER 784.

'since the permutations are too various to admit of universally appropriate labels' (58).
Lord Cross said, perhaps more helpfully (59):

> If I am charged with a sexual offence why should it make any difference to the
> admissibility or non-admissibility of similar fact evidence whether my case is that the
> meeting at which the offence is said to have been committed never took place or that I
> committed no offence in the course of it? In each case I am saying that my accuser is
> lying. . . . In *R v Chandor* and *R v Flack* the Court of Appeal approved the distinction
> between the two types of defence for the purposes of the admission of similar-fact
> evidence. But though the decisions in these two cases may well have been correct, I
> cannot, as at present advised, agree with that part of the reasoning in them.

It is submitted that the view of Lord Cross is to be preferred, although the nature of
the defence may well influence the judge in the exercise of his discretion in any case
where the probative value was less than extremely cogent. The risk of prejudice in the
case of a literal total denial, is obvious and serious (60).

The other problem lies in the admissibility of incriminating articles found in the
possession of the accused. The decision in the case of *Thompson v R* (61) is clearly open
to criticism in the light of the more modern approach to evidence of disposition and
similar facts, but has never been abrogated. It has indeed been followed in a number of
cases. The justification in *Thompson's* case was principally that the finding of the articles
went to rebut the defence of mistaken identity, but it may be that if the rule is still in
force, such evidence has now become generally admissible from the outset. In *R v
Reading and Others* (62) the articles were such as to connect the defendant with a certain
robbery, and there was admitted evidence of possession of articles stolen in the course of
such robbery, which clearly linked the defendant with the robbery. And more recently,
in *R v Mustafa* (63) the principle was used to justify the reception of evidence that a
stolen Access card had been found (in a Barclaycard holder) at the defendant's home, a
week after two successful thefts which it was alleged the defendant had committed by
using a stolen Barclaycard and forging the signature of its holder.

The rationale of *Reading* and *Mustafa* is no doubt the specific probative value afforded
by evidence of the possession of the articles in question. The real criticism of *Thompson*
may be, not the time at which the evidence would now become admissible, but the
likelihood that the evidence itself might now be regarded as doing no more than showing
a fairly general disposition. It is submitted that the case should not now be followed.

5.7 Forms of similar-fact evidence

It is immaterial whether the defendant has been charged with or convicted of any offence
in relation to the matters offered as similar fact, and indeed, if he has been tried, what the
verdict may have been, as long as evidence of the facts is relevant. Whether the evidence
is accepted is a matter for the jury, and, as we have seen in *R v Rance; R v Herron* (64) the
mere fact that the evidence is the subject of some dispute does not affect its admissibility.
Of course, in civil cases, the conduct will commonly not amount to a criminal offence,

58 [1975] AC 421 at 452.   59   [1975] AC 421 at 458.
60 This view is also held by the editors of Phipson, 12th ed., para. 457.
61 (HL) [1918] AC 221.   62   (CCA) [1966] 1 WLR 836.   63   (CA) (1976) 65 Cr App R 26.
64 (1975) 62 Cr App R 118; see 5.3.2, ante.

but to some similar tort, breach of contract or trust, or infringement. Where the conduct does amount to a criminal offence, and the defendant has been convicted of such offence, it is submitted that, contrary to the view sometimes expressed, the prosecution are entitled to prove the fact of conviction in addition to the facts alleged, whether or not the defendant pleaded guilty to the former charge.

The test of admissibility being what it is, evidence of facts which occurred subsequent to those forming the subject-matter of the instant charge are equally capable of having a probative value, and may accordingly be admitted. Thus in *R* v *Geering* (65), on a charge of murder by the defendant of her husband using arsenic, evidence was rightly admitted of the subsequent death by arsenic poisoning of two of the defendant's sons and the illness of a third from the same cause, the defendant being responsible for the food of all the victims during the relevant period.

The similar-fact evidence can and should be proved as part of the prosecution case. If the defendant gives evidence, he may be cross-examined as provided by s. 1 of the Criminal Evidence Act 1898 (proviso) (*e*) and (*f*)(i).

5.8   Questions for counsel

1   Is there some striking similarity in Coke's previous conviction for rape, which would give rise to probative value on the present charge?

2   If so, of what does it consist?

3   Is it of importance for any purpose that Coke's defence is one of consent?

4   Is the judge likely to exercise his discretion to exclude the evidence?

5   At what stage would the prosecution be entitled to lead the evidence, and would it make any difference that Coke would be shown to have a previous conviction?

6   If Margaret Blackstone had previously had sexual intercourse with Coke, but denied this in cross-examination, could Coke adduce evidence of such acts as part of his case?

7   Can Coke prove as part of his case that last year, Margaret threatened to complain falsely that she had been raped by his mate, Kevin?

6 The Rule Against Hearsay — I

A: THE RULE AGAINST HEARSAY

6.1 Statement and application of the rule

The rule against hearsay is one of the most important and commonly applied rules of the law of evidence, and yet at the same time, the least understood by students, the profession and the judiciary. Almost all the major problems which it seems to cause in practice stem from a failure to observe that the definition of hearsay contains, not one, but two elements and that only if both are present can the rule operate to exclude evidence. The rule against hearsay is that evidence is inadmissible if (a) it consists of any statement made by a person other than while giving evidence in the instant proceedings, *and* (b) it is tendered for the purpose of proving any fact contained in the statement. To restate the rule in pithy, if not entirely comprehensive terms: if you wish to prove the truth of some fact, you can call A to say that from his own knowledge or observation it is true, but you cannot call B to say that A told him that the fact is true.

The rule derives from considerations of policy, which in turn proceed from an awareness that hearsay, if admitted, would carry with it at least two formidable difficulties: first, that evidence consisting of a communication made to the witness by someone else has the inherent danger of unreliability through repetition, the danger increasing in proportion to the number of communications involved before the ultimate recipient gives evidence; second, that hearsay evidence cannot usefully be challenged in cross-examination, except on the inadequate basis of the veracity or reliability of the source of the communication, and therefore the court cannot see and hear the evidence directly tested. Both difficulties arise from the lack of direct evidence. Neither of these objections is theoretically fatal to the actual reception of hearsay evidence, because the view might equally well be taken that hearsay should be admitted, but should ordinarily be given little weight, or should not be acted upon in the absence of corroboration. Not all hearsay is unreliable. Frequently, it comes from an unimpeachable source, and is manifestly cogent, and it may be the best or the only available evidence of the fact to be proved. In such cases, there is no reason of theory why it should not be admitted and accorded full weight. This is often true in the case of documentary hearsay statements.

When there is added to these objections, however, the risk of concoction — which Professor Cross has described as 'one aspect of the great pathological dread of manufactured evidence which beset English lawyers of the late eighteenth and early nineteenth centuries' (1) — one can see why the common law set its face firmly against the admission of hearsay evidence. Had matters stopped there, the consideration of the rule would be a

---

1 *Evidence*, 5th ed. p. 479.

short and relatively simple matter. But even at common law, it was recognised that the sheer indispensability of hearsay to the determination of the truth in many cases meant that there had to be some exceptions. Where necessary witnesses were dead, where acts were hopelessly ambiguous without some contemporary explanation by those who performed them, where facts otherwise incapable of proof were stated in records kept, for the express purpose of future reference, by public officials acting under a duty, the law allowed hearsay to be admitted, subject to exacting and sometimes excessively rigorous safeguards. In very recent times, important exceptions applicable to criminal trials began to be enacted by statute, to supplement the rules at common law. By far the most significant was the Criminal Evidence Act 1965, passed in panic, after the House of Lords in *Myers* v *DPP* (2) had shrunk from the prospect of legislating judicially for a wholesale exception in favour of the admission of hearsay commercial records, in the absence of which prosecutions for offences of serious dishonesty might have come to an abrupt end.

The emergence of ever-widening exceptions to the rule at common law, and the gradual acceptance of the desirability of a general rule of inclusion rather than exclusion of evidence, have led to the most important and far-reaching inroad of all into the common-law rule. In civil proceedings, the Civil Evidence Act 1968 has, within certain limits and with extensive safeguards, adopted the view that hearsay is a question of weight, rather than a question of admissibility. Although the Act is often spoken of as an 'exception' to the rule against hearsay and arguably is so, it is true to say that it has created a wholly new rule for civil proceedings in favour of the admission of certain hearsay, while maintaining a sceptical vigilance over the weight of evidence so admitted. The Act has also given statutory force, for civil cases, to certain of the common-law exceptions referred to above. The reason, undoubtedly, why this step has been taken in civil cases but not in criminal, is that it has been felt safer to entrust the sifting and weighing of hearsay evidence to the trained, critical mind of a judge sitting alone as a tribunal of fact, than to a jury of laymen who may be accustomed in their daily lives to acting uncritically on what they are told by others. But it may be doubted whether such a task, though admittedly difficult, is any more so than that of applying the rule that an out-of-court confession made by A implicating both himself and B is evidence against A but not against B, or the rule that a recent complaint in a sexual case is evidence confirming the complainant's story, but not evidence of the facts stated in it and is incapable of affording corroboration of the complainant's evidence, or for that matter than many other feats which juries are commonly called on to perform. Both the Law Reform Committee and the Criminal Law Revision Committee have recommended corresponding reforms in criminal cases, although there is much disagreement about how far such change should be permitted to go, and it may be that something short of the position in civil cases would be wise (3).

The rule against hearsay will, therefore, occupy a great deal of space. The remainder of this chapter is taken up by consideration, in this section, of the scope of the common-law rule itself and in section B of the minor common-law exceptions applicable to criminal cases. Chapter 7 is concerned with the major common-law exceptions of admissions and confessions and statements made by and in the presence of defendants. Chapter 8 deals with the statutory exceptions, principally the Criminal Evidence Act 1965 and the Civil Evidence Act 1968.

2   (HL) [1965] AC 1001.
3   Law Reform Committee, 13th report, paras. 48–52; Criminal Law Revision Committee, 11th report, paras. 229–48.

The common-law rule against hearsay (as modified peripherally by statute) applies to all adversarial proceedings which are not affected by the Civil Evidence Act 1968, that is to say to criminal proceedings, and to all proceedings in magistrates' courts, since the 1968 Act has not yet been applied to the civil jurisdiction of those courts. There is sometimes a tendency in criminal cases to permit limited relaxations of the rule in relation to evidence tendered by the defence, but the practice is contrary to authority and has been deprecated. In *R* v *Turner and Others* (4) the trial judge was held to have been correct in refusing to admit evidence to the effect that a person not called as a witness had admitted having committed the offence charged. The person concerned had withdrawn the admission after making it, but this should not have affected the admissibility of what he had said. Only by calling him as a witness (when their difficulties would have included his privilege against self-incrimination) could the defence have properly put the evidence before the court. And in *Sparks* v *R* (5), the sort of case which feeds the desire for reform, where the defendant was charged with indecently assaulting a girl aged just under four years, who did not give evidence and was presumably incompetent to do so, the Privy Council held that the evidence of the girl's mother to the effect that the girl had told her that the attacker was coloured (the defendant being white) had been rightly rejected. Dealing with this point, Lord Morris of Borth-y-Gest, giving the reasons for the committee's advice, said (6):

> It was said that 'it was manifestly unjust for the jury to be left throughout the whole trial with the impression that the child could not give any clue to the identity of her assailant'. The cause of justice is, however, best served by adherence to rules which have long been recognised and settled. If the girl had made a remark to her mother (not in the presence of the appellant) to the effect that it was the appellant who had assaulted her and if the girl was not to be a witness at the trial, evidence as to what she had said would be the merest hearsay. In such circumstances it would be the defence who would wish to challenge a contention, if advanced, that it would be 'manifestly unjust' for the jury not to know that the girl had given a clue to the identity of her assailant.

Later, after rejecting a contention that the evidence was admissible under the res gestae exception to the hearsay rule (section B, post) Lord Morris pointed out that, if the evidence had been of an incriminating statement which had been admitted for the prosecution as part of a recent complaint, it would not have been evidence of the truth of what the girl had said. He added:

> Their Lordships can see no basis upon which evidence concerning a remark made by her to her mother could be admitted. Even if any basis for its admission could be found the evidence of the making of the remark would not be any evidence of the truth of the remark. Evidence of the making of the remark could not in any event possess a higher probative value than would attach to evidence of the making of a complaint in a case where the complainant gives evidence or to evidence of an accusation made to or in the presence of an accused. Nor can the principle of the matter vary according as to whether a remark is helpful to or hurtful to an accused person.

Happily, the appeal was allowed for other reasons, but the result of the application of

4   (1975) 61 Cr App R 67.   5   (PC, Bermuda) [1964] AC 964.   6   Ibid at 978.

the rule in such cases, though logically impeccable, is to say the least disturbing.

It is important to note that the rule against hearsay is not appropriate to non-adversarial proceedings, where the purpose of the proceedings is not to determine a dispute between parties but to investigate questions such as the welfare of children on an inquisitorial basis. Hence, in *Humberside County Council* v *R* (7), where evidence existed that the guardian of a child, who was not a party to proceedings to determine whether a care order should be made, had made admissions of his ill-treatment of the child, such statements were admissible when related by other witnesses, despite their apparently hearsay character, because they were relevant to the object of the court's inquiry. The ratio of the decision appears to be a relatively narrow one, in that the court was faced with a statutory duty under s. 1(2) of the Children and Young Persons Act 1969 to determine whether it was satisfied that certain conditions were shown to exist. Lord Widgery CJ emphasised that the rule against hearsay is of general application to proceedings in juvenile courts, which are of an adversarial nature, and the same would be true of contested custody proceedings, which involve a dispute between parties, notwithstanding that the court must first and foremost consider what is in the best interests of the child.

Reverting to the statement of the rule against hearsay given on page 123, it will be recalled that much of the difficulty often experienced with regard to the working of the rule can be avoided by remembering that a piece of evidence does not cease to be direct (and so become hearsay) merely because it consists of a statement made other than while giving evidence. For this to occur, the second element of the rule (that the statement is tendered with a view to proving the truth of its contents) must also be present. The fact that statements may be direct evidence, where the very fact of their being made is sought to be proved as relevant, must be borne in mind throughout the remainder of this section. In order to ascertain whether it is direct or hearsay, evidence must always be tested by two questions: (a) What is the source of the statement? and (b) For what purpose is it tendered?

6.2   Question (a): the source of the statement

The rule against hearsay applies to all statements and assertions made by any person other than while giving evidence in the proceedings in question (8). The exclusion, therefore, applies to statements made in the course of giving evidence on other occasions (9), so that a deposition made at committal proceedings is hearsay for the purposes of the trial. It applies also to statements made by a witness himself, on an occasion prior to giving evidence and repeated by him in evidence as a previous statement. These so-called self-serving or previous consistent statements are undoubtedly hearsay, but are subject to somewhat specialised rules, discussed in detail in 13.3, post.

The way in which the statement was expressed is immaterial. In addition to oral statements, there may be many other possibilities. Signs or gestures may be treated as hearsay, as where a dying woman pointed in such a way as to suggest the identity of her assailant (10).

Documents are a most important source of hearsay statements, and it must be emphasised that documentary statements are subject to the rule against hearsay as they

---

7   (DC) [1977] 1 WLR 1251.
8   Though the proper production of a document may be a statement made while giving evidence.
9   *R* v *Eriswell (Inhabitants)* (1790) 3 TR 707; *Haines* v *Guthrie* (1884) (CA) 13 QBD 818.
10   *Chandrasekera* v *R* (PC, Ceylon) [1937] AC 220.

are to the rules of evidence generally. The point was brought home in alarming circumstances in *Myers* v *DPP* (11). In this case, the defendant was convicted of offences of dishonesty in relation to motor vehicles. His practice was to buy up wrecked cars with their log-books, to disguise stolen cars so that they corresponded as nearly as possible with the wrecks and their log-books, and to sell the stolen cars as if they were the wrecks, repaired by him. In order to prove their case, the prosecution adduced evidence from a witness in charge of records which were kept on microfilm, containing details of every car made at the works of a certain manufacturer. The microfilm was prepared from records compiled by workmen on cards, which were destroyed after being filmed, and which recorded the cylinder-block number of each car. Since the cylinder-block number was stamped indelibly on the engine of each vehicle, the evidence was of some value to the prosecution in proving the true identity of the cars in question. The House of Lords were unanimous in holding that the evidence contained in the records was hearsay, and that it could not be admitted under any recognised exception to the rule, and also that it would be eminently reasonable and convenient that it should be admitted if possible. But while the minority (Lords Pearce and Donovan) were prepared to extend the range of exceptions to deal with the admissibility of some records, the majority (Lords Reid, Morris of Borth-y-Gest and Hodson) held that such a change was one to be made, if at all, by the legislature.

The implications of the decision were at once compelling and horrific. Many prosecutions for offences of dishonesty depend upon trade or business records being admitted as evidence of the facts recorded in them, which may have been compiled, as were those in *Myers,* by large numbers of persons, who may be dead, unavailable or unable to remember their contents; they may extend over a long period of time. It would be by the sheerest good fortune only that any relevant facts could be proved from them by admissible evidence. The legislature, as has been noted, responded by introducing a statutory basis for the admission of trade or business records under certain circumstances.

But the principle of *Myers* v *DPP* has survived the reversal of the actual result in terms of admissibility on the facts of that case. Many documents cannot be brought within the terms of the Criminal Evidence Act 1965; some doubt has recently been raised about the very working of that Act (12); and there remain many cases where private documents containing statements which are highly relevant and obviously reliable evidence, must be excluded for the purposes of proving the truth of the facts stated in them (13).

Statements may also be made by conduct. In the cases referred to of signs and gestures, the conduct is indistinguishable in effect from an oral statement; both are intended to, and do in fact convey information. But some difficulty has arisen where the conduct, while not intended to communicate a fact, nonetheless has that effect, by necessary implication. In *Wright* v *Doe* d *Tatham* (14) Parke B refused to admit, on the issue of the sanity of the testator, letters written to him by businessmen during the relevant period of his life, which were said to be of such a nature that they would have been written only to a person in command of his mental faculties. Some of the difficulties stemmed from the character of the evidence as a kind of non-expert opinion, which would be inadmissible on the issue. Parke B likened the case interestingly to that of a sea

---

11   (HL) [1965] AC 1001.
12   See *R* v *Pettigrew* (CA) [1980] Crim LR 239; and 8.3.5, post.
13   Private documents are, of course, not admissible under the exception in favour of the contents of public documents: see 6.8, post.
14   (Exch) (1837) 7 A & E 313.

captain, who having inspected a ship, embarked on it with his family, which evidence he thought would be inadmissible on the issue of the seaworthiness of the vessel at that time. But there are also objections based on hearsay, in that the court is being asked to accept that the act of the businessmen in writing, or of the sea captain in embarking, go to prove the truth of the fact, sanity or seaworthiness, which that conduct may be thought necessarily to imply. For this purpose, words may equally amount to or involve an unintended communication of information. In *Teper* v *R* (15) the conviction of the defendant on a charge of arson of his shop was set aside, where in order to contradict his alibi, the prosecution had been allowed to adduce evidence that a woman at the scene of the blaze had been heard to shout to a passing motorist, who bore some resemblance to the defendant, 'Your place burning down, and you going away from the fire.'

It is submitted that such statements must indeed be within the rule against hearsay: it is their actual, rather than their intended effect which is of significance. Some confusion has been caused by cases where a statement may be admissible by virtue of the res gestae exception, which are dealt with in 6.6, post. But an exception can only be considered where the statement falls, on the face of it, to be excluded under the principal rule, and it seems that these cases confirm the view stated above. If A is charged with an offence, evidence that a bystander, or the victim, shouts: 'A, why did you do such a thing?' may in certain circumstances be admissible either under the res gestae principle, or as a statement made in the defendant's presence, but if it cannot be brought under a recognised exceptional case, it is surely no different from evidence that the bystander or the victim told the police that A had committed the offence, which is inadmissible hearsay. In either case, the evidence is clearly tendered with a view to inviting the jury to draw the conclusion that A was the person who committed the offence.

6.3   Question (b): the purpose for which the statement is tendered

It has already been emphasised that the source of the statement alone does not determine whether it offends against the rule against hearsay. A statement made other than while giving evidence will be inadmissible only if it is tendered with a view to proving the truth of any relevant fact stated therein. Failure to appreciate this element of the rule has led to the wrongful exclusion of perfectly good, direct and admissible evidence tendered for the purpose of proving, where it is relevant to do so, that the statement was in fact made, or what its contents in fact were, or the state of mind of the maker of the statement at that time. Such errors are a result of what Professor Cross has called the 'superstitious awe . . . about having any truck with evidence which involves A's telling the court what B said' (16). In order to distinguish between admissible and inadmissible statements, it is really necessary to do no more than identify correctly the issue in support of which the statement is tendered, and to ask the question: Is the tribunal of fact being asked to accept the statement as evidence of the truth of a fact stated therein? If the answer to that question is yes, the statement is inadmissible for that purpose, as being hearsay. If, conversely, the court is being invited to consider the statement for a relevant purpose unrelated to the truth or falsity of its contents, the statement is admissible for that purpose. The examples which follow in 6.3.1, 6.3.2 and 6.3.3 are given only to illustrate the working of the rule in common situations. It should be remembered throughout that it is hearsay which is inadmissible, and not evidence of what A said to B.

15 (PC, British Guiana) [1952] AC 480.
16 [1965] Crim LR 68 at 82.

6.3.1 *To prove the truth of relevant facts stated: inadmissible*

In *R* v *Gibson* (17) an unidentified woman had said to the prosecutor at the scene of the wounding charged, 'The man who threw the stone went in there,' indicating a house in which the defendant was found. The woman's statement to the prosecutor was not made while giving evidence in the proceedings, and was obviously tendered for the purpose of suggesting that the person found in the house was the culprit, i.e. that the fact stated was true. The statement was inadmissible hearsay; evidence of the identity of the defendant should have been given by calling the woman. Cases where statements are tendered for the purpose of proving identity, and which plainly cannot be justified as having relevance to any other issue, are a common instance of the working of the rule. In *Jones* v *Metcalfe* (18) an eyewitness to a road traffic accident took the registration number of a lorry, the bad driving of which was said to have caused a collision between two other vehicles. The eyewitness reported the number to the police, who as a result interviewed the defendant, and obtained his admission that he had been driving a lorry of that number on the relevant day. He denied, however, that his driving had been such as to cause any accident. By the time the defendant was tried by the magistrates for driving without due care and attention, the eyewitness was unable to remember what the number of the lorry was. The police officer's evidence, which included an account of what he had been told by the eyewitness, was hearsay and inadmissible on the issue of the identity of the lorry, because it consisted of a statement made by the eyewitness other than while giving evidence at the trial and was clearly relevant only to the issue of identity, the Bench being invited to accept the truth of what the eyewitness had said to the officer about what the registration number was. The conviction was quashed by the Divisional Court, on the ground that there was no evidence upon which the justices were entitled to find that a lorry of the number recorded was that responsible for the accident.

It will be noticed that it makes no difference that, in *Gibson*, the woman was unable to be called to give evidence at all, whereas in *Jones* v *Metcalfe* the eyewitness was called, but was unable to deal with the question of identity. Yet, there is obviously a considerable qualitative difference between the pieces of evidence in the two cases, in that the eyewitness in *Jones* v *Metcalfe* afforded evidence of everything except the actual link of the number, and that he would have been able to give evidence even of this, by refreshing his memory from the police officer's note, had he verified it contemporaneously (19). The artificiality of this position produced expressions of reluctance in the decision of the Divisional Court, on the part of all three members. In particular, Diplock LJ said (20):

I reluctantly agree. Like [Lord Parker CJ] I have every sympathy with the magistrates because the inference of fact that the appellant was the driver of the lorry at the time of the accident is irresistible as a matter of common sense. But this is a branch of the law which has little to do with common sense. The inference that the appellant was the driver of the lorry was really an inference of what the independent witness said to the police when he gave them the lorry number, and since what he had said to the police would have been inadmissible as hearsay, to infer what he said to the police is inadmissible also. What makes it even more absurd is, as [Lord Parker CJ] pointed out, that if when the independent witness gave the number of the lorry to the police

17   (CCR) (1887) 18 QBD 537.   18   (DC) [1967] 1 WLR 1286.
19   As to refreshing the memory from contemporaneous notes, see 13.2 post.
20   (DC) [1967] 1 WLR 1286 at 1290–1.

officer, the latter had written it down in his presence, then the police officer's note could have been shown to the independent witness and he could have used it, not to tell the justices what he told the police officer, but to refresh his memory. This case does illustrate . . . the need to reform the law of evidence.

The reform which Diplock LJ had in mind was that advocated in the 13th report of the Law Reform Committee, but as we have seen, reform in criminal cases of the common-law rule against hearsay has not yet been subjected to any general change. Indeed, *Jones* v *Metcalfe* has been followed since (21), and undoubtedly represents the present law. An interesting, but it is submitted tenuous, distinction was made in *R* v *Smith* (22). The defendant was charged with attempting to murder M at her home. An eyewitness, who had seen a man in the vicinity of M's home at the material time, described the man to a police officer who made a sketch following her directions. The sketch was admitted in evidence. It was argued on appeal that the sketch was hearsay, in that it represented, albeit in visual rather than written form, a statement of what the eyewitness had said to the officer, and that what the eyewitness had said to the officer was necessarily reproduced in the sketch, which was obviously tendered to prove the identity of the offender, i.e. that its contents were true. This argument was rejected, the Court of Appeal holding that the sketch was one in effect made by the eyewitness, employing the skilled hand of the officer. The logic thus far can hardly be disputed, but the very point seems to establish the contention made for the appellant. If the eyewitness had made a written statement of the man's description to the police, such statement would have amounted to a previous consistent statement, and would not have been admissible. It is true that, if contemporaneous, she might have used it to refresh her memory while giving evidence, and this would surely apply equally to the sketch; but it is hard to see why the sketch should itself be admissible, whether made by the eyewitness or by the officer at her direction. One can hardly fail to sympathise with the plight of any court which is obliged to apply such inconvenient and surely unnecessary rules of law, but piecemeal judicial reform of such a fundamental topic often involves, as here, a process of reasoning which is not at all happy.

The identity cases are only one example of the working of the rule excluding non-evidential statements for the purpose of proof of the facts stated. The rule operates to exclude any evidence directed to establishing a relevant fact, by reference to what a person has said about it other than while giving evidence in the instant proceedings. In *R* v *Attard* (23), for instance, the prosecution sought to prove the substance of an interview which had taken place between the defendant and a police officer, relating to the offence charged. The interview had been conducted through the medium of an interpreter, because the defendant, who was Maltese, was unable to speak English. All would have been well, had the interpreter been called to prove the conversation, but the officer purported to give evidence of what had been said between the defendant and himself. It was held that his evidence as to what had been said was hearsay. Whatever was said in English by the officer (which could not be understood by the defendant) was in any case inadmissible to prove its truth, but more importantly, the officer could not give direct evidence of the substance of what had been said in Maltese by the defendant or the

21   See *R* v *McLean* (CA) (1967) 52 Cr App R 80; *Cattermole* v *Millar* (DC) [1978] RTR 258.
22   [1976] Crim LR 511.
23   (1958) 43 Cr App R 90. The decision led to the universal practice of calling interpreters in such cases.

interpreter; he was relating what the interpreter had said the conversation had been, with a view to proving what it had in fact been.

Where hearsay evidence would be inadmissible to prove the truth of a fact, it would seem to follow, and has been held, that any admission made by a party against his interest, based solely upon that hearsay and not upon matters within his own knowledge, should be rejected as having no more evidential value than the hearsay on which it was based (24). Thus, in *Surujpaul* v *R* (25) the defendant was charged with murder as an accessory before the fact. He made an admission that the murder in question had in fact been committed. It was held that this admission should not have been received in evidence, because the defendant had not been present at the murder, had no personal knowledge of the facts which he was purporting to admit and was relying entirely upon what he had been told by another. In *Comptroller of Customs* v *Western Lectric Co. Ltd* (26), the respondents were charged with making a false declaration on a customs import entry produced to a customs officer, the false declaration relating to the country of origin of certain goods. The articles were entered as having their origin either in Australia or the United Kingdom, and if this was true, they would have been subject to a preferential tariff. Inspection of the goods by a customs officer revealed that the articles were labelled respectively, 'Denmark' and 'Made in USA', and in the light of this, the respondents' agent filed a further entry stating the origin of the goods to be Denmark and the United States. This further entry was subsequently relied on as an admission by the respondents of the true origin of the goods. The Privy Council held that a conviction could not be based upon an admission so clearly made solely in reliance on the hearsay markings of the goods (27). Lord Hodson, delivering the judgment of their Lordships, observed that:

> If a man admits something of which he knows nothing it is of no real evidential value. The admission made by the respondents' agent was an admission made upon reading the marks and labels on those goods and was of no more evidential value than those marks and labels themselves.

For very similar reasons, in *R* v *Marshall* (28) the trial judge accepted a submission of no case to answer where, on a charge of handling stolen goods, the only evidence from which the jury could infer that the goods were stolen was an admission made to the police by the defendant that this was the case. This admission was based solely on what the defendant had been told by a man who sold him the goods. The decision is an excellent illustration of the extent of the hearsay rule, because although the admission was not evidence that the goods were stolen, had there been other evidence of that fact, the admission would have been admissible and cogent evidence that the defendant knew or believed them to be stolen, i.e. of his state of mind at the time when he received them.

6.3.2   For purposes other than proof of the truth of facts stated: admissible
Where a statement is tendered for its evidential value as such, and there is no issue as to the truth of any fact stated therein, the statement is admissible. In this context, its 'evidential value as such' means that the very fact that the statement has been made or

---

24   For the admissibility of admissions against interest, see Chapter 7.
25   (PC, British Guiana) [1958] 1 WLR 1050.   26   (PC, Fiji) [1966] AC 367.
27   As to which see *Patel* v *Comptroller of Customs* (PC, Fiji) [1966] AC 356. *Quaere* whether the marks and labels would be admissible by virtue of the Criminal Evidence Act 1965: see Chapter 8, *post*. Where the defendant has some personal knowledge of the facts which he admits, his admission may be prima facie evidence of the facts admitted even though based solely upon his past experience: see *R* v *Chatwood* [1980] 1 All ER 467.
28   [1977] Crim LR 106.

has been made in a certain form is either itself in issue in the case, or is relevant to some fact in issue in the case.

6.3.2.1   Cases where the making of the statement is itself in issue.   The fact that a statement has been made may itself be in issue, as where a plaintiff sets out to prove that he has been defamed, or a prosecutor to prove that the defendant has uttered a seditious speech, or used threatening words. In these cases, it must be proved that the defendant did in fact make a statement in a certain form, or having certain contents, and whether what he said was true is not, at that stage in issue. In *R* v *Chapman* (29) the defendant was charged with driving with excess alcohol, following a road traffic accident which had resulted in his being taken to hospital. Under those circumstances, the Road Safety Act 1967 provided that before he was required to supply a specimen of breath, the police officer should ascertain from the doctor in charge of the defendant that the former had no objection to such specimen being required. The officer gave evidence that he had asked the doctor, who had offered no objection. It was argued on appeal that the doctor should have been called to state that he had had no objection, but the Court of Appeal rejected the suggestion that the officer's evidence was hearsay. The only issue was whether the doctor had or had not in fact given his consent to the sample being required. Whether what the doctor said was true or not was not in issue.

6.3.2.2   Cases where the making of the statement is itself relevant.   The making of a statement may be of great relevance to the essential issues in a case, even though it may not itself be an issue. In *Subramaniam* v *Public Prosecutor* (30) the defendant was charged with unlawful possession of firearms, contrary to certain regulations then in force. It would have been a defence that the defendant had a lawful excuse for his possession, and he sought to give evidence that he had been threatened by terrorists and only had the weapons under duress. It was held on appeal that he had wrongly been prevented from stating what the terrorists had said to him. The issue was not the truth of anything which the terrorists had said, but the fact that they had made threats which caused the defendant to be in a particular state of mind, which was clearly relevant to the question of his guilt. The case is a classic example of error through failure to consider both elements of the hearsay rule. Similarly, in *R* v *Willis* (31) where the defendant was charged with larceny of a drum of metal cable, and had given answers to questions put by the police which might have been seen as incriminating, it was held that he had been wrongly prevented from relating a conversation which he had held with his employee which showed his subsequent answers to the police in a quite different light. Again, there was no issue of the truth of anything said by the employee, but only the effect of what was said on the defendant's mind at the time when he spoke to the police.

A particularly interesting example, which explores a slender part of the dividing line between hearsay and admissible statements, is *Mawaz Khan and Amanat Khan* v *R* (32). The defendants were charged with the murder of another man on a certain day. Each made a statement to the police, independently of the other, giving an alibi according to which they had been together at a club and had sustained their injuries in the course of fighting each other there. Neither defendant gave evidence at the trial, and they subsequently appealed on the ground that the trial judge had invited the jury to view the statements as evidence against both of them, if satisfied that they were fabrications. This,

29   (CA) [1969] 2 QB 436.   30   (PC, Malaya) [1956] 1 WLR 965.
31   (CCA) [1960] 1 WLR 55.   32   (PC, Hong Kong) [1967] 1 AC 454.

would be contrary to the rule in the case of hearsay statements made by defendants admitted as confessions as evidence of the facts admitted in them (see Chapter 7), according to which such a statement is evidence only against the maker, and not against anyone else affected by its contents (33). If the statements in this case were hearsay, therefore, the trial judge was guilty of a serious misdirection. The Privy Council, upholding the majority view of the Supreme Court of Hong Kong, held that the statements were not hearsay. The trial judge had directed the jury as follows:

> The Crown's case here is not that these statements are true and that what one says ought to be considered as evidence of what actually happened. What the Crown say is that these statements have been shown to be a tissue of lies and that they disclose an attempt to fabricate a joint story. Now . . . if you come to that conclusion then the fabrication of a joint story would be evidence against both. It would be evidence that they had co-operated after the alleged crime.

Holding this direction to be a proper one, Lord Hodson said (34):

> Their Lordships agree with Hogan CJ and Rigby AJ in accepting the generality of the proposition maintained by the text writers and to be found in *Subramaniam's* case that a statement is not hearsay and is admissible when it is proposed to establish by the evidence, not the truth of the statement, but the fact that it was made. Not only therefore can the statements of each appellant be used against each appellant individually . . . but they can without any breach of the hearsay rule be used, not for the purpose of establishing the truth of the assertions contained therein, but for the purpose of asking the jury to hold the assertions false and to draw inferences from their falsity.
>
> The statements were relevant as tending to show that the makers were acting in concert and that such action indicated a common guilt.

What was of relevance to the issue was not the truth of any fact actually contained in either statement, but the fact that two statements had been made, apparently independently of each other, but asserting in detail the same innocent account of the matter. If the jury rejected this account, having heard the whole of the evidence, then it was relevant for them to consider the implications of having before them two statements obviously fabricated as part of a prearranged plan, and to draw inferences about the guilt of the defendants. If, as happens frequently, the prosecution had tendered the statements as confessions, then because they would have been tendered as falling within an exception to the rule against hearsay (and not as non-hearsay statements) they would have been admitted as evidence of the truth of the facts stated in them, but only against the maker in each case.

6.3.3 *Where the true purpose of tendering is doubtful: admissible?*

There can be no doubt that at common law, the rule against hearsay was intended to cover, and does cover, any case where the party tendering a statement, made other than

---

33 The statements could be said to be evidence 'against' the defendants only in so far as the jury rejected them as statements of truth. As they were entirely self-serving, they could otherwise have no evidential value in a case where the makers did not give evidence, but where a jury concludes that a defendant has deliberately lied in order to seek to exculpate himself, they are entitled to draw adverse inferences from that conclusion: see 7.10.3 and 7.11, post.

34 [1967] 1 AC 454 at 462.

in the course of evidence in the proceedings, must in reality be doing so with a view to the statement being acted upon as evidence of facts stated in it. In the cases dealt with in 6.3.1 and 6.3.2, the identification of this purpose was straightforward, and so accordingly was the classification of the statement as hearsay or non-hearsay. Not all the cases at common law are so straightforward, and in the examples which follow, it is difficult to avoid the conclusion that, although the statements were admitted as non-hearsay, as being relevant as such to some issue in the case, their relevance must ultimately have depended upon the assumption that facts stated in them were true. There can be little doubt but that such cases are a result of the growing pains of this branch of the law, in the sense that, given the more relaxed approach to hearsay embodied in the modern statutory exceptions, it would surely have been unnecessary for the hearsay character of the statements to be brushed aside. They must, however, be mentioned because in criminal cases, the prevalence of the common-law rule still occasions such problems, as will appear below from the decisions in *R* v *Rice and Others* and *Ratten* v *R*.

In some earlier cases, statements were received for the purpose of explaining some act or event which might otherwise have been ambiguous or at least unexplained. These cases do much to support the analysis offered above, in that the natural way of looking at the statements concerned is to regard them as hearsay admissible, if at all, by virtue of the res gestae principle (or in more modern times, by virtue of the Civil Evidence Act 1968). But because there were objections to their admission under the res gestae principle as it then stood, the court was evidently anxious to find some other basis of admission, and this could only be done by reaching the conclusion that the statements were not hearsay, because they were tendered as being relevant as such to some issue in the case, and not for the purpose of proving any facts stated in them. In *Attorney-General* v *Good* (35) the demonstrably untrue statement of the wife of a debtor, to the effect that her husband was away from home, was admitted to show the husband's intention of defrauding his creditors. The statement was not evidence of the fact that the husband was, or was not at home, but was evidence tending to support the allegation that he was setting up a false story as to his whereabouts. Similarly, in *Hayslep* v *Gymer* (36) where the housekeeper of the deceased was able to produce a written note stating that she had received certain goods as a gift from her late employer, the statement was admitted to qualify and explain her act of handing the goods over to another, and so to rebut the apparent significance of that act as an admission that she was not entitled to them. It was not, however, evidence that the goods were a gift. This unattractive and artificial logic has been rendered obsolete by the Civil Evidence Act 1968 on those particular facts. But the problem remains that it is not easy to see how the fact of the making of the statements assisted the court in these cases, except with some assumption about the truth of the statements themselves. It is true to say that it was the state of mind of the husband and the housekeeper respectively that was in issue, but this could hardly be demonstrated unless the court took the view, at least implicitly, that the facts contained in the statements tendered as going to that issue were true.

The process of logic involved in these decisions was applied to cases where the making of the statement was regarded, in effect, as itself being an act on the part of the maker of the statement relevant to the issues. The statement was, therefore, admissible as direct evidence on the issues. In *Lloyd* v *Powell Duffryn Steam Coal Co. Ltd* (37) it was sought to show that the plaintiff and her child were dependants of a workman who had been

---

35   (1825) M'Cle & Yo 286.   36   (1834) 1 A & E 162.
37   [1914] AC 733.

killed, it was alleged, through the fault of the defendants. In order to show this, the plaintiff had to prove that the deceased was the father of her child, and had promised and intended to marry her. The plaintiff's evidence of paternity and of the deceased's intentions towards her, was held by the House of Lords to be capable of being supported by evidence of statements made by the deceased during his lifetime, which were to the effect that he regarded the plaintiff as his fiancée and the child as his. The words were a form of treatment of the plaintiff and the child as such, and could only have been spoken on the basis that the deceased believed himself to be the father of the child and that he intended to support the plaintiff and the child as his dependants. Since the deceased's statements were rejected as statements by a person, since deceased, against his interest (which would have rendered them admissible, exceptionally, even if hearsay: see section B of this chapter, post) they could not be evidence that the child was his, and their admissibility was, therefore, confined to support of what the plaintiff had said. But the distinction is plainly tenuous. It surely cannot be realistically maintained that the belief or statement of the deceased could support the evidence of the plaintiff, unless at least some assumption were made that such belief or statement was the truth; the fact that the belief was held, or the statement made, taken alone, assists not at all. The same result was reached in *Re Jenion, Jenion v Wynne* (38) where, the declarations of a deceased mother being admissible at common law (as an exception to the hearsay rule) for the purpose of proving that her children were illegitimate, the statements of the putative father that the children were his, were held admissible for the purpose, not of proving the illegitimacy, but of supporting the declarations of the mother.

It is submitted that these admittedly ingenious efforts to invest apparently hearsay evidence with the character of direct evidence, have caused considerable confusion about the extent of the common-law rule against hearsay. Nowhere is this confusion better exemplified than in the decision of the Court of Criminal Appeal in *R v Rice and Others* (39). On a charge of conspiracy, part of the prosecution case against Rice was that he had taken a flight to Manchester on or about a certain date, in the company of a co-defendant, Hoather. This was denied. The prosecution produced an airline ticket to Manchester in respect of a date at about the relevant time, affording two seats in the names of Rice and Moore (another co-defendant). The prosecution suggested that Hoather flew in place of Moore. The ticket was put to Rice in cross-examination, and, he having denied all knowledge of it, it was exhibited and shown to the jury. On appeal it was argued, understandably, that the ticket could have been tendered for no purpose except that of suggesting to the jury that it was evidence of the fact that Rice (at least) had flown to Manchester on the day shown, and that it was accordingly hearsay and had been wrongly admitted. The Court rejected the argument on the basis that the ticket was relevant, by its very existence in that form, to the issue of whether Rice had flown to Manchester. The following extraordinary passages were taken from the judgment of the court delivered by Winn J (40):

> The court thinks that it would have been more accurate had the recorder said that the production of the ticket from the place where used tickets would properly be kept was a fact from which the jury might infer that probably two people had flown on the particular flight and that it might or might not seem to them by applying their common

38   (CA) [1952] Ch 454.   39   [1963] 1 QB 857.
40   Ibid at 872–3; cf the more reasonable earlier decision in *R v Podmore* (1930) 22 Cr App R 36; (finding of documents partly in handwriting of deceased admissible to prove dishonest relationship between defendant and deceased, precise nature of which was immaterial).

knowledge of such matters that the passengers bore the surnames which were written on the ticket.

It is plain that the latter inference was not one to be readily accepted in a case where it was not suggested that [the appellant] Moore, whose name was on the ticket, had actually flown; indeed it is obvious that pro tanto the potential inference was excluded. Nevertheless it remained open for partial acceptance in respect of [the appellant] Rice. . . .

So far as Rice was concerned the ticket was treated differently and assumed importance from the direction given that the jury might, if they saw fit, regard it as corroboration of Hoather's evidence that Rice flew with him to Manchester and that Rice booked the ticket. . . .

The court finds no misdirection in that passage. . . .

The court doubts whether the air ticket could constitute admissible evidence that the booking was affected either by Rice or even by any man of that name but it does not think that for relevant purposes the distinction between the booking of the ticket and the use of it was material with regard either to the case against Rice or to his defence.

It may be that the explanation of this judgment is that the Court of Criminal Appeal appreciated and shied away from the awful truth which was finally conceded by the House of Lords in *Myers* v *DPP*, that the exclusion of such a document paved the way for a coach and four to be driven through the whole process of prosecution for many offences. Certainly, the air ticket might well now be admissible under the provisions of the Criminal Evidence Act 1965. The reasoning also found some support from the Court of Appeal, and the minority of the House of Lords, in *Myers* (41), but the terms of that support lack conviction. It is submitted that it is indefensible and nonsensical to tell a jury that they can consider whether 'the passengers bore the surnames which were written on the ticket', while also telling them that they are not to consider the ticket as evidence of any fact stated in it. Hopefully, the 1965 Act has prevented many similar counsels of desperation, but it has not removed the problem altogether.

On somewhat stronger ground is the decision of the Privy Council in *Ratten* v *R* (42). The defendant was charged with the murder of his wife by shooting. His defence was that the gun had gone off accidentally while he was cleaning it. A telephone operator gave evidence that about five minutes before a time when the wife was known to be dead, she received a call from a hysterical woman, made from the defendant's telephone number, in which the woman said, 'Get me the police,' and gave the defendant's address. The question was, whether the detail of this call was admissible. The Privy Council held that the evidence was not hearsay, despite the nature of the words spoken by (as it must have been) the wife, because the call was relevant to prove that the wife had made such a call shortly before her death, and, if the jury wished to draw the inference, that she was at that time in a state of emotion or fear. These matters tended to refute the defendant's account of the episode and in particular his defence of accident (43). It is perhaps arguable that this object could have been achieved without giving in evidence what had

41   See [1965] AC 1001, per Widgery J at 1007–8; Lord Pearce at 1044–5; Lord Donovan at 1048, all of whom saw *Rice* and *Myers* as involving the same problem. The argument makes the ticket into a piece of 'real evidence', and so seeks to circumvent the rule against hearsay: see the very similar reasoning of Sir Jocelyn Simon P in *The Statue of Liberty* [1968] 1 WLR 739, considered in 16.4.5.

42   (PC, Victoria) [1972] AC 378.

43   It was held alternatively that even if the statement by the wife were hearsay, it was admissible under the res gestae principle (see 6.6, post).

been said by the wife during the call, a point which may be emphasised by considering what the position should have been if the wife had instead said, 'My husband is trying to kill me' or something else directly incriminating of that kind. But Lord Wilberforce regarded the words as a part of the 'composite act' of a telephone call, and held that to confine evidence to part only of the call 'would be to deprive the act of most of its significance' (44). It is certainly quite tenable to contend that the circumstances prevailing immediately before the wife's death were of great relevance to the defence raised by the defendant, and to that extent there was clearly a perfectly legitimate use to be made of the evidence as a piece of direct evidence on that issue. Its hearsay character is of far less importance than in a case such as *Rice*.

6.4 Practical considerations: avoidance and evasion

Witnesses hardly ever appreciate the demands of the rule against hearsay, unless they are witnesses such as police officers who have some professional acquaintance with the rule. It is therefore of some importance to scrutinise witness statements (and, in less leisurely circumstances, oral evidence as it is given) with a view to testing any evidence which appears to consist of an account of what the witness was told by someone else. When the two questions (page 126) have been asked, the evidence under scrutiny will emerge as falling into either the category of direct evidence (in which case it is admissible from the witness) or hearsay (in which case it is not). If the evidence is hearsay, it must also be further examined with a view to seeing whether it can be brought within some exception, but discussion of this further step must await section B and Chapters 7 and 8.

Most criminal cases abound with examples of each category, and despite the attention given above to the difficult cases, the distinction, though vital, is not usually too difficult. Let us take, for example, the following passages from the depositions in the case of Coke and Littleton:

(a) Statement of Margaret Blackstone: 'We all started talking and Henry said that he had a new album by a band we liked, and invited us to his flat to listen to it.'

(b) Statement of WPC Raymond: 'I asked her [Margaret] various questions, in reply to which she gave me an account of her having been raped by a young man known to her called Henry Coke.'

Both pieces of evidence, proposed to be given by the witnesses from whose depositions they are taken, clearly consist of statements made to the witness by others when not giving evidence in these proceedings. Question (a) therefore answers itself. As to question (b), a moment's thought dictates different results in the two instances given. In the first, the purpose and relevance of the evidence has nothing whatsoever to do with the truth of what Coke said. It is to be adduced for the purpose of showing the means by which Coke succeeded in persuading the girls to come to his flat. It is therefore a piece of direct evidence going to an element of the prosecution case. The second is quite different. The only possible purpose of adducing evidence of what Margaret said to WPC Raymond is to suggest that what was said was true. The mere making of such a statement can have no relevance in itself, and unless it can be brought within an exception, the statement is hearsay and inadmissible (45).

44 Ibid at 388.
45 The distinction arose in what appears to be the earliest ever reported criminal case: *Adam and Others* Gen 3: 9–19. The Man, the Woman and the Serpent were charged with eating the fruit of the Tree of the Knowledge of Good and Evil. On being questioned about her part in the offence, the Woman replied, 'The Serpent beguiled me,

The strictures of the rule against hearsay produce, not infrequently, a sense of frustration in practitioners and witnesses at not being able to adduce evidence which would tend to reveal clearly the truth of a case. This frustration has led to the widespread use of devices, some legitimate others less so, designed to minimise the effect of the rule's restrictiveness. The ideal avoidance is, of course, to call direct evidence of the fact or event to be proved, from a witness who perceived it. But this desirable possibility is not always present. A witness can, of course, be asked to say, answering merely yes or no, whether he had a conversation with someone or looked at some document, but such evidence is usually neither very relevant nor very useful. In practice, devices are habitually tolerated which necessarily involve the tacit assertion by a witness of what he has been told by another, but which give meaning and sequence to his evidence of what he himself saw or did. The classic instance is the evidence of a police officer, beginning with the words, 'acting on information received'. Of course, the jury are bound to infer a connection of common sense between what the officer was told, and the inquiries he thereafter made, and in many cases it will inevitably appear that the officer was told something about the defendant. But in practice, there can really be little objection; no jury is likely to think that the officer commenced his inquiries through some telepathy or divine revelation, and in many cases if the information seems to have been inaccurate, it may actually assist the defence. Certainly, the jury are unlikely to give any weight at all to a communication whose details are unknown, made by someone about whom they are told nothing (46).

There are, however, other devices which are less harmless, which have been deprecated by the appellate courts, but which continue to enjoy a surprising degree of liberty in practice. They may be illustrated by the following examples:

    (a)   On a charge of theft:
Q. Did you have a conversation with X?
A. Yes.
Q. Then what did you do?
A. As a result of that conversation, I arrested the defendant for theft.
    (b)   On a charge of obtaining by false pretences (taken from *R* v *Saunders* (47)):
Q. Did you make inquiries as to whether any trade had been done by the prisoners?
A. I did.
Q. Did you as the result of such inquiries find that any had been done?
A. I did not.

Both passages may be thought objectionable because, although neither reveals the exact terms of the conversation or enquiry which took place, each reveals the substance of it by necessary implication. In each case, the first question and answer is undoubtedly admissible, so far as it goes. But at the stage of the second question and answer, it may be that the two diverge. In the first example, the passage may perhaps be justified as a slight extension of the 'acting on information received' sequence, whose dangers are more

and I did eat.' This reply would be inadmissible hearsay against the Serpent, charged as a counsellor or procurer; but would be admissible, direct evidence that the Woman was beguiled, if beguilement were her defence. It is noteworthy that the report contains no suggestion that there was any other evidence against the Serpent, and it is difficult to avoid the conclusion that he was wrongly convicted.

---

46   But *quaere* whether the relaxation should be permitted further than really necessary to account for what is subsequently done. Should, for instance, 'as a result of an emergency call' be allowed?
47   (CCR) [1899] 1 QB 490.

formidable in theory than in practice; the jury may simply think that the officer should have made further inquiries by questioning the defendant. But in the second, the passage is a naked evasion of the rule, in that the witness is being asked, in effect to relate the substance of what he was told, even though the question is framed so as to seem to ask him what he did. Quite separate problems arise where a witness states that, having spoken to X, he said to the defendant, 'X tells me that you have stolen his property. What do you say?' If the defendant adopts the truth of what X has said, by admitting his guilt, then all is well: his admission will be evidence against him. But if he denies it, or refuses to answer, the admissibility of the passage can be a difficult matter, which is explored in Chapter 7. It is certain, however, that the witness's assertion of what X said is not evidence against the defendant of itself.

The lesson to be learnt from these examples is a sound one in every evidential question, that it is the actual effect and not the form of the question and answer which matters, and that one has to look at the whole passage in order to gauge this, and not just at individual questions and answers. Evidence is not admissible if it in fact consists of hearsay, whether or not a question seems to be framed so as to deal with direct evidence of what the witness perceived or did. In the analogous context of privilege, the use of such devices was the subject of adverse comment by Lord Devlin in *Glinski* v *McIver* (48) in the following terms:

> But it was thought . . . that privilege would be claimed. . . . So the customary devices were employed which are popularly supposed, though I do not understand why, to evade objections of inadmissibility based on hearsay or privilege or the like. The first consists in not asking what was said in a conversation or written in a document but in asking what the conversation or document was about; it is apparently thought that what would be objectionable if fully exposed is permissible if decently veiled. . . . The other device is to ask by means of 'Yes' or 'No' questions what was done. (Just answer 'Yes' or 'No': Did you go to see counsel? Do not tell us what he said but as a result of it did you do something? What did you do?) This device is commonly defended on the ground that counsel is asking only about what was done and not about what was said. But in truth what was done is relevant only because from it there can be inferred something about what was said. Such evidence seems to me to be clearly objectionable. If there is nothing in it, it is irrelevant; if there is something in it, what there is in it is inadmissible.

This deprecation notwithstanding, in practice witnesses continue to be permitted to state that they had conversations with others and that as a result of such conversations, took certain steps or acted in certain ways, and it may be that in most cases, no or little harm can result, while the evidence is made easier for the jury to follow. The judge has, undoubtedly, ample power to exclude in a case where harm may be done. For example, there could be no objection of substance to D/I Glanvil or D/S Bracton stating that he began his inquiries as a result of information received. Nothing is added to the direct evidence given by other witnesses, and of course the jury may and will expect to hear that Mrs Blackstone contacted the police after Margaret's complaint.

48   (HL) [1962] AC 726 at 780.

B: MINOR COMMON-LAW EXCEPTIONS

6.5 Introduction

At the beginning of the preceding section, it was said that the rigidity of the rule against hearsay at common law inevitably gave rise to exceptions. The exceptions were narrowly construed in the period of their most important development during the nineteenth century, and by means of such restrictive construction, the domain of the rule against hearsay was jealously guarded. For this reason alone, the common-law exceptions failed to achieve the prominence which they may have merited. And in more modern times, when a more liberal interpretation might have been expected to prevail, and indeed has prevailed in the relatively few cases when it has been given the opportunity, their importance has been overshadowed by the emergence of more general statutory exceptions. Consequently, it is unnecessary to consider them in great detail, and what follows is a reasonably concise account of the working of the three exceptions of general significance, namely (a) the res gestae principle, (b) declarations by persons since deceased and (c) statements contained in public documents. There were, no doubt, several other small exceptions recognised by the common law, applicable to more specific situations. These were by no means finally settled in their operation and extent, were of importance in relation to civil cases, have now been superseded by the Civil Evidence Act 1968 and need not be considered.

It is to be observed that each of the exceptions referred to below has two characteristics. The first is that each is justified by the consideration that, did the exception not exist, the facts to be proved would be difficult, and often impossible to prove at all, and there would be a serious hindrance to the administration of justice. The res gestae principle is called for by the ambiguity of many facts standing alone without contemporary explanation or qualification; declarations by persons since deceased are rendered necessary by the finality of the grave; statements in public documents gained acceptance because of the proliferation of important facts recorded in them, which neither informant nor recorder could be expected to recall, even if available to give evidence. The second, and equally important, characteristic is that each is closely circumscribed by stringent safeguards which severely limit their application in the interests of ensuring, so far as possible, the reliability of the statements admitted. Under the res gestae principle, the safeguard is the spontaneity of the statement, the absence of concoction; in the case of declarations by persons since deceased, it lies in adversity to the interests of the maker, or in his duty or in his certainty of impending death; in the case of public documents, it lies in the orderly and prompt making of a record by a public official pursuant to his duty, and for the purpose of future public reference. In the nineteenth-century cases, the safeguards were insisted upon to a degree which sometimes threatened the very life of the exception; in more recent times, a more lenient approach is to be seen, though the spirit of the safeguards remains.

It is also important to stress that because the evidence admitted under exceptions to the rule is hearsay in character, where it is admitted, it is admitted as evidence of the truth of the facts contained in the statement, i.e. admitted for the purpose for which, but for the exception, it would be inadmissible. There is no question here of evidence being divested of its hearsay character, and being admitted as relevant to some other issue. As we have seen, direct evidence has no need of an exception because it is unaffected by the rule.

6.6   The res gestae principle

The actual expression 'res gestae' is probably best ignored, save for the amusement it has afforded to writers and judges. It is a piece of grammatical nonsense, in that if the phrase is to be employed at all, it should certainly appear, not in its plural form, but in the singular *'pars rei gestae'*, in which it might arguably be marginally more useful. It has been unkindly but correctly dealt with by Lord Wilberforce, who has said that 'the expression "res gestae", like many Latin phrases, is often used to cover situations insufficently analysed in clear English terms' (49). It connotes simply that there are of necessity many facts and events, of which evidence is to be given, of which accompanying, contemporaneous statements are an integral constituent part; so that the fact or event, if narrated without reference to the statement, would be ambiguous, meaningless or misleading. Despite some assertions to the contrary (50), the accompanying, integral statement may be narrated as evidence of the truth of the facts stated in it, but the essential factor in each case is that of spontaneity or contemporaneity, without which the statement could hardly be described as an integral part of the fact or event to be proved. The cases in which the principle has been applied are various, and various ways of classifying them have been suggested. In any event, the main theme of the res gestae principle runs through them all alike, and classification is not of critical importance. That adopted in producing the three categories below is a slightly truncated version of that used by Professor Cross (51). The categories themselves are no more than identifiable situations to which the principle has been applied, and whatever their differences of fact, they all alike fall aptly within the words of Grove J in *Howe* v *Malkin* (52) that: 'Though you cannot give in evidence a declaration per se, yet when there is an act accompanied by a statement which is so mixed up with it as to become part of the res gestae, evidence of such a statement may be given.'

6.6.1   *Statements accompanying and explaining relevant acts*
Where the true signficance of a relevant act falls to be proved, the statement of the actor on that subject may be the best evidence of it, provided that the statement is not a calculated justification, and provided that the statement actually relates and refers to the act which it is said to explain. These provisos dictate the conditions under which such cases may be brought within the rule. Firstly, the statement must be contemporaneous with the act; whether it is so is a question of fact and degree in every case, and the test seems to be whether the the statement does in reality accompany and explain the act, as opposed to being no more than a subsequent apologia for it, made after reflection. Where the act is a continuing one, however, the statement may be one made during its continuance, as where the stated intentions of a bankrupt in going or remaining abroad are admitted to show his intention *vis-á-vis* his creditors. His intention may be equivocal at the time of his departure, and may only become apparent by his statements made while abroad (53). Secondly, the statement must relate to the act; in *R* v *Bliss* (54) evidence that, when planting a tree, a tenant of land (since deceased) had said that the tree was being planted on the boundary of his estate, was rejected as evidence of the

---

49   In *Ratten* v *R* (PC, Victoria) [1972] AC 378 at 388.
50   For example, by Lord Atkinson in *R* v *Christie* (HL) [1914] AC 545 at 553. Certain statements may, of course, also have some value as direct evidence, and be admissible also for that purpose.
51   *Evidence*, 5th ed. p. 576 et seq.
52   (1878) 40 LT 196.
53   See, e.g., *Rouch* v *Great Western Railway Co.* (1841) 1 QB 51.   54   (1837) 7 A & E 550.

location of the boundary. Had the tree been planted as a deliberate act of demarcation of the boundary, the case might have been different; but the statement as an observation coincidental to any possible question of the boundary's limits at the time when it was made could not be said to explain the planting of the tree. In cases falling under this head, the statement to be admitted must be that of the actor, who can explain his act by direct evidence, and not the (opinion) evidence of someone who witnessed the act.

6.6.2   Spontaneous statements by participants in or observers of events

The common law recognised that an event might also be explained by some spontaneous statement in the nature of an uncalculated outburst, as it were, in the heat of the moment, made by someone who either played some part in the event in question or who witnessed it. The obvious need in cases of this kind was for a safeguard against concoction to the advantage of the maker of the statement, and this was achieved by a rule in favour of strict proof of spontaneity. The rule is one of some antiquity, as may be seen from the decision in *Thompson* v *Trevanion* (55), which was an action by the plaintiff for an assault on his wife. Holt CJ held that 'that what the wife said immediately upon the hurt received, and before that she had time to devise or contrive any thing for her own advantage, might be given in evidence.' The dictum struck exactly the right note, in stressing the rationale of the requirement of spontaneity, and it would have been as well if it had been adhered to in the spirit, rather than the letter. But in the nineteenth century, the concept of spontaneity was carried to absurd lengths for its own sake, rather than for the purpose of ensuring the necessary degree of reliability. There is usually cited, as the apotheosis of this trend, the grotesque case of *R* v *Bedingfield* (56), in which evidence that when the victim of an alleged murder stumbled from a room where she had been alone with the defendant, her throat cut by a mortal wound, she said, 'See what Harry has done!', was rejected by Cockburn CJ as being admissible under the res gestae principle, on the ground that the statement was insufficiently spontaneous.

The decision in *Bedingfield* was not dictated by earlier authority. Indeed, it was plainly contrary to that in *R* v *Foster* (57), in which on a charge of manslaughter by the reckless driving of a cabriolet, a statement made by the deceased after the event was admitted to prove the nature of the vehicle which had run him down. The absurdity of the decision in *Bedingfield* has been realised and departed from, and it is almost certain that it no longer represents the law. Commenting on *Bedingfield* in *Ratten* v *R* (58), Lord Wilberforce observed that 'there could hardly be a case where the words uttered carried more clearly the mark of spontaneity and intense involvement.' The facts of *Ratten* have been dealt with in 6.3, ante, when we concentrated on the primary ground of the decision of the Privy Council that the substance of the telephone call made by the wife very shortly before her death at the hands of the defendant was not hearsay because it represented direct evidence of the state of affairs then prevailing at the defendant's house, and powerfully contradicted his defence of accident. But as an alternative (and perhaps sounder) basis for their decision, the Privy Council held that, even had the evidence of the call been hearsay, it would have been admissible by virtue of the res gestae principle. On a strict application of *Bedingfield*, the evidence must have been rejected, but the Privy Council did not view this approach as the correct one. Lord Wilberforce proposed

55   (1693) Skin 402.
56   (1879) 14 Cox CC 341.
57   (1834) 6 C & P 325.
58   (PC, Victoria) [1972] AC 378 at 390. The decision has also been doubted elsewhere: see, e.g., *R* v *Taylor* (Supreme Court of South Africa) 1961 (3) SA 616.

a quite different test, which, it is submitted, would restore the original common-law position, and indeed the spirit of the rule (59):

> The possibility of concoction, or fabrication, where it exists, is on the other hand an entirely valid reason for exclusion, and is probably the real test which judges in fact apply. In their Lordships opinion this should be recognised and applied directly as the relevant test: the test should not be the uncertain one whether the making of the statement was in some sense part of the event or transaction. This may often be difficult to establish: such external matters as the time which elapses between the events and the speaking of the words (or vice versa), and differences in location being relevant factors but not, taken by themselves, decisive criteria. As regards statements made after the event it must be for the judge, by preliminary ruling, to satisfy himself that the statement was so clearly made in circumstances of spontaneity or involvement in the event that the possibility of concoction can be disregarded. Conversely, if he considers that the statement was made by way of narrative of a detached prior event so that the speaker was so disengaged from it as to be able to construct or adapt his account, he should exclude it. And the same must in principle be true of statements made before the event. The test should be not the uncertain one, whether the making of the statement should be regarded as part of the event or transaction. This may often be difficult to show. But if the drama, leading up to the climax, has commenced and assumed such intensity and pressure that the utterance can safely be regarded as a true reflection of what was unrolling or actually happening, it ought to be received. The expression 'res gestae' may conveniently sum up these criteria, but the reality of them must always be kept in mind: it is this that lies behind the best reasoned of the judges' rulings.

The emphasis on the reliability of the statement, rather than on the quest for literal spontaneity, is surely to be welcomed as breathing fresh life into a source of evidence that had almost been strangled by the nineteenth-century cases, but it seems that the pendulum may more recently have swung too far in the opposite direction to *Bedingfield*. In *R* v *Nye and Loan* (60) the driver of a vehicle involved in a road traffic accident was assaulted by a passenger in another vehicle. He then sat in his car, recovering from the effect of the assault, and some minutes later, when the police arrived, identified his assailant to them. The words which he spoke were held to have been properly admitted under the res gestae principle. Although it is true that the *Ratten* test makes it a matter essentially for the judge to determine whether the words are a 'true reflection' of what had happened, spoken under 'intensity and pressure', and although consequently it will be only in comparatively rare cases that their admission will provide the foundation for an appeal, it must be said that the decision is a very difficult one to justify. Whatever the effect of the assault in rendering concoction during a period of recovery less likely, it does not appear that there was any real element of spontaneity which would have excluded the possibility of it in real terms, and it is almost certainly impossible to reconcile this decision with the sound statement of the common law in *Thompson* v *Trevanion*.

59   [1972] AC 378 at 389.
60   (CA) (1977) 66 Cr App R 252.

6.6.3   Contemporaneous declarations of the physical or mental state of the speaker
Statements narrating the contemporaneous physical or mental state of the speaker, including his emotions and feelings, are admitted as part of the res gestae, on an assumption of spontaniety and involvement. Thus, in *R* v *Conde* (61), on a charge of neglect of a child by depriving it of food, the child's complaints of feeling hungry were held to be admissible. The rule permits a statement of what the condition was, but not of its cause, unless the cause is itself admissible by virtue of the res gestae principle or some other exception to the hearsay rule, for example as a dying declaration. In *R* v *Horsford* (62), the deceased had made a statement to a doctor in the terms, 'I have taken poison; [the defendant] sent it to me.' On the trial of the defendant for murder, the first part of the statement was admitted, but the second rejected.

The statement must concern the contemporaneous condition of the speaker. In *R* v *Parker* (63) it was held to be wrong to admit evidence that the defendant's wife (with whose unlawful wounding the defendant was charged) had said to a neighbour, 'He shot me; he said he would.'

6.7   Declarations by persons since deceased

The intervention of death between the making of a statement and the trial of proceedings to which facts contained in the statement are relevant, quite obviously produces unique problems, to which the usual rules of hearsay are not altogether appropriate. The rules which grew up at common law to deal with such cases reflect the stark truth that in the absence of some provision it would have been impossible to prove many facts of great importance, which had occurred some fairly long time in the past and which were not the subject of any admissible record. In modern times, there is at least one statutory exception designed to meet the same difficulty. The rules at common law show that declarations made by persons since deceased are admissible, exceptionally, to prove the facts contained in them, in four kinds of case, which may be examined briefly. None of them is of very great contemporary importance, because of the growth of more general exceptions to the rule against hearsay, particularly in civil cases, and, in the case of dying declarations, because of the growing practice (hardly to be disapproved of, despite its damage to one of the common law's most romantic rules) of incapacitating by anaesthesia those who are in a state of mind which would allow their declarations, if they could be made, to be admitted under the rule (64). In each case considered, the declaration may have been made orally or in writing.

6.7.1   Matters of public concern
In order to prove matters of custom, prescriptive rights, public rights, pedigree and the like the declarations of persons since deceased are admissible (65). Public rights may be those which affect the public at large, for example the right to take tolls on part of a highway, or those which are 'general' rights, which affect the inhabitants of a particular district, or some other class of people, for example rights of common. In civil cases, such declarations would almost always now be admissible under part 1 of the Civil Evidence Act 1968, and in criminal cases their occurrence must now be very rare.

---

61   (1868) 10 Cox CC 547.   62   *The Times*, 2 June, 1898.   63   (CCA) (1960) 45 Cr App R 1.
64   For this reason, these exceptions are here described in outline only. For fuller accounts, see Cross, *Evidence*, 5th ed. p. 503 et seq, p. 551 et seq; Phipson, *Evidence*, 12th ed., para. 881 et seq.
65   Matters of this sort may also be proved at common law by evidence of general reputation and family tradition: see 9.2, post; Civil Evidence Act 1968, s. 9(3) and (4).

6.7.2 Declarations against interest

The fears of the common law regarding manufactured evidence in the context of the rule against hearsay subsided where the statement sought to be admitted was one contrary to the interests of the maker. Indeed, we shall see in the next chapter the extent to which adverse admissions and confessions by the living may be important. Similarly, a declaration made by a person since deceased is admissible to prove the facts it states if its contents were against the interests of the maker. It seems that the interests so affected may be either pecuniary, as where the maker acknowledges his indebtedness, or proprietary, as where the maker acknowledges that he is not the owner of property or that he holds property upon certain terms. It would seem, however, that the fact that the statement would have tended to expose the maker to criminal prosecution will not be sufficient (66). Whether it would be sufficient that the statement would have tended to expose the maker to tortious liability is not clear, but it is certainly possible to regard this as an example of a statement against the pecuniary interest of the maker (67). The statement must have been against the interests of the maker at the time when it was made; the maker must have known it to be against his interests when he made the statement; and, although there has been considerable conflict of authority (68), the better view is that the maker must have had personal knowledge of the facts stated by him. These conditions, of course, seek to ensure that the statement is to be relied on, so far as possible.

The facts which may be proved by declarations against interest are in no way limited to those which might have been contemplated by the maker when making the statement, and the court may use the statement as evidence of facts which the maker would have regarded as incidental to or even irrelevant to the purpose of the statement. In *Higham* v *Ridgway* (69) a statement made by a deceased midwife that he had delivered a child on a certain day and acknowledging payment of his fees, was held to be admissible evidence of the child's date of birth. The importance of the statement to the midwife was that it showed that he had been paid, and being accordingly against his pecuniary interest, it would have been admissible to prove that fact. But it was admitted for a quite different, and incidental, purpose, to prove a fact which, while not in itself against the maker's interest, was contained in a statement which, taken as a whole, had that effect.

6.7.3 Declarations in the course of duty

Declarations by persons since deceased are admissible if they consist of declarations of the acts of the maker of the statement which he owed a specific duty to record, and if the acts recorded were actually performed by him. The duty must be one owed by the maker to another. It seems that the duty in this context should be a legal or at least professional one (70), but though the cases point in this direction, moral duties do not seem to have been excluded specifically, and to include them would be in keeping with the scope of duty envisaged by s. 4 of the Civil Evidence Act 1968, under which such statements are

---

66 See the *Sussex Peerage Case* (HL) (1844) 11 Cl & F 85. Apart from the difficulty of squeezing such cases within the scope of the rule, there is the formidable practical objection that to do so would produce cases where confessions made by accomplices who died before trial might be admitted as evidence against the defendant, whereas statements of the same kind made by living accomplices are evidence only against the maker. As to statements tending to show adultery, see *B* v *Attorney-General* [1965] P 278. At one time, co-respondents bore a risk of having to pay damages for adultery, as well as costs.

67 An acknowledgement of a moral obligation to pay seems to be enough, even if the obligation could not have been enforced: *Coward* v *Motor Insurers' Bureau* (CA) (1963) 1 QB 259. If this is right, there must be a basis for admitting statements of fact which might have rendered the maker liable to an award of damages against him.

68 Summarised by Professor Cross, *Evidence*, 5th ed. p. 559.   69 (1808) 10 East 109.

70 *Mills* v *Mills* (1920) 36 TLR 772; *Simon* v *Simon and Others* [1936] P 17.

surely now equally admissible in civil cases. The record must have been made contemporaneously with the performance of the act, but this requirement is not literal and is, as in other contexts (71), one of fact and degree. The declaration must no doubt be made within a period of time consistent with the proper execution of the duty to record, and it may be supposed, while the facts were fresh in the mind of the recorder. But it appears that there may be no objection where the declaration was made prior to the act being performed, provided that the act was performed and provided that it was performed contemporaneously with the declaration. In *R v Buckley* (72), on a charge of murdering a police constable, an oral declaration by the constable to his superior that he was about to go to keep observation on the defendant was held to be admissible as evidence of what the constable was doing when he met his death, and therefore as evidence, in effect, of the identity of the murderer. The requirements are, again, imposed in the interests of ensuring that the statements admitted are reliable as being made promptly and under a duty, and therefore as presumptively accurate. In *Price v Earl of Torrington* (73) a record made in the evening of the day on which the acts were done was sufficient, whereas in *The Henry Coxon* (74) the delay of an entry in a ship's log-book made two days after the acts recorded was fatal. But these times are not absolute. The duty may involve recording at, say, weekly intervals, on a time-sheet or in a book of accounts, and it is submitted that a prompt entry in accordance with that duty would be acceptable. Specific cases dealing with questions of contemporaneity are probably best regarded as examples of the working of the principle and not as laying down hard and fast rules on maximum intervals of time.

6.7.4 Dying declarations in homicide cases
On an indictment for murder or manslaughter, the dying declarations of the victim are admissible to prove the cause and circumstances of the death. The rule is a specific one, applying only to the criminal cases stated, and allowing the evidence only for the limited purpose stated. Attempts were at one time made to extend the rule to other offences, for example on a trial for the rape of a deceased person (75), but these were firmly rejected, even in fairly plausible cases such as *R v Hutchinson* (76), a charge of using an instrument with intent to procure a miscarriage, where the offence had actually resulted in the death of the deceased. But the true rule may be that the death of the deceased must itself be the subject-matter of the charge, in which case there would seem to be no reason why dying declarations should not be admitted in cases of causing death by reckless driving, or aiding and abetting suicide. As to this, there is as yet no authority. It appears that the declaration is admissible equally whether it is favourable or unfavourable to the defendant, as in *R v Scaife* (77) where the declaration tended to suggest that the deceased had provoked the defendant.

The rationale of the rule is that the reliability of the declaration is assured by the imminence of death, and the consequent lack of motivation to tell anything other than the truth. It is doubtful whether the principle has ever been expressed more forcibly than it was by Eyre CB in the following celebrated exposition in *R v Woodcock* (78):

71   Cf. the position with regard to documents used to refresh the memory, where a similar condition is imposed so as to ensure accuracy, so far as possible: see 13.2, post.
72   (1873) 13 Cox CC 293. One would think that this decision represents the outer limits of the rule, and might not necessarily be followed today.
73   (1703) 1 Salk 285.   74   (1878) 3 PD 156.   75   *R v Newton and Carpenter* (1859) 1 F & F 641.
76   (1822) cited in 2 B & C 608n; and see *R v Hind* (CCR) (1860) 8 Cox CC 300 (procuring abortion).
77   (1836) 2 Lew CC 150.   78   (1789) 1 Leach 500 at 502.

Now the general principle on which this species of evidence is admitted is, that they are declarations made in extremity, when the party is at the point of death, and when every hope of this world has gone: when every motive to falsehood is silenced, and the mind is induced by the most powerful considerations to speak the truth.

The situation gave rise, the Chief Baron added, to an 'obligation equal to a positive oath administered in a court of justice'.

Like the requirement of contemporaneity in the res gestae cases (with which the present rule often overlaps) that of a 'settled, hopeless expectation of death', which developed from the dicta in *Woodcock* and elsewhere, having started as a sensible enough check on the reliability of the declaration, achieved a high degree of artificiality and technicality and was enforced more for its own sake than anything else. What matters is the state of mind in which the maker of the statement was when he made it. If he was under a settled, hopeless expectation of death, the declaration will be admissible, even where the deceased's belief was contradicted by his surgeon (79), and even where the deceased did not die for some eleven days after making the declaration, during which time he was repeatedly assured that he would recover (80). But if the deceased appears from the available evidence to have entertained any hope of recovery at all, and was under no certainty of death, the declaration must be rejected. Thus where the deceased merely thought himself to be in great danger (81), or said that he had 'no hope of recovery at present' (82), the evidence was rejected on the basis that the expectation of death could not be said to be settled and hopeless.

The proof of statements made by persons since deceased is often a matter of some difficulty if such statements are made orally, and can be so in the case of written statements. It appears that although the evidence tendered will not necessarily be inadmissible merely because the witness from whom it comes cannot remember literally every word of the statement, if the witness cannot at least swear that what he remembers is substantially the complete and accurate statement, it should be rejected. So too where the deceased was incoherent, or died before the statement was finished, as in the dramatic instance of *Waugh* v *R* (83), where the deceased said, referring to the defendant, 'The man has an old grudge for me simply because . . .', and died before he could complete the sentence. The Privy Council held that the declaration, tendered as a dying declaration in a prosecution of the defendant for the murder of the deceased, should not have been admitted. Even where a statement is complete, it must be right for the trial judge to warn the jury of any danger of incoherence or inaccuracy which appears from the face the evidence, and he must, it is submitted, have some degree of discretion to exclude, even where the statement is prima facie admissible, where there appears to be an appreciable risk of unreliability arising from the circumstances in which the deceased was at the relevant time.

6.8 Facts contained in public documents

Statements made in public documents are, at common law, admissible as prima facie, though not conclusive, evidence of the facts contained in them (84). This exception to

79   *R* v *Peel* (1860) 2 F & F 21.
80   *R* v *Mosley and Morrill* (CCR) (1825) 1 Mood CC 97.
81   *R* v *Errington and Others* (1838) 2 Lew CC 150.
82   *R* v *Jenkins* (CCR) (1869) LR 1 CCR 187.   83   [1950] AC 203.
84   See generally *Irish Society* v *Bishop of Derry* (HL) (1846) 12 Cl & F 641, *Sturla* v *Freccia* (HL) (1880) 5 App Cas 623. A certified copy is sufficient proof of such a document.

the rule against hearsay is justified by the formidable problems which might otherwise arise of proving a multiplicity of facts of public concern or interest, recorded over considerable periods of time, by a variety of public officials charged with the duty of recording certain matters for the purpose of future public reference, who, even if not dead or unavailable, could not be expected to have any recollection of the matters recorded. The number and types of public documents falling within the rule is, of course, immense and continually growing, but the common-law rule has diminished considerably in significance because of massive interventions by statute in favour of the admissibility of specific classes of document. Quite apart from the many specific provisions in particular statutes, in civil cases the rule has been superseded entirely by the provisions of the Civil Evidence Act 1968. Almost all public documents would now fall within the provisions of s. 4 of that Act, dealing with the admissibility of hearsay statements contained in records made by persons acting under a duty to do so, which provision is wide enough to encompass also private documents, which were excluded by the common-law rule. But in addition, the effect of s. 9(1) and (2) of the Act is that any statements made in public documents which, but for part 1 of the Act, would have been admissible as evidence of the facts contained in them by virtue of the common-law rule, are now admissible for that purpose by virtue of that section.

The safeguard at common law, the equivalent of contemporaneity or the settled, hopeless expectation of death elsewhere, lay in the circumstances in which the document was compiled. It was originally the position at common law that the conditions of admissibility under the rule were (a) that the document must have been made and preserved for public use and must contain matters of public interest; (b) that it must be open to public inspection; (c) that the entry or record sought to be proved must have been made promptly after the events which it purports to record; and (d) that the entry or record sought to be proved must have been made by a person having a duty to inquire into and satisfy himself of the truth of the facts recorded.

The first two conditions ensure that the rule is limited to documents which are truly made for public purposes and contain matters of public interest or concern, and which are truly documents of public reference to which the public have access. The rule therefore necessarily excludes documents brought into being for a private purpose, or which contain only facts of purely private interest. However, the term 'public' does not require that the document should be of concern to the whole world, and is apt to include what might be called matters of 'general' concern, in the sense that that term is employed to denote the interests of sections of the public. Thus a document which concerns the inhabitants of a given district or city, or those having certain proprietary interests, will be public for the purposes of the rule (85). The third condition, while probably originally a condition of admissibility, is now to be regarded as a question of weight (86).

It is the fourth condition which has given rise to difficulty in modern times, because of the changing nature of public records. The most important part of the common-law safeguard was the duty to inquire into the facts, which lay upon a public official charged with compiling a document for public reference. But the whole theory of the safeguard depended upon the premise that records made for public use were in earlier times compiled by local officers, who would habitually either officiate at or have personal knowledge of the events which they recorded, or who could at least reasonably be

---

85   See *Sturla* v *Freccia* (HL) (1880) 5 App Cas 623 per Lord Blackburn at 643. Lord Blackburn cites the books of a manor, which would be of concern to those interested in the manor.
86   See *R* v *Halpin* [1975] QB 907 per Geoffrey Lane LJ at 913.

expected to make any necessary inquiries from those immediately concerned. The classic illustration is that of the vicar who kept records of baptisms, marriages and burials within the parish. In an uncomplicated and localised society, such records might reasonably be trusted on that basis. But in a complex, more diverse and much larger society, the reality is very different, and public officers are now charged with making many records for public use, the contents of which they could not possibly personally know or verify. This has exposed a serious deficiency in the original rule, when applied to modern records, a deficiency which was clearly and forcibly demonstrated in *R v Halpin* (87). Halpin and others were charged with conspiracy to defraud a local authority, and corruption, arising from the performance of a service contract for the supply and renewal of paving stones for the local authority. It was material for the prosecution to prove that, during the period of the conspiracy, the defendant and his wife were in effect the sole shareholders and directors of the company which had the contract with the local authority, from which the jury might be invited to infer that the defendant was in a position to, and did in fact, exercise control over the transactions which were said to be fraudulent. In order to prove this, the prosecution adduced the contents of the file from the Companies Register containing the annual statutory returns of the company, which were required to be made by the company and submitted to the Registrar by virtue of s. 124 of the Companies Act 1948. Although such returns were required to be made and submitted, there was no statutory provision for the admissibility of the statements contained in them, so that, being hearsay, they could be admitted for the purposes desired by the prosecution only if they were admissible under the public documents rule. It was cogently argued on appeal that the returns offended by failing to satisfy the fourth condition, in that the file was not made by a person having a duty to inquire into and satisfy himself of the truth of the facts recorded. To this argument, there was really no answer, but the Court of Appeal, holding that the common law must, 'move with the times', were content to modify the condition judicially to suit modern conditions. Geoffrey Lane LJ, delivering the judgment of the court, said (88):

> . . . the common law should move with the times and should recognise the fact that the official charged with recording matters of public import can no longer in this highly complicated world, as like as not, have personal knowledge of their accuracy.
>
> What has happened now is that the function originally performed by one man has had to be shared between two: the first having the knowledge and the statutory duty to record that knowledge and forward it to the Registrar of Companies, the second having the duty to preserve that document and to show it to members of the public under proper conditions as required.
>
> Where a duty is cast upon a limited company by statute to make accurate returns of company matters to the Registrar of Companies, so that those returns can be filed and inspected by members of the public, the necessary conditions, in the judgment of this court, have been fulfilled for that document to have been admissible.

There is an obvious convenience in this approach in modern conditions, and whatever one's reservations (and they are surely legitimate) about this wholesale judicial legislation in a case where the Court was minded to apply the proviso (to s. 2(1) of the Criminal Appeal Act 1968) in any event, the judgment seems to bring the public-document exception into line with the statutory position in civil cases, under s. 4 of the Civil

87   [1975] QB 907.   88   Ibid at 915.

Evidence Act 1968. This specifically provides that the record made admissible may be compiled by a person acting under a duty (to make it) acting on information supplied to him by another who has, or may reasonably be supposed to have, personal knowledge of the facts. Although some legislative tidying-up is no doubt desirable, the fourth condition is therefore likely in future to stand as modified by *Halpin*.

The kinds and classes of public document capable of falling within the rule are too numerous and diverse to permit of any detailed discussion in this work (89). Those documents, however, which are of relevance to criminal cases, to which the common-law exception is now confined, are probably small in number, and will ordinarily be company records, extracts from registers and the like, where no statutory basis for admission exists. The categories of public documents are conveniently grouped under the following heads, which may be commented on very shortly.

(a) *Public papers.*   Statements and public recitals in state and official papers dealing with matters properly before either House of Parliament are admissible evidence of the facts stated in them. These may be royal proclamations, addresses to the Crown, state papers, or documents printed by authority of either House, for example an extract from the register of divisions to prove the casting of votes (90). Public facts contained in the government *Gazettes* of London, Edinburgh and Belfast may be proved by production of the *Gazette*. This would include the details of proclamations and orders in Council.

(b) *Public registers and records.*   Facts contained in many registers and records, notably those relating to births, marriages and deaths, are now admissible by virtue of specific statutory provisions. But the common-law rule is still occasionally of importance in relation to less usual records, and in relation to foreign registers and records, which are admissible evidence at common law of the facts stated in them, provided that it is first proved that they are public documents required to be kept for public reference by the law of the country of their origin (91). The register is evidence of the facts stated in it, so that a register of births is evidence of the fact and date of birth, and a register of deaths of the fact and date of death (though at common law, not of the cause of death, which is a statement of opinion). And in the case of a marriage celebrated outside England and Wales, the fact and the date of the marriage may be proved by a properly proved foreign marriage certificate or extract from a register, unless the existence or validity of the marriage is in dispute in the proceedings (92).

A note of caution must, however, be sounded in the use of facts contained in public registers and records. Although the fact and date of, for example, a birth or marriage may be proved in this way, the register cannot prove the identity of any person before the court as being a person named in the register. Thus, where it is material to prove this additional fact, for example to show that the defendant before the court is the person named as having been married on a certain day to A, and whose subsequent 'marriage' to B was accordingly bigamous; or to show that a person with whom the defendant is alleged to have committed incest is the person named as having been born to certain parents proved to be the parents of the defendant; this fact must be proved by other

---

89   The subject is exhaustively reviewed in Phipson, *Evidence*, 12th ed., para. 1051 et seq. The classification which follows in the text is gratefully based on that used by Phipson.

90   But not *Hansard,* which does not have the authority of Parliamentary Journals. Statutes must be treated separately. Public statutes are judicially noticed in all proceedings. Facts stated in private statutes are not evidence against strangers to the statute of the truth of any fact recited therein.

91   *Lyell* v *Kennedy; Kennedy* v *Lyell* (HL) (1889) 14 App Cas 437. As to the distinction between public and private records of this sort, see *Re Butler's Settlement Trusts* [1942] Ch 403.

92   See the Matrimonial Causes Rules 1977, r. 40.

evidence, for example by calling a person who was present at the marriage or birth in question (93).

(c) *Public inquisitions, surveys, etc.* Where there is a quasi-judicial duty to inquire into public facts, the findings of a public inquisition, survey, inquiry or similar under-taking are admissible to prove the public facts so found. These cases are chiefly of importance in relation to findings of public, general or customary rights and the like, but have also been held to include the findings of a coroner's inquest and its verdict *super visum corporis,* admitted to prove in libel proceedings that a certain person had been murdered (94), and the findings of the disciplinary committee of the General Dental Council, admitted to prove the misconduct of a dentist for the purposes of an action by his partner to dissolve the partnership (95).

(d) *Official certificates, etc.* Official certificates, letters and returns, made by public officers under some legal authority to do so, are admissible evidence of any authorised fact stated in them. In many cases, for example the proof of previous convictions and fingerprint records, the admissibility of the relevant certificates is governed by statute. But certain certificates continue to be admissible at common law, for example those supplied by members of the government dealing with the recognition of foreign states, the status of foreign sovereigns or governments, the existence of states of war and the like (96).

(e) *Company books.* Although statute, especially the Companies Act 1948, has made many records relating to companies admissible (97), we saw from *R v Halpin* that there is a residue which falls within the common-law rule. The rule is that entries in the public books of a corporation or public company are admissible evidence of the facts stated therein, in so far as those facts relate to the public acts of the company. The entries must have been duly made by the proper officer of the company, and must have been authenticated by an authorised signature or stamp. The public acts of the company would be those relating to the appointment of officers, and the acts and transactions of the company in the course of its public business, as opposed, for example to records of private proceedings taken by the company or its entitlement to property.

(f) *Published public works.* Reference may be made, for ease and convenience, to published works of an authoritative nature, for the purpose of proving, or enabling the court to take judicial notice of facts of a public nature recorded therein as matters of knowledge. Thus, histories may be referred to for ancient public facts not otherwise provable, or to enable the court to notice judicially facts concerned with governmental or constitutional matters. Maps may be used to show facts of geographical notoriety. Dictionaries may be resorted to for the meaning of English words in general usage, though not to show the meaning of foreign or technical words, which ought to be the subject of expert evidence. Scientific tables may be used to show demonstrable mathe-matical and scientific facts, or even it seems, statistical probabilities which are generally accepted, for example where the Carlisle tables are employed to show anticipated lifespan in actions in tort.

---

93 At common law, even the admission of a party against his interest would be of doubtful value to prove his birth, as the admission would be founded on hearsay. But such facts may sometimes be proved by extrinsic, circumstantial evidence, as for example where the age of a girl was proved by evidence of a long course of treatment of her as being of a certain age, including her admission to and stay in a home where girls of over sixteen were not permitted: *R v Bellis* (CCA) (1911) 6 Cr App R 283.
94 *R v Gregory* (1846) 8 QB 508.   95 *Hill v Clifford* (CA) [1907] 2 Ch 236.
96 *The Parlement Belge* (CA) (1880) 5 PD 197; *Mighell v Sultan of Johore* (CA) [1894] 1 QB 149.
97 See, e.g., s. 118 (register of members); s. 145(2) (minutes of meetings of directors and general meetings).

6.9   Questions for counsel

1   In the depositions and defence proofs of evidence in the case of Coke and Littleton, identify and distinguish any examples you can find of:
   (a)   Evidence of statements as direct evidence.
   (b)   Evidence of statements inadmissible as hearsay.
   (c)   Evidence of statements admissible only by virtue of a common-law exception to the rule against hearsay.
2   Consider specifically the admissibility of exhibit GG1 (the suspected handwriting of Coke found at his flat by D/I Glanvil).

7 The Rule Against Hearsay — II

A: ADMISSIONS

7.1 Principles of admissibility

In 6.7.2, ante, it was said that the common law was prepared to allow evidence of a statement by a deceased person to be admitted, despite its hearsay character, if its effect was adverse to the interests of the maker of the statement. The putative absence of risk of concoction and exaggeration in such statements, contrasted with that obviously present in the case of self-serving or previous consistent statements, removes one of the important objections to hearsay evidence. As with the dead, so with the living. At common law, statements adverse to the case of the maker are admissible, as an exception to the rule against hearsay, to prove the truth of the facts admitted. The safeguard inherent in this exception is simply that a party has no motive to admit facts which are prejudicial to his case, unless such facts are true.

The admissions dealt with in this chapter are properly referred to as informal admissions. This term serves to distinguish them from formal admissions (1), which are concessions made *inter partes* for the purpose of the proceedings, having the effect (as if made on the pleadings) of establishing the facts formally admitted without the need for recourse to evidence and which cannot be withdrawn without leave.

Informal admissions are statements made by a party (or by some person by whose admission a party is bound as a matter of law) from which the court would be entitled to, but is not bound to, find facts or draw inferences adverse to the case of that party. An informal admission is, therefore, merely one piece of evidence to which the court may have regard when considering the facts to which it relates. Its weight will depend upon the circumstances in which it is made, and the clarity or ambiguity of the contents of the statement. Evidence may be given to explain away or contradict the admission, or to show that because of the circumstances in which it was made, no weight should be attached to it. An admission may be inferred from a statement in any form, whether oral, in writing or by some conduct which can only be interpreted as an acknowledgement of a weakness or defect in a party's case, such as evidence of a conspiracy between a relative of the party and a solicitor's clerk to suborn false witnesses at the trial (2).

The common-law rule has been much modified by practice, particularly in relation to criminal cases, in which specialised rules of admissibility have been developed. Admissions relevant to the issue of guilt in criminal cases are known as confessions, and if made to persons in authority are subject to additional conditions of admissibility, which are

---

1 See 1.9, ante; and see the subject of judicial confessions, dealt with in 11.7, post. Certain admissions may also have effect as estoppels by conduct (outside the scope of this work) or per rem judicatam: see Chapter 10, Section B, post.
2 *Moriarty and Another* v *London, Chatham & Dover Railway Co.* (1870) LR 5 QB 314.

considered in section B of this chapter. In civil cases, the common-law rules prevail, although they now enjoy a statutory basis by virtue of s. 9 of the Civil Evidence Act 1968 which, so far as material, provides that:

(1) In any civil proceedings, a statement which, if this Part of this Act had not been passed, would by virtue of any rule of law mentioned in subsection (2) below have been admissible as evidence of any fact stated therein shall be admissible as evidence of that fact by virtue of this subsection.

(2) The rules of law referred to in subsection (1) above are the following, that is to say any rule of law —

(a) whereby in any civil proceedings an admission adverse to a party to the proceedings, whether made by that party or by another person, may be given in evidence against that party for the purpose of proving any fact stated in the admission . . .

Because an informal admission is no more than a piece of evidence relevant to the determination of the truth or probability of certain facts, and because consequently its effect and weight (if any) are questions of fact, the proper interpretation of the statement is of great importance. It is, therefore, a fundamental principle that the whole of a statement said to contain an admission adverse to the case of the maker should be looked at by the court. It would be quite wrong to isolate, and perhaps take out of context, some part of a statement which appears on the face of it to constitute an admission. The statement read as a whole may have a quite different effect, which may modify or altogether nullify the appearance of an adverse admission. The evidential value of statements partly favourable and party adverse to the maker has given rise to considerable problems in criminal cases, in which self-serving statements are inadmissible to prove the truth of any relevant facts stated therein. This is considered further in 7.11, post. But in civil cases, there seems to be no reason why those parts of the statement favourable to the maker should not be admissible to prove the truth of the facts stated, in the same was as those parts which are adverse. Be this as it may, the whole statement must be put before the court (3).

The important rules at common law concern the circumstances in which a party may be bound by admissions made by other persons, or made by himself while acting in a different capacity, and the extent of the facts which may be proved by adverse admission. These matters will now be considered.

7.2 What admissions may bind a party

In addition to the simple case where a party makes in his personal capacity a statement adverse to his interests, an admission made in other circumstances or by other persons may bind the party, in the sense of being admissible evidence of the facts admitted adverse to his case. The admissibility in such cases depends upon the relationship between the party and the maker of the statement, which is sometimes, though not altogether happily, described as one of 'privity'. This imports some identity of interest in the litigation, or in the subject-matter of the litigation, which suggests that an admission from the maker of the statement is tantamount to, or should be regarded as if it were, an

---

3   In criminal cases, statements may sometimes be edited, so as to exclude matters which are inadmissible and prejudicial, for example revelations of bad character. See 7.10.2, post.

admission by the party himself. In some cases, the identity is one imputed by the law rather than having any realistic basis of fact. The cases which call for consideration, from a practical point of view, are those referred to below.

7.2.1   Parties in other capacities

Wherever a party litigates in his personal capacity, either as plaintiff or defendant or otherwise, any admission made by him on another occasion may be proved against him, even though it may have been made by him in a representative or other capacity, such as in proceedings in which he represented a person under disability (4), or acted on behalf of beneficiaries or dependants.

At common law, however, the converse proposition would not hold good, there being no justification, in the absence of some other relationship of privity, for holding that a party to proceedings in which he is necessarily represented by another, should be prejudiced by any admission made by that representative elsewhere in his personal capacity. Thus, in *Legge* v *Edmonds* (5), where the issue was the legitimacy or illegitimacy of a child of the plaintiff who was suing as administratrix of her husband's estate, admissions made by the plaintiff tending to show that she had committed adultery were held to be inadmissible, although in any proceedings involving the plaintiff in her personal capacity, they would clearly have been admissible on the same issue. In civil cases, it may be that such statements could now be admitted under s. 2 of the Civil Evidence Act 1968, even if not under s. 9, and there is some authority to suggest that the court might exempt such admissions from the notice procedure in the interests of securing a fair trial, to avoid what might otherwise be the consequence that the party relying on such admissions might be obliged to call an opposite party (6). Since representative proceedings refer in reality only to civil cases, it may be that the common law has now been wholly superseded by statute to this extent, though the weight of admissions received in such circumstances may not always be very great. The position of private prosecutors in criminal cases may, however, prompt some academic speculation.

7.2.2   Other parties

At common law, an admission made by one party is evidence against the maker of the statement, but not against any other party implicated by it. This principle is of considerable practical importance in relation to confessions in criminal cases, and is further considered in 7.10.3, post. In civil cases, admissions made by other parties may now be rendered admissible under s. 2 of the Civil Evidence Act 1968. The common-law rule has the logical, though curious, result that if A and B are jointly charged with the same offence, for example with conspiring together unlawfully, A may be convicted upon his admission that he and B were guilty of the conspiracy, while B may have to be acquitted because of the lack of admissible evidence against him, A's admission being of no evidential value against B (7).

This rule must be carefully distinguished from a very different rule, with which it is sometimes confused, according to which, where A and B are jointly charged and the prosecution allege a common design, the acts and declarations of A and B, even though

4   *Stanton* v *Percival* (HL) (1855) 5 HL Cas 257.
5   (1855) 25 LJCh 125.
6   See *Tremelbye (Selangor) Rubber Co. Ltd* v *Stekel and Others* [1971] 1 WLR 226; 8.9.4, post.
7   Cf *DPP* v *Shannon* (HL) [1975] AC 717. Before the passing of the Civil Evidence Act 1968, the same result frequently obtained in divorce cases, where A obtained a decree on the ground of adultery by Mrs A with B, on the admission of Mrs A, while B was dismissed from the suit for lack of evidence against him.

made by one in the absence of the other, are admissible evidence against both to prove the existence and carrying out of the common design (8). This rule has been beset by serious misconceptions. It is sometimes said, quite wrongly, that it applies only to cases of conspiracy. While the rule clearly does apply to cases of conspiracy, it is by no means limited to cases where conspiracy is charged as such, but extends to all cases where an agreement to engage in a common design is implicit in the·charge. Thus, whether a number of defendants are charged with conspiracy, or with a number of substantive offences committed pursuant to a conspiracy, should not affect the principle, and it is submitted that dicta in some cases such as *R* v *Dawson; R* v *Wenlock* (9), to the effect that charges of conspiracy may work injustice by rendering admissible evidence which would be inadmissible on equivalent substantive charges, are ill-founded. However, it is also submitted that this misconception flows from another and more fundamental misconception, namely that declarations in furtherance of a common design are hearsay in character, and therefore are admitted by virtue of the exception in favour of admissions. In fact, it is submitted, such declarations are direct evidence of the common design. If A and B combine together to rob a bank, and while A waits in the getaway car, B enters the bank and says to the cashier, 'I've got a gun; give me the money', it is absurd to suggest that A can object to a witness relating B's words on the ground that the witness would be giving hearsay evidence. Words can amount to conduct, and B's words are just as much direct evidence of the carrying out of the common design as would be the fact that B actually produced a gun and silently threatened the cashier with it. Of course, once the common design has come to an end, evidence of any declarations made subsequently by individual defendants would be hearsay, and admissible only by virtue of an exception, if at all. Thus, if the design is ended by the arrest of the defendants, and A makes admissions to the police implicating both himself and B, what he says can be treated as evidence only against himself and not against B. And even during the continuance of the common design, declarations which are in no way in furtherance of it, and therefore have no value as direct evidence, may equally be hearsay. In *R* v *Blake and Tye* (10), where Tye made entries in two books which tended to incriminate both himself and Blake in a conspiracy to evade customs duty, the entries in one book, which were part of the mechanics of the conspiracy, were admissible against both Tye and Blake as being declarations in furtherance of it. However, those in the second book, which were pure matters of record made for Tye's personal convenience and unrelated to the carrying out of the common design, were admissible against Tye as an admission, but inadmissible hearsay against Blake.

7.2.3   Witnesses in other proceedings

At common law there was some controversy over the position of a person who was a party in two successive legal actions. What view should be taken of evidence which such a person had relied on in the first action but which could be taken as an admission on an issue in the second action? It was clear that, in general, unless the same witness would give the same evidence in the second action, it was not possible to use in the second action evidence given only in the first without breaking the rule against hearsay (11).

8   The rule is one of some antiquity at common law, and admits, for example, the individual speeches, placards and printed leaflets of various defendants, made for the purposes of the common design, as evidence against each of them: see, e.g., *R* v *Duffield* (1851) 5 Cox CC 404.
9   (CCA) [1960] 1 WLR 163 at 170.   10   (1844) 6 QB 126.
11   See generally *British Thomson-Houston Co. Ltd* v *British Insulated & Helsby Cables Ltd* (CA) [1924] 2 Ch 160. The rule was confused by the possibility of using such admissions to prove knowledge or agency, and by the possibility of estoppel.

However, in some cases, the courts permitted reliance upon admissions contained in affidavits of witnesses previously relied upon by a party (12). Happily, the position has been clarified by s. 2 of the Civil Evidence Act 1968, which expressly provides for the admissibility in civil cases of statements made in evidence in other proceedings. In criminal cases, while it is theoretically possible that recourse might be had to the common-law rules, it is difficult to dispute the view of Professor Cross (13) that it is highly improbable that a criminal court would permit the use against a defendant of admissions contained in affidavits made by third parties, even where the defendant had relied upon them in some earlier proceedings.

7.2.4 Agents

Admissions made by an agent acting within the scope of his authority are admissible against his principal. The agent acts within his authority, for this purpose, not only when he is authorised to make such admissions expressly, but also when he is authorised to represent the principal for any purpose and the admissions are made in the proper course of that representation. It is, therefore, unlikely that admissions made by an agent relating to transactions prior to the commencement of the agency will be admissible, but there is no reason why the agent should not be given authority to deal with them. Similarly, it is unlikely that a servant of the principal should be able to make admissions which may be received against his employer, but it is a question of fact whether he has received any proper authority. In civil cases, statements made by agents or employees may now be admitted under s. 2 of the Civil Evidence Act 1968, thus removing a number of difficult questions concerning the scope of the agency (14).

The agency must be shown to exist and to extend to authorise the agent sufficiently before the admission made by the agent can be received. The agency may be proved by direct evidence, or in a civil case presumably by the hearsay statement of the agent. But there seems to be no reason why the court should not infer the existence and scope of the agency from the facts before it, for example where a person, in response to a request to see someone able to deal authoritatively with a certain matter, comes forward and purports to deal with the enquirer (15).

Admissions by agents admissible for present purposes are those made by the agent to third parties, and not those contained in statements made by the agent to the principal. Thus, although the directors of a company may make admissions admissible against the company during the course of proper dealings on the company's behalf with third parties, their statements made, for example, to a meeting of the shareholders, cannot be received as admissions against the company (16).

It is worth commenting specifically upon two particular instances of the many conceivable forms of agency which may be likely to result in useful admissions, namely those of legal representatives and spouses of parties.

(a)   *Legal representatives.* In civil cases, a solicitor has an implied authority, arising from his general instructions, to make on behalf of his client either a formal admission dispensing with the need for further proof of the facts admitted, or statements on the client's behalf within the proper scope of his instructions which may subsequently prove

---

12   *Evans* v *Merthyr Tydfil UDC* (CA) [1899] 1 Ch 241.
13   *Evidence,* 5th ed. p.523–4.
14   In civil cases such as *Burr* v *Ware RDC* (CA) [1939] 2 All ER 688, statements made by employees would now be admitted under s. 2. As to the notice procedure applying to such cases, see 7.2.1, ante.
15   *Edwards* v *Brookes (Milk) Ltd* (DC) [1963] 1 WLR 795.
16   *Re Devala Provident Gold Mining Co.* (1883) 22 ChD 593.

to be adverse to the client's case and so become admissible under the present rule. Such statements may be made in court or in chambers, or in correspondence or documents written in connection with the subject-matter of the proceedings (17). After, though not before, the issue of proceedings, the solicitor may compromise a claim on behalf of the client. But it appears that an admission made by the solicitor to a person other than an adverse party to the proceedings, or outside his proper conduct of the proceedings, or by way of fraud on his client, cannot be received.

In criminal cases, formal admissions may now also be made, by virtue of s. 10 of the Criminal Justice Act 1967, and these have, broadly, the same effect as they would in civil cases. But statements which may later prove adverse will be admissible only where they are made upon the express instructions of the client, and not where they are made only upon the basis of a solicitor's general instructions (18), although by s. 11(5) of the Criminal Justice Act 1967 a notice of alibi given pursuant to that section by a solicitor is deemed to have been given with the authority of the defendant, unless the contrary is proved.

Counsel may likewise made admissions, both formal and informal, which may later be admitted against his client, although his authority is narrower than that of the solicitor, in that he must have been acting within the terms of his brief or instructions in relation to the matter in question. Nonetheless, counsel's authority pursuant to his instructions is that of conducting the case in every respect, and this includes the power, in civil cases, to consent to judgment, call no evidence or to compromise the suit. Statements made in court or in chambers by counsel, or assented to by signing an endorsement on his opponent's brief, may be relied upon by the court as admissions. However, admissions made in such ways will be admissible only for the purposes of the proceedings in which they are made, and admissions made in interlocutory proceedings will, it seems, not bind the client on the hearing of the main suit, at least where there is no estoppel and the other side would not be prejudiced by the rejection of the admission (19). In criminal cases also, statements made by counsel in open court may be admitted against the defendant, because of counsel's general authority to speak on his client's behalf and on his instructions, and in *R* v *Turner and Others* (20), an admission of an offence made by counsel in the course of mitigation of another offence, was held to be admissible on the prosecution of the defendant for the offence so admitted.

(b)   *Spouses.* It is also worthy of note that the law does not impute any agency capable of permitting evidence of admissions against the 'principal', merely because of the relationship of husband and wife. There may on the facts of a given case be evidence that one spouse gave sufficient authority to the other, for example to conduct his business, but in the absence of such evidence, admissions made by one spouse will not be evidence against the other. The same principle applies to other relationships, for example that of parent and child (21).

7.3   What may be proved by admission

Informal admissions may be received on matters of fact or law, or on both together. So

---

17   An admission by letter that the client has no defence may be proved with a view to obtaining immediate judgment: *Ellis* v *Allen* [1914] 1 Ch 904. This does not of course apply to without-prejudice communications: see 11.10, post.

18   See, e.g., *R* v *Downer* (CCR) (1880) 14 Cox CC 486.

19   *H. Clark (Doncaster) Ltd* v *Wilkinson* (CA) [1965] Ch 694. Whether this ought to be the position seems, to say the least, open to question.

20   (CA) (1975) 61 Cr App R 67.   21   *G(A)* v *G(T)* (CA) [1970] 2 QB 643.

far as matters of fact are concerned, we have seen (22) that admissions should be founded upon the personal knowledge of the maker of the statement, and will be rejected as evidence of the facts admitted where the admission is based upon pure hearsay as to which the maker has no personal knowledge. But where the maker of the statement is speaking about matters perceived by him, his admission may be prima facie evidence of the facts admitted, even where further evidence, such as expert evidence, ought to be tendered in order to prove the facts more specifically. Thus, in *R* v *Chatwood and Others* (23), the admission of an experienced drug user was admitted as prima facie evidence that the substance with which he injected himself was a dangerous drug. There would seem to be no conflict between this decision and those in such cases as *Comptroller of Customs* v *Western Lectric Co. Ltd* because in the *Chatwood* case, the identity of the drug was in any event a matter to be proved by evidence of opinion, and although expert opinion might be of more value, that of an experienced user was by no means to be disregarded, and was evidence upon which the jury was entitled to act. And there have been instances where facts within the peculiar competence of the defendant have been proved by his own admission, even though necessarily based upon hearsay, as for example his age (24). The explanation of these decisions seems to be one of convenience and the unlikelihood of injustice to the defendant. The weight of admissions of fact is, as we have seen a question of fact depending upon the circumstances and terms of the statement. In some cases, particularly in divorce cases where the maker of the statement may have some interest to serve in making it, the court will scrutinise the admission with care, as it will if there appears to be any doubt about the reliability of the statement, having regard to the maker's state of mind at the time.

Admissions of matters of law, though admissible, are usually of little weight, being founded on (generally uninformed) opinion. Indeed, an admission on a question of foreign law, for instance the validity of a marriage celebrated abroad, where the prosecution is for bigamy, will be rejected altogether (25). But admissions of the validity of English marriages are admissible (26), and the cases show a variety of other matters of law which have been established by admission, including the existence of a nuisance (27). There is no objection to the reception of an admission of law which seems even to conclude the very point which the jury have to decide, for example an admission that the defendant stole the property, the subject of the indictment, though the weight of such admission must still be considered: there may be cases where the defendant's apparently clear admission is nullified by evidence that did not understand the legal nature of theft, and intended only to admit a perhaps innocent taking of the property. But of course, such admissions, particularly when dealing with non-technical and common offences, are often of very great weight, and may in fact conclude the case against the defendant in themselves. There is, of course, an obvious danger in acting on an admission of a matter of law where the matter is a technical one or may be open to debate, and there will be cases where the only safe course is to reject the admission altogether, as was done in *R* v *Philp* (28), where the defendant's admission of the prosecutor's title to property met precisely that fate.

22   6.3.1, ante; *Comptroller of Customs* v *Western Lectric Co. Ltd (PC, Fiji)* [1966] AC 367; *R* v *Marshall* [1977] Crim LR 106.
23   (CA) [1980] 1 All ER 467.
24   *R* v *Walker* (1884) 1 Cox CC 99; *R* v *Turner* (CCA) [1910] 1 KB 346.
25   *R* v *Naguib* (CCA) [1917] 1 KB 359.
26   *R* v *Flaherty* (1847) 2 Car & Kir 782; though the admission would not of itself justify a conviction for bigamy.
27   *R* v *Neville* (NP) (1791) 1 Peake 91.   28   (1830) 1 Mood CC 263.

B: CONFESSIONS

7.4 Confessions to persons in authority

In criminal cases, admissions are of recurring importance because of the habitual practice of interrogation of suspects employed by the police and other prosecuting authorities. It would be no exaggeration to say that the exception to the hearsay rule involving admissions is of importance in almost every criminal case of any significance and is the most important of all exceptions in criminal cases. The degree of emphasis placed upon the oral and written admissions in the papers in the case of Coke and Littleton is by no means untypical, and would probably be greater in actual practice. In criminal cases, admissions made by a defendant relevant to his guilt are known as confessions, and although they are subject to the rules governing admissions generally, discussed in section A above, their admissibility may also depend upon the satisfaction of additional conditions, if, as is usually the case, they are made to persons in authority (29).

A person in authority is one who is concerned in the arrest, detention, interrogation or prosecution of the defendant, and who, therefore, has, or may properly be thought by the defendant to have, some influence or control over the case against the defendant, or the manner in which the defendant is to be treated during the course of the investigation or the prosecution. This definition itself suggests that confessions made to persons in authority should be examined carefully because of the obvious risk that the defendant may make a confession, not for the purpose of freely admitting his guilt, but because of some hope or fear, supposed or actual, which he may entertain with regard to the powers of the person in authority; and indeed, it is from this consideration that the additional conditions of admissibility flow.

The question of whether a given person is a person in authority is one of fact in every case, though there are some persons, notably police officers and other professional investigators who will inevitably be so if they appear to the defendant to be playing some role in the investigation in which he is implicated. There are, however, cases in which the question is less simple. The case of a uniformed officer acting in a purely administrative capacity at a police station, who may do no more than supply the defendant with refreshments while he is detained for the purpose of interrogation, is one such. Although there is old authority in *R* v *Shepherd* (30), that an officer having a prisoner in custody is a person in authority, it may not follow that every police officer acting under the direction of the officer in charge of the station in some routine matter should be so. A doctor called by the police to examine a person in custody has been held to be an independent expert and in no sense the agent of the police (31), but while this may be acceptable where the doctor does no more than examine the defendant because of some suspected illness, or to ascertain whether he is fit to be detained, it is surely open to question when the doctor is called to examine the defendant with a view to giving evidence subsequently on behalf of the prosecution (32). An officer of the Customs and Excise investigating alleged drugs

---

29 The use of the word 'confession' does not connote, in the popular sense, a full and comprehensive acknowledgement of guilt. Any admission relevant to the issue of guilt in a criminal case is a 'confession' for present purposes, and, if made to a person in authority is subject to the additional conditions of admissibility: see *Commissioners of Customs & Excise* v *Harz and Another* (HL) [1967] 1 AC 760 at 817–8 per Lord Reid.

30 (1836) 7 C & P 579.

31 *R* v *Nowell* (CCA) [1948] 1 All ER 794. The case raises the wider problem of persons generally used in ancillary roles by investigating bodies.

32 In Scotland, a police surgeon is seen as acting on behalf of the police, and would be a person in authority; it is submitted that this view is more realistic than that prevailing in England, and should be followed.

offences (33), or any similar person authorised to undertake investigations on behalf of a public authority, for example the Inland Revenue (34) or the Department of Health and Social Security, will stand upon the same footing as a police officer. And where the defendant is himself subject to some personal discipline or authority, it may be that a superior who undertakes some investigation of the defendant's conduct is a person in authority for present purposes. In *R* v *Smith* (35), it was assumed, no doubt rightly, that a regimental sergeant-major, who threatened to keep a number of soldiers on parade until he received a confession from one of them, was a person in authority.

The mere fact that a person to whom a confession has been made subsequently gives evidence for the prosecution does not make him a person in authority. In *Deokinanan* v *R,* (36) the Privy Council rejected an argument that a man whom the defendant regarded as his friend, and who was placed in custody with the defendant by the police in the hope of obtaining information from the defendant, was a person in authority. Viscount Dilhorne cited the words of Lord Parker CJ in *R* v *Wilson; R* v *Marshall-Graham* (37) that:

> [Counsel for the appellant Marshall-Graham] in the course of the argument sought to put forward the principle that a person in authority is anyone who can reasonably be considered to be concerned or connected with the prosecution, whether as initiator, conductor or witness. The court find it unnecessary to accept or reject the definition, save to say that they think that the extension to a witness is going very much too far.

Of course, investigators do habitually give evidence for the prosecution. But it seems that in order that a witness should be a person in authority, there must be something over and above the fact of being a witness. It is obvious that many prosecution witnesses have and can appear to have no influence whatsoever over the treatment or prosecution of the defendant. Conversely, some witnesses who are personally interested in the subject-matter of the prosecution may be persons in authority, despite the fact that they are not involved as a matter of duty in the investigation, because of their apparent and sometimes actual power to influence the course of events. Into this category may fall the defendant's employer if the offence is one against the employer's property (38), the householder with burglary of whose property the defendant is charged (39), or, presumably in any case, the prosecutor (40), complainant or victim (41). These are no more than illustrations of the principle that the appearance to the defendant is just as important as the reality. If a person to whom the defendant makes a confession reasonably appears to the defendant to be capable of influencing his treatment, or the bringing or conduct of the prosecution, then that person is a person in authority, even though the matter may be altogether out of his hands, for example because the police are determined or bound to prosecute in any

33 *R* v *Grewal* [1975] Crim L.R. 159.
34 Though by s. 105 of the Taxes Management Act 1970 a statutory modification of the rules of admissibility has been introduced for confessions made to officers of the Inland Revenue. See 7.5, post.
35 [1959] 2 QB 35.   36   (PC, Guyana) [1969] 1 AC 20.
37 (CA) [1967] 2 QB 406 at 415.
38 *R* v *Moore* (CCR) (1852) 2 Den CC 522.
39 *R* v *Wilson; R* v *Marshall-Graham* (CA) [1967] 2 QB 406. The same principle no doubt applies to confessions made to store detectives, security officers and the like.
40 *R* v *Jenkins* (CCR) (1822) Russ & Ry 492. In *R* v *Upchurch* (CCR) (1836) 1 Mood CC 465, the principle was extended (on the facts) to the wife of the prosecutor; and from *R* v *Warringham* (1851) 2 Den CC 447, it would seem to apply to the defendant's partner or the partner's spouse, where the alleged offence is one against partnership property.
41 See, e.g., the Nova Scotia decision of *Downey* v *R* (1977) 38 CRNS 57, where the victim of a robbery interviewed the defendant at the instigation of the police.

event, or because there are other persons who may be interested in the bringing of the prosecution.

Where the defendant wrongly believes that a person is one who is capable of influencing his treatment or prosecution, when that person cannot on any reasonable view be supposed to be in authority, it has been held that the confession is not subject to the additional conditions of admissibility (42) and it may be that this would today be the case where the defendant's belief was wholly unreasonable; but it is submitted that, since it is the appearance to the defendant which is the crucial factor, the matter must be looked at through the defendant's eyes, and bearing in mind that under the stress of being suspected, the defendant may be tempted to take an unduly optimistic or pessimistic view of the persons who could affect him, favourably or adversely, in relation to the case.

A confession is also subject to the additional conditions of admissibility, if it is made by the defendant to a third party in the presence of a person in authority who tacitly assents to the proceedings by taking no part in them, or by failing to dissent or dissociate himself from them. In *R* v *Moore* (43) a father said to his son, aged sixteen, in the presence of a police officer, 'You had better make a statement, and then we can go home.' It was held that the officer's presence had lent to that remark by the father the tacit approval of a person in authority, even though the officer had himself said nothing, and that accordingly, the son's resulting confession must be treated as if made at the suggestion of the officer himself. The same result obtained in *R* v *Hume* (44) where an officer remained silent while two persons arrested with the defendant tried to persuade the defendant to admit responsibility for certain stolen prescriptions, on the ground that whereas they were on bail in respect of other matters, the defendant was of previous good character. In such cases, the effect on the defendant's mind must be the same as it is where the confession is made to the person in authority without intervention, because the reality or appearance of influence over his treatment or prosecution is just as great as in the cases where the person in authority invites the confession by his own words, or merely by his own presence combined with the circumstances of the case.

Confessions made to persons other than persons in authority are admissible in accordance with the rules applicable to admissions generally, dealt with in section A, and are not subject to the additional conditions about to be discussed, although it has been suggested that the trial judge has some discretion to exclude a confession in such a case if the circumstances in which it was obtained were such as to deprive the defendant of any real freedom of decision (45). Confessions made to other persons in custody (46) or to relations or friends of the defendant are, therefore, admissible for the prosecution, subject to any discretion to exclude. Turning to the case of Coke and Littleton, the oral and written confessions said to have been made by Coke to D/I Glanvil were clearly made to a person in authority, whereas equally clearly, that made by Littleton to his wife was not, because although it was overheard and recorded by D/I Glanvil, the inspector was not present when the statement was made.

Confessions made to persons in authority are subject to the special conditions of admissibility that (a) they must have been made voluntarily, and (b) they must not have

42 *R* v *Frewin* (1855) 6 Cox CC 530, though the confession was excluded on the facts.
43 (CA) (1972) 56 Cr App R 373; and see *R* v *Cleary* (CCA) (1963) 48 Cr App R 116.
44 [1979] Crim LR 724.
45 This is presumably an exercise of the normal judicial discretion to exclude where the prejudicial effect of evidence greatly exceeds any possible probative value. Winn LJ in *R* v *Richards* (CA) [1967] 1 WLR 653, and in *R* v *Northam* (CA) (1967) 52 Cr App R 97 at 103 suggested that such confessions also require the further conditions to be admissible in law, but this seems plainly contrary to authority, going back to *R* v *Taylor* (1839) 8 C & P 733.
46 *R* v *Ali; R* v *Hussain* [1966] 1 QB 688.

been obtained by oppression (47). The burden of proving that each of these conditions is satisfied rests upon the prosecution and, if in dispute, must be proved to the standard required of the prosecution on the main issue, i.e. beyond reasonable doubt. The admissibility of confessions, when disputed, is determined by the trial judge as a question of law in the absence of the jury. The practice relating to such determination is dealt with in 7.9, post. These conditions, which are of the utmost importance in practice, will now be considered in detail.

7.5 Voluntariness

The rule that confessions to persons in authority should be voluntary has a considerable history, and in 1914, Lord Sumner was able to speak of it as 'long established' and 'as old as Hale'. The word has a specialised meaning in this context, a meaning which was authoritatively pronounced upon by Lord Sumner in the course of his speech in *Ibrahim* v *R* (48). The facts of *Ibrahim's* case are not in themselves of significance. There fell to be considered the terms of an unambiguous confession to murder made by a serving soldier to his commanding officer on a question-and-answer basis. The evidence generally against the defendant was overwhelming. Lord Sumner expressed the requirement of voluntariness in the following words:

> It has long been established . . . that no statement by an accused is admissible in evidence against him unless it is shown by the prosecution to have been a voluntary statement, in the sense that it has not been obtained from him either by fear of prejudice or hope of advantage exercised [(49)] or held out by a person in authority.

The 'fear of prejudice' and 'hope of advantage' are habitually spoken of respectively as involving 'threats' and 'inducements', although these terms are not to be derived from Lord Sumner's words (50). Useful as such terms may be as a form of shorthand, their use has occasioned some difficulty by tending to confuse the state of the defendant's mind at the time when the confession was made, with the state of mind or intention of the person in authority. This confusion led the Court of Appeal in *R* v *Isequilla* (51) to the erroneous conclusion that:

> . . . under the existing law the exclusion of a confession as a matter of law because it is not voluntary is always related to some conduct on the part of authority which is improper or unjustified. Included in the phrase 'improper or unjustified' of course must be the offering of an inducement, because it is improper in this context for those in authority to try to induce a suspect to make a confession. Counsel for the Crown says, and we agree, that if one looks to the authorities there is no case in the books

---

47   These requirements are not affected by the decision of the House of Lords in *R* v *Sang* [1979] 3 WLR 263 that, in general, the manner in which evidence is obtained is irrelevant to the question of its admissibility. The House of Lords expressly held that the rules relating to confessions remained separate. See also 1.6, ante.

48   (PC, Hong Kong) [1914] AC 599 at 609. For the position where statements are obtained by misrepresentation or deception, see 1.6; 7.5.

49   'In passing, I must say that the word "exercised" in the above quotation though repeatedly reproduced is, I believe, meaningless and corrupt in the report. I believe that Lord Sumner really said "excited" and that he was quoting from the almost equally well known and authoritative judgment of Cave J in *R* v *Thompson*. However that may be, the sense is obvious and unaffected.' Lord Hailsham of St Marylebone in *DPP* v *Ping Lin* [1976] AC 574 at 597–8.

50   Though they may properly be derived from the judgment of Cave J in *R* v *Thompson* (CCR) [1893] 2 QB 12 at 15, referred to by Lord Hailsham in *Ping Lin,* quoted in the previous note.

51   [1975] 1 WLR 716, per Lord Widgery CJ at 721–2.

which indicates that a confession can be regarded as not voluntary by reason of the present grounds, unless there is some element of impropriety on the part of those in authority. That seems to be the case, and we can see no justification for extending the principle today.

The facts of *Isequilla*, which turned on the state of mind of the defendant at the time when his confession was made, did not make for a meritorious appeal in a case where it was conceded that the police officers had acted with perfect propriety throughout, but the judgment of the Court of Appeal had the result that the requirement of voluntariness would be satisfied by evidence that there had been no improper or unjustified behaviour on the part of the police officers, and left unprovided for the possibility that a person in authority might unintentionally suggest to a suspect some fear of prejudice or hope of advantage, in consequence of which he might make a confession. Certainly, this would have been a curious omission from any requirement of law that the confession should be proved beyond reasonable doubt to be voluntary, and it was by no means an inevitable deduction from the words of Lord Sumner in *Ibrahim*. In due course, the matter was considered by the House of Lords in *DPP* v *Ping Lin* (52). The defendant was discovered by police officers smoking heroin in his flat, and substantial quantities of the drug were found there. The defendant, when questioned, maintained that he was a user of, but not a dealer in, the drug, and offered to help the police to find those higher up in the chain of supply, in return for being 'let out' or helped by the police. The officer conducting the interview refused to make any such agreement, but on one occasion added, 'If you show the judge that you have helped the police to trace bigger drug people, I am sure he will bear it in mind when he sentences you.' The defendant then disclosed the name of his supplier, and was later charged with conspiracy to contravene the Misuse of Drugs Act 1971. It was clear that the officer did not intentionally hold out any 'inducement' to the defendant. Lord Kilbrandon said of his words:

> Although, looking back on it, one can agree with the Court of Appeal that much trouble would have been saved if [the officer] had not used the words he did, his policy in trying to induce the lesser man in the chain to implicate the larger was wholly justifiable.

The House of Lords had, therefore, to decide whether what mattered was the intention of the officer, or the effect of his words on the mind of the defendant at the time when he made his statement. The House held, disapproving the passage from the judgment of the Court of Appeal in *Isequilla* cited above, that it was the mind of the defendant that was more important, and that it was not enough for the prosecution to show that the officer had not intended to obtain a confession by improper means or that he had not acted improperly. In the words of Lord Salmon (53):

> In the context of the question raised by this appeal it is difficult to understand the relevance of the references to impropriety in some of the cases to which we have been referred. No doubt, for anyone to obtain a confession or statement in breach of the established rule is ex hypothesi improper. Indeed it is impossible to imagine how the rule could be breached with propriety. It would seem, therefore, that the references to

52 [1976] AC 574.
53 Ibid at 606. See also *R* v *Allerton and Others* [1979] Crim LR 725.

impropriety add nothing. They may, however, have been intended to cover instances in which a person in authority has obtained a confession by subjecting an accused to inhuman treatment; but in my view, the rule as stated by Lord Sumner already covers such cases. In any event, no authority can be needed for the self-evident proposition that a confession or statement so obtained could not be voluntary.

In my opinion, the intention of a person in authority who makes a threat or a promise or offers any inducement prior to an accused making a confession or statement is irrelevant. So is the fact that the threat is gentle or the promise or inducement slight save in so far as this may throw any light on the vital question — was the confession or statement procured by the express or implicit threat, promise or inducement.

The trial judge must, therefore, look at what was done and said and weigh the effect of what was done and said on the mind of the defendant at the relevant time. The members of the House of Lords in *Ping Lin* were agreed also that it is an unprofitable exercise to search for reported cases, which might appear superficially to resemble the case under scrutiny. Each case turns on its own facts. This approach usefully highlights the important truths that there are many potential fears of prejudice excited and many potential hopes of advantage held out by persons in authority, and that each one of these will have a different effect upon the mind of each defendant in whom it may be excited or to whom it may be held out. To decide that conduct is capable of amounting to excitement of a fear or holding out a hope is to answer only half the question. It remains to consider whether that conduct may in fact have operated in that way on the mind of that defendant, and whether he may in fact have made a confession or statement in response to that conduct. The final answer will depend not only upon the nature of the conduct, but also the circumstances and characteristics of the defendant. Although it has been said that the court will be 'at pains to hold that even the most gentle . . . threats or slight inducements will taint a confession' (54), the reality is that what will induce a man of previous good character, unacquainted with procedure in a police station or the practice of interrogation, to rush to confess will perhaps leave unmoved a man with numerous previous convictions, who has been through it all before. As Lord Reid said in *Commissioners of Customs & Excise* v *Harz and Another* (55).

> It is true that many of the so-called inducements have been so vague that no reasonable man would have been influenced by them, but one must remember that not all accused are reasonable men or women: they may be very ignorant and terrified by the predicament in which they find themselves. So it may have been right to err on the safe side.

Whether or not a confession is proved to have been made voluntarily is, therefore, a question of fact in every case, and no attempt should be made to restrict aritificially the sort of threat or inducement which may render a confession involuntary. It is true that, at one extreme, there are cases such as those where the confession is extracted by means of violence, where no court could conceivably hold it to be voluntary, and at the other there are cases where what is put forward as a threat or inducement is so nebulous or slight that no court could entertain serious doubt that the statement was voluntary. But these are

54 By Lord Parker CJ in *R* v *Smith* [1959] 2 QB 35 at 39.
55 (HL) [1967] 1 AC 760 at 820.

matters of evidence, and should not be allowed to obscure the true test. In *R* v *Middleton* (56), it was alleged that a threat was made to the defendant that a woman who was known to, but unrelated to, the defendant, and in whose house stolen goods had been found, would be kept in custody and her children taken into care. The Court of Appeal held that the trial judge had erred in ruling that such a threat was incapable of amounting to the holding out of a fear of prejudice. The judge had held that such matters affecting 'strangers', as opposed to the defendant, his family or close friends, could not fall within Lord Sumner's proposition. In the Court of Appeal, Edmund Davies LJ disposed of this attempt at restriction, as follows:

> The courts reprehend the resorting to threats or inducements in order to extort a confession. But if such extortion is used, what does it matter to whom the inducement or the threat relates? As a matter of common sense, of course, the more remote the person involved in the threat is from the person or close circle of the accused man the more difficult it may be to establish that the confession was improperly obtained; but that is a consideration which goes to the weight of the evidence that a threat was made and not to the admissibility of a confession if the threat was, in fact, established. . . .
>
> The law, as we understand it, is not confined in the way submitted to and accepted by the recorder. The categories of inducement are not closed.

The principle that the categories are not closed had already been accepted by the House of Lords in *Commissioners of Customs & Excise* v *Harz and Another* (57), when rejecting a contention that a fear of prejudice or hope of advantage should only be capable of operating to exclude a confession if it consisted of a threat or promise related to the charge or contemplated charge against the defendant. Lord Reid demonstrated the illogicality of such a restriction, and concluded that it had never been part of the law of England. Of course, if the threat or promise is wholly unrelated to the charge or contemplated charge, then like the threat to a stranger, less weight may be put on it as evidence that the confession may not have been voluntary. There is older authority, which appears not to have been overruled expressly, to the effect that a moral, spiritual or religious inducement or threat should not be capable of operating to exclude a confession, and that some temporal or material benefit or consequence must be promised or threatened (58). But although the rule gave rise to some delightful episodes of melodrama, in which masters and mistresses implored their servants not to add the sin of falsehood to that of the offence to be charged, it may be doubted whether the cases which laid it down have survived the more modern authorities discussed above. Like many other factors, it is now probably a matter of weight, rather than law.

In *R* v *Kwabena Poku* (59), Melford Stevenson J excluded a confession, apparently as involuntary, where a police officer had told the defendant, in good faith, but mistakenly, that he would be incriminated by forensic evidence of semen found on the clothing of a girl with whose attempted rape he was charged, whereas there was in fact no such evidence. The defendant had been misled. It is submitted that ordinarily, this must be the correct approach, unless the false statement cannot have had any real effect on the

56   [1975] QB 191 at 197.
57   (HL) [1967] 1 AC 760.
58   See, e.g., *R* v *Wild* (CCR) (1835) 1 Mood CC 452; *R* v *Sleeman* (1853) 6 Cox CC 245. It seemed to be immaterial whether the confession was made to a minister of religion or not: *R* v *Gilham* (CCR) (1828) 1 Mood CC 186.
59 . [1978] Crim LR 488; and see 7.7.4, post.

defendant's mind. The decision contrasts with some older authorities in which it was held that even the deliberate administration of drink to the defendant, designed to produce a confession, would not render such confession inadmissible.

Counsel for Coke will undoubtedly wish to challenge the admissibility of the oral and written confessions which, according to D/I Glanvil, were made voluntarily by Coke at the police station. If the confessions were obtained in the circumstances set out in Coke's proof of evidence then clearly they must be excluded. In the light of *Commissioners of Customs & Excise* v *Harz and Another,* it does not matter that the threat said to have been made by D/I Glanvil related to a charge not brought against Coke and which, on the evidence, could probably not have been brought against him. And in this case, although he has been involved in a police investigation before, and may therefore be taken not to be wholly unacquainted with police procedure and the practice of interrogation, it may be argued with some force that the threat, if made, would have held a peculiar terror for one who had previously been convicted of a sexual offence and who appears to have some abhorrence for offences against children. In this latter respect, the words of Coke's statement under caution may assist him. Threats to charge the defendant with other offences if he does not confess, threats to charge some other person with the offence, and threats to withhold bail are all examples of fears of prejudice which may, if made, mean that a subsequent confession cannot be regarded as voluntary. Each of them may just as easily appear in the guise of a promise: to release the defendant on bail from the police station, to forbear from opposing bail at court, to forbear from preferring further charges, to allow the defendant to have other offences taken into consideration, and so on. And it does not appear to matter that the initial suggestion of some advantage may have come from the defendant, rather than from the officer; indeed, in *DPP* v *Ping Lin* (60) it was the defendant who first raised the possibility of his giving information in return for some benefit. If the suggestion is taken up or pursued by the officer, then a hope of advantage is held out (61). Had D/I Glanvil, in response to Littleton's request for bail, replied, 'Tell me the truth, and we'll see about it,' or some words to that effect, such words would undoubtedly have been capable of amounting to a hope of advantage.

Two specific matters should be dealt with. The first is that a mere exhortation to a defendant to 'tell the truth' is not in itself either an excitement of a fear of prejudice or the holding out of a hope of advantage. But depending on the context in which, and the way in which, the exhortation is made, it may certainly take on that appearance. The words, 'You had better tell the truth' (62), or, 'I think it would be better for you if you made a statement and told me exactly what happened' (63), may be construed as containing some implied promise or threat. As Cave J pointed out in *R* v *Thompson* (64), the danger is that the defendant may be left with the impression that it is incumbent on him, for reasons of self-interest, if for no other reason, to say something when he is in fact entitled, without risk of prejudice, to remain silent. The second is that in one important case, the common-law rules have been modified by statute, to prevent the exclusion of certain confessions made in proceedings against a person for fraud or wilful default in relation to tax, or in proceedings for recovery or penalty in tax matters. In such proceedings, it is provided by s. 105 of the Taxes Management Act 1970 that:

---

60   [1976] AC 574.
61   As was the case in *R* v *Zaveckas* (CA) [1970] 1 WLR 516 (bail); *R* v *Northam* (1967) 52 Cr App R 97 (offences to be taken into consideration).
62   *R* v *Fennell* (CCR) (1881) 7 QBD 147.   63   *R* v *Richards* (CA) [1967] 1 WLR 653.
64   (CCR) [1893] 2 QB 12 at 16.

(1)   Statements made or documents produced by or on behalf of a person shall not be inadmissible . . . by reason only that it has been drawn to his attention that —

(*a*)   in relation to tax, the Board [i.e., the Commissioners of Inland Revenue] may accept pecuniary settlements instead of instituting proceedings, and

(*b*)   though no undertaking can be given as to whether or not the Board will accept such a settlement in the case of any particular person, it is the practice of the Board to be influenced by the fact that a person has made a full confession of any fraud or default to which he has been a party and has given full facilities for investigation,

and that he was or may have been induced thereby to make the statements or produce the documents.

This provision was introduced by s. 34 of the Finance Act 1942 to combat what was otherwise as clear an inducement as could possibly be wished for, and to reverse, on its facts though not in principle, the decision to that effect in *R* v *Barker* (65). The provision is to be construed strictly in favour of the defendant, and will not affect a case where a confession is obtained by any other inducement.

The effect produced upon the mind of the defendant by any fear of prejudice or hope of advantage may be removed either by the passage of time, or by a specific contradiction of it by some other person in authority. If the defendant makes a confession after this has occurred, then it will be admissible. Whether the fear or hope has been removed is a question of fact, but in general, it would be difficult to establish to the required standard of proof that all effect had gone from the defendant's mind. In *R* v *Smith* (66), although the first confession made by the defendant was rejected because it was made to the defendant's regimental sergeant-major, who had threatened to keep a number of soldiers on parade until a confession was forthcoming from one of them, his subsequent oral and written confessions to regular investigating officers were admitted, because by that time the original threat which had tainted the first confession had obviously passed beyond recall. However, this was an unusual case, and where a police officer wrongly excites some fear or holds out some hope, it is unlikely that it could be wholly removed while the defendant is in the custody of the police. There is authority that this could only be done where the contradiction of the threat or promise is made by an officer higher in rank than the first (67), and it would seem that very clear terms would be called for.

7.6   Absence of oppression

The absence of oppression was not referred to by Lord Sumner in the passage from his speech in *Ibrahim* v *R* quoted on page 163. But when the Judges' Rules appeared in revised form in 1964, the introduction stated that they did not affect the principle, described as 'overriding and applicable in all cases', that:

. . . it is a fundamental condition of the admissibility in evidence against any person, equally of any oral answer given by that person to a question put by a police officer and of any statement made by that person, that it shall have been voluntary, in the sense that it has not been obtained from him by fear of prejudice or hope of advantage, exercised or held out by a person in authority, or by oppression.

65   (CCA) [1941] 2 KB 381.
66   [1959] 2 QB 35.
67   See, e.g., *R* v *Doherty* (1874) 13 Cox CC 23.

The origin of this addendum to Lord Sumner's words is to be found in those of Lord Parker CJ in *Callis* v *Gunn* (68), in which the Lord Chief Justice observed (obiter, because the case was concerned with the admissibility of fingerprint evidence obtained without caution) that:

There is a fundamental principle of law that no answer to a question and no statement is admissible unless it is shown by the prosecution not to have been obtained in an oppressive manner and to have been voluntary in the sense that it has not been obtained by threats or inducements.

Whatever the origin of the addendum, it is now generally accepted that the absence of oppression in the obtaining of a confession is a condition of admissibility (69), though opinion differs on whether the lack of oppression is an independent requirement in itself, or merely one aspect of the requirement of voluntariness. It is unlikely that this question is of any significance in practice, any more than the view sometimes heard that oppressive circumstances are not a factor affecting admissibility as a matter of law, but go only to the question whether the judge should exclude the statement in the exercise of his discretion. Despite the apparent significance of the question flowing from the burden of proof, the reality is that if there is any real probability that a confession has been obtained oppressively, it should be excluded in any event. But it is submitted, nonetheless, that the absence of oppression has now become a requirement of law which must be satisfied before a confession can be admitted, whatever may have been the position in 1914.

Whether there have been oppressive circumstances, and whether a confession has been obtained in oppressive circumstances, are questions of fact in every case, and the facts nearly always involve the length of time for which, or conditions under which, the defendant has been held in detention during interrogation, whether he has been permitted access to advice or to visitors, whether due regard has been paid to his health and general circumstances, and the like. It is pointless to seek to enumerate or define the many factors which go to make up a picture of oppressive circumstances, at which the court must look. As in the case of voluntariness, much depends upon the effect produced upon an individual defendant; what one man may find intolerably oppressive, another may find a matter of no consequence, so that although there are no doubt circumstances which anyone must find oppressive, the ultimate question of fact is whether those circumstances in fact induced this defendant to make a confession. The categories of oppression, like those of threats or inducements, may properly be said not to be closed.

Nonetheless, some definition of oppression has been arrived at, and now seems to have received the blessing of the courts in much the same way as that provided by Lord Sumner for voluntariness. In *R* v *Prager* (70) the term fell to be considered by the Court of Appeal, in response to argument on appeal that a confession ought to have been excluded at the trial because it had been obtained oppressively. Edmund Davies LJ giving the judgment of the court, said:

The only reported judicial consideration of 'oppression' in the Judges' Rules of which we are aware is that of Sachs J in *R* v *Priestly* [(71)] where he said:

68   (DC) [1964] 1 QB 495 at 501.
69   See, e.g., *Commissioners of Customs & Excise* v *Harz and Another* (HL) [1967] 1 AC 760, per Lord Reid at 818.
70   [1972] 1 WLR 260 at 266.   71   (1965) 51 Cr App R 1.

. . . to my mind, this word, in the context of the principles under consideration imports something which tends to sap, and has sapped, that free will which must exist before a confession is voluntary. . . . Whether or not there is oppression in an individual case depends upon many elements. I am not going into all of them. They include such things as the length of time of any individual period of questioning, the length of time intervening between periods of questioning, whether the accused person had been given proper refreshment or not, and the characteristics of the person who makes the statement. What may be oppressive as regards a child, an invalid or an old man or somebody inexperienced in the ways of this world may turn out not to be oppressive when one finds that the accused person is of a tough character and an experienced man of the world.

In an address to the Bentham Club in 1968 [(72)], Lord MacDermott described 'oppressive questioning' as

> questioning which by its nature, duration, or other attendant circumstances (including the fact of custody) excites hopes (such as the hope of release) or fears, or so affects the mind of the subject that his will crumbles and he speaks when otherwise he would have stayed silent.

We adopt these definitions or descriptions and apply them to the present case.

7.7   Judicial discretion: the Judges' Rules

The Judges' Rules are rules, which were laid down for the first time by the judges of the King's Bench Division in 1912 and subsequently revised by their successors of the Queen's Bench Division in 1964 (73), for the purpose of offering guidance to police officers and other professional investigators involved in the conduct of investigations, with particular reference to the treatment and interrogation of suspects. The rules are not rules of law, and do not in any way indicate that the judiciary will attempt to control the way in which investigations are carried out or interrogations conducted. The import of the rules must be clearly understood. Their due observance is not in itself a guarantee that any confession obtained will be admissible; their breach is not in itself a guarantee that a confession will be excluded. The rules do not alter or modify the principle of law that confessions and statements must, in order to be admissible, be shown to be voluntary and to have been obtained without oppression. But if it is demonstrated that some breach of the rules has occurred, the trial judge may, in the exercise of his discretion, exclude the resulting confessions, notwithstanding (and assuming) that the confession is admissible as a matter of law. The matter is entirely one for the trial judge, who must consider whether any unfairness or prejudice has been occasioned to the defendant by reason of the breach (74). The exercise of discretion will rarely be interfered with on appeal, unless the trial judge has clearly been guilty of a serious error

72   (1968) 21 Current Legal Problems 10.
73   And reissued from time to time by the Home Secretary. The present document is Home Office Circular 74/1978, which reproduces the 1964 rules without change. A fuller history of the rules is contained in appendix A to the circular. The rules are also reproduced as a practice note at [1964] 1 All ER 237.
74   The existence of this discretion is not affected by the decision of the House of Lords in *R* v *Sang* [1979] 3 WLR 263 that, in general, the trial judge has no discretion to exclude otherwise admissible evidence merely because it has been illegally or unfairly obtained. The law on confessions was expressly left unchanged by the House. See also 1.6, ante.

of judgment. The judge's task, in short, is to weigh the gravity and circumstances of the breach against the seriousness of the charge, the evidence as a whole and the apparent cogency of the confession, and so to decide whether it would be unjust to the defendant to allow the confession to go before the jury. But the extent of the judge's discretion is amply demonstrated by *R v Prager* (75). The defendant, who was charged with serious offences contrary to the Official Secrets Acts, was interrogated without being cautioned as required by rule r. 2 of the Judges' Rules. There could be no doubt that the defendant should have been cautioned pursuant to the rule at a certain stage, but he had not been cautioned because of a deliberate decision taken in advance by the interrogating officers, a decision said to be justified by the serious nature of the case. The trial judge, having concluded that the defendant's confession was voluntary, declined to consider the question of discretion separately, and held the confession to be admissible. This approach was strongly criticised in argument on appeal, but was upheld by the Court of Appeal. Edmund Davies LJ said (76):

> [Counsel] submitted before us that it was imperative that Lord Widgery CJ decided first whether r. 2 had or had not been breached, for, if it had been, the confession should not have been admitted unless there emerged 'some compelling reason why the breach should have been overlooked'. He cited no authority for that proposition, which, he claimed, involved a point of law of very great importance. This 'complete lack of authority' (to use [counsel's] phrase) is not surprising, for in our judgment, the proposition advanced involves no point of law and is manifestly unsound. Its acceptance would exalt the Judges' Rules into rules of law. That they do not purport to be, and there is abundant authority for saying that they are nothing of the kind. Their non-observance may, and at times does, lead to the exclusion of an alleged confession; but ultimately all turns on the judge's decision whether, breach or no breach, it has been shown to have been made voluntarily. In the present case, Lord Widgery CJ was, without deciding the point, prepared to assume in the accused's favour that there *had* been a breach of r. 2, and then proceeded to consider whether its voluntary nature had nevertheless been established. In our judgment, no valid criticism of that approach can be made. On the contrary, it appears to us entirely sound.

It does not follow from the judgment of the Court of Appeal that a confession cannot be excluded unless the breach has led to a lack of voluntariness, or to the existence of oppressive circumstances; if this were so, consideration of the rules would be altogether otiose. Many of the provisions of the rules have nothing to do with potential questions of voluntariness or oppression. But the case does show that the legal question of admissibility is, indeed, overriding. The preamble to the rules makes the same point:

> The principle [that confessions must have been voluntary and obtained without oppression] is overriding and applicable in all cases. Within that principle the following rules are put forward as a guide to police officers conducting investigations. Non-conformity with these rules may render answers and statements liable to be excluded from evidence in subsequent criminal proceedings.

And in *R v May* (77), Lord Goddard CJ said:

75 [1972] 1 WLR 260.   76 Ibid at 265–6.
77 (1952) 36 Cr App R 91 at 93. See also *R v Sang* (HL) [1979] 3 WLR 263, per Lord Scarman at 288.

The test of the admissibility of a statement is whether it is a voluntary statement. There are certain rules known as the Judges' Rules which are not rules of law but rules of practice drawn up for the guidance of police officers; and if a statement has been made in circumstances not in accordance with the Rules, in law that statement is not made inadmissible if it is a voluntary statement, although in its discretion the court can always refuse to admit it if the court thinks there has been a breach of the Rules.

The document known in practice as the Judges' Rules consists in fact of four parts: (a) Appendix A, a note dealing with the history and general purpose of the rules; (b) The preamble (78), containing a statement of relevant rules of law within the framework of which the Judges' Rules operate; (c) The Judges' Rules themselves; and (d) Appendix B, containing various administrative directions to the police on interrogation and the taking of statements.

7.7.1   Appendix A: general note
This, as already stated, is historical and explanatory. It may be noted that the appendix disclaims for the rules any intention of dealing with or describing the 'many varieties of conduct which might render answers and statements involuntary and therefore inadmissible'.

7.7.2   The preamble
The preamble sets out five rules of law which are unaffected by the Judges' Rules. Of these, we have already seen that the most important, certainly from an evidential point of view, is that concerned with the admissibility of confessions, that is to say the principle that confessions must be shown to have been voluntary and obtained without oppression. This 'overriding' principle is placed, for emphasis, last in the list, and requires no further comment. The remainder of the preamble reads as follows:

These rules do not affect the principles:
(a)   That citizens have a duty to help a police officer to discover and apprehend offenders;
(b)   That police officers, otherwise than by arrest, cannot compel any person against his will to come to or remain in any police station;
(c)   That every person at any stage of an investigation should be able to communicate and to consult privately with a solicitor. This is so even if he is in custody provided that in such a case no unreasonable delay or hindrance is caused to the processes of investigation or the administration of justice by his doing so;
(d)   That when a police officer who is making inquiries of any person about an offence has enough evidence to prefer a charge against that person for the offence, he should without delay cause that person to be charged or informed that he may be prosecuted for the offence;
(e)   [Principles of admissibility]

Whatever the implications of these 'principles' for other purposes, it is necessary here only to comment upon them briefly in so far as they may affect the admission or exclusion of confessions. Principles (b) and (c) came to the attention of the Court of Appeal under

---

78   This section is not given a name in the document, and the term 'preamble' is here adopted purely for convenience.

striking circumstances in *R* v *Lemsatef* (79), in which the defendant was detained by officers of the Customs and Excise at about 12.40 a.m. in connection with suspected drugs offences, and was interrogated until 4.20 a.m. when he asked to see a solicitor, a request which was refused for reasons found by the Court to be wholly inadequate. Although the defendant's wife later instructed a solicitor, the solicitor was not permitted by the officers to see the defendant until 6.18 p.m. that day, by which time the defendant had made both oral and written confessions. The trial judge, treating the question as one of discretion, since he found the confessions to be voluntary and therefore admissible in law, allowed them to go before the jury. The Court of Appeal, while criticising in scathing terms the conduct of the officers in detaining the defendant without making it clear that he was under arrest, and in refusing him access to his solicitor without proper cause, found no reason to interfere with the judge's exercise of discretion, even though they proposed to allow the appeal on other grounds. It is difficult not to conclude from this decision that attempts to enforce principle (c) have failed. It would be hard to imagine a case more deserving of the exercise of discretion in favour of exclusion. It is to be hoped, however, that the following passages taken from the judgment of the court, delivered by Lawton LJ will nonetheless encourage some rejuvenation of judicial scrutiny in future cases (80):

The law is clear. Neither arrest nor detention can properly be carried out without the accused person being told the offence for which he is being arrested. There is no such offence as 'helping police with their inquiries'. This is a phrase which has crept into use, largely because of the need for the press to be careful about how they report what has happened when somebody has been arrested but not charged. If the idea is getting around amongst either Customs and Excise officers or police officers that they can arrest or detain people, as the case may be, for this particular purpose, the sooner they disabuse themselves of that idea, the better. . . .

If detaining or arresting officers are going to refuse to allow solicitors to advise a man under detention or arrest, it is no use their mouthing the words of the Judges' Rules: they must be prepared, if asked, to justify what they are doing. . . .

This court wishes to stress that it is not a good reason for refusing to allow a suspect, under arrest or detention to see his solicitor, that he has not made any oral or written admission.

Principle (d) has been held to be such that any breach of it will be a factor to be taken into account in deciding whether any confession made after such a breach was made voluntarily (81), but while this is clearly so, presumably it may also be considered on the question of discretion in a case where the confession is held to have been voluntary.

---

79 [1977] 1 WLR 812.
80 Ibid at 816–7. In *R* v *Allen* [1977] Crim LR 163, MacKenna J exercised his discretion to exclude a confession where the only reason advanced for refusing the defendant access to his solicitor was that he might be advised to remain silent. But in *R* v *Elliott* [1977] Crim LR 551, on similar if not stronger facts, Kilner Brown J took the opposite course. Hopes that some statutory rights might be conceded by the Criminal Law Act 1977 were not realised; s. 62 falls far short of such reform.
81 *R* v *Collier and Stenning* (CCA) [1965] 1 WLR 1470.

7.7.3   The Judges' Rules proper
Rule 1

When a police officer is trying to discover whether, or by whom, an offence has been committed he is entitled to question any person, whether suspected or not, from whom he thinks that useful information may be obtained. This is so whether or not the person in question has been taken into custody so long as he has not been charged with the offence or informed that he may be prosecuted for it.

This rule may in due course have to be recast somewhat in the light of the observations of the Court of Appeal in *R* v *Lemsatef,* which would tend to suggest that the officer's powers are rather more closely confined, unless he is prepared to make an arrest, or, of course, unless the defendant freely consents to answer in any event. There would seem to be no objection to a defendant, who is in custody in respect of an offence, being questioned with regard to other offences in respect of which he is not then in custody (82).

Rule 2

As soon as a police officer has evidence which would afford reasonable grounds for suspecting that a person has committed an offence, he shall caution that person or cause him to be cautioned before putting to him any questions, or further questions, relating to that offence.

The caution shall be in the following terms:

> 'You are not obliged to say anything unless you wish to do so, but what you say may be put into writing and given in evidence.'

When after being cautioned a person is being questioned, or elects to make a statement, a record shall be kept of the time and place at which any such questioning or statement began and ended and of the persons present.

The moment when it becomes appropriate to administer a rule 2 caution is not always easy to pin-point, even in retrospect, as must be attempted when the trial judge is invited to exercise his discretion in favour of exclusion of a confession because of the absence of a caution. It is, of course, often a matter of considerable difficulty for an officer in the course of an investigation. At what stage in the investigation of Coke's alleged rape of Margaret Blackstone should D/I Glanvil have administered a rule 2 caution? There are obviously a number of possibilities: immediately on arrival at Coke's flat; on finding the pieces of paper bearing writing, exhibit GG1; when Coke made his first incriminating reply at the police station? One sees from the inspector's deposition that he will say he decided to arrest and caution at the first possible opportunity. Coke's account is wholly different, in that he suggests that he was not cautioned until the stage of making his written statement under caution.

Despite some authority in older cases for the proposition that a rule 2 caution is required at the stage where the officer has some suspicion that the suspect has committed an offence, such a view would tend to dictate a caution at a very early stage, and is hardly supported by the use of the word 'evidence' in the rule itself. As Lord Devlin said in

---

82   *R* v *Buchan* (CCA) [1964] 1 WLR 365.

Shaaban bin Hussien and Others v *Chong Fook Kam and Another* (83), 'suspicion arises at or near the starting point of an investigation of which the obtaining of prima facie proof is the end'. The view that rule 2 comes into play at so early a stage was decisively rejected by the Court of Appeal in *R* v *Osbourne; R* v *Virtue* (84). The defendants were arrested on suspicion of robbery, and were interrogated without caution. At the time of the interrogation, the officer had no admissible evidence against the defendants, but had reason to suspect their involvement in the robbery. Later, evidence was forthcoming when the defendants were identified on an identification parade. It was necessary to determine the moment when a rule 2 caution should have been administered. The Court of Appeal was clearly of the view that the officer was under no obligation to caution until he had at least some admissible evidence, as opposed to mere suspicion, of the defendant's involvement in the offence. Lawton LJ said (85):

The first problem which arises in this case is what is meant by 'evidence' in this context.

It is important for the court to remind itself that the Judges' Rules are intended for the guidance of police officers. They have to comply with the rules. If a police officer looks at the rules and asks himself the question 'what do they mean?', he would answer in the light of his own police experience. In police experience, evidence means information which can be put before a court; . . .

There are other indications in the rules that that is the right way for them to be construed. The rules contemplate three stages in the investigation leading up to somebody being brought before a court for a criminal offence. The first is the gathering of information, and that can be gathered from anybody, including persons in custody provided they have not been charged. At the gathering of information stage, no caution of any kind need be administered. The final stage, the one contemplated by Rule III of the Judges' Rules, is when the police officer has got enough (and I stress the word 'enough') evidence to prefer a charge. That is clear from the introduction to the Judges' Rules which sets out the principle. But a police officer when carrying out an investigation meets a stage in between the mere gathering of information and the getting of enough evidence to prefer the charge. He reaches a stage where he has got the beginnings of evidence. It is at that stage that he must caution. In the judgment of this court, he is not bound to caution until he has got some information which he can put before the court as the beginnings of a case.

On this basis, one can perhaps see the force of the decision of D/I Glanvil to caution at once. His decision was no doubt assisted by the fact that he proposed to arrest Coke 'for raping Margaret Blackstone', and indeed since Margaret had already provided admissible and strong evidence against Coke, it is difficult to see that the inspector's decision could properly have been any different. If this evidence is to accepted, therefore, there has been a proper compliance with the rule. Of course, if Coke is right, and there was no caution until a much later stage, then a breach of rule 2 would have been clearly established, and the judge would have to consider whether he ought to exclude Coke's resulting oral confessions, if such they be. The judge would have to weigh the apparent lack of reason for the breach with the likelihood or otherwise of prejudice to Coke arising from the lack of caution.

83 (PC, Malaysia) [1970] AC 942 at 948. Although dealing with a point unconnected with the Judges' Rules, the advice of the Privy Council in this case, delivered by Lord Devlin, contains a most instructive analysis of the difference between suspicion and evidence.
84 [1973] QB 678.   85 Ibid at 687–8.

Rule 3

(a)   Where a person is charged with or informed that he may be prosecuted for an offence he shall be cautioned in the following terms:

> 'Do you wish to say anything? You are not obliged to say anything unless you wish to do so but whatever you say will be taken down in writing and may be given in evidence.'

(b)   It is only in exceptional cases that questions relating to the offence should be put to the accused person after he has been charged or informed that he may be prosecuted. Such questions may be put where they are necessary for the purpose of preventing or minimising harm or loss to some other person or to the public or for clearing up an ambiguity in a previous answer or statement.

Before any such questions are put the accused should be cautioned in these terms:

> 'I wish to put some questions to you about the offence with which you have been charged (or: about the offence for which you may be prosecuted). You are not obliged to answer any of these questions, but if you do the questions and answers will be taken down in writing and may be given in evidence.'

Any questions put and answers given relating to the offence must be contemporaneously recorded in full and the record signed by that person or if he refuses by the interrogating officer.

(c)   When such a person is being questioned, or elects to make a statement, a record shall be kept of the time and place at which any questioning or statement began and ended and of the persons present.

This rule governs the conduct of the third stage referred to by Lawton LJ in the passage from his judgment in *R* v *Osbourne; R* v *Virtue* cited above. Where the officer has sufficient evidence to warrant preferring an actual charge or informing a person that he may be prosecuted for an offence, it is a sound and salutary rule that no further interrogation should be permitted, except in the circumstances envisaged by the rule. 'Charged', for the purpose of rule 3, means formally charged with the offence (86). However, in *Conway* v *Hotten* (87), the defendant was told that he 'would be charged' with an offence and was invited to 'think about it', and it was held that what had been said had the same effect as the preferment of a formal charge, and that the subsequent interrogation of the defendant was a breach of rule 3. But the words 'informed that he may be prosecuted' refer only to a case where the defendant has not been arrested, and where the police contemplate the issue of a summons; it does not refer to a case where a suspect is arrested and where he may be charged after further consideration (88). The difference between being 'informed that he may be prosecuted' and what occurred in *Conway* v *Hotten* is that in the former situation, there is no question of any step by way of

86   *R* v *Brackenbury* [1965] 1 WLR 1475n; [1965] 1 All ER 960.
87   (DC) [1976] 2 All ER 213.
88   *R* v *Collier amd Stenning* (CCA) [1965] 1 WLR 1470, differing on this point from *R* v *Brackenbury* [1965] 1 WLR 1475n.

charge; the defendant is merely told that application will or may be made for summary process to issue out of and at the discretion of the court. In *Conway* v *Hotten,* the officer had unequivocally indicated his intention formally to charge the defendant within the near future, and because of the undoubted power of the police to cause this to be done, the charge was as inevitable and certain in the mind of the defendant as if it has already been preferred; the officer had committed himself to that course, and therefore to the third stage of his investigation.

Rule 4

This rule deals in detail with the procedure for taking written statements under caution. Although this procedure is extremely important in practice, it is too long and detailed to reproduce in full here. But the statement under caution is designed to enable a suspect to put in writing, as a formal record and under monitored conditions, what he wishes to say, and to do so in his own words. Such a statement under caution is almost always preferable as a piece of evidence to an oral statement, for exactly those reasons. If a statement under caution is tendered as a confession, having been taken in breach of rule 4 in any respect, then even if the judge is sure that it was made voluntarily, he may exclude it in the exercise of his discretion, following the usual rule. Coke made a statement under caution to the police, exhibit GG2, and this is given as an illustration of how the requirements of the rule are complied with habitually in practice. What is important is not so much by whom the physical act of writing the body of the statement was carried out, whether by Coke himself or by D/I Glanvil at his dictation, but that the statement should have been made in Coke's own words. For this reason, the circumstances under which the officer may ask questions during the taking of the statement are also closely controlled by the rule.

Rule 5

If at any time after a person has been charged with, or has been informed that he may be prosecuted for an offence a police officer wishes to bring to the notice of that person any written statement made by another person who in respect of the same offence has also been charged or informed that he may be prosecuted, he shall hand to that person a true copy of such written statement, but nothing shall be said or done to invite any reply or comment. If that person says that he would like to make a statement in reply, or starts to say something, he shall at once be cautioned or further cautioned as prescribed by rule 3(a).

The use of statements made by co-defendants or potential co-defendants causes a number of problems of practice. While a statement made by A, implicating both himself and B, is evidence against A, in so far as it amounts to a voluntary confession, it is not evidence against B. But if the statement of A implicates B, it may be both useful and fair to show B the statement at an early stage. There is an obvious danger that, if B makes some comment on or reply to the statement, which it is later sought to tender as a confession by B, such comment or reply will be unintelligible without reference to A's statement, which may in effect become incorporated into evidence against B. If B accepts the truth of what A says, then he adopts A's confession as his own, and there is no danger. But it is obvious that great care must be taken to see that a suspect does not, by some spontaneous and ill-judged reaction to what another has said about him, prejudice his case, and accordingly the use of statements by other suspects is closely controlled by this rule. Provided the rule is followed, such use may be made of statements, and it is often the fairest course to take where allegations are made by one against another. There could be no objection to Littleton being shown Coke's statement and allowed to read it, though he must be cautioned, and if he chose to say nothing, Coke's statement could not be evidence against Littleton for any purpose.

Rule 6

Persons other than police officers charged with the duty of investigating offences or charging offenders shall, so far as may be practicable, comply with these Rules.

The rules are intended to apply to professional investigators acting on behalf of a public body, be it the police, the Commissioners of Customs and Excise or any other body which has the duty of investigating or prosecuting offences. It has been held that the rules do not bind foreign police officers questioning a suspect in England about charges that are intended to be the basis of an application for extradition from England to stand trial abroad (89). The rules do, however, apply to professional investigators employed by private persons or concerns for the purpose of investigation and prosecution, for example store detectives (90) and security officers (91). The meaning of the words 'so far as may be practicable' is unclear, but they would appear to refer to the fact that professional facilities outside the ranks of the police or similar bodies may be inadequate to permit the literal observation of the rules in all respects. Where they are not observed for such a reason, the trial judge may have to consider whether the defendant has been prejudiced, and whether the investigator has done all that could reasonably be expected of him in the circumstances.

7.7.4 The administrative directions

The last part of the document known as the Judges' Rules is a set of administrative directions to the police, concerned with interrogation and the taking of statements in particular respects. Most of the content of the directions is purely regulatory and of no significance in relation to the law of evidence, and the directions are not reproduced here. It should be noted, however, that they do contain important guidelines for the interrogation of and the taking of statements from children and young persons, and foreigners speaking in their native language. Failure to observe the directions may well have a bearing on whether any resulting confession can be shown to be voluntary. The provisions for affording a suspect reasonable comfort and refreshment may also be significant, particularly where it is subsequently alleged that a statement was not voluntary or should be excluded in the exercise of the judge's discretion because of some temporary disability to which the defendant was subject which might have been overcome by reasonable means, or because of some permanent disability which might have been compensated for by taking a statement in a certain way. In *R* v *Davis* (92) the trial judge excluded, in the exercise of his discretion, a confession made by a defendant, the reliability of which was in doubt because of the possibility that he was still affected by a

89   *R* v *Governor of Ashford Remand Centre, ex parte Beese* (DC) [1973] 1 WLR 969.
90   Though not other employees of the store: *R* v *Nichols* (CA) (1967) 51 Cr App R 233.
91   *R* v *Fallon* [1975] Crim LR 341.
92   [1979]Crim LR 167; cf the unsuccessful attempt to exclude made in *R* v *Isequilla* [1975] 1 WLR 716.

dose of the drug pethidine, administered some hours previously. The obtaining of medical aid or refreshment, the mere lapse of time, the procuring of some person qualified to help a suspect to express himself, or even the securing of the presence of some member of a suspect's family may be enough to show a voluntary statement, and these steps are all plainly within the spirit, if not the letter, of the directions.

7.8 Challenging confessions as a question of fact

Like any other evidence, the circumstances or contents of a confession may be disputed as a question of fact. In other words, as in Coke's case, a defendant may dispute that he made a confession at all, or that what he did say has been properly and accurately recorded (93); or he may allege that the circumstances in which he made the confession are quite different from those related by the officer. We have already seen that a defendant may dispute, as a matter of law, the admissibility of a confession. This is a matter for the judge to determine in the absence of the jury. The defendant may also invite the judge, similarly a matter of law to be decided in the absence of the jury, to exclude the confession in the exercise of his discretion. If the judge decides, at this stage, that the confession should be admitted, because he holds it to be voluntary and made without oppression, and because there are no circumstances warranting the exercise of the discretion to exclude, the result is that the confession may be proved in the presence of the jury and becomes evidence in the case for them to consider. But the weight to be attached to the confession is a question of fact for the jury, and although the jury are not concerned with voluntariness or oppression as such, it is both proper and necessary for the defence to raise in front of the jury the allegations which they make about the confession. Those allegations, having been relevant to the issue of law of admissibility, are equally relevant at a later stage to the weight, if any, to be accorded to the confession. If the jury think that the defendant may not have made the confession at all, or may not have made the confession in the way alleged, or that the confession may have been obtained other than by an exercise of the defendant's free will, then the admissibility of the confession will not matter; the jury will accord it little or no weight, and will not act on it to convict. Another good reason for renewing the defence case in front of the jury is that should further evidence come to light, even at that late stage, from which the judge may infer that his earlier ruling was wrong, he may reconsider it and withdraw the confession from the jury (94).

Counsel for Coke may make, as it were, a three-pronged attack on the oral and written confessions related by D/I Glanvil. He may (a) dispute admissibility, (b) invite the exercise of the discretion to exclude; and if unsuccessful (c) attack the inspector's evidence as an issue of fact in front of the jury. Each of these prongs of the attack involves putting Coke's case and, probably, his giving evidence of what occurred at the police station. There is nothing inconsistent in his disputing the admissibility of, or inviting the judge to exclude, the alleged oral confession ('Yes, I may as well . . .') while later maintaining as a question of fact, if it is admitted, that he never said those words.

---

93   Usually, though not inevitably, such allegations will involve an imputation on the character of the officer concerned, because they suggest fabrication of evidence; this, subject to the judge's discretion, will expose the defendant to cross-examination under s. 1 (*f*)(ii) of the Criminal Evidence Act 1898 should he later give evidence before the jury: see 4.12, ante.

94   *R v Watson* (CA) [1980] 2 All ER 293. Ordinarily, this will result in the discharge of the jury and an order for a new trial, because of the risk of prejudice to the defendant arising from the jury's having been exposed to inadmissible evidence. But in his discretion, the judge may decide to continue and give the jury a strongly worded warning in the summing-up, particularly if the confession would in any event have carried little weight.

The question of admissibility must be judged on the footing that it was said. If the confession is ruled to be admissible but the jury do not accept that it was then they will disregard it. Coke may, with complete consistency, adopt each of the three methods of attack, or any or all of them, and in view of the nature of his case, it seems inevitable that he would combine them in the circumstances of the present case. As to the written confession, Coke may raise the circumstances in which he says it was obtained, firstly so as to dispute its admissibility, and secondly, if it is admitted, to suggest to the jury that no weight should be accorded to it.

7.9   Practice: proof of confessions

The practice relating to the proof of confessions may be conveniently summarised as follows, bearing in mind the points made in the preceding paragraphs.

(a)   If admissibility of the confession is not in dispute, it may be opened to and proved before the jury; its weight is then a matter of fact for them.

(b)   If admissibility is disputed, or if the defence intend to invite the judge to exclude the confession in the exercise of his discretion, counsel for the defence should inform counsel for the prosecution of this intention at the outset of the trial, and the confession should not be opened to the jury or referred to in their presence. At the moment when the subject arises naturally for the first time in evidence (95), the jury should be asked to withdraw, and the questions of law are then resolved by the judge in a 'trial within a trial', properly known as the 'voire dire' (96). The procedure on the voire dire is that the prosecution (on whom, it will be recalled, the burden of proof lies) call the evidence that the confession was made voluntarily, and this is open to cross-examination. The defendant is entitled to give evidence in his turn, if he wishes. He may be cross-examined. He may call witnesses. Counsel then address the judge.

It is necessary to add one or two words concerning evidence given by the defendant on the voire dire, because of the decision of the Privy Council in *Wong Kam Ming* v *R* (97) which has clarified (albeit not entirely happily) various matters of practice which had previously been obscure. The defendant was charged with murder and malicious wounding arising from a violent attack by a group of men against a massage parlour in Hong Kong, for which the motive was apparently revenge. The only evidence against him was his own confession in writing that he had been present at the scene of the attack, and had 'chopped' someone with a knife. As a result of an objection by the defence, heard on the voire dire, the trial judge held the statement to be inadmissible and excluded it. But in the course of giving evidence on the voire dire, the defendant had been asked in cross-examination whether the contents of his statement were in fact true, and had admitted that he had been present and that he had played some part in the attack. The Crown applied for, and were given, leave to prove before the jury the defendant's admissions on the voire dire, and later, when the defendant gave evidence before the jury, to cross-examine him with regard to discrepancies between his evidence in front of the jury and his evidence on the voire dire. It fell to the Privy Council to answer three

95   If the opening cannot be made intelligible without the confession, e.g. because it is the only evidence, the matter may be dealt with as a preliminary point.
96   Sometimes found in the form 'voir dire', and deriving from the proper form of oath for the decision of secondary issues. In magistrates' courts, the Bench must determine the issue, and, if they exclude the confession, dismiss it from their minds. This is a formidable problem of summary procedure which often results in the defence forgoing the legal issue, and limiting their challenge to the factual issue of weight.
97   [1980] AC 247.

principal questions: (a) may the defendant properly be asked, on the voire dire, whether the contents of his confession are true? (b) may the prosecution prove, as part of their case before the jury, incriminating evidence given by the defendant on the voire dire? and (c) may the prosecution cross-examine the defendant in front of the jury with regard to his previous inconsistent evidence on the voire dire? The first two of these questions carried the subsidiary questions, whether, if the answer to the principal question was in the affirmative, any judicial discretion lay to exclude such evidence. To the first two questions, the first by a majority (98), the second unanimously, the Privy Council gave the answer no; to the third, unanimously, they answered, 'only if the confession has been admitted after the voire dire'. The two subsdiary questions, therefore, did not require an answer.

There are a number of practical criticisms which may be made of the decision. On the first question, while as the majority held, the trial judge is not concerned on the voire dire with the truth of the confession, but only with its admissibility, it is often relevant to enquire whether the confession is true, simply because this may affect the issue of how it came to be made. Did the defendant involuntarily or while under oppression invent a pack of lies, or blurt out the truth? If it is alleged (as it often is) that the words of the confession are those, not of the defendant, but of the officer, does the confession contain some element of truth which the officer could not then have known? In *R v Hammond* (99) the Court of Criminal Appeal expressly sanctioned cross-examination of a defendant concerning the truth of a confession alleged not to be voluntary, although it was there put on the less satisfactory basis that such questions went to credit. On the second question, while some rule of policy may be thought to protect the defendant from having exposed to the jury what he has said on the voire dire, it is not entirely clear why the interests of justice may require the jury to be kept in ignorance, and perhaps to acquit in ignorance of the fact that the defendant has admitted on oath during the trial that the whole or part of the case against him is true. Certainly, the position on the voire dire must, if it is the correct position, for some reason be different from that with regard to other forms of judicial confession. The answer to the third question is perhaps the strangest of all. It is not easy to see how the answer can be reconciled with the fact that counsel for the prosecution is entitled by statute (100) to cross-examine the defendant with regard to previous statements made by him inconsistent with his evidence before the jury.

(c)   If the confession is excluded, then it may not be referred to in the presence of the jury for any purpose (101). If it is held to be admissible then, as we have seen, it will be proved in the presence of the jury and may be challenged in any way. The jury are not concerned with any question of 'voluntariness' and should not be directed in such terms (102) but may consider all matters affecting the weight of the confession, which is entirely a question of fact for them.

98   Lords Diplock, Salmon; Edmund Davies and Keith; Lord Hailsham of St Marylebone dissenting.
99   (CCA) [1941] 3 All ER 318. The majority view of the Privy Council in *Wong Kam Ming* was that this case should be 'treated as overruled'.
100   Criminal Procedure Act 1865, s. 4. In *Wong Kam Ming,* the Privy Council was concerned with a provision of the Hong Kong Evidence Ordinance to the same effect.
101   *R v Treacy* (CCA) [1944] 2 All ER 229.
102   *Chan Wei Keung v R* (PC, Hong Kong) [1967] 2 AC 160; *R v Ovenell; R v Walter A. Cartwright Ltd* [1969] (CA) 1 QB 17.

7.10   Practice: use of confessions

7.10.1   Against the maker
A confession, proved as an exception to the rule against hearsay, is admitted as evidence
of the truth of the matters adverse to the defendant contained therein. It may, if the jury
think it right, be relied upon to convict, even in the absence of other evidence. As Erle J
said in *R* v *Baldry* (103), a 'confession . . . well proved . . . is the best evidence that can be
produced'. Because the weight of a confession is a question of fact, the Court of Appeal
will rarely interfere with a conviction based upon such evidence, even where it is
unsupported. The general principle, although from time to time subjected to sceptical
judicial comment, has fairly recently been restated by the Court of Appeal (104).
However, where the terms of the confession are such that no reasonable jury could safely
draw the necessary inference of guilt from it, the conviction may be quashed as being
unsafe and unsatisfactory; this may occur where the defendant's words are wholly
ambiguous, as where he merely says in answer to an allegation, 'All right', which may
amount to no more than acknowledgement that it has been made, or as in *R* v *Schofield*
(105), 'Just my luck', which may indicate no more than an expression of dismay at being
wrongly suspected. The confession should, it is submitted, be clear and compelling
before a jury are invited to act on it, unsupported, to convict, but if it is so, then it must
be left to them on that basis.

7.10.2   Editing of confessions
Confessions are subject to the rule regarding admissions generally that the whole
statement must be put before the court, to be looked at as a whole and in context. This
means that where a statement is partly adverse to, and partly favourable to, the
defendant, he is entitled to have both parts placed before the jury, although this may
cause problems of evidential value which are considered in para 7.11, post. But there are
occasions when confessions must be placed before the jury in an 'edited' form, in order
to prevent the jury from being exposed to prejudicial and inadmissible material. When a
confession is made, it is important that it should be recorded in the defendant's words,
exactly as it is made. Frequently, confessions contain some allusion to the defendant's
bad character. The answer said to have been given by Coke, when invited to tell D/I
Glanvil what had happened, 'Yes, I may as well. With form for the same thing, I reckon
I'm going down for a while. Will you write a statement for me?' is not an uncommon
example. Clearly, the jury are entitled to hear what Coke said to the inspector, but any
probative value in the allusion to his previous conviction, in the context of his confession,
is more than outweighed by the prejudicial effect which the answer might have in the
minds of the jury. The answer should, therefore, be edited to omit the offending
passage, provided that this can be done without doing a fatal degree of violence to the
sense (in which case the judge may have to exclude altogether). The inspector should,
therefore, be asked (before giving evidence) to limit his account of the answer to 'Yes, I
may as well . . . Will you write a statement for me?' or, arguably, to those words and 'I
reckon I'm going down for a while', but certainly omitting the reference to 'form for the
same thing'. If this is not done, and the inadmissible and prejudicial part is given in

103   (CCR) (1852) 1 Den CC 430.
104   In *R* v *Mallinson* [1977] Crim LR 161; but see the observations of Cave J in *R* v *Thompson* [1893] 2 QB 12
at 18.
105   (1917) 12 Cr App R 191.

evidence, the conviction will almost certainly be quashed (106). With a written confession, the same principle applies, and edited copies of the statement should be produced for the use of the jury, with no marks of editing (107).

7.10.3 Confessions implicating co-defendants

At common law, it is a fundamental principle of the use of admissions and confessions that an admission or confession is evidence against the maker of the confession only, and not against any other person implicated by it. This is a rule applicable to statements made in all circumstances by way of admission, including a plea of guilty in the face of the court. It is sometimes said that the co-defendant may make the statement evidence against him if he is present when it is made, and does not dissent from it, or adopts it as his own. However, this is an apparent exception only, in that if, on the whole of the evidence, the jury think that the co-defendant has adopted what was said, then it is in reality his own confession and no longer merely that of the maker of the statement. The rule has no exception at common law; a confession is inadmissible hearsay against all but the maker of it. This is ,of course, in stark contrast to the position when a defendant gives evidence from the witness-box in the course of the trial, when, like any other evidence, what he says is evidence in the case for all purposes, whether or not it implicates the co-defendant. In the light of the reference to Littleton by Coke in his statement under caution, the implications of the rule must be carefully examined in their case.

The rule involves important difficulties of practice. Confessions by one defendant implicating another are one of the hazards of joint trial, which must be accepted. The mere fact that the situation arises is no ground, in itself, for separate trials. Where defendants are jointly charged they should ordinarily be tried together. In *R* v *Lake* (108) the defendant and two others were charged with conspiracy to burgle. Both co-defendants made statements to the police which implicated Lake very seriously in the offence. Despite the risk of prejudice arising from the volume of inadmissible material against Lake, the Court of Appeal refused to interfere with the decision of the trial judge to refuse an application for separate trial. But the Court of Appeal recognised that there would be exceptional cases, where the probative value of a confession is very considerable against the maker, while the prejudicial effect is equally considerable against the co-defendant, where such an order may be necessary.

Frequently, the problem can be solved, or at least minimised by editing. This course is not always available, because both the prosecution and the maker of the statement may have reasons for wanting the whole statement to go to the jury. If A says that B was wholly or partly to blame, this may in some cases be cogent evidence against A. But where the reference to B is of little or no significance to the case against A, the judge can and should order A's statement to be edited (109).

What is vital, in any case where A's statement implicates his co-defendant B, is that

---

106   However, the rule is one of practice, rather than law. If the defendant makes an incriminating reply to an allegation put to him, it is probably admissible in strict law, even though it would tend to expose some aspect of his character; and in *Turner* v *Underwood* (DC) [1948] 2 KB 284, a reply in terms similar to Coke's was held to have been properly admitted as a matter of law. But the court emphasised that as a matter of almost invariable practice, it should be excluded, at least in jury cases. (*Turner* v *Underwood* was an appeal from a magistrates' court.) In *R* v *Knight and Thompson* (1946) 31 Cr App R 52, a conviction on indictment was quashed because of a failure to edit out details of previous convictions, and it is submitted that this must be correct in almost every case.

107   This is sometimes said to involve a degree of deception of the jury, but in reality is no more so than the exclusion of any other evidence on legal grounds. The practice enjoys the clear sanction and approval of the courts: see *R* v *Weaver; R* v *Weaver* (CA) [1968] 1 QB 353.

108   (1976) 64 Cr App R 172; and see the observations of the Court of Appeal in *R* v *Josephs and Christie* (1977) 65 Cr App R 253.

109   See, e.g., *R* v *Rogers and Tarran* [1971] Crim LR 413.

the judge should direct the jury that the statement is evidence against A only and not against B. Whether juries succeed in this exercise in mental gymnastics is a moot point, but they are frequently assisted by the observation that it is clearly unfair to hold against B a statement made in his absence by A, who may have his own reasons for implicating B, and to which B had no chance of replying. Be that as it may, the absence of a clear direction on the point will be fatal to B's conviction (110). The statement cannot be evidence against B for any purpose. In *R* v *Dibble* (111) this applied even where A offered to give evidence for the prosecution against B, was treated as hostile and cross-examined on his statement. A's statement implicated B, but was evidence going only to A's credit, and the failure of the trial judge to direct the jury not to regard it as evidence against B was fatal to B's conviction.

7.10.4   *Evidence yielded by information contained in confessions*
Confessions are often useful to the prosecution for reasons other than the possibility of tendering them as evidence in themselves. It may be that as a result of information supplied in the confession, the police are enabled to obtain further evidence, for example the recovery of stolen goods or the discovery of a body. Such evidence is, of course, direct and admissible. But where the confession is at the trial held to be inadmissible, a problem does arise which has been accorded in the textbooks more attention than it probably deserves. The problem is simply whether the evidence thus yielded is 'tainted' by the inadmissiblity of the confession, and ought itself to be excluded, or whether its existence as direct evidence independently of the confession dictates that it should be admissible.

There are cases where the evidence, while ostensibly independent of the confession, is in reality so bound up with it that the two must stand or fall together. Such a case was *R* v *Barker* (112) where, because of inducements held out by officers of the Inland Revenue, the defendant produced books which contained evidence of fraud. The defendant's actual confession of fraud was excluded because of the inducements, but it was argued, that the books were admissible in their own right. It was held that the books were part and parcel of the confession, produced solely for the purpose of explaining and amplifying the confession, and could not be admitted.

But in the ordinary case, evidence of an independent discovery will be admissible. The difficulty is one of communication more than anything else, because it is obviously important that the jury should hear no reference to an inadmissible confession, yet without hearing of the confession, the discovery may be difficult to understand. It may be doubted whether the problem is any greater than the commonly accepted one of the 'gap' in the jury's information caused by the operation of the hearsay rule, when evidence is given by an officer of what he did after 'information received'. In both cases, the jury are faced with a gap in the evidence, but usually it is not important. Ordinarily, the independent evidence will be admitted, and this has been the rule at least since *R* v *Warickshall* (113), when the finding of stolen goods as a result of an inadmissible confession was received in evidence. The court held that the test was that the independent evidence should be capable of being 'fully and satisfactorily' proved without reference to the confession, and this seems to be correct today. The trial judge has, presumably, power to exclude where it seems that admission would inevitably reveal something

---

110   *R* v *Gunewardene* (CCA) [1951] 2 KB 600.   111   (CCA) (1908) 1 Cr App R 155.
112   (CCA) [1941] 2 KB 381. It will be recalled that the actual result of this case (though not the principle) was reversed by statute: see 7.5, ante.
113   (1783) 1 Leach 263.

of the confession to the jury. It was suggested in *R* v *Gould* (114) that the part of the confession which related to the yielding of the evidence could be isolated from the remainder, and could be received to explain the independent evidence, but such a course would seem unsatisfactory and has since been rejected (115).

There would be little point in proving that, by reason of an inadmissible confession, a fruitless search was made, and such evidence was held to be inadmissible in *R* v *Jenkins* (116). It has never been decided whether, if the defendant makes a confession indicating for example that stolen goods are to be found in a certain place and after search, those goods are discovered in a different place, evidence of such discovery will be admissible. It is difficult to think of any coherent reason for exclusion, given that the jury should not be told what the defendant said in his confession, in any event.

7.11 Partly adverse statements

It happens very frequently that a defendant will make a written or oral statement which, while partly adverse to his case, also contains exculpatory or self-serving passages. We have already seen that the whole of the statement must in general go to the jury, and that the weight of the statement as a confession is a matter of fact for the jury. The latter proposition involves the further conclusion that it is for the jury to say whether the statement tendered amounts to a confession at all. Unless it does, the jury will not act on it as evidence against the defendant. But the undoubtedly proper admission of entire statements also involves a problem of evidential value in criminal cases, in that self-serving statements are not evidence of the truth of the facts contained in them, whereas confessions are so (117).

The rules which have been developed for the treatment of partly adverse statements are consistent and logical, but their appeal to juries as a matter of common sense must be open to considerable doubt. If the prosecution tender as a confession a statement containing both adverse and exculpatory passages, the jury will look at the statement as a whole and decide whether, taken as a whole, it constitutes a confession, and if it does, what weight it should be given. For this purpose, the defence are entitled to suggest that the exculpatory passages qualify or nullify those parts which appear to be adverse. Thus, in *R* v *McGregor* (118) where the prosecution, at a retrial, proved, as part of their case, statements made in evidence by the defendant at the first trial, the defendant was entitled to bring to the attention of the jury those passages in the same evidence which were consistent with his case on the retrial, and the jury were then to consider the defendant's alleged admission as a whole. But as the defendant did not give evidence at the retrial, the exculpatory passages in his previous statement in evidence at the first trial were not verified on oath before the jury, and had not been tested before them in cross-examination, and it was therefore natural that the jury should give more weight to the adverse passages, and conclude that, read as a whole, the defendant's evidence at the first trial amounted to a confession.

In addition to qualifying or nullifying apparently adverse passages, exculpatory passages may also be relevant as showing the defendant's reaction when first taxed with the offence, or indeed, when taxed with it at any stage. It would, therefore, be a misdirection to suggest to the jury that exculpatory passages have no value as evidence. But in a

114 (1840) 9 C & P 364.   115 See, e.g., *R* v *Berriman* (1854) 6 Cox CC 388.   116 (1822) Russ & Ry 492.
117 In civil cases, s. 2 of the Civil Evidence Act 1968 is wide enough to admit self-serving statements as evidence of the truth of the facts stated in them, so that, except in relation to weight, the problem is avoided.
118 [1968] 1 QB 371.

criminal case, what the jury cannot do is to regard a statement or passage consistent with the defence as evidence of the truth of the facts stated. In *R* v *Storey; R* v *Anwar* (119), where the prosecution made out a prima facie case of possession of cannabis by the defendant, who did not give evidence, she could not rely upon a statement made by her to the police, consistent with innocence, in order to sustain a submission of no case to answer. No criticism could, therefore, be made of a passage in the summing-up to the effect that the statement could not prove the truth of the matters contained in it which might (if proved on oath) have assisted the defence.

From these cases may be derived the proper approach to partly adverse statements, which was expressed by James LJ in *R* v *Donaldson; R* v *Watson; R* v *Reed* (120) in the following terms;

> In our view there is a clear distinction to be made between statements of admission adduced by the Crown as part of the case against the defendant and statements made entirely of a self-serving nature made and sought to be relied upon by a defendant. When the Crown adduce a statement relied upon as an admission it is for the jury to consider the whole statement including any passages that contain qualifications or explanations favourable to the defendant, that bear upon the passages relied upon by the prosecution as an admission, and it is for the jury to decide whether the statement viewed as a whole constitutes an admission. To this extent, the statement may be said to be evidence of the facts stated therein. . . .
>
> When the Crown adduce evidence in the form of a statement by the defendant which is not relied on as an admission of the offence charged such a statement is evidence in the trial in that it is evidence that the defendant made the statement and of his reaction which is part of the general picture which the jury have to consider but it is not evidence of facts stated.

The court held that the trial judge had been guilty of a misdirection, in directing the jury that a statement made by the defendant could be evidence only in so far as it amounted to an admission. It might be thought suprising at first sight that statements which are not relied upon as admissions should be adduced by the prosecution at all, except perhaps in the case where the prosecution allege that the defendant has in the statement given a false account, albeit one consistent with innocence, so that the making of such a statement is in itself evidence against him. But whatever the theoretical position is on admitting statements which do no more than show reaction or form 'part of the general picture', it is now well established as a matter of practice that the jury should be told and should assess whatever the defendant may say when taxed with the offence. In *R* v *Pearce* (121), the defendant made two written statements consistent with his case, when interviewed on two consecutive days. The statements were excluded by the trial judge on the ground that they were made after consultation between the defendant and his solicitor, could not therefore be said to be evidence of the defendant's reaction when taxed with the offence, and accordingly had no evidential value. The Court of Appeal held that the exclusion had been wrong. The rule was not confined to evidence of the defendant's reaction when first taxed, although the later the statement, the less likely it will be to command any real weight. The court added, somewhat mysteriously, that a statement might properly be excluded where it was made for the purpose of becoming

119   (CA) (1968) 52 Cr App R 334.   120   (CA) (1976) 64 Cr App R 59 at 65.
121   [1979] Crim LR 658.

part of the prosecution case, and as 'a deliberate attempt to infiltrate the prosecution case'.

The proper direction to the jury, therefore, is one which will surely sound strange and is difficult to justify in terms of common sense: it is that the whole statement must be considered in assessing whether it is to be regarded as a confession; if so, the adverse parts of the statement are evidence against the defendant of the facts stated in them; any parts consistent with the defence (or the whole of a self-serving statement) may be evidence of the defendant's reaction, and of the 'general picture', but not of the facts stated in them.

C: STATEMENTS IN THE PRESENCE OF THE DEFENDANT

7.12   Principles of admissibility

Where statements relevant to the issues in a case are made in the presence of a party, such statements may be admitted in order to explain the reaction of that party to the statements or, if the party accepts or adopts the truth of the statements, as part of any adverse admission made by him. The rule applies at common law to civil and criminal cases alike, but has lost its identity in civil cases because of the breadth of s. 2 of the Civil Evidence Act 1968. The critical area of the rule, in modern practice, lies in the treatment of statements made by way of taxing the defendant with the offence charged in criminal cases. The practice of interrogation is, of course, based upon putting to the defendant allegations, and therefore the repetition to him of hearsay statements, in order to elicit his reaction to them. If the defendant acknowledges the truth of such allegations, they merge into his confession, and no separate problem of the admissibility of the allegations will arise. But difficulties do present themselves where the defendant denies the allegations, or remains silent.

7.12.1   The defendant's denials

Where the defendant denies the allegations put to him, although as a matter of law the statements remain admissible for the limited purpose of showing his reaction, they gain no further force from what the defendant says, and in some cases, because of the risk, of prejudice, it may be right to exclude the interrogation altogether. Otherwise, the prosecution may in effect be permitted to put before the jury the substance of their case in a hearsay form, which would plainly be inadmissible in any other circumstances unless the defendant accepted its truth. An interrogation consisting of a series of hearsay allegations, followed by the defendant's denial of each seriatim is of no evidential value to the prosecution (or, on the present state of the law, to the defence, except as evidence of consistency) but may be prejudicial to the defence. It does not follow that this will always be the case, because it may be that the prosecution are entitled to rely upon the manner of the denial, for example where the defendant gives a demonstrably untrue explanation which, though on the face of it consistent with innocence, becomes incriminating when disproved. The trial judge may in some cases have to hear argument, or decide the question on the voire dire.

There is clear authority that, as a matter of practice, statements made in the defendant's presence should be excluded if, in the opinion of the judge, there is no material on which the jury could properly find that the defendant accepted the truth of what was being put to him, and accordingly adopted the allegations by the way of confession. If the jury may properly draw that conclusion, then it must be left to them as a question of fact. In *R* v *Norton* (122) the conviction was quashed when a hearsay statement was narrated to the jury, there being no evidence that the defendant had in any way accepted it, and the soundness of the general proposition was accepted by the House of Lords in *R* v *Christie* (123). The defendant was charged with indecent assault on a small boy. The boy was called to give evidence unsworn, but although he described the assault, he did not speak to the fact that shortly afterwards, he had identified the defendant to his mother and a police officer. The mother and the officer were called to give evidence of the identification, and the evidence was that when confronted in this way, the defendant said, 'I am innocent' — an account which he maintained from first to last. One of the matters canvassed on appeal was that the boy's statement should have been excluded in view of the reaction of the defendant to it. Ultimately, the House determined to quash the conviction because of a misdirection on corroboration, but the argument mentioned drew some sympathy. Lord Reading said (124):

> In general, such evidence can have little or no value in its direct bearing on the case unless the accused, upon hearing the statement, by conduct and demeanour, or by the answer made by him, or in certain circumstances by the refraining from an answer, acknowledged the truth of the statement either in whole or in part, or did or said something from which the jury could infer such an acknowledgement, for if he acknowledged its truth, he accepted it as his own statement of the facts.

Lord Moulton referred to the rule of exclusion, in the absence of some evidence of acceptance by the defendant, as 'a practice of a very salutary nature', and indicated that the hearsay statement could have no evidential value unless somehow adopted (125).

As a matter of practice, it will be apparent that in many cases there will be no risk of prejudice simply because there is other, direct evidence of the nature of the prosecution's allegations, and for the jury to hear it repeated with a denial can do no real harm; indeed, the evidence of consistency with the defence offered at trial may actually assist the defendant. But where there is no direct evidence, or no direct evidence of that precise kind, or where the jury may be misled into looking for corroboration where it cannot exist, the risk is very great. Even where this risk is not present, if the allegations are numerous or very grave, there is some danger that the jury may unconsciously adopt them as fact. In all such cases, and where there is any possibility of prejudice, it is submitted that such hearsay evidence is better excluded (126).

7.12.2   The defendant's silence

If statements made in the defendant's presence should be excluded as mere hearsay, unless there is evidence from which it can be inferred that the defendant acknowledged the truth of the allegations contained in them, it would seem to follow that it should only be in exceptional circumstances that the defendant's silence should be held to constitute an acknowledgement of the kind required. The caution prescribed by r. 2 of the Judges' Rules serves, not to create a right which the defendant did not previously enjoy, but to remind him of the right which he enjoys at every stage of an investigation. The principle

---

122   (CCA) [1910] 2 KB 496.
123   [1914] AC 545.   124   Ibid at 565.
125   Ibid at 559–60. See also per Lord Atkinson at 553–4.
126   For an instance of extreme prejudice, see *R* v *Taylor* (CA) [1978] Crim LR 92; and cf Judges' Rules, r. 5.

was applied in *Hall* v *R* (127), where the defendant was charged with possession of a controlled drug. The evidence against him was that, the drug having been found on premises which he occupied jointly with others, but not in his room, he was told by an officer that another defendant had said that the drug belonged to him, and that the defendant made no reply to this allegation. The Privy Council held that the defendant's conviction could not be sustained. Lord Diplock said (128):

> It is a clear and widely known principle of the common law . . . that a person is entitled to refrain from answering a question put to him for the purpose of discovering whether he has committed a criminal offence. A fortiori he is under no obligation to comment when he is informed that someone else has accused him of an offence. It may be that in very exceptional circumstances an inference may be drawn from a failure to give an explanation or a disclaimer, but in their Lordships' view silence alone on being informed by a police officer that someone else has made an accusation against him cannot give rise to an inference that the person to whom this information is communicated accepts the truth of the accusation. . . .
>
> The caution merely serves to remind the accused of a right which he already possesses at common law. The fact that in a particular case he has not been reminded of it is no ground for inferring that his silence was not in exercise of that right, but was an acknowledgement of the truth of the accusation.

Lord Diplock's reference to 'very exceptional circumstances', in which silence might be held to constitute some form of admission may have been based on what Cave J had said in *R* v *Mitchell* (129), although *Mitchell* may not have been cited in argument in *Hall*. It is important to put the dictum of Cave J into context. The defendant in *Mitchell* was charged with procuring a miscarriage by unlawful means, and so causing the death of the woman concerned. A statement made by the deceased woman was held not to be admissible as a dying declaration, and the taking of her deposition by a magistrate had to be stopped when the deceased became too ill to continue, and before the defendant's solicitor had had any opportunity to cross-examime her; it was accordingly inadmissible in evidence, as it might have been by statute if completed. It was sought to admit what there was of the deposition as a statement made in the presence of the defendant. Cave J rejected the attempt, holding that the defendant, who was legally represented, could not reasonably have been expected to make any reply in the circumstances. Against that background, the learned judge said:

> Now the whole admissibility of statements of this kind rests upon the consideration that if a charge is made against a person in that person's presence, it is reasonable to expect that he or she will immediately deny it, and that the absence of such a denial is some evidence of an admission on the part of the person charged, and of the truth of the charge. Undoubtedly, when persons are speaking on even terms and a charge is made, and the person charged says nothing, and expresses no indignation, and does nothing to repel the charge, that is some evidence to show that he admits the charge to be true.

The important emphases in this dictum are firstly, the circumstance that the defendant and his accuser should have been 'on even terms', and secondly, that it must have been

127 (PC, Jamaica) [1971] 1 WLR 298.   128 Ibid at 301.   129 (1892) 17 Cox CC 503 at 508.

reasonable to expect some reaction, in the way of indignation or refutation of the charge. It seems that what Cave J must have had in mind was a situation where some spontaneous accusation was made, to which some reply was available which, on the basis that the defendant was innocent, might naturally have been expected by way of spontaneous riposte. In such a context, the principle seems unobjectionable, and indeed has been applied in cases where its use could hardly be questioned (130). But it fits uneasily in more modern times into the context of a formal interview between defendant and police officer, where more mature consideration has supervened upon the heat of the moment. It is tempting to add that the dictum seems to fit especially uneasily where the defendant has been cautioned, but remembering the words of Lord Diplock in *Hall,* that the caution is a reminder, not a creator, of the right of silence, perhaps this should not, of itself, matter. Nonetheless, in *R v Chandler* (131), the Court of Appeal applied the dictum to just such a case. The 'even terms' were said to result from the fact that the defendant was in the company of his solicitor when interviewed. But even on the basis that this may produce even terms within the meaning of the dictum, it is difficult to see that the situation could have been such that the defendant might reasonably have been expected to seek to rebut the charge. Indeed, the facts of *R v Mitchell* and the decision of Cave J on those facts, seem to suggest exactly the opposite. Lawton LJ said (132):

> Some comment on the defendant's lack of frankness before he was cautioned was justified provided the jury's attention was directed to the right issue, which was whether in the circumstances the defendant's silence amount to an acceptance by him of what the detective sergeant had said. If he accepted what had been said, then the next question should have been whether guilt could reasonably be inferred from what he had accepted. To suggest, as the judge did, that the defendant's silence could indicate guilt was to short-circuit the intellectual process which has to be followed.

With respect, the intellectual process advocated by Lawton LJ seems to be just as suspect as that advocated by the trial judge. It was apparently pointed out in argument to the Court of Appeal that no distinction could properly be drawn between pre- and post-caution interrogation, if the right of silence was to prevail, and the words of Lord Diplock in *Hall* were drawn to the Court's attention. But these were stigmatised by Lawton LJ as seeming 'to conflict with *R v Christie* and with earlier cases and authorities'. A passage from the speech of Lord Atkinson in *Christie* (133) was cited to lend weight to this proposition. But the House of Lords in *Christie* was not concerned with such a situation, because the defendant did rebut the charge, and the passage cited bears no obvious relation to the facts which the Court of Appeal had to consider in *Hall.* If *Chandler* was rightly decided, it would seem to follow that a solicitor who is present when his client is interviewed can no longer safely advise his client to exercise his right of silence. It may be, and indeed it has been strenuously advocated in many quarters, that the position of the defendant at common law is too favourable under modern conditions, and that a jury should be entitled to draw some inference from his silence. But if so, such a step surely requires the intervention of statute.

Some support for *Chandler* is sometimes claimed in the decision of the Privy Council in *Parkes v R* (134), in which the advice was delivered by Lord Diplock. *Parkes* was decided after *Chandler,* but the latter case appears not to have been cited. The defend-

130 See, e.g., *Bessela v Stern* (CA) (1877) 2 CPD 265.   131 [1976] 1 WLR 585.
132 Ibid at 590.   133 [1914] AC 545 at 554.   134 (PC, Jamaica) [1976] 1 WLR 1251.

ant was charged with the murder of a girl. The girl's mother found her bleeding very shortly after the infliction of the wound, and saw the defendant nearby holding a knife. The mother twice accused the defendant of stabbing her daughter, and to these accusations he made no reply, but when the mother said that she intended to detain him until the police arrived, the defendant attempted to stab her with the knife. Lord Diplock based himself upon the dictum of Cave J in *Mitchell,* and held that the trial judge had been 'perfectly entitled to instruct the jury that the defendant's reactions to the accusations including his silence were matters which they could take into account along with other evidence in deciding whether the defendant in fact committed the act with which he was charged'. It is submitted that this must be correct. It was precisely the sort of case which Cave J presumably had in mind. One might perhaps go further, and say that the silence of the defendant was a relatively small part of an obviously guilty reaction, which the jury were entitled to consider, to the mother's accusation. His action in attacking the mother could be considered as some form of admission that there was truth in her accusations. *Parkes* could hardly be further away from *Chandler* on the facts.

It is submitted that the true rule on the present law is that unless the defendant's silence can properly be left to the jury as a form of admission of the allegation, in the very exceptional circumstances envisaged in *Mitchell* and exemplified in *Parkes,* the statements made to the defendant ought to be viewed in the same way as if the allegations had been denied.

7.13 Questions for counsel

1 On what principles will the admissibility of the oral and written confessions of Coke as a matter of law be decided?

2 What is your view of the admissibility in law of:
(a) Coke's reply to D/I Glanvil on his arrest at his flat;
(b) Coke's oral replies at the police station;
(c) Coke's written statement under caution?

3 Assuming the admissibility of these statements as a matter of law, are there any grounds on which the trial judge might be invited to exclude any of them.
(a) on D/I Glanvil's account;
(b) on Coke's own account?

4 What steps should counsel for Coke take in order to challenge the statements and to safeguard Coke's interests generally?

5 What is your view on the admissibility of the words 'That's him', spoken by Angela Blackstone when identifying Littleton, in the light of his reply and subsequent answers to the police before being arrested? Would it have altered your view if Littleton had made no reply?

6 What is your view of the admissibility of Littleton's apparent confession to his wife while at the police station (leaving aside any question of privilege)?

7 If the confession is admissible in law, is there any room for the exercise of judicial discretion to exclude?

8 How should you deal with that confession on Littleton's behalf?

9 In view of the references in Coke's statement under caution to Littleton, how should Littleton's position be safeguarded if that statement is to be put before the jury?

8 The Rule Against Hearsay — III

A: STATUTORY EXCEPTIONS IN CRIMINAL CASES

8.1 Introduction

In criminal cases, the concern of the common law to shield juries from forms of evidence traditionally regarded with suspicion, has proved long-lived and comprehensive. We have seen in Chapter 6 that the common law was obliged in certain cases, from the sheer necessity of allowing the proof of important facts which otherwise could not be proved, to permit some exceptions to the rule against hearsay. We also saw that those exceptions were jealously and restrictively construed, and that they have proved to be too narrow and too unsystematic to cope adequately with many aspects of modern practice. The decision in *Myers* v *DPP* (1), while coming in some respects like a bolt from the blue, in another sense operated merely to confirm a nagging fear in the common lawyers that the day of reform could not be delayed indefinitely. It has, nonetheless, been delayed so far as any comprehensive measures are concerned. A measure of reform was hurriedly conceded, in the face of the refusal of the House of Lords to undertake the task of formulating fresh exceptions of such major dimensions, in the form of the Criminal Evidence Act 1965, but even that has recently been threatened by a decision whose importance may not have been fully recognised (2). The Law Reform Committee and the Criminal Law Revision Committee have appealed in vain for a rational and thorough recasting of the subject (3), but the work awaits the calming of the traditional fears that juries will prove incapable of weighing up the new areas of evidence which might be opened up to them. The only comment one can make is that their task would seem much lighter than many of those which have been imposed on them by the common law already; reference is made elsewhere in this book to the rule that a confession made by A implicating B is evidence against A, but not against B, and to the rule that a recent complaint in a sexual case, while admissible to confirm the complainant's evidence, is not evidence of the truth of the facts stated in the complaint and cannot provide the corroboration required of the complainant's evidence. It is a curious logic indeed according to which juries are happily permitted to undertake such feats as these, but are forbidden to undertake that of sifting and weighing simple matters of hearsay, a concept familiar to them in their daily lives.

---

1   (HL) [1965] AC 1001. See generally, 6.1, ante.
2   *R* v *Pettigrew* [1980] Crim LR 239.
3   Law Reform Committee, 13th report, paras 48–52; Criminal Law Revision Committee, 11th report, paras 229–48.

8.2 Minor exceptions

Even before the wider attempt at reform prompted by *Myers* v *DPP* a number of statutory provisions had been found to be both salutary and capable of operation without injustice. Some were so unobtrusive that they hardly attracted attention as being exceptions to the rule against hearsay at all, and all work in practice habitually and conveniently. It is necessary in this work only to give an outline of the most important. Some provisions not considered here, for example s. 27(4) of the Theft Act 1968, render admissible specific pieces of hearsay evidence as such.

In committal proceedings, the deposition of a person able and willing to give material information, but dangerously ill and unlikely to recover, may be taken out of court, and will be admissible, subject to certain conditions, both at those proceedings and at any subsequent trial of the defendant for the offences charged as a result of the committal proceedings (4). A somewhat similar provision exists for the admission of the deposition of a child or young person in committal proceedings relating to an offence involving bodily injury alleged to have been committed against that child or young person, where the court is satisfied on medical evidence that the attendance of the child or young person before the court would involve serious danger to his or her life or health (5). On committal proceedings for a sexual offence alleged to have been committed against a child or young person, there is a mandatory provision that the child shall not be called as a witness for the prosecution, except in the cases mentioned in the section, and that the statement of the child or young person shall be 'admissible in evidence of any matter of which his oral testimony would be admissible' (6). For this purpose, a sexual offence is any offence under the Sexual Offences Act 1956 or the Indecency with Children Act 1960 or any attempt to commit such an offence.

It has long been the rule in criminal trials on indictment that the deposition of a witness who was conditionally bound at the committal proceedings, and who has not since been notified that he is required to attend, may be read as evidence. The same applies to that of a witness who is 'proved at the trial by the oath of a credible witness' to be dead, insane, too ill to be able to travel or 'kept out of the way by means of the procurement of the accused or on his behalf' (7). This provision does not apply, at a retrial, to the deposition of any person who gave evidence at the original trial or to the written statement of such a person tendered at the original committal proceedings, but in such a case a transcript of the evidence given by any witness at the original trial may, with the leave of the judge, be read as evidence at the retrial, either by agreement between the prosecution and the defence or where the judge is satisfied that such witness is dead, unfit to give evidence or to attend for that purpose, or that all reasonable efforts to find him or secure his attendance have been made without success (8).

Of general importance are the provisions of s. 2 and s. 9 of the Criminal Justice Act 1967. S. 2, which applies to committal proceedings, provides that:

4   Magistrates' Courts Act 1952, s. 41; Criminal Law Amendment Act 1867 as amended. The defendant must have the opportunity of attending and cross-examining, and the statement taken must be served on him before it can be admitted at the trial.
5   Children and Young Persons Act 1933, s. 42 and s. 43. The defendant must have been given notice of the taking of the deposition and have had the opportunity to attend and cross-examine.
6   Children and Young Persons Act 1963, s. 27; the provision does not apply where the defence object, or in identification cases.
7   Criminal Justice Act 1925, s. 13(3); it must be proved that the deposition was taken in the presence of the defendant and that he had full opportunity to cross-examine. The provisions of s. 13(3) apply, without this requirement, to written statements tendered at committal under s. 2 of the Criminal Justice Act 1967, by s. 2(7) of that Act.
8   Criminal Appeal Act 1968, sch. 2, which is not restricted to retrials ordered by the Court of Appeal.

(1) . . . a written statement by any person shall, if the conditions mentioned in the next following subsection are satisfied, be admissible as evidence to the like extent as oral evidence to the like effect by that person.

The conditions referred to are designed to ensure the authenticity of the statement, to ensure that the maker of the statement has had drawn to his attention the penalties for giving false evidence and, most importantly of all, to ensure that the party or parties against whom the evidence is tendered shall first have had copies of such statements served on them, and that they may object to the admission of the statement. They or the court may insist upon the maker being called to give oral evidence (9). If the statement refers to and identifies any exhibit, that exhibit shall be treated as if it had been produced in evidence, and a copy of any documentary exhibit referred to must be served with the copy of the statement on the other parties. The clear meaning of the section is that the written statements, if tendered without objection, are to be regarded as evidence for all purposes, so that the court may commit for trial even where all the evidence tendered consists of s. 2 statements.

S. 9 makes the same provision for admissibility of written statements 'in any criminal proceedings, other than committal proceedings', subject to broadly the same conditions as s. 2. In particular, s. 9(4) provides that the party who has served the statement, or the court of its own motion or on the application of any other party, may require the witness to attend to give oral evidence. It is, however, often overlooked that s. 9(2)(*d*) (unlike the corresponding provision of s. 2) lays down a time-limit of seven days from service of the statement, during which a party on whom a statement is served must object by notice if the statement is not to be admissible by virtue of the section. Should this time limit not be complied with, the statement is admissible, although the court may presumably exercise its own power to require the attendance of the witness in any case where the interests of a fair trial seem to dictate this course.

The effect of s. 9 is that the statement tendered in any criminal trial under the section becomes evidence in the case, and the jury should be directed accordingly. The practice laid down by the Act is that the statement shall be read aloud, or if the court so directs, an account shall be given of its contents, at the trial (10); this is usually done by the clerk in a straightforward case of reading aloud, though where an account is to be given or where the references to exhibits are complex and may need to be explained to the jury, it should be left to counsel for the party calling the evidence. The purpose of the section (as of s. 2) is to save the time of the court and of the witness in a case where the evidence is not challenged, and would have been given orally in chief without cross-examination. Its importance is greater in summary trials, where no other service of the prosecution statements will have been made, than in trials on indictment where the statements will have been served prior to committal and where there is, as we have seen, other statutory provision for the reading of the depositions of conditionally bound witnesses. But s. 9 is of importance where evidence comes to light after committal, or was not in the form required by s. 2 at the committal stage. In such a case the statements concerned, when reduced into the form prescribed, may be served on the defence with a notice of additional evidence, under s. 9 and are subject to the provisions of the section. Although evidence tendered without objection under s. 9 is unchallenged evidence, it nonetheless falls to be considered by the jury and is not conclusive of the facts stated as would be the case if those facts had been formally admitted under s. 10 of the Act (11).

9 Criminal Justice Act 1967, s. 2(4).   10 Ibid s. 9(6); cf s. 2(5).   11 See 1.9, ante.

Statements prepared for use in criminal proceedings are now prepared in the form required by s. 2 and s. 9, and this may be seen from the depositions in the case of Coke and Littleton.

8.3 Criminal Evidence Act 1965

We have already noted that the decision of the House of Lords in *Myers* v *DPP* caused Parliament to react quickly to introduce some measure of admissibility for hearsay evidence of commercial records in criminal cases, in order to avoid what might well have been the result that very many prosecutions for serious offences of dishonesty would be rendered impossible to conduct (12). No witness can reasonably be expected to carry in his head the records of a modern business, even if he is alive and fit and available to give evidence at the time of the trial (13), and naturally, the problem increases with the lapse of time in any given case, and with the ever-growing complexity of modern commercial concerns and their records generally. The Act went a certain way towards remedying the immediate problem occasioned by the decision in *Myers* itself, but as already noted, was a hurried and piecemeal reform which remains unsatisfactory as a general provision for such an important area of the law. Some of its weaknesses and lacunae have been exposed, and it is hoped to indicate these as the Act is considered below, but it is impossible to rule out the discovery of yet others. It is high time Parliament gave the matter further attention.

The Act has at least the merit of being concise. S. 1 provides for admissibility as follows:

(1) In any criminal proceedings where direct oral evidence of a fact would be admissible, any statement contained in a document and tending to establish that fact shall, on production of the document, be admissible as evidence of that fact if —

(*a*) the document is, or forms part of, a record relating to any trade or business and compiled, in the course of that trade or business, from information supplied (whether directly or indirectly) by persons who have, or may reasonably be supposed to have, personal knowledge of the matters dealt with in the information they supply; and

(*b*) the person who supplied the information recorded in the statement in question is dead, or beyond the seas, or unfit by reason of his bodily or mental condition to attend as a witness, or cannot with reasonable diligence be identified or found, or cannot reasonably be expected (having regard to the time which has elapsed since he supplied the information and to all the circumstances) to have any recollection of the matters dealt with in the information he supplied. . . .

(4) In this section 'statement' includes any representation of fact, whether made in words or otherwise, 'document' includes any device by means of which information is recorded or stored and 'business' includes any public transport, public utility or similar undertaking carried on by a local authority and the activities of the Post Office.

8.3.1 'Statement contained in a document'

The terms 'statement' and 'document' are both defined partially by s. 1(4); neither

12 See 6.1 and 6.2, *ante*, where the facts of the case are discussed.
13 In some cases, the witness may be able to refresh his memory using a note which he made or verified personally, contemporaneously with the events dealt with.

definition is expressed as exclusive. It is clearly intended that it should not matter whether the statement is made by words, figures, diagrams or in any other form, provided that it is a representation of fact. In contrast to civil cases, in which hearsay statements of opinion may now be given by virtue of the Civil Evidence Act 1972, such statements are not admissible in criminal proceedings under this Act, and any admissible evidence of opinion must be the subject of oral evidence by a competent witness.

The definition of a document is intended to encompass not only traditional books, ledgers and other paper records commonly kept in commerce, but also such contemporary phenomena as records kept on tape, videotape, microfilm, or stored in computers (14). The equivalent definition contained in s. 10(1) of the Civil Evidence Act 1968 enumerates a number of such other devices specifically as being included in the term 'document' for the purpose of that Act, and adds, in the cases of audio and video recordings in whatever form, that they are 'documents' even if it is necessary to use equipment in order to produce from them an aural or visual image. This part of the definition was not included in the 1965 Act for criminal cases, but whether this omission is signficant has yet to be revealed. Reading together the definitions of 'statement' and 'document', it would appear that plans, maps, graphs, drawings and photographs and the like may be regarded as 'documents' within the meaning of the Act, as they are expressly declared to be for the purposes of the Civil Evidence Act 1968.

8.3.2 'Tending to establish that fact'

The requirement here seems to be that the statement shall have some relevance to the proof of the fact, and not that it shall be of any particular weight for that purpose. The words were so construed by the Court of Appeal for the purposes of the Evidence Act 1938 in *Dass v Massih* (15), in which expert-opinion evidence on the handwriting of part of a letter, which was relied upon by the plaintiff as being an acknowledgement by the defendant of his indebtedness to the plaintiff, was held to 'tend to establish' that that part of the letter was not written by the defendant. As such it was admissible, but its weight was a matter for the trial judge. Although the words have not been the subject of authority for the purposes of criminal cases under the 1965 Act, there would seem to be no good reason for adopting any different view.

8.3.3 'Is, or forms part of, a record'

In *R v Tirado* (16), the Court of Appeal expressed 'some hesitation' in deciding that a file of correspondence, maintained simply as a repository for letters as and when they came in, was capable of amounting to a 'record' for the purposes of the Act, although the case turned on other factors, and the point may be regarded as open. It is submitted that there is considerable force in the objection. Certainly, the words 'compiled . . . from information supplied' suggest some element of deliberation in the making of a source of future reference, though they probably imply no necessary element of method or quality which may go only to weight. Nonetheless, the Act does not prescribe that the information received shall be dealt with in any particular way beyond 'compilation', and in many cases the regular adding to a file may be enough if no other steps could reasonably be thought necessary to produce a sufficient source of future reference. Records admissible

14   A microfilm record has been held to be capable of being a 'banker's book' for the purpose of the Bankers' Books Evidence Act 1879: *Barker* v *Wilson* (DC) [1980] 2 All ER 81. See also 16.1, post.
15   (CA) [1968] 1 WLR 756.
16   (1974) 59 Cr App R 80 at 89. The Court of Appeal's doubts in this case were shared by a different court in *R v Jones; R v Sullivan* [1978] 1 WLR 195 at 198–9.

in civil cases under s. 4 of the Civil Evidence Act 1968 must be compiled by persons 'acting under a duty', which may contrast with the requirement of the 1965 Act that the compilation should be 'in the course of that trade or business', the latter perhaps suggesting a lesser degree of formality. It would appear to be contrary to the spirit of the 1965 Act to exclude a source of information which has been conserved deliberately for business purposes, although clearly its weight may be very slight where the degree of effort in the compilation is unimpressive. None of this involves the acceptance as a record of the letters in *Tirado,* which were an apparently random collection received from various people. There was for a time some question whether a single document, or to be more precise, materials relating to one transaction only, could be a record or part of a record, and in *R* v *Gwilliam* (17) the Court of Appeal appears to have doubted whether a single Home Office consignment note could enjoy such status, for the purpose of proving that a breathalyser device used to test a specimen of the defendant's breath was a device approved for the purpose by the Home Secretary. But Lord Parker CJ expressly declined to decide the case on that basis. It is submitted that the matter has now been concluded by the more recent decision of the Court of Appeal in *R* v *Jones; R* v *Sullivan* (18). The defendants were directors of a transport business, and were charged with conspiracy to steal from containers. The containers broken into had been packed in the Far East and then shipped to England. It was necessary for the prosecution to prove the original contents of the containers, and for this purpose they put in evidence bills of lading and other documents made out in Hong Kong. It was argued that each set of documents merely dealt with a single shipment of goods and, having a limited life-span, could not be or form part of a record. The court, having considered *Gwilliam,* saw no reason why either consideration should prevent the documents from constituting a record. Geoffrey Lane LJ, giving the judgment of the court, said (19):

> Although it is not an exhaustive definition of the word, 'record' in this context means a history of events in some form which is not evanescent. How long the record is likely to be kept is immaterial: it may be something which will not survive the end of the transaction in question, it may be something which is indeed more lasting than bronze, but the degree of permanence does not seem to us to make or mar the fulfilment of the definition of the word 'record'. The record in each individual case will last as long as commercial necessity may demand.
>
> The documents in the present case seem to us to fall precisely into that category. They are the written records of the particular transaction. They are documents containing the history of this particular transaction, where the goods started from, the method of transport, the name of the ship, the port of arrival and the container depot destination on the one hand and the final consignee's destination on the other. They are carefully and deliberately compiled for the information of those in this country who are going to be the recipients of the goods. There is no necessity, as we see it, for the contents of these documents to be entered into a book or a ledger as was suggested in one of the cases; indeed these very documents themselves might have been copied into a ledger but how, one asks, could that make them any more or less a record than they are at the moment?

17 [1968] 1 WLR 1839.   18 [1978] 1 WLR 195.
19 Ibid at 199. The court also considered and rejected an argument that the documents could not be admitted because they had not been compiled in England.

198 The Rule Against Hearsay — III

8.3.4 'Relating to any trade or business'

Once again, s. 1(4) provides a partial and non-exclusive definition; the word 'business' is somewhat curiously dealt with as including a number of public activities, but what common factor it is which unites them under that heading is not really clear. It may be that the intention is to include any enterprise of a private or public nature which trades on a commercial basis, with a view to making a profit. But while this would presumably be a reasonable view of the matter, it cannot be asserted with any confidence. In civil cases, s. 4 of the Civil Evidence Act 1968 is not so constrained, and the records of any body may be admitted, as long as there was a duty to compile them. While it is to be appreciated that Parliament had in mind the dictates of commercial documents in the light of *Myers* v *DPP*, it is surely somewhat regrettable that the Act is to be confined in such an artificial way. The potential for absurdity is illustrated by the doubtless correct decision in *R* v *Crayden* (20), in which the Court of Appeal, having clearly shared the sense of puzzlement expressed above, held that medical records kept by a hospital operating within the framework of the National Health Service were not records of a trade or business. Lawton LJ pointed to the wider definition of the word 'business' which seemed to be permissible in other contexts (in civil cases, which cannot assist directly) (21) and held that the wording of s. 1(4) precluded its adoption for the purposes of the 1965 Act, firstly because, had a wider meaning been intended, the words of enlargement in the subsection would have been unnecessary, and secondly because, had the Act intended to make records of governmental or public activities generally admissible, some words of limitation, for example to prevent the revelation of confidential information, would surely have been included. Lawton LJ concluded (22):

> Every one of the activities specified by the enlarging words in the Act of 1965 relates to an activity which has an element in it of supplying services or goods although it may not be the only element. The supply of goods or services by the bodies specified in s. 1(4) is a form of commercial activity carried on for the public benefit, but not for the private profit. It follows, in our judgment, that the word 'business' as used in this Act has a commercial connotation. We do not find it necessary to construe this word in more precise terms since our only task is to say whether the medical records of the [hospital] produced by [its chief medical records officer] related to a trade or business. Whether a hospital outside the National Health Service should be adjudged to be a business for the purposes of the Act of 1965 does not arise for decision in this appeal.

Lawton LJ then considered the various activities of a National Health Service hospital, and said: 'In our judgment the provision of such a service cannot be a business within the meaning of that word as used in this Act.'

The result of this is that on a prosecution of a doctor for the manslaughter of a patient by gross negligence, the compilers of the relevant medical records having gone abroad, the records would be inadmissible if the doctor worked in a National Health Service hospital; whereas in a civil action brought by the personal representatives of the patient on behalf of his estate and dependants, the same records would clearly be admissible. If the doctor worked in a privately run hospital, the same result would obtain in the civil action, but it may be that the records could also be admitted in the criminal prosecution.

20   [1978] 1 WLR 604.
21   See, e.g., *Rolls* v *Miller* (CA) (1884) 27 ChD 71; *Town Investments Ltd* v *Department of the Environment* (HL) [1978] AC 359.
22   [1978] 1 WLR 604 at 609.

Viewed in this light, the requirement of a commercial connotation, while lending some meaning to the wording of the Act, can hardly be said to have put the law on a very rational basis, and there seems to be every justification for removing this restriction and substituting some test along the lines of that of duty employed in the Civil Evidence Act 1968. It is, for the time being, difficult to find any fault with the judgment of the Court of Appeal in *Crayden,* and indeed it derives some support from that in *R* v *Gwilliam,* to which reference has already been made. In *Gwilliam* the issue was whether a Home Office consignment note, relating to the delivery of a breathalyser device from a Home Office Supply and Transport Store to the police, was admissible to show that the device used to test the defendant's breath was one approved by the Home Secretary. It was held that the Home Office Supply and Transport Department was not a business for the purpose of the Act. It seems that the commercial element was missing, in contrast to the examples provided by s. 1(4), but the judgment delivered by Lord Parker CJ does not go into the court's reasons for so holding. If this is right, then a commercial undertaking, for example a nationalised industry, is within the Act, but an administrative or governmental activity, and perhaps even a charity, must be excluded.

8.3.5 The requirement of personal knowledge

The requirement that the supplier of the information from which the record is compiled have, or may reasonably be supposed to have personal knowledge of the matters dealt with in the information so supplied is intended to offer some safeguard of the accuracy of the records admitted under the Act. Much the same safeguard is employed by s.4 of the Civil Evidence Act 1968, where it is combined with the requirement of a duty on the part of the compiler of the record and of any intermediaries by whom the information may be transmitted from the supplier to the compiler. It may be that the expression in parentheses in the 1965 Act, 'whether directly or indirectly', is intended to cover the use of intermediaries. If so, given the risk of distortion in the course of repetition which has always been a major danger of introducing hearsay, the 1965 Act falls down in its safeguard. There is no control over that part of the transmission of the information corresponding to that in the 1968 Act for civil cases. Another problem arises when one considers the circumstances in which personal knowledge by the supplier may reasonably be presumed to have been present. In civil cases under the 1968 Act, there is authority that this will readily be presumed, even where the information has been supplied some considerable time ago, where the supplier was acting under a public duty (23), but it may be doubted whether the same latitude can be expected where the information is supplied for private, commercial purposes. It will probably be a matter for evidence in any given case.

More recently, a yet more serious lacuna in the Act has come to light, following the decision of the Court of Appeal in *R* v *Pettigrew* (24). Shortly after a burglary in which some £650 in new £5 notes was stolen from a house, the defendant was found in possession of three new £5 notes. The prosecution wished to prove that the notes found in his possession could have come from the sequence of notes stolen, which could be traced by a series of steps from the Bank of England to the loser. In order to do this, the prosecution put in evidence a print-out produced at the Bank of England (25) by a

---

23 *Knight and Others* v *David and Others* [1971] 1 WLR 1671; see 8.6, post.

24 [1980] Crim LR 239; the case may cause some revision of the fairly optimistic view taken of the working of the Act by Tapper, *Computer Law* (1978), p. 159–60.

25 At first instance, it was also argued that the Bank of England was not a trade or business for the purpose of the Act. For some reason, this interesting and very arguable point was not pressed on appeal.

machine operated by an employee of the Bank. The operator fed into the machine bundles of printed and serially numbered notes, and himself noted the first number of the series. The machine then recorded the number of each note in the bundle. The Court was prepared to hold that, had this been the machine's sole function, the operator could fairly be said to have personal knowledge of the serial numbers in each bundle, having access to the means of such knowledge because he had recorded the number of the first note and knew how many notes were in the bundle. But the machine had the additional function of destroying defective notes and recording the numbers of the notes destroyed by it. These numbers could not be said to have been within the personal knowledge of any person, because they were selected and recorded automatically by the machine. On this 'highly artificial' ground, the Court allowed the appeal. But it would seem to be the Act, rather than the point, which is to be condemned for artificiality, and it is difficult to resist the conclusion that the implications of this decision go far beyond the facts upon which is was made. It would appear to exclude from the ambit of the Act any process of an entirely mechanical nature, any process automatically carried out, where a machine is entrusted with the task of sifting, collating, arranging or putting into a different form any information, and must exclude any process other than mere recording or storing which is carried out by mechanical means, it being at least arguable in any other case that the operator has personal knowledge only of the data supplied to the machine and not of that which the machine produces. The Court of Appeal appears not to have considered the possibility that the operator might reasonably have been supposed to have personal knowledge, and although he might presumably have checked the bundles when they emerged, such a view is hardly appealing. Even the Court's readiness to accept that personal knowledge might be equated with having access to the means of such knowledge flies somewhat in the face of the words of the statute. In civil cases, the wide definition of a 'computer' as 'any device for storing and processing information', contained in s. 5(6) of the Civil Evidence Act 1968 makes a more realistic concession to the technological age, and presumably no objection could have been taken to the admission of the evidence in *Pettigrew* under that section. The 1965 Act has dealt with the problem by making the minimum possible derogation from the rules of Common Law, which were never designed for, and are quite inadequate to deal with, records stored in and information processed by modern machines.

8.3.6 *Determination of admissibility*
By s. 1(2) of the Act:

> For the purpose of deciding whether or not a statement is admissible as evidence by virtue of this section, the court may draw any reasonable inference from the form or content of the document in which the statement is contained, and may, in deciding whether or not a person is fit to attend as a witness, act on a certificate purporting to be a certificate of a fully registered medical practitioner.

With the aid of the matters referred to in this subsection, the trial judge must satisfy himself that all the requirements of s. 1(1)(a) and (b) are met, before the evidence tendered can be admitted by virtue of the Act. Although the judge may look at the document in order to assist him, he must hear evidence if it appears to be necessary in order to resolve the issue, and the resolution of the issues proposed by s. 1(1)(b) may present quite difficult problems of evidence, according to the age and nature of the document. It will not be possible in every case to identify the supplier of the information, or to produce a sufficient account of him at trial. The judge must be able to draw a reasonable inference to the effect that the conditions are met, and the party seeking to adduce the evidence must therefore be prepared to lay a proper foundation of evidence justifying its reception. In *R v Nicholls* (26), where the judge admitted evidence without first taking proper steps to satisfy himself of its admissibility, the Court of Appeal quashed the conviction, holding that:

> There was nothing to indicate in the state of the evidence whether those who might have been called as witnesses in relation to the information compiled on the document were alive or dead, whether in this country or beyond the seas, whether unfit or fit to attend as witnesses or would or would not have a reasonable expectation of being able to recollect the information which they provided and which was contained in the documents. . . . The defendant was entitled to have the matter investigated as in a trial within a trial in order to ascertain whether or not the evidence can properly be admitted pursuant to the Act.

There must be some investigation of whether oral evidence may on a reasonable view be forthcoming, presumably bearing in mind the possibility of the use of any document made or verified contemporaneously by such witness being used to refresh his memory. But the older and more complex and more technically recorded or stored the information, the more likely it may be to demonstrate that the document should be admitted. The view taken by the court is in line with the general policy of the Act to admit evidence only where necessary in the light of the inadequacy of the rules of common law. Indeed, s. 2(2) provides that: 'Nothing in this Act shall prejudice the admissibility of any evidence which would be admissible apart from the provisions of this Act,' a provision which contrasts starkly with the policy of the Civil Evidence Act 1968, which supersedes the common-law rules entirely.

8.3.7 *Weight*
By s. 1(3) of the Act:

> In estimating the weight, if any, to be attached to a statement admissible as evidence by virtue of this section regard shall be had to all the circumstances from which any inference can reasonably be drawn as to the accuracy or otherwise of the statement, and, in particular, to the question whether or not the person who supplied the information recorded in the statement did so contemporaneously with the occurrence or existence of the facts stated, and to the question whether or not that person, or any person concerned with making or keeping the record containing the statement, had any incentive to conceal or misrepresent the facts.

This subsection does not call for comment, save that the trial judge ought to draw to the attention of the jury any matters of evidence which bear on the view which they may take about the statement, and explain to them in straightforward terms the strengths and weaknesses of the statement as evidence in the case, in the light of any other evidence which may have been given.

26   (1976) 63 Cr App R 187.

B: STATUTORY EXCEPTIONS IN CIVIL CASES

8.4   Civil Evidence Act 1968: introduction

The comparative rarity of jury trial in civil cases in modern times is one of the principal factors, if not the principal factor, which led to a willingness in the legislature to seek to update the rules of evidence in such cases. It has already been seen that the common-law exceptions to the rule against hearsay, developed piecemeal and restrictively construed, became wholly inadequate to cope with the needs of modern litigation, and it has been suggested in section A of this chapter that criminal cases continue to suffer quite drastically from the reliance which they must place on those rules, modified only peripherally by statute. The Civil Evidence Act 1968 was not the first attempt to rationalise the rules. The Evidence Act 1938, for example, made a surprisingly radical bid (considered in its time) to relax the strictness of the common law. But today it appears not to concede very much. It was considerably circumscribed by conditions of admissibility, and applied in any event only to documentary evidence. It need not be further considered here, except to recognise its value as a formative stage of advancement (27).

Although the 1968 Act is often referred to as an 'exception' to the rule against hearsay, and although it too has its limitations on admissibility of hearsay evidence, the reality is that the Act has in effect swept away, so far as civil cases are concerned, the common-law rule against hearsay, and substituted for it a statutory code which provides for the general admissibility of hearsay evidence subject to important evidential and procedural safeguards. The code is contained in part 1 of the Act, which consists of ss. 1–10 inclusive, and which must be read together with the important related procedural provisions contained in RSC, Ord. 38 rr. 21–31, made pursuant to s. 8.

The purpose and effect of the Act is stated in direct terms in s. 1:

(1)   In any civil proceedings a statement other than one made by a person while giving oral evidence in those proceedings shall be admissible as evidence of any fact stated therein to the extent that it is so admissible by virtue of any provision of this part of this Act or by virtue of any other statutory provision or by agreement of the parties, but not otherwise.

(2)   In this section 'statutory provision' means any provision contained in, or in an instrument made under, this or any other Act, including any Act passed after this Act.

The meaning of 'civil proceedings' is explained by the interpretation section, s. 18, as follows:

(1)   In this Act 'civil proceedings' includes, in addition to civil proceedings in any of the ordinary courts of law —

(a)   civil proceedings before any other tribunal, being proceedings in relation to which the strict rules of evidence apply; and

---

27   The substantive parts of the Evidence Act 1938 are repealed by the 1968 Act, in respect of all proceedings to which the latter applies. The 1968 Act has not yet been extended to civil proceedings in magistrates' courts, and in such proceedings, the 1938 Act may still be resorted to.

(*b*)   an arbitration or reference, whether under an enactment or not,
but does not include civil proceedings in relation to which the strict rules of evidence
do not apply.

The bulk of the Act was, by s. 20(4), to be brought into effect by statutory instrument
made by the Lord Chancellor, and as observed in note (27), the Act does not as yet apply
to proceedings within the civil jurisdiction of the magistrates' courts. To these
proceedings, the provisions of the Evidence Act 1938 continue to apply where appropriate, and only at such time as the 1968 Act is extended will the 1938 Act be repealed in
relation to such proceedings, as it has in relation to the other 'civil proceedings' referred
to in s. 18 of the 1968 Act. The exclusion of proceedings to which the strict rules of
evidence do not apply reflects the fact that in such proceedings, no authority is needed
for the admission of the kinds of evidence for which provision is made by the Act.

It is important to note that s. 1 permits the admission of hearsay evidence only in the
three circumstances set out, that is to say, (a) by virtue of one of the provisions of the
Act, (b) by virtue of any other statutory provision, or (c) by agreement between the
parties. The section expressly excludes any other possibility of admission of hearsay
evidence in civil proceedings, and must therefore be taken to have abrogated, in relation
to civil proceedings, the common-law exceptions to the rule against hearsay, although as
we saw in Chapter 6, certain of the common-law rules have been 'adopted' and given
statutory force by s. 9 (28). Whether evidence is admissible by virtue of 'any other
statutory provision', in addition to being admissible by virtue of s. 2, s. 4 or s. 5 of the
1968 Act, may be of importance inasmuch as the notice procedure, which applies to
evidence admissible under those sections by virtue of RSC, Ord. 38, does not apply to
evidence which can be admitted otherwise (29). It may therefore be avoided in such
cases. The power of the parties in civil cases to make an agreement at any time about
evidence which is to be admissible, generally or for any particular purpose, in those
proceedings, is expressly preserved by s. 18(5)(*b*) of the 1968 Act.

The only defect of evidence cured by the Act is that of its hearsay character. Nothing in
the Act gives any licence to admit evidence which is, for any other reason, inadmissible
under the general law of evidence. Clearly, a party tendering evidence cannot be in a
more favourable position because he proposes to have the evidence admitted in a
hearsay form by virtue of the Act than if he proposed to call direct evidence of the same
facts. The major sections providing for admission of specific categories of hearsay
statement, that is to say, s. 2, s. 4 and s. 5, each provide expressly that the admissibility
shall be of evidence 'of any fact stated therein of which direct oral evidence would be
admissible'. These provisions are reinforced by s. 18(5)(*a*), which preserves the power of
the court in any case to exclude evidence in the exercise of its discretion; this is of course
in addition to the power of the court to exclude evidence as a matter of law, where it is for
any reason inadmissible.

Leaving aside s. 1, which has already been dealt with, it is now proposed to indicate
briefly the structure of the remaining sections of part 1 of the Act, and the places in which
they are to be dealt with.

The major provisions within the general framework of s. 1, providing for the admissi-

28   See 6.7 et seq, ante; see also 7.1, ante, and 9.2, post.
29   For this purpose, s. 9 of the 1968 Act is itself an 'other statutory provision', in the sense that s. 9(5) and Ord.
38, r. 21(2) exclude from the notice procedure evidence admissible under that section, even though it may also be
admissible under s. 2, s. 4 or s. 5.

bility of hearsay evidence in particular cases or of particular kinds are s. 2 (statements made other than while giving evidence in the instant proceedings), s. 4 (statements contained in documents which are, or are parts of, records) and s. 5 (statements produced by computers). These sections are considered further in this chapter.

S. 3 deals with the evidential value of previous consistent or inconsistent statements and of documents used by a witness to refresh his memory while giving evidence, and is dealt with in relation to those matters in 13.2, 13.3, 13.4 and 14.6, post.

S. 6 deals with various questions relating to the determination of admissibility of, and proof of, statements tendered under the Act, and with the assessment of the weight of statements admitted under certain sections, which matters are dealt with in this chapter, and with the position of hearsay statements in relation to the rules of corroboration, which is dealt with in 15.4, post.

S. 7 provides for the admissibility of evidence tending to discredit evidence given under s. 2 or s. 4, where the maker of a hearsay statement is not called to give evidence, and is dealt with in 14.11, post.

S. 8 requires or gives authority for the making of the various rules of court necessary to give effect to the proposed procedural framework within which part 1 is to operate. The rules concerned, contained in RSC, Ord. 38, are considered in this chapter, and s. 8 requires no further comment.

S. 9, as we have seen, adopts and gives statutory force to a number of rules of the common law permitting the use of hearsay evidence for various purposes, without changing the substance of the law in those cases. The different rules so adopted are referred to in the context of their operation at common law, in the places where they arise naturally: admissions in 7.1, public documents in 6.7, evidence of reputation in 9.2.

S. 10 deals with a number of important definitions and interpretations relevant to part 1, and these are considered in this chapter, so far as material.

8.5 Statements admissible under s. 2

S. 2 of the Act provides as follows:

(1)   In any civil proceedings a statement made, whether orally or in a document or otherwise, by any person, whether called as a witness in those proceedings or not, shall, subject to this section and to rules of court, be admissible as evidence of any fact stated therein of which direct oral evidence by him would be admissible.

(2)   Where in any civil proceedings a party desiring to give a statement in evidence by virtue of this section has called or intends to call as a witness in the proceedings the person by whom the statement was made, the statement —

(*a*)   shall not be given in evidence by virtue of this section on behalf of that party without the leave of the court; and
(*b*)   without prejudice to paragraph (*a*) above, shall not be given in evidence by virtue of this section on behalf of that party before the conclusion of the examination-in-chief of the person by whom it was made, except —
   (i)   where before that person is called the court allows evidence of the making of the statement to be given on behalf of that party by some other person; or
   (ii)   in so far as the court allows the person by whom the statement was made to

narrate it in the course of his examination-in-chief on the ground that to prevent him from doing so would adversely affect the intelligibility of his evidence.

(3) Where in any civil proceedings a statement which was made otherwise than in a document is admissible by virtue of this section, no evidence other than direct oral evidence by the person who made the statement or any person who heard or otherwise perceived it being made shall be admissible for the purpose of proving it:

Provided that if the statement in question was made by a person while giving oral evidence in some other legal proceedings (whether civil or criminal), it may be proved in any manner authorised by the court.

8.5.1 S. 2(1)

This subsection provides for the general admissibility of statements made by persons other than while giving evidence in the instant proceedings as evidence of the truth of the facts stated therein — a literal reversal of the position with regard to hearsay at common law. It should be noted firstly that the subsection permits the admission of such hearsay statements, whether or not the maker of the statement is also called as a witness, though if he is called, the statement is admissible in its own right only with leave and subject to the other conditions laid down by s. 2(2) (30). Secondly, it is to be observed that the section, like the remainder of part 1 of the 1968 Act, applies only to statements of fact. The principle has been extended to hearsay statements of opinion, where such evidence is admissible under the general law of evidence, by the Civil Evidence Act 1972. This is considered briefly in 8.10 and at greater length in Chapter 9, post. Thirdly, as we have observed, the phrase, 'evidence of any fact stated therein of which direct oral evidence by him would be admissible', makes the obvious limitation that the evidence admitted under the section must be such that it would be unobjectionable by reference to the rules of evidence generally if it were given orally by the maker of the statement, apart from the consideration of hearsay.

Some question arises as to the limits of the kind of 'statement' which may fall within the subsection. For the purposes of part 1 of the Act, s. 10(1) provides that ' "statement" includes any representation of fact, whether made in words or otherwise'.

S. 2(1) provides that it should not matter whether the statement is made 'orally or in a document or otherwise', although statements made otherwise than in a document are made subject to further provisions under s. 2(3). It seems fairly clear, therefore, that the subsection includes statements made in the form of conduct, for example that which was rejected on the common-law rules against previous consistent statements in *Corke* v *Corke and Cooke* (31) where the wife and the co-respondent were not permitted to give evidence that, on being discovered in a compromising situation together, they telephoned a doctor with a view to being examined and so disproving the suggestion of adultery. What is less clear is whether the subsection can be construed so as to permit the reception of statements not intended to be assertive, but from which the court might be enabled to draw inferences of fact. The shout of the bystander in *Teper* v *R* (32), 'Your place burning and you going away from the fire', the letters in *Wright* v *Doe* d *Tatham*

30 Where the maker of the statement is also called as a witness, his admissible hearsay statement is incapable in law of corroborating his evidence: Civil Evidence Act 1968, s. 6(4)(*a*).
31 (CA) [1958] P 93; see 13.3, post.
32 (PC, British Guiana) [1952] AC 480; the facts are easily translatable into those of a civil case, and may refer to matters other than identification, for example in an action for personal injuries where a bystander shouts in the direction of the plaintiff, 'Don't go in there without a safety helmet'; see also 6.2, ante.

written by businessmen to the testator, indicative of his mental capacity at the time they
were written, which was disputed in the proceedings (33), the action of the mythical
sea-captain postulated by Parke B in that case, who, after inspecting a ship for seaworthiness, embarked upon it with his family, were all rejected at common law, and
must all be reconsidered in the light of s. 2(1). Professor Cross (34) argues that
statements made orally (or, presumably, in writing) may be within the subsection as
being implied representations of fact, even if not intended by the maker as communica-
tive of the facts stated, but rejects the idea that statements made by conduct and not
intended to be assertive can fall within it. But it may be that the distinction is one of
weight rather than admissibility. The use of the word 'representation' is not felicitous to
give effect to either case, and it is to be regretted that the Act did not make the point
clear.

8.5.2   S. 2(2)

The provisions of s. 2(2) refer to cases where the maker of the hearsay statement is to be
called or has been called as a witness, and it is proposed to adduce his hearsay statement
also, either by way of supplement to his evidence or as a previous consistent statement or
both, such courses being specifically envisaged by the wording of s. 2(1). There is no
limitation as such on the reasons for what may appear to be a duplication of evidence, but
while the weight of a previous consistent statement which has no other function may be
very slight, even if admitted, there are cases where it is necessary or desirable for the
proper presentation of the case that the oral evidence of the witness should be supple-
mented by the evidence of a hearsay statement made by him. Such a case would be one
where, because of illness, age or the sheer lapse of time, the witness's evidence would be
less reliable or even literally unintelligible without the earlier statement. This use of the
statutory provisions was grudgingly accepted as almost an unfortunate consequence of
the corresponding provisions of the Evidence Act 1938 (35), but is now clearly intended
to follow and is to be welcomed. The granting and refusal of leave under s. 2(2)(a) will be
based on the judge's view of what would be fair to both sides, and it is by no means to be
assessed only with regard to the interests of the party seeking to adduce the evidence.
There may be cases where the judge deems it unjust to the other side to allow a witness's
hearsay statement to be given, having regard to the importance of his evidence to the
case, the circumstances of the making of the statement, or its apparent lack of reliability.
He will no doubt exercise his powers to allow the evidence in a case where to do so would
promote a fair trial by helping the court to discover the truth, and where no injustice can
be caused by that course.

The requirement of leave is the most important difference between cases where the
maker of the statement is to be called (when leave is needed to adduce the hearsay
statement) and cases where the maker is not called (when leave is not needed). The
remaining provisions of s. 2(2) are self-explanatory; s. 2(2)(b) is designed to ensure that
the cross-examiner of a witness, whose hearsay statement is to be adduced in addition to
his oral evidence, is enabled, as far as may be possible having regard to the interests of all
the parties, to cross-examine the witness on the basis of unprompted oral evidence given
before the adduction of the hearsay statement. This is of particular importance where
the hearsay statement is in writing, and is not a document from which the witness would
be entitled to refresh his memory while giving evidence. The provision is actually of

33 (Exch) (1837) 7 A & E 313.   34 *Evidence*, 5th ed. p. 495–6.
35 See *Harvey* v *Smith-Wood* [1964] 2 QB 171; a proper case, if ever there was one.

benefit to both sides, inasmuch as if the witness cannot be cross-examined properly on what oral evidence he is able to give, the weight of his evidence may be seriously affected. It would also appear to be proper and appropriate for the judge to delay his decision whether or not to grant leave for the admission of the hearsay statement until the natural moment arrives for it under s. 2(2)(*b*), when he will usually be able to form a more complete view of the matter, in the light of the evidence in chief.

8.5.3   S. 2(3)

This part of the section creates a signficant distinction between statements made in a document and statements made otherwise. With the exception referred to in the proviso to the subsection, statements made otherwise than in documents must be proved by the direct oral evidence of the maker of the statement or a person who perceived (usually, but not necessarily, heard) the statement being made. The provision accords recognition to the evident truth that statements contained in documents can be proved with greater certainty and accuracy than those made in transient form.

Before expanding on the importance of the distinction, it will be convenient to observe the kinds of statements which will fall into either camp. S. 10(1) provides that, for the purposes of part 1 of the Act:

'document' includes, in addition to a document in writing —

(*a*)   any map, plan, graph or drawing;

(*b*)   any photograph;

(*c*)   any disc, tape, sound track or other device in which sounds or other data (not being visual images) are embodied so as to be capable (with or without the aid of some other equipment) of being reproduced therefrom; and

(*d*)   any film, negative, tape or other device in which one or more visual images are embodied so as to be capable (as aforesaid) of being reproduced therefrom;

What seems to be intended is a statement made in a form which is permanent, to the extent of being capable of being produced to the court in its original form at the time of trial, either by being produced as such, or by being played back to the court by the use of appropriate equipment, such as a projector or tape-recorder. It would, therefore, seem that the kinds of statement which will fall within the provisions of s. 2(3) are those in transient form, that is to say statements made orally, or by conduct.

It is sometimes said that s. 2(3) limits the contents of statements not made in documents to 'first-hand hearsay', whereas those made in documents are admissible also when they contain 'second-hand hearsay'. By the expressions 'first-hand' and 'second-hand' hearsay, is meant simply that if A perceives an event and makes a statement about it to B, then evidence from either A or B about what A said in his statement is at one remove only from the direct evidence of the event (first-hand); whereas if B repeats A's statement to C, who was not present when it was made, then coming from C, it is at second remove from the direct evidence (second-hand). At the risk of splitting hairs, the Act does not in fact say that second-hand hearsay is, as such, inadmissible, but that in the case of a statement not made in a document, such statement (while admissible) may only be proved by the evidence of the maker or of a person who perceived it being made. It is a question of means of proof and no more. The result is that if A's statement is made orally, A himself or B may give evidence to prove it, but C may not; if A's statement is contained in a document, it may be proved (subject to s. 6(1), see 8.8, post) by C or by anyone who is able to prove that it is A's statement. This is a preferable and more accurate way of expressing the requirement of s. 2(3). The customary use of the terms 'first-hand' and 'second-hand' may occasionally brand as inadmissible a statement which is arguably quite capable of being admitted, as where B makes a contemporaneous note of what A says, or even secretly records it on tape, and later gives the writing or tape to C. It may be an interesting semantic question whether this is first or second-hand, but it seems perfectly arguable that A's statement was made in a document and so may be proved by C. If B merely later writes down his recollection of what A said and gives the writing to C, C cannot prove the statement, not because it is second-hand, but because the Act say that his evidence is inadmissible for that purpose; the statement may be proved quite properly either by A or B.

Statements made by a person while giving oral evidence in other legal proceedings are admissible under s. 2 (36) and are exempted from the evidential requirements of s. 2(3) notwithstanding that they are made otherwise than in a document. Indeed, the proviso to the subsection allows a considerable degree of latitude in the manner of proof. It should be observed that, while the court is free to permit proof of the statement concerned in any manner which seems to be appropriate, the Court of Appeal were prepared to hold in *Taylor* v *Taylor* (37) that with regard to a criminal trial on indictment, the transcript of evidence was admissible under s. 2. It would probably have been more precise to say that the transcript was a proper manner of proving the statements made in the course of giving evidence, which statements were admissible under s. 2, but clearly, the practice is the most satisfactory and accurate available to the court. In courts where no such record is taken as will enable an exact transcript to be produced, resort may be had to notes taken by the Bench or the clerk, or even by a legal representative. In view of the wording of the proviso, it would be open to the court, in the last resort, to permit a witness to narrate what evidence he had himself given in other proceedings, or to call another person who heard the former evidence being given. An application for the court to rule on this matter in advance may be made by any party under RSC, Ord.38, r. 28.

8.6 Statements admissible under s. 4

By s. 4 of the Act:

(1) Without prejudice to section 5 of this Act, in any civil proceedings a statement contained in a document shall, subject to this section and to rules of court, be admissible as evidence of any fact stated therein of which direct oral evidence would be admissible, if the document is, or forms part of, a record compiled by a person acting under a duty from information which was supplied by a person (whether acting under a duty or not) who had, or may reasonably be supposed to have had, personal knowledge of the matters dealt with in that information and which, if not supplied by that person to the compiler of the record directly, was supplied by him to the compiler of the record indirectly through one or more intermediaries each acting under a duty.

36 Though their admissibility and the conditions on which they are admitted are governed by RSC, Ord. 38, r. 28 (made under the authority of s. 8(3)(*b*) of the Act) which gives the court wide powers to regulate their admission and proof; see 8.9, post.

37 [1970] 1 WLR 1148. The court thought that the transcript of the summing-up might have to be admitted under s. 4 of the Act as part of a record compiled by the shorthand writer acting under a duty, as opposed to s. 2.

(2) Where in any civil proceedings a party desiring to give a statement in evidence by virtue of this section has called or intends to call as a witness in the proceedings the person who originally supplied the information from which the record containing the statement was compiled, the statement —

(*a*) shall not be given in evidence by virtue of this section on behalf of that party without the leave of the court; and

(*b*) without prejudice to paragraph (*a*) above, shall not without the leave of the court be given in evidence by virtue of this section on behalf of that party before the conclusion of the examination-in-chief of the person who originally supplied the said information.

(3) Any reference in this section to a person acting under a duty includes a reference to a person acting in the course of any trade, business, profession or other occupation in which he is engaged or employed or for the purposes of any paid or unpaid office held by him.

This section, which relates to the admissibility of records, is to some extent equivalent to, though much wider than, s. 1 of the Criminal Evidence Act 1965 in criminal cases. S. 4 applies only to statements contained in 'documents' within the meaning of s. 10(1), which was discussed in 8.5.3, and like s. 2, preserves the requirement of general admissibility under the rules of evidence, by the limitation that the statement may be evidence, 'of any fact stated therein of which direct oral evidence would be admissible'. Various matters require some further consideration.

8.6.1 'Record'

Curiously, the Act contains no definition of 'record', perhaps because it had not at the time become apparent that the term could be the subject of debate. But as we have seen, the same word employed in s. 1 of the Criminal Evidence Act 1965 has not been altogether free from difficulty. The matter is considered, together with the relevant cases decided under the 1965 Act in 8.3.3, ante, and there being no authority on the point specifically under the 1968 Act, it is reasonable to assume that the observations made in that paragraph apply equally to the word 'record' here. It is submitted that some element of deliberate accumulation or preservation of material for future reference is envisaged, although its quality or method probably goes only to the weight of the evidence.

8.6.2 'Acting under a duty'

The records rendered admissible by s. 4 are not confined to those of a trade or business, as are those admissible under s. 1 of the 1965 Act in criminal cases, but instead, a safeguard is introduced to ensure some degree of accuracy in the records admitted by requiring that the record shall have been made by a person acting under a 'duty', and thus carrying some measure of personal responsibility for that which he records. The duty requirement does not apply to the person who originally supplied the information from which the record is compiled, though his conduct is subject to the separate safeguard of the requirement of personal knowledge. But the duty requirement does apply to 'intermediaries', that is to say, anyone who acts as a link in the chain of communication or supply of the information from the original supplier to the eventual compiler of the record. This is a sensible provision, which avoids the obvious lacuna in the corresponding safeguard of the Criminal Evidence Act 1965 (see 8.3.5, ante).

The non-exclusive definition of 'duty' provided by s. 4(3) shows that a wide approach is intended. The duty need not relate only to commercial matters, and need not even relate to any function for which the compiler is paid, but would include duties arising from public or even private, honorary offices, and so would appear to cover not only legal duties, but also social or moral ones. The term has not as yet given rise to difficulty.

8.6.3   The requirement of personal knowledge
The original supplier of the information is subject to the requirement that he had, or may reasonably be supposed to have had, personal knowledge of the matters dealt with in the information which he supplied. The existence of a wide, separate provision, in s. 5, for the admissibility of statements produced by computers has probably obviated the problems which have recently come to light in relation to the corresponding provisions in the Criminal Evidence Act 1965 (see 8.3.5, ante). The trial judge is entitled, under s. 6(2), in deciding the admissibility of statements tendered under s. 4, to have regard to the circumstances in which the statement was made or to its form and contents and to draw any reasonable inference from those matters. It may be that in many cases, the actual or probable state of personal knowledge of the supplier will be readily apparent once reference is made to them. But it appears that the court will be ready to hold that the supplier may reasonably be supposed to have had such knowledge in a case where lapse of time has rendered such a finding necessary, at least where the supplier was carrying out a public or official function. In *Knight and Others* v *David and Others* (38), a claim by the plaintiffs to certain land depended upon events which occurred in 1886, and for the purpose of establishing that claim, the plaintiffs sought to put in evidence a tithe map and tithe apportionment survey, made under the provisions of the Tithe Act 1836. Goulding J, while holding that these documents were admissible at common law as proving public or general rights (39), was prepared to infer also that the supplier of the information contained in them, acting as he was in an important public capacity, might be reasonably supposed to have had personal knowledge of the matters dealt with in the information which he supplied with a view to those documents being compiled.

8.6.4   S. 4(2)
This subsection makes provision, similar but not exactly identical to that in s. 2(2), for cases where the party tendering admissible evidence contained in a record proposes also to call as a witness the original supplier of the information. The purpose of the provisions is the same as that of s. 2(2) (see 8.5.2, ante). But it is both interesting and important to note that, while the same requirement of leave and the same limitation on the time when the statement may be put in evidence are imposed, the latter is in this section absolute, and is not capable of being relieved by the exceptions provided for in s. 2.

8.7   Statements admissible under s. 5

It is not proposed to consider here the detailed provisions of s. 5, which, though not unimportant and indeed likely to become more so as technology advances, have not yet attracted the attention of the courts. The section provides that in civil proceedings, subject to various safeguards relating to proof of the proper supply of information to, and the proper working of the computer, and to rules of court, statements produced by

---

38   [1971] 1 WLR 1671.
39   Strictly, this seems to be incorrect, because the rule referred to by Goulding J is one incorporated into the Civil Evidence Act 1968 by s. 9; but this makes no difference of substance in its operation, and the learned judge's view seems plainly right in principle.

computers are to be admissible 'as evidence of any fact stated therein of which direct oral evidence would be admissible'. The section is clearly designed to permit the introduction of a certain degree of mechanically and automatically produced evidence, and so would seem to avoid the problems which have arisen under the Criminal Evidence Act 1965 with regard to the requirement in that Act that in every case an element of personal knowledge is to be looked for which the operator of an automatic machine may well not· have (40). It is to be noticed that, in s. 4 of the Civil Evidence Act 1968, the operation of that section (in which there is also a requirement of personal knowledge) is expressly said to be 'without prejudice to s. 5'.

By s. 5(6), for the purposes of part 1 of the Act: '"computer" means any device for storing and processing information, and any reference to information being derived from other information is a reference to its being derived therefrom by calculation, comparison or any other process.'

8.8   S.6: proof, admissibility, weight

S.6 deals with matters ancillary to the admission of statements tendered under s. 2, s. 4 or s. 5 (and, in the case of the provisions for the determination of weight, those tendered under s. 3) of the Act. The provisions of s. 6(4) dealing with such statements in the context of corroboration, are dealt with in 15.4, post. The matters considered here concern the mode of proof of admissible hearsay statements (s. 6(1)), the determination of the admissibility of such statements (s. 6(2)) and their weight when admitted (s. 6(3)).

8.8.1.   S. 6(1)
This subsection provides for the proof of statements tendered under s. 2, s. 4 or s. 5 of the Act and contained in documents (within the meaning of s. 10(1)). It will be recalled that statements admissible under s. 2 which are not made in documents are subject to the special rule of proof set out in s. 2(3). S. 6(1) provides that:

> Where in any civil proceedings a statement contained in a document is proposed to be given in evidence by virtue of section 2, 4 or 5 of this Act it may, subject to any rules of court, be proved by the production of that document or (whether or not that document is still in existence) by the production of a copy of that document, or of the material part thereof, authenticated in such manner as the court may approve.

The subsection must be read together with s. 10(2), which provides that:

> In this part of this Act any reference to a copy of a document includes —
>
> (*a*)   in the case of a document falling within paragraph (*c*) but not (*d*) of the definition of 'document' in the foregoing subsection [(41)], a transcript of the sounds or other data embodied therein;
> (*b*)   in the case of a document falling within paragraph (*d*) and not (*c*) of that definition [(42)], a reproduction or still reproduction of the image or images embodied therein, whether enlarged or not;

40   *R v Pettigrew* [1980] Crim LR 239; see 8.3.5, ante.
41   Paragraph (*c*) is concerned with sounds and aural data capable of being reproduced: see 8.5.3, ante.
42   Paragraph (*d*) is concerned with visual images on film and the like capable of being reproduced: see 8.5.3, ante.

(c)   in the case of a document falling within both those paragraphs, such a transcript together with such a still reproduction; and

(d)   in the case of a document falling within the said paragraph (d) of which a visual image is embodied in a document falling within that paragraph, a reproduction of that image, whether enlarged or not,

any any reference to a copy of the material part of a document shall be construed accordingly.

In the case of documents in written form, including for this purpose the maps, plans, graphs and drawings referred to in s. 10(1)(a) and (b), the absence of any mandatory requirement would appear to indicate that any form of manual, automatic or photographic copy will suffice, provided that it is capable of being properly authenticated. The term 'authenticated' in s. 6(1) presumably means no more than that the copy should be shown to be a true copy of the original, however and whenever made, and the evidence required to prove this is not specified, the matter being one for the court in every case.

This permissive code of proof of admissible hearsay contained in documents contrasts vividly with the strict requirements at common law for the proof of the contents of documents tendered as direct evidence, in which case the production of the original is required, except in certain cases, and secondary evidence is inadmissible. Reference should be made in this connection to 16.2, post.

8.8.2   S. 6(2)

S. 6(2) relates to the determination of admissibility of a statement under s. 2, s. 4 or s. 5, and provides for reference to the circumstances in which the statement was made and to its form and contents, if made in a document. The provision corresponds to those of s. 1(2) of the Criminal Evidence Act 1965, in respect of the necessarily documentary statements with which that Act is concerned. Clearly, the matters referred to in s. 6(2) are those which are likely to assist the judge in the assessment of the various conditions of admissibility which he may have to consider for the purposes of s. 2, s. 4 or s. 5. As with s. 1(2) of the 1965 Act (see 8.3.6, ante) it would appear that a party who disputes the admissibility of such a statement is entitled to have the matter investigated, and as we shall see in 8.9, the rules of court are designed to ensure that this process can be effected at an interlocutory stage of the proceedings, so that the trial itself is not subject to undue interruption because of disputes over admissibility. Nonetheless, there will be unforeseen matters which require and must be given attention, and if necessary decided by the judge, at the trial stage. S. 6(2) provides that:

For the purpose of deciding whether or not a statement is admissible in evidence by virtue of section 2, 4 or 5 of this Act, the court may draw any reasonable inference from the circumstances in which the statement was made or otherwise came into being or from any other circumstances, including, in the case of a statement contained in a document, the form and contents of that document.

8.8.3   S. 6(3)

By this subsection:

In estimating the weight, if any, to be attached to a statement admissible in evidence by virtue of section 2, 3, 4 or 5 of this Act regard shall be had to all the circumstances from which any inference can reasonably be drawn as to the accuracy or otherwise of the statement and, in particular —

(*a*)   in the case of a statement falling within section 2(1) or 3(1) or (2) of this Act, to the question whether or not the statement was made contemporaneously with the occurrence or existence of the facts stated, and to the question whether or not the maker of the statement had any incentive to conceal or misrepresent the facts;
(*b*)   in the case of a statement falling within section 4(1) of this Act, to the question whether or not the person who originally supplied the information from which the record containing the statement was compiled did so contemporaneously with the occurrence or existence of the facts dealt with in that information, and to the question whether or not that person, or any person concerned with compiling or keeping the record containing the statement, had any incentive to conceal or misrepresent the facts; and
(*c*)   [makes equivalent provision for statements admissible under s. 5].

The subsection does not call for comment, except that the question of weight is much easier to deal with in civil cases, where the judge will inevitably form his own view at an early stage, and where, in some cases, his view of the likely weight may even lead him to refuse leave where leave is required for admission. Certainly, there is no need for adherence to the terms of the subsection in quite the same way as there may be in criminal cases, where the trial judge may well be obliged to direct the jury with regard to the weight of evidence admitted under the Criminal Evidence Act 1965, in the terms of s. 1(3) of that Act (see 8.3.7, ante). Although it is a ground of appeal in civil cases that a decision was against the weight of the evidence, a judge cannot be tied to the literal wording of s. 6(3), and it is to be noticed that the paragraphs of the subsection are expressed to be merely particular instances of 'all the circumstances from which any inference can reasonably be drawn as to the accuracy or otherwise of the statement', to which the judge is to have regard.

8.9   The notice procedure

S. 8 of the Civil Evidence Act 1968 provides statutory authority for the creation of a substantial body of rules of court within the framework of which s. 2, s. 4 and s. 5 shall operate. S. 8(1) provides:

Provision shall be made by rules of court as to the procedure which, subject to any exceptions provided for in the rules, must be followed and the other conditions which, subject as aforesaid, must be fulfilled before a statement can be given in evidence in civil proceedings by virtue of section 2, 4 or 5 of this Act.

The remainder of the section provides specifically for various kinds of rule, sometimes in mandatory form and sometimes by way of an enabling provision. The resulting rules governing practice in the High Court are to be found in RSC, Ord. 38, rr. 21–31 (43).

43   The corresponding practice in the County Court is to be found in CCR, Ord. 20, rr. 20–32. These are not considered separately here, but may be found in the *County Court Practice*. RSC, Ord. 38, rr. 30–31, relating to evidence admissible under s. 7 of the Act, are also not considered here.

They will be examined here only in their general effect, and so as to highlight the evidential points which they raise. For the more detailed practical working of the rules, reference should be made to the *Supreme Court Practice*. The overriding purpose of the rules is to bring about and enforce a system of notice, that is to say a procedure of general application that, as a requirement of practice, a party wishing to give in evidence a hearsay statement admissible by virtue of s. 2, s. 4 or s. 5 must first give to each other party notice of that intention, indicating the nature and substance of the evidence which is sought to be adduced. The opponent is then enabled, by himself giving notice, to compel the party seeking to adduce the evidence to call as a witness the maker of the statement, unless for one of a number of reasons the maker is not available to be called, or there would be no point in calling him to deal with the evidence in question. In effect, the rules impose a further condition of admissibility upon statements tendered under these sections, albeit a condition of practice rather than law, and albeit that the court is given a general discretion to admit despite non-compliance with the rules. The provisions may be summarised as follows, in a convenient and much appreviated form, before being considered in more detail:

(a)   By r. 21, a party wishing to adduce hearsay evidence under s. 2, s. 4 or s. 5 must, within certain time-limits, serve notice of his intention to do so, the form of such notice differing with the section applicable to the evidence.

(b)   On receipt of such notice, any other party may serve, under r. 26, a counter-notice requiring the party wishing to adduce the evidence to call as a witness any person named in the original notice as being a person involved in the making or receiving of the hearsay statement in question. Subject to the Court's discretion, failure to comply with a counter-notice will result in the hearsay evidence being inadmissible.

(c)   A counter-notice may be ineffective, however, where the party wishing to adduce the evidence states in his notice that for any one of the reasons enumerated in r. 25, it is not possible, or is pointless, to call the person in respect of whom the counter-notice was to be given. The opponent must then either accept this position, or invite the court to determine whether the reason alleged does in fact apply to the person concerned, having served a counter-notice indicating that he disputes the applicability of the reason given. The court will then decide whether the counter-notice may take effect so as to require the attendance of that person. If the reason given is held to apply to that person, the hearsay statement is admissible and he need not be called.

(d)   The court has an overriding discretion, by virtue of r. 29, to receive evidence under s. 2, s. 4 or s. 5, notwithstanding any non-compliance with the rules. This discretion must, of course, be exercised judicially so as to do justice between the parties and ensure a fair trial, having regard to all the circumstances.

These provisions must now be considered in a little more detail.

8.9.1   Notice of intention
By r. 21:

(1)   Subject to the provisions of this rule, a party to a cause or matter who desires to give in evidence at the trial or hearing of the cause or matter any statement which is admissible in evidence by virtue of section 2, 4 or 5 of the Act must —

(*a*)   in the case of a cause or matter which is required to be set down for trial or hearing or adjourned into court, within 21 days after it is set down or so adjourned, or within such other period as the Court may specify, and

(*b*)   in the case of any other cause or matter, within 21 days after the date on which an appointment for the first hearing of the cause or matter is obtained, or within such other period as the Court may specify,

serve on every other party to the cause or matter notice of his desire to do so, and the notice must comply with the provisions of rule 22, 23 or 24, as the circumstances of the case require.

(2)   Paragraph (1) shall not apply in relation to any statement which is admissible as evidence of any fact stated therein by virtue not only of the said section 2, 4 or 5 but by virtue also of any other statutory provision within the meaning of section 1 of the Act. [(44).]

The time-limits imposed, within which notice must be given, are intended to ensure that, so far as possible, every other party is given an adequate length of time to determine whether he accepts the admissibility of the statement, or whether he wishes to take any steps to dispute it. It is also important that any such issues as may arise should be considered and dealt with, as far as possible, at the interlocutory stage, so that the smooth and expeditious conduct of the trial is not affected by unnecessary applications relating to the admissibility of evidence.

The form of the notice varies according to which section applies to the statement sought to be admitted. The form is governed in the case of statements admissible under s. 2 by r. 22, in the case of those admissible under s. 4 by r. 23 (45) and in the case of those admissible under s. 5 by r. 24. Rule 24 is not considered further in detail. The principal provisions of r. 22 and r. 23 are as follows:

22. — (1)   If the statement is admissible by virtue of section 2 of the Act and was made otherwise than in a document, the notice must contain particulars of —

(*a*)   the time, place and circumstances at or in which the statement was made;
(*b*)   the person by whom, and the person to whom, the statement was made; and
(*c*)   the substance of the statement or, if material, the words used.

(2)   If the statement is admissible by virtue of the said section 2 and was made in a document, a copy or transcript of the document, or of the relevant part thereof, must be annexed to the notice and the notice must contain such (if any) of the particulars mentioned in paragraph (1)(*a*) and (*b*) as are not apparent on the face of the document or part. . . .

23. — (1)   If the statement is admissible by virtue of section 4 of the Act, the notice

44   For self-evident reasons, r. 21(3) provides that no notice need be given where the hearsay statement sought to be admitted is alleged to have been made by a deceased and is to be admitted in a probate action the subject of which is the deceased's estate.
45   If the statement tendered as admissible by virtue of s. 2 or s. 4 is one consisting of evidence given (orally or in a document) in other legal proceedings, or is contained in a record of direct oral evidence so given, the notice under r. 21 makes available the procedure under r. 28, as an alternative to a r. 26 counter-notice in such cases: see 8.9.2, post.

must have annexed to it a copy or transcript of the document containing the statement, or of the relevant part thereof, and must contain —

(*a*)   particulars of —

(i)   the person by whom the record containing the statement was compiled; and
(ii)   the person who originally supplied the information from which the record was compiled; and
(iii)   any other person through whom that information was supplied to the compiler of that record;

and, in the case of any such person as is referred to in (i) or (iii) above, a description of the duty under which that person was acting when compiling that record or supplying information from which that record was compiled, as the case may be;
(*b*)   if not apparent on the face of the document annexed to the notice, a description of the nature of the record which, or part of which, contains the statement; and
(*c*)   particulars of the time, place and circumstances at or in which that record or part was compiled.

In addition, rules 22, 23 and 24 each provide that if the party giving the notice alleges that any person, particulars of whom are contained in the notice, cannot or should not be called as a witness, at the trial or hearing, for any of the reasons specified in r. 25, then the notice must contain a statement to that effect specifying the reason relied on. This is to enable other parties to refer such reason to the court under r. 27. The object of having notices in the forms indicated in these rules is, of course, to ensure that the other party's disadvantage in being faced with hearsay evidence is balanced by his knowing in advance as much about that evidence as he can, and by his being enabled, in consequence, to decide whether a counter-notice should be served under r. 26. The degree of detail insisted upon by the rules does in fact provide a real measure of compensation for having to accept, if it must be accepted, evidence admissible under one of the sections to which the rules apply. It also illustrates the advantage to a party in being able to justify, if he can, the admission of hearsay statements other than under s. 2, s. 4 or s. 5, for example under s. 9; in such a case, he escapes the notice procedure altogether, and not only avoids giving his hand away before trial, but also avoids the possibility of a counter-notice. This is made clear by r. 21(2). Hearsay evidence admitted by agreement of the parties, as it may be under s. 1, would present no practical problem in this context but in order to dispense with notice altogether every party affected must agree to its admission, any party who does not agree being entitled to notice under r. 21.

The provisions of r. 21 are to be enforced assiduously. Any party wishing to adduce hearsay evidence under s. 2, s. 4 or s. 5 must serve a notice in his own right. Thus in *Letraset International Ltd* v *Dymo Ltd* (46) where the plaintiffs served notice of their intention to adduce hearsay statements admissible under s. 2, consisting of evidence given on their behalf at a previous hearing, but later abandoned their intention to adduce them, the defendants were held not to be entitled to adduce such statements as part of their case without first serving notice on the plaintiffs under r. 21 in their own right; they were not entitled to rely for that purpose on the notice given by the plaintiffs because the

46   [1976] RPC 65. The point was not considered on appeal.

plaintiffs were not able to infer from their own notice the exact nature and extent of the evidence which the defendants intended to adduce. The rule also applies to a case where a party intends to adduce in evidence hearsay statements made in documents disclosed to him on discovery (47).

8.9.2 Counter-notice
R. 26 provides that:

(1) Subject to paragraphs (2) and (3), any party to a cause or matter on whom a notice under rule 21 is served may within 21 days after service of the notice on him serve on the party who gave the notice a counter-notice requiring that party to call as a witness at the trial or hearing of the cause or matter any person (naming him) particulars of whom are contained in the notice. . . .

(4) If the party to a cause or matter by whom a notice under rule 21 is served fails to comply with a counter-notice duly served on him under this rule, then, unless any of the reasons specified in rule 25 applies in relation to the person named in the counter-notice, and without prejudice to the powers of the Court under rule 29, the statement to which the notice under rule 21 relates shall not be admissible at the trial or hearing of the cause or matter as evidence of any fact stated therein by virtue of section 2, 4 or 5 of the Act, as the case may be.

It is important to note the effect of a counter-notice. It does not oblige the party on whom it is served to call the person referred to as a witness. The effect of r. 26(4) is that if such person is not called, the statement, the subject of the r. 21 notice, will not be admissible by virtue of s. 2, s. 4 or s. 5, unless either r. 25 applies or the judge exercises his discretion to admit it under r. 29. It does not necessarily mean that the statement cannot be admitted, and nothing in the rule precludes the admission of the statement under some other statutory provision, or as a piece of direct evidence for a purpose other than to prove the truth of the facts stated in it. If the witness is called, as required by the counter-notice, the effect is not that his hearsay statement is thereby rendered inadmissible (48), but that it will be admissible only subject to the requirement of leave, and to the other requirements of s. 2(2) or s. 4(2), as the case may be.

Apart from the cases to which r. 25 applies, counter-notice should be served wherever it is wished to require the attendance of a person referred to in the r. 21 notice, except in cases falling within r. 28. These are cases where the r. 21 notice expresses a wish to give in evidence a statement, admissible under s. 2, consisting of evidence given (orally or in a document) in other legal proceedings, or a statement, admissible under s. 4, contained in a record of any direct oral evidence so given. In such cases, r. 28, made under the authority of s. 8(3)(*b*) of the Act, confers on the court a wide power to permit such evidence to be given, to impose conditions on its admissibility and to give general directions with respect to it. In such cases, r. 26(3) provides that no counter-notice should be served, but instead, an application made to the court for directions under r. 28.

While a party is at liberty to serve a counter-notice in any case except those mentioned above, it is pertinent to observe that the court has ample power to deal by way of costs with unnecessary requirements for witnesses to attend, and with any waste of the court's

---

47 *Minnesota Mining & Manufacturing Co.* v *Johnson & Johnson Ltd* (CA) [1976] FSR 6.
48 *Pace* the *Supreme Court Practice,* which in the commentary on r. 26 appears to suggest the contrary.

time. The procedure should, therefore, be used with some discretion, bearing in mind not only the nature but also the likely weight of the evidence to be adduced on the other side, and remembering that there are cases where a witness giving oral evidence may invest part of the case with a force which may be wholly lacking in a hearsay document.

8.9.3 *Witnesses who cannot or should not be called*

As we have seen, r. 22, r. 23 and r. 24 provide that r. 21 notices given in the cases to which, they are appropriate may and should contain any allegation made that a person named in the notice cannot or should not be called as a witness, and the reason relied on for that allegation should be set out. The reasons upon which reliance may be placed for this purpose are laid down in r. 25, and no other reasons may be resorted to. R. 25 provides that:

> The reasons referred to in rules 22(3), 23(2) and 24(3) are that the person in question is dead, or beyond the seas, or unfit by reason of his bodily or mental condition to attend as a witness or that despite the exercise of reasonable diligence it has not been possible to identify or find him or that he cannot reasonably be expected to have any recollection of matters relevant to the accuracy or otherwise of the statement to which the notice relates.

The inclusion of such an allegation in a r. 21 notice has an immediate effect on the subsequent procedure. Firstly, it imposes restrictions on the service and effect of a counter-notice. By r. 26(2):

> Where any notice under rule 21 contains a statement that any person particulars of whom are contained in the notice cannot or should not be called as a witness for the reason specified therein, a party shall not be entitled to serve a counter-notice under this rule requiring that person to be called as a witness at the trial or hearing of the cause or matter unless he contends that that person can or, as the case may be, should be called, and in that case he must include in his counter-notice a statement to that effect.

There may, of course, be cases where even the limited use which may be made of a counter-notice in these circumstances is useless, as where it can readily be demonstrated that the person referred to is dead or beyond the seas, but the other reasons may easily give rise to considerable dispute. In such case, any party may refer such dispute to the court under r. 27 for determination of the question whether any of the reasons specified in r. 25 applies to the person in question. The court may, and will if possible, determine this issue before trial, and where this is done, no further application may be made at trial unless fresh evidence comes to light, which could not, with reasonable diligence, have been adduced at the original application: r. 27(3). If the court determines that a r. 25 reason applies, the party seeking to adduce the hearsay evidence is entitled to do so in any event. If no r. 25 reason is found to apply, the counter-notice will take effect in the normal way.

Any one of the r. 25 reasons, standing alone, will suffice if shown to apply. In *Rasool* v *West Midlands Passenger Transport Executive* (49), the defendants wished to adduce the

---

49 [1974] 3 All ER 638. Of interest are Finer J's observations at 642 as to the possible consequences to the defendants of not seeking to find the witness.

hearsay statement of a person who, according to their r. 21 notice, had 'left her former address . . . and cannot at present be found. It is understood that she is now beyond the seas and is probably resident in Jamaica'. On the available evidence, this account appeared to be accurate, although the defendants had made no effort to trace the potential witness. It was argued for the plaintiffs that the statement was not admissible, because even if the missing witness was beyond the seas, it was still for the defendants to show that despite the exercise of reasonable diligence, she could not be found. Finer J rejected the plaintiff's argument, holding that the reasons given in r. 25 were disjunctive, and that the provision that the witness could not be found with reasonable diligence was simply one of them. If the defendants established any one reason, as they had, the balance of probabilities being the appropriate standard of proof in the matter, the statement was admissible. This decision was approved by the Court of Appeal in *Piermay Shipping Co. SA and Another v Chester* (50).

8.9.4 The court's discretion

By s. 8(3)(*a*) of the Act, the rules of court to be made were empowered to confer on the court a discretion to allow the admission of a statement under s. 2, s. 4 or s. 5 despite the non-compliance in any particular case with the rules concerning admissibility. The court was not, however, to be given any discretion to exclude admissible evidence, where the rules had been complied with, save in the sole instance of statements falling within what later became r. 28, consisting of evidence given, or the record of oral evidence given, in other proceedings. The existence of a wide inclusionary discretion was felt to be necessary to prevent the new law from being encumbered or even strangled by excessive technicality. The discretion is conferred by r. 29, which provides that:

(1) Without prejudice to section 2(2)(*a*) and 4(2)(*a*) of the Act and rule 28, the Court may, if it thinks it just to do so, allow a statement falling within section 2(1), 4(1) or 5(1) of the Act to be given in evidence at the trial or hearing of a cause or matter notwithstanding —

(*a*) that the statement is one in relation to which rule 21(1) applies and that the party desiring to give the statement in evidence has failed to comply with that rule, or
(*b*) that that party has failed to comply with any requirement of a counter-notice relating to that statement which was served on him in accordance with rule 26.

(2) Without prejudice to the generality of paragraph (1), the Court may exercise its power under that paragraph to allow a statement to be given in evidence at the trial or hearing of a cause or matter if a refusal to exercise that power might oblige the party desiring to give the statement in evidence to call as a witness at the trial or hearing an opposite party or a person who is or was at the material time the servant or agent of an opposite party.

The discretion must be exercised judicially, with a view to doing justice between the parties and securing a fair trial. The operation of the general discretion under r. 29(1)

---

50   [1978] 1 WLR 411. Whether this ought to be the position is open to some question. Both Finer J in *Rasool* and Donaldson J at first instance in *Piermay* recognised that the construction left something to be desired. But it was evidently a deliberate step by Parliament, which as Eveleigh LJ pointed out in *Piermay*, departed from the position under the Evidence Act 1938 under which being beyond the seas was insufficient unless it was also shown that a person could not be found with reasonable diligence.

may be aptly illustrated by contrasting the cases of *Ford* v *Lewis* (51) and *Morris* v *Stratford-on-Avon RDC* (52). In *Ford* v *Lewis,* the infant plaintiff was struck by a vehicle driven by the defendant. The plaintiff was, at the material time, in the charge of her parents, and the defendant (who by the time of the trial was a mental patient and incapable of giving evidence) wished to put in evidence, *inter alia,* statements made in medical records and in a document which he himself had made, which tended to show that the plaintiff's father was very drunk at the time of the accident. No notices under r. 21 had been served in respect of such statements. The reason for non-compliance with the rule emerged for the first time in the Court of Appeal, and was that notice had been withheld on the advice of counsel, apparently on the purported ground that it was not known how the plaintiff's case was to be put, and whether it would be necessary to use the statements in evidence. The Court of Appeal were, therefore, faced with the situation that the trial judge had been unaware of the true reason why the rules had not been complied with, and had to decide whether the request for exercise of discretion under r. 29 could be upheld. The whole court condemned the course which had been adopted on behalf of the defendant, and while Davies LJ was against the granting of a new trial because of the already considerable delay and because it seemed to him that the ultimate result must be the same, the majority (Edmund Davies and Karminski LJJ) held that the order was inevitable. Edmund Davies LJ said (53):

> In these most unfortunate circumstances, it seems to me impossible that the defendant should be permitted to rely upon the judge's purported exercise of his discretion under r. 29. I hold that there can be no valid exercise of such discretion if there has (for any reason) been a deliberate withholding from the court of the reason for non-compliance. Had Veale J known that this was the result of a deliberate decision based upon the tactical value of surprise, I regard it as inconceivable that he would have ruled in favour of admitting the statement. But, with the profoundest respect to Davies LJ I go so far as to say that, even if he had, such an attitude ought not to be countenanced by this court. A suitor who deliberately flouts the rules has no right to ask the court to exercise in his favour a discretionary indulgence created by those very same rules. Furthermore, a judge who, to his knowledge, finds himself confronted by such a situation would not, as I think, be acting judicially if he nevertheless exercised his discretion in favour of the recalcitrant suitor. The rules are there to be respected, and those who defy them should not be indulged or excused. Slackness is one thing; deliberate disobedience another. The former may be overlooked: the latter never, even though, as here, it derives from mistaken zeal on the client's behalf. To tolerate it would be dangerous to justice.

In *Morris* v *Stratford-on-Avon RDC,* on the other hand, the facts were entirely different. At the trial of an action for personal injury some five years after the event, a witness gave evidence for the defendants. At the conclusion of his examination in chief, it became apparent for the first time to counsel for the defendants that it would be desirable that an application should be made to the trial judge to admit, in the exercise of his discretion, a statement made by the witness some nine months only after the event. The judge admitted the statement, despite objection on behalf of the plaintiff. No notice had, of course, been served under r. 21. The Court of Appeal upheld the judge's exercise of discretion. Megaw LJ said (54):

51   (CA) [1971] 1 WLR 623.   52   (CA) [1973] 1 WLR 1059.   53   [1971] 1 WLR 623 at 633.
54   [1973] 1 WLR 1059 at 1063.

Nothing that I say must be taken in any way as suggesting that non-compliance with the rules as to notices is a matter that can be lightly overlooked. On the other hand, there must be cases in which there is, sensibly and reasonably, no ground for supposing that a statement which is in existence is going to be used by a party. It would perhaps be unfortunate if the matter were to be so interpreted that, in every case, those who are advising a party felt it necessary to advise him that, if there is any possibility, however remote, that as a result of something which may happen hereafter, an application might be sought to be made, then notice should be given in advance. But, quite clearly, if there is reason to suppose, on proper consideration of the evidence, that such an application may be made, then care must be taken that the proper notices should be given.

Megaw LJ then held that no blame whatsoever could attach to counsel in the instant case, considered *Ford* v *Lewis,* and concluded (55):

It is perfectly apparent that that is not this case, and that this case bears no conceivable relationship to the matters which motivated the court to take the course that it did in that case. However, it is right that careful consideration should always be given, on an application of this sort, to matters such as those that were stressed before us by counsel for the plaintiff: for example, that the statement was taken as a proof of evidence and that it was not closely contemporary with the time of the accident but was taken some nine months later. Those are matters which of course go to weight; but they can also be relevant on the question of a decision as to the exercise of discretion. Another matter which in my judgment must always be carefully watched, when an application of this sort is made under the Civil Evidence Act 1968 without proper notices having been given, is for the judge to make sure, so far as he can, that no injustice will be done to the other party by reason of the statement being allowed to be put in evidence. If there is ground to suppose that there will be any injustice caused, or that the other party will be materially prejudiced or embarrassed, then the judge should either refuse to allow the document to be admitted or, in his discretion, allow it on terms, such as an adjournment at the cost of the party seeking to put in the statement.

It would be difficult to elaborate usefully on those very clear guidelines offered by the Court of Appeal on the exercise of the discretion under r. 29.

Without prejudice to the general discretion under r. 29(1), there is a more specific discretion under r. 29(2), designed to avoid the possibility that the notice procedure might actually lead to the result that a party who serves a notice under r. 21 might, by reason of the service on him of a counter-notice (or an application under r. 28), be compelled as the price of putting in a hearsay statement, to call as a witness an opposite party or a person who is, or was at a material time, the servant or agent of an opposite party. This is a real danger when it is proposed to use against a party, quite legitimately under the Act, a hearsay statement made by such a person on another occasion. The discretion is there to guard against the possibility, in effect, that a party might be forced to call a foreseeably hostile, or at least foreseeably unreliable, witness. Its proper use is illustrated by the decision of Pennycuick V-C in *Tremelbye (Selangor) Rubber Co. Ltd* v *Stekel and Others* (56). The plaintiff company brought an action alleging that the various defendants had been party to a dishonest transaction whereby the plaintiff company's money had been used in the purchase of its own shares. One defendant and three

55   Ibid at 1064–5.   56   [1971] 1 WLR 226.

employees of another defendant (a bank) had given evidence for the prosecution in criminal proceedings arising from a Board of Trade inquiry in respect of the same matters. The plaintiffs sought to put in evidence the statements of those persons contained in the transcript of the evidence in the criminal proceedings. It was held that the interests of justice required that the plaintiffs be permitted to adduce the transcript. Failing such a direction, the plaintiffs would be placed in the obviously invidious position of having either to call witnesses who could not be expected to give favourable evidence, or to forgo the use of relevant and perhaps cogent evidence in their favour. The evidence was allowed to be admitted on terms that the defendants should have the opportunity to cross-examine the witnesses, and the plaintiffs to re-examine without the limitation on the questions which could ordinarily be put to 'their own' witnesses. Although the decision turned on an application for leave under r. 28, it would appear that the result must have been the same in the case of a counter-notice. The situation was that contemplated expressly by r. 29(2).

8.10   Civil Evidence Act 1972

It will be recalled that the Civil Evidence Act 1968 applies only to statements of fact, a provision that excludes statements of opinion, when contained in hearsay statements, even where such opinion would be admissible by the general law of evidence, if given in evidence orally. The Civil Evidence Act 1972 extended the application of the 1968 Act to statements of opinion by the following words contained in s. 1(1):

> Subject to the provisions of this section, part 1 . . . of the Civil Evidence Act 1968, except s. 5, . . . shall apply in relation to statements of opinion as it applies in relation to statements of fact, subject to the necessary modifications and in particular the modification that any reference to a fact stated in a statement shall be construed as a reference to a matter dealt with therein.

This subsection applies alike to statements admissible under s. 2 and those admissible under s. 4 of the 1968 Act but the particular exigencies of the latter section called for more precise definition of the circumstances in which hearsay statements of opinion' might properly be admitted as contained in records, and accordingly s. 1(2) of the 1972 Act provides that:

> Section 4 . . . of the Civil Evidence Act 1968, as applied by subsection (1) above, shall not render admissible in any civil proceedings a statement of opinion contained in a record unless that statement would be admissible in those proceedings if made in the course of giving oral evidence by the person who originally supplied the information from which the record was compiled; but where a statement of opinion contained in a record deals with a matter on which the person who originally supplied the information from which the record was compiled is (or would if living be) qualified to give oral expert evidence, the said section 4, as applied by subsection (1) above, shall have the effect in relation to that statement as if so much of subsection (1) of that section as requires personal knowledge on the part of that person were omitted.

This provision achieves two important results. Firstly, it removes what would otherwise have been a serious ambiguity by providing that it is not the opinion evidence of everyone concerned in the making of a record which may be admitted under s. 4. The opinion evidence of the compiler of the record, or of an intermediary by whom the information was transmitted from the original supplier to the compiler, is not admissible even though contained in the record unless, coincidentally, it would also be admissible if given in the course of oral evidence by the original supplier of the information. This must, of course, be looked at by reference to the general law of opinion evidence, dealt with in Chapter 9, post. But it may be worth observing that by s. 3(2) of the 1972 Act, Parliament also provided that:

> It is hereby declared that where a person is called as a witness in any civil proceedings, a statement of opinion by him on any relevant matter on which he is not qualified to give expert evidence, if made as a way of conveying relevant facts personally perceived by him, is admissible as evidence of what he perceived.

Secondly, the subsection removes the requirement of personal knowledge in s. 4, in so far as the supplier of the information is dealing with a matter on which he is, or would have been, qualified to give expert-opinion evidence. The safeguard of personal knowledge, which is apposite to statements of fact, would have no real meaning in relation to statements of opinion. But the competence of the supplier as an expert is in itself some safeguard, and must be established to the court's satisfaction if asserted.

The consequence of the extension of part 1 of the 1968 Act to statements of opinion is, on the face of it, that such statements should be subject to the notice procedure as if they were statements of fact. In relation to non-expert opinion, this is indeed the result (57). But, in the case of expert-opinion evidence, the 1972 Act itself provided a separate statutory authority for the making of different rules of court, designed to promote general, early disclosure of such evidence to the other parties as a condition of being permitted to adduce it. The rules of court dealing with expert evidence are, accordingly, quite distinct from those relating to statements of fact and non-expert opinion. The rules for expert-opinion evidence are to be found in RSC, Ord. 38, rr. 36–44, and are dealt with in detail in 9.4, post, but it may be observed here that they are not confined to hearsay statements, but deal with the treatment of expert evidence generally in civil proceedings. Where a party calls as a witness the maker of an expert report, such report may be put in evidence at the commencement of the maker's examination in chief or at such other time as the court may direct: Ord. 38, r. 43. This departure from the rule for other witnesses in s. 2(2) and s. 4(2) of the 1968 Act, authorised by s. 2(1) of the 1972 Act, is obviously justified by the nature of the evidence.

8.11 Affidavits

It is not possible, within the scope of the present work, to consider in detail the practice relating to affidavits, but it should be noted that by RSC, Ord. 41, r. 5, an affidavit to be used in interlocutory proceedings may state the opinion information or belief of the deponent, together with the source of that opinion information or belief. Subject to the operation of that rule, and of Ord. 38, r. 3 (which gives the court wide powers to deal with the proof of relevant matters generally), r. 21(4) provides that the requirement of notice under r. 21 shall not apply to statements which a party to such proceedings desires

---

57 RSC, Ord. 38, r. 34, extends to such cases the provisions of rr. 20–23 and 25–33, 'with such modifications as the court may direct or the circumstances of the case may require'.

to have included in his affidavit or an affidavit to be used on his behalf in those proceedings. But where it is proper for evidence to be given on affidavit in any final proceedings, in the sense of proceedings in which the substantive merits of the case are to be determined, Ord. 41, r. 5, does not apply, and the notice procedure under r. 21 then operates as in the case of any other admissible hearsay evidence tendered under s. 2, s. 4 or s. 5. The exemption, therefore, applies only to affidavits used in interlocutory proceedings (58). Moreover, no rule permits the inclusion of hearsay statements without notice in any document exhibited to an affidavit, whether in final or interlocutory proceedings. The rule covers the affidavit itself and no more (59).

8.12   Questions for counsel

1   What rules would apply at the committal proceedings with respect to the use as evidence of witness statements made by prosecution witnesses? What safeguards are offered to the defence?

2   What steps should the prosecution take at the committal proceedings with regard to the evidence of Angela Blackstone? What steps may the defence take at this stage with regard to that evidence?

3   If, between committal and trial, Angela tells D/I Glanvil that she has become too frightened of Coke and Littleton to give evidence against them, may her deposition in any circumstances be read in evidence?

4   What steps should the prosecution take if:
  (a)   between committal and trial, fresh relevant evidence comes into their hands?
  (b)   a fully bound witness dies?

5   Assume the following facts: instead of asserting that he spent the morning at home, Littleton asserts as an alibi that he was working alone in a certain place, for one of his part-time employers. The only material available to support his alibi is an entry in the employer's wages book, made by the employer, which purports to show that Littleton was working at that time and place. The employer has since died. Are there any, and if so what circumstances in which the entry in the wages book can be used in evidence by Littleton?

58   *Nationwide Building Society* v *Bateman* [1978] 1 WLR 394.
59   *Re Koscot Interplanetary (UK) Ltd* [1972] 3 All ER 829.

9 Opinion Evidence

9.1 General rule

The general rule of common law was that the opinions, beliefs and inferences of a witness were inadmissible to prove the truth of the matters believed or inferred if such matters were in issue or relevant to facts in issue in the case. Apart from the question of the relevance and reliability of opinion evidence it was held to offend by upsurping the function of the court, to form an opinion on the facts in issue, on the basis of the facts proved by the evidence placed before it.

This did not, of course, prevent the admission of such evidence for other purposes, notably for the purpose of proving what the state of mind of the holder of an opinion was, at a certain time, if relevant to do so. Thus, in *Sheen* v *Bumpstead* (1) the belief of a party who represented that a trader was solvent was held admissible on the question whether the representation was made in good faith. And the belief of a defendant charged with handling stolen goods will be admitted to show that he knew or believed, or did not know or believe, that the goods were stolen, but will be inadmissible to prove that the goods were in fact stolen (2).

The same rule applied to evidence of general reputation, or public opinion, which is no more than an extended form of opinion evidence. Such evidence will be inadmissible to prove the truth of the matters generally reputed or believed to be true, but will be admissible to prove what the general reputation of a matter, or the state of public opinion on that matter, in fact was at a given time, if relevant to do so (3).

The common-law rule was and is subject to three important exceptions, but otherwise remains in full effect. The exceptions are:

(a) General reputation will be admissible as a weapon of last resort to prove matters of public concern, which would otherwise be impossible or very difficult to prove.

(b) Expert-opinion evidence is admissible to prove matters of specialised knowledge, on which the court would be unable properly to reach a conclusion unaided.

(c) Non-expert-opinion evidence may be received on matters within the competence and experience of people generally.

Before examining the detail of these exceptions, it is worth observing that wherever opinion evidence is admissible in civil cases it may be given in the form of hearsay statements according to and subject to the provisions of part 1 of the Civil Evidence Act

---

1 (ExCh) (1863) 2 H & C 193. 2 Cf *R* v *Marshall* [1977] Crim LR 106.
3 In contemporary practice such matters may be easier to prove in certain cases. Public opinion may, for example, be proved by evidence of a survey carried out scientifically: *Customglass Boats Ltd and Another* v *Salthouse Brothers Ltd and Another* (Supreme Court of New Zealand) [1976] RPC 589.

1968 (4). That Act did not originally apply to statements of opinion, but it was envisaged that it should be extended, and by s. 1 of the Civil Evidence Act 1972:

(1)   Subject to the provisions of this section, part 1 (hearsay evidence) of the Civil Evidence Act 1968, except s. 5 (statements produced by computers), shall apply in relation to statements of opinion as it applies in relation to statements of fact, subject to the necessary modifications and in particular the modification that any reference to a fact stated in a statement shall be construed as a reference to a matter dealt with therein.

S. 1(2) provides that where the statement of opinion is contained in a record, and it is sought to admit it under s. 4 of the 1968 Act, the statement must be one which would be admissible if made in direct oral evidence by the original supplier of the information from which the record was compiled. But where the statement would be admissible because the original supplier is or was qualified to give expert opinion evidence to that effect, s. 4 of the 1968 Act applies without any requirement of personal knowledge, which would be inapposite to such evidence.

Statements of opinion may, therefore, be admitted under either s. 2 or s. 4 of the 1968 Act, as the circumstances permit. In all cases except that of expert-opinion evidence, for which separate provision is made by s. 2 of the 1972 Act, a party wishing to adduce hearsay evidence of opinion, must comply with the notice procedure, laid down, pursuant to s. 8 of the 1968 Act, by RSC, Ord.38, rr. 21–31 (5).

A: GENERAL REPUTATION

9.2   Principles of admissibility

We have already observed that the common law succeeded in overcoming its objections to certain forms of evidence, based upon unreliability, in cases where, unless such evidence were admitted, no evidence would be available, or where the relevant facts would be impossible, or in practical terms impossible, to prove. It was accordingly accepted that in cases where direct evidence was difficult or impossible to obtain with regard to matters of public concern, such matters might, as a last resort, be proved by evidence of general reputation. Subject to the observation made in note (3) ante, it is obvious that matters of public concern are often difficult to prove, either because of the difficulty of physically marshalling the necessary volume of evidence, or because relevant witnesses are dead or unavailable. Happily, the increasing availability and reliability of records has rendered the task progressively easier, but resort is still had to the common-law rule in some circumstances.

These circumstances may be categorised as follows:

(a)   To establish matters of pedigree or the existence of a marriage. The contemporary importance of the rule lies in the proof of such questions of some antiquity, as matters of marriage and descent are, increasingly, capable of proof by official records.

(b)   To identify or show a reference to a person or thing, or to prove the existence of a public or general right. The question of identification or reference here is one of

---

4   The provisions of part 1 of the 1968 Act are considered in detail in 8.1, 8.5 and 8.6, ante.
5   The notice procedure is considered in detail in 8.9, ante. For s. 2 of the 1972 Act, see 9.4, post.

identification or reference in the mind of the public generally. Thus, in an action for defamation, it is necessary to show that the matter complained of referred to the plaintiff. This may be proved by evidence that the matter was taken, by the public generally, as referring to the plaintiff for which purpose evidence, e.g., that the plaintiff was publicly jeered at after publication, may be admitted to prove the reference (6). And in the rather strange case of *Re Steel, Wappett* v *Robinson* (7), the extent of a devise of land in a will was proved by evidence that certain fields were known locally as 'customary freeholds', and so correspond with the words of the devise of 'my freehold lands and hereditaments at Morland Field', although the fields in question were, in fact, privileged copyholds.

(c)   To prove good or bad character. In *R* v *Rowton* (8) it was held that 'character' should be equated with the general reputation of a person in his locality, so that at common law such evidence was not only admissible, but was the only admissible evidence for this purpose. In modern times, it is generally accepted that 'character' is a wider concept than one of reputation, and indeed the use of evidence of reputation has been criticised as tending to show, not the actual character but merely the generally accepted character of a person. Nonetheless, such evidence is certainly admissible whenever it is relevant to prove character, and is of considerable importance where the defendant in a criminal case seeks to establish his good character (9).

In all the above cases, the admissibility of evidence of reputation in civil cases is expressly provided for by s. 9(3) of the Civil Evidence Act 1968. The section does not change the rules stated above (10) but provides that the evidence shall be admissible by virtue of the section, where previously it would have been admissible by virtue of any of the common-law rules referred to. The section adds to the idea of reputation that of 'family tradition', which is a more specific and limited version of the idea of reputation and is of particular relevance in cases of pedigree and marriage. The section is additional to the provisions of s. 2 and s. 4, under which some statements might also be admissible as hearsay statements of the matters contained in them, but where evidence is admissible by virtue of s. 9(3) it may be adduced free of the restrictions of law in ss. 2–7 of the 1968 Act, and of the notice procedure laid down by RSC Ord.38 rr. 21–31 (11).

B: EXPERT-OPINION EVIDENCE

9.3   Principles of admissibility

It is an ancient rule of the common law that on a subject requiring special knowledge and competence, evidence is admissible from witnesses who have acquired, by study or practice, the necessary expertise on the subject. Such witnesses are known as 'experts'. The evidence is justified by the fact that the court would be unable, unaided, to draw proper inferences and form proper opinions from such specialised facts as were proved before it, and even perhaps to judge what facts have been satisfactorily proved. As long ago as 1782, Lord Mansfield said in *Folkes* v *Chadd and Others* (12) that the opinion of scientific men upon proven facts may be given by men of science within their own science. Today, the variety of matters upon which expert evidence is required is constantly growing, and the role of expert witnesses is expanding continually. A number of

6   See, e.g., *Cook* v *Ward* (1830) 6 Bing 409.   7   [1903] 1 Ch 135.   8   (CCR) (1865) Le & Ca 520.
9   The admissibility of character evidence is dealt with fully in Chapter 4. See in particular 4.1 and 4.8.
10   Civil Evidence Act 1968, s. 9(6).   11   Ibid s. 9(5).   12   (1782) 3 Doug 157.

important and common applications of the rule in modern practice will be referred to individually in 9.6, post.

9.3.1 Competence and weight

Qualification to give expert evidence is technically a matter of competence, and the court should investigate the credentials of a proposed witness before permitting him to give expert evidence. No doubt, a witness who lacked any apparent qualification would not be heard, but if the witness has some claim to expertise, the modern practice is to receive his evidence, though its weight may be open to serious adverse comment if the apparent expertise is not translated into reality. The court is concerned with actual expertise, not with the means by which that expertise is acquired. Paper qualifications by themselves may not be a guarantee of actual skills relevant to the questions before the court, and expertise gained by substantial relevant experience certainly renders an expert witness competent, and may invest his evidence with considerable weight. In *R* v *Silverlock* (13) a solicitor, who had made a study of handwriting, was allowed to give evidence as an expert, notwithstanding his lack of formal qualification on the subject, because of his demonstrable actual skill.

An expert witness, if competent, is, like any other witness, also compellable. In *Harmony Shipping Co. SA* v *Saudi Europe Line Ltd and Others* (14) a handwriting expert, having been consulted on behalf of the plaintiffs, was later consulted by solicitors for the defendants. After giving them his opinion on certain documents relevant to the action, the expert realised that he had inadvertently advised both sides and, in accordance with his professional rules, declined to accept further instructions from the defendants. The defendants served on him a *subpoena ad testificandum*, which he sought to have set aside. The Court of Appeal held that he was compellable to give evidence for the defendants, and that there was no contractual relationship between the expert and the plaintiff which would (even if enforceable, which must be doubtful (15)) bind the expert not to appear for the defendants. Of course, some of the communications passing between the expert and the plaintiffs would be protected by legal professional privilege, subject to any waiver by the plaintiffs.

Expert opinion may be contradicted and cross-examined, like any other evidence, and the attack may include cross-examination going to credit. The position of an expert is that he must be regarded as any other independent witness, and although he enjoys such weight as may follow from his peculiar ability to assist the court, it will be a misdirection to direct the jury that his evidence should be accepted unless the witness himself betrays reasons for rejecting it (16). The tribunal of fact must obviously retain control over the findings of fact, which are its ultimate responsibility. This does not mean that expert evidence of a categorical nature, which is effectively unchallenged, may be disregarded capriciously in favour of unaided lay opinion, and it would be equally wrong to invite the jury to take this course (17) or to content themselves with unaided observation on a matter calling for expert evidence (18). But there will be occasions where the tribunal of fact will be driven to reject expert evidence, and occasions where the tribunal will have to choose between conflicting opinions from experts dealing with the same matters. The

---

13   (CCR) [1894] 2 QB 766. Cf *R* v *Murphy* (CA) [1980] 2 WLR 743.   14   [1979] 1 WLR 1380.
15   As Lord Denning MR pointed out at 1386, such a contract would probably be held to be contrary to public policy. Indeed, if the decision in the case had been otherwise, one party might, by instructing every reputable expert, effectively deprive his opponent of expert advice, and create 'property' in expert witnesses.
16   *R* v *Lanfear* (CA) [1968] 2 QB 77.   17   *Anderson* v *R* (PC, Jamaica) [1972] AC 100.
18   *R* v *Tilley; R* v *Tilley* (CCA) [1961] 1 WLR 1309.

courts have not always accorded to expert evidence the recognition it deserves, perhaps because of the risk of a witness tending to render an opinion favourable to the party calling him, although there is no greater risk, and possibly less, of this than with other kinds of witness. It seems that the present emphasis on the independent status of experts may have reversed the older preference for direct evidence, which was sometimes taken to unrealistic lengths (19).

9.3.2 Function of expert evidence

The function of an expert is to assist the court by giving evidence of his opinion on the matters of specialised knowledge on which his assistance is sought. At common law, this was held to mean that the expert might not be asked his opinion on the 'ultimate question', or in other words he might not be asked directly his opinion on an issue in the case. The reason was that he would thereby usurp the function of the court. Thus, the witness might describe to the court the mental condition of the defendant, but might not be asked whether the defendant was insane if that was the issue which the court had to decide (20). This rule was never satisfactory and seems to have disappeared in modern practice. It has been expressly reversed in civil cases by s. 3 of the Civil Evidence Act 1972, which provides:

(1)   Subject to any rules of court . . . where a person is called as a witness in any civil proceedings, his opinion on any relevant matter on which he is qualified to give expert evidence, shall be admissible in evidence. . . .

(3)   In this section 'relevant matter' includes an issue in the proceedings in question.

It is generally considered that the same principle now applies in criminal cases. Certainly, great artificiality was produced by the previously supposed limitation. It is not suggested that the new approach binds the court in any way to accept any evidence given, so there is no good reason why the expert should not be asked to deal with the point which everyone knows he is called to prove or disprove.

There is, however, a somewhat different rule, of great importance, that expert-opinion evidence will not be admitted if it relates only to a question on which the lay opinion of the tribunal of fact is equally valid. This is to state no more than the obvious proposition that expert evidence is confined to those matters on which it is necessary in order to assist the court to determine the issues. Thus, where the question is one of the intent of a defendant, in a case where there is no question of mental illness, the evidence of psychiatrists will not assist the jury to determine that issue, the matter being one within the jury's experience of everyday affairs (21). And it has been said, with reference to an issue of provocation, that psychiatric evidence 'has not yet become a satisfactory substitute for the common sense of juries or magistrates on matters within their experience of life' (22). The reaction of the defendant to certain provoking circumstances, and the reasonableness of that reaction, have been held to be issues determinable without expert assistance (23). On the other hand, defences which fall outside the ordinary

19   As in *Bowden* v *Bowden* (1917) 62 SJ 105 where the direct evidence of the mother of the paternity of a child born to her 307 days after her last intercourse with her husband was preferred to the opinion of several doctors to the contrary.
20   *Daniel M'Naghten's Case* (HL) (1843) 10 Cl & F 200.   21   *R* v *Chard* (CA) (1971) 56 Cr App R 268.
22   *R* v *Turner* (CA) [1975] QB 834 per Lawton LJ at 843.
23   This rule is said to be unaffected by the decision in *DPP* v *Camplin* (HL) [1978] AC 705, *sed quaere* whether the jury could never be assisted by evidence of the likely reaction of persons with certain characteristics.

experience of jurors, such as insanity and diminished responsibility, are proper subjects of expert medical evidence, and although the jury are not bound to accept such evidence, and must look at all the evidence in the case including any conflict in the medical evidence (24) they should act on the evidence before them, and the Court of Apeal will quash a verdict of guilty of murder, where the unchallenged medical evidence suggests that such a verdict is wrong, and is itself uncontradicted by other evidence (25). Similarly, the defence of automatism is one outside the normal experience of juries, and is a proper subject of expert evidence. In *R* v *Smith* (26) the Court of Appeal upheld the admission of expert evidence tending to show that the evidence of the defendant, consistent with his defence of automatism, that he had killed in his sleep, was scientifically impossible.

In the case of *Lowery* v *R* (27), which is generally thought to turn upon its own facts, two defendants were charged with the murder of a girl, in circumstances from which it was clear that one or other of them, or possibly both, must have been guilty of the murder. There was no motive for the murder except the sheer, sadistic pleasure of committing it. In order to show that his co-defendant was the more likely of the two to have committed the murder, one defendant called evidence from a psychiatrist, tending to show that the co-defencant had a character and disposition which rendered him likely to behave in the way alleged, certainly more so than the defendant. The co-defendant contended on appeal that the evidence of character was wrongly admitted. Although on the face of it, the evidence was open to considerable question, both because it was evidence of character whose relevance to prove guilt was doubtful, and because it was an attempt to adduce expert-opinion evidence on the very subject which the jury had to decide and which seemed to be a matter within their competence, the Privy Council dismissed the appeal. It was held that on the specific issue before the jury, which required a decision as between two defendants, the evidence was relevant and admissible and assisted the jury, if they accepted it, to resolve that question. The decision is probably best regarded as applying only to such specific circumstances, and not as any general exception to the usual rule.

9.3.3 *Presentation of expert evidence*
Expert evidence will almost always be found, on analysis, to combine some evidence of fact with evidence of opinion. This is quite acceptable, and is in some respects unavoidable, in so far as the expert may have to relate his investigation of the facts of the case, or his familiarity with the exhibits, in order to explain his opinion. The expertise and knowledge of the witness is, in any event, likely to have been based upon many other events or transactions with which he has been concerned, and the opinions of others, accumulated as experience over a considerable time, and therefore must contain some element of what may loosely be termed hearsay. This is no objection to the admission of the evidence, although it is important to note that, while the expert may refer to other facts or transactions in order to explain his opinion, he may not by his evidence prove those facts as such, and if such other facts are material to the case, they must be proved by proper factual evidence. Into the latter category would fit valuations of other similar properties referred to by an expert valuer to explain his opinion in respect of the property in question (28).

24   *Walton* v *R* (PC, Barbados) [1978] AC 788; *R* v *Kiszko* (CA) (1978) 68 Cr App R 62.
25   *R* v *Matheson* (CCA) [1958] 1 WLR 474.   26   [1979] 1 WLR 1445.
27   (PC, Victoria) [1974] AC 85.
28   *English Exporters (London) Ltd* v *Eldonwall Ltd* [1973] Ch 415.

There appears at one time to have been a rule that an expert witness might not state the reasons for his opinion in chief, although he might be asked for them in cross-examination, but the rule has now become obsolete, and the practice is for the evidence to be presented in any convenient way, and to be fully explained in chief. It is worth observing that it is quite proper for counsel to consult an expert witness directly, while advising in conference, on all matters of expert-opinion evidence, although not on unrelated questions of fact. This can assist greatly in presentation. An expert witness may be asked any question, even hypothetical, necessary to develop and explain his opinion. He may refer for the same purpose to any work of authority on the subject, although the court should not look at passages not referred to in evidence. He may also relate the results of any tests or experiments which he has made, either for the purposes of the case or, if relevant, generally, and may, with the permission of the court, demonstrate any matter in court or during a view, although the conduct of demonstrations must be carefully controlled in the interests of relevance and fairness to other parties.

9.4 Disclosure of expert evidence in civil cases

As we have seen, with the exception of expert evidence, opinion evidence consisting of hearsay statements, which are sought to be admitted by virtue of s. 2 or s. 4 of the Civil Evidence Act 1968, as extended by the Act of 1972, is subject to the notice procedure contained in RSC, Ord. 38, rr. 21–31 (29). In respect of expert-opinion evidence, Parliament determined to lay down a separate and much more far-reaching code, which in effect requires pre-trial disclosure of expert evidence proposed to be adduced in civil cases. Power to establish the code was given by s. 2 of the Civil Evidence Act 1972 and it has been promulgated in RSC, Ord. 38, rr. 36–44. It is vital to stress that the code applies to expert evidence generally and not just to evidence admissible as hearsay by virtue of the Act. The purpose of the code is to save time and costs. It recognises that in the majority of cases there is a wide area of agreement between experts, and if that area can be identified at an early stage then evidence can be shortened and attention concentrated on the areas of disagreement. In many cases, it may lead to complete agreement of all relevant expert evidence before the trial begins.

There is no doubt that the code has been effective in its aim, and there are indications that the courts will insist upon its observation (30). However, the very extent and nature of the provisions require proper safeguards for the parties affected by them, and there are powers to restrict the evidence which may be ordered to be disclosed, and to admit evidence despite disclosure in a proper case. The court is given power to override the rules by giving leave to adduce evidence, notwithstanding failure to comply. Reference must, however, be made at once to one important matter. Expert reports, which may later form the basis of the evidence called, are very frequently, if not usually, the subject of legal professional privilege. The Act provides that such privilege shall not prevent the operation of the code (31) but does not operate to remove such documents from the protection of privilege, which continues to attach to them within the usual rules (32). A

---

29   See 8.9 and 9.1, *ante*. The notice procedure may be applied by the court, as a matter of discretion, in the limited cases dealt with by RSC, Ord. 38, r. 41 (post).
30   See *Ollett* v *Bristol Aerojet Ltd* [1979] 1 WLR 1197.
31   Civil Evidence Act 1972, s. 2(3).
32   *Causton* v *Mann Egerton (Johnsons) Ltd* (CA) [1974] 1 WLR 162. For legal professional privilege, see 11.8, post.

party is not, therefore, compellable to disclose privileged expert reports in his possession, but is precluded (subject to safeguards) from adducing in evidence the matters contained in them unless they are disclosed.

9.4.1   The statute
S. 2(2) of the Civil Evidence Act 1972 provides that the notice procedure of RSC, Ord. 38, rr. 21–31 shall not apply to statements of fact or opinion contained in expert reports (33) that are proposed to be admitted as hearsay under s. 2 of the 1968 Act. In place of the notice procedure, s 2(3)(*a*) of the 1972 Act permits rules to be made enabling the court to direct disclosure by a party to the other parties, in the form of expert reports, of the expert evidence proposed to be adduced by that party at trial. S. 2(3)(*b*) adds that the rules may prohibit the adducing of evidence, which is the subject of a direction, without leave, if the direction has not been complied with.

In addition to the provisions dealing with admissible hearsay, s. 2(4) provides that enabling rules may be made dealing with oral expert evidence, so as to provide conditions subject to which it may be given. S. 2(5) provides that the rules may prohibit the adducing, without leave, of any oral expert evidence whatsoever, if any direction given under s. 2(3) is not complied with. Where a party calls or intends to call as a witness the maker of a (hearsay) expert report, admissible under s. 2 of the 1968 Act, s. 2(1) of the 1972 Act and RSC, Ord. 38, r. 43, exempt that party from the restrictions imposed in respect of other witnesses by s. 2(2) of the 1968 Act, and allow the report to be put in evidence at the commencement of its maker's evidence in chief, or at such other time as the court may direct.

9.4.2   The rules
The rules made in pursuance of these wide enabling provisions have taken full advantage of the powers provided. The principal rule is Ord. 38, r. 36, which provides that:

> (1)   Except with the leave of the court or where all parties agree, no expert evidence may be adduced at the trial or hearing of any cause or matter unless the party seeking to adduce the evidence has applied to the court to determine whether a direction should be given under rule 37, 38 or 41 (whichever is appropriate) and has complied with any direction given on the application. [(34).]

The existence of three separate rules (37, 38 and 41) under which directions may be given in different cases is authorised by s. 2(6) of the 1972 Act which provides that the rules may make different provisions for different classes of case, for expert reports dealing with matters of different classes and for other different circumstances. Similarly, Ord. 38, r. 39, allows the court to limit a direction given under rr. 37 or 38 (it would be inappropriate under r. 41) to part only of the evidence sought to be adduced. R. 36 clearly places the onus upon a party wishing to adduce expert-opinion evidence to apply for directions, and to see that the directions are complied with.

The three rules under which directions may be given have somewhat different provisions, and apply to different types of evidence, as follows. Rr. 37 and 38 apply to proposed oral evidence and r. 41 to proposed evidence contained in statements.

---

33   An 'expert report' is a 'written report by a person dealing wholly or mainly with matters on which he is (or would if living be) qualified to give expert evidence': Civil Evidence Act 1972, s. 2(7).
34   R. 36(2) contains an exception for matters which are permitted to be stated in affidavits: see Ord. 41, r. 5.

9.4.2.1   R. 37: oral medical evidence in actions for personal injuries.   The emphasis in this type of evidence is in favour of mandatory disclosure, in all but certain exceptional cases. Where an application is made under r. 36, in respect of oral expert evidence relating to medical matters, the court shall direct disclosure in the form of written reports, unless there is 'sufficient reason' for not doing so. By r. 37(2), the court may treat as a sufficient reason the fact that the pleadings contain an allegation of medical negligence, or that the expert evidence may express an opinion on the manner in which injuries were sustained, or on the genuineness of symptoms. In these cases, disclosure would effectively force a premature disclosure of the strength of a party's case on the facts directly in issue. The rule does not suggest that these facts are the only ones capable of amounting to sufficient reason, and the matter appears to be a discretionary one, subject to the obvious mandatory intention of the rule.

9.4.2.2   R. 38: other oral expert evidence.   In cases of oral expert evidence to which r. 37 does not apply, the emphasis is rather different. R. 38 provides in such cases that the court may, if satisfied that it is desirable to do so, direct that the substance of the proposed evidence be disclosed in written reports. Strangely, however, r. 38(2) refers to 'sufficient reason for not giving such a direction', and mentions under that head evidence based upon a version of the facts in dispute between the parties, and upon matters outside the personal observation and professional expertise of the expert.

9.4.2.3   R. 41: expert evidence contained in statements.   This rule provides for cases where the expert evidence, of whatever nature, is contained in an (admissible hearsay) statement and the party seeking to adduce it alleges that the maker of the statement cannot or should not be called as a witness (35). In such a case, the court may, but evidently need not, direct that the evidence be subject to the notice procedure under rr. 21–31, with any necessary modifications.

It is also necessary to observe one further provision, under which directions are subject to absolute mandatory disclosure. By virtue of Ord. 38, r. 40, where a party intends to apply under r. 36 in an action arising out of an accident on land due to a collision or apprehended collision, in respect of the expert evidence of an engineer in connection with motor vehicles, that party must, before the hearing of the summons for directions make available to all other parties a report by the engineer containing the substance of his evidence.

9.4.3   Time for application

Applications under r. 36 should, wherever possible, be dealt with on the summons for directions (36). The master has power to limit the number of witnesses who may be called on either side (37), and the exercise of this power should be considered in the interests of saving time and costs. The task is much simplified if proper disclosure has been made. The master may also direct agreement of expert reports, but only in a case where this is clearly appropriate (38).

---

35   This is a muted echo of Ord. 38, r. 25 (see 8.9, ante). It lacks the complication of the mandatory application of the notice procedure, but enables the court to apply that procedure in a proper case, presumably where it would be unjust not to do so, having regard to the nature of the evidence.
36   Practice Direction (QBD) [1974] 2 All ER 966.
37   See RSC, Ord. 38, r. 4; Ord. 25, r. 3.
38   *Proctor* v *Peebles (Papermakers) Ltd* [1941] 2 All ER 80.

9.4.4   Effect of disclosure

The consequences of disclosure of expert reports for the purposes of the proceedings are starkly stated by Ord. 38, r. 42: 'A party to any cause or matter may put in evidence any expert report disclosed to him by any other party in accordance with this part [i.e. rr. 35–44] of this Order.'

It follows, therefore, that once disclosure has been made, the report cannot be kept out, if another party wishes to put it in, merely because the party who produced it has decided not to rely upon it or not to call the evidence in question. It is essential to decide before the application for directions, whether the evidence should be disclosed, or whether the report should be used only for assistance in the conduct and assessment of the case, in which case its privilege can and should be protected.

9.5   Expert evidence called by the court

In civil actions in the High Court, the court may, in any non-jury case (39), and on the application of any party, appoint an independent expert (the 'court expert') to inquire and report upon any question of fact or opinion, where any question for an expert arises (40). The question may not be one of law or construction. An 'expert' for this purpose is defined as: 'any person who has such knowledge or experience of or in connection with [the] question that his opinion on it would be admissible in evidence' (41). The expert makes and sends to the court a report. Any party may apply for leave to cross-examine the court expert, and there is limited provision for the parties to call· evidence to contradict him (42). If the report is agreed, it may clearly be treated as evidence in the case, but Ord. 40, r. 2(3) provides, somewhat mysteriously, that: 'Any part of a court expert's report which is not accepted by all the parties . . . shall be treated as information furnished to the Court and be given such weight as the Court thinks fit.'

It has been suggested that the court has an inherent power to appoint an expert, even in the absence of an application, where it is in need of assistance (43) and apparently even where a party objects to such a course (44).

In certain very limited cases, 'assessors' may sit with the judge (45). Their function is not that of witnesses; they sit to advise the judge with regard to specialised questions of fact, and are members of the court, although their views may be overruled by the judge. The principal use of assessors is in Admiralty cases.

9.6   Common subjects of expert evidence

Although there is a considerable number of subjects upon which expert-opinion evidence may be admitted, the following are of common occurrence in practice, and merit some individual mention.

39   No such provision exists for criminal cases or in magistrates' courts, although for the use of reports of probation officers in domestic proceedings, see Magistrates' Courts Act 1952, s. 59, s. 60; *Higgs* v *Higgs* (DC) [1941] P 27.
40   RSC, Ord. 40, r. 1. See also the corresponding provisions of Ord. 32, r. 16 (Judge in chambers) and Ord. 103, r. 27 (appointment of scientific advisers in patent actions). The 'question' and the identity of the court expert shall be agreed if possible, or otherwise settled by the court: Ord. 40, r. 1(2), (3).
41   Ord. 40, r. 1(4).   42   Ord. 40, r. 4 and r. 6.
43   *Colls* v *Home & Colonial Stores Ltd* (HL) [1904] AC 179 per Lord Macnaghten at 192; *Badische Anilin und Soda Fabrik* v *Levinstein* (1883) 24 ChD 156.
44   *Attorney-General* v *Birmingham, Tame & Rea District Drainage Board* (HL) [1912] AC 788.
45   Supreme Court of Judicature (Consolidation) Act 1925, s. 98; RSC, Ord. 33, r. 6.

9.6.1 Scientific and technical matters

Reference has already been made to the existence of specific rules of court, which relate to the treatment of medical evidence in personal injury cases and the evidence of engineers in motor-vehicle collision cases. These rules are, perhaps, sufficient testimony in themselves to the everyday importance of such evidence. There are also many other areas of scientific and technological evidence, and the field is an expanding one. In Coke's case, we see an example of the evidence produced by a forensic scientist, Dr Espinasse. Forensic science ranges over a very wide range of matters, of particular though not exclusive significance in criminal cases, matters such as the presence and age of fingerprints and blood stains; the examination of weapons and ammunition; the identification of drugs, poisons and chemicals, fibres and paint. Dr Espinasse's evidence will, no doubt, be agreed in the present case, as Coke does not dispute having had sexual intercourse with Margaret Blackstone. But it is noteworthy how significant the evidence would be, were that matter to be challenged. The witness states his examination of the exhibit, 'SGV1' as a piece of factual evidence, and goes on to give his opinion and his reasons. Of course, no forensic evidence is beyond challenge, and it is a matter for the jury; but the evidence remains formidable, and as we have seen, the judge should not invite the jury to disregard it capriciously. The evidence of Dr Espinasse can, of course, go no further than to indicate the occurrence, within a certain time, of sexual intercourse. The medical evidence of Dr Vesey could go further, by suggesting that such intercourse was forcible, and this too would be a matter of expert opinion by the doctor based upon her observation and examination of Margaret. In fact, Dr Vesey's evidence is far from damning in this respect.

It is vital, in all cases involving any examination of exhibits that there should be evidence accounting for the safe-keeping and treatment of each exhibit from the moment of its creation or appropriation, until the moment of its examination by the expert, and indeed, if it is to be produced as evidence in court, until trial. It may be noted that there is a 'chain' of possession of exhibit SGV1 from Dr Vesey to D/S Bracton to Dr Espinasse, and it is important that this chain should be unbroken. There is a similar chain in respect of the handwriting exhibits GG1 and GG3 from D/I Glanvil to D/S Bracton to Mr Hale. The safe-keeping is of considerable importance in relation to the tape-recording of the conversation between Littleton and his wife. Before admitting the tape in evidence, the judge will have to satisfy himself that there is a prima facie case in favour of the tape being original and admissible. For this purpose, D/I Glanvil will have to account for his keeping of the cassette, exhibit GG4, from the moment of the recording, until its production in court (46). Should there be any doubt as to its originality, or any question of interference with it, expert evidence may be highly valuable, after forensic examination.

9.6.2 Documents and handwriting

The scientific examination of documents and handwriting is a specialised branch of forensic science. The detailed legal basis for evidence of examination and comparison of documents and handwriting is considered in 16.3, post, to which reference should be made. It will be seen that the first task of the prosecution is to prove the genuineness of the sample of handwriting provided by Coke (exhibit GG3). By genuineness is meant authorship by Coke, and this can be proved by the evidence of D/I Glanvil, if not

---

46   *R* v *Robson; R* v *Harris* [1972] 1 WLR 651. See 16.4, post.

admitted. Once this is established (47) evidence of a comparison with the disputed writing (exhibit GG1) becomes admissible (48) and Mr Hale may state both his examination of and comparison of the exhibits, and his consequent opinion. The disputed question of authorship, and its significance, if proved, are of course matters of fact for the jury. It may be seen that Mr Hale's evidence, though not conclusive, is certainly strong, and it may be that cross-examination would have to involve analysis of the chart produced by him, perhaps with the aid of expert advice for the defence on the technical questions raised.

Evidence of this sort is, of course, of great importance in many criminal and civil cases, where the authenticity of a document or signature, or due execution, falls to be proved, and is particularly relevant to cases involving fraud or forgery.

9.6.3   Art, literature, learning, etc.

Expert evidence on these subjects may be adduced where matters concerning specialised fields fall to be proved. There may be various uses of it, but one which tends to occur frequently is in relation to the defence of 'public good' under s. 4 of the Obscene Publications Act 1959, as amended. The defence provides that a person shall not be convicted of an offence under s. 2 in relation to an obscene article, 'if it is proved that publication of the article in question is justified as being for the public good on the ground that it is in the interests of science, literature, art or learning, or of other objects of general concern.' The phrase 'other objects of general concern' is restricted to the specific matters alluded to in s. 4 and does not permit of a wider interpretation, for instance the relief of sexual tension in the context of the general psychiatric health of the community (49).

Expert evidence is admissible to prove or disprove the defence under s. 4 which is clearly a matter upon which the jury will require guidance, in order to arrive at a proper opinion. However, the defence will only arise on the assumption that the jury consider the article to be obscene, which is a question of fact for them, and upon which expert evidence is not admissible (50).

9.6.4   Professional and trade practices and standards

Evidence from members of a profession or trade, either generally or in a particular field of reference or a particular geographical area, will be admissible as expert-opinion evidence to show the practice of the profession or trade, or the standards expected of reasonably competent members generally. Such evidence is relevant to establish customary terms of contracts of various sorts, the existence of trade practices, the reasonableness of covenants in restraint of trade, the standard of professional competence reasonably expected of a person against whom negligence is alleged in the exercise of his profession, and a variety of other matters.

9.6.5   Foreign law

Questions of foreign law, which for this purpose means the law prevailing in any jurisdiction other than England and Wales, are questions of fact, and should, where

47   On a balance of probabilities: *R* v *Angeli* (CA) [1979] 1 WLR 26.
48   Criminal Procedure Act 1865, s. 8.   49   *DPP* v *Jordan* (HL) [1977] AC 699.
50   *Attorney-General's Reference (No. 3 of 1977)* (CA) [1978] 1 WLR 1123. In an exceptional case, a jury may be assisted by expert evidence on the likely effect of material on special classes of reader, e.g. children, in their task of deciding whether the material would be likely to deprave or corrupt: *DPP* v *A & B C Chewing Gum Ltd* (DC) [1968] 1 QB 159.

relevant, be proved by evidence, like any other question of fact (51). It is obviously desirable, and has always been the practice, that foreign law should be proved by expert evidence from a witness who has knowledge or experience of the law concerned. In relation to civil proceedings, s. 4(1) of the Civil Evidence Act 1972 now provides that:

> It is hereby declared that in civil proceedings a person who is suitably qualified to do so on account of his knowledge or experience is competent to give expert evidence as to the law of any country or territory outside [England and Wales] irrespective of whether he has acted or is entitled to act as a legal practitioner there.

The form of the section as a declaration suggests that it is intended to confirm what was thought to be the position at common law, and indeed, there is authority to support the proposition (52).

S. 4(2), designed to avoid the embarrassing prospect of different decisions by English courts on identical points of foreign law, provides for proof of such points by reference to reported decisions of superior courts in England in which they have previously been decided. Such evidence, of which notice must be given, may be contradicted, but will otherwise be accepted as proving the point of foreign law concerned (53).

C: NON-EXPERT-OPINION EVIDENCE

9.7 Principles of admissibility

As was observed at the outset of this chapter, opinion evidence was rejected at common law as evidence of the truth of the matters believed, at least partly because it tended to usurp the function of the court. Nowhere is this defect more apparent than in relation to the opinion of persons not qualified as experts on matters directly in issue in the proceedings.

By s. 3(2) of the Civil Evidence Act 1972:

> It is hereby declared that where a person is called as a witness in any civil proceedings, a statement of opinion by him on any relevant matter on which he is not qualified to give expert evidence, if made as a way of conveying relevant facts personally perceived by him, is admissible as evidence of what he perceived.

Much controversy has raged as to whether this declaration accurately represents the state of the common law, and therefore whether it may apply in effect to criminal cases also (54). It is submitted that this is and should be the case. The admissibility is confined to matters of the general competence and experience of people generally, which they are able and accustomed to appreciate by a process of observation of commonplace facts, and which require no process of conscious deduction. They are in reality matters of

51 However, the jury should not be left to decide it without a definitive direction. The judge may have to decide between conflicting opinions: *Re Duke of Wellington, Glentanar v Wellington* [1947] Ch 506; affirmed (CA) [1948] Ch 118.
52 *Brailey v Rhodesia Consolidated Ltd* [1910] 2 Ch 95 (Reader in Roman-Dutch Law in the Inns of Court).
53 Civil Evidence Act 1972, s. 4(2)(*b*).
54 The point was apparently not adverted to in *Rasool v West Midlands Passenger Transport Executive* [1974] 3 All ER 638, where a statement made by the defendants' witness (admissible otherwise under s. 2 of the Civil Evidence Act 1968) contained the words: 'The bus driver was in no way to blame for the accident.' This statement was, it seems, not called into question by the way in which it was expressed, the witness seeking to explain what she had seen, but the decision is hardly satisfactory.

perception, perceived directly by the witness while using his ordinary senses, so that while in an abstract sense it may be said that the witness is expressing an opinion, he is in fact merely using natural language to convey facts which he perceived, and which would otherwise be difficult, if not impossible, to relate.

There can be no final rule on where the line of admissibility may be drawn. In any case tried without a jury, the matter is likely to be resolved by the judge taking a realistic view of what the witness is trying to say. The following cases are examples only of the use of non-expert-opinion evidence.

9.7.1 Identity and resemblance

A witness may state that a person, thing or document is the same as, or bears a resemblance to, one that he has seen on a previous occasion. The matter is one of perception, and there would be formidable difficulties of proof in very many cases if this were not permitted (55). Both the identifying witness and any other person who witnessed a previous indentification, may give evidence of what transpired on that occasion (56). This is subject, in criminal cases, to the safeguards required in the interests of preventing potentially misleading or incorrect evidence being given of identification, and to the various administrative requirements for the proper treatment of evidence of identification (57). But in general, a witness may give evidence of matters within this category, and may be referred to any photograph or other exhibit necessary to enable him to explain what he perceived.

9.7.2 Mental or physical condition

The rule applies to observable conditions, in so far as expert evidence is not required of them. The condition of the witness himself is admissible as well as that of others, and he may state his reaction to events or circumstances, or his reasons for his acts, provided that he does not infringe the rule against previous consistent statements (58). He may not, however, state his opinion of the intentions of others (59), which must be objectionable as inadmissible opinion or hearsay, or both. Wherever the condition of a person must be proved as a matter of some precision, so that the court must have expert evidence of it, the opinion of a witness other than an expert is inadmissible. A good illustration is *R* v *Davies* (60) where it was held that, although a lay witness could state that a person had been drinking, which was a matter of general competence, he might not state that that person was unfit to drive through drink, which was a matter of expert medical evidence. For the same reason, a lay witness may not be called to prove the sanity of another (61) although his evidence is apparently admissible on the issue of his own sanity (62).

9.7.3 Age, speed, value

These matters are usually assumed to be within ordinary human experience, although evidence can obviously prove them only to a reasonable approximation (63). The weight of such evidence will depend, *inter alia*, on the apparent experience of the witness, e.g. as

55 See, e.g., *Fryer* v *Gathercole* (1849) 4 Exch 262 per Pollock CB. The rule also applies to handwriting with which the witness is personally familiar.
56 *R* v *Osbourne; R* v *Virtue* (CA) [1973] QB 678.
57 *R* v *Turnbull* (CA) [1977] QB 224. Home Office Circular No. 109/78. See generally, 13.3.3.2, post.
58 See Chapter 13.   59 *Townsend* v *Moore* (CA) [1905] P 66.   60 (CMAC) [1962] 1 WLR 1111.
61 *R* v *Neville* (1837) Craw & D 96; *Greenslade* v *Dare* (1855) 20 Beav 284.
62 *Hunter* v *Edney* (1885) 10 PD 93.
63 No one is liable to be convicted of speeding on the uncorroborated evidence of opinion of one witness as to speed: Road Traffic Regulation Act 1967, s. 78A(2).

a driver or passenger if his evidence relates to speed. It would seem to be right that evidence of value would be admissible only in respect of objects in common use or knowledge, and not where the object is, for example, an antique or otherwise of special value, upon which expert evidence would be required (64).

9.8 Affidavits

Although evidence permitted to be given by affidavit is, like other evidence, subject to the ordinary rules of admissibility, it is provided by RSC, Ord. 41, r. 5(2), that: 'An affidavit sworn for the purpose of being used in interlocutory proceedings may contain statements of information or belief with the sources and grounds thereof.'

The rule is confined to interlocutory proceedings, where the rights and liabilities of the parties are not decided. Thus, in *Nationwide Building Society* v *Bateman* (65) an affidavit which was permitted to be sworn for the purposes of a mortgage action, and was used in final proceedings, was held to be irregular, where it contained matters which the deponent was unable to prove of his own knowledge.

It is also essential that the affidavit state the sources and grounds of the belief deposed to. Although in practice, the requirement appears often to be ignored, the courts occasionally comment strongly on the matter (66) and there is power to strike the affidavit out.

The purpose of the rule is to permit the introduction of admissible hearsay evidence in interlocutory matters, where it might have been given in the course of evidence in final proceedings.

64   *R* v *Beckett* (CCA) (1913) 8 Cr App R 204.   65   [1978] 1 WLR 394.
66   See, e.g., *Re J.L. Young Manufacturing Co. Ltd, Young* v *J.L. Young Manufacturing Co. Ltd* (CA) [1900] 2 Ch 753.

Part 3   Questions of Policy

10 Evidential Value of Previous Judgments

10.1 Introduction

There are at least two objections of theory to the use of previous judgments to prove the truth of facts upon which they were based. The first is that such evidence would be mere evidence of opinion by which strangers to the judgment should not be prejudiced. The second is that a judgment so used, is in effect, hearsay. And so the common law adopted the position, albeit not without some hesitation, that previous judgments should not be admissible as evidence of the truth of the facts on which they are based, as against strangers to the judgment.

However, the position was by no means as simple as that. Although the common-law rules precluded reliance on a judgment for the purpose of proving the truth of facts on which it was based, there could be no objection based on hearsay to relying on a judgment to prove, if relevant to do so, the existence and formal details of the judgment itself, its contents or its legal effect. Moreover, even if it were sought to use the judgment for the purpose of proving the truth of facts on which it was based, the position would plainly be different in a case where the parties to the instant proceedings had also been the parties to the previous proceedings. The policy of the law, of preventing repetitious and oppressive litigation, had a clear interest in maintaining the binding nature of a final judgment of a court of competent jurisdiction, as a definitive finding of the facts in issue as between those parties. A judgment should be relied upon if the issues are reopened in subsequent proceedings between the same parties or those claiming through them. Persons claiming through a party to previous proceedings are known for this purpose as that party's 'privies'. Privity may arise in various relationships, for example 'in estate', between lessor and lessee, vendor and purchaser; 'in blood', between ancestor and heir; or 'in law', between testator and executor. In these and other cases of privity the privy stands, as it were, in the shoes of the party with respect to the instant proceedings.

In considering the evidential value of previous judgments, therefore, the following cases must be distinguished:

  (a) Judgments as evidence of their own existence, contents and legal effect.
  (b) Judgments as evidence of the truth of facts on which they are based, as between the parties to the proceedings in which the judgment was given, and their privies.
  (c) Judgments as evidence of the truth of facts on which they are based, as between strangers to the proceedings in which the judgment was given, or as between parties to the proceedings (or their privies) and strangers.

A: JUDGMENTS AS EVIDENCE OF THEIR EXISTENCE, CONTENTS AND LEGAL EFFECT

10.2 Introduction

Judgments of courts of competent jurisdiction are public transactions, and so presumed to be faithfully made and recorded. Thus, at common law, all such judgments were not only evidence, but conclusive evidence of their own existence, contents and legal effect, both against parties or their privies, and against strangers; whereas they were not even admissible evidence of any facts on which the judgment was based. Thus, in an action for malicious prosecution, the record of the verdict of the jury acquitting the plaintiff was conclusive of the prosecution of him by the defendant and of his acquittal, but was inadmissible to prove either the plaintiff's innocence of the offence charged or malice on the part of the defendant (1). Similarly, where an action was brought against a master in respect of the negligence of his servant and a verdict was entered for the plaintiff, in a subsequent action by the master against the servant, the first judgment was conclusive of the amount of damages awarded against the master, but was inadmissible to prove that the servant had been negligent (2).

It also followed from the conclusive nature of the contents and legal effect of the judgment, that a witness could not be heard to give evidence which had the effect of contradicting any such matter, so that although the judgment was inadmissible to prove the truth of any facts on which it was based, it was admissible for the purpose of contradicting a witness who sought to give evidence conflicting with its formal parts. In *Watson* v *Little* (3) a witness gave evidence that a son was born to her on a certain day, being five days after her marriage. Evidence was received to contradict her in the form of an affiliation order made by justices, since deceased, reciting that they had found on the evidence of the witness that the child had been born on a day prior to her marriage. This evidence, though admissible to contradict the witness, was not evidence that the child was illegitimate. And on the trial of a defendant on a charge of handling stolen goods, the evidence of a witness that he stole the goods in question may apparently be contradicted by evidence of the witness's acquittal on that charge (4).

10.3 Judgments in rem and in personam

The position is somewhat more complicated where the judgment in question is a judgment '*in rem*'. A judgment *in rem* may be defined as one which has the effect of declaring the status of a person or thing for all legal purposes and hence as against all the world, as opposed to a judgment ('*in personam*') which has effect merely to establish the rights and obligations, in respect of the subject-matter of the proceedings, of the parties and their privies.

The important feature of a judgment *in rem* is that its contents are as a matter of law declaratory of a state of affairs, so that the facts on which the judgment is based are in effect determined conclusively against parties, privies and strangers alike. The legal effect of the judgment is to declare the truth of the facts on which it is based. This rule is, therefore, wider than and distinct from any rule of estoppel operating between the

1 *Purcell* v *M'Namara* (1808) 1 Camp 199.   2   *Green* v *New River Co.* (1792) 4 TR 590.
3   (1860) 5 H & N 572.   4   *R* v *M'Cue* (1831) Jebb CC 120.

parties and their privies, and from any rule concerning the admissibility or otherwise of judgments as evidence of the truth of facts on which they are based.

Whether a judgment is one *in rem* is a matter of law, to be decided having regard to the jurisdiction of the court to utter such a judgment, and to the nature and form of the judgment itself. The most obvious example is a decree of divorce or nullity of marriage, which has the effect of declaring the personal status of the parties in addition to deciding their rights and obligations as litigants *vis-à-vis* each other (5). Similarly, a grant of probate is declaratory of the status of the executor to whom it is granted, as may be seen from the rather striking facts of *Allen* v *Dundas* (6). The defendant owed a debt to the deceased, which after the death, he paid to the deceased's executor. Subsequently, the plaintiff succeeded in having the will set aside in his own favour, on the ground that it had been forged. The plaintiff sought to recover the debt (which had not been accounted for by the original executor) from the defendant. It was held that the plaintiff could not be heard to challenge the original executorship as that status subsisted until the will was set aside. Accordingly, the defendant, who had paid the debt to a person who at the material time had the status of executor, had discharged the debt properly and was not liable further. Other examples of judgments *in rem* are adjudications in bankruptcy (7), adjudications of the General Medical and Dental Councils striking off a practitioner (8) and judgments of a prize court condemning a ship and her cargo on the ground that the cargo did not enjoy neutral status (9). A noteworthy 'exception' in the sense that the judgment appears on the face of it to have a declaratory effect, is that of judgments affecting legitimacy or illegitimacy. Thus, an affiliation order affects only the parties to the proceedings in which it is pronounced (10), and by s. 45(5) of the Matrimonial Causes Act 1973 a declaration of legitimacy shall not prejudice any person who has not been given notice of or made a party to the proceedings and who is not the privy of a person who has so been given notice or made a party.

B: JUDGMENTS AS EVIDENCE OF THE FACTS ON WHICH THEY WERE BASED: PARTIES AND PRIVIES

10.4 Introduction

In respect of judgments whose effect is called into question in subsequent proceedings for or against the original parties or their privies, any objections based on opinion or hearsay, are held to be outweighed by other factors of policy. The policy of the law is expressed in the maxims, *'Interest reipublicae ut sit finis litium'* and *'Nemo debet bis vexari pro eadem causa'*. If issues already litigated and decided between parties or their privies were allowed to be reopened there would be no finality in litigation and the way would be opened for numerous vexatious, frivolous and oppressive suits.

For this reason, the rule affecting parties and their privies goes much further than a mere question of admissibility of a previous judgment in instant proceedings. There arises by reason of the judgment an estoppel called 'estoppel *per rem judicatam*', which operates to prevent either party and their privies, litigating in the same capacity, from

---

5 See, e.g., *Salvesen* v *Administrator of Austrian Property* (HL, Scotland) [1927] AC 641. In the case of divorce, the reference is of course to a decree absolute, and not to a decree nisi, which may be set aside on cause being shown, and which does not alter the status of the parties: *Travers* v *Holley* (CA) [1953] P 246.
6 (1789) 3 TR 125. 7 Bankruptcy Act 1914, s. 138(2). 8 *Hill* v *Clifford* (CA) [1907] 2 Ch 236.
9 *Geyer* v *Aguilar* (1798) 7 TR 681. 10 *Anderson* v *Collinson (DC)* [1901] 2 KB 107.

disputing any matter of fact or law which has necessarily been decided finally as between them by the judgment, and from adducing any evidence inconsistent with the decision of any such matter (11). Estoppel *per rem judicatam* operates in substantially different ways in civil cases, in which it is becoming a highly developed doctrine, matrimonial causes, in which its operation is confused, and criminal cases, in which it is now said that it is not applicable as such. These types of case must therefore be examined separately.

10.5   Civil cases

In civil cases, it is now clear that there are two sorts of estoppel *per rem judicatam,* that is to say 'cause-of-action estoppel' and 'issue estoppel' (12).

10.5.1   Cause-of-action estoppel

Cause-of-action estoppel arises from the principle that the cause of action in a suit merges in the judgment given upon it. If, therefore, the parties litigating in the same capacity have obtained a final judgment in which it is held that the cause of action lies or does not lie, their rights and obligations are determined in relation to that cause of action, and the matter ends there (13). It follows that the parties (and their privies) may not litigate the same cause of action a second time between themselves, because they are estopped from asserting any fact inconsistent with the merger of the cause of action in the judgment. The rule is of course apt to protect the parties, especially the defendant, against unnecessarily disjoined proceedings, but the results can sometimes appear bizarre. In *Conquer* v *Boot* (14) the plaintiff successfully sued the defendant and recovered judgment in respect of a breach of warranty to build a house in a good and workmanlike manner. Subsequently, by reason of the same breach of warranty (albeit the plaintiff sought to describe it differently) the plaintiff suffered further loss, which might not have been apparent at the time of the first action. It was held that the cause of action was *res judicata* and that the plaintiff was estopped from asserting it for a second time.

The rule has no application where the parties agree or intend to obtain a series of individual decisions, usually by means of successive arbitrations, upon a number of disputed matters as and when they may occur in the execution of a contract or other transactions in which they may be involved (15). In these circumstances it is no doubt envisaged that the cause of action is not to be regarded as finally determined until all relevant matters have been determined, and it is submitted that this way of viewing the matter would often produce more obviously just results than *Conquer* v *Boot.* The court always retains power to prevent oppressive suits and abuses of its process, and there is no doubt that the rule can work hardship when taken to its logical conclusion.

Nonetheless, in order to prevent multiplicity of actions, cause-of-action estoppel has been extended to apply to all causes of action which a party exercising reasonable

11 An 'estoppel' may be defined as a rule which prevents ('estops') a party from asserting or denying certain facts. Estoppels arise in various circumstances, and much inconsequential controversy rages about whether they are to be regarded as rules of evidence or of substantive law.

12 For an instructive description of the two, see the judgment of Diplock LJ in *Thoday* v *Thoday* (CA) [1964] P 181 at 197 et seq.

13 See *Fidelitas Shipping Co. Ltd* v *V/O Exportchleb* (CA) [1966] 1 QB 630, per Lord Denning MR at 640. As against defendants alleged to be jointly and severally liable, no estoppel will arise unless liability is satisfied completely as against at least one of them.

14 (DC) [1928] 2 KB 336.

15 *Purser & Co. (Hillingdon) Ltd* v *Jackson and Another* [1977] QB 166. The judgment of Forbes J contains interesting observations on the application of the rule generally, particulary in relation to arbitrations.

diligence should have asserted in the action in which judgment was given, as well as those which he did assert. This extension of the rule is designed to ensure that, as far as possible, all matters on which either side can properly rely, are considered together in litigation. The result is that if a party omits, whether deliberately or inadvertently, to bring forward a matter on which he could have sought to rely in the proceedings then he will be estopped from asserting that matter as a cause of action after judgment has been given (16). This part of the rule, too, can have drastic consequences. In *L.E. Walwin & Partners Ltd* v *West Sussex County Council* (17) the plaintiffs maintained a barrier to vehicular traffic along a highway which linked their residential estate with the sea. This they claimed the right to do, asserting that the dedication of the road as a highway had been partial only and had reserved the right to maintain the barrier. The defendants proposed to remove the barrier as an obstruction of the highway, and the plaintiffs brought an action to restrain them from so doing. In 1958, the plaintiffs predecessors in title (to whom the plaintiffs were therefore privy) had been party to proceedings before Quarter Sessions in which the status of the road had been in question. The question of the barrier had not been raised in those proceedings, although it might have been raised as a proper matter for the court to take into account. It was held that the failure by their privies estopped the plaintiffs from asserting that the dedication of the highway had been partial as they said, and the action failed.

10.5.2 Issue estoppel

Issue estoppel also applies to the parties or their privies litigating in the same capacity. If parties obtain a final judgment which necessarily decides certain issues between them then, in later proceedings between the same parties, they are estopped from disputing that decision, and from adducing any evidence inconsistent with it. It is said, although very far from being definitively established, that issue estoppel differs from cause-of-action estoppel in two respects: firstly that the rule applies only to issues actually decided by the judgment, and not to issues which might or ought to have been canvassed by the parties; and secondly that the estoppel will not bind a party who can adduce fresh evidence which may make the finding on the issue questionable.

The first proposition was not supported by the Court of Appeal in *Fidelitas Shipping Co. Ltd* v *V/O Exportchleb* (18), but it is submitted that there is much force in Professor Cross's view that the difference should be adhered to, because of the formidable difficulty of ascertaining what issues a reasonably diligent party should be expected to assert. Often, the presentation of a case depends on considerations other than purely legal ones (19).

The second proposition is confirmed by a dictum of Diplock LJ in *Mills* v *Cooper* (20), though it is said that a party cannot rely on it if, had he exercised reasonable diligence, he could have adduced the evidence in the original proceedings. It is submitted with respect that this proposition (which is admittedly supported by earlier authority) is inconsistent with the basis of *res judicata,* although clearly the emergence of fresh evidence may be relevant as enabling a party to challenge a decision on appeal, or to avoid the estoppel altogether by showing that the judgment was obtained by fraud or collusion.

16   See *Henderson* v *Henderson* (1843) 3 Hare 100 per Wigram VC at 114.
17   [1975] 3 All ER 604. See also *Public Trustee* v *Kenward* [1967] 1 WLR 1062.
18   [1966] 1 QB 630.
19   Cross, *Evidence*, 5th ed., p. 333. See also the speech of Lord Upjohn in *Carl Zeiss Stiftung* v *Rayner & Keeler Ltd and Others; Rayner & Keeler Ltd and Others* v *Courts and Others* (HL) [1967] 1 AC 853 at 947.
20   (DC) [1967] 2 QB 459 at 468.

10.5.3   Necessary conditions of estoppel

Whatever may be the position with regard to those supposed differences, which require
further clarification, there is no doubt that the operation of estoppel *per rem judicatam* of
either kind is subject to the following conditions:

   (a)   Finality of judgment.
   (b)   Identity of parties.
   (c)   Identity of capacity.
   (d)   Identity of issues.

These may be described as the substantive conditions. The estoppel is also subject to the
condition that the judgment cannot be impeached in itself as being given without
jurisdiction, or other than on the merits, or as having been obtained by fraud or
collusion, and to the procedural requirement that estoppels must be pleaded. These
matters are dealt with in 10.8 and 10.12, post.

10.5.3.1   Finality of judgment.

In this context the word 'final' indicates that the
judgment is one which (subject to an appeal) decides the issues between the parties
necessary to the determination of the proceedings (in other words, 'final' as opposed to
'interlocutory'). Provided the judgment in fact has this effect, it is irrelevant that the
judgment was pronounced in the course of a hearing that was interlocutory in form, for
example on summons, motion or application (21). The possibility of an appeal does not
affect the finality of the judgment, nor indeed does the fact that an appeal is pending.
However, it seems that if the judgment is one given by an inferior court, no estoppel is
created unless the judgment is one from which an appeal lay; whether or not an appeal
was actually pursued being irrelevant (22).

   A judgment is not final if the action is discontinued, withdrawn or stayed on payment
of a sum of money, or, it seems, is dismissed for want of jurisdiction (23). But a judgment
obtained by default may be final, if it necessarily and with complete precision decides the
issue between the parties (24) as may a judgment which determines the liability of one
party to the other, even though the relief to be granted has not been pronounced upon
(25).

10.5.3.2   Identity of parties.

Estoppel will only arise when the parties to the instant
proceedings are identical(apart from privity) with those to the previous proceedings. In
Townsend v *Bishop* (26), Townsend had been injured while driving his father's car,
which collided with a lorry driven by the defendant. In an action by Townsend's father
against the defendant in respect of the damage to the car, the defendant succeeded on a
plea of contributory negligence, which before 1945 was a complete defence. In a
subsequent action by Townsend himself against the defendant, it was held that
Townsend could dispute that he had been negligent. He was not estopped from denying

21 *Midland Bank Trust Co. Ltd and Another* v *Green and Another* [1978] 3 WLR 149; reversed (CA) on other
grounds [1979] 3 WLR 167. Issue estoppel may be created by an admission made in the face of the court or in a
consent order, as well as in the terms of a controverted judgment: *Khan* v *Goleccha International Ltd* (CA) [1980]
2 All ER 259.
22 *Concha* v *Concha* (HL) (1886) 11 App Cas 541.
23 *Tak Ming Co. Ltd* v *Yee Sang Metal Supplies Co.* (PC, Hong Kong) [1973] 1 WLR 300.
24 *New Brunswick Railway Co.* v *British & French Trust Corporation Ltd* (HL) [1939] AC 1.
25 *Jowett* v *Earl of Bradford* (EAT) [1977] ICR 342. The decision has met with considerable criticism, on the
basis that it could not be said that there was a judgment at all, let alone a final one.
26 [1939] 1 All ER 805.

the contributory negligence that had been established in the previous action because the parties in the two cases were different.

The requirement of identity is narrowly and restrictively construed, as may be seen from the somewhat complicated decision in *Carl Zeiss Stiftung* v *Rayner & Keeler Ltd and Others; Rayner & Keeler Ltd and Others* v *Courts and Others* (27). The plaintiffs (Carl Zeiss Stiftung), who manufactured glass and optical equipment, had been established on a charitable basis in 1896 in what is now the German Democratic Republic. Following numerous political events after the Second World War, the Council of the district of Gera, a body set up by a decree of the government of the German Democratic Republic (which was not then recognised by the British government), claimed to represent the plaintiffs as their governing body. The Council brought an action in the West German courts to restrain the alleged passing off of their goods, but were defeated on a preliminary motion, it being held that the Council were not authorised to represent the plaintiffs before the West German court. The plaintiffs thereupon commenced similar proceedings in England, and were countered with an application to strike the action out as having been commenced by their English solicitors, Courts & Co., without proper authority. It was argued that the solicitors were estopped from asserting that they were duly authorised to act on behalf of the plaintiffs, because of the decision that the Council (by whom they were instructed) was incompetent to represent the plaintiffs. The House of Lords held that no estoppel arose. The Council of Gera had been the effective plaintiff in the West German action; the English solicitors had not been parties to that action and there was no question of privity.

In the light of the consistent policy of the courts in favour of narrow construction, some disquiet may be occasioned by the decision of a majority of the Court of Appeal in *McIlkenny* v *Chief Constable of the West Midlands and Another* (28). This was one of four appeals heard together. The plaintiffs had been convicted of murder by causing explosions and sentenced to life imprisonment. They brought actions in respect of alleged assaults made on them by police officers, for whose actions the defendants were responsible, while in police custody before their trial. There was no dispute that the plaintiffs had been assaulted on other occasions, near in time to those complained of, by prison officers, for whose actions the Home Office admitted liability. The question of alleged assaults by the police had been raised by the plaintiffs at their criminal trial, with a view to showing that certain statements made by them to the police were not voluntary. The trial judge found that the statements were voluntary, and admitted them in evidence. The plaintiffs were convicted by the jury. The plaintiffs claimed to have fresh evidence tending to show that they were assaulted on occasions other than when in the custody of the prison officers. The Court of Appeal struck the action out. Lord Denning MR held that the plaintiffs were estopped from alleging the assaults complained of, such estoppel being created by a combination of the finding of the judge on the voire dire and the verdict of the jury, the latter showing that the jury had agreed with the judge. It is submitted, with respect, that this judgment is plainly wrong. In his dissenting judgment, Goff LJ pointed out that, even on the questionable assumption that the voire dire and verdict together constituted a final judgment (29), the prosecution in the criminal case

---

27 [1967] 1 AC 853. In addition to the *ratio* given in the text, the House of Lords was evidently not satisfied with the evidence that the West German judgment was a final one.
28 [1980] 2 WLR 689.
29 Technically, the jury were not concerned with the voluntariness of the statements, and even though they were entitled to consider how the statements were obtained, for the purpose of deciding what weight to give to them, the inscrutability of the general verdict of guilty makes it impossible to say positively what view the jury

was not identical with the defendants in the instant action, and no privity could arise between them. The dangers of equating, as parties, prosecuting authorities and prosecution witnesses who may be personally implicated in subsequent civil proceedings by the events decided on a general verdict of guilty or not guilty, are surely too obvious to require elaboration (30).

10.5.3.3 Identity of capacity. Even where the parties are ostensibly identical, no estoppel will arise if any party in fact litigates in a capacity distinct from that in which he litigated in the previous proceedings. The classic example is *Marginson* v *Blackburn Borough Council* (31). A collision occurred between the plaintiff's car, driven by his wife as his agent, and an omnibus driven by a servant of the defendants. The plaintiff's wife was killed, he was injured and damage was caused to property situated near the scene of the collision. In an earlier action by the property owners against the owners of both vehicles, it was found that both drivers had been negligent and damages were awarded against both vehicle owners. In this second action the car owner sued the owners of the bus, claiming both in respect of his own injuries (suing in person) and on behalf of the wife's estate and dependants (suing as her personal representative). In the claim brought in his personal capacity, the plaintiff was held to be estopped from denying negligence on the part of the wife, which prior to 1945 was a complete answer to the action. In his representative capacity, however, no estoppel arose because he sued in a capacity different to that in which the finding in the first action had been made against him.

10.5.3.4 Identity of issue. It is of course fundamental, if estoppel *per rem judicatam* is to arise, that the issue sought to be raised in the instant proceedings should be identical to that decided in the previous proceedings. There are two possible approaches to the problem of identification of issues. One, which may be termed the narrow approach, is to examine the issue strictly and insist that precisely the same matters of law and fact in every respect should be identifiable. The other, termed by way of contrast the broad approach, would have recourse to the substantial coincidence of the factors on which the issue is in reality based, and would ignore peripheral matters of distinction. It is impossible on the present authorities to state which approach the courts prefer, and examples of both are common. To take two widely cited illustrations, in *Hoystead and Others* v *Commissioner of Taxation* (32) the broad approach prevailed, so that the respondent commissioner was estopped from supporting his assessment of the appellants for the tax year 1920/21 because the same principle of tax law had already been decided in the appellants' favour by the High Court of Australia in respect of the tax year 1918/19; the issue in respect of 1920/21 was not of course literally the same as that in respect of 1918/19 but was identical save for the differing tax year. However, in *Society of Medical Officers of Health* v *Hope* (33), a valuation officer was not estopped by the decision of a local valuation court which had decided in 1951 that the society's premises were exempt from rating, but this did not estop the valuation officer from listing the premises as non-exempt when he carried out his statutory duty of compiling a new list in 1956, there having admittedly been no change of user in the intervening period. On the

took. This consideration has led the House of Lords to reject issue estoppel as such in criminal cases: see *DPP* v *Humphrys* [1977] AC 1. The decision of the judge on the voire dire was clearly not final in this sense.
30   The Court of Appeal, on marginally sounder ground, also held unanimously that the action should be struck out as an abuse of the process of the court.
31   (CA) [1939] 2 KB 426.   32   (PC, Australia) [1926] AC 155.
33   (HL) [1960] AC 551.

narrow approach, the officer was carrying out a periodic statutory duty of preparing a list for rating purposes, and the issue in respect of the premises in 1956 was held to be distinct from that prevailing in 1951. A restrictive approach was also preferred by Walton J in *Re Manly's Will Trusts (No. 2)* (34) where the devolution of a part of the property of the testator had been determined on a point of construction in previous proceedings. It was held that no estoppel arose in relation to the question of the devolution of different property of the testator, even though the result depended upon the identical point of construction.

Particularly difficult problems of identification arise in considering cases of negligence. In *Marginson* v *Blackburn Borough Council,* to which reference has already been made, the court took a broad approach: negligence and contributory negligence are technically distinct issues in law and, on a narrow view, no estoppel should have arisen. However, the authority of the case on this point is not strong, because of the pre-1945 consequences of contributory negligence. There is later and stronger authority in favour of the broad approach in *Bell* v *Holmes* (35) and *Wood* v *Luscombe* (36). In both cases, A's liability for contributory negligence when suing B was held to be the same issue as that of A and B's respective liabilities to C arising from the same collision. A and B were therefore estopped from disputing a previous apportionment of liability *inter se* when the question arose of their liability to C. Of the argument that the issues were different, in that the duty of care was owed and the damage caused to different persons, McNair J said in *Bell* v *Holmes* (37):

Those are different legal issues, of course, in a sense, but I do not feel the fact that they are technically different legal issues should prevent them from giving effect to the plea of estoppel in a case where, having examined the pleadings in the county court action and compared them with the pleadings in the present action, I am satisfied that the issues of fact, and the evidence to support them in respect of liability, would be identically the same.

It is submitted that this view accords both with common sense and with the policy of the law of restraining repetitive litigation. Nonetheless, it has not passed unchallenged. In *Randolph* v *Tuck and Others* (38) Lawton J declined to follow McNair J in *Bell* v *Holmes,* holding that a finding, in an action between the first defendant and the third defendant, that the former was solely to blame for the collision was not the same issue as that of the liability of either to the plaintiff arising from the same collision. Accordingly, the first defendant was not estopped from denying his sole liability in an action brought against him and the third defendant by the plaintiff. *Randolph* v *Tuck* in its turn, was not followed by Streatfield J, who in *Wood* v *Luscombe* preferred the reasoning of *Bell* v *Holmes.* Since no realistic distinction can be made on the facts of these various cases, it is to be hoped that some more authoritative guidance will in due course be offered by an appellate court. There will, of course be cases where the determination of liability as between A and B does not effectively determine the liability of either to C; the question must depend on the facts of each case. Evidently, Lawton J thought that *Marginson* v *Blackburn Borough Council* was such a case. But it is submitted that it must rarely be satisfactory that apportionment should be re-litigated in respect of each aspect of the

---

34 [1976] 1 All ER 673.   35 [1956] 1 WLR 1359.
36 [1966] 1 QB 169.   37 [1956] 1 WLR 1359 at 1366.
38 [1962] 1 QB 175.

damage flowing from the same tortious act (the logical result of *Randolph* v *Tuck*); and that it must be even more rarely satisfactory to invite conflicting judicial apportionments of liability for the same tortious act. In cases where this was justified, it would surely be because differences of substance, not merely of form, arise on a sensible analysis of the legal issues.

Happily, one matter which does seem clear is that in the often complex task of identifying and comparing issues, the judge is entitled to pray in aid as far as necessary the pleadings, evidence, argument and judgment in the previous proceedings, and to draw any proper conclusions from such materials about what the issues were. Thus, in *Randolph* v *Tuck,* Lawton J had regard to the notes of the county court judge, which he admitted in evidence despite objection from the Bar; and the practice of comparing pleadings now appears to be well established.

10.6 Matrimonial causes

Matrimonial causes are civil proceedings of a specialised kind, and accordingly are subject to estoppel *per rem judicatam,* whether cause-of-action estoppel or issue estoppel, with qualifications of a specialised kind. Such qualifications arise not only because decrees of divorce and nullity operate *in rem,* but also and more significantly because the conduct of matrimonial proceedings is circumscribed by statutory duties cast upon the court to inquire into the facts alleged, irrespective of the manner in which the case may be conducted by the parties.

It has long been established that no estoppel binding the parties can operate to prevent the court from carrying out its duty to inquire into the facts alleged, even where one of the parties or even both, objects (39). In relation to divorce matters, the duty is now laid down by s. 1(3) of the Matrimonial Causes Act 1973, which provides that:

> On a petition for divorce it shall be the duty of the court to inquire, so far as it reasonably can, into the facts alleged by the petitioner and into any facts alleged by the respondent.

It certainly appears that the duty of inquiry precludes the operation of estoppel in proceedings in the High Court or divorce county court, arising from a finding by magistrates in the exercise of their matrimonial jurisdiction. In *Hudson* v *Hudson* (40) precisely this reason was advanced for the rule, and it is difficult to see why, but for the duty, an estoppel should not arise, because the status of the court is not generally relevant to estoppel *per rem judicatam* unless the judgment is one of an inferior court and not subject to a right of appeal. It seems estoppel does operate to prevent a matter decided by a magistrates' court being reopened in a magistrates' court. In *Stokes* v *Stokes* (41) the wife, having failed in her allegation of desertion in the magistrates' court, was estopped from asserting the same desertion in fresh proceedings before a different magistrates' court.

In the higher courts, the position is somewhat different. The fact that issues may have been litigated previously in a court having divorce jurisdiction should not, on the face of

---

39   *Harriman* v *Harriman* (CA) [1909] P 123; *Thompson* v *Thompson* (CA) [1957] P 19, per Denning LJ at 29. In *Hudson* v *Hudson* [1948] P 292 the interesting point was made that the inquiry may most efficiently be made by allowing the parties to fight the case.
40   [1948] P 292. The duty of inquiry in this case was imposed by the Matrimonial Causes Act 1937, s. 4.
41   (DC) [1911] P 195.

it, affect the duty of the court to inquire. But in *Finney* v *Finney* (42), it was held that where the wife's petition for judicial separation on the ground of cruelty was dismissed by the Court of Divorce and Matrimonial Causes (now the Family Division of the High Court), the wife was thereafter estopped from presenting a petition for divorce based upon the same allegations. It was suggested in *James* v *James* (43) that there was a difference between a case in which a charge was dismissed by the High Court, and a case in which there was a duty to inquire into facts already proved elsewhere. Certainly, the authorities indicate that the dismissal of a charge by the High Court is to be regarded as giving rise to an estoppel, but it is not easy to see why the distinction should be made in that form, and it may be that the true rule is that the estoppel will arise only where the duty to inquire applied to the court giving the previous judgment. The facts of *James* v *James* and other decisions show that justices should apply an estoppel in respect of charges dismissed by the High Court. In *James* v *James* the husband's charge of adultery had failed in defended divorce proceedings before a judge of assize. When the wife subsequently applied to a magistrates' court for matrimonial relief, it was refused on the ground, as the court found it to be, of the same alleged adultery. The Divisional Court held that the issue of adultery was *res judicata*. For present purposes, it seems that no distinction is to be made between decisions of the High Court and those of the divorce county court, which exercises in most respects, an equivalent jurisdiction (44).

Whatever the position may be, Parliament thought it necessary, with regard to allegations already proved elsewhere, to make express provision for the multiple use of successful charges. The reason for this is that a party may frequently wish to use the same allegations before different tribunals for the purpose of obtaining different relief, as where a party who has been granted relief in a magistrates' court, or a decree of judicial separation, wishes to present a petition for divorce, relying on the same or substantially the same allegations. As a matter of strict law, applying the narrow approach, it is likely that no estoppel could arise to prevent such a course, because the actual ground for divorce is irretrievable breakdown, which is an issue distinct from any ground of other relief based on conduct. But on a broad view, irretrievable breakdown is in practice evidenced by reference to conduct which will correspond with that upon which a previous tribunal had adjudicated. Hence, s. 4(1) of the Matrimonial Causes Act 1973 provides:

A person shall not be prevented from presenting a petition for divorce, or the court from granting a decree of divorce, by reason only that the petitioner or respondent has at any time, on the same facts or substantially the same facts as those proved in support of the petition, been granted a decree of judicial separation or [relief in a magistrates' court].

S. 4(2) provides for the admissibility of the previous order or decree as sufficient proof of any adultery, desertion or other fact by reference to which it was granted, but requires the court to take, in addition, evidence from the petitioner, before granting a decree.

The question of the grant of decrees of divorce and nullity is, of course, of particular significance to the duty to inquire, because of the operation of such decrees *in rem* as declaring the status of the parties. For this reason, it is especially unlikely that the court would ever regard itself as precluded from the inquiry by any estoppel which might bind

42　(CDMC) (1868) LR 1 P & D 483.　　43　(DC) [1948] 1 All ER 214.
44　*Razelos* v *Razelos* (No. 1) [1970] 1 WLR 390.

the parties. This is dramatically illustrated by the facts of *Hayward* v *Hayward* (45). In proceedings in a magistrates' court, the husband had asserted the validity of the marriage, although the evidence suggested that both he and the wife had reason to believe that the marriage may have been void *ab initio* because it was bigamous. On a subsequent petition for nullity based on the bigamous nature of the marriage, it was held that the husband was not estopped from asserting that the marriage was void. Phillimore J specifically discounted the operation of estoppel *per rem judicatam* on the basis that the previous proceedings were in a magistrates' court, but held that when hearing the present petition the High Court had a clear duty to inquire, a ground which must surely have prevailed even if the earlier relief had been sought in the higher court.

A matter of great importance in modern times is the developing rule that, while judgment on the main suit in the divorce county court or the High Court will create an estoppel precluding the parties from disputing the decision in the main suit, and therefore also the issues necessarily decided finally by that decision, the estoppel will not prevent the parties from raising issues of fact afresh in ancillary proceedings where to do so is relevant to an issue in those proceedings, and where it is not sought to deny the basis of the decision in the main suit. In the narrow sense, the *'res'* or issue is of course a different one in ancillary proceedings, despite the close similarity of the factual matters involved; they are raised for a different purpose. This is sometimes said to be the justification for the rule, and certainly, there is authority that factual issues can be pleaded and fought for a purpose different to that involved in the previous proceedings (46). But the true justification is probably one of policy. The courts have set their face against contested divorces based on allegations of conduct, and are anxious that a party who forbears from defending or cross-praying in a suit shall not be inhibited from raising any relevant matter in subsequent proceedings for ancillary relief. Thus, in *Tumath* v *Tumath* (47), a husband who chose not to defend the wife's petition for divorce, or to oppose her plea for the exercise of the court's discretion was held not to be estopped, in subsequent proceedings for ancillary relief, from denying allegations made in her discretion statement, of which he had been given notice in the main suit, that his behaviour had conduced to her adultery and that he had admitted his own adultery. Neither was the husband estopped from alleging that the wife had deserted him, even though this allegation might have been raised in the main suit. And in *Porter* v *Porter* (48) a wife who allowed the husband's petition based on desertion to go undefended, while estopped from setting up the allegations of cruelty pleaded in her answer as just cause for her desertion (an issue necessarily determined by the judgment and decree in the main suit) was not estopped from raising them in ancillary proceedings with a view to mitigating the apparent significance of the decree as pronounced.

The rule operates with particular force where the court is concerned with the welfare of children, and it has been doubted judicially whether, in modern times, an estoppel can ever preclude the court from investigating any issue which appears to be relevant to the welfare of the children. In *Rowe* v *Rowe* (49) the respondent husband did not defend the wife's petition for divorce, and so the wife obtained a decree and an order for custody of the children. The latter order was based on the assumption that the children were 'children of the family' within the meaning of the Matrimonial Causes Act 1973 and this fact was not disputed by the husband when returning the acknowledgement of service of the petition in the form prescribed by the rules. It was held that the husband was not

45   [1961] P 152.   46   See, e.g., *Thoday* v *Thoday* (CA) [1964] P 181.   47   (CA) [1970] P 78.
48   [1971] P 282.   49   (CA) [1980] Fam 47.

estopped from denying in subsequent proceedings that the children were children of the family. No doubt even in proceedings relating to children, no party would be entitled to dispute the basis of the decision in the main suit itself, but on the other hand, this would rarely, if ever, now be of direct relevance to the subsequent proceedings.

The rule in favour of a lenient approach to questions of estoppel in ancillary proceedings is of recent origin, and stems from the new philosophy of matrimonial law which has developed since the Divorce Reform Act 1969 came into force. There was previously considerable authority for a strict view of estoppel in such cases, but it is submitted that the more lenient approach is now becoming firmly established, and should be followed in future as being consistent with the spirit of the law generally (50).

10.7 Criminal cases

In relation to criminal cases, the doctrine of estoppel *per rem judicatam* has had a chequered career, and has at various times been confused with, and been made to defer to, the quite distinct question of pleas in bar. The difficulties of applying the estoppel to criminal cases must be conceded. A broader approach to the law has always been necessary in view of the comparative informality of procedure; it is not easy to fit a precise doctrine of previous judgments into a system of rudimentary written pleadings and general, oral pleas to the issue. In particular, however, two distinctive characteristics of criminal law have combined to militate against the doctrine.

Firstly, there is the very inscrutability of a general verdict of guilty or not guilty. Although the delivery of a general verdict may theoretically be regarded as creating something analogous to cause-of-action estoppel, the prevalence from an early time of the pleas in bar has rendered the concept otiose. And the very nature of the verdict, pronounced on the general issue of guilt or innocence, without any expression of the reasoning underlying it, makes it impossible, in the majority of cases, to identify the precise issues determined by the jury and therefore to ascertain the limits of any issue estoppel which the verdict may be thought to create. It is true that in some cases, where, for example, the verdict of guilty can safely be assumed to have involved the rejection of the only defence open to the defendant on the facts of the case, it may be possible to identify at least some area of final decision of issues. But in general it will not be possible to do so with any sufficient degree of precision, and in cases where the verdict is one of not guilty, it is submitted that this must almost always be so.

Secondly, the incidence of the burden and standard of proof renders it dangerous to attempt to draw conclusions from the verdict with regard to individual issues. The jury may be satisfied of guilt beyond reasonable doubt, so that the truth of each element of the offence would seem to have been decided in favour of the prosecution. But within that area of certainty, it will frequently be unclear what precise issues of fact the jury have decided in their favour. And where the verdict is one of not guilty, it is actually unnecessary for the jury to decide issues of fact at all, beyond the bare assertion that they do not find them proved, on the evidence available, beyond reasonable doubt.

For these reasons, finality in criminal cases has been achieved by other means, centred principally upon the desire to safeguard the defendant against double jeopardy. Three areas of limitation have been explored by the courts, with varying levels of acceptance. These are:

---

50   The court's approach to ancillary matters in modern law is authoritatively set forth in *Wachtel* v *Wachtel* (CA) [1973] Fam 72. Cf *Humberside County Council* v *R* (DC) [1977] 1 WLR 1251 on cases where the welfare of children is concerned.

(a) The operation of pleas in bar: accepted.

(b) The prevention of contradiction of earlier verdicts for any purpose: apparently accepted.

(c) The operation of issue estoppel: rejected.

10.7.1 Pleas in bar

It is unnecessary for present purposes to consider the detail of the practice relating to pleas in bar (51). The principle of the criminal law is that a man shall not be proceeded against and stand in peril twice in respect of the same, or substantially the same, offence. The special pleas of autrefois convict and autrefois acquit may therefore be successfully tendered to prevent prosecution if the defendant has on a previous occasion been lawfully convicted or acquitted of the offence in respect of which it is sought to try him, or if he could lawfully have been convicted in a previous indictment of that offence, or if the offence for which it is sought to try him is in effect the same, or substantially the same, as one of which he has previously been lawfully convicted or acquitted, or of which he might lawfully have been convicted on a previous indictment (52).

Thus, if Coke should be acquitted in due course of the charge of raping Margaret Blackstone, the result will be that he may not be proceeded against further for that alleged offence, even if further incriminating evidence subsequently comes to light. However, the bar goes further than that, and would also operate to prevent his being prosecuted for attempted rape or indecent assault arising from the same facts, because the jury in a trial for rape is entitled to return an alternative verdict of guilty of either of those offences. On the other hand, there would be no bar to his being tried, for instance, on a charge of stealing some article of her clothing abandoned by her when she fled, because when being tried for rape Coke is not in jeopardy of conviction on such a charge.

Pleas in bar are evidently wider than, and distinct from, any principle of estoppel *per rem judicatam*. It is true that the pleas form some rough analogy to cause-of-action estoppel. But pleas in bar are very different from issue estoppel, firstly because no amount of fresh evidence can in any way limit the operation of the plea. And secondly, because it is clear that the pleas operate regardless of the circumstances of the previous verdict, so that it need not have been obtained on the merits. In *R* v *Pressick* (53) a charge was dismissed because the prosecution were not ready to proceed and an adjournment was refused, whereupon the prosecution offered no evidence. It was not thereafter open to the prosecution to proceed against the defendant in respect of the charge dismissed. There must, however, be a determination of guilt or innocence, so that no plea can be offered where the examining justices refuse to commit for trial and discharge the defendant, or where a charge is withdrawn or allowed to be taken into consideration.

10.7.2 Rule against contradiction of previous verdict

The consequences of a verdict may, however, be more far-reaching than merely to prevent renewed efforts to prosecute the defendant. It has been held that the verdict itself may not be contradicted subsequently, for example by the prosecution suggesting

---

51 See generally Archbold, *Criminal Pleading, Evidence and Practice,* 40th ed. paras 373 et seq; *Connelly* v *DPP* (HL) [1964] AC 1254.

52 This third category is sometimes regarded as falling outside the scope of pleas in bar and as being a function of the court's general power to restrain oppressive prosecutions. In *Connelly* v *DPP* (HL) [1964] AC 1254, Lords Morris of Borth-y-Gest and Hodson favoured the extended-plea-in-bar view, Lords Devlin and Pearce the oppression view.

53 [1978] Crim LR 377.

in other proceedings against the defendant that he is guilty of an offence of which he has been acquitted. In *Sambasivam* v *Public Prosecutor, Federation of Malaya* (54), the defendant was charged with two offences, possessing a firearm and possessing ammunition, contrary to certain emergency regulations of the Federated Malay States. Under the emergency regulations the case was tried by a judge and two assessors. At his trial, the defendant was acquitted of possessing the ammunition, and on the charge of possessing the firearm, the court being unable to agree, there was a new trial with different assessors. In the course of the new trial, the prosecution sought to rely upon a confession, allegedly made by the defendant, to both offences. No warning was given to the assessors that there would be a reference to the ammunition charge. The Privy Council quashed the conviction on the new trial. The prosecution were not entitled to introduce the reference to the charge on which the defendant had been acquitted without making it plain that the defendant was not guilty of that charge, which had obvious consequences affecting the reliability of the confession as a whole. The Judicial Committee said (55):

> The effect of a verdict of acquittal pronounced by a competent court on a lawful charge and after a lawful trial is not completely stated by saying that the person acquitted cannot be tried again for the same offence. To that it must be added that the verdict is binding and conclusive in all subsequent proceedings between the parties to the adjudication. The maxim *Res judicata pro veritate accipitur* is no less applicable to criminal than to civil proceedings.

It was argued in *DPP* v *Humphrys* (56) that this decision was authority for the proposition that issue estoppel might apply to criminal cases, but the argument was rejected by the House of Lords. It was not an issue which the prosecution sought to contradict by the use made of the confession, but the fact of the defendant's acquittal as demonstrated by the verdict, and therefore also his innocence of the offence. What was therefore objectionable was the suggestion of the defendant's guilt of an offence of which he had been acquitted, in order to promote the assertion of his guilt of the offence being tried. If, therefore, the facts of a charge on which the defendant has been acquitted are material to further charges, not as asserting his guilt on the original charge, but as being relevant to the defendant's state of mind in relation to the further charges, it seems that those facts may be proved as long as this can be done without asserting his guilt of, and thereby contradicting the verdict on, the original charge. The distinction is employed to justify the decision in *R* v *Ollis* (57), in which the defendant had been acquitted on a charge of obtaining money by false pretences by passing a worthless cheque knowing that it would not be met. He was then prosecuted for exactly similar alleged offences, and his defence was that he believed that funds would be available to enable the cheques to be met. The prosecution adduced the evidence in respect of the cheque passed on the previous charge with a view to suggesting that he knew the later cheques would similarly be dishonoured. It was held that the evidence was admissible for the purpose of proving the defendant's state of mind when he passed the subsequent cheques, and thus leading to the conclusion that he had a fraudulent intention. It was said that the evidence was relevant to the defendant's state of mind, and was not adduced for the purpose of contradicting the earlier verdict. While the distinction is no doubt sound in principle, its application to *Ollis*'s case is unconvincing. Unless he was guilty of

---

54 [1950] AC 458.   55 Ibid at 479.   56 (HL) [1977] AC 1.   57 (CCR) [1900] 2 QB 758.

the previous offence, the prosecution were surely bound to accept that his state of mind at that time was innocent, and it cannot have been legitimate to infer more than knowledge that one cheque had been dishonoured. The reality was that the prosecution were seeking to admit similar-fact evidence in circumstances where it was not open to them to do so.

R v *Ollis* was relied upon with a view to upholding the conviction in *G* v *Coltart* (58). The defendant (G), a domestic servant in the house of Mr and Mrs T, was charged with theft of goods belonging to Mrs D, a guest in the Ts' house. Because the prosecution were unable to call Mrs D, who had returned to South Africa, the charge was, by consent, dismissed. The defendant was then prosecuted for the theft of goods found at the same time, belonging to Mrs T. The defence was that she intended to return the goods and, to rebut this defence, the prosecution proved that the defendant had not returned the goods belonging to Mrs D, even though told that Mrs D was returning to South Africa the next day. The conviction was quashed. It was held that the necessary inference was that the prosecution were seeking to obtain some benefit from contradicting the verdict on the previous charge, and not merely to show the state of mind of the defendant. Although the court was loyal to the decision in *Ollis,* it is clear from the judgment of Salmon LJ that some unhappiness was felt about it, and the distinction made by the court is far from compelling. It is submitted that the cases where such evidence can be adduced without in effect contradicting the previous verdict must be rare.

Since this line of authority was held by the House of Lords in *DPP* v *Humphrys* not to depend upon any question of issue estoppel, it would seem that it continues to represent the law, despite the decision in that case. There seems also to be no reason of principle why the defendant should be permitted to contradict a verdict of guilty against him in previous proceedings, or, for that matter, to contradict a verdict of not guilty in previous proceedings against a co-defendant or a witness for the prosecution.

10.7.3 Issue estoppel

In *DPP* v *Humphrys* (59) the defendant had been acquitted of a charge of driving a motor cycle on 18 July 1972 while disqualified. The defendant admitted that he was disqualified on that date, but denied that he was driving, althought the evidence of a police officer was that he had stopped the defendant while the defendant was driving. The defendant gave evidence that he had not driven at all during 1972. Subsequently, further evidence came to light, which cast doubt on the evidence given by the defendant, and he was charged with perjury and convicted. In the course of the trial for perjury, the same police officer repeated his evidence about having stopped the defendant on 18 July 1972. The Court of Appeal allowed an appeal against conviction, on the ground that the verdict in the first trial had created an estoppel on the issue whether the defendant had been driving on 18 July 1972 and that accordingly the officer's evidence was inadmissible to support the charge of falsely swearing that the defendant had not driven during 1972. The prosecution appealed to the House of Lords.

The purpose of calling the officer's evidence afresh was said to be that it tended to show that the defendant's evidence at the first trial was false, and not in any way to contradict the verdict at the first trial. This distinction, which seems reasonable on the facts of the case, meant that the evidence was unexceptionable on the *Sambasivam* principle, and of course there was no question of a plea in bar. Unless, therefore, the

58   (DC) [1967] 1 QB 432.   59   [1977] AC 1.

principle of issue estoppel applied, the evidence was admissible. The House of Lords held unanimously that the doctrine of issue estoppel had no application to criminal proceedings.

The argument in favour of issue estoppel in criminal proceedings had, for the reasons discussed earlier, a relatively short history. The possibility was canvassed in *Connelly* v *DPP* (60), where the matter was clearly obiter. Lords Morris, Hodson and Pearce appear to have been favourably inclined to the doctrine, Lord Devlin to have been opposed to it, and Lord Reid to have expressed no opinion. The difficulties of application to criminal cases were not overlooked, and it was recognised that the doctrine, if it applied at all, must apply to the defendant as much as to the prosecution. The latter point was squarely faced by Lawson J in *R* v *Hogan* (61). The defendant was charged with causing grievous bodily harm with intent. His only defence was lawful self-defence. The jury convicted. Subsequently, the victim of the offence died, allegedly as a result of his injuries, and the defendant was charged with his murder. It was held that the defendant was estopped from denying that he had caused grievous bodily harm to the deceased with intent to do so, and from asserting that he had done so in self-defence. The only issues for the jury on the charge of murder were, therefore, that of causation of death, and that of provocation, which would have been no defence to the previous charge but would be a partial defence to murder. The decision has, it is submitted, an unassailable logic and is a particularly good example of the limited kind of criminal case in which conclusions may safely be drawn with regard to the issues decided by the jury in the first trial. Nonetheless, the decision in *Humphrys* overrules that in *Hogan*.

It is submitted that the outright rejection, by the House of Lords in *Humphrys,* of issue estoppel in criminal cases was unnecessary and unfortunate, despite the obvious difficulties of application, to which reference has already been made and which weighed heavily with the House (62). A party asserting issue estoppel cannot justify his claim unless the issues are specifically identifiable in terms of what the first jury must necessarily, by their verdict, have decided finally between the prosecution and the defendant. This limitation alone would be sufficient safeguard against the possibility of unfairness, while leaving untouched the manifest logic of cases such as *Hogan*. The argument of Lord Fraser (63) that it would be a 'public scandal' if a defendant could not be charged with perjury, where it later appeared that he had given false evidence, may be met by the rejoinders that issue estoppel would not produce this result, that estoppel would not operate on the basis of a judgment obtained by fraud, and that perjury must in any event be regarded in a special light when considering judgments obtained by means of it. The result in *Humphrys* was, no doubt, quite reasonable on its own facts.

In the result, however, nothing presently remains of the doctrine, and whatever the powers of judges of superior courts to prevent oppressive process, on which their Lordships expressed differing views, there is undeniably something of a hole in the law.

10.8 Pleading

Estoppels of all kinds may not be relied upon unless pleaded, and the rule applies to estoppel *per rem judicatam* (64). It is now unnecessary to consider the implications of this rule, if any, in criminal proceedings. A party may waive reliance upon an estoppel, and

60 (HL) [1964] AC 1254. 61 [1974] QB 398.
62 See, e.g., the speech of Lord Salmon, [1977] AC 1 at 43. 63 Ibid at 58.
64 *Vooght* v *Winch* (1819) 2 B & Ald 662.

may be taken to have waived it unless he pleads it. Where, however, a writ was issued to commence an action before judgment was given for the plaintiffs in an earlier action against the defendants, there was no reason why the plaintiffs should not, upon judgment being given in the first action, amend their pleadings in the second so as to allege the estoppel. No waiver could arise unless the plaintiffs had had an opportunity to plead the estoppel (65).

C: JUDGMENTS AS EVIDENCE OF THE FACTS ON WHICH THEY WERE BASED: STRANGERS

10.9   Introduction

At common law there was no fixed view on the admissibility of a judgment as evidence, of the facts upon which it was based, for or against strangers to the judgment. There was some authority either way, and it was certainly possible to find examples of cases where, with obviously convenient results, the courts overcame the apparent stumbling blocks of theory and allowed reliance on previous judgments. Thus, in *Re Crippen* (66) a husband, who was subsequently executed for the murder of his wife, made a will, and the executrix thereby appointed sought to administer the estate of the murdered wife. Application was made to vest the wife's estate elsewhere, on the ground that the husband's estate should not be permitted to benefit from his crime. It was argued that the conviction of the husband was not admissible to prove that he had murdered the wife. But the court held that, where there was an issue of rights accruing as a result of crime, the conviction was admissible as prima facie evidence of the commission of such crime. And in *Partington* v *Partington and Atkinson* (67) a finding of adultery against a husband made in a suit in which the husband was co-respondent, and to which the wife was not a party, was admissible for the wife, in a subsequent suit brought by her against the husband, as prima facie evidence of his adultery.

It seems from these cases that there was a limited recognition of previous judgments as evidence of facts but that, unlike the position when only the formal fact of judgment is relied on, the evidence could be only prima facie, and was certainly not conclusive. The question was further complicated by confusion in some authorities between this question, and the question of the operation of judgments *in rem*, and questions of other exceptional rules of evidence concerned with such matters as custom and public rights, which might sometimes be established by judgments.

10.10   The rule in Hollington v Hewthorn

At length, it was apparent that the balance of authority lay against the admissibility of judgments for or against strangers, and the rule was authoritatively laid down by the Court of Appeal in *Hollington* v *F. Hewthorn & Co. Ltd* (68). In an action for negligence by the plaintiff against an individual defendant and his employer, arising from a road traffic accident, the conviction of the individual defendant of the offence of driving without due care and attention was not admissible to prove that the individual defendant had been negligent. Despite the superficial attraction of the close similarity of issues in the different proceedings, and of the argument that the plaintiff, although not a party to

---

65   *Morrison, Rose & Partners* v *Hillman* (CA) [1961] 2 QB 266..
66   [1911] P 108.   67   [1925] P 34.   68   [1943] KB 587.

the prosecution, could hardly be prejudiced by admission of the conviction, the evidence was rejected for three formidable reasons: that the opinion of the previous tribunal was irrelevant; that findings of fact by the justices, especially in an uncontested case, might be qualitatively different from those which should prevail in a contested action in the High Court; and that it would be extremely difficult, if possible at all, to identify the facts upon which the conviction was based.

10.11 Reversal of the rule in civil cases

In civil cases in which several different plaintiffs or defendants may be entitled to recover or may be liable for the consequences of the same wrongful civil act, procedural provisions permit joinder of all necessary parties and consolidation of actions. This means that closely related civil claims can usually be adjudicated together and so that the need for reliance upon previous judgments given in civil proceedings can often be avoided. However, problems may still arise with previous criminal convictions and findings of adultery or paternity. Three kinds of case are principally concerned:

(a)   Where the plaintiff wishes to prove the conviction of the defendant of a criminal offence, relevant to the plaintiff's cause of action or to an issue in civil proceedings.

(b)   Where a party to an action for defamation wishes to prove that another has been convicted of a criminal offence, where the commission or otherwise of such offence is relevant to the action.

(c)   Where a party to civil proceedings (e.g. divorce) wishes to rely upon a finding of adultery or paternity made against another in previous proceedings relevant to his cause of action or an issue in the instant proceedings.

In these kinds of case, Parliament has decided that the convenience of permitting proof to be made in the manner described above outweighs even the cogent reservations expressed in *Hollington* v *Hewthorn*, and by ss. 11–13 of the Civil Evidence Act 1968 has made previous judgments admissible, but in these kinds of case only. In criminal cases, and in the small number of civil cases which are not covered by the Act, it would seem that *Hollington* v *Hewthorn* remains good law, and should be followed (69).

10.11.1   Convictions relevant to civil proceedings
S. 11 of the Civil Evidence Act 1968, provides as follows:

(1)   In any civil proceedings the fact that a person has been convicted of an offence by or before any court in the United Kingdom or by a court-martial there or elsewhere shall . . . be admissible in evidence for the purpose of proving, where to do so is relevant to any issue in those proceedings, that he committed that offence, whether he was so convicted upon a plea of guilty or otherwise and whether or not he is a party to the civil proceedings; but no conviction other than a subsisting one shall be admissible in evidence by virtue of this section.

(2)   In any civil proceedings in which by virtue of this section a person is proved to

69   So that as against a handler of stolen goods, the conviction of the thief is not evidence that the goods are stolen. Many inconveniences could be avoided in criminal cases, where the commission of an offence by a person other than the defendant falls to be proved, if the statutory relaxation were to be extended to cover them, and little injustice, if any, could result.

have been convicted of an offence by or before any court in the United Kingdom or by a court-martial there or elsewhere —

(a)   he shall be taken to have committed that offence unless the contrary is proved; and

(b)   without prejudice to the reception of any other admissible evidence for the purpose of identifying the facts on which the conviction was based, the contents of any document which is admissible as evidence of the conviction, and the contents of the information, complaint, indictment or charge-sheet on which the person in question was convicted, shall be admissible in evidence for that purpose.

So far as s. 11(1) is concerned, the following points should be noted:

(a)   The expression 'civil proceedings' is defined by s. 18(1), for all purposes of the Act, including ss. 11–13 (see 8.4, ante).

(b)   The section has no application to a conviction by a court outside the United Kingdom, other than a court martial.

(c)   It is irrelevant whether or not the person convicted is a party to the civil proceedings, for example the servant or agent of the defendant for whose acts the defendant is vicariously liable; it is also irrelevant whether or not the criminal proceedings were contested.

(d)   A 'subsisting' conviction means one which has not been quashed on appeal, and will include a conviction substituted by an appellate court for the original conviction. But the mere fact that an appeal is pending against a conviction does not mean that the conviction is not 'subsisting' for the purpose of s. 11; in such a case, any civil proceedings to which the conviction is said to be relevant should be adjourned, if necessary, pending the outcome of the appeal (70).

The construction of s. 11(2)(a) has given rise to differences of opinion among those judges who have been called upon to consider it. It is generally accepted that where a conviction is proved by virtue of s. 11, it has the effect of reversing the burden of proof, so that the party seeking to assert that the offence was not committed would bear the burden of proving that fact, apparently on the balance of probabilities. Where the commission of the offence is an issue central to the cause of action or defence, the burden of proof so reversed will be the legal burden. Thus in *Wauchope* v *Mordecai* (71) the plaintiff had been knocked off his bicycle when the defendant opened the door of a car as the plaintiff was passing. The defendant was later convicted of the offence of opening the door so as to cause injury or danger. By an oversight, the trial judge was not referred to s. 11 and found for the defendant, basing his decision on the incidence of the legal burden of proof. The Court of Appeal allowed the plaintiff's appeal. The burden lay on the defendant to prove that he had not opened the door negligently, and if the judge had considered s. 11, he must have found that that burden had not been discharged.

The decision in *Wauchope* v *Mordecai* left open, however, the question of the weight which should be attached to the conviction, once admitted, as evidence of the commission of the offence. In *Taylor* v *Taylor* (72) a wife petitioned for divorce on the ground of her husband's adultery. The adultery complained of was incestuous, in that it had been committed with the daughter of the family. The husband had been convicted of the

70   *Re Raphael, Raphael* v *d'Antin and Another* [1973] 1 WLR 998.
71   [1970] 1 WLR 317.   72   [1970] WLR 1148.

relevant incest, and his application for leave to appeal against conviction was refused. The wife tendered evidence of the conviction in the divorce proceedings under s. 11, and the husband sought to prove that he had not committed the offence. The trial judge found, on the basis of the depositions used at the trial and on the basis of oral evidence taken before him, which the Court of Appeal found to be unsatisfactory, that the husband had discharged the burden on him and had proved that he had not committed incest. The Court of Appeal allowed an appeal by the wife. In the words of Davies LJ, '. . . . it . . . is obvious that, when a man has been convicted by twelve of his fellow countrymen and countrywomen at a criminal trial, the verdict of the jury is a matter which is entitled to very great weight when the convicted person is seeking, in the words of the statute, to prove the contrary' (73). The trial judge should, accordingly, have obtained a transcript, or otherwise satisfied himself with regard to the evidence and details of the criminal trial and thus embarked upon a full and searching investigation of the husband's case, to see whether the burden of proof was discharged. There was not sufficient evidence upon which his conclusion could have been based (74).

The Court of Appeal in *Taylor* v *Taylor* were referred to the decision at first instance of Paull J in *Stupple* v *Royal Insurance Co. Ltd; Stupple* v *Same* (75), which had not then reached the Court of Appeal. That case involved a claim and counterclaim in respect of sums of money, said to be the proceeds of a robbery, of which Mr Stupple had been convicted. The issue, in effect, was whether his conviction was correct. Paull J asked himself the question, what his view would have been if he had sat as a juryman on the criminal trial. Though this approach won some support in *Taylor* v *Taylor,* it won none from the differently constituted Court of Appeal that heard the Stupples' case. But the court upheld the judge's view that the conviction, and its affirmation by the Court of Criminal Appeal, were: 'from a practical point of view . . . conculsive' (76). The Court of Appeal was, however, unable to agree on the precise effect of s. 11(2)(*a*) in terms of weight. Lord Denning MR thought that the evidence went further than merely shifting the burden of proof, and was 'a weighty piece of evidence in itself'. The conviction 'itself tells in the scale in the civil action.' Conversely Buckley LJ said: 'In my judgment, proof of conviction under this section gives rise to the statutory presumption laid down in s. 11(2)(*a*), which, like any other presumption, will give way to evidence establishing the contrary on the balance of probability, without itself affording any evidential weight to be taken into account in determining whether that onus has been discharged' (77). The third member of the court, Winn LJ, expressed no opinion on the point. It is submitted that the intention and wording of the section are alike better served by the view of Lord Denning MR.

Whatever the position, there now seems to be no reason why a conviction, admitted under s. 11, should not corroborate other evidence called for the party tendering it. Such

73   Ibid at 1152.
74   The limits of the means by which a party may discharge the burden of disproving a conviction cannot be said to be settled. In *Stupple* v *Royal Insurance Co. Ltd; Stupple* v *Same* (CA) [1971] 1 QB 50, Lord Denning MR conceived of a broad range of weapons, by calling fresh evidence, discrediting evidence given at the trial, and even by explaining a plea of guilty or a failure to appeal, to rebut the obvious inference. But it seems, as Paull J held at first instance, that the court is not entitled to consider, as if it were a criminal appellate court, the circumstances of the conduct of the trial; it must confine itself to the evidence and papers, and the formal record. In *Taylor* v *Taylor,* the Court postulated that the evidence at the trial would be admissible (presumably as evidence of truth) under either s. 2(1) or s. 4(1) of the Act, though the summing up would more probably be admissible under s. 4(1) as a record made by the shorthand writer acting under a duty.
75   [1971] 1 QB 50.
76   Lord Denning MR has since said (in *McIlkenny* v *Chief Constable of the West Midlands and Another* [1980] 2 WLR 689 that evidence adduced to disprove a conviction must be decisive: *sed quaere.*
77   See [1971] 1 QB 50 at 76.

a result had been approved in *Mash* v *Darley* (78) but had necessarily perished under the rule in *Hollington* v *Hewthorn*. The decision was that the conviction of a respondent to affiliation proceedings, for unlawful sexual intercourse with the applicant, was capable of corroborating her evidence, as required in such proceedings. It is submitted that the case is now sound law, once again.

10.11.2   Findings of adultery and paternity relevant to civil proceedings
S. 12 of the Civil Evidence Act, 1968 provides:

(1)   In any civil proceedings —

(a)   the fact that a person has been found guilty of adultery in any matrimonial proceedings; and
(b)   the fact that a person has been adjudged to be the father of a child in affiliation proceedings before any court in the United Kingdom,

shall . . . be admissible in evidence for the purpose of proving, where to do so is relevant to any issue in those civil proceedings, that he committed the adultery to which the finding relates or, as the case may be, is (or was) the father of that child, whether or not he offered any defence to the allegation of adultery or paternity and whether or not he is a party to the civil proceedings; but no finding or adjudication other than a subsisting one shall be admissible in evidence by virtue of this section.

(2)   In any civil proceedings in which by virtue of this section a person is proved to have been found guilty of adultery as mentioned in subsection (1)(a) above or to have been adjudged to be the father of a child as mentioned in subsection (1)(b) above —

(a)   he shall be taken to have committed the adultery to which the finding relates or, as the case may be, to be (or have been) the father of that child, unless the contrary is proved; and
(b)   [provides for the admissibility of evidence to show the facts on which the finding or adjudication was based]

It will be observed that the section follows closely the provisions of s. 11, and it would appear that the law relating to s. 11, as set out above, will apply with any necessary modifications to this section also. Certainly, it has been held that the effect of the section is to reverse the burden of proof and to require the party seeking to disprove the finding or adjudication to do so, on a balance of probabilities (79). The expression 'matrimonial proceedings' does not include matrimonial proceedings in a magistrates' court, and is confined to proceedings in England and Wales (s. 12(5)).

10.11.3   Convictions relevant to defamation actions
S. 13 of the Civil Evidence Act 1968 provides:

(1)   In an action for libel or slander in which the question whether a person did or did

---

78   (DC) [1914] 1 KB 1.
79   *Sutton* v *Sutton* [1970] 1 WLR 183. For the use of transcripts of previous matrimonial proceedings, see Practice Direction of 13 June 1969 [1969] 1 WLR 1192.

not commit a criminal offence is relevant to an issue arising in the action, proof that at the time when that issue falls to be determined, that person stands convicted of that offence shall be conclusive evidence that he committed that offence; and his conviction thereof shall be admissible in evidence accordingly.

The operation of s. 13 differs greatly from that of s. 11, in that the conviction is conclusive evidence of the commission of the offence. The reason for this wording of the section is to prevent the abuse of defamation proceedings for the purpose of attempting to reopen convictions, even when they may have been affirmed on appeal, and also to protect those concerned in writing or publishing justifiable material, relying upon the conviction for the truth of what they write or publish. It must, therefore, follow that a statement of claim, which does no more than complain of a statement, accurate in itself,, which asserts and fairly comments upon the fact that a person has committed an offence of which he has been lawfully convicted, must be struck out; though where the statement complained of also alleges matter not covered by s. 13, it may be right to leave the whole statement of claim intact (80).

By s. 13(3), a person stands convicted of an offence only if there is against him a subsisting conviction of the offence by or before a court in the United Kingdom or a court martial there or elsewhere.

10.11.4 *Ss. 11–13: general considerations*
Where any document is admissible to identify the facts upon which a conviction, finding or adjudication is based, a certified or authenticated copy of such document shall be admissible in evidence, and shall be taken to be a true copy, unless the contrary is shown (s. 11(4), 12(4), 13(4)).

By RSC, Ord.18, r. 7A, in an action tried with pleadings, a party who wishes to rely on evidence pursuant to s. 11 or s. 12 must plead his intention, specifying the facts relied upon, and must indicate the issue in the case to which it is relevant. The rule does not apply to evidence admissible under s. 13, presumably because the evidence is not open to challenge except to deny that there is a subsisting conviction. There would appear to be no reason why such evidence should not be pleaded, in view of its effect in law.

D: IMPEACHMENT OF JUDGMENTS

10.12 Principles and grounds

All that has gone before has proceeded on the assumption that the judgment is one which cannot be challenged on behalf of a party prejudiced by it. In most cases, this assumption will be a proper one. The effect of a judgment may be nullified if it is shown not to be final, and any judgment may be nullified or varied on appeal, though only at the instance of a party, a privy or a person entitled to intervene.

In addition to these matters, however, a person prejudiced by a judgment, which is said to have evidential value against him, or by which he is said to be estopped, may seek to 'impeach' the judgment on one of the following grounds:

(a)   That the judgment was not obtained on the merits. If, for example, the judgment

80   *Levene v Roxhan and Others* (CA) [1970] 1 WLR 1322.

was obtained by some technical objection, in default of pleading (81) or by some temporary disability of a party, error of the court or by want of prosecution (82). The rationale of these cases is, of course, that no investigation of any relevant issues has taken place, so that no evidential conclusion could safely be drawn from the judgment.

(b)   That the judgment was obtained in circumstances where the court had no jurisdiction to pronounce it.

(c)   That it was obtained by fraud, collusion or forgery. The objection on the ground of collusion does not, of course, apply where there has been a genuine compromise of litigation on the merits of the case, or a proper settlement sanctioned by the court. Impeachment of a judgment on these grounds may be made only by a person who is not privy to the defect alleged.

10.13   Questions for counsel

1   Assuming that Coke is acquitted of raping Margaret Blackstone:

(a)   Could he be charged with that offence again, should new evidence come to light?

(b)   May he be charged later with attempted rape or indecent assault, arising from the same facts?

2   If Littleton gives evidence in support of his alibi, and is acquitted of indecently assaulting Angela Blackstone, and thereafter further evidence comes to light which disproves the alibi, may Littleton be charged with perjury in respect of his evidence, and if so, are there any limits on the evidence the prosecution may call? In particular, what would be the position with regard to Littleton's alleged tape-recorded confession to his wife?

3   If Coke is convicted of raping Margaret Blackstone, what would be the significance of such conviction if:

(a)   Margaret Blackstone thereafter brings an action in the High Court against Coke for assault and battery?

(b)   Coke brings an action for libel against Mrs Blackstone for having written and published an article in a magazine about the rape of Margaret, stating that Coke was a rapist?

(c)   Margaret Blackstone becomes pregnant, allegedly as a result of the act of rape, and brings affiliation proceedings against Coke, for which purposes her evidence requires to be corroborated?

4   In question 3, would it matter for any purposes that at the material time Coke's conviction was subject to an appeal against conviction pending in the Court of Appeal, Criminal Division?

81   *Re Orrell Colliery & Fire-Brick Co.* (1879) 12 ChD 681.   82   *Pople v Evans* [1969] 2 Ch 255.

11 Public Policy and Privilege

11.1 Public policy and privilege contrasted

One of the major principles recognised by the law in the conduct of litigation is that of disclosure of evidence. By this expression is meant that the parties should disclose, to each other and for the purposes of the proceedings (1), any and all evidence, relevant to the issues in those proceedings, which is or has been in their possession, custody and power. The object of the principle is simply that all such relevant evidence in the case should be available to be inspected by all parties, and that the parties should be free to place before the court any evidence which will assist it in determining the truth and in doing justice between the parties. The idea of inspection of evidence in the possession of another party is primarily of importance in the field of documentary and real evidence, and most of the battles in the field of public policy and privilege have been fought in relation to such evidence. But the principle of disclosure and its object of enabling the parties to place before the court all relevant and admissible evidence, applies to evidence in whatever form, and the rules of privilege in particular are of considerable significance in relation to certain kinds of oral evidence.

The principle has as a necessary corollary the rule that no party should be entitled to frustrate or hinder the doing of justice in any proceedings by withholding from his opponent or from the court evidence which is relevant and admissible for that purpose. But this cannot be an absolute rule. It may be overriden by some important public interest that certain evidence should not be disclosed to a party because of the likelihood of danger to the national interest or of impairment of the working of some aspect of the public service. In such a case, as Lord Reid pointed out in *Conway* v *Rimmer and Another* (2), the public interest in the doing of justice as between the parties to litigation has to be balanced against a different but equally demanding public interest:

> It is universally recognised that here there are two kinds of public interest which may clash. There is the public interest that harm shall not be done to the nation or the public service by disclosure of certain documents, and there is the public interest that the administration of justice shall not be frustrated by the withholding of documents which must be produced if justice is to be done. There are many cases where the nature of the injury which would or might be done to the nation or the public service is of so

---

1   The court will not countenance the abuse of its process, which results from the improper use of evidence ordered to be disclosed, i.e. the use of such evidence for purposes other than the proper conduct of the proceedings: *Riddick* v *Thames Board Mills Ltd* (CA) [1977] QB 881; *Church of Scientology* v *DHSS* (CA) [1979] 1 WLR 723.
2   (HL) [1968] AC 910 at 940.

grave a character that no other interest, public or private, can be allowed to prevail over it.

The result of such considerations may, therefore, be that facts of undoubted relevance to proceedings, which may indeed sometimes be potentially conclusive of such proceedings, will not be permitted to be proved. Such facts are said to be excluded by public policy.

Even outside this sphere, the rule of disclosure has never been an absolute one. The law recognises that other considerations may enter the field, even where they appear to be of a purely private nature. Although most private interests must bow to the requirement of a fair and open trial, some are important enough to override it. Certain rules may prevent evidence being given, e.g.: the insistence that no person should be compelled to divulge what has passed between him and his legal advisers in the course of seeking and giving legal advice; that communications between husband and wife during the marriage should not be elicited under compulsion. Evidence which enjoys a measure of protection for a reason of this kind is said to be privileged. Again, evidence of undoubted relevance, and sometimes potentially conclusive evidence, may be withheld, and the interests of other parties are affected accordingly.

The fact that evidence which is relevant (3) and otherwise admissible may be excluded by public policy or privilege, lends to the two subjects of this chapter an appearance of similarity which is misleading. The rules and their operation are quite distinct, and any superficial identity of result is more than outweighed by substantial and far-reaching differences (4). The principal differences are worth considering in a little detail before the individual rules themselves are examined.

11.1.1   Sphere of application

Where facts are excluded by public policy, they are excluded regardless of the nature of the proceedings. Private privileges, on the other hand, may sometimes apply only to particular kinds of proceedings, as with matrimonial communications where the privilege now applies only to criminal proceedings and has always terminated with the marriage.

11.1.2   Possibility of waiver

Private privilege has always been a rule against compulsion, and has never prevented the voluntary disclosure or giving of privileged evidence by a person entitled to insist on the privilege. A person who voluntarily discloses in such circumstances is said to waive his privilege. Privilege may, according to the circumstances in which it arises, apply to evidence in the possession of, or capable of being given by, a party to proceedings, or any witness in the proceedings. The privilege is personal to that party or witness, and he alone can waive it (5). Conversely, the onus of asserting the privilege also rests on the party or witness entitled to it, and evidence disclosed or given other than under unlawful compulsion will be admissible for all purposes, even though privilege might with advice or diligence have been asserted in respect of it (6).

3   If evidence is not relevant then no question of public policy or privilege will arise: *R v Cheltenham Justices, ex parte Secretary of State for Trade* (DC) [1977] 1 WLR 95.
4   The distinction is not assisted by the use of the misleading term 'Crown privilege' to describe some aspects of public policy. For criticism of this usage, see *Rogers v Home Secretary; Gaming Board for Great Britain v Rogers* (HL) [1973] AC 388 per Lord Reid at 400 and Lord Pearson at 406.
5   It seems to follow, and has been held, that a party cannot in general found an appeal on the upholding or rejection of a privilege attaching to his witness: *R v Kinglake* (1870), 22 LT 335. But no adverse inference may be drawn from a proper insistence on a privilege: *Wentworth v Lloyd* (HL) (1864) 10 HL Cas 589.
6   See, e.g., *R v Noel* (CCA) [1914] 3 KB 848.

However, an objection based on public policy may be asserted by any person, whether a witness or a party, or indeed any person interested for any reason in withholding the evidence. The objection will also, where appropriate, be taken by the court of its own motion. It is generally held that no waiver can be made of an objection based on public policy and that evidence must sometimes be withheld even where all the parties are content that it be disclosed, although Lord Denning MR has powerfully questioned this as an invariable proposition (7).

11.1.3 Use of secondary evidence

Where facts are excluded by public policy, not only are the documents which are the immediate subject of the exclusion affected, but the result is that the contents of such documents cannot be proved in evidence by secondary means. This excludes copies of such documents, oral evidence of their contents and even their use by a witness to refresh his memory (8).

On the other hand, privilege attaches only to an original document or communication as such and although secondary evidence of such documents or communications is, in law, confidential, it is nonetheless admissible to prove the facts contained therein. It follows, therefore, that an opponent may prove facts contained in a privileged document by producing a copy of the document or by adducing oral evidence of its contents (9). Thus, in *Calcraft* v *Guest* (10) the defendant was held to be entitled to put in evidence copies of proofs of evidence of witnesses of the plaintiff's predecessor in title, relating to a previous action, the originals of these documents (which were plainly privileged under the legal professional privilege rule) having been returned to the plaintiff. The privilege attached only to the original, and did not inhibit the proof of the contents by other means, even though the plaintiff could not be compelled to produce the original or to disclose it to the defendant. In *Rumping* v *DPP* (11) the House of Lords held that a letter written by the defendant to his wife, which amounted to a confession to the murder with which he was charged, could be put in evidence by the prosecution, it having been handed over to the police by a person to whom it had been entrusted for posting. The letter would have been privileged in the wife's hands as a matrimonial communication, and the decision illustrates an even wider rule than that in *Calcraft* v *Guest*, namely that privilege attaching to the original can be lost by its actual disclosure, even where no waiver is intended.

The lesson to be learnt from these examples is that privilege must be jealously guarded: it ceases to exist if waived or lost, and is rendered impotent by copying unless prompt action can be taken to restrain the copier. The lesson was learnt the hard way in *R* v *Tompkins* (12) where, the defendant having given certain evidence in chief, there was put to him during cross-examination a note which he had earlier written to his counsel which contradicted his evidence. The contents of the note were not read out, but on seeing it, the defendant admitted that he had not told the truth in chief and altered his

7 Dissenting in the Court of Appeal in *Burmah Oil Co. Ltd* v *Bank of England* [1979] 1 WLR 473 at 487.
8 See *Gain* v *Gain* [1961] 1 WLR 1469. Any course which expressly or by necessary implication involves the revelation of the contents seems to be prohibited.
9 In accordance with the usual rule (see 1.6, ante, and *R* v *Sang* (HL) [1979] 3 WLR 263), the means by which the secondary evidence is obtained, even if improper or illegal, is irrelevant to the question of its admissibility. However, an injunction will be granted to restore to proper possession privileged or confidential documents, and to restrain their use by persons not entitled to have them, if proceedings are brought for this purpose: *Lord Ashburton* v *Pape* (CA) [1913] 2 Ch 469. However, no injunction will be granted to restrain the use of relevant evidence by the Crown in a public prosecution: *Butler* v *Board of Trade* [1971] Ch 680.
10 (CA) [1898] 1 QB 759.   11 [1964] AC 814.
12 (1977) 67 Cr App R 181.

evidence. He was subsequently convicted. The Court of Appeal rejected an argument
that the prosecution had not been entitled to make use of the note as, in effect, a
previous inconsistent statement. Although originally privileged, as a communication
between client and legal adviser, its loss entitled the prosecution to make use of it, once it
was in their hands. Ormrod LJ observed, perhaps a little unkindly, that it would require
'a remarkable exercise in moral philosophy' to conclude that perjury should not be
exposed where such means came to hand.

11.1.4   Taking the objection

Where the Crown is a party to proceedings and proposes to withhold documentary
evidence on the ground of public policy, the documents concerned can be included in the
part of the list of documents that deals with the items that are subject to an objection to
production. The matter will then be dealt with on a summons for discovery. Where the
Crown is not a party, and in cases where the process of discovery is not available (13), the
objection should be taken at trial, after notice. In any event, the objection should be
supported by evidence, usually given by affidavit, sworn by the relevant minister or a
subordinate of sufficient authority and responsibility (14). The court has power to
regulate the manner in which the objection can be made, and may require to be satisfied
by further evidence. However, a certificate signed by the minister is habitually accepted,
provided that, like an affidavit, it deals with the material matters. The requirements are
that the identity and nature of the documents are described with sufficient particularity,
that the grounds of the objection are stated and that the affidavit or certificate should
state that the maker has personally examined the documents in question, before reaching the conclusion that they should be withheld in the public interest (15).

The claim on the ground of public policy may legitimately be made either on a
'contents basis' or a 'class basis', that is to say, the objection may relate to specific facts
contained in specific documents, or to the entirety of a certain class of documents
because of their collective character. The court is more likely to be sympathetic if an
objection is based on the specific contents of a document than if it is based only on the
document's classification, especially where the class appears to the court to consist of
'routine communications' (16).

A claim to privilege may be made in the list of documents, and argued on a summons
for discovery, if it relates to documents within the possession or power of the party
claiming privilege. In many cases, however, the claim is made at trial in the course of
evidence, at the moment when a question is asked to which objection is taken. This
course is appropriate, for example, when the privilege claimed is that against self-
incrimination, and generally where the privilege is that of a witness, rather than a party.
The judge must then rule on the matter before allowing the evidence to proceed. In a
criminal case, he should do so in the absence of the jury, and may do so in camera if
necessary, for example to test a claim to the privilege against self-incrimination. The
ruling may require evidence to support or resist the claim, or legal argument or both.

---

13   Discovery is not available in criminal cases, and is not invariably used in actions in the county courts: see
RSC, Ord. 24; CCR, Ord. 14. Discovery may be ordered by an industrial tribunal when appropriate. For cases to
which the Crown is a party see the Crown Proceedings Act 1947, s. 28.
14   *Alfred Crompton Amusement Machines Ltd* v *Commissioners of Customs & Excise (No. 2)* (CA) [1972] 2
QB 102. The point was not considered in the House of Lords.
15   See *Re Grosvenor Hotel, London (No. 2)* (CA) [1965] Ch 1210 per Lord Denning MR at 1244.
16   See the comments of Lord Reid in *Conway* v *Rimmer and Another* (HL) [1968] AC 910 at 940–1.

A: PUBLIC POLICY

11.2 Affairs of state

The most compelling and basic of the grounds on which public policy may be asserted is that of direct national interest, in the sense that disclosure would prejudice the safety or good order of the realm. Perhaps the most obvious instances are provided by the wartime cases. In *Asiatic Petroleum Co. Ltd* v *Anglo-Persian Co. Ltd* (17) disclosure of the documents in question would have revealed details of military plans during wartime, and of course public policy operated to prevent this. Similarly, in the leading case of *Duncan* v *Cammell Laird & Co. Ltd* (18) the plaintiff in an action for damages for personal injury was refused discovery of the plans and specifications of, and the contract for, the construction of the submarine *Thetis*, on which he had been working. The First Lord of the Admiralty ordered the defendants to object to their production, on the clear ground of direct damage to the national interest during wartime.

But the ambit of public policy has never been confined to such extreme examples. There are many ways in which damage of some description may be done in some area of national concern, and as the process of government becomes more complex and far-reaching, so correspondingly does the potential for claims to withhold based on public policy expand and widen. The vast progress in the technology of storing and reproducing information, and the consequent explosion of documents and records, have also contributed to the growing difficulty felt by the courts in separating the genuine possibility of harm from specious attempts to conceal routine bureaucratic communications. This chapter can do no more than indicate the various directions in which the claim has been recognised (19).

It has been recognised that there are matters of great importance, which may aptly be termed 'affairs of state'. An objection to disclosure of documents relating to such matters should almost always be allowed, even on a class basis. Such documents relate to the workings of inner government, the formulation of national policy and similarly high matters. These were dealt with by Lord Reid in his speech in *Conway* v *Rimmer* (20):

> I do not doubt that there are certain classes of documents which ought not to be disclosed whatever their content may be. Virtually everyone agrees that cabinet minutes and the like ought not to be disclosed until such time as they are only of historical interest.

The most important reason for this was that:

> ... such disclosure would create or fan ill-informed or captious public or political criticism. The business of government is difficult enough as it is, and no government could contemplate with equanimity the inner workings of the government machine

---

17   (CA) [1916] 1 KB 822.

18   (HL) [1942] AC 624. None of the strictures cast on this decision in *Conway* v *Rimmer* appear to call into question its correctness on its own facts.

19   The better view is probably that public policy develops within the categories suggested in this section, rather than that new categories can be recognised by the courts. In *Fender* v *St John-Mildmay* (HL) [1938] AC 1, Lord Atkin at 10 and Lord Thaukerton at 23 saw any extension of the categories as a matter for Parliament, not the courts. The contrary view of Lord Hailsham of St Marylebone expressed in *D* v *NSPCC* (HL) [1978] AC 171 at 230, that the courts may extend the categories as conditions change, has not received universal agreement. However, given the scope for expanding the existing categories, the point may be only of academic interest.

20   [1968] AC 910 at 952.

being exposed to the gaze of those ready to criticise without adequate knowledge of the background and perhaps with some axe to grind.

In Lord Reid's view, this would apply to:

> ... all documents concerned with policy making within departments including, it may be, minutes and the like by quite junior officials and correspondence with outside bodies.

And significantly, Lord Reid added:

> Further it may be that deliberations about a particular case require protection as much as deliberations about policy.

Lord Reid's sentiments were echoed in respect of documents such as cabinet minutes, dispatches from ambassadors and communications between departmental heads, by the other members of the House (21). But these documents figure comparatively rarely in private litigation, and have occasioned no real difficulty. The conduct of military affairs (22), the government's activities in the administration of colonies (23), the good relations of the United Kingdom with foreign powers (24) and other similar affairs of state in the strictest sense, have always been recognised as entitled to protection (25). But there remain unanswered two questions of the utmost importance:

(a) Are the courts able or entitled to question the assertion by the minister that documents should be withheld on the ground of public policy?

(b) If the answer to question (a) be yes, by what criterion should the minister's claim be judged?

Both questions were answered by the House of Lords in *Conway v Rimmer*. The appellant had been a probationer police officer in the Cheshire Constabulary, but had been dismissed as unlikely to become an efficient police officer. During his term of service, he had been charged with, but acquitted of, theft, the allegation being that he had stolen a torch belonging to a colleague. Being dissatisfied with his treatment, he brought an action for malicious prosecution against the chief constable. At the stage of discovery, the Home Secretary claimed that certain reports, relating to the appellant's qualities as a probationer officer and to the decision to prosecute him, should be withheld on the ground of public policy. The reports were undoubtedly relevant to the action, and an interesting facet of the case was that the chief constable had no objection to their disclosure. The ground advanced by the Home Secretary was simply that the production of the documents would be 'injurious to the public interest'.

On the question whether the court had any power to question the view of the minister, the House acknowledged, as it had to, that the minister was far better placed than the court to assess what was in the public interest. This consideration had led an earlier

---

21   See the speeches of Lord Hodson at 973 and Lord Pearce at 987.
22   *Beatson v Skene* (1860) 5 H & N 838; *HMS Bellerophon* (1874) 44 LJ Adm 5.
23   *Hennessy v Wright* (DC) (1888) 21 QBD 509.
24   *R v Governor of Brixton Prison, ex parte Soblen* (CA) [1963] 2 QB 243 at 273–4. See also *Buttes Gas & Oil Co. v Hammer and Another* (CA) *The Times* 28 June 1980.
25   See the list of examples given in Phipson, *Evidence*, 12th ed., para 564. However, many of the older cases might have been decided differently if they had been heard after *Conway v Rimmer*.

House of Lords, in *Duncan* v *Cammell Laird & Co. Ltd*, to hold that the minister's certificate should be conclusive and binding on the court, so that the trial judge had no power to admit or order disclosure of documents protected, in effect, by executive decision. For a variety of reasons, the later House in *Conway* v *Rimmer* had no compunction about departing from the previous, though comparatively recent, ruling. The exhaustive review of the authorities undertaken by Lords Reid and Morris of Borth-y-Gest shows that the conclusion reached in *Duncan* v *Cammell Laird & Co. Ltd* was founded in part on an erroneous belief that the law of Scotland regarded ministerial objections as conclusive, and that in such a respect the law of England ought not to differ from that of Scotland. Given the correctness of the first proposition, the second would surely also be correct, but as Lord Morris was able to show, the first was incorrect and in need of revision. This too prompted in itself a reversal of *Duncan* v *Cammell Laird & Co. Ltd*.

Undoubtedly the most cogent reason of all for the decision in *Conway* v *Rimmer* was the dissatisfaction felt almost universally with the former rule, because of the ease with which it could be used to provide a blanket immunity from production for documents of no more than marginal importance to any identifiable national interest. After *Duncan* v *Cammell Laird & Co. Ltd* there had been a number of cases which had given rise to a strongly expressed judicial disquiet. In *Broome* v *Broome* (26) the minister objected to the admission in divorce proceedings of documents relating to efforts by a Service welfare organisation to reconcile the parties, on the ground that its disclosure might 'prejudice the morale of the armed forces'. The court, scathing in its impotence, commented on the lack of discernible public interest in the matter and remarked that the matter was one which properly fell under the head of private privilege and no more. In *Ellis* v *Home Office* (27) Devlin J, faced with an objection from the Home Office to the disclosure of reports by doctors and prison officers on the mental condition of a prisoner and dealing with his assault on a fellow prisoner, who sought damages against the Home Office, referred to an 'uneasy feeling' that justice had not been done and more than an uneasy feeling that justice had not been seen to be done.

Weighing these considerations against the undoubtedly greater competence of the minister in assessing the dictates of public interest, Lord Reid reached the following conclusion (28):

> I would therefore propose that the House ought now to decide that courts have and are entitled to exercise a power and duty to hold a balance between the public interest, as expressed by a minister, to withhold certain documents or other evidence, and the public interest in ensuring the proper administration of justice. That does not mean that a court would reject a minister's view: full weight must be given to it in every case, and if the minister's reasons are of a character which judicial experience is not competent to weigh, then the minister's view must prevail. But experience has shown that reasons given for withholding whole classes of documents are often not of that character.

Lord Pearce said (29):

26   [1955] P 190. Much the same thing happened in *Gain* v *Gain* [1961] 1 WLR 1469 in respect of a medical report of a naval surgeon commander.
27   [1953] 2 QB 135.
28   [1968] AC 910 at 952. This conclusion had been contended for in untested decisions of the Court of Appeal: see *Re Grosvenor Hotel, London (No. 2)* [1965] Ch 1210.
29   Ibid at 987. the 'candour' argument in favour of withholding documents has never recovered from the

It is conceded that under the existing practice there can be no weighing of injustice in particular cases against the general public disadvantage of disclosure and its effect on candour. But it is argued that a judge, who is the only person who can properly weigh the former, is incapable of properly weighing the latter. I do not understand why he cannot do so, especially if the ministry gives some specific details of the type of document in question and some specific reasons why it is undesirable to allow production. It is a judge's constant task to weigh human behaviour and the points that tell for or against candour. He knows full well that in general a report will be less inhibited if it will never see the light of public scrutiny, and that in some cases and on some subjects this may be wholly desirable. He also knows that on many subjects this fact has little if any important effect. Against this he can consider whether the documents in question are of much or little weight in the litigation, whether their absence will result in a complete or partial denial of justice to one or other of the parties or perhaps to both, and what is the importance of the particular litigation to the parties and the public. All these are matters which should be considered if the court is to decide where the public interest lies.

On the second question of the criterion by which the minister's claim should be judged, the House held that the duty of the court was to decide on balance whether the documents are to be disclosed. But at the same time, there is to be a distinction between a 'contents' claim, in which case the court would comparatively rarely be disposed to dissent from the view of the minister, if given proper reasons, and a 'class' claim, particularly where the class appeared to be of routine documents. In this latter case, Lord Reid said that the test was to be whether the withholding of documents was 'really necessary for the proper functioning of the public service' (30). The process of holding the balance means that the court must be free to inspect the documents in question privately, without in the first instance disclosing them to the parties (31). In *Conway* v *Rimmer* the House of Lords regarded the reports as routine on an inspection of them, and ordered their disclosure to the appellant.

11.3 Governmental and administrative matters generally

Nothing in the authorities on affairs of state limits the area of governmental activity to the comparatively dramatic circumstances of the wartime cases, or to the lofty foreign-policy cases. Government policy is nowadays formulated and carried out in relation to a wide and ever-increasing sphere of activity, and the principles laid down in *Conway* v *Rimmer* apply over the whole spectrum. It is no doubt true to say that the more mundane and essentially administrative the subject, the less likely it is that a class of documents will satisfy the test propounded by Lord Reid, or that the contents of any given document will be of sufficient delicacy and gravity to warrant its exclusion; but each case will be examined on its merits.

blows dealt to it in *Conway* v *Rimmer,* and is demonstrably less valid than the similar, but distinct, argument in relation to informers.

---

30   Ibid at 952. The words cited were adopted from the speech of Lord Simon in *Duncan* v *Cammell Laird & Co. Ltd* (HL) [1942] AC 624 at 642, and the test was reiterated by Lord Reid in *Rogers* v *Home Secretary* (HL) [1973] AC 388 at 400–1.

31   The House rejected the argument that the inspection by the court without reference to the parties was contrary to the rules of natural justice, whether or not the Crown is a party. Lord Morris, more cautious, held that there was a power to inspect which should be exercised sparingly. And see the observations of Lord Wilberforce in *Burmah Oil Co. Ltd* v *Bank of England* (HL) [1979] 3 WLR 722 at 733.

A good illustration in modern times is that of documents relating to the government's economic policy. It was at one time doubted whether economic questions *per se* would suffice to give rise to a claim based on public policy at all. Thus, in *Smith* v *East India Co.* (32), in what was essentially a commercial action, despite the fact that the company played a vital role in the political government of India, documents passing between the court of directors and the British government commissioners for India were held to be the subject of public-policy immunity, solely by virtue of their political content. But as it became more and more clear that it is an important function of government to regulate, if not to participate in, economic and commercial activity, the mood changed. In *M. Isaacs & Sons Ltd and Others* v *Cook* (33) it was held that communications passing between the Prime Minister of Australia and the Australian High Commissioner in London, which were said to contain matter defamatory of the plaintiff, were to be withheld on the ground of public policy, even though the contents of such communications were plainly commercial in character.

In *Burmah Oil Co. Ltd* v *Bank of England* (34) the company sought a declaration against the Bank that a sale by the company to the Bank of certain stock at a price required by the government, pursuant to an agreement made in 1975, was inequitable and unfair, and claimed an order for the transfer back of the stock at the 1975 price. The company had, at the time of the agreement, been in dire financial straits because of an international oil crisis, and the agreement had been designed to 'rescue' the company, under the very close control of the government working through the Bank. The company sought discovery of all relevant documents. The Crown intervened and objected to the production of some sixty-two documents, which for this purpose were divided into three categories. Categories A and B both related to the formulation of government economic policy, at ministerial level and at a lower level (35). The majority of the Court of Appeal (36) were in favour of upholding the objection taken by the Crown. Lord Denning MR, dissenting, did not accept that the 'rescue' operation was a matter of policy. He said (37):

Now I can understand that privilege in regard to high questions of state policy, such as those dealing with foreign affairs or the defence or security of the realm. But I do not think it should be extended to commercial transactions undertaken by the government or the Bank of England. This rescue operation of Burmah was *par excellence* a commercial transaction. Such as those which the City of London has undertaken many a time in recent years.

The House of Lords upheld the majority of the Court of Appeal. Lord Wilberforce saw no need to inspect the documents, in view of the clear and detailed certificate of the minister. The other Lords, having inspected the documents, held that none of them contained matter of such evidential value as to make an order for their disclosure necessary to dispose fairly of the case. Lord Scarman (38) described the documents as '"high level". They are concerned with the formulation of policy. They are part of the inner working of the government machine.'

---

32 (LC) (1841) 1 Ph 50.
33 [1925] 2 KB 391. In a case of a commercial nature, there is no doubt that the court will scrutinise a claim based on public policy with great care: see, e.g., *Robinson* v *State of South Australia (No. 2)* (PC, South Australia) [1931] AC 704 at 715–6.
34 (CA) [1979] 1 WLR 473; affirmed (HL) [1979] 3 WLR 722.
35 Category C was classified as 'confidential'. As to this, see 11.5, post.
36 Bridge and Templeman LJJ (Upholding Foster J at first instance), Lord Denning MR dissenting.
37 [1979] 1 WLR 473 at 486.   38 [1979] 3 WLR at 758.

It is, therefore, the nature of the documents, and not the area of government to which they relate, which will determine whether or not public-interest immunity will be applied. It is not necessary that the matter should relate to an aspect of central government, or that the body or department on whose behalf public policy is claimed should be an organ of central government. In *D* v *NSPCC* (39) the society, a voluntary body incorporated by royal charter, had power under the Children and Young Persons Act 1969 to bring care proceedings in a juvenile court, although it was under no duty to do so. The society sought help from members of the public in supplying it with information' about children who might be ill-treated, and offered a guarantee of confidentiality to informants. Someone informed the society that the plaintiff's daughter had been ill-treated, information which proved to be without foundation. The plaintiff brought an action for damages for negligence on the part of the society, alleging that it had exercised insufficient care in investigating the complaint before sending an inspector to her home to see the child. The plaintiff sought discovery of, *inter alia*, the identity of the informant and the society claimed that the identity ought to be withheld on the ground of public policy.

The Court of Appeal by a majority (40) held that the plaintiff was entitled to discovery of the identity, Scarman LJ and Sir John Pennycuick holding specifically that public-policy immunity was confined to matters of central government. The House of Lords reversed the ruling. The decision turned primarily on the analogy of the immunity accorded to police informers (see 11.4 post) but the House also disposed of the point that the society was not an organ of central government. Lord Simon of Glaisdale, in the course of a careful refutation of any such requirement, observed (41):

> . . . 'the state' cannot on any sensible political theory be restricted to the Crown and the departments of central government (which are, indeed, part of the Crown in constitutional law). The state is the whole organisation of the body politic for supreme civil rule and government – the whole political organisation which is the basis of civil government. As such it certainly extends to local – and, as I think, also statutory – bodies in so far as they are exercising autonomous rule . . . There is a recurrent transfer of functions between central, local and statutory authorities. For example, near the heart of the issue before your Lordships, the Crown as parens patriae had traditionally a general jurisdiction over children; a residue is now exercised in the High Court, but the bulk has been devolved by statute on local authorities.

Lord Simon regarded *Conway* v *Rimmer* and *Re D* (42) as existing authority for the proposition which the House now recognised, although the objection in the former was taken by the Home Secretary, and the decision in the latter owed as much to an express statutory provision and the practice of the court against discovery in cases relating to children, as to any general principle of public policy. Nonetheless, *Rogers* v *Home Secretary* (43) is clear authority for the application of the rule to statutory bodies, and there is also authority before *Conway* v *Rimmer* against a restriction to central govern-

39   [1978] AC 171.
40   Scarman LJ and Sir John Pennycuick, Lord Denning MR dissenting.
41   [1978] AC 171 at 235–6.
42   (CA) [1970] 1 WLR 599. Local-authority and other reports regarding the welfare of children are sometimes said to be the subject of public-policy immunity, but their use seems more often to be viewed by the courts as a matter of practice in the light of any relevant statutory provisions, as in *Re D*. See also *Official Solicitor* v *K* (HL) [1965] AC 201.
43   (HL) [1973] AC 388.

ment, albeit such cases must be treated cautiously in the light of the then general acceptance of the conclusiveness of ministerial objections. The decision in *D* v *NSPCC* has put the matter beyond doubt: public policy may be claimed for documents of a local authority or statutory body, where it is appropriate, although the cases in which this claim will prevail over the principle of disclosure will presumably be comparatively rare (44).

11.4   Information given for the detection of crime etc.

It has long been a rule of English law that in any public prosecution, or information for fraud against the revenue laws, or in any civil proceedings arising from either of these, no question may be asked and no evidence may be given which would tend to reveal the identity of any person who has given information leading to the institution of the prosecution or information. There is said to be an overriding public interest in preserving the anonymity of informants, because of the obvious likelihood of sources of information drying up otherwise. A public prosecution is, in modern law, likely to include any case brought by or after investigation by the police, or any executive body having police powers for any purpose, and indeed the police informer is the classic example of the species. But the rule should, it is submitted, and might now well be held to, apply also to private prosecutions, there being no obvious ground of public policy for distinguishing private from public prosecutions for this purpose. The rule prevents any question, direct or indirect, which would tend to reveal the identity of an informant or the channel of information.

In *Marks* v *Beyfus* (45) the rule was stated for modern practice by Lord Esher MR. The plaintiff, who had brought an action alleging a conspiracy to prosecute maliciously, sought to elicit from the Director of Public Prosecutions the name of his informant. The refusal of the Director to answer was upheld. But Lord Esher did recognise that there must be one exceptional case (46):

> . . . if upon the trial of a prisoner the judge should be of opinion that the disclosure of the name of the informant is necessary or right in order to show the prisoner's innocence, then one public policy is in conflict with another public policy, and that which says that an innocent man is not to be condemned when his innocence can be proved is the policy that must prevail.

It is accepted that this exceptional case is still a proper one, although the number of cases in which the information is necessary to show the defendant's innocence is not likely to be great. The evidence of what is said by an informant is the purest form of hearsay, and even if it were not, the calling of an informant would be self-defeating in all but the gravest cases.

The police informer supplying information about crime is, of course, not the only source of information upon which public bodies may act and indeed depend for their ability to act. The identity of informers on matters involving possible frauds against the revenue laws has long been regarded as meriting protection under the rule, and in a

---

44   For an example of minimal public interest in withholding information being defeated by the clear likelihood of serious injustice, see *Norwich Pharmacal Co. and Others* v *Commissioners of Customs & Excise* (HL) [1974] AC 133.
45   (CA) (1890) 25 QBD 494.
46   Ibid at 498.

modern context this application of the rule was confirmed in *Alfred Crompton Amusement Machines Ltd* v *Commissioners of Customs & Excise (No. 2)* (47) where the
commissioners had obtained information from customers of the company and others,
relevant to assessments of the company's liability for purchase tax, which were the
subject of an intended arbitration. It was held that the commissioners were entitled to
withhold documents which would reveal the sources of their information, since if
became known that sources of information could not be kept secret, the working of the
legislation under which the commissioners' powers were exercised in relation to the tax
would be harmed by a lack of information. Lord Cross of Chelsea, with whom the other
members of the House, on this point, agreed said (48):

> Here . . . one can well see that the third parties who have supplied this information to
> the commissioners because of the existence of their statutory powers would very much
> resent its disclosure by the commissioners to the appellants and that it is not at all
> fanciful . . . to say that the knowlege that the commissioners cannot keep such infor-
> mation secret may be harmful to the efficient working of the Act. In a case where the
> considerations for and against disclosure appear to be fairly evenly balanced the courts
> should I think, uphold a claim to privilege on the ground of public interest and trust to
> the head of the department concerned to do whatever he can to mitigate the ill-effects
> of non-disclosure.

The obvious importance of a free supply of information to the working of various
public bodies has been instrumental in the extension of the informant rule to situations
beyond, but analogous to the original example of the detection of crime. In *Rogers* v
Home Secretary; *Gaming Board for Great Britain* v *Rogers* (49) the Gaming Board
refused applications by Rogers for certificates of consent to the grant to him of licences
under the Gaming Act 1968 to operate certain gaming establishments. The refusal
followed a letter to the board from the Assistant Chief Constable of Sussex concerning
Rogers. In some unexplained way, Rogers obtained a copy of the letter, and laid an
information against the Assistant Chief Constable, alleging criminal libel. The proceedings resulted from the issue by Rogers of witness summonses against the Chief Constable
of Sussex and the secretary of the board, to attend at the magistrates' court and produce
documents, including copies of the letter. The House of Lords held that the witness
summonses should be set aside. Lord Reid said (50):

> I do not think that 'the public service' should be construed narrowly. Here the question
> is whether the withholding of this class of documents is really necessary to enable the
> board adequately to perform its statutory duties. If it is, then we are enabling the will
> of Parliament to be carried out.
>   There are very unusual features about this case. The board require the fullest
> information they can get in order to identify and exclude persons of dubious character
> and reputation from the privilege of obtaining a licence to conduct a gaming establish-
> ment. There is no obligation on anyone to give any information to the board. No
> doubt many law-abiding citizens would tell what they know even if there was some risk

---

47   (HL) [1974] AC 405.
48   Ibid at 434. The remarks contained in the last sentence cited from the speech of Lord Cross on the 'burden
of proof' point, should be read in conjunction with those of Lord Reid in *Conway* v *Rimmer* [1968] AC 910 at 952;
see 11.2, ante.
49   [1973] AC 388.   50   Ibid at 401.

of their identity becoming known, although many perfectly honourable people do not want to be thought to be mixed up in such affairs. But it is obvious that the best source of information about dubious characters must often be persons of dubious character themselves. It has long been recognised that the identity of police informers must in the public interest be kept secret and the same considerations must apply to those who volunteer information to the board. Indeed, it is in evidence that many refuse to speak unless assured of absolute secrecy.

It is to be noticed that *Rogers's* case was a not inconsiderable extension of the rule as expounded in *Marks* v *Beyfus*, because not only did it involve applying the rule to administrative rather than judicial proceedings but it extended the rule to cover information which need not involve criminal or dishonest conduct at all, but could be general observations on character or reputation, based perhaps in part on opinion. It seems, therefore, that the doctrine may have been extended to cover information given secretly for the benefit of the suppression of undesirable behaviour generally, or the promotion of any necessary vigilance over the conduct of public affairs, if those objects are at least partly dependent on the free flow of information.

This impression is supported by the (obiter) remarks of Lord Widgery CJ on the subject of evidence and correspondence given and supplied to inspectors who carried out a statutory investigation into the affairs of a company (51). It is convincingly confirmed by the decision of the House of Lords in *D* v *NSPCC* (52) the facts of which were examined in 11.3 ante. The House was perfectly prepared to draw an analogy between information supplied to the police, and that supplied to the society for the purpose of enabling it to carry out its duties and to take decisions whether to exercise its powers to institute care proceedings. Lord Simon of Glaisdale said (53):

> I have already cited long-standing and approved authority to the effect that sources of police information are not subject to forensic investigation. This is because liability to general disclosure would cause those sources of information to dry up, so that police protection of the community would be impaired. Exactly the same argument applies in the instant case if for 'police' you read 'NSPCC' and for 'community' you read 'that part of the community which consists of children who may be in peril'. There can be no material distinction between police and/or local authorities on the one hand and the appellants on the other as regards protection of children. It follows that, on the strictest analogical approach and as a matter of legal rule, the appellants are bound to refuse to disclose their sources of information.

Lord Diplock, having observed engagingly, that (54):

> My Lords, in [*Rogers* v *Home Secretary; Gaming Board for Great Britain* v *Rogers*] this House did not hesitate to extend to persons from whom the Gaming Board received information for the purposes of the exercise of their statutory functions under the Gaming Act 1968 immunity from disclosure of their identity analogous to that which the law had previously accorded to police informers. Your Lordships' sense of values might well be open to reproach if this House were to treat the confidentiality of information given to those who are authorised by statute to institute proceedings for

51 *R* v *Cheltenham Justices, ex parte Secretary of State for Trade* (DC) [1977] 1 WLR 95 at 100.
52 [1978] AC 171.   53 Ibid at 241.   54 Ibid at 218–19.

the protection of neglected or ill-treated children as entitled to less favourable treatment in a court of law than information given to the Gaming Board . . .

saw the same analogy as Lord Simon:

> The anonymity of those who tell the police of their suspicions of neglect or ill-treatment of a child would be preserved without any extension of the existing law. To draw a distinction in this respect between information given to the police and that passed on directly to a local authority or to the NSPCC would seem much too irrational a consequence to have been within the contemplation of Parliament when enacting the Children and Young Persons Act 1969.

It is true that the neglect and ill-treatment of children may well amount to a criminal offence, but the information passed to the society is not given primarily for this purpose, but in order to enable suitable steps to be taken on behalf of any children found to be neglected or ill-treated. It would appear that the way is now open for further extensions of the informant rule in suitable cases, along the lines which have been suggested.

11.5 Confidentiality

If A supplies to B documents or information under some promise, express or implied, of confidentiality, the question whether B may subsequently be compelled to disclose or produce such documents or information has given rise to considerable debate. Attempts to avoid such a result may be, and have been, asserted in two guises. First, it may be said that confidential information is in itself a separate ground of private privilege, which attaches to documents and information in certain circumstances and is subject to the usual rules of private privilege. As to this, it now seems to be established that, except (a) in cases to which legal professional privilege applies, and (b) in cases where confidential information is imparted in the course of bona fide 'without-prejudice' negotiations (in which cases the material is privileged irrespective of any question of confidentiality as such), no privilege arises in respect of material imparted in confidence (55).

Secondly, it may be said that imparting confidential information may involve questions of public policy, and may enable an objection to be taken upon that basis. This argument has met with rather more success. It is true that it cannot be in every case that the mere fact of confidentiality will outweigh the public interest in disclosure for the purposes of litigation, but in certain cases it may as part of the overall picture have that effect. In *Alfred Crompton Amusement Machines Ltd* v *Commissioners of Customs & Excise (No. 2)* (56) the House of Lords considered, and rejected, the argument for the commissioners that the fact of receipt of information from customers of the company relating to the company's liability for purchase tax, in circumstances obviously intended to be confidential, of itself entitled the commissioners (and indeed bound them) to withhold that information on the ground of public policy. But Lord Cross of Chelsea said (57):

> 'Confidentiality' is not a separate head of privilege, but it may be a very material

---

55 *Chantrey Martin & Co.* v *Martin* (CA) [1953] 2 QB 286. The separate privilege point was briefly revived by Lord Denning MR in the Court of Appeal in the *Alfred Crompton* case, [1972] 2 QB 102 at 134, once again tapping the stream of Equity. But it was laid to rest in the House of Lords in the same case: see [1974] AC 405 at 429, per Lord Cross of Chelsea.
56 [1974] AC 405.   57 Ibid at 433–4.

consideration to bear in mind when privilege is claimed on the ground of public interest. What the court has to do is to weigh on the one hand the considerations which suggest that it is in the public interest that the documents in question should be disclosed and on the other hand those which suggest that it is in the public interest that they should not be disclosed and to balance one against the other.

This approach has been approved and followed in subsequent decisions (58). Although the circumstances in which confidential information is imparted vary considerably from case to case, it is no doubt true, as Browne LJ observed in *Science Research Council* v *Nassé* (59) that 'the courts should and will do all they can to uphold the moral and social duty not to break confidences'. But unless there is some compelling public interest in the confidence, it will not prevail over the public interest in disclosure. A misleading impression is sometimes given by references in the context of confidentiality to such cases as *Rogers, Alfred Crompton* and *D* v *NSPCC*. Although it is true that the information given in those cases was given in confidence, and though the phrase was canvassed, the real ground of decision in each was that the information was necessary for the efficient running of some part of the public service, be it the collection of tax, the management of gaming establishments or the protection of neglected children, and that disclosure would be likely to result, not only in a breach of confidence, but in information not being given in future. Balancing the public interests, as Lord Cross of Chelsea proposed, led accordingly to a decision against disclosure, but to see such a decision as giving effect to confidentiality *per se* would be to miss the point.

The most searching testing ground for the element of confidentiality may, therefore, prove to be cases concerned with official reports, memoranda, correspondence and the like which are called into question in subsequent proceedings. These are documents for which qualified privilege might, perhaps, be claimed in proceedings for defamation, written under a duty, but quite distinct from the informant or quasi-informant cases. Such were the police reports in *Conway* v *Rimmer* (see 11.2). The argument that protection was necessary in such cases, in order to ensure candour in what was written, was dealt a blow from which it has never recovered, and confidential or not, if the documents are routine and there is no compelling reason to withhold them, they must be disclosed. There are instances where the subject-matter of the reports or other documents fully justify a decision to withhold, for example those dealing, within a local-authority department, with the welfare of children (60). But the decision will not always be straightforward and will always depend on the facts. In *Burmah Oil Co. Ltd* v *Bank of England* despite the clear view of the Court of Appeal that the category C documents should be withheld, Lord Edmund Davies was prepared to entertain the contrary view (61).

The law relating to confidential reports was much discussed in the Court of Appeal and the House of Lords in *Science Research Council* v *Nassé; Leyland Cars (BL Cars Ltd)* v *Vyas* (62). These two appeals, which were heard together, concerned employees who alleged that refusal of promotion by their employers was motivated by unlawful discrimination. They wanted discovery of confidential reports by their employers con-

58 See, e.g., *D* v *NSPCC* [1978] AC 171; *Science Research Council* v *Nassé* (HL) [1979] 3 WLR 762. The view was not entirely new: see, e.g., *Wheeler* v *Le Marchant* (CA) (1881) 17 Ch D 675, per Sir George Jessel MR at 681.
59 (CA) [1979] QB 144 at 179, affirmed by the House of Lords [1979] 3 WLR 762.
60 *Re D* (CA) [1970] 1 WLR 599; see 11.3, ante.
61 See note 35 and 11.3, ante. The dictum was plainly obiter, the company having abandoned its claim for discovery of the category C documents for the purposes of the appeal to the House of Lords.
62 (CA) [1979] QB 144; affirmed (HL) [1979] 3 WLR 762.

cerning both themselves and the other employees who were considered for promotion at the same time.

The employers in each case did not object to disclosure of the reports relating to the applicants, but did object to discovery of those dealing with the rivals. Both the Court of Appeal and the House of Lords accepted Lord Cross of Chelsea's treatment of confidentiality as the correct one. It was argued for the applicants that the reports were necessary for disposing fairly of the case, and that once it was shown that they were relevant, no element of confidentiality could protect them from disclosure. The argument was rejected, and although much of the decision turned on the particular practice of discovery in industrial tribunals, both the Court of Appeal and the House of Lords were prepared to view the case in a wider context. The Court of Appeal, balancing the arguments for and against disclosure, came down against it on the facts of the cases before them. Lord Denning MR thought that the applications for discovery went 'beyond what is necessary'. Lawton LJ, differing in terms of emphasis, said:

> In my judgment, when balancing the interest of the applicant against the desirability of preserving confidentiality, the judge or chairman must remember that Parliament has created new causes of action which it has enacted are to be tried like actions in tort. If among the defendants' documents there are some (albeit confidential ones) which will help the applicant to prove his case, he is entitled to see them.

But he also pointed out the interest of the public generally in, 'the maintenance of efficient and fair procedures for taking on and promoting employees, allotting places in universities and for the granting of housing accommodation and services', and added: 'I am satisfied that general orders for discovery such as are commonly made in the High Court are not necessary' (63).

In the House of Lords, it was said, while upholding the actual decision of the Court of Appeal, that the tribunal should inspect the documents in order to determine whether discovery was necessary for disposing fairly of the case. While reiterating that confidentiality itself would be insufficient to create public-interest immunity, the House also rejected the notion that confidentiality should be ignored once the relevance of the documents was established. The true position was clearly stated by Lord Edmund Davies, who may have had in mind the observation of Browne LJ in the Court of Appeal on the duty of the courts to uphold the 'moral and social duty not to break confidences' (64):

> Learned counsel for the appellants went so far as to submit that the confidential nature of the documents here in question is totally irrelevant to the matter of discovery, and that the tribunal or court should therefore wholly ignore the protests of third parties against the disclosure of information furnished by them in the belief that neither it nor its sources would ever be revealed. .... But for myself I am wholly unable to spell out from the absence of [statutory provision] the conclusion that confidentiality is an irrelevance. It is true that it cannot of *itself* ensure protection from disclosure [his Lordship referred to the *Crompton* case and *D* v *NSPCC*], but confidentiality may nevertheless properly play a potent part in the way in which a tribunal or court exercises its discretion in the matter of discovery.

There was ample evidence supporting the view expressed by the Court of Appeal

63   [1979] QB 144 at 177.
64   [1979] 3 WLR 762 at 777.

that the disclosure to inspection of confidential reports could well create upsets and unrest which would have a general deleterious effect. And a court, mindful of that risk, may understandably – and properly – think it right to scrutinise with particular care a request for their inspection. That is not to say, however, that the fear of possible unrest should deter the court from ordering discovery where the demands of justice clearly require it, but it serves to counsel caution in such cases.

It may well be necessary to apply these principles in future to a large and varied number of problems in many fields. It is submitted that any balancing of the issues must in future comprehend firstly, the nature of the documents themselves and their relevance to the proceedings, secondly, the nature of the confidence given in the particular case and the probable effects on the future supply of information of disclosure, and thirdly, in the light of those considerations, what the overall requirements of the interests of justice are.

The willingness of the courts to give effect to confidentiality, so far as they properly can in the overall exercise of their judgment, has been demonstrated by decisions in other areas in which confidentiality has played an important part. An important area comprises relationships which, although essentially confidential, enjoy no private privilege such as that attaching to the relationship of lawyer and client. Such relationships are those of doctor and patient, priest and penitent, probation officer or social worker and client, journalist and informant. Such confidential information as changes hands in the proper working of these relationships is often imparted orally, rather than in documents, but this operates only to shift the battleground from discovery to examination in the witness box. The courts recognise the public interest in the free exercise of confidential relationships, and will not lightly compel answers which may result in the damaging of an individual relationship, or of the standing of a professional man or his profession generally. In *Attorney-General v Mulholland* (65) Donovan LJ said:

While the journalist has no privilege entitling him as of right to refuse to disclose the source, so I think the interrogator has no absolute right to require such disclosure. In the first place the question has to be relevant to be admissible at all: in the second place it ought to be one the answer to which will serve a useful purpose in relation to the proceedings in hand – I prefer that expression to the term 'necessary'. Both these matters are for the consideration and, if need be, the decision of the judge. And over and above these two requirements, there may be other considerations, impossible to define in advance, but arising out of the infinite variety of fact and circumstance which a court encounters, which may lead a judge to conclude that more harm than good would result from compelling a disclosure or punishing a refusal to answer.

These words are all the more striking for having been delivered in the course of a case in which Donovan LJ, like the other members of the Court of Appeal, found unhesitatingly that two journalists had been guilty of a grave contempt in refusing to answer questions properly put to them at a public inquiry dealing with matters of high national security. In another case arising from the same inquiry, *Attorney-General v Clough* (66) Lord Parker CJ said that: ' ... it still ... would remain open to this court to say in the

65 (CA) [1963] 2 QB 477 at 492.
66 [1963] 1 QB 773 at 792.

special circumstances of any particular case that public policy did demand that the
journalist should be immune.'

The effect of these views was summarised by Lord Denning MR in *Mulholland* in the
following terms (67):

> Take the clergyman, the banker or the medical man. None of these is entitled to refuse
> to answer when directed by a judge. Let me not be mistaken. The judge will respect
> the confidences which each member of these honourable professions receives in the
> course of it, and will not direct him to answer unless not only it is relevant but also it is a
> proper and, indeed, necessary question in the course of justice to be put and answered.
> A judge is the person entrusted, on behalf of the community, to weigh these conflict-
> ing interests.

So, in cases of this kind also, there must be a balancing process, a weighing of the
competing interests, and the interest of the public in confidences of the kind before the
court, is an important matter to be put into the balance. It may be that, for example,
journalistic confidences will appear much stronger, when concerned with investigative
journalism which exposes wrongdoing or highlights matters of public concern, but even
in such a case, any wrongdoing or irresponsibility on the part of the journalist, is likely to
tell in the balance the other way (68).

The important cases on this subject have concerned journalists but there is no reason
to suppose that the position of other persons whose calling involves the receipt of
confidential information differs, and indeed the passage cited from the judgment of
Lord Denning MR in *Mulholland* seems to confirm this.

11.6   Judicial disclosures

It is contrary to public policy that a judge should be compelled to give evidence or to
make any disclosure of a matter affecting the substance of any proceeding in which he
has been engaged judicially. It appears that the rule applies strictly only to superior
judges (69), that is to say judges of the Crown Court when hearing cases charged on
indictment, puisne judges and above, although any judicial officer, even when willing,
should be called only as a last resort (70). The rule does not apply to matters collateral to
the proceedings, for example the events surrounding the escape of a prisoner from court
(71).

Arbitrators are in a somewhat different position, in that it is only their judicial
reasoning to which the rule applies. Hence, it seems that an arbitrator may be
examined in evidence on the facts and history of a case, with a view to showing that he
has made an error of fact, but not on the details or grounds of his award which are
matters within his judicial consideration (72). This distinction seems to make it possible
to compel an arbitrator to prove that he made an error of fact, went outside his terms of
reference or even was guilty of some misconduct.

---

67   [1963] 2 QB 477 at 489. See also *Senior v Holdsworth, ex parte Independent Television News Ltd* (CA)
[1976] QB 23.
68   *British Steel Corporation v Granada Television Ltd* (CA) *The Times* 8 May 1980; affirmed (HL) *The Times*
31 July 1980.
69   *R v Harvey* (1858) 8 Cox CC 99.
70   Such evidence is competent, and may be received unsworn. As to the practice, see 12.13, post.
71   *R v Thanet (Earl) and Others* (1799) 27 St Tr 821.
72   *Re Whiteley and Roberts' Arbitration* [1891] 1 Ch 558. See also *Bourgeois v Weddell & Co.* (DC) [1924] 1
KB 539.

Jurors present a particular problem. So far as their conduct in court is concerned, any irregularity can be dealt with by the trial judge, even if it involves the revelation of some difference of opinion among the members of the jury. Thus in *Ellis* v *Deheer* (73) evidence was received from members of the jury who had been unable to get into court to hear the verdict, and later said that the verdict delivered was not that of the whole jury. But such cases are not unlike those where members of the jury are improperly approached or become separated after retirement. These cases are within the province of the trial judge, as being irregularities in the conduct of the case, and the verdict can be reviewed on appeal, without reference to judicial disclosures as such.

The rule about judicial disclosures applies also to the deliberations of the jury during their retirement. The appellate courts have consistently refused to entertain, let alone compel, the evidence of individual jurors for the purpose of impeaching the verdict. The reason is that the verdict, stated without dissent in open court to be that of the whole jury or of an acceptable majority, cannot as a matter of public policy thereafter be challenged on an individual basis; the time for challenge has passed on its delivery with apparent assent, and to allow jurors to squabble subsequently over it would produce many difficulties.

However, the rule has produced some alarming cases. In *R* v *Roads* (74) evidence from a juror was rejected, in which the juror stated that she did not agree with the verdict of guilty delivered in court, but had been too frightened to say so. In *Jackson* v *Williamson* (75) the evidence of the entire jury to the effect that they had made a mistake about the amount of damages was similarly rejected, as was that of two jurors in *R* v *Thomas* (76) who, after a criminal trial held in Wales, tendered affidavits stating that they were able only to understand Welsh, and had been unable to follow the evidence at the trial, which had been given in English (77).

B: PRIVATE EVIDENTIAL PRIVILEGES

11.7 Self-incrimination

11.7.1 Judicial confessions: the need for privilege
In order to appreciate the need for a privilege against self-incrimination, it is important to understand that a person who, in the course of giving evidence in judicial or quasi-judicial proceedings, gives an answer which may be construed as an admission of some offence or wrongdoing, is liable to have that answer used as evidence against him in subsequent proceedings in respect of the offence or wrongdoing. An answer which may be used in this way is sometimes described as a 'judicial confession'.

The simplest and most obvious form of judicial confession is when a defendant admits he is guilty of the offence for which he is being tried. This form is irrelevant to the subject of privilege, because no privilege exists which protects a party from questions directed to show that he is guilty of the offence or wrongdoing with which he is charged in the instant proceedings. If this were not so, no party could usefully be cross-examined by an opponent, and the need for freedom to establish one's case by cross-examination of the

---

73   (CA) [1922] 2 KB 113.
74   (CA) [1967] 2 QB 108. See also *Nesbitt* v *Parrett* (CA) (1902) 18 TLR 510 (juror unable to speak in protest in court because of shock at amount of damages awarded, with which he disagreed).
75   (1788) 2 TR 281. *Sed quaere.*   76   (CCA) [1933] 2 KB 489.
77   As to voluntary disclosure by jurors for other purposes, see *Attorney-General* v *New Statesman & Nation Publishing Co. Ltd* (DC) [1980] 2 WLR 246.

opponent has been recognised and enforced for as long as parties have been competent witnesses. Despite the heavy armour otherwise afforded to the defendant in a criminal case, s. 1(e) and (f)(i) of the Criminal Evidence Act 1898 specifically permits the Crown to take this course, and the defendant may be asked any question notwithstanding that it may incriminate him in the offence for which he is being tried.

Consequently, the defendant may admit his guilt in various ways. The most obvious and most cogent is by means of a free and voluntary plea of guilty in the face of the court. Where such a plea is tendered, further proof of guilt is unnecessary, and the court may proceed to sentence. He may freely admit his guilt while giving evidence at the trial. But he may also have admitted against him a confession or adverse admission made at an earlier stage of the proceedings, for example when the defendant is asked at committal proceedings whether he wishes to say anything in answer to the charge. In such a case, it is specifically provided by statute that his statement is to be admissible in evidence at the trial (78). Where the defendant pleads guilty at a summary trial of an offence triable either way, and later with the leave of the court withdraws his plea and elects trial at the Crown Court, the status of the withdrawn plea causes some difficulty. The judge may at the trial permit the plea to be proved by the prosecution as a judicial confession, and exclude it if it appears to lack that quality, for example because it was entered by the defendant while unrepresented and under a mistake of law, or because of some pressure exerted on him to plead guilty (79).

What is more material for present purposes is putting to a witness any question, the truthful answer to which will or may incriminate him in respect of some offence with which he is *not* then charged. The answer itself may lead to his being charged, or, if the charge is already contemplated, may provide evidence against him to support it. In this case, too, the rule is that an answer given on oath will be admissible in the subsequent proceedings as a judicial confession. Thus in *R* v *Chapman* (80), when the defendant was before examining justices charged with unlawful carnal knowledge of a girl aged between thirteen and sixteen, he admitted that he had had carnal knowledge of the girl while she was under thirteen, and that admission was received on a subsequent indictment for that offence. The precise nature of the proceedings is immaterial, provided that they are of a judicial or quasi-judicial kind, at which evidence is lawfully taken under oath. Thus, in addition to any civil or criminal proceedings, answers given at a coroner's inquest (81) or at a military tribunal of inquiry (82) will, equally, be admissible subsequently.

However, where evidence is being given at an inquiry or before a tribunal which is the creature of statute and therefore exercises purely statutory powers to receive evidence, the admissibility of answers given will depend principally upon the wording or apparent intention of the statute. Many such provisions deal with the question expressly (83) but where they do not, the general rule seems to be that answers will be admissible in subsequent proceedings, unless the witness was by the statute under compulsion to answer even incriminating questions. However, even where a statute provides for

78   See Criminal Justice Act 1925, s. 12, as amended; Magistrates' Courts Rules 1968, r. 4. The rule on judicial confessions does not apply to answers given at trial on the voire dire: *Wong Kam-Ming* v *R* (PC, Hong Kong) [1980] AC 247.
79   *R* v *Rimmer* (CA) [1972] 1 WLR 268.
80   (1912) 29 TLR 117.
81   The importance of evidence given at inquests has diminished with the powers of the court, which is no longer able to take depositions or to return verdicts implicating named persons in an offence. See Criminal Law Act 1977, s. 56.
82   *R* v *Colpus and Boorman; R* v *White* (CCA) [1917] 1 KB 574.
83   See, e.g., Bankruptcy Act 1914, s. 15, s. 166; Companies Act 1948, s. 167(4), s. 270(7); Companies Act 1967, s. 50. For statutory restrictions on the use of evidence given in certain ordinary proceedings see Theft Act 1968, s. 31; Criminal Damage Act 1971, s. 9. See also Civil Evidence Act 1968, s. 14(4), and 11.7.4, post.

admissibility in subsequent proceedings, answers will be excluded if the questions put fall outside the scope of the statute and thus outside the power of the questioner (84).

For various historical reasons, including, according to many writers, the dark memory of the compulsory examinations of the Star Chamber, the law has always leaned in favour of the rule that no one should be compelled to incriminate himself in an offence with which he is not charged, or to provide evidence against himself (85). Hence, except in the cases where statute otherwise provides expressly, every witness is entitled to the privilege against self-incrimination.

11.7.2 Scope of the privilege
No witness is bound to answer any question if the answer thereto would, in the opinion of the judge, have a tendency to expose the witness to any criminal charge, penalty or, in a criminal case, forfeiture which the judge regards as reasonably likely to be preferred or sued for.

In practice, it is the exposure to possible criminal charges which is of importance. The rare and unimportant cases of liability to penalties and forfeitures seem to have had their origin in what are now remote and old rules of practice that equity would not, by discovery or interrogatories, aid either common informers or proceedings for forfeiture. The courts now have wide powers to give relief from forfeiture, and that part of the privilege has been abolished except in relation to criminal proceedings by s. 16(1)(*a*) of the Civil Evidence Act 1968.

There is no privilege with regard to questions the answer to which would tend to expose the witness to the risk of civil proceedings, even at the suit of the Crown (86) except in the rare instance of proceedings for a penalty. It was at one time thought that the common-law privilege included the right to refuse to answer a question tending to show that the witness had committed adultery. The view was never supported by any basis more substantial than that the ecclesiastical courts had some power, purely notional in modern history, to impose forfeiture on lay offenders, and although it was asserted as recently as 1891 by Bowen LJ in *Redfern* v *Redfern* (87), it was demolished beyond recall as 'fanciful' by a more secularly inclined Court of Appeal in *Blunt* v *Park Lane Hotel Ltd and Briscoe* (88). There was, indeed, a statutory privilege to the like effect, by virtue of s. 3 of the Evidence Further Amendment Act 1869 but it applied only to 'proceedings instituted in consequence of adultery' and was abolished for all purposes by s. 16(5) of the Civil Evidence Act 1968 (89).

Where the rule does apply, it permits the witness to refuse to answer, not only questions which may be incriminating directly, but also questions the answers to which are clearly capable of use in providing evidence against him. Thus, in *R* v *Slaney* (90) a witness in a prosecution for criminal libel, by advertisement in newspapers, stated in evidence that he knew who had written to a newspaper with an advertisement. He was permitted to refuse to answer a further question about the identity of this person, on the ground that the information could have enabled evidence of his own possible complicity to be obtained. And in *Rank Film Distributors Ltd and Others* v *Video Information*

---

84 *Commissioners of Customs & Excise* v *Harz and Another* (HL) [1967] 1 AC 760; *Karak Rubber Co. Ltd* v *Burden and Others* [1971] 1 WLR 1748.
85 The use of the breathalyser seems to be a notable modern exception.
86 Witnesses Act 1806.
87 (CA) [1891] P 139.
88 (CA) [1942] 2 KB 253.
89 So a witness may be asked or interrogated directly about his commission of adultery: *Nast* v *Nast and Walker* (CA) [1972] Fam 142.
90 (NP) (1832) 5 C & P 213.

Centre and Others (91) it was held that defendants, against whom an Anton Piller order (92) was made, could not be obliged by the order to disclose to the plaintiffs' solicitors information which would enable evidence to be obtained against them in connection with a possible prosecution under s. 21 of the Copyright Act 1956.

But there is a judicial function of some importance of deciding whether the privilege should be allowed, or whether a witness must be compelled to answer an incriminating question. The judge must satisfy himself of two matters. First, by taking evidence in the absence of the jury and, if necessary, in camera, that the answer to the question would tend to expose the witness to a criminal charge. This is a process of legal inquiry, in the sense that the judge must look at the elements of the apprehended charge, and see whether the witness's fears are justified as a matter of law. Second, that the institution of the proceedings is not just 'a remote or insubstantial risk' but that there is a 'real and appreciable' danger to the witness, having regard to the ordinary operation of the law (93).

This second requirement is sometimes far from easy. There are obvious cases where there would be clear evidence of a serious offence which in the ordinary way could not be overlooked. There are equally clear cases where no danger is involved, as in *Blunt* v *Park Lane Hotel Ltd and Briscoe* (94) where the Court of Appeal saw not the remotest prospect of a witness being exposed, in 1942, to an ecclesiastical forfeiture in respect of her adultery, and *R* v *Boyes* (95) where although the defendant's possession of a royal pardon under the Great Seal would have been no answer to a prosecution by impeachment, it was unthinkable that such proceedings would be instituted against him. It was said in this last case that, once it appears that a witness is at risk, 'great latitude should be allowed to him in judging for himself of the effect of any particular question.' But this does not deprive the judge of the duty to rule on the privilege, and he must do so on the basis of what appear to be the practical realities of the situation.

It may be right to disallow the claim to privilege where the witness has already jeopardised himself by making a similar statement to the police, and is already in peril (96). The judge can also take into account the apparent rarity of certain prosecutions, the trivial nature of the offence or the lapse of time since its commission, in assessing the likelihood of proceedings. But these matters must be weighed with great care (97). The rarity of prosecutions seems to have influenced the argument in such cases as *Rio Tinto Zinc Corporation and Others* v *Westinghouse Electric Corporation* (98), where it was contended that because the European Commission had failed to impose fines (under art. 85 of the EEC Treaty) in respect of a cartel, of which it had knowledge, companies thought to be implicated in establishing or operating the cartel could be required to produce documents which might have the effect of incriminating them. Both the Court of Appeal and the House of Lords held that the argument was fallacious. Although there might be cases where such an inference could safely be drawn, in the present circumstances it was likely that production would increase the prospect of proceedings, by offering evidence upon which the Commission might be disposed, at last, to act. It would

91   (CA) [1980] 2 All ER 273.
92   An order obtained in ex parte proceedings to permit premises to be searched to find articles infringing copyright. See *Anton Piller KG* v *Manufacturing Processes Ltd and Others* (CA) [1976] Ch 55.
93   *Rio Tinto Zinc Corporation and Others* v *Westinghouse Electric Corporation; et e contra* [1978] AC 547 per Lord Denning MR at 574.
94   [1942] 2 KB 253.
95   (1861) 1 B & S 311. The passage quoted appears at 330.
96   *Brebner* v *Perry* [1961] SASR 177.
97   *Triplex Safety Glass Co. Ltd* v *Lancegaye Safety Glass (1934) Ltd* (CA) [1939] 2 KB 395.
98   [1978] AC 547.

seem, therefore, that the judge should take into account an increase in the danger to the witness, which would result from making available evidence whose previous absence may have inhibited the institution of proceedings. Some limited forbearance on the part of an authority empowered to commence proceedings cannot necessarily be equated with inaction or unconcern.

Where a witness is wrongly compelled to answer a question in breach of the privilege against self-incrimination, his answer will be inadmissible in subsequent proceedings against him (99). Herein lies, of course, the significance of the privilege in relation to judicial confessions.

11.7.3 Foreign law

Curiously, it was never decided at common law to what extent, if at all, the privilege may be claimed in response to a question which might have the effect of exposing the witness to some charge or penalty under the law of another country. There were dicta against the application of the privilege, unless the provisions of the relevant foreign law (a question of fact) were admitted on the pleadings, which suggests that it was felt inappropriate for the judge to attempt to assess the likelihood of proceedings being commenced in another jurisdiction (100). There is clearly much force in this, as the judge must otherwise try to weigh, not only the substantive law but also the practice of the foreign court or prosecuting authority in order to assess whether the risk is real and appreciable.

In civil cases, a compromise formula has been laid down, and it is almost certain that the common law would follow the same approach, were the matter to arise in a criminal case. By s. 14(1) of the Civil Evidence Act 1968:

> The right of a person in any legal proceedings other than criminal proceedings to refuse to answer any question or produce any document or thing if to do so would tend to expose that person to proceedings for an offence or for the recovery of a penalty —

> (a) shall apply only as regards criminal offences under the law of any part of the United Kingdom and penalties provided for by such law.

It should be noted that, by virtue of the European Communities Act 1972 the law of the EEC is a part of the law of England. Accordingly, in the *Westinghouse* case, it was not disputed in the House of Lords that fines which the European Commission could impose under art. 85, and which were recoverable by proceedings under English law, were, 'a penalty provided for by such law', within the meaning of the subsection.

While the subsection does extend the privilege to charges and penalties which may arise under law which is technically foreign, for instance the law of Scotland, it limits the sphere of operation territorially to that which an English judge is plainly competent to assess.

11.7.4 Incrimination of spouses

It was also never really clear at common law whether the privilege extended to refusal to answer questions which would tend to expose the spouse of the witness to some charge or penalty. There were dicta to the effect that it did extend thus far, but no further (101).

---

99   *R* v *Garbett* (ExCh) (1847) 1 Den CC 236.
100 *USA* v *McRae* (LC) (1868) LR 3 Ch App 79.
101 *R* v *All Saints, Worcester (Inhabitants)* (1817) 6 M & S 194 per Bayley J at 201.

Again, statute has intervened in civil cases, and it must be assumed that the common law would now reach the same result in a criminal case: s. 14(1) of the Civil Evidence Act 1968 provides:

> The right of a person in any legal proceedings other than criminal proceedings to refuse to answer any question or produce any document or thing if to do so would tend to expose that person to proceedings for an offence or for the recovery of a penalty —
> ...
> (b) shall include a like right to refuse to answer any question or produce any document or thing if to do so would tend to expose the husband or wife of that person to proceedings for any such criminal offence or for the recovery of any such penalty.

The intention of the Act is that the privilege of the witness and that of the witness's spouse shall be coextensive. That is the effect of the word 'like', and is reinforced by the provisions of the remainder of the section. S. 14(2) applies the same immunity to statutory rights not to give self-incriminating answers in proceedings under statutory powers of inspection and investigation. S. 14(3) provides that where, by statute, a witness is compellable to answer even incriminating questions, such compulsion applies to answers which would incriminate the spouse as well as those which would incriminate the witness himself. And s. 14(4) provides that any statutory provision that answers given by a witness shall not be admissible against him in any given proceedings, shall be construed as providing also that such answers shall not be admissible in such proceedings against the spouse of the witness.

These provisions should be read together with those of s. 18(2) that references to the husband or wife of a person in the Act or in any amendment made by the Act do not include references to a person who is no longer married to that person.

11.8 Legal professional privilege

The relationship of lawyer and client, and the preparation of materials for litigation enjoy at common law a special position in their entitlement to privilege. The term 'legal professional privilege', which is not entirely satisfactory, is used to comprehend two distinct rules. The first is the rule that communications between lawyer and client, made in the course of seeking and giving advice within the normal scope of legal practice, are privileged in all cases, at the instance of the client. The second is the rule that communications passing between a client or his legal adviser and third parties in contemplation of actual litigation are privileged, provided that use for the purposes of litigation is at least the dominant purpose of the communication; in this case too, the privilege is that of the client. In both cases, it is immaterial whether the communication is with advisers or third parties in England or elsewhere, or whether the contemplated litigation may take place in England or elsewhere (102).

11.8.1 *Lawyer and client*
All communications passing between a legal adviser and his client, in the course of seeking and giving legal advice within the proper scope of the professional work of the legal adviser, are privileged at the instance of the client (not of the adviser). It is

---

102   *Re Duncan, Garfield v Fay* [1968] P 306.

irrelevant in this case whether or not the advice is immediately connected with litigation then in contemplation, though it is probably true to say that all legal advice is concerned with a possible ultimate resort to litigation, even if (as is almost always the case) the advice is directed to avoiding it wherever possible (103). The rule applies to solicitor and counsel alike, and so covers any advice given orally or in writing and any instructions given for the purposes of such advice. The rule applies also to advice sought of and given by salaried legal advisers, and it has been suggested, though not decided, that it may extend to the so-called 'McKenzie friend' who may appear to advise a layman in the presentation of a case, or to argue before a tribunal to which restrictions on rights of audience do not apply (104). As we have seen (11.5, ante) no other confidential relationship is privileged in this way (105).

The communications, if they are to be the subject of privilege, must have been made within the proper scope of the adviser's work, and during the continuance of the lawyer–client relationship, i.e. during the currency of the lawyer's professional retainer on behalf of the client. This will, of course, include any communications necessary to bring the relationship into existence, such as an initial consultation or instructions. But no communication is privileged merely because one party to it is a lawyer, and where no professional relationship comes into being no privilege can arise. In *Minter* v *Priest* (106) where the defendant refused to act as a solicitor in a transaction relating to land, and was alleged to have defamed the plaintiff in the course of giving his reasons for so refusing, it was held that the relationship of solicitor and client had not been established, and that the communication, not being made for the purpose of establishing the relationship, was not privileged. But it seems that where documents are delivered to a solicitor for his consideration and subsequent advice, such delivery may amount to a privileged communication. Indeed, this will surely be so wherever the documents are brought into existence for the purpose of obtaining advice. However, in *Frank Truman Export Ltd and Others* v *Commissioner of Police of the Metropolis* (107) it was held that pre-existing documents, which might have held some evidential value against the owner as evidence of fraud, were privileged in the hands of the plaintiff's solicitor to whom they had been delivered for his consideration and advice in relation to likely criminal charges based on the apparent fraud. If this decision is right, it would mean that by placing incriminating material in the hands of a solicitor at the crucial moment, a person may protect such material from an otherwise likely exposure by search warrant (108). Such a course would certainly not be a proper means of avoiding discovery in a civil case.

On the other hand, in any case where the relationship of lawyer and client clearly does exist, the privilege is not inhibited by the fact that the lawyer is advising professionally a body of persons of which he happens also to be a member, for example a tenants' association, voluntary organisation or board of trustees (109).

By what might perhaps be described as an evidential application of the maxim, '*Nemo dat quod non habet*', it is clear law that a client who could himself maintain no privilege in

---

103   See *Greenhough* v *Gaskell* (LC) (1833) 1 My & K 98.
104   *M. & W. Grazebrook Ltd* v *Wallens* (NIRC) [1973] ICR 256. In the case of a layman in such a position, the privilege may extend only to the conduct of the case itself. This is an increasingly important question, which requires clarification.
105   Though for certain limited purposes, a form of the privilege exists in relation to patent agents: Civil Evidence Act 1968, s. 15.
106   (HL) [1930] AC 558.
107   [1977] QB 952.
108   This result did not follow on the facts of the case, because the plaintiff's solicitor had voluntarily permitted the police to take the documents in question away, and on the issue whether an injunction would be granted against the police, this was conclusive against: cf *Butler* v *Board of Trade* [1971] Ch 680.
109   *O'Rourke* v *Darbishire* (HL) [1920] AC 581.

respect of documents of a given class cannot better his position merely by handing them over to his solicitor. Thus, in *R* v *Peterborough Justices, ex parte Hicks* (110), where the client could not have prevented the seizure by the police of a document, such seizure being properly made by virtue of a warrant under the Forgery Act 1913, his solicitors were in no better position to resist seizure of the document when in their hands, even though the defendant had placed it there in connection with the preparation of his defence.

No privilege will arise where the relationship of lawyer and client is in reality a front for the commission or furtherance of some fraudulent or dishonest act. It may be that the lawyer is an accomplice of the client, but the rule applies equally where the lawyer is made the innocent tool of the fraud. In *R* v *Jones* (111) the client deviously inserted a forged will into a bundle of documents relating to title, which he had delivered to an attorney, in the hope that the attorney would find and act on the forgery. The rule applies to any fraud or dishonesty which the client seeks to further under cover of legal advice, where the advice is intended by the client to assist or guide him in his dishonest designs (112). It extends similarly to tortious acts involving deceit or conspiracy, which are later made the subject of civil actions, but not to other civil wrongs which cannot fairly be said to involve fraud or dishonesty. There must be at least a prima facie appearance of fraud or dishonesty before the judge questions an apparent case of legal professional privilege (113).

If two or more clients jointly retain the professional services of a solicitor then it may be difficult to determine how the privilege should operate in subsequent litigation between the clients. A typical instance is that of the family solicitor who receives confidences from both husband and wife while helping them towards reconciliation or over some family arrangement. In later divorce proceedings, one party may wish to inquire about admissions made by the other to the solicitor. The rule appears to be a simple enough one, namely that matters arising in the course of and within the scope of a joint retainer must be disclosed to any of the joint clients. But if the solicitor acts or advises any one client outside the scope of the joint retainer, the usual privilege will attach. All that can be said within the ambit of the present work is that the task of distinguishing these areas is usually more difficult than that of stating the rule (114).

11.8.2 Communications with third parties
Communications made between a party (or his legal adviser on his behalf)and a third party are privileged at the instance of the party if, but only if, they are made for the specific purpose of pending or contemplated litigation. This part of the rule is apt to cover communications with witnesses and their proofs of evidence, and is particularly important in relation to communications with potential expert witnesses, from whom it may be desired to obtain an opinion, but who are not legal advisers. Nothing in the provisions of RSC, Ord. 38, rr. 36–44, which impose certain obligations of disclosure of expert reports as a condition of calling the expert evidence concerned, affects the operation of the privilege; but a party may have to elect whether to disclose a report and call evidence of its contents, or to stand on the privilege, use the report as an opinion only and not call it in evidence (115).

110   (DC) [1977] 1 WLR 1371. And see the *Frank Truman Export* case, ante.
111   (CCR) (1846) 1 Den CC 166.   112   *R* v *Cox and Railton* (CCR) (1884) 14 QBD 153.
113   *Crescent Farm (Sidcup) Sports Ltd* v *Sterling Offices Ltd and Another* [1972] Ch 553. And see *Williams* v *Quebrada Railway, Land & Copper Co.* [1895] 2 Ch 751; *O'Rourke* v *Darbishire* (HL) [1920] AC 581.
114   See, e.g., *Harris* v *Harris* (DC) [1931] P 10.
115   For the detailed provisions of the rules and their operation, see 9.4, ante.

The requirement that the communication be made for the purposes of pending or contemplated litigation is one which limits very considerably the material which is so privileged, and represents an important distinction between this and the case of communications between client and legal adviser. In *Wheeler* v *Le Marchant* (116) the defendant was obliged to produce reports made to his solicitor by a surveyor, because although the reports related to the subject-matter of the litigation, they had been made at a time when no litigation was contemplated by the defendant.

There is considerable uncertainty about whether the communication must have been made solely for the purposes of pending or contemplated litigation, whether it must have been a major, but need not have been the only purpose, or whether litigation need have been no more than one of a number of possible purposes. The debate which raged on this topic in the older cases, many of which seem very unsatisfactory (117) may at last have been resolved by the House of Lords in *Waugh* v *British Railways Board* (118). The plaintiff's husband, who was employed by the defendants, was killed in a collision between two trains, and she brought an action under the Fatal Accidents Act 1976 in respect of his death. The board denied negligence and alleged contributory negligence on the part of the deceased. The plaintiff sought discovery of an internal report, prepared by the board for submission to the railway inspectorate and the ministry. The report was also a valuable, and probably the best, source of evidence of the causes of the accident, containing as it did the statements of witnesses and a technical account of the collision. But the report was also designed, according to its heading, 'for the information of the board's solicitor: this form is to be used by every person reporting an occurrence when litigation by or against the BRB is anticipated. It is . . . to be sent to the solicitor for the purpose of enabling him to advise the BRB in regard thereto.' The board claimed that it was a privileged document. The House of Lords held that the public interest in the due administration of justice strongly required the disclosure of such a cogent piece of evidence, and that this requirement could be defeated only where preparation for the purposes of litigation was shown to be 'at least the dominant purpose' for which it was prepared. The fact that the report purported on the face of it to have been made for such a purpose, since litigation was clearly foreseeable after such an event, was not conclusive in itself of the dominant purpose of the document, and the court was entitled to look behind the claim made for itself by the document by its own wording. On the facts of the case, the House of Lords held that the report had other major purposes in relation to the safe running of the railways, and that submission to the solicitor was not shown to be the dominant purpose of preparation; the report must accordingly be disclosed.

11.9 Matrimonial communications

The learned judgments of the Court of Appeal in *Shenton* v *Tyler* (119) demonstrate that the common law had no rule that communications passing between spouses during the marriage were the subject of privilege. This may have been because during the formative years of the common-law rules, the spouses of parties were incompetent, although the possibility of privilege could be and indeed must have been of relevance in some cases to which the incompetence did not apply, or where the spouse was not giving evidence *qua*

116   (CA) (1881) 17 ChD 675.
117   See, e.g., *Jones* v *Great Central Railway Co* (HL) [1910] AC 4; *Seabrook* v *British Transport Commission* [1959] 1 WLR 509.
118   [1979] 3 WLR 150.
119   [1939] Ch 620.

spouse. The origin of the privilege which now exists is in fact both modern and statutory. S. 3 of the Evidence Amendment Act 1853 provided that: 'No husband shall be compellable to disclose any communication made to him by his wife during the marriage, and no wife shall be compellable to disclose any communication made to her by her husband during the marriage.

Although to some extent the privilege is bound up historically with the much broader question of the competence of spouses generally, it is and must remain entirely distinct (120). It has, of course, nothing to do with competence as such, but operates only as a restriction on the compellability which would ordinarily accompany competence, and then in relation only to specific matters. Further, the option is that of the spouse to whom the communication is made, so that a competent spouse may presumably give evidence of such communications, and no objection can be taken by the communicating spouse.

The 1853 enactment applied to all cases in which the spouse was competent in the proceedings but has been specifically reaffirmed in subsequent Acts which have extended the areas of the spouse's competence as a witness against or for his or her spouse when charged with a criminal offence. S. 1(d) of the Criminal Evidence Act 1898 (which had a revolutionary effect upon the evidence of spouses in criminal cases) provided expressly that nothing in the Act should render a spouse compellable to disclose communications made by the other spouse during the marriage. In similar vein have followed s. 39 of the Sexual Offences Act 1956 and s. 30 of the Theft Act 1968 which materially widened, in their turn, the areas of competence of spouses in criminal cases. The necessity of these provisions is in no way lessened by the various decisions which have established that the spouse, though competent, is not a compellable witness for the prosecution because the privilege relates, not to evidence generally, but to particular matters which may arise during the course of evidence (121).

Thus stated, the privilege continues to apply to criminal cases. But it has been abolished as anachronistic, 'except in relation to criminal proceedings', by s. 16(3) of the Civil Evidence Act 1968 (122).

The use of the words 'husband' and 'wife' in s. 3 of the 1853 Act has been construed to mean that the restriction on compellability comes to an end with the marriage itself, so that a widowed or divorced former spouse has no privilege against disclosure of communications made during the marriage. In *Shenton* v *Tyler*, therefore, it was held that a widow could be interrogated to elicit evidence of the setting up of a secret trust in the plaintiff's favour by reference to the intentions of the widow's deceased husband expressed during his lifetime. Whatever the merits of this construction, on which opinion varies, it has undoubtedly caused problems in the construction of the same words for the purposes of the question of the competence of spouses; these problems are examined in 12.7, post. But in the light of the general view of the privilege as somewhat anachronistic, it seems unlikely that the decision in *Shenton* v *Tyler* would be departed from in a criminal case, even though, because of *R* v *Algar* (123), a different interpretation may have to be given to s. 1(d) of the Criminal Evidence Act 1898 than to other parts of the Act in which the words 'husband' and 'wife' occur (124). It would seem most desirable to resolve the position by statute.

120   This part of this chapter should be read in conjunction with 12.5 et seq dealing with the competence of spouses.
121   See the authorities cited in 12.6, post.
122   As, by s. 16(4), was a more recent yet more anachronistic privilege relating to evidence of the occurrence or non-occurrence of sexual intercourse during the marriage.
123   (CCA) [1954] 1 QB 279.
124   If the problem could still arise in civil cases, the point would be settled by s. 18(2) of the Civil Evidence

11.10 Without-prejudice negotiations

Because of the obvious public interest in the proper compromise of civil litigation whenever this can be achieved, the law offers a measure of protection to communications designed to arrive at this result. The danger of making or responding to any offer in settlement of litigation is that the gesture may later be construed as some admission of liability. For this reason, communications with an opponent may be made 'without prejudice'. The effect of this is that they may not, at trial, be referred to on the issue of liability or willingness to settle. Without-prejudice negotiations (usually contained in correspondence) will not be ordered to be disclosed on discovery, and will not form part of the bundle of correspondence, referred to by way of contrast as 'open', which is placed before the court in the normal course of events.

The privilege attaching to without-prejudice correspondence covers all bona fide offers of settlement or compromise, whether the litigation is pending or contemplated. The words 'without prejudice' need not actually appear on a letter designed to have the effect described, but the practice of using them by way of heading is both usual and desirable. Conversely, the mere insertion of the words will not assist a letter which is not a bona fide approach within the scope of the rule. Once negotiations have commenced, the rule obviously protects not only offers of settlement, but also responses by way of acceptance or counter-offer.

Although without-prejudice negotiations are usually carried on by correspondence, there is nothing to preclude their conduct by other means, such as oral attempts at settlement by the parties or their advisers. In particular, in matrimonial cases, negotiations may have taken place through the good offices of a mediator or counsellor. Where this occurs, and offers and suggestions are relayed to the parties via a third party, it has been held that the substance of the negotiations are privileged as if they were made in correspondence. Thus, in *McTaggart* v *McTaggart* (125) where an interview between the spouses had been arranged by a probation officer on a 'without-prejudice' basis, either spouse was entitled to object to evidence of what had been said being received at trial. However, the privilege is that of the parties, so that the probation officer is not entitled to object, and where the privilege had been waived by the parties, the judge was bound to admit the evidence. In *Mole* v *Mole* (126) it was held that the principle applies equally where one party only is interviewed by the probation officer with a view to reconciliation, and that where any person acting in the same capacity arranges an interview which is in fact intended to be without prejudice, the same result obtains. However, it must be noted that without-prejudice negotiations can only be conducted where the parties or those acting on their behalf engage in discussions aimed at a settlement. Where, therefore, a case worker spoke to the respondent to affiliation proceedings with a view to possible adoption of the child, and was not acting as the agent of either party, the respondent's admissions to the worker of paternity were not privileged, and were

---

Act 1968, which adopts the rule that the words 'husband' and 'wife' do not include persons who are no longer married to a person. This is to apply to 'this Act and . . . any amendment made by this Act in any other enactment'. Could it be argued that the provisions of s. 16(3) restricting the operation of s. 3 of the 1853 Act to criminal proceedings may be said to be an 'amendment' of that section of the purpose of s. 18(2)? It would solve one or two problems! Cf 12.7, post.

---

125   (CA) [1949] P 94. See the judgment of Cohen LJ at 96.
126   (CA) [1951] P 21. The rule would also apply to communications made between the parties themselves for the same purpose; see *Theodoropoulas* v *Theodoropoulas* [1964] P 311. The suggestion in *Bostock* v *Bostock* [1950] P 154 that the rule does not apply to meetings between the parties and their solicitors can hardly be correct.

admitted on the issue of paternity (127).

Although without-prejudice correspondence is not admissible at trial on the issue of liability or willingness to settle, it may be admissible, the issue of liability having been determined, on other issues, for example on the question of costs where delay or unreasonable refusal to settle may be material (128). And since an agreement to compromise litigation is one made for good consideration and fully enforceable, without-prejudice correspondence is admissible to show that an agreement was reached and what the terms of such agreement were in any subsequent proceedings with reference to it.

11.11   Questions for counsel

1 Of the various papers set out in Chapter 2, which may be the subject of privilege, and for what reasons?
2 If the defence papers in the case of Littleton are by inadvertence sent by his solicitors to the solicitor for the prosecution and are copied by him, what is the position with regard to (a) the originals; (b) the copies; (c) the information contained in those papers?
3 Would the position differ if, instead of being sent, the papers were seized from the offices of Littleton's solicitors by police officers?
4 May counsel for Littleton object to the admission of the tape-recording of the conversation between Littleton and his wife, as being privileged?
5 If Mrs Littleton is called to give evidence for her husband, may she object to answering questions which:
   (a) would tend to incriminate Littleton in the offence of indecently assaulting Angela Blackstone?
   (b) would involve her revealing anything which Littleton may have said to her privately about the alleged offence?
6 If Coke and Littleton give evidence in their defence, may they object to answering questions tending to show that they are guilty of the offences charged in the indictment?

---

127   *R v Nottingham Justices, ex parte Bostock* (DC) [1970] 1 WLR 1117. In the case of industrial conciliators, Parliament has provided for a statutory privilege in the Employment Protection (Consolidation) Act 1978, s. 133(6).
128   Particularly in cases where payment in is not possible: see *Calderbank v Calderbank* (CA) [1976] Fam 93.

Part 4 The Mechanics of Evidence

12 Preliminaries: Competence and Compellability; Oaths and Affirmations

A: COMPETENCE AND COMPELLABILITY

12.1 General rule

Any treatment of the subject of the handling of witnesses must begin by considering whether there are any restrictions on who may be called to give evidence, and whether giving evidence should be regarded as an optional activity, in which the proposed witness may decline to engage, or as an obligation enforceable by the court. These questions are referred to respectively as those of competence and compellability. A witness is said to be competent if, by the existing rules of law, his evidence is receivable by the court in the proceedings concerned. A witness is said to be compellable if he is not only competent, but may lawfully be required by the court, under sanction of penalty as a contemnor, to give his evidence (1).

These questions are, and must remain, quite distinct from that of whether individual pieces of evidence enjoy some privilege in the hands of the witness, a matter considered in the preceding chapter. We are now concerned with the evidence of the witness as a whole, and so with his competence and compellability concerning all the matters material to the case on which he could speak.

The general rule of English law is that all witnesses are both competent and compellable, a rule justified by the need to make available to the court, as far as possible, all relevant and admissible evidence which may assist it in the determination of the issues (2). At common law, this consideration was counterbalanced, and probably more than counterbalanced, by the emergence of an important body of exceptional cases in which various witnesses were held not to be competent, for reasons which will be referred to in the next paragraph. The exceptions have gradually been reduced and simplified by a series of judicial and statutory reforms, but continue to play a significant role in the conduct, particularly, of criminal cases. Unfortunately, the piecemeal nature of the reform, which has occupied nearly two centuries, has left certain areas of ambiguity in a field which has no obvious need for complexity, and it is submitted that a comprehensive statutory statement of the rules would be both fairly simple and highly desirable.

---

1 In appropriate cases, particularly where the witness is a party or has some interest in the outcome of the proceedings, a refusal to give evidence will lead to the drawing by the tribunal of fact of adverse inferences.
2 The rule applies to all witnesses, including experts: *Harmony Shipping Co. SA* v *Saudi Europe Line Ltd and Others* (CA) [1979] 1 WLR 1380.

12.2 Exceptions

It is, happily, unnecessary to consider in detail the scope of the various historical exceptions which grew up at common law, although it is certainly instructive to understand and bear in mind the justifications which the common law advanced for them, some of which continue to underlie the exceptions which survive. It is possible to identify two particular fears which led to the wholesale rejection of the evidence of certain potential witnesses, and it must be said that these fears were so seriously regarded, that very sound reasons for admitting the evidence, based on its obvious cogency and on clear considerations of convenience, were rejected out of hand. There can be no doubt that the fears blinded the law to many cases of grave injustice which resulted from incompetence imposed in these cases.

The first fear may be described broadly as a fear of manufactured or exaggerated evidence resulting from self-interest. This fear led to the rejection of the evidence of the parties to the proceedings and of that of their spouses, though curiously not of other relatives of the parties, and of the evidence of any proposed witness personally interested in the outcome of the proceedings. The second fear may be described broadly as a fear of the evidence of certain persons as such, because of personal characteristics which supposedly rendered of no account any evidence which they might give, in whatever circumstances. Into this category of incompetence fell children of tender years and persons of defective intellect, whose condition in life was thought to dictate incompetence; those convicted of 'infamous crimes' whose conduct was thought to disqualify them as acceptable witnesses; and, most extravagantly of all in modern eyes, non-Christians, whose inability to be properly sworn was held to remove the essential sanction of the oath, without which evidence was not to be received.

The most exaggerated and unnecessary incompetences have long since gone, whittled away and finally removed by statute during the nineteenth century. Thus, although at common law the evidence of atheists and believers other than Christians could not be received, the rule was modified by the middle of the eighteenth century. In *Omychund v Barker* (3) the evidence of non-Christians who held a belief in the 'Governor of the Universe' was held to be receivable. The problem of atheists, who held no belief capable of providing a sanction against untruthfulness caused greater concern, but they were rendered competent by the Evidence Further Amendment Act 1869. The incompetence of those convicted of infamous crimes was modified in 1828 to make the incompetence only coextensive with their period of sentence, and was abolished by the Evidence Act 1843. The same Act abolished incompetence stemming only from interest in the outcome of the proceedings.

The cases which, despite some measure of reform and simplification, still call for detailed attention are: the parties and their spouses (in which the difficulties appear to be confined to defendants in criminal cases and their spouses), and children of tender years. These matters will be fully examined in the paragraphs which follow, after which mention will be made of persons of defective intellect, an incompetence which survives in much modified form, and of one or two minor incompetences of little practical importance.

---

3   (LC) (1745) 1 Atk 21.

12.3   Parties to the proceedings

The abolition of incompetence through interest in 1843 paved the way for abolishing the incompetence of the parties themselves, who are no doubt the most striking example of the species of interested persons. For civil proceedings, the abolition was effected by the Evidence Act 1851, with the exception of proceedings instituted in consequence of adultery and actions for breach of promise of marriage, in which cases the incompetence survived until the Evidence Further Amendment Act 1869. The result of the abolition was that the parties became competent witnesses in every case, and, following the general rule, compellable. This is the position in the present law, and it involves the proposition that a party to civil proceedings may both give evidence himself and, if he thinks it wise, subpoena any other party to give evidence also. The rule as it now stands is one of obvious convenience.

The position in criminal cases was complicated by a variety of historical considerations. The issue was, of course, whether the defendant was to be regarded as a competent witness. Although in one sense, it might be thought desirable that his position should be equated to that of a party to civil proceedings, the consequence of his being thereby rendered compellable gave rise to much heart-searching. Dark references abounded in the nineteenth centry, when the matter received attention, to a reversion to the in-quisitorial practices of Star Chamber and the evil of defendants being compelled to provide evidence against themselves by being forced into the witness-box. There were also technical problems of reconciling the idea of a compellable defendant with the incidence of the burden of proof in criminal cases. In the end, the matter was resolved by compromise, in a series of statutory provisions culminating in the Criminal Evidence Act 1898. The compromise was, in essence, that the defendant was rendered competent only for the defence, and was expressly made non-compellable (4). This unique deviation from the traditional rules rendered necessary a series of supplementary provisions dealing with evidence given by the defendant. The prosecution may not comment upon the failure of the defendant to give evidence in his defence pursuant to the Act (5). If the defendant elects to give evidence, although he may be asked any question tending to criminate him in the offence charged, he may not be cross-examined about his character or about any offences not charged, except in the limited circumstances prescribed by the Act (6). The defendant is, unless otherwise ordered, to give his evidence from the witness-box (7). This provision reflects the fact that if the defendant elects to give evidence, his evidence is evidence in the case for all purposes, even if it has the effect of incriminating him or a co-defendant (8), and he is to be regarded in the same way as any other witness called for the prosecution or the defence. Lastly, the Act specifically preserved the right of the defendant to make an unsworn statement from the dock (9), a practice which had grown up in the nineteenth century to compensate the defendant for his incompetence as a witness. The co-existence of this right with his competence to give evidence has caused a number of problems, which are considered in detail in 12.14, post.

4   Criminal Evidence Act 1898, s. 1 and proviso (*a*). The rule applies to all criminal cases, with the unimportant exception of prosecutions for public nuisance under the Evidence Act 1877 in which the defendant is both competent and compellable.
5   Criminal Evidence Act 1898, s. 1 proviso (*b*). The necessity for this provision has been doubted. Nothing in the Act prevents the judge from commenting on the matter, but he must do so in a balanced way, and in particular must not suggest to the jury that they are entitled to infer guilt from the defendant's failure to give evidence. See *R* v *Rhodes* (CCR) [1899] 1 QB 77; *R* v *Mutch* (CA) [1973] 1 All ER 178; *R* v *Sparrow* (CA) [1973] 1 WLR 488. Stronger comment is permissible in some cases than in others, but great caution must be exercised.
6   Criminal Evidence Act 1898, s. 1 provisos (*e*) and (*f*). See 4.9 et seq, ante.
7   Criminal Evidence Act 1898, s. 1 proviso (*g*).   8   *R* v *Rudd* (CCA) (1948) 32 Cr App R 138.
9   Criminal Evidence Act 1898, s. 1 proviso (*h*).

12.4   A defendant in a criminal case

The position which resulted from the provisions of s. 1 of the Criminal Evidence Act 1898 must now be examined in detail. It will be convenient to look at the defendant as a potential witness (a) for the prosecution; (b) on his own behalf; and (c) for a co-defendant.

12.4.1   For the prosecution

The Act left unaffected the common-law rule of incompetence so far as the prosecution are concerned. The important consequence of this is to prevent the prosecution from calling a defendant to give evidence for the prosecution against a co-defendant. In *R v Grant and Others* (10) indictments were quashed where, in the course of committal proceedings, the prosecution called persons jointly charged, and others charged with offences intended to form part of the same indictment, to give evidence against their co-defendants. It follows, therefore, that if the prosecution think it desirable to call a person in such a position, they must first ensure that he ceases, before giving evidence, to be a defendant. This will be the position if he has already been acquitted of all the matters alleged against him or if he has pleaded guilty to all the matters alleged against him in the indictment. If neither of these has happened before he is required as a witness, then the prosecution must either (a) offer no evidence against him (or enter a *nolle prosequi*) or (b) accept his plea of guilty to a part of the indictment to which it is offered, and agree to formal verdicts of not guilty, or to leave other charges on the file, as may be appropriate. The effect is that the former defendant is no longer a party to any proceedings before the jury, and is therefore both competent and compellable for the prosecution (11).

The practice whereby former defendants give evidence for the prosecution, having pleaded guilty, in the hope of attracting a lenient sentence, is a common one. There is a rule of practice that one who 'turns Queen's evidence' in this way, should be sentenced before giving evidence, so as to avoid the risk and the appearance of his tailoring his evidence for his own ends (12). This is, of course, contrary to the usual practice of sentencing those who have pleaded guilty at the end of the trial, when the judge has a fuller picture of the roles of the various defendants individually. However, it has been made clear recently that the time of sentence is a matter for the discretion of the judge, who may decide that he has insufficient material on which to determine sentence at the outset of the trial (13).

An accomplice, whether or not jointly charged, against whom proceedings are pending but who is not being tried in the instant proceedings, for example because the indictment has been ordered to be severed, should not be called for the prosecution unless an undertaking is given by the prosecution that proceedings will be discontinued against the accomplice (14). This appears to be a rule of practice, rather than of law, because the accomplice is not a party to the proceedings before the jury. The purpose of the rule is to prevent the possibility of a conviction being obtained by the tactical use of separate trials, when evidence would have been incompetent on a joint trial. In *R v Pipe* (14), it

10   (CCA) [1944] 2 All ER 311. See also *R v Sharrock and Others* [1948] 1 All ER 145. The actual result in *Grant* might be affected now by the rule that committals for trial are not bad merely because some inadmissible evidence is received, but the principle remains: *R v Norfolk Quarter Sessions, ex parte Brunson* (DC) [1953] 1 QB 503.
11   *R v Boal; R v Cordrey* (CCA) [1965] 1 QB 402 at 411. But since he is an accomplice, the jury must be warned of the danger of acting on his uncorroborated evidence. See 15.6, post.
12   *R v Payne* (CCA) [1950] 1 All ER 102.
13   See the authorities set out in Archbold, 40th ed., para. 401a.   14   *R v Pipe* (CA) (1966) 51 Cr App R 17.

was held to be wholly irregular to call for the prosecution a receiver of stolen goods, who had been charged and against whom proceedings were about to start, to give evidence against the thief from whom he had received the stolen goods. But the matter appears, ultimately to be a matter of judicial discretion (15).

12.4.2 On his own behalf
As we have seen in outline, the Criminal Evidence Act 1898 provides that the defendant is to be a competent, but not compellable, witness for the defence. This is achieved by the following wording of s. 1:

Every person charged with an offence . . . shall be a competent witness for the defence at every stage of the proceedings, whether the person so charged is charged solely or jointly with any other person. Provided as follows:—

(a) A person so charged shall not be called as a witness in pursuance of this Act except on his own application.

It has already been observed that the defendant, if called upon his own application, is to be treated in all respects as any other witness in the case, subject only to the remaining provisos to s. 1. The evidence which he gives must therefore be considered by the jury and given such weight as they think fit. If the defendant elects to give evidence, he may accordingly be cross-examined freely to show his guilt, or that of any co-defendant, subject only to provisos (e) and (f); his evidence is evidence in the case for all purposes. Even where his own evidence in chief is limited to an admission of his own guilt and does not advance his own case, he may be cross-examined to show the guilt of his co-defendant (16).

The provision for competence 'at every stage of the proceedings' is wide enough to include evidence at the committal proceedings, at which the defendant is competent by virtue of the section (17). It also comprehends not only evidence given in his defence before the jury, but evidence given by the defendant for any other purposes in the trial, for example on the trial of an issue of admissibility on the voire dire (18), and during the course of mitigation. In *R v Wheeler* (19) it was argued that the defendant was not liable to be convicted of perjury in respect of his false evidence during mitigation, because a conviction for perjury is only possible if the defendant has been 'lawfully sworn', and the defendant was not a competent witness after conviction, the issue in the case having been determined. The argument was rejected. Mitigation is a 'stage of the proceedings'.

12.4.3 For a co-defendant
The circumstances will be rare indeed in which a defendant before the jury is called to give evidence for a co-defendant, where he does not propose to do so in his own defence, since he would thereby expose himself to cross-examination on his own case, and since, being a defendant, he is not compellable to give evidence at the instance of a co-defendant, any more than he is on his own behalf. There is no doubt, however, that the

15 *R v Pipe* (ante) and *R v Turner and Others* (1975) 61 Cr App R 67, per Lord Parker CJ at 78–9. And see 12.4.3, post. The point is a serious lacuna in s. 1 as it now stands.
16 *R v Paul; R v McFarlane* (CCA) [1920] 2 KB 183; *R v Rudd* (CCA) (1948) 32 Cr App R 138.
17 *R v Rhodes* (CCR) [1899] 1 QB 77.
18 *R v Cowell* (CCA) [1940] 2 KB 49.
19 (CCA) [1917] 1 KB 283.

phrase 'for the defence' is wide enough to allow of his competence for a co-defendant, and there seems to be no reason why in a proper case, one defendant should not give evidence for another, for example on the voire dire. It may also be observed that if one defendant gives evidence in his own defence, he may be cross-examined on behalf of a co-defendant, even though he has not given evidence adverse to that co-defendant, for the purpose of eliciting any matters favourable to the case of the co-defendant (20).

Of course, a person who ceases to be a defendant, before his co-defendant is called upon to make his defence, for example where the case against him has been withdrawn from the jury at the close of the prosecution case, becomes both competent and compellable for the co-defendant in accordance with the usual rule (21). However, the serious lacuna in s. 1 referred to in note 15 was aggravated as regards co-defendants by the decision of Lawton J at first instance on a preliminary point in *R v Richardson and Others* (22). H, M and others had originally been jointly charged, but at the beginning of the trial, an application was made and acceded to on behalf of M that because of the state of his health, he should be tried separately. The effect of this was to sever the indictment to that extent. H then applied for a witness summons against M, to compel M to give evidence on behalf of H. M was clearly a competent witness for H, but it was argued that he was not compellable because of s. 1. Lawton J held M to be compellable, holding that the word 'proceedings' in s. 1 means 'a trial which is going on' (23). It is of course true that M was not a defendant then before the jury, and it must be conceded that the Act does not expressly cover the point raised. However, it is submitted that the decision is highly unsatisfactory as a matter of practice, and that the lacuna should be filled by statute. The authority for the pre-1898 position at common law is both tenuous and ambiguous (24). The result of *Richardson* is to conflict with the rule of practice generally imposed on the prosecution in the same lacuna, by *R v Pipe* (25); indeed, it presumably allowed the prosecution to enjoy an even more favourable position than if they had been permitted to call M themselves, because they were free to cross-examine him. It seems quite indefensible that questions of compellability should be determined by references to procedural matters in this way (26).

It seems most unlikely that the prosecution would wish to seek to call either Coke or Littleton against the other, unless one voluntarily decides to plead guilty to the charge against him. Where serious charges are involved against both, it would not be right to think of dropping the case against either, and there is no real room for accepting pleas to lesser charges here. Thus, it follows that Coke and Littleton will remain incompetent witnesses for the prosecution, but will be competent (not of course compellable) in their own defence and in that of each other; in the circumstances of this case, the last possibility hardly arises. If either gives evidence in his defence, he may be freely cross-examined about both offences as a witness in the case for all purposes. The circumstances illustrate the advantage of being last on the indictment, and so being called upon last to make one's defence. Coke, being first on the indictment, must take his decision whether or not to give evidence before he knows what is likely to be said in

20   *R v Hilton* (CA) [1972] 1 QB 421.
21   *R v Boal; R v Cordrey* (CCA) [1965] 1 QB 402 at 411.
22   (1967) 51 Cr App R 381.   23   Ibid at 385.
24   *R v Payne* (CCA) (1872) LR 1 CCR 349; *R v Bradlaugh* (1883) 15 Cox CC 217, in neither of which can any firm rule at common law be fairly said to have been established.
25   See 12.4.2, ante.
26   It is, however, to be noticed that the witness will enjoy the privilege against self-incrimination, which as a defendant would not be available to him in respect of the offence charged because of proviso (e) to s. 1. In many cases, this may well render his evidence valueless to the party calling him, if the privilege is properly enforced from the bench.

evidence by Littleton, either in chief or in cross-examination. Littleton may hear Coke's evidence before deciding. If Coke elects not to give evidence, he has lost his chance of contradicting in evidence anything said against him subsequently by Littleton, though he may seek to repair the damage by cross-examination. The point has some relevance for the prosecution, in deciding the order in which to indict. It is best from their point of view to order the defendants so that those against whom the case seems weakest appear as early in the indictment as their involvement in the offences will properly allow, so that they cannot rely upon not having the case against them made stronger by the evidence of their co-defendants.

12.5 Spouses of parties

We have seen that the abolition of incompetence through interest by the Evidence Act 1843 paved the way for the competence of the parties themselves. For the same reason, the competence of the spouses of parties was rendered inevitable. It was enacted for civil cases by the Evidence Amendment Act 1853, subject to the exceptions of proceedings instituted in consequence of adultery and breach of promise of marriage which the Act of 1851 had left in respect of parties, and these exceptions were likewise removed for spouses by the Evidence Further Amendment Act 1869. Consequently, in civil cases, the spouse of the parties are now both competent and compellable, in accordance with the general rule.

As with the parties themselves, very different considerations prevailed in relation to criminal cases. The issue here was the extent to which the defendant's spouse might be competent either for the prosecution or for the defence. The position at common law was far from satisfactory. On the one hand, there had always been felt a sense of natural repugnance at the thought of spouses giving evidence against each other (27) and of apprehension at the obvious dangers of perjured and exaggerated evidence. Coupled with these factors was the compelling influence of the legal fiction that husband and wife were one person in law, a fiction which died only with reluctance towards the end of the nineteenth century. Taken together with the privilege against self-incrimination, which because of the fiction extended to the spouse, it provided a formidable barrier to competence (28). But on the other hand, despite these powerful inducements to incompetence, it had been recognised as early as the seventeenth century, that the enforcement of the law demanded some degree of deviation from the strict rule. The precise limits of the deviation were never certain. However, it came to be recognised that a defendant's spouse might be a competent witness for the prosecution in some instances. Treason, for reasons of policy, was thought to be one; offences of violence against the spouse, because of the habitual absence of any other evidence in many cases, another.

The Criminal Evidence Act 1898 had, therefore, to deal with the spouse, both as a potential prosecution witness and, following the new policy of the nineteenth century reforms, as a potential defence witness. As a defence witness, the Act allied the spouse closely with the defendant, rendering the spouse competent for the defence, but only

---

27 Such feeling of repugnance as has manifested itself in recent times has been directed generally to the idea of compelling spouses, rather than rendering them competent. But even as to this, there is more than one view. See, e.g., the powerful dissenting speech of Lord Edmund-Davies in *Hoskyn* v *Commissioner of Police of the Metropolis* (HL) [1979] AC 474 at 501.

28 `. . . it hath been resolved by the justices, that a wife cannot be produced either against or for her husband, *quia sunt duae animae in carne una;* and it might be a cause of implacable discord and dissention between the husband and the wife, and a means of great inconvenience'. Co. Litt. 6b.

capable of being called on the application of the defendant (29). In relation to the prosecution, the Act preserved (but failed, regrettably, to define) the competence of the spouse, where, exceptionally, it existed at common law. The Act also provided that a defendant's spouse was to be competent for the prosecution if the offence charged was one of those specified in the Act (30). Subsequent enactments notably the Sexual Offences Act 1956 and the Theft Act 1968, have continued to extend the range of statutory competences, and it is now a moot point whether the spouse is not, in modern law, competent for the prosecution in all cases where his or her evidence is likely to be of any real significance (31). Unhappily, the position of the spouse so far as compellability is concerned was neglected both by the common law, and by the 1898 Act, in so far as it made the spouse competent for the prosecution. In all probability, this is because it was assumed that the usual rule in favour of compellability of competent witnesses would apply, although there were indications to the contrary (32).

12.6   Spouse of a defendant in a criminal case

We may now examine the position of spouses in modern law as witnesses (a) for the prosecution, (b) for the defendant to whom they are married, and (c) for a co-defendant.

12.6.1   For the prosecution

Despite the observations made in note 31, it remains true to say that the rule is that the spouse of the defendant is an incompetent witness for the prosecution, other than in certain exceptional cases. This incompetence applies whether the defendant is charged alone or jointly with others, so that in *R* v *Mount*; *R* v *Metcalfe* (33), where three defendants were charged with shop-breaking, and the wife of one of them was called for the prosecution, the reception of her evidence was fatal to the conviction of all three. In *R* v *Deacon* (34), the defendant was charged with the murder of his brother-in-law (count 1) and with the attempted murder of his wife (count 2). No application was made for separate trials of the counts, which arose from the defendant's use of a shotgun on a single occasion. The wife was called to give evidence for the prosecution. The jury convicted on count 1 and were then discharged from returning a verdict on count 2. The defendant appealed. It was common ground on appeal that the wife was not a competent witness on count 1, although she was so on count 2, which was an offence of violence against herself. The conviction was quashed because her evidence had been wrongly received on count 1, even though it was properly received on count 2. The evidence was such that it necessarily went to prove count 1, as to which it was incompetent.

The general rule is subject to four important classes of exceptional case, in which the spouse is competent for the prosecution. These are: (a) exceptions at common law; (b) exceptions falling within s. 4 and the schedule to the Criminal Evidence Act 1898 as amended; (c) exceptions falling within s. 39 of the Sexual Offences Act 1956 and related

---

29   Criminal Evidence Act 1898, s. 1 and proviso (*c*). Proviso (*d*) ensures that the privilege against being compelled to disclose matrimonial communications shall not be affected by the Act. The prosecution may not comment on the failure of the spouse to give evidence: proviso (*b*).
30   Ibid. s. 4 and sch.
31   This comment is directed particularly to the two statutes in the text, which between them cover the overwhelming majority of what might be called 'domestic offences' in which the evidence of a spouse is often crucial, if not indeed the only evidence.
32   Some of which are set out in the speech of Lord Wilberforce in *Hoskyn* v *Commissioner of Police of the Metropolis* (HL) [1974] AC 474 at 485 et seq. The question of compellability has given rise, consequently, to considerable problems.
33   (CCA) (1934) 24 Cr App R 135.   34   (CA) [1973] 1 WLR 696.

provisions; and (d) exceptions falling within s. 30(2) and (3) of the Theft Act 1968. These must be examined individually.

12.6.1.1 Exceptions at common law It was thought, though never really established, that the spouse was competent for the prosecution in cases of high treason. The point was one of some controversy among writers on the common law, and cannot be regarded as finally decided. Further discussion of the subject is outside the scope of this work.

The only class of case clearly established as an exception at common law is where the defendant is charged with an offence of violence against the spouse. The rule may be traced back at least as far as *Lord Audley's Case* (35) where the defendant was charged with aiding and abetting his footman to commit rape on his wife, in the defendant's presence. It was held that the wife was a competent witness for the prosecution on this charge. The rule was also extended to cover the admissible dying declaration of the deceased wife, on a charge against the husband of murdering her, in *R* v *Woodcock* (36). The exception is now clearly established. It seems to have been applied also to cases where the defendant forcibly abducted and married the victim, so as to prevent the gross result that the defendant, by his very criminal act, might succeed in rendering incompetent the only witness against him, but again, it is unnecessary to pursue this subject here.

The question of what amounts to an offence of violence against the spouse causes occasional difficulties. For example, in *R* v *Yeo* (37), Gorman J held that a charge of maliciously sending to the wife, 'knowing the contents thereof a letter threatening to murder her', contrary to s. 16 of the Offences against the Person Act 1861 was not within the exception and that the wife was incompetent. The *ratio* of the decision was that no actual personal injury was sustained by the wife, but it is difficult to see why this should be the crucial factor in all cases. In *R* v *Verolla* (38) Melford Stevenson J was prepared to hold that the wife was competent on a charge of attempting to murder her by poisoning her milk, even though no personal injury was in fact sustained, although it is clearly possible to distinguish the two cases. The answer now in cases of doubt could well be that the wording of s. 30 of the Theft Act 1968 seems wide enough to overlap substantially with the common-law rule, and the question of how far that provision has trespassed upon the common-law preserve is still an open one. Certainly, the facts of *Yeo* might be held to fall within the wording of s. 30(3) as being an offence 'with reference to that person's wife or husband'.

Strangely, little attention was paid to whether a wife who was competent within the common-law exception was also compellable. When the issue was raised in modern times, the search for authority proved to be almost fruitless. In *R* v *Lapworth* (39) the Court of Criminal Appeal answered the question by a simple application of the equation, competent = compellable, one rule of common law following logically from another. In so doing, however, the court was departing (as it was entitled to do) from the view taken by the House of Lords in *Leach* v *R* (40), of the analogous problem in relation to s. 4 of the Criminal Evidence Act 1898 which had remained silent on the matter of the compellability of a spouse rendered competent by that section. As Lord Wilberforce has powerfully demonstrated since (41), the decision in *Leach* is not satisfactorily disposed

35 (HL) (1632) 3 St Tr 402.   36   (1789) 1 Leach 500.
37 [1951] 1 All ER 864n.   38 [1963] 1 QB 285.
39 (CCA) [1931] 1 KB 117. See also *R* v *Algar* (CCA) [1954] 1 QB 279.
40 [1912] AC 305.
41 *Hoskyn* v *Commissioner of Police of the Metropolis* (HL) [1979] AC 474 at 488.

of by the bland distinction that it was a matter of construction of s. 4 as opposed to the common law. If the 1898 Act was silent on the subject, then the rules of common law cannot be taken to have been interfered with, and the speeches in *Leach* show quite unmistakably that the Lords thought themselves to be applying the fundamental rule of common law to a new category of competent witness, a category which happened to have been created by statute. This rule, they perceived as being different for a spouse giving evidence in a criminal case, as opposed to witnesses falling within other categories of competence. Earl Loreburn LC described it as a 'fundamental and old principle . . . that you ought not to compel a wife to give evidence against her husband in matters of a criminal kind' (42). Lord Atkinson said that the same principle was 'deep seated in the common law of this country' (43).

Against this background, which had produced the absurdity of two different rules about compellability, dependent upon the accident of the reason for the wife's competence, the matter was reviewed by the House of Lords in *Hoskyn* v *Commissioner of Police of the Metropolis* (44). The defendant was charged with wounding one Janis Scrimshaw with intent to do her grievous bodily harm. Two days before the start of the trial, the defendant and Janis Scrimshaw were married. Mrs Hoskyn, as she now was, was reluctant to give evidence and being compelled to do so by the trial judge, who was bound by *Lapworth*, was treated as hostile. Her evidence nonetheless assisted in the conviction of the defendant. On appeal, the House of Lords held (45) that, though competent, she was not compellable.

Lord Salmon put the matter as follows (46):

The main argument on behalf of the Crown is that all persons who are competent witnesses, normally are also compellable witnesses. And therefore, so the argument runs, in cases in which wives are competent witnesses it follows that they also must be compellable witnesses. This seems to me to be a complete non sequitur, for it takes no account of the especial importance which the common law attaches to the status of marriage. Clearly, it was for the wife's own protection that the common law made an exception to its general rule by making the wife a competent witness in respect of any charge against her husband for a crime of violence against her. But if she does not want to avail herself of this protection, there is, in my view, no ground for holding that the common law forces it upon her.

In many such cases, the wife is not a reluctant or unwilling witness; she may indeed sometimes be an enthusiastic witness against her husband. On the other hand, there must also be many cases when a wife who loved her husband completely forgave him, had no fear of further violence, and wished the marriage to continue and the pending prosecution to fail. It seems to me altogether inconsistent with the common law's attitude towards marriage that it should compel such a wife to give evidence against her husband and thereby probably destroy the marriage. It is indeed remarkable that if a wife were a compellable witness, no single authority to that effect (prior to *R* v *Lapworth*) has been drawn to the attention of this House.

The decision in *Hoskyn* has undoubtedly settled an age-old gap in the law, and has the

---

42   [1912] AC 305 at 309. Equally strong were the words of the Earl of Halsbury at 311.
43   Ibid at 311   44   [1979] AC 474.
45   Lord Wilberforce, Viscount Dilhorne, Lords Salmon and Keith of Kinkel; Lord Edmund-Davies dissenting.
46   Ibid at 495. So also Lord Wilberforce at 488, who also regarded the argument for the Crown as a 'complete *non sequitur*'.

merit of unifying the law in respect of spouses competent for any reason for the prosecution in a criminal case, and clearly, good reasons are to be found for exemption from the general rule (47).

12.6.1.2 Exceptions under the Criminal Evidence Act 1898 By s. 4 of the Criminal Evidence Act 1898:

(1) The wife or husband of a person charged with an offence under any enactment mentioned in the schedule to this Act may be called as a witness either for the prosecution or defence and without the consent of the person charged.

(2) Nothing in this Act shall affect a case where the wife or husband of a person charged with an offence may at common law be called as a witness without the consent of that person.

The contents of the schedule have varied from time to time, and some offences originally included have now been made the subject of competence elsewhere, notably under the Sexual Offences Act 1956. The contents of the schedule are now: (a) child destruction, contrary to the Infant Life (Preservation) Act 1929; (b) the various offences against children and young persons set out in the first schedule to the Children and Young Persons Act 1933 (which relate to offences against the person and sexual offences); (c) persistent refusal or neglect to maintain, contrary to s. 51 of the National Assistance Act 1948.

In these cases, as we have seen, the House of Lords has held, in *Leach* v *R*, that the spouse, though competent, is not compellable.

12.6.1.3 Exceptions under the Sexual Offences Act 1956 and related provisions By s. 39 of the Sexual Offences Act 1956:

(1) Where this section applies, the wife or husband of the accused shall be competent to give evidence at every stage of the proceedings, whether for the defence or for the prosecution, and whether the accused is charged solely or jointly with any other person.

Subsection (2) applies the section to all offences under the Act, except buggery (s. 12), indecent assault on a man (s. 15), and assault with intent to commit buggery (s. 16). Offences against the wife under s. 12 or s. 16 would presumably fall within the scope of the exception at common law. The offences covered by the section were originally included in the schedule to the Criminal Evidence Act 1898.

Subsection (1) has two provisos, which mirror the provisions of the 1898 Act in preserving privilege for matrimonial communications and in forbidding the prosecution to comment on the failure of the spouse to give evidence.

---

47 It would not be right to assume that all the arguments are one way. There are at least three powerful arguments which militate against the majority view: (a) In the absence of authority, there is some logic in law in assuming that the usual rule applies, i.e., competent = compellable; (b) some offences are too grave to be, in effect, compromised just because a wife changes here mind about giving evidence; lesser offences would probably not be pursued by prosecuting authorities in such circumstances; (c) being compellable is a useful protection against a wife witness who is willing, but is subject to intimidation. These matters are forcefully dealt with in the dissenting speech of Lord Edmund-Davies at 499. See also 11th Report of Criminal Law Revision Committee, para. 149.

Section 39(3) provides: 'This section shall not affect section 1 of the Criminal Evidence Act 1898, or any case where the wife or husband of the accused may at common law be called as a witness without the consent of the accused.'

There are corresponding provisions for the competence of spouses by statute in the following related enactments, which may be said to cover offences within a broadly similar field:

(a) In cases of bigamy: Criminal Justice Administration Act 1914, s. 28(3).
(b) In offences under the Indecency with Children Act 1960: see s. 1(2).
(c) In offences contrary to the Protection of Children Act 1978: see s. 2(1).

In the cases dealt with under these enactments (with the exception of the Criminal Justice Administration Act 1914 which is probably subject to the rule in *Leach* v *R*) Parliament wisely decided to pre-empt the possibility of renewed battle on the front of compellability. Each of the sections referred to provides expressly in the course of a proviso that the spouse is not to be compellable to give evidence.

12.6.1.4   Exceptions under the Theft Act 1968   S. 30 of the Theft Act 1968 contains a remarkably misplaced piece of legislative engineering, couched as it is in the context of a reforming statute dealing comprehensively with the enactment of a new body of substantive law. The section contains two extremely important subsections, which have a far-reaching effect on the law relating to the competence of spouses, and which, despite their inclusion in the Act, are not confined to offences under the Act, nor necessarily to offences of the kind dealt with by the Act. The subsections are s. 30(2) and (3), which provide as follows:

(2) . . . a person shall have the same right to bring proceedings against that person's wife or husband for any offence (whether under this Act or otherwise) as if they were not married, and a person bringing any such proceedings shall be competent to give evidence for the prosecution at every stage of the proceedings. [(48).]

(3) Where a person is charged in proceedings not brought by that person's wife or husband with having committed any offence with reference to that person's wife or husband or to property belonging to the wife or husband, the wife or husband shall be competent to give evidence at every stage of the proceedings, whether for the defence or for the prosecution, and whether the accused is charged solely or jointly with any other person . . .

The scope of s. 30(3) calls for some comment. The phrase 'with reference to' is capable of encompassing a wide variety of offences, which may well overlap wholly or partially with the scope of the competence exception at common law. To this extent, it may provide a useful escape from the borderline cases under that exception. There is no doubt, however, that coupled with the absence of restriction to offences of any particular kind, it has effected a massive extension of the previous law on the subject. As Professor Cross has observed (49), the full implications of the subsection have probably yet to be

48 S. 30(4) provides that in some cases, prosecutions brought by virtue of this subsection shall be instituted only by or with the consent of the Director of Public Prosecutions.
49 Cross, *Evidence*, 5th ed. p. 175.

recognised. It has already been established that the phrase 'with reference to' is wider than, for example, 'against', and is apt to include any offence which affects the rights or obligations of the other spouse. In *R* v *Noble* (50), a wife forged her husband's signature on documents intended for a finance company, which would not have considered the application for an advance solely on the strength of the wife's own signature. It was held that this was an offence committed 'with reference to' the husband. His position *vis-à-vis* the company was affected by the forgery, and that was sufficient to bring the case within the subsection.

The position with regard to compellability is not as simple as the framers of the Act probably intended. S. 30(3) is followed by a proviso, which appears to refer only to subsection (3) and not to subsection (2) in these terms: 'Provided that (*a*) the wife or husband (unless compellable at common law) shall not be compellable... to give evidence. ...'

The reference in parentheses to compellability at common law was designed to give effect to the law as it was thought to be in the light of *Lapworth*. Since the decision of the House of Lords in *Hoskyn*, the words are meaningless, there being no case at common law in which the spouse is compellable. It is not entirely clear why the proviso was not applied to subsection (2) but the likelihood must be that, where proceedings are instituted by the spouse, who afterwards becomes unwilling to give evidence, the proceedings would not be pursued. This is, however, by no means conclusive. The court may not agree with the proposal to discontinue, and it is regrettable that this possibility was not catered for by the simple rearrangement of punctuation which would have sufficed for the purpose. Although it seems, as Professor Smith has pointed out (51), that it would be open to the court, under subsection (2), to hold the spouse to be compellable, it is surely inconceivable that such a result, conflicting both with subsection (3) and with *Leach* v *R* in the case of the 1898 Act, should be arrived at in the present state of the law.

12.6.2   *For the defendant to whom married*
The position of the spouse as a defence witness for a husband or wife charged with an offence is provided for by the Criminal Evidence Act 1898. We have already observed the operation of s. 1 in relation to the defendant, and we then omitted the reference to the spouse. The full text of s. 1 together with proviso (*c*) dealing with the spouse, is as follows:

> Every person charged with an offence, and the wife or husband, as the case may be, of the person so charged, shall be a competent witness for the defence at every stage of the proceedings, whether the person so charged is charged solely or jointly with any other person. Provided as follows:— . . .

> (*c*) The wife or husband of the person charged shall not, save as in this Act mentioned, be called as a witness in pursuance of this Act except upon the application of the person so charged. [(52).]

The exceptive phrase in the proviso, 'save as in this Act mentioned' refers to the provisions of s. 4(1) (see 12.6.1.2, ante), that in cases falling within the schedule to the

---

50   (CA) [1974] 1 WLR 894.
51   *The Law of Theft*, 4th ed. para. 457. Professor Griew, *The Theft Acts 1968 and 1978*, 3rd ed para. 12-04, supports the view stated in the text, as, with rather less certainty, does Professor Smith.
52   For the meaning of 'at every stage of the proceedings' see 12.4.2, ante.

Act, the spouse is a competent witness for the prosecution or for the defence without the consent of the defendant.

The wording of proviso (*c*) contains a problem, at least in theory, concerning compellability. The matter has, apparently, hardly been adverted to by learned writers on the subject (53) who have asserted that the spouse is competent, but not compellable, as a witness for the defendant. This result naturally follows, in the case of the defendant himself, from the words 'except on his own application', in proviso (*a*). But it is not apparent that the same result follows at all from the wording of proviso (*c*) that the spouse shall not be called except on the application of the defendant (not on the application of the spouse). It is certainly unlikely in practice that any defendant would wish to call a reluctant spouse to give evidence on his behalf, especially if the reluctance stems from questions which might be put to the spouse in cross-examination. But the problem remains whether a defendant might appeal, if refused a witness summons in such a case. And the problem did arise in a realistic context in *R* v *Boal*; *R* v *Cordrey* (54) where it was argued on appeal by Boal that he should be allowed to call on the appeal evidence from his wife, dealing with an alibi, which had not been called at the trial. The appeal was dismissed on this point, virtually without discussion, on the ground that the wife had been competent, though not compellable, for the defence at the trial and that her evidence was accordingly not 'fresh evidence'. But it is submitted that the issue should have been whether she was compellable, and if it were shown that she had declined to give evidence at the trial, interesting questions might arise.

The intention of the legislature has been more clearly expressed in subsequent Acts. Both s. 39 of the Sexual Offences Act 1956 and s. 30(3) of the Theft Act 1968 expressly provide by their provisos that the spouse is not to be compellable to give evidence when rendered competent by the section to do so, and since the competence relates to evidence both for the prosecution and the defence, the position seems reasonably clear (55). It is surely likely that this approach would be followed in future cases falling within the exceptions at common law and s. 4 of the Criminal Evidence Act 1898, where the decisions in *Hoskyn* and *Leach* are not directly in point. However, the considerations which prevent a spouse from being compellable at the instance of the prosecution are not necessarily to be applied to the question whether he or she should be so for the husband or wife charged with an offence.

12.6.3   *For a co-defendant*

Although the spouse of one defendant may be unaffected in theory by that relationship, so far as co-defendants are concerned, the common law saw and recognised the difficulties of treating the spouse of one defendant as subject to the ordinary rules as a witness on behalf of another. The risk of evidence adverse to the witness's wife or husband would in most cases be very great. At common law there was a rule, accordingly, that the spouse was competent for the co-defendant with the consent of the wife or husband charged, but not otherwise (56). In the exceptional case of offences of violence against the spouse, however, he or she was competent always for the co-defendant, as for the prosecution.

The Criminal Evidence Act 1898 preserved this state of affairs as the basic rule. The wording of s. 1 rendering the spouse competent 'for the defence' is wide enough to

---

53   Phipson, *Evidence*, 12th ed., para. 1507 et seq; Heydon, *Evidence: Cases and Materials*, p. 385; Archbold, 40th ed., para. 503 et seq; Professor Cross (*Evidence*, 5th ed., p 178) mentions the matter without discussion.
54   [1965] 1 QB 402. See also the hardly compelling dicta of Darling J in *R* v *Acaster* (CCA) (1912) 7 Cr App R 187, which purport to be based upon the decision in *Leach* v *R* (HL) [1912] AC 305.
55   But see note 57, post.   56   *R* v *Thompson* (CCR) (1872) LR 1 CCR 377.

include co-defendants, as it is in the case of a person charged. But the competence is, in this case too, subject to the limitation of proviso (*c*) that the spouse may be called only on the application of the husband or wife charged. It would seem to follow, therefore, that the spouse is always competent for the co-defendant with the consent of the husband or wife charged.

The Act further provided, however, by s. 4(1) that in the scheduled cases, the spouse was to be competent for the defence 'and without the consent of the person charged'. And by s. 4(2), there were preserved the cases at common law in which the spouse might be called without the consent of the person charged. Subsequent Acts providing for statutory competence followed the pattern of s. 4(1). Both s. 39 of the Sexual Offences Act 1956 and s. 30(3) of the Theft Act 1968 provide that the spouse shall be competent for the defence, and make no reservation about consent. The former gives rise to a little difficulty by providing that s. 39, 'shall not affect s. 1 of the Criminal Evidence Act 1898 or any case where the wife or husband of the accused may at common law be called as a witness without the consent of the accused' (s. 39(3)). One reading of this provision might be that proviso (*c*) to s. 1 of the 1898 Act applies to the cases falling within s. 39, so that the spouse is competent only with the consent of the person charged. But it has generally been assumed that the provision was not intended to alter the law which prevailed when these offences fell within the provisions of s. 4 of the Criminal Evidence Act 1898. Whatever the true position, it would appear that the argument postulated in note 57 would be considerably stronger in this instance than in relation to s. 30(3) of the Theft Act 1968 (57).

So far as compellability of a spouse for a co-defendant is concerned (a question to be distinguished carefully from that of competence with or without the consent of the person charged) the specific provisions of s. 39 of the Sexual Offences Act 1956 and s. 30(3) of the Theft Act 1968 apply to prevent compellability in the cases to which they apply as they do where the spouse is proposed to be called for the husband or wife charged. The position in other cases may safely be assumed to be governed by *Leach* and *Hoskyn*. The objections recognised by the common law apply with a force almost equal to that in the case where the spouse is proposed to be called for the prosecution.

12.7 Former spouses

The effect of the termination of the marriage, by death or dissolution, upon a witness who, had the marriage survived, would have been incompetent by virtue of the relationship, has always been somewhat obscure. It has somehow escaped the attention of the legislature, and still depends upon authority which because of its age, leaves the present position doubtful.

At common law, the incompetence of a spouse survived the termination of the marriage, in respect of matters which occurred during the marriage. In *Monroe* v *Twistleton* (58) the plaintiff was held not to be entitled to call the divorced wife of the defendant in order to prove a contract allegedly made between the defendant and himself during the marriage. The rule was followed in *O'Connor* v *Marjoribanks* (59) in which personal representatives suing in respect of the alleged conversion of part of an

---

57 It would be interesting to hear it argued that the provision in favour of competence for the defence, in any statute enacted after 1898, is strictly otiose, and should therefore be read subject to proviso (*c*) of that Act. The result of this would be to require consent in all cases; and indeed, the wording of s. 4(1) expressly negativing the need for consent in the scheduled cases, suggests that the omission of any reference in the later Acts to consent may have been a significant error.

58 (NP) (1802) Peake Add Cas 219.   59 (1842) 4 Man & G 435.

estate were not permitted to call the widow of the deceased with a view to proving what instructions about the disposal of the estate had been given by the deceased during his lifetime. A former spouse was, of course, competent to give evidence concerning events that occurred after the termination of the marriage. Whether or not the incompetence of a former spouse relates also to events which occurred prior to the marriage appears never to have been decided.

The termination of the marriage may be, and in the older cases more commonly was, effected by a decree of nullity. If a decree of nullity is based on a ground which renders the marriage voidable only, so that there has been a valid marriage up to the date of the decree then it does not affect incompetence with respect to events before the decree (60). However a technical distinction, no doubt soundly rooted in theory, was made in cases where the decree was based on a ground which rendered the 'marriage' void *ab initio*. In such a case, there had never been, in law, a valid marriage, and no rule of incompetence could therefore arise, let alone survive (61). This distinction, whatever its merits as an exercise in logic, is of questionable value in modern law as a basis for a rule of evidence, and it is to be hoped that it will be abrogated in due course.

The mere fact that the parties to a marriage are not cohabiting has no effect on the existence of incompetence due to the relationship of marriage. This applies whether the parties are living apart without any express arrangement, or pursuant to a separation agreement, or even pursuant to a decree of judicial separation or non-cohabitation order made by a court. In *Moss* v *Moss* (62) the Divisional Court rejected an argument that the word 'coverture' used in the older cases to describe the duration of the incompetence connoted cohabitation only, so as to render a spouse competent to give evidence of events which occurred after the spouses had ceased to cohabit. While the marriage endured, so did the 'coverture', and a spouse was incompetent in respect of matters during such period.

The rule in *Monroe* v *Twistleton* has never been formally abrogated, but at least in civil cases, its position has become exceedingly tenuous, and it might profitably be decently buried if and when the opportunity arises. Its main problem has been the intervention of statute all around it. In s. 1 of the Evidence Amendment Act 1853, which rendered competent the spouses of the parties in almost all civil cases, the words used to describe those so made competent were 'husband' and 'wife'. If the incompetence of former spouses survives, therefore, it must be because those words exclude former husbands and wives. This would produce the preposterous result that while existing spouses are competent and compellable in respect of events during the marriage, former spouses are not. For this reason alone, it has probably been assumed that the Act effectively abrogated *Monroe* v *Twistleton*, so far as civil cases are concerned. This convenient construction is, unfortunately, difficult to justify by hard facts, especially in view of *Shenton* v *Tyler* (63) a decision on the identical words in s. 3 of the same Act (relating to matrimonial privilege) in which a strong Court of Appeal held, after an exhaustive

---

60   *R* v *Algar* (CCA) [1954] 1 QB 279.   61   *Wells* v *Fisher* (NP) (1831) 1 Mood & R 99.

62   [1963] 2 QB 799, a case whose complications would now be avoided by resort to s. 30 of the Theft Act 1968. Some concession at least has been made to the changed circumstances, after cohabitation has ceased, by the exemption from the need for institution of proceedings by or with the consent of the Director of Public Prosecutions, of cases against a person for theft of or criminal damage to property belonging to that person's spouse, where they are, by virtue of any court order, under no obligation to cohabit at the time of the offence: Theft Act 1968, s. 30(4) proviso (*a*)(ii).

63   [1939] Ch 620. The decision in this case is in effect adopted by s. 18(2) of the Civil Evidence Act 1968 for the purposes of that Act and any provision amended by that Act. While this is not material in relation to competence and compellability generally, it does have repercussions in the law of privilege in which the same problem occurs; see 11.7 and 11.9, ante.

review of the authorities (including *Monroe* v *Twistleton* and *O'Connor* v *Marjoribanks*) that the words 'husband' and 'wife' could not be construed so as to include widowers and widows. The truth is that *Monroe* v *Twistleton* depends on a premise (the incompetence of spouses) which, in civil cases, is no longer valid.

In criminal cases, where the history of the competence of spouses has taken a very different course, *Monroe* v *Twistleton* has enjoyed a more vigorous old age. In *R* v *Algar* (64) the defendant was charged with the forgery of his wife's signature on cheques drawn on her bank account during 1947 and 1948. In 1949, the marriage was annulled because of the impotence of the defendant, a ground which rendered the marriage voidable only. The former wife was called at the defendant's trial in 1953. The Court of Criminal Appeal quashed the conviction, holding that she remained incompetent following *Monroe* v *Twistleton*. It seems, therefore, although the decision has not gone uncriticised, that in criminal cases where an existing spouse would be incompetent, then in respect of matters occurring during the marriage, the incompetence survives the termination of the marriage. Where, of course, an existing spouse is competent, there can be no basis for any incompetence when the marriage has ended.

It appears that the evidence of Mrs Littleton will play some significant part in the trial of Coke and Littleton. She would be competent (though not compellable) for the prosecution against Littleton, or equally for the defence, by virtue of s. 39 of the Sexual Offences Act 1956. It is hardly likely that the prosecution will seek to call her, since they have in any event a tape-recording of the conversation to which they would wish her to speak, and since she would almost certainly either refuse to give evidence, or turn hostile. Assuming, however, that the prosecution make use of the tape-recording, Littleton will no doubt be anxious to call her to deal with the true circumstances of the conversation, and to give evidence additionally of his good character. These considerations will not be affected if, before the trial, Mrs Littleton leaves her husband because of the events in question, or even obtains a decree of divorce against him.

12.8 Children of tender years

The concern of the common law with regard to the competence of young children is based upon very different considerations to those discussed earlier in this chapter. The question here is one of reliability at a young age of a child witness. It affects civil and criminal cases alike, and little or no difference is to be observed in the courts approach to them.

The competence of a child of tender years is based entirely on the opinion of the judge, who must examine the child with a view to establishing whether or not he may be relied upon, in the sense that he understands the importance of telling the truth, and the consequences of falsehood. The judge has a positive duty to embark upon the inquiry, irrespective of the views of the parties. He must do so, even though, in a criminal case, the examining justices have taken a view that the child is competent (65), and the inquiry must be held in open court in the presence of the jury (66).

There is no set age at which a child ceases to be 'of tender years' or becomes competent to give evidence. In the recent leading case of *R* v *Hayes* (67) it was said by the Court of

---

64 [1954] 1 QB 279. The case would now fall within s. 30(3) of the Theft Act 1968. It could not have been brought within a similar, through narrower, provision of the Married Women's Property Act 1884 because the bank, which had reimbursed the former wife's account, was the party defrauded, not the former wife herself.
65 *R* v *Surgenor* (CCA) [1940] 2 All ER 249.
66 *R* v *Reynolds* (CCA) [1950] 1 KB 606.
67 [1977] 1 WLR 234. The passage cited is at 237.

Appeal that 'the watershed dividing children who are normally considered old enough to take the oath and children normally considered too young to take the oath, probably falls between the ages of eight and ten.' But the range of ages of the children accepted or rejected by the court as competent witnesses, in the considerable number of reported cases, is greater than that, and little profit can be derived from accumulating statistics on the subject (68). Indeed, to do so would be to miss the point. The question is not the precise age of the child, but whether the judge, after his inquiry, forms the view that the child has the necessary degree of intelligence and understanding. The Court of Appeal in *Hayes* observed (69) that '. . . we think it right also to approach the matter on the footing that this is very much a matter within the discretion of the trial judge and we think that this court, although having jurisdiction to interfere if clearly satisfied that the trial judge's discretion was wrongly exercised, should hesitate long before doing so. The judge sees and hears the boy or girl. which means very much more than the bare written word.'

The important question is, on what basis the judge should make his assessment of the child's intelligence and understanding. Here, the recent cases diverge from the old. Originally, at common law, the main and overriding question was whether the child understood the oath. Unless he did, and showed appreciation of the nature of an oath and the divine sanction against falsehood, he was not to be regarded as competent. Competence and the taking of the oath went hand in hand (70). Therefore, the questions posed by the judge to the child were primarily directed to his understanding of the oath itself. In *R v Brasier* (71), which was formerly a leading authority, the judges, having noted that evidence could lawfully be given only on oath, held that there was no 'precise or fixed rule' about age, and continued: '. . . their admissibility depends upon the sense and reason they entertain of the danger and impiety of falsehood, which is to be collected from their answers to questions propounded to them by the court.'

The difficulties of enforcing the proper application of this requirement were onerous, and led to such extreme results as the interruption of trials to allow children to be instructed about the oath, or even, in certain instances, to receive some basic religious training, in order to give evidence. In due course, frustration with this manifestly unrealistic way of treating child witnesses led Parliament to enact that in criminal cases, children might, subject to proper inquiry concerning their intelligence, be permitted to give evidence unsworn. This avoided the equation of competence and oath by removing the child from the duty of being sworn altogether. By s. 38(1) of the Children and Young Persons Act 1933:

Where, in any proceedings against any person for any offence, any child of tender years called as a witness does not in the opinion of the court understand the nature of an oath, his evidence may be received, though not given upon oath, if, in the opinion of the court, he is possessed of sufficient intelligence to justify the reception of the evidence, and understands the duty of speaking the truth.

The section, which succeeds earlier provisions, has the great advantage of pointing

68 A selection of examples is given in Phipson, *Evidence,* 12th ed., para. 1500.
69 [1977] 1 WLR 234 at 237.
70 This equation was not at all restricted to children. At common law, atheists and 'infidels' were originally incompetent, becuase of their inability to be properly sworn. The importance of the oath was very great, and was central to the competence of any witness.
71 (CCR) (1779) 1 Leach 199, 1 East PC 443. The child witness in the case is variously reported as having been 'five' and 'under seven'. Cf *R v Wallwork* (CCA) (1958) 42 Cr App R 153.

the court in a direction more calculated to further the ends of justice than that of inquiry into a child's religious state. It also has, however, the disadvantage that because of the absence of the oath, special provision had to be made to emulate the usual conse-·quences of sworn evidence. Thus, a new offence akin to perjury was built in by s. 38(2), because perjury itself required the defendant to have been 'lawfully sworn' in the proceedings. More significantly, whereas the common law had required the jury, as a matter of practice, to look for corroboration of the evidence of a child of tender years, a stricter requirement was made for unsworn evidence, and by the proviso to s. 38(1), where such unsworn evidence is given for the prosecution, the defendant, 'shall not be liable to be convicted of the offence unless that evidence is corroborated by some other material evidence in support thereof implicating him' (72).

The two kinds of evidence receivable from children, sworn and unsworn, have continued to coexist somewhat uncomfortably because of these distinctions, and it has not been at all easy to identify the frontiers of each. Happily, the criterion suggested to the courts by s. 38(1), based on the intelligence of the child and his understanding of the duty to speak the truth, has now been found to correspond with what the law sees as the true test of competence. In *R* v *Hayes* (73) the defendant was charged with inciting three boys to commit acts of gross indecency with him, and with committing such an act with one of the boys. At the time of the trial, the boys were aged twelve, eleven and nine respectively. The youngest boy gave unsworn evidence under s. 38(1). The judge, after an exchange of questions and answers, allowed the two older boys to be sworn. The appeal was based on certain answers which led to doubt about whether the oldest boy called had any belief in God, or in the divine sanction of an oath. The appeal raised, in effect, the question whether the view propounded in *Brasier* should continue to stand as a proper test of competence in modern law. The Court of Appeal, dismissing the application for leave to appeal, dealt with the matter thus (74):

> The court is not convinced that that is really the essence of the court's duty in the difficult situation where the court has to determine whether a young person can or cannot properly be permitted to take an oath before giving evidence. It is unrealistic not to recognise that, in the present state of society, amongst the adult population the divine sanction of an oath is probably not generally recognised. The important consideration, we think, when a judge has to decide whether a child should properly be sworn, is whether the child has a sufficient appreciation of the solemnity of the occasion and the added responsibility to tell the truth, which is involved in taking an oath, over and above the duty to tell the truth which is an ordinary duty of normal social conduct.

It now appears that the test of competence is, in reality, not far removed from that laid down for the giving of unsworn evidence under s. 38(1). It is submitted that this is a healthy development in the law. It may be that there is an added maturity which comes with the advance of age, which enables a child to appreciate the solemnity of the proceedings and so be enabled to take the oath, but there can be no doubt that it is desirable that the reception of evidence should be based upon the test of intelligence and appreciation of the duty of telling the truth.

It is, of course, far more satisfactory that a child should be sworn, wherever this course may properly be taken. There seems little doubt that Angela Blackstone may give

72 See 15.5 and 15.6, post.   73 [1977] 1 WLR 234.   74 Ibid at 236–7.

evidence on oath, although the judge must, briefly, establish this fact to his satisfaction, by framing questions suitable to elicit her view of the seriousness of the proceedings, and attitude to speaking the truth, not just in a social context, but in the context of the proceedings.

12.9   Persons of defective intellect

There was, at common law, an undeveloped view that 'lunacy' was a bar to competence. The view probably resulted both from the dangers of unreliability and from doubtful capacity to appreciate the nature of an oath. It is, of course, a fairly modern tendency in the law to seek to recognise and accommodate the more sophisticated diagnosis and treatment of mental illness, and the law has not always kept pace with the consequences of the obsolescence of the generic classification of mental patients under the heading of lunacy (75).

Although the position in contemporary law is largely unexplored, it seems that the court will take a pragmatic view, and accord competence to a person of defective intellect, which corresponds with the judge's view of his capacity to understand the nature of the proceedings and to speak the truth to the best of his ability. The question is whether the proposed witness is, at the time of being called, capable of giving proper evidence. If his lack of capacity is a temporary one, his evidence may be receivable after a suitable adjournment, as may be the case with a witness who arrives at court drunk. Incapacity will not be accepted if the witness's evidence can be taken with reasonably practicable precautions, particularly if the evidence may be important (76).

The matter is, therefore, one for the judge, who should, if necessary, inquire into the capacity of the witness in open court and in the presence of the jury. If the witness is declared to be competent, he may give evidence on any relevant issue (77), and is subject to the normal rules of evidence.

12.10   Miscellaneous exceptions to the rule of compellability

Apart from the defendant and the defendant's spouse in criminal cases, the general rule is that all competent witnesses are compellable to give evidence. There are a number of comparatively unimportant further exceptions, which are noted here, primarily for the sake of completeness.

The Sovereign and foreign heads of state, though competent, are not compellable. By various statutory provisions, certain persons who are accredited diplomats or officers of international organisations, enjoy a greater or lesser degree of immunity from compellability, according to their accredited status as such (78).

The position of judges and counsel as witnesses to the facts of or incidents surrounding the trial of cases in which they are judicially or professionally engaged, is dealt with in 11.6, ante.

By s. 6 of the Bankers' Books Evidence Act 1879:

A banker or officer of a bank shall not in any legal proceeding to which the bank is not

75   As witness the continued existence of the M'Naghten Rules.
76   Cf *R* v *Hill* (CCR) (1851) 2 Den CC 254, where an inmate of an asylum, whose 'only delusion' (sic) was that spirits occasionally talked to him, was permitted to give evidence in a prosecution for manslaughter.
77   Including, it seems, that of his own sanity: *Hunter* v *Edney* (1885) 10 PD 93.
78   Diplomatic Privileges Act 1964; Consular Relations Act 1968; International Organisations Act 1968; Diplomatic and Other Privileges Act 1971.

a party, be compellable to produce any banker's book the contents of which can be proved under this Act, or to appear as a witness to prove the matters, transactions, and accounts therein recorded, unless by order of a judge made for special cause.

The purpose of the provision is to protect bankers and their officers from the onerous requirements which might otherwise follow from the frequent recourse of the courts to evidence contained in bankers' books. The Act provides sufficient modes of proof of entries in such books, and a procedure for obtaining orders for their discovery and inspection. These are dealt with in 16.2.3, post.

B: OATHS AND AFFIRMATIONS

12.11 The requirement of sworn evidence

We saw in the preceding section of this chapter that the ability to take the oath was, at common law, a central and probably the central element of competence as a witness. It was, historically, and is today a fundamental rule that evidence given to the court for any purpose shall be sworn, though more modern times have countenanced exceptional cases, which would not have been admitted in earlier days. Evidence is sworn if the witness is first required to take a lawful oath or affirmation, which carries with it the sanction of the law against false evidence.

Evidence given unsworn is, unless given in one of the cases recognised as exceptional, a nullity, and any conviction or judgment based on it will be set aside on appeal. In *R v Marsham, ex parte Pethick Lawrence* (79) where the magistrates' court, by error, conducted a case on the basis of unsworn evidence and thereafter re-heard the case in the proper manner on the same day, an appeal was brought on the ground that the defendant had stood in jeopardy twice because of the procedure adopted by the court. The appeal failed. The first hearing, based on unsworn evidence, had been a nullity, and the defendant had not then stood in jeopardy. And in *Birch v Somerville* (80) where the Lord Lieutenant of Ireland was permitted (irregularly) to give evidence 'on my honour as a peer', it was held that, but for acquiescence at the time, the irregularity would have grounded an order for a new trial.

Witnesses may be sworn either by taking the oath in a lawful form, or by affirming. The rules relating to both were formerly complex, but have happily been simplified and rationalised by the Oaths Act 1978. Both possibilities may now be considered shortly.

12.11.1 Oaths

By s. 1(1) of the Oaths Act 1978, any oath may be administered and taken by the witness holding the book in his uplifted hand, and repeating the words of the oath prescribed by law (81). S. 1(2) goes on to provide that the oath shall be administered in this manner, unless the witness voluntarily objects thereto, or is physically incapable of taking the oath in the prescribed way. This is a significant provision, in that it places the onus on the

---

79 (DC) [1912] KB 362.
80 (1852) 2 ICLR 253.
81 The forms of oath were at one time diverse. In 1927, the judges of the King's Bench Division approved by resolution the following form for all civil and criminal proceedings in the courts over which they presided, and it has now passed into universal usage: 'I swear by Almighty God that the evidence I shall give shall be the truth, the whole ruth and nothing but the truth.'

witness to notify the court of any objection which he may have to being sworn in the prescribed manner, except in the case of physical incapacity. Formerly, the witness was asked his religion, and if, being neither a Christian nor a Jew, it was inappropriate to swear him on the New or Old Testament, the court embarked of its own motion upon an inquiry to find a suitable book, or determine whether the witness should affirm. If no objection is made, it now follows from s. 1 that the witness has been lawfully sworn.

The Act does, however, provide fully for proper objections by witnesses, and clearly it is right that a witness should be sworn in a manner which he regards as binding, wherever this may be done without undue delay or inconvenience. By s. 1(3) of the Act: 'In the case of a person who is neither a Christian nor a Jew, the oath shall be administered in any lawful manner.'

The 'lawful manners' referred to are various (82), and have grown up haphazardly over a period of time. Members of non-Christian religions (other than Jews) are permitted to be sworn upon a book regarded in their religion as holy, although the appropriateness of holy books has been judged, not always accurately, by the law's view of the dictates of witnesses' beliefs. There are special forms of oath appropriate to Quakers and Moravians. The ancient practice of swearing by kissing the Testament is permitted, while the Scots practice of swearing by the uplifted hand is specifically preserved as a lawful form by s. 3 of the Act.

12.11.2 Affirmations
By the Oaths Act 1978, s. 5:

(1) Any person who objects to being sworn shall be permitted to make his solemn affirmation instead of taking the oath. [(83).] . . .

(4) A solemn affirmation shall be of the same force and effect as an oath.

The section has the welcome result that any witness may choose to affirm, as a voluntary alternative to being sworn. Previously, the judge was required to be satisfied after inquiry, either that the witness had no religious belief, or that being sworn would be contrary to his religious belief, although the letter of the law was frequently ignored in practice.

In addition to those who object to being sworn, a person may be permitted to affirm if 'it is not reasonably practicable without inconvenience or delay to administer an oath in the manner appropriate to his religious belief' (s. 5(2)). This provision is designed to cater for oaths of an unusual nature which might find the court administration unprepared and ill-equipped. It happens that witnesses occasionally insist upon some form of unusual oath, for the purpose of embarrassing the court, or of seeking to avoid giving evidence, and in order to meet this possibility, s. 5(2) is made enforceable by s. 5(3): 'A person who may be permitted under subsection (2) . . . to make his solemn affirmation may also be required to do so.'

82   There is a fascinating compendium to be found in Phipson, *Evidence*, 12th ed., paras. 1519–22.
83   The form of affirmation, which was provided by the Oaths Act 1888, s. 2 (now the Oaths Act 1978, s. 6(1)), is as follows: 'I [full name] do solemnly, sincerely, and truly declare and affirm that the evidence I shall give shall be the truth, the whole truth and nothing but the truth.'

12.12   Effect of oaths and affirmations

In *R* v *Hayes* (84) the Court of Appeal observed that it would be unrealistic to suppose that in contemporary society, the divine sanction of an oath was generally recognised. The case was concerned with child witnesses, but the observation was directed also to adults and it can hardly be denied that more temporal sanctions probably have more effect in ensuring, so far as it can be ensured, that witnesses are under some influence to speak the truth.

The Oaths Act 1978 recognises the trend by implication, by providing that the formal taking of the oath in court is to be the binding and effective act, for legal purposes, rather than the belief or conscience which may or may not lie behind the oath in the case of any individual witness. In other words, a witness is not to be permitted to escape the consequences of having been sworn simply by claiming subsequently that the oath was not such as to bind him, having regard to his beliefs. S. 4 of the Act provides:

(1) In any case in which an oath may lawfully be and has been administered to any person, if it has been administered in a form and manner other than that prescribed by law, he is bound by it if it has been administered in such form and with such ceremonies as he may have declared to be binding.

(2) Where an oath has been duly administered and taken, the fact that the person to whom it was administered had, at the time of taking it, no religious belief, shall not for any purpose affect the validity of the oath.

The real sanction against false evidence given on oath is, of course, prosecution for perjury. By s. 1 of the Perjury Act 1911, perjury in a judicial proceeding is committed: 'If any person lawfully sworn as a witness... in a judicial proceeding wilfully makes a statement material in that proceeding, which he knows to be false or does not believe to be true' (85). The importance of the lawful swearing of witnesses is clearly apparent, because this offence, providing the sanction, cannot be committed otherwise. But it would be sufficient if the oath were taken in the circumstances envisaged by s. 4 of the Oaths Act 1978, and because, by s. 5(4) of the 1978 Act, an affirmation is 'of the same force and effect as an oath', false evidence on affirmation falls within the scope of perjury.

12.13   Minor exceptions to the requirement of sworn evidence

We must give some little attention to the major problem of unsworn statements from the dock in criminal cases, but it will be convenient first to notice some less important cases in which evidence may be received unsworn, and one case, the evidence of children, of greater importance, to which reference has already been made.

(a) The evidence of children of tender years may be received unsworn, where the provisions of s. 38(1) of the Children and Young Persons Act 1933 apply: see 12.8, ante.
(b) The evidence of a witness called merely to produce a document may be received

---

84   [1977] 1 WLR 234. And see para. 12.8, ante.
85   As to the law concerning perjury generally, see Archbold, 40th ed., para. 3501 et seq.

unsworn, provided that the document can be identified, or its identity is not in dispute (86).

(c) Where a judge or counsel is asked to explain some aspect of a case in which he has been judicially or professionally engaged, he may appear and speak unsworn from his proper place in court (87).

(d) On licensing applications, evidence may be received unsworn, although the court may refuse to accept unsworn evidence, if the application is opposed (88).

12.14 Unsworn statements from the dock

Unsworn statements made from the dock by the defendant in a criminal case have traditionally been regarded as an exception to the requirement of sworn evidence, although this is rather misleading because such statements are not really 'evidence' in the true sense. The right of a defendant to make an unsworn statement grew up in the course of the nineteenth century, in order to compensate for his inability to give evidence in his defence (before 1898), and for his inability, in cases of felony, to be represented by counsel (before 1836) (89). The rule evolved that the defendant might put his case to the jury in his own words without being liable to cross-examination, and it seems to have been analogous to counsel's closing speech, rather than to the giving of evidence. However, it has come to occupy a position in the order of trial which aligns it procedurally with the giving of evidence, namely as part of the case of the defendant in question, before the speeches of counsel. When the disabilities of the defendant were at length removed, it would have been logical, and probably wise, to abolish the practice as obsolete, at least in the case of a represented defendant. No doubt out of considerations of fairness to the defence, this was not done, and indeed the Criminal Evidence Act 1898, s. 1 proviso (*h*) specifically provided that: 'Nothing in this Act shall affect ... any right of the person charged to make a statement without being sworn.'

The result is that the right survives and coexists uneasily with both the right to give evidence on oath and with the speech to the jury by counsel for the defence (90). The unsworn statement is, in practice, an alternative to evidence on oath by the defendant, and is often resorted to where the defendant does not wish to be subjected to cross-examination. Formidable problems have arisen with regard to the status of unsworn statements in modern criminal practice, and in particular to the way in which the jury should be directed to treat them.

In *R* v *Shimmin* (91) a pre-1898 case, Cave J had held that the effect of an unsworn statement was essentially a matter of 'weight', and was 'entitled to such considerations as the jury might think it deserved'. The formulation suggested that the statement had at least some evidential value, in that 'weight' is a term associated with the evaluation of evidence. The confusion was not relieved by the subsequent observation in *R* v *Dunn*; *R* v *O'Sullivan* (92) that the statement must be 'relevant' to the issues in the case, or by that

86   *Perry* v *Gibson* (1834) 1 A & E 48.
87   The practice is one of last resort, for obvious reasons of avoiding embarrassment: see 12.10 and 11.6, ante. The practice of the Court of Appeal, Criminal Division, is now to prefer evidence from counsel on affidavit, where necessary, dealing with his conduct of a case at trial.
88   *R* v *Sharman and Others, ex parte Denton* (DC) [1898] 1 QB 578.
89   A defendant was from an early date entitled to counsel in cases of misdemeanour, and in cases of treason, after 1695.
90   The statement should be in the defendant's own words, and should not be written by counsel, although there is no objection to counsel advising the defendant on matters of weight and relevance of its contents.
91   (1882) 15 Cox CC 122.   92   (CCA) (1922) 17 Cr App R 12.

in *R* v *Frost*; *R* v *Hale* (93) that it is 'certainly more than mere comment and, in so far as it is stating facts, it is clearly something more and different from comments in counsels' speeches.'

In *R* v *Coughlan* (94) what might have been a useful opportunity to settle the question finally was not fully exploited. M and C were charged with conspiracy. M made an unsworn statement from the dock, while C gave evidence in his defence. The trial judge directed the jury that the statement by M was not evidence in the case, although they were entitled to consider the statement in evaluating the evidence before them. On appeal, C contended that the direction had deprived him of the support which his evidence had received from favourable passages in M's statement. The Court of Appeal, upholding the direction, pointed out that the Criminal Evidence Act 1898 had 'tacitly indicated that something of possible value to the defendant was being retained', and went on to make the following observations:

(a) What was said in an unsworn statement was not to be 'altogether brushed aside', but was of 'persuasive rather than evidential value'.

(b) An unsworn statement could not prove facts not otherwise proved by evidence, but 'might show the evidence in a different light'.

(c) The jury should, therefore, be directed to consider the statement in relation to the evidence as a whole. They need not be told that the statement is evidence in the strict sense, but they should be told that it had 'less cogency' than sworn evidence.

The court refused leave to appeal, as subsequently did the House of Lords, on the basis of the following question certified by the Court of Appeal as being one of general public importance: 'Is an unsworn statement from the dock by an accused in accordance with s. 1(*h*) of the 1898 Act part of the evidence upon which the jury has to found its verdict in the case?'

The question has still not finally received an answer, and the judgment in *Coughlan* failed to decide categorically between what may be termed the 'persuasive' and 'evidential' schools. It is submitted that the true nature of the statement is persuasive, as the tenor of *Coughlan* suggests. The effect of an unsworn statement on the case for a co-defendant throws the problem into a sharp focus, and makes it one of some urgency. It would seem that the Court of Appeal has decided that the statement cannot of itself prove relevant facts. In *R* v *George* (95) G and H were charged with murder. After G had closed his case, H made an unsworn statement, in which he said that G was wholly responsible for the offence. G appealed against his conviction, relying on the refusal of the trial judge to allow him to call evidence in rebuttal of this statement, to the effect that H had, during an adjournment of the trial, said that he was prepared to withdraw it. The Court of Appeal dismissed the appeal, holding that H's statement was not evidence against G, and should be treated in the same way as an out-of-court statement, which would have been inadmissible hearsay against G. With respect, the comparison is not a happy one. It is one thing to direct the jury that what A says to the police out of court is evidence against A, but not against B who is implicated by it; it is quite another to direct them so to regard what A says to them, albeit not on oath, when conducting his case in court. Nonetheless, it is submitted that it is a sound principle that an unsworn statement should not be

93   (CCA) (1964) 48 Cr App R 284.
94   (CA) (1976) 64 Cr App R 11.
95   (1978) 68 Cr App R 210.

capable of being evidence against a co-defendant.

It is submitted that the question should be definitively decided. if the right to make unsworn statements is to remain part of the practice in criminal trials. But it would seem preferable to abrogate the right as obsolete and unnecessary, except perhaps where a defendant is unrepresented.

The immunity of the defendant from cross-examination on an unsworn statement is complete, even where he implicates a co-defendant in the offence charged, or makes imputations on the character of the prosecutor or a witness for the prosecution. However, the Court of Appeal has been prepared to hold that, where the defendant makes an assertion about his good character in the course of an unsworn statement, the prosecution may lead evidence in rebuttal of what is said (96). Whether there are any other circumstances in which rebuttal evidence may be tendered in response to an unsworn statement is unclear, but on the authority of *George*, it appears unlikely.

12.15   Questions for counsel

1 In what circumstances might Coke and Littleton be competent witnesses (a) for the prosecution; (b) in their own defence; (c) for each other? Would they be compellable in any such case?

2 In what circumstances may Mrs Littleton be a competent witness (a) for the prosecution; (b) for her husband; (c) for Coke? Will she be compellable in any such case?

3 How should the competence of Angela Blackstone as a witness be determined? What options are open to the court with regard to her evidence, and what are their advantages or disadvantages to the prosecution and defence respectively?

4 If after Coke has given evidence in his defence, Littleton makes an unsworn statement from the dock implicating Coke in the rape of Margaret Blackstone, how should the jury be directed about it?

96   *R v Campbell; R v Lear; R v Nicholls* (CA) (1978) 69 Cr App R 221.

13 Examination in Chief

13.1 Nature and conduct of examination in chief

Examination in chief is the process whereby a party, who has called a witness to give evidence on his behalf, elicits from that witness evidence relevant to the issues and favourable to the examiner's case. The examination can be conducted safely only on the basis of a signed proof of evidence supplied by the witness, dealing with the matters on which he can speak, but of course the examination need not be confined to the contents of the proof, and may range over any matters relevant to the issues which transpire to be within the competence of the witness. The proof of evidence should be taken by a solicitor, since it is improper in general for counsel to interview a witness, other than an expert (1). In a criminal case, examination in chief of the prosecution witnesses is conducted on the basis of, but is not restricted to, the contents of the deposition made by the witness.

With the exception of the parties themselves, and of expert witnesses, who are never excluded from court, the judge may require that a witness withdraw from court until called to give evidence. In criminal cases, this is the general rule for all witnesses, although the police officer in charge of the case is usually permitted to remain in court, at least until the start of police evidence, in the absence of any specific objection to his presence. In civil cases, the witnesses are usually present, unless specifically ordered to withdraw upon the application of any party. The matter is one for the discretion of the judge, and no question of natural justice is involved. If a witness deliberately remains in court after being ordered to leave, his evidence may not be admitted, but a judge has no discretion to exclude evidence on the sole ground that the witness has been present in court before giving evidence (2).

It is important that evidence in chief should be given in the words of the witness, not those of the examiner, and consequently leading questions are not permitted (3). A leading question is one which puts words into the witness's mouth, or suggests directly the answer which the examiner expects of him (4). It is, however, permissible to lead the witness on the following matters:

---

1 The Senate of the Inns of Court and the Bar has now recognised that in cases in a magistrates court, where counsel is not attended by a solicitor, it may be necessary and permissible for counsel to take a proof of evidence.
2 See generally *Moore* v *Registrar of Lambeth County Court* (CA) [1969] 1 WLR 141; *R* v *Briggs* (CCA) (1930) 22 Cr App R 68; *Tomlinson* v *Tomlinson* [1980] 1 WLR 323.
3 Evidence elicited in chief by leading questions appears not to be inadmissible, but its weight is often very slight: *Moor* v *Moor* (CA) [1954] 1 WLR 927.
4 The avoidance of leading questions is not an easy technique to acquire. If, for example, it is sought to elicit that Littleton touched Angela Blackstone on the leg, it would be leading to ask: 'Did he touch you on the leg?' or even: 'Did he touch you?' The proper way would be: Q: 'Did Littleton do anything to you?' A: 'Yes.' Q: 'What was that?' or some formula to the same effect.

(a)   On preliminary matters, preparatory to questions about the facts in issue. It is usual, for example to lead the witness's name and address (5).

(b)   On any matters which are not in dispute.

(c)   Where a witness is called to deal with some fact already in evidence, he may be asked directly about that fact.

(d)   Where leave has been granted to treat the witness as hostile: see 13.4, post.

(e)   By agreement between all concerned. It is common and good practice for an advocate to indicate to his opponent over what area the opponent may lead a given witness without objection.

Every witness called is required to identify himself to the court by giving his name and address. In a case where disclosure of the name and address of the witness might endanger the witness, or where it is necessary to the proper administration of justice, the judge has power to allow the details to be written down (6). There are statutory provisions to ensure the anonymity of complainants and defendants in rape offences, and of children and young persons in proceedings of any kind (7).

The detailed procedural considerations of the calling of evidence are outside the scope of this work, and reference should be made to texts dealing with procedure. There are, however, three important matters of evidential significance, which arise commonly in the course of evidence in chief, and which must be treated in some depth. These are:

(a)   The use by witnesses of documents to refresh the memory, while giving evidence.

(b)   The admissibility of previous consistent, or self-serving statements made by the witness.

(c)   The treatment of adverse and hostile witnesses.

13.2   Refreshing the memory

All too often, a considerable time elapses between the occurrence of events relevant to proceedings, and the trial of the proceedings themselves. It would be unrealistic to expect that a witness will always be able to give accurate and reliable evidence about events unless he is able to refresh his memory by looking at some note or document. This is true particularly of witnesses such as police officers, who have to give evidence in many different cases. On the other hand, a document cannot refresh the memory accurately unless its own accuracy can be vouched for, a factor which in effect dictates the making of the document as soon as possible after the events with which it deals.

The rule is that a witness may, while giving evidence, refresh his memory by reference to any document which was (a) made or verified by the witness, (b) contemporaneously with the events to which it relates. These limitations on the origin of the documents which may be referred to are treated seriously, and before a witness is permitted to refer, an application must be made to the judge, who should inquire of the witness whether the conditions are satisfied. The judge should satisfy himself of this, whether or not any objection is taken, and if the conditions are not fulfilled, should not allow the reference; if they are fulfilled, the witness is entitled to refer (8).

It is worth emphasising that the conditions of reference apply only to the use by the

5   Unless the address is in itself relevant, e.g., to the question of jurisdiction in a divorce case.
6   *R* v *The Socialist Worker Printers & Publishers Ltd and Another, ex parte Attorney-General* (DC) [1975] QB 637.
7   See the Sexual Offences (Amendment) Act 1976 s. 4 and s. 6; Children and Young Persons Act 1933, s. 39.
8   The question is one for the judge rather than the other side, although cross-examination on the origin of the document is often permitted.

witness of the document to refresh his memory while giving evidence in the witness-box. Before giving evidence, there is nothing to prevent a proposed witness from looking at any document available to him, whatever its origin. In *R* v *Richardson* (9) it was argued that it was improper for a witness to look, outside court, at a document which could not be used in court because of its lack of contemporaneity, in this case a statement made to the police some time after the event. The Court of Appeal rejected the argument. Quite apart from the apparent reasonableness of the principle that any witness, whether for the prosecution or the defence, ought not to be denied access to a statement made by him for the purpose of the proceedings, to seek to deny such access would create a highly artificial situation. The court pointed out that the view contended for would tend to turn the giving of evidence into a test more of memory than reliability; that it would do nothing to deter the dishonest witness, because it would be effectively unenforceable, but it would place substantial difficulties in the way of an honest and conscientious witness. It is, therefore, perfectly proper, not only for a witness to look at his statement or proof of evidence outside court before giving evidence, but also for counsel to take steps to see that the witnesses on his side have access to such documents as will help them, and it seems that this should be done in a case where lapse of time may otherwise mar the evidence of a witness. Opinion differs on whether counsel has any duty to inform his opponent when his witnesses have, to his knowledge, seen their statements, but there appears to be no rule of law to this effect; such a course is desirable, because the weight to be attached to the evidence of the witness may well be affected (10).

In whatever way the witness may assist his recollection before giving evidence, once he enters the witness-box, he must observe the far narrower rules and be subject to the judge's ruling. We may now consider in more detail, firstly the conditions of reference to and secondly, the treatment of memory-refreshing documents including such evidential value as they may have.

13.2.1 Qualities of memory-refreshing documents

13.2.1.1 Made or verified by the witness. The best and most reliable memory refresher is a note made at the time of the events referred to, and compiled for the express purpose of subsequent use in the witness-box. The archetype is, of course, the police officer's notebook. However, the requirement of law does not go so far. There is no rule that the document must have been compiled for any particular purpose. It need not even be in the handwriting of the witness, or made by him personally; but he must at least have verified it, that is to say that he must have seen the document while it was being compiled by another (or soon enough afterwards to make his verification contemporaneous: see 13.2.1.2, post), he must have checked its contents at that time and acknowledged them to be accurate, while the events were still fresh in his memory. It is preferable that he should have recorded his verification, for example by signing the document. This is not a legal requirement, but renders more likely the judge's finding that the witness is entitled to refer. A good illustration of the making and verification of a document is *Anderson* v *Whalley* (11) in which a ship's log-book, kept by the mate and later checked and authenticated by the captain, was said to be a document from which either was entitled to refresh his memory.

9 [1971] 2 QB 484.
10 *Worley* v *Bentley* (DC) [1976] 2 All ER 449; *R* v *Westwell* (CA) [1976] 2 All ER 812. If there is any such duty, it is evidently one founded in professional etiquette, and no more. The safe course for any advocate is probably to assume that his opponent's witnesses have seen their statements or proofs outside court.
11 (1852) 3 Car & Kir 54.

A memory-refreshing document is not required to be in any particular form, as long as it complies with the conditions. A witness may, therefore, make a document in any convenient form. In *R* v *Mills; R* v *Rose* (12) a police officer was allowed to refresh his memory from a note which was, in effect, a partial transcription of a tape-recording of incriminating conversations which took place between the defendants while in custody at the police station. The tape-recording itself was not used in evidence, but the officer was able, relying partly on his own recollection and partly on the note, to give evidence of what was said in the conversation. Quite apart from the admissibility of the tape-recording as such, as a piece of real evidence, there is similarly no reason why D/I Glanvil should not give evidence from any contemporaneous note made by him from the recording of the conversation between Littleton and his wife. Because there is no requirement of form, a statement made to the police may be referred to, if it satisfies the requirement of contemporaneity.

The making and verification of a document or note is proper and sufficient if effected by two or more witnesses pooling their recollections, in order to produce the best possible record of the events. This is a standard practice of police officers and was specifically approved in *R* v *Bass* (13) as being the most efficient method of producing an accurate memory refresher. When delivering the judgment of the Court of Criminal Appeal, Byrne J said:

> This court has observed that police officers nearly always deny that they have col-
> laborated in the making of notes, and we cannot help wondering why they are the only
> class of society who do not collaborate in such a matter.

The judge went on to observe that such collaboration was the most natural and best explanation for two identical notebooks made by officers dealing with the same events, a phenomenon which is, from time to time, treated with some suspicion in cross-examination of the officers. The practice of collaboration is natural and useful. To seek to forbid it would not deter the dishonest witness, but would place unnecessary difficulties in the way of the honest and conscientious. It matters not at all whether the result of the collaboration is the production of two or more notes made by the witnesses individually, or one note made physically by one witness and verified by the others. Each is entitled to refer to the note which he has either made or verified. It would, therefore, be natural, rather than surprising, if at the trial of Coke and Littleton, the notebooks of D/I Glanvil and D/S Bracton are identical in their treatment of events which both officers witnessed. Since the officers would make use of their notebooks to make their witness statements, the same observation applies equally to the statements.

13.2.1.2   Contemporaneous with the events to which it relates.   The requirement of contemporaneity is the safest means of vouching for, at least, the substantial accuracy of the document. The word 'contemporaneous' is not, of course to be applied literally in every case, as many events provide no opportunity for a note to be made as they actually occur. In some instances, this is feasible, for example where a police officer makes a note during an interview taking place between the defendant and another officer, but in general the word is given an extended meaning, in order to make the rule workable in practice.

In order to be contemporaneous with the events to which it relates, a document will in practice probably have been made at the first practicable opportunity, but the rule of law is that if not made literally contemporaneously, it must certainly have been made while the events are still fresh in the mind of the witness. In *Richardson,* the Court of Appeal commented that 'this definition does provide a measure of elasticity and should not be taken to confine witnesses to an over-short period'. There is no set time beyond which a document cannot be a contemporaneous record; it is a matter of fact and degree for the judge in every case (14). In *R* v *Langton* (15), the defendant had compiled a document over a period of a fortnight, on the basis of which a witness had paid over sums of money to workmen at the end of the fortnight. The witness was allowed to look at the document in order to refresh his memory about what sums he had paid. But the longer the period, the less the likelihood that the court will accept that the document is within the rule (16).

The older rule was that the original contemporaneous document should be referred to, if in existence, and that where the witness had no independent recollection of the events and so was dependent upon being permitted to refresh his memory, the original alone might be used unless any copy available was itself contemporaneous (17). However, in modern practice, there would seem to be no reason why a later copy should not be referred to, provided that it can be shown to be a true copy of the contemporaneous original. It would appear unnecessary and pedantic to apply to memory refreshers the rules relating to strict proof of the contents of documents as evidence in their own right. The question is of importance in the not uncommon circumstances which arose in *R* v *Cheng* (18). The defendant was arrested in February 1972 but subsequently absconded. The trial did not take place until March 1975 and in the intervening period of time, the police officer's notebook had been lost. The officer was allowed to refresh his memory by reference to his witness statement, upon it being shown to the court's satisfaction, firstly that the original (lost) notebook had been contemporaneous, and secondly, that the officer had made his statement by copying the relevant part of his notes. And where an officer makes, contemporaneously, rough notes of an interview, which he shortly afterwards incorporates into a full note, expanding them with the aid of his recollection, he should be allowed to refresh his memory from the full note, and not just from the rough, even though the contents of the two are not identical (19). It would be possible to extract from these cases the principle that where a contemporaneous original is made, the witness should be permitted to refresh his memory from a newer copy of, or derivation from, the original, provided that the copy or derivation is compiled exclusively from the contents of the original, the actual and fresh recollection of the witness, or a combination of the two.

13.2.2 *Treatment of memory-refreshing documents*
Reference by a witness to a document while giving evidence may have one of two results. It may revive or refresh his memory, so as to enable him to give oral evidence, from his refreshed recollection, of what he actually perceived or did. On the other hand, it may be that the memory of the witness is not assisted, and that consequently, he is unable to do more than say, 'I do not remember. But I can say that the document was made at the

14   *R* v *Simmonds* (CA) [1969] 1 QB 685; *R* v *Richardson* (ante).
15   (CCR) (1876) 2 QBD 296.
16   The matter is one very much for the discretion of the trial judge. Though periods much longer than *Langton* would be unlikely to satisfy the rule, there will always be exceptional cases, where the events will be assumed to have been fresh enough. In *R* v *Fotheringham* (CA) [1975] Crim LR 710, a witness who was an accomplice was allowed to refer to his statement to the police made some twenty-two days after the event. This must surely be close to the outer limit of the rule.
17   *R* v *Harvey* (1869) 11 Cox CC 546.   18   (1976) 63 Cr App R 20.
19   *Attorney-General's Reference (No. 3 of 1979)* (CA) (1979) 69 Cr App R 411.

time, and that it is accurate.' It is vital to observe that, at the outset, a document used to refresh the memory is not evidence. Indeed, it will frequently, if not usually, be inadmissible hearsay, unless in a civil case it might be admitted under Part 1 of the Civil Evidence Act 1968. What is evidence is what the witness states from the witness-box by way of giving oral evidence (20). Nonetheless, a memory-refreshing document may attain some evidential status, depending on the course taken in cross-examination, since cross-examination may lend relevance to and thus render admissible a piece of evidence, which would not otherwise have been admissible as part of the case of the party calling a witness.

The opposing party is entitled to inspect a document used by a witness, while in the witness-box, for the purpose of refreshing his memory (21). The opposing party may further cross-examine the witness with regard to any part of the document used by the witness to refresh his memory, without making the document evidence for the party calling the witness (22). If, however, cross-examination takes place on other parts of the document, the rule is that the party calling the witness is entitled to put the document in evidence as part of his case (23). The reason is that matters falling outside the use of the document as a memory refresher have been raised, and the jury are entitled to see the subject-matter of the cross-examination; whereas cross-examination restricted to the portions referred to by the witness amounts to no more than questioning on his oral evidence.

The putting of the document in evidence, where this occurs, involves its production for the inspection of the jury, or other tribunal of fact. The jury must, therefore, be directed as to the evidential use which they are entitled to make of the document, and its relationship to the oral evidence given by the witness. Here there is a manifest divergence between the rule at common law, which continues to govern criminal cases, and the provisions of the Civil Evidence Act 1968 which have deliberately modified the position in civil cases (24).

At common law, where a memory-refreshing document is put in evidence, it is evidence only of the consistency of the witness, and goes only to his credit. In *R* v *Virgo* (25) the conviction was quashed where the trial judge directed the jury, by necessary implication, that the diary of a prosecution witness, used by the witness to refresh his memory, could be regarded as evidence of the truth of the facts contained in it. The witness had been cross-examined extensively on the document in a way which clearly justified the putting of it in evidence, on the issue of the credit of the witness, which was the subject of the cross-examination; but it could have no other evidential value, and the jury were to try the case on the evidence before them, including the oral evidence of the witness. The point is that the jury's assessment of the weight to be accorded to the evidence may be affected by its consistency with the document.

---

20   Thus there is no objection to a witness reading from a contemporaneous note when he himself has failed to recollect the incident concerned. However, evidence of that kind is unlikely to carry much weight.
21   *Burgess* v *Bennett* (1872) 20 WR 720. The inspection must be confined to matters relevant to the case, though it need not be confined to the parts used by the witness to refresh his memory. It is undecided whether the opponent may call for a document that the witness has admitted looking at outside court but has not used while giving evidence. The question has been answered in the negative in Scotland: *Hinshelwood* v *Auld* 1926 SC(J) 4, but Archbold, 40th ed., para. 531 doubts whether the same view would prevail in England.
22   This should not be confused with the rule that calling in cross-examination for a document in the possession of the opponent (not one used as a memory refresher) involves putting the document in evidence if called upon to do so. See 14.8 post. Contrast *Senat* v *Senat* [1965] P 172 with *Stroud* v *Stroud* [1965] 1 WLR 1080.
23   *Gregory* v *Tavernor* (NP) (1833) 6 C & P 280; *Senat* v *Senat* [1965] P 172.
24   This is not the only instance of the divergence of the 1968 Act from the rules of common law. See, e.g., s. 3 and s. 7, and 14.6 and 14.11, post.
25   (1978) 67 Cr App R 323.

In civil cases, the position is governed by s. 3(2) of the Civil Evidence Act 1968 which is in the following terms:

> Nothing in this Act shall affect any of the rules of law relating to the circumstances in which, where a person called as a witness in any civil proceedings is cross-examined on a document used by him to refresh his memory, that document may be made evidence in those proceedings; and where a document or any part of a document is received in evidence in any such proceedings by virtue of any such rule of law, any statement made in that document or part by the person using the document to refresh his memory shall by virtue of this subsection be admissible as evidence of any fact stated therein of which direct oral evidence by him would be admissible.

The provision is part of the overall structure of part 1 of the Act, dealt with in detail in Chapter 8, ante, the object of which is to transfer the emphasis of the rules of evidence from questions of admissibility to those of weight. It follows that in a civil case, the judge may always consider a memory-refreshing document as evidence of the facts contained therein, provided that oral evidence by the witness would be admissible of such facts by virtue of the rules of evidence generally. He may act on the facts revealed by the document for any proper purpose, although clearly it is not in every case that a memory-refreshing document would command that degree of weight. The judge may, of course, also use the document for the purpose of assessing the credit of the witness, but is not confined to this use of it, as would be the position at common law.

13.3 Previous consistent or self-serving statements

At common law, a witness may not give evidence that he has, on a previous occasion, made a statement consistent with his present evidence. Variously called the rule against previous consistent statements, the rule against self-serving statements and the rule against narrative, the rule is soundly based on the proposition that such a statement can have no improving effect on the evidence of the witness given on oath in court. Such statements are also objectionable as hearsay. At common law, they are excluded, subject to reasoned exceptions, as evidence of consistency as they are as evidence of the truth of the facts stated.

Thus, in *R v Roberts* (26) where the defendant was charged with murder, he was not permitted to state in evidence that two days after the killing, he had told his father that his defence would be one of accident, as it indeed was at the trial. The rule applies to statements in any form, including what might be termed indirect statements by conduct. In *Corke v Corke and Cook* (27), a suit for divorce, the wife and co-respondent, who had been found together in compromising circumstances, but had denied adultery, were not permitted to give evidence that they had telephoned a doctor to ask for a medical examination (which did not take place), with a view to confirming their denial of adultery.

Before coming to the exceptional cases at common law, it will be convenient to observe that in this instance too, the Civil Evidence Act 1968 has radically altered the position in relation to civil cases. By s. 2(1):

---

26 (CCA) [1942] 1 All ER 187.
27 (CA) [1958] P 93.

In any civil proceedings a statement made, whether orally or in a document or otherwise, by any person, whether called as a witness in those proceedings or not, shall . . . be admissible as evidence of any fact stated therein of which direct oral evidence by him would be admissible.

This appears to be quite wide enough to include previous consistent statements, and is generally accepted as having this effect (28). Such evidence will be subject to the provisions of s. 2(2), relating to cases where the maker of a hearsay statement proposed to be tendered in evidence is called as a witness; so that the leave of the court will be required before evidence may be given of the previous consistent statement, and such evidence shall not be given before the conclusion of the evidence in chief of the witness, except in the cases stipulated by s. 2(2)(*b*)(i) and (ii). Such statements, where admitted, are by virtue of the section, evidence of the truth of the facts stated therein, provided that oral evidence by the witness would be admissible of such facts under the general rules of evidence. In many cases, if not the great majority, the admission of a previous consistent statement made by a witness called to give oral evidence will be of no, or no appreciable, value to a party. In such a case, the judge may refuse to leave under s. 2(2), or treat the evidence as having some, probably slight, value as showing consistency and thus going to credit. But there are cases, for example those corresponding to the common-law exceptions by virtue of which they are admitted under the res gestae rule or to rebut a suggestion of recent fabrication, where a previous consistent statement may be of substantial value; so too where the recollection of the witness may legitimately be supposed to have suffered since the making of the statement, by reason of lapse of time, illness or some other such cause.

By s. 6(4) of the Act, a previous consistent statement admitted under s. 2 is incapable of corroborating the evidence of the maker. This result would also follow at common law, because of the absence of the essential requirement of an independent source (29).

At common law, previous consistent statements are admissible in the following exceptional cases, each of which, happily, may be justified by circumstances which lend to the statement a relevance which ordinarily, it would not enjoy (30). As we have seen, in the ordinary case, a witness's story is not enhanced by the fact that it has been rehearsed out of court, prior to being given in evidence. The common law rules are still in full force in criminal cases. The exceptions, which are considered in detail either here, or in an appropriate place in another chapter, are:

(a) Where a statement is admissible by virtue of the res gestae rule.

(b) Where a wholly or partially self-serving statement is made by the defendant, in relation to an offence charged, when questioned about the offence.

(c) Where a witness gives evidence of a previous identification of the defendant.

(d) Where a statement is admissible as a recent complaint in a sexual case.

(e) Where a statement is admissible to rebut a suggestion of recent fabrication.

---

28 Phipson (12th ed., para. 643) contends that s. 2 does not render admissible statements implied by conduct, as in *Corke* v *Corke and Cook* [1958] P 93. But the words 'orally or in a document or otherwise' do not, it is submitted, in themselves exclude the possibility, and admission is more in keeping with the policy of the Act.

29 See 15.4, post.

30 No writer on the subject of previous consistent statements can fail to acknowledge his indebtedness to the seminal article on the subject by Mr R. N. Gooderson [1968] CLJ 64, which explores perceptively the various cases of admissibility at common law.

13.3.1 Statements admissible under the res gestae rule

The res gestae rule is one of the common-law exceptions to the rule against hearsay, and in effect allows evidence, otherwise objectionable as hearsay, to be given, where a statement is an integral part of the transaction to which it relates, and so ought to be given in evidence, so as to invest the evidence of the transaction with a completeness, in the absence of which the evidence might be ambiguous or misleading. The normal case is of a spontaneous statement made contemporaneously with the transaction by a partici- pant or bystander. Habitually, therefore, the rule operates to admit what are in reality previous consistent statements, although they are also often given in evidence by other witnesses, who heard them being made. The subject of the res gestae rule is considered in detail in 6.6, ante.

13.3.2 Statements made by the defendant when questioned about the offence

Statements made by the defendant, concerning the offence charged, in response to questioning, occasion great difficulty. Such statements occupy, in their own right, the entirety of Chapter 7. The defendant may, of course, admit the offence charged; conversely, he may deny it in a manner consistent with his defence at trial, in which case the statement which he makes is self-serving within the meaning of the present rule. Very frequently, he makes a statement, which the jury may regard as partly incriminating and partly self-serving. It seems that, with the exception of statements of a self-serving nature made with the express intention of ensuring their inclusion in the evidence given for the prosecution, by way of 'infiltration' of the prosecution case, the jury ought to hear whatever the defendant may say about the allegation made against him. It is true that the evidential value of a self-serving statement is materially less than that of a confession of guilt or an adverse admission, but at least as a matter of practice designed to ensure fairness to the defendant, his out-of-court statements are admitted in evidence, as evidence of his reaction when charged with the offence and, if he gives evidence to the same effect, as evidence of consistency (31).

13.3.3 Evidence of previous identification

Evidence of identification of the defendant, as the person who committed the offence charged, has been the subject of considerable controversy and anxiety. The danger of conviction on the basis of inaccurate evidence of identification has haunted the courts throughout modern criminal practice, particularly since the case of Adolf Beck, early in the century, and has found recent expression in the guidance provided for cases turning on identification evidence in *R* v *Turnbull* (32). The subject must be approached both from the standpoint of admissibility, and from that of the treatment of identification evidence generally, and with regard to the factors affecting its weight.

13.3.3.1 Admissibility of evidence of previous identification. A witness may, of course, give evidence that he saw the defendant commit the offence charged, or that he saw the defendant in circumstances from which the jury would be entitled to draw that inference. This would be direct evidence implicating the defendant, albeit its treatment must be subject to the guidelines discussed in 13.3.3.2, post. But there are theoretical objections to evidence that the witness, on an occasion subsequent to the commission of the offence, but before giving evidence, made an out-of-court identification of the

---

31　The matter is fully explored in Chapter 7, ante.
32　(CA) [1977] QB 224.

defendant (a 'previous identification'). If given by the person who made the previous
identification, such evidence would appear to be self-serving when tendered in support
of his evidence given at the trial identifying the defendant as the person who committed
the offence. If given by any other person who witnessed the previous identification, for
example a police officer who conducted an identification parade, it is exceptionable as
hearsay. It is no answer to the objection to say that the use made of such evidence might
be limited to that of consistency with the witness's identification evidence at trial.
Nonetheless, there is no doubt that evidence of previous identifications is admissible
both from the identifying witness and, unless the evidence would contradict that of the
identifying witness directly, from another witness who perceived the identification being
made (33). Despite the observation of Lawton LJ in this case, that it would be wrong 'to set
up artificial rules of evidence, which hinder the administration of justice', it is manifest
that the admission of evidence of this kind must be regarded as an exception to the
general rule. It is, however, equally true that the exception is based upon cogent and
important considerations.

Where a question of identification arises, it is obviously in the interests of the
defendant, no less than that of the prosecution, that the matter should be investigated at
the earliest possible moment after the offence, by allowing the prospective witness the
opportunity, under properly controlled conditions, to confirm or repudiate any initial
identification implicating the defendant, who is at that stage a suspect. The longer this
process is delayed, the greater the risk of error, and to wait until trial would almost
always increase that risk to unacceptable proportions. But while these considerations
militate in favour of evidence of previous identifications being received, they do not
assist on the question whether such evidence is to be admitted for the purpose of proving
that the defendant is the person who committed the offence or only for the purpose of
confirming evidence of identification given at the trial. This is a distinction which does
not appear always to have been appreciated in the authorities (34).

In *R* v *Christie* (35) the defendant was charged with indecent assault on a small boy.
Shortly after the alleged offence, the boy, together with his mother and a police officer,
approached the defendant, and the boy said, 'That is the man,' and went on to describe
what had been done to him. The defendant said in reply, 'I am innocent,' and the issue
was one of identification. The boy, giving evidence unsworn, identified the defendant in
court. He was not asked about the identification at the time of the defendant's arrest but
evidence to that effect was elicited from the other witnesses. The House of Lords held
that the evidence was admissible. Although the members of the House were not *ad idem*
in their reasons (36), it is submitted that it is possible to extract from the various speeches
that the evidence of what had taken place out of court was admissible for the purpose of
confirming the evidence of the boy identifying the defendant as the man who had
committed the offence. The objections of Viscount Haldane LC and Lord Moulton seem
to have been based primarily on the failure of the prosecution to elicit the boy's words
from the boy himself, an objection even then disavowed by Lord Atkinson and which
would be unlikely to be heeded in modern times. And Lord Reading held that the
evidence of the prior identification would have been admissible from the boy himself.

33 *R* v *Osbourne; R* v *Virtue* (CA) [1973] 1 QB 678.
34 See Libling, [1977] Crim LR 268 et seq.
35 [1914] AC 545.
36 It is essential to bear in mind that the decision in *Christie* was concerned primarily with the admissibility of
the boy's words as words spoken in the presence of the defendant, having regard to the defendant's reaction to
them. Also that in 1914, the words were not admissible as a recent complaint in a case such as that charged,
whereas they would now certainly be so.

The relevance of the evidence was indeed asserted by Viscount Haldane as being 'to show that the boy was able to identify at the time and to exclude the idea that the identification of the prisoner in the dock was an afterthought or a mistake' (37).

But the proposition that evidence of identification is admissible only for the purpose of confirming the identification made in court can only be tested against decisions in cases where the identifying witness is not available to give evidence at trial, or where such witness is called, but is unable or unwilling to identify the defendant (or anyone) as being the subject of the earlier identification. Although such cases are more properly dealt with as a problem of the rule against hearsay, because the previous identification can hardly be described as self-serving where there is no evidence for it to serve, it is instructive to mention the position here for the assistance it may offer as to the purpose of the admissibility of such evidence generally. In *R* v *Burke and Kelly* (38) a witness had previously identified a man as being one of two who had robbed him two days previously, but was unable at trial to say that the defendant Kelly had been that man. The prosecution were permitted to call a police officer to give evidence that the witness had, on the previous occasion, identified Kelly. This was a case where the witness was able to say that he had identified someone, and another witness was called to supplement that evidence by plugging the gap in the first witness's memory of who had been identified. Even without making the obvious comment on the weight of such evidence (39), the admissibility of the evidence of the police officer seems tenuous. If it was designed merely to confirm that the witness had identified someone, a fact unlikely to be disputed in itself, then no mention of Kelly should have been made. Even if the witness were able to say at trial that, although now unable to say whom he had identified, he was sure that he had been correct at the time, it is difficult to say in what way the evidence of the officer could be said to 'confirm' this. It seems little different from allowing the officer to say, 'The witness told me it was Kelly,' and it is not easy to envisage any court admitting that as evidence of the truth of what the witness had said.

The Court of Appeal was prepared, however, to follow and even extend the principle in *R* v *Osbourne; R* v *Virtue* (40). Both defendants had been picked out on identification parades, the defendant O by Mrs B, and the defendant V by Mrs H. At the trial, both witnesses failed to confirm their previous identification. Mrs B stated that she was unable to remember having picked anyone out, while Mrs H's evidence was so unsatisfactory that it could not properly be regarded as an identification of V in court. Evidence from a police officer was then called for the prosecution, over an objection made on behalf of O, that the witnesses had previously identified O and V respectively. The Court of Appeal upheld the admission of the evidence, holding that the decision in *Christie* justified the rather tersely stated principle that: '. . . evidence of identification other than identification in the witness-box is admissible.' In the case of Mrs H, the matter was probably little different to that of *Burke and Kelly*. In the case of Mrs B, however, it was argued that the evidence of the officer was inadmissible, because it contradicted the evidence of Mrs B, who was not a hostile witness. The argument seems sound in principle, but was rejected on the actual substance of what Mrs B had said. Presumably,

37   Ibid at 551.
38   (1847) 2 Cox CC 295.
39   The weight may not always be open to such comment. As Lawton LJ said in *Osbourne and Virtue*, '. . . if the experience of this court is anything to go by, accused persons often look much smarter in the dock than they do when they are first arrested' [1973] 1 QB 678, at 690.
40   [1973] 1 QB 678. It should be said, in fairness, that the word 'follow' in the text is subject to the observation that the court did not apparently hear any argument based on hearsay, and *Burke and Kelly* was not cited to them.

had she stated, wrongly, that she had picked out someone other than O, the result might have been different. The decision has been much criticised, and it is certainly unfortunate that the hearsay problem of the officer's evidence, and the purposes of its admissibility were not considered (41).

It is submitted that the view taken by the Court of Appeal of *Christie* is simplistic and misleading, and that the true view of it is that evidence of previous identification is permitted, by way of an exception, because if it were not, the administration of justice would suffer the dual perils that the strength of a good identification would seep away with time, and that a bad identification would carry an ever-increasing risk to the defendant, perhaps culminating in an assumption by the witness that his poor memory is somehow confirmed by the mere fact that the defendant is in the dock, charged with the offence. The true rule is surely that evidence of previous identification is to be restricted to the case where a witness is able to give evidence in court of the identity of the offender, and is admissible only for the purpose of confirming the evidence, in which role it has a cogency normally missing from self-serving statements. In addition, it may, subject to the not inconsiderable reservations to *Burke and Kelly* made earlier, be permissible to extend the rule to cases where the witness, although unable to state in evidence whom he identified previously, can say that he identified someone and that he was sure at the time that his identification was correct. As Libling (42) points out, such evidence can be cross-examined on effectively as to accuracy at the time of the previous identification, and is free from the major danger inherent in hearsay evidence. In these cases, *Osbourne and Virtue* is surely correct in holding that evidence may be given by a witness who perceived the previous identification being made.

It may be doubted whether, in practice, a jury may be expected to exhibit any reaction to evidence of previous identification, other than to say, 'It must be the right man,' and certainly very careful guidance is required, if any extension to the original rule is to be contemplated. It is submitted that the following words, taken from the speech of Lord Moulton in *Christie* (43), are as forceful now as when they were first uttered:

> Identification is an act of the mind, and the primary evidence of what was passing in the mind of a man is his own testimony, where it can be obtained. It would be very dangerous to allow evidence to be given of a man's words and actions, in order to show by this extrinsic evidence that he identified the prisoner, if he was capable of being called as a witness and was not called to prove by direct evidence that he had thus identified him.

13.3.3.2   Treatment of identification evidence.   Admissibility is only the first facet of evidence of identification, and has probably given rise to less concern than the vexed question of the weight and reliability of such evidence. Periodically, cases where some miscarriage of justice appears to have occurred because of mistaken evidence of identification reopen the problems of trying to ensure the detection of faulty evidence in a field more open to error than most. In *R* v *Turnbull* (44) a five-member Court of Appeal considered four separate appeals against conviction, and laid down guidelines for the

---

41   The court might also have been assisted by the observations of the Privy Council in *Sparks* v *R* [1964] AC 964, in which, dealing with evidence of identification which exculpated the defendant (in that the victim said that her attacker was coloured, while the defendant was white) Lord Morris of Borth-y-Gest said, at 981: 'There is no rule which permits the giving of hearsay evidence merely because it relates to identity.'
42   [1977] Crim LR, p. 277.
43   [1914] AC 545 at 558.
44   [1977] QB 224. Lord Widgery CJ, Roskill and Lawton LJJ, Cusack and May JJ.

treatment of cases which depend wholly or substantially on the correctness of one or more identifications of the defendant. The guidelines were said to 'involve only changes of practice, not law', but the court also emphasised that failure to follow them is likely to lead to a conviction being quashed, and will do so where the failure results in the conviction being regarded by the Court of Appeal as unsafe or unsatisfactory. The guidelines may be summarised as follows:

(a) The judge should always warn the jury of the special need for caution before convicting the accused in reliance upon the correctness of identification evidence, drawing their attention to the possibilities of error.

(b) The judge should invite the attention of the jury to examine closely the circumstances in which the identification was made: the conditions under which and the length of time for which the observation took place. Was the defendant known to the witness, or was there any particular reason why the witness might be expected to remember the defendant? How soon after the event did the witness give a description to the police?

(c) The judge should remind the jury specifically of any weaknesses which have appeared in the identification evidence.

(d) If the prosecution have reason to believe that there is any material discrepancy between the description of the defendant given at first to the police, and his actual appearance, or in any case where the defence so request, they should supply the defence with particulars of the description first supplied to the police.

(e) Where the quality of identification evidence is good, the jury may safely be left to assess it, and may convict on that basis. Conversely, where the quality of the evidence is poor, the judge should withdraw the case from the jury, and direct an acquittal, unless there is other evidence which goes to support the correctness of the identification. The judge should tell the jury what evidence there is which may support the identification (45). In particular, he must direct them that the fact that the defendant elects not to give evidence, cannot of itself support it, although he may, of course, point out that the identification evidence is uncontradicted by evidence from the defendant. Where the defendant puts forward an alibi, a defence which is of course crucial to the correctness of identification evidence, the jury may regard its falsity as supporting the identification, but should only do so if they think that the false alibi was put forward for the purpose of deceiving them, and not, for example out of stupidity or panic.

In addition to the guidelines laid down in *Turnbull* for the treatment of evidence actually before the court, there are rules for the guidance of the police, covering the conduct of identification parades and the use of photographs for the purpose of identifying suspects. The detailed provisions of these rules are outside the scope of the present work (46), but it may be observed that following the report of Lord Devlin's Committee on Evidence of Identification, the Attorney-General, in a written answer to the House of Commons (47), stated that the Director of Public Prosecutions would attach very considerable importance to the proper working of the rules when deciding whether or not to institute proceedings. Moreover, in any committal proceedings or subsequent

45   Such evidence need not amount technically to corroboration; for instance, it need not come from a source independent of the witness. See generally 15.7, post.
46   The rules are contained in Home Office Circular No. 109/1978, set out *in extenso* in Archbold, 40th ed., paras 1351 et seq.
47   Although the answer relates strictly only to cases of which the Director has the conduct, the hope was expressed that other prosecuting authorities would follow his lead, and this seems to have been the case. Hansard, May 27, 1976, Vol. 912. No. 115.

trial, the prosecution would not invite a witness to make a 'dock identification', where the witness had not previously identified the defendant at an identification parade. The importance of this statement of principle is very great, if only because it encourages identification in properly controlled circumstances, and discourages identification by means of a one-to-one 'confrontation' or in court while the defendant is in the dock, because of the danger that the witness will feel that his identification is supported by the presence of a suspect at the police station, or as defendant in the dock (48).

From similar considerations, the Director proposed that in cases where evidence of identification was involved, the identifying witnesses would be called at committal, and that the procedure under s. 1 of the Criminal Justice Act 1967 would not be followed in such cases. By this means it is hoped to evaluate the evidence at an early stage, and allow the presentation of an alibi, if the defence wish to put one forward (49).

13.3.4 Recent complaints in sexual cases

Although it has been stated elsewhere in this chapter that the exceptions to the rule against previous consistent statements are reasoned, it must be confessed that, if ever there was some reasoned basis for the exception about to be discussed, it has become well hidden in the mists of time. Bracton tells us somewhat enigmatically that a woman who complains of rape should 'go to the next town and there make discovery to some credible persons of the injury she has suffered' (50). The reason for this may lie in some early recognition of the undoubted suspicion which fell at common law on a woman who failed to complain within a short time of an outrage done to her, but almost certainly Oliver Wendell Holmes J. is correct in his unkind stigmatisation of the recent complaint as 'a perverted survival of the ancient requirement that a woman should make hue and cry as a preliminary to an appeal of rape' (51).

Whatever its origin, the phenomenon survives into modern law, and fits uneasily into the role of admissible evidence, though any requirement for a complaint as a matter of law has long since perished. The exception is that in sexual cases, evidence may be given by the complainant and by any person to whom the complaint was made, of a complaint made voluntarily, and at the first opportunity reasonably afforded, of the offence. The complaint is admissible only for either of two purposes: (a) to confirm the evidence of the complainant relating to the offence, and/or (b) to rebut or disprove consent on the part of the complainant, if that is an issue in the case.

With regard to the first purpose, it should be noted that a recent complaint, although it may confirm the complainant's evidence, is not capable of corroborating that evidence, and the corroboration which is to be looked for of the complainant's evidence in a sexual case as a matter of practice, must be sought elsewhere. This is because the complaint lacks the necessary element of an independent source (52).

The exception applies only to sexual cases. From the older authorities, it is clear that it was for a long period of history doubtful whether there was a more general application to

48   This principle may be departed from where it is impracticable to hold a proper identification parade, for example because the defendant is of very unusual physical appearance, *R* v *Hunter* (CA) [1969] Crim LR 262, or refuses to attend a parade or to take part, *R* v *John* (CA) [1973] Crim LR 113. The appellate courts have in the past quashed convictions where the method of obtaining identification evidence was irregular and unsafe: *R* v *Cartwright* (CCA) (1914) 10 Cr App R 219.
49   The practice has since been modified because of the pressure on the courts. Now s. 1 may be used by consent and with the approval of the court to avoid inordinate delay or to spare, for example, child witnesses the ordeal of giving evidence twice where the defence do not require it.
50   *De Corona*, b. 3, fol. 147; expounded in Blackstone's Commentaries, vol. 4, c. 15, 211.
51   *Commonwealth* v *Cleary* (1898) 172 Mass 175.
52   See, e.g., *R* v *Lovell* (CCA) (1923) 17 Cr App R 163. See also 15.4, post.

offences of violence, and there were certain cases in which the exception does appear to have been applied. Thus, in *R* v *Wink* (53), a complaint was admitted, apparently under this rule, in a case of robbery. And perhaps on a closer analogy, there was some suggestion that a recent complaint could be admitted in a matrimonial case, to support a charge of cruelty (54). But it must be remembered that recent complaints may at times overlap with statements made in the defendant's presence, with statements admissible under the res gestae rule, and with dying declarations, and the older cases do not always distinguish adequately between these various heads of admissibility, simply because the distinctions did not crystallise until comparatively modern times. But the older cases cannot really survive the decisions in *R* v *Lillyman* (55) and *R* v *Osborne* (56) which have, by necessary implication, restricted the rule to sexual cases.

For some time after these decisions, it was thought that the rule applied only to offences against females, but in *R* v *Camelleri* (57) it was held that recent complaints might be admitted in sexual cases generally, and in that case the exception was accordingly applied to a charge of indecent assault on a male.

The complaint may be admissible even if it was not made in the defendant's presence. Indeed, if made in his presence, the complaint may well be admissible for other reasons, depending upon his reaction to it. Whether a complaint was 'recent' is a question of fact and degree in every case. Certainly it is not necessary that it was made within the comparatively short period required for admissibility under the res gestae rule. On the other hand, the complaint must have been made at the first opportunity which reasonably presented itself. Thus, it is not a question of the length of time *per se*. The availability of persons to whom the complainant might reasonably be expected to speak, her age, her emotional state and the nature of the offence may all be relevant, and it is a matter for the judge to rule on, having regard to all the circumstances (58).

The 'recent' element is not only a safeguard against concocted self-serving complaints, but also some guarantee that the complaint has at least some value as evidence of the matters in respect of which it is admissible. For the same reason, it is a requirement that the complaint must have been voluntary and spontaneous. This does not rule out a complaint made in response to questioning, but if it is, in effect, dragged out of a reluctant complainant by leading or threatening questions or, even worse, by force, it will not be made voluntarily and is likely to be rejected. In *R* v *Osborne* (59) where the owner of a fried fish shop was alleged to have indecently assaulted a girl under thirteen who had come to the shop with friends, a complaint was upheld where it was induced by a friend with the question, 'Why are you going home?' It seems that non-leading questions, designed to inquire about the complainant's distress, will not offend against the rule, but the question for the judge is not who spoke first, but was it a voluntary and spontaneous complaint. It was succinctly stated by Ridley J in *Osborne* as follows (60):

If the circumstances indicate that, but for the questioning there probably would have been no voluntary complaint, the answer is inadmissible. If the question merely

53   (NP) (1834) 6 C & P 397.
54   *Berry* v *Berry and Carpenter* (1898) 78 LT 688. The attempt to establish this rule in this and other civil cases was probably due to the incompetence of the parties at that time. However, the question was raised as recently as *Fromhold* v *Fromhold* (CA) [1952] 1 TLR 1526. The possibility must be obsolete since the Civil Evidence Act 1968 came into force.
55   (CCR) [1896] 2 QB 167.   56   (CCR) [1905] 1 KB 551.   57   (CCA) [1922] 2 KB 122.
58   *R* v *Cummings* (CCA) [1948] 1 All ER 551. Some examples are collected in Archbold, 40th ed., para. 523a, but no rule can be laid down based on the passage of time alone.
59   [1905] 1 KB 551.   60   Ibid at 556.

anticipates a statement which the complainant was about to make, it is not rendered inadmissible by the fact that the questioner happens to speak first.

In earlier cases it was held, not without some logical force, that although the complainant might relate that she had made a recent complaint, for the purpose of confirming her evidence, she was not to be permitted to relate the details of what she had said. The distinction is an important one, in that if the substance of the complaint could be given, in addition to the fact of its having been made, then particulars of the offence, including the identity of the defendant, might be placed before the jury as confirmatory evidence, which would be wholly inadmissible to prove the truth of the facts stated. It might have been expected that the evidence would be restricted to the fact of the complaint being made, in the light of this difficulty, but in *R* v *Lillyman* (61) the Court for Crown Cases Reserved came down firmly on the other side. The victim of an alleged indecent assault and attempted rape was held to be entitled to relate not only the fact that she had made a recent complaint to her mistress, but also the substance of what she had said.

The jury must, nonetheless, be directed that the only relevance of the complaint lies in its confirmatory value of the complainant's evidence, and in its value on the issue of consent, if that is in issue in the case, and that they are not entitled to regard the complaint as evidence of the truth of the matters stated by the complainant in it. It is one of those directions which juries must, to say the least, find very confusing, especially as they must also be told that even if it is confirmatory of the complainant's evidence in court, the complaint cannot in law corroborate that evidence. The dangers of admitting detailed evidence of a previous consistent statement are very great, particularly where identity is in issue, and it is submitted that *Lillyman* is by no means a necessarily desirable decision. No doubt it is now too late to reverse the decision, except by statute.

It follows, of course, that if consent is not in issue, and the complainant does not give evidence, there is no ground upon which a recent complaint can be admitted. In *R* v *Wallwork* (62) the defendant was charged with incest with his daughter, aged five. The little girl went into the witness-box, but proved unable to give evidence. Evidence was then admitted from the grandmother of a complaint made to her by the girl, in which she had stated that the defendant was the perpetrator of the act. It was held that the evidence was inadmissible, there being no function for it to perform. Consent was obviously not in issue, and there was no evidence which the complaint could confirm. Lord Goddard CJ suggested that in such a case, the fact of the complaint might be given, as opposed to its substance, but this seems contrary both to principle and authority, and has not found acceptance in other cases.

The two exceptions which have just been discussed, relating to previous identifications and recent complaints, are likely to be of great importance to the case of Coke and Littleton. In the case of Margaret Blackstone, there is no difficulty of identification; Coke does not dispute it, and even if he did, where the witness is able to state that she knows the defendant personally, much of the danger inherent in evidence of identification is removed. In such a case, the judge would remind the jury of the fact, and the other circumstances of the identification, and would no doubt feel it to be quite safe to leave the matter to the jury. But Margaret's complaint to her mother is quite another matter. Although it was made shortly afterwards, it seems that Margaret did not take the first reasonably practicable opportunity to make it. This in itself would not conclude the matter, because account must obviously be taken of her age, and very distressed condition, arising not only from what had happened to her, but to her younger sister while in a sense under Margaret's protection. But it is more worrying that Margaret's mother found so much difficulty in extracting the story from her, and the judge would have to take account of the possibility that the complaint might have been devised to cover what might otherwise seem to be her lack of responsibility. It is clear that the judge has a very difficult task to perform. It may be that evidence of both Mrs Blackstone and Dr Vesey of Margaret's extreme distress may tip the scales in favour of admission, provided that, following *Osborne*, the judge takes the view that a complaint would inevitably have been made.

Angela's case presents less of a problem, so far as her complaint is concerned. Clearly, it was voluntary and spontaneous, and made at the first practicable opportunity. No one would reasonably expect a young girl to complain to the first person she meets, and her waiting until her arrival home would not affect the issue. This will have the consequence that evidence both from Angela, and from her mother will be admissible both of the fact that a complaint was made, and of its substance, i.e. the detail of the offence which she gave. But there is a more difficult and crucial problem in the evidence of identification. The fact that Littleton's defence is one of mistaken identity, and an alibi, gives rise to very serious issues indeed. The circumstances of the identification are very similar to those in *Christie*, where the boy's words, 'That is the man,' were admitted as evidence of a previous identification. There was, however, a good deal of disagreement about whether the detail of the offence, related by the boy in the defendant's presence, formed part of the act of identification, as Lord Atkinson was prepared to hold, or whether the identification was limited to the words, 'That is the man,' as Viscount Haldane LC and Lord Moulton thought. It may well be that Lord Atkinson's view was based on the consideration that, at the time of *Christie*, the words could not be admitted as a recent complaint on the offence charged.

But it will be clear to the jury, if evidence of the identification is admitted, that Angela was identifying Littleton as the man who assaulted her, and evidence of the details will emerge from the recent complaint and from her evidence in court. It is, therefore, imperative for the judge to consider the nature of the evidence of identification, from the standpoint of the *Turnbull* guidelines, a matter with which the House of Lords in *Christie* was not, of course, concerned. Certainly, the judge would have to take into account that the identification was not made in accordance with the guidelines relating to the proper conduct of identification parades. The judge would also have to remind the jury that she gave no verbal description of her assailant, and of the fact that Angela's attention may have been focused as much on the music, and on her sister, as on Littleton himself. On the other hand, she had a fairly long time, with no physical obstruction and in good conditions, in which to observe him. It may be that one satisfactory step would be to ask Littleton to stand on an identification parade, to see whether Margaret can identify the man who assaulted her sister, as she suggests in her statement. This would be quite likely to be decisive one way or the other. Certainly, if Margaret picked out Littleton, the evidence of identification would appear to be formidable.

The jury would also be entitled to take into account, as confirming the evidence of identification, the conversation between Littleton and his wife, if they accept it as an adverse admission. The judge would be entitled, provided that a prima facie case exists at the close of the prosecution case, to direct the jury to consider any evidence given by Coke from the witness-box implicating Littleton, though not Coke's statement under caution, which is, of course, inadmissible against Littleton.

13.3.5   Rebuttal of suggestions of recent fabrication
Although the final exception to be considered is one which arises in cross-examination or
re-examination, rather than examination in chief, it is convenient to deal with it in the
present context as being a recognised exception to the rule against previous consistent
statements. The exception is that where, in cross-examination it is suggested that the
witness has fabricated his evidence within some ascertainable period of time, he may
rebut the suggestion by showing that before that time, he had made a statement
consistent with his evidence to another person. The relevance of the previous statement
in such circumstances is readily apparent.

Where, therefore, a witness gave evidence that a will had been forged, and it was
suggested to him that he had invented his evidence out of enmity towards the defendant,
the witness was permitted to prove that he had made the same statement to a third
person, at a time before the cause of the enmity arose (63). And in *R* v *Oyesiku* (64)
where it was put to the defendant's wife that she had prepared her evidence in collusion
with her husband, she was likewise allowed to prove that, after the defendant's arrest
and before she had any opportunity to speak to him, she had made to his solicitor a
statement to the same effect.

The suggestion, must however, be in the terms set out above. A general cross-
examination designed to show that the evidence is unreliable, or even untruthful, will
not let in a previous consistent statement. In *Fox* v *General Medical Council* (65) a doctor
was charged with infamous conduct, in relation to his adulterous association with a
woman patient, who subsequently committed suicide. The Privy Council upheld the
decision of the GMC that the evidence of a friend of the doctor, stating that the doctor
had, after the patient's death, made to him a statement consistent with his case, was not
admissible merely because the doctor's evidence was challenged as being generally
untrue. Lord Radcliffe stated the rule in the following terms:

> If in cross-examination a witness's account of some incident or set of facts is challenged
> as being a recent invention, thus presenting a clear issue as to whether at some
> previous time he said or thought what he has been saying at the trial, he may support
> himself by evidence of earlier statements by him to the same effect. Plainly the rule
> that sets up the exception cannot be formulated with any great precision, since its
> application will depend on the nature of the challenge offered by the course of
> cross-examination and the relative cogency of the evidence tendered to repel it.

Lord Radcliffe then considered the nature of the cross-examination which had taken
place, and concluded that it was directed to showing the general untruthfulness of the
doctor's evidence and that his answers were consistent with either view of the case. His
Lordship went on:

> Could it have made any contribution to the [Disciplinary Committee's] judgment on
> the veracity of his whole account for them to know that in such a situation he had told

---

63   *Flanagan* v *Fahy* [1918] 2 IR 361. The oft-cited case of *R* v *Coll* (CCR, Ireland) (1889) 24 IR 522 appears to
be rather an example of an explanation in re-examination of an apparent inconsistency exposed in cross-
examination. The witness was asked why no reference had appeared in his statement to the defendant, when he
had implicated the defendant in his evidence. He was allowed, having admitted that the statement made no such
reference, to explain the inconsistency in terms of an omission, and to point out that an earlier statement made by
him had referred to the defendant. See also *R* v *Benjamin* (CCA) (1913) 8 Cr App R 146.
64   (CA) (1971) 56 Cr App R 240.
65   (PC, Disciplinary Committee of the GMC) [1960] 1 WLR 1017.

the old friend substantially the same story as to his innocence of the matters charged as he was now telling at the hearing? Their Lordships do not think that it could. In their view, the challenge to the appellant's evidence that was raised by the cross-examination was not of the order that could be affected by proof of statements made by him of that kind at that date. No tribunal that was not otherwise prepared to accept the appellant's general story could have been led to do so by hearing what he had told [the friend] on April 15. So regarded, the evidence rejected is no more than the previous assertion of the defence story told at the trial, which Humphreys J pointed out in *R v Roberts* is clearly inadmissible.

It seems that it must be possible for the court to detect a specific time at or after which it is suggested that the fabrication took place. This and this alone lends cogency to a statement made before that time, tending to negative the suggestion.

Because of the purpose for which the previous statement is admitted, at common law, its evidential effect is limited to the rebutting of the suggestion made of recent fabrication, and it cannot be used as evidence of the truth of what the witness then said. In this respect, it runs parallel to the general rule affecting admissible previous consistent statements, for example recent complaints, and for the same reason it may not amount to corroboration of the evidence of the witness. This is the position in criminal cases.

In civil cases, not for the first time, we must note that the position has been altered by statute. S. 3(1)(*b*) of the Civil Evidence Act 1968 provides that:

(1) Where in any civil proceedings — . . .

(b) a previous statement made by a person called as [a witness in those proceedings] is proved for the purpose of rebutting a suggestion that his evidence has been fabricated,

that statement shall by virtue of this subsection be admissible as evidence of any fact stated therein of which direct oral evidence by him would be admissible.

It may be doubted whether this provision is as radical a change as it appears to be. If the statement is consistent with the evidence given then the judge will be unlikely to give more weight to it as evidence of the truth of the facts stated in it than he would be inclined to give to the evidence of the witness itself. The role of statements admitted for this purpose will continue to be one of rebuttal, in which, if properly admitted, they may of course be very cogent. S. 6(4) preserves the common-law position that statements admitted for the present purpose are incapable in law of corroborating the evidence of the maker.

13.4 Unfavourable and hostile witnesses

Witnesses who 'fail to come up to proof', in other words who are unfavourable in their evidence to the party calling them, or less favourable than might have been expected, are one of the hazards of litigation. It by no means follows that a witness in this position is dishonest, or motivated by malice towards the party calling him. It may be that his knowledge or recollection are not as great as was supposed, or as was once the case. The tenor of what he is able to say may have been misunderstood or exaggerated in the course of taking his proof of evidence. It may, however, be that the witness is dishonest or malicious, and he may actually set out to sabotage the case of the party calling him. Given that a party may not, generally, in evidence in chief put leading questions to his own witness, or in effect cross-examine him, what is that party entitled to do in order to repair any damage caused to his case? The answer involves consideration of two possible remedies, which are: (a) the acceptance of the evidence, combined with calling other admissible evidence in favour of the party's case; and (b) direct discrediting of the witness by reference to previous statements made by him inconsistent with his evidence.

13.4.1   Use of other evidence
Any party to litigation is entitled to call all the admissible evidence at his disposal which may assist him in proving his case. This principle is not affected by the fact that part of that evidence turns out to be unfavourable or insufficiently favourable. Consequently, the mere fact that a witness proves unfavourable does not prevent the calling of any other available evidence dealing with the matters which the witness was supposed to prove (66). Indeed, if the rule were otherwise, the quantity of evidence which could be called, would depend upon the accidental factor of whether the unfavourable witness was called first or last.

Within the category of other available evidence must now be counted, in civil cases, admissible hearsay statements made by the witness himself. While nothing in the Civil Evidence Act 1968 operates to allow a party to discredit directly a witness who is not hostile, the wording of s. 2 undoubtedly permits the putting in evidence of hearsay statements, in addition to the oral evidence of the witness, and (subject to the provisions of s. 2(2)) for the purpose of supplementing the oral evidence given by the witness. The course suggested is possible only with leave, by virtue of s. 2(2), and the putting in of the statement must wait until the end of examination in chief, subject to the power of the judge to allow the statement to be narrated in chief 'on the ground that to prevent him from doing so would adversely affect the intelligibility of his evidence': s. 2(2)(b)(ii).

It is submitted that this course is appropriate to cases where a witness is unfavourable, or insufficiently favourable because of his inability properly to deal with the matters put to him as a result of failing recollection caused by age, illness or the lapse of time. Hearsay evidence would no doubt be an inappropriate subject of leave (and would anyway be devoid of weight) where it was sought to bolster up an inherently unreliable or reluctant witness. The use of hearsay evidence to supplement unfavourable evidence in proper cases was recognised even before the 1968 Act. In *Harvey* v *Smith-Wood* (67), an elderly witness was called for the plaintiff on the trial of her action in March 1963. The witness was unable to deal, to the plaintiff's satisfaction, with certain crucial events, which had occurred in January 1951, by reason of his own age and the considerable lapse of time. Lawton J 'with some regret' acceded to an application to admit in evidence a written statement made by the witness in 1956, dealing with those events, under s. 1(1) of the Evidence Act 1938 (68). The regret expressed was 'because it seems to me that it is an unfortunate situation if counsel can call a witness and, when that witness does not come up to proof, counsel should be allowed to produce some earlier document which shows that on some other occasion the witness made a different statement.' Lawton J went on

66   *Ewer* v *Ambrose* (1825) 3 B & C 746, where the defendant had the misfortune to call a witness who proved the exact opposite of the proposition which he had been called to support.
67   [1964] 2 QB 171.
68   This section differed in important respects from s. 2 of the 1968 Act, but it is necessary only to refer to the fact that, under the 1938 Act, the statement was admissible without leave on the facts of *Harvey* v *Smith-Wood*.

to say that counsel should hesitate to adopt such a course 'except in very special circumstances'.

It is submitted, with respect, that the reservations alluded to by Lawton J may more happily be applied to questions of weight, than to those of admissibility (69) and under the 1968 Act, subject always to questions of weight, it would seem proper to build up a case by the admission of all the available evidence. Where it is foreseeable that evidence may not be as favourable as might otherwise be expected, having regard to the character-istics of the witness and to the lapse of time, it would no doubt be wise to serve appropriate notices in compliance with RSC Ord. 38, r. 21, but where the defect in the evidence arises *ex improviso* at the trial, the court may waive the requirement if no injustice is caused to the other side (70).

13.4.2 Direct discrediting

It is obviously embarrassing and undesirable that a party should be permitted to impeach directly the evidence of a witness whom he has tendered to the court as a witness of truth. And it is clear that he may do so, only where the witness is not simply unfavourable, but is 'hostile' in the sense that he displays some hostile animus towards the party calling him, and evinces no desire to give evidence fairly or to tell the truth. Hostility may stem from malice, bribery, intimidation or a mere indisposition to co-operate.

The position at common law was never developed to any satisfactory extent, beyond the principle stated above. The judge always enjoys a residual power to put any question which he thinks necessary in the interests of justice, even though such questioning may take the form of cross-examination (71). But the real problem was whether a party could ever impeach a hostile witness called by him, by putting to the witness a statement previously made by him inconsistent with his evidence. There were dicta that this course was permissible, based mainly upon policy considerations of preventing bribery and other dishonest acts of interference with the administration of justice (72). But it was left to Parliament to lay down a general rule to that effect, and the need grew in urgency with the growth of the practice of taking proofs of evidence in all forms of litigation.

The provision now in force is s. 3 of the Criminal Procedure Act 1865 which provides that:

A party producing a witness shall not be allowed to impeach his credit by general evidence of bad character; but he may, in case the witness shall in the opinion of the judge prove adverse, contradict him by other evidence, or, by leave of the judge, prove that he has made at other times a statement inconsistent with his present testimony; but before such last-mentioned proof can be given the circumstances of the supposed statement, sufficient to designate the particular occasion, must be mentioned to the witness, and he must be asked whether or not he has made such statement.

The construction of this inelegantly worded enactment has caused great difficulty. It is clear enough that the section applies alike to civil and criminal proceedings, and that proof of a previous inconsistent statement requires leave of the judge. But what is the

69 This view had received judicial support previously, e.g., in *Bearman's Ltd v Metropolitan Police District Receiver* (CA) [1961] 1 WLR 634 per Devlin LJ at 655. This case was cited to Lawton J and must have been in his mind, as he had himself appeared as counsel on that occasion, though it turned on a different point.
70 *Morris v Stratford-on-Avon RDC* (CA) [1973] 1 WLR 1059.
71 *Bastin v Carew* (NP) (1824) Ry & M 127.
72 *Melhuish v Collier* (1850) 15 QB 878 per Erle CJ at 890 is an example.

meaning of 'adverse' which the judge is required to assess? It is unfortunate that the draftsmen of the 1865 Act did not heed the comments made in *Greenough* v *Eccles and Others* (73) when there fell to be construed the identically worded s. 22 of the Common Law Procedure Act 1854. The court held that the word 'adverse' must be construed to mean 'hostile', on the somewhat desperate reasoning that, if the word signified no more than 'unfavourable', it was hard to see how the judge should be able to form any opinion on that matter; whereas hostility could be demonstrated to him by reference to the previous statement and the demeanour of the witness.

An application must be made in every case in which it is sought to treat a witness as hostile, and the judge must be shown the statement proposed to be proved (74). In a criminal case, it is the duty of prosecuting counsel to show the statement to the judge in any case where the witness is clearly hostile, and to ask for leave to cross-examine the witness as hostile (75). The treatment of a hostile witness must be confined to the courses permitted by the section, that is to say contradiction by other evidence (as might be done with an unfavourable witness) and (with leave) proof of a previous inconsistent statement, subject to the preliminary questions required by the section to establish authorship of such a statement. It is not permissible to attack the credit of a party's own witness by general evidence of bad character.

It seems that the Act has not, however, removed the power of the judge at common law to allow any question to be put which seems to him to be necessary in the interests of justice. In *R* v *Thompson* (76) the victim of an alleged offence of incest was called for the prosecution, but refused to give evidence. The trial judge permitted her to be treated as hostile. It was argued on appeal that this course was not open, at least in so far as the proof of her previous statement was concerned, because the witness having given no evidence, there was no 'present testimony' with which the previous statement could be said to be 'inconsistent,' under s. 3. This attractive argument failed, the Court of Appeal holding that, whatever the position might be under the statute, the judge retained a power at common law to satisfy the interests of justice by requiring the witness to answer any question directed to that end.

It remains to consider the evidential effect of a previous inconsistent statement proved by virtue of s. 3 of the Criminal Procedure Act 1865, and yet again, the picture is of a limited effect applicable to criminal cases at common law, modified for civil cases by statute. At common law, if the hostile witness, being shown his statement, admits that it is true, then his adoption of it becomes his evidence, and no separate question of the evidential value of the statement as such arises. But where the witness admits that he made the statement, but continues to give evidence inconsistent with it, the jury must be directed to try the case upon his evidence. They may use the statement only as evidence going to the credit of the witness, and it will be a serious misdirection to invite them to act

<hr/>

73 (1859) 5 CB(NS) 786 per Williams and Willes JJ. The section reduced Cockburn CJ to the anguished cry: 'The solution by my learned brothers is a solution of a difficulty, otherwise incapable of any solution, but I am not satisfied therewith, and without actually dissenting from their judgment, I do not altogether assent to it.' As reported in 28 LJCP 160 at 164. The section also causes problems over the words, 'contradict him by other evidence', which at common law, might have been done in the case even of a merely unfavourable witness; the phrase is generally assumed to restate this right, which involves reading into the section the parenthesis, 'as he might have done heretofore, and also . . . [to prove . . . etc.]'. This is a drastic piece of construction, but it is difficult to make sense of it otherwise.
74 Even where the witness is a party called by his opponent, there must be a ruling on hostility: *Price* v *Manning* (CA) (1889) 42 ChD 372.
75 *R* v *Fraser; R* v *Warren* (CCA) (1956) 40 Cr App R 160. Where a witness turns hostile at committal proceedings, the prosecution may wait until the trial before treating him as such; *R* v *Mann* (1972) 56 Cr App R 750.
76 (1976) 64 Cr App R 96.

upon the contents of the statement as evidence of guilt (77). It is immaterial whether the inconsistent statement is an unsworn statement, or one such as a deposition, made on oath in other proceedings (78). In *R v Harris* (79), the Court of Criminal Appeal said:

> ... it was permissible to cross-examine this girl upon the assertions she had previously made, not for the purpose of substituting those unsworn assertions for her sworn testimony, but for the purpose of showing that her sworn testimony, in the light of those unsworn assertions, could not be regarded as being of importance.

In such a case, the jury must, therefore, assess the evidence of the witness in the light of the statement put to him, to show inconsistency, and if the inconsistency is substantial and is unexplained to their satisfaction, the statement may altogether destroy the effect of the evidence. Be that as it may, the jury cannot substitute the statement for the evidence.

In civil cases, the position is now governed by s. 3(1) of the Civil Evidence Act 1968:

> Where in any civil proceedings —
>
> (*a*) a previous inconsistent or contradictory statement made by a person called as a witness in those proceedings is proved by virtue of section 3 ... of the Criminal Procedure Act 1865; ...
>
> that statement shall by virtue of this subsection be admissible as evidence of any fact stated therein of which direct oral evidence by him would be admissible.

Unlike the corresponding provision under s. 3(1)(*b*), dealing with previous consistent statements admitted to rebut suggestions of recent fabrication, this does create a radical change in the use of previous statements. The judge in a civil case may now elect to act on the previous statement, sworn or unsworn, of the hostile witness, in preference to his evidence from the witness-box. It is submitted that this a useful provision, which might well be extended in modified form to criminal cases, perhaps limited to cases where the previous statement is sworn (as it often is). Where a witness is hostile, it is not infrequently the case that he has been intimidated, or otherwise interfered with, and it is by no means unthinkable that a jury should be able to consider what he said on oath about the matter previously, at a time before his evidence was subjected to pressure, and perhaps accept it as evidence of the truth of what he then said.

13.5 Questions for counsel

1 Devise a series of questions to take Margaret and Angela Blackstone through their evidence in chief, without leading them.
2 If D/I Glanvil and D/S Bracton apply to refresh their memories from their notebooks, what must the judge take into account before permitting this?

---

77 *R v Golder and Others* (CCA) [1960] 1 WLR 1169. Though where the evidence is otherwise strong, the proviso may be applied: *R v Oliva* (CCA) [1965] 1 WLR 1028.
78 *R v Birch* (CCA) (1924) 18 Cr App R 26; and *R v Golder and Others* (CCA) [1960] 1 WLR 1169 were both concerned with sworn evidence at a magistrates' court in the committal proceedings.
79 (1927) 20 Cr App R 144, at 147. The helpful phrase forbidding 'substitution of the statement for the evidence also appears in *R v White* (CCA) (1922) 17 Cr App R 60 at 64.

3 Under what circumstances may the officers' notebooks be put in evidence? What evidential value would they have?

4 May Angela Blackstone, her mother or the officers give evidence of the identification of Littleton in the street? What considerations apply generally to the evidence of identification of Littleton?

5 May evidence be given of the accounts given to their mother by Margaret and Angela of what had happened at Coke's flat? If so, what evidence may be given, and to what effect?

6 If at the committal proceedings, Margaret refuses to give evidence, or asserts that she consented to the act of intercourse, what should counsel for the prosecution do?

14   Cross-examination and Beyond

14.1   Introduction

Consideration of the course of evidence, following the discussion of examination in chief in the last chapter, must take into account both cross-examination by the party against whom a witness is called, and re-examination by the party calling the witness, where necessary in the light of cross-examination. But it will also be convenient to deal, in this chapter, with two subjects falling outside what might be termed the routine course of evidence. These are evidence called in rebuttal, and witnesses called by the judge of his own motion. These topics will each be examined in the sections which follow, and, as with examination in chief, we shall be concerned with their evidential rather than procedural aspects, although some comment on the latter will be helpful, and will be made where the practice of calling witnesses bears upon the evidential questions which arise.

A: CROSS-EXAMINATION

14.2   Liability to cross-examination

Any witness who has been sworn on behalf of any party is liable to be cross-examined on behalf of any other party to the proceedings. The liability does not depend upon whether the witness has given evidence adverse to the case of the cross-examining party, because it is perfectly proper for cross-examination to take place for the purpose of eliciting facts favourable to the cross-examiner's case, irrespective of the nature of the witness's evidence in chief. The right to cross-examine exists even where the witness has given no evidence in chief, either because counsel calling him decides, once he has been sworn, not to ask any questions of him (1), or because, as frequently happens in the case of witnesses who exactly corroborate witnesses already called, he is sworn solely for the purpose of being tendered for cross-examination. The latter practice is common in the case of police officers whose evidence in chief will be identical, any one of whom can give the relevant evidence in chief, but all of whom may be required for cross-examination by the defence.

Cross-examination is, however, like any other questioning, subject to the rules of evidence, one of which is that the answers elicited must be directly relevant to an issue in the case, or indirectly so, as in the case of questions going to credit. Where it appears that a witness is unable to give relevant evidence, it would seem that no question of

---

1   *R* v *Brooke* (NP) (1819) 2 Stark (NP) 472. If a witness gives no evidence in chief then there can be no cross-examination concerning his credit because it cannot be relevant: *Hobbs* v *C.T. Tinling & Co. Ltd; Hobbs* v *Nottingham Journal Ltd* (CA) [1929] 2 KB 1.

cross-examination can arise, and the same result obtains where examination in chief is stopped by the judge for any reason properly within his power, before any relevant question has been put (2).

It seems that where a witness, who has given evidence in chief, becomes unavailable to be cross-examined, his evidence in chief remains admissible, but is unlikely to carry very much weight (3). If his absence from the witness-box is temporary, for instance because of illness, it is obviously desirable that an adjournment should be granted, wherever this can be done without undue inconvenience or delay, in order to allow cross-examination to take place. However, if a witness absconds with a view to avoiding cross-examination, an obvious inference is to be drawn by the tribunal of fact, which would be justified in rejecting the witness's evidence altogether (4).

If a witness gives evidence unsworn (see 12.13 and 12.14, ante), he is liable to cross-examination, except, apparently, where a witness is called only to produce a document whose identity is otherwise proved, and where a judge or counsel speaks from his place in court about a case in which he has been judicially or professionally engaged (5).

14.3 Effect of omission to cross-examine

Failure to cross-examine a witness who has given relevant evidence for the other side is held technically to amount to an acceptance of the witness's evidence in chief. It is, therefore, not open to a party to impugn in a closing speech, or otherwise, the unchallenged evidence of a witness called by his opponent, or even to seek to explain to the tribunal of fact the reason for the failure to cross-examine. In *R* v *Bircham* (6), for example, counsel for the defendant was not permitted to suggest to the jury that the co-defendant and a witness for the prosecution were the perpetrators of the offence charged, where that allegation had not been put to either in cross-examination. Accordingly, it is counsel's duty, in every case, (a) to challenge every part of a witness's evidence which runs contrary to his own instructions; (b) to put to the witness, in terms, any allegation against him which must be made in the proper conduct of the defence: and (c) to put to the witness counsel's own case, in so far as the witness is apparently able to assist with relevant matters, or would be so able, given the truth of counsel's case. The duty is, of course, not to be interpreted as a licence to introduce irrelevant matters, and is to be carried out with due regard to the undoubted discretion of counsel to omit reference to matters of an apparently trivial or minor significance in the context of the case as a whole. This paragraph should be read in conjunction with the observations made in 14.4, post, with regard to counsel's duty in the conduct of cross-examination.

The second consequence of failure to cross-examine is a tactical one, but no less important for that. Where part of a party's case has not been put to witnesses called for the other side, who might reasonably have been expected to be able to deal with it, that party himself will probably be asked in cross-examination why he is giving evidence about matters which were never put in cross-examination on his behalf. The implication of the question is that the party is fabricating evidence in the witness-box, because if he

2 *Creevy* v *Carr* (NP) (1835) 7 C & P 64.
3 For example, where the witness dies after giving evidence in chief: see *R* v *Doolin* (1832) Jebb CC 123 (in which the witness fainted and was 'supposed by many to be dead').
4 *Shea* v *Green* (DN) (1886) 2 TLR 533.
5 A defendant who makes an unsworn statement from the dock in a criminal trial, is not giving evidence, and cannot be cross-examined on it: see 12.14, ante.
6 (CA) [1972] Crim LR 430.

had ever mentioned the matters in question to his legal advisers, then they would have been put on his behalf at the proper time. The point is one much beloved of prosecuting counsel in criminal cases, though quite what weight juries attach to it, if they follow it at all, is unclear. However, there is some risk that the defendant's credit as a witness may be affected by failure to cross-examine fully on his behalf. If counsel has, by inadvertence, omitted to put some part of the case which should have been put, it is accordingly his duty, at the first possible moment, to mention that fact to the judge and apply for any necessary witness to be recalled for that purpose. The judge has a discretion in every case, whether or not to allow any witness to be recalled for further cross-examination (7), and will ordinarily permit this if it can be done without undue inconvenience, delay or injustice to another defendant.

The duty to cross-examine is habitually and sensibly dealt with by agreement between counsel that no adverse inference will be suggested, if counsel forbear from putting to corroborative witnesses, matters which have clearly been put to at least one witness, and where it is not to be expected that the corroborative witness will contradict the first. The device saves much time, and can be employed for yet more laudable purposes, where the putting of issues is confined to one witness, for the purpose of sparing children or other vulnerable witnesses the ordeal of dealing with delicate questions. Where the device is properly employed, no point will be taken on a failure to put every matter to every witness. However, counsel for a defendant must consider with great care how far he may properly refrain from cross-examination. Frequently the forbearance is confined to the corroborative evidence of police officers, whose evidence may safely be expected to correspond with their depositions, and even then often to relatively minor matters, unless it is clear that the witness intends to do no more than reassert his evidence in chief, and to make no concession to the cross-examination.

14.4 Nature and conduct of cross-examination

Cross-examination is the process whereby a party seeks (a) to test the veracity and accuracy of evidence in chief, given by a witness called for another party, and (b) to elicit from that witness any relevant facts which may be favourable to the case for the cross-examiner.

A witness who has been sworn is compellable to answer any proper question put in cross-examination, whether directed to an issue in the case (i.e. to the substance of his evidence) or to his credit as a witness. With the exception of the defendant in a criminal case, whose position is governed by s. 1 of the Criminal Evidence Act 1898, a witness may be compelled to answer even questions directed to showing his bad character, for the purpose of impugning his credit as a witness. The credit of a witness depends upon the view which the tribunal of fact ultimately take of (a) his knowledge of the facts, (b) his impartiality, (c) his truthfulness and (d) his respect for his oath or affirmation. These qualities may, therefore, be attacked to the extent necessary to dissuade the tribunal from relying on the witness's evidence, but counsel has a duty not to exceed what is required, and the judge may restrain unnecessary cross-examination, even where some basis for the questions can be found as a matter of law (8).

---

7 In *R v Wilson* [1977] Crim LR 553, the Court of Appeal refused to interfere with the discretion of the trial judge, who had allowed the defendant to be recalled for the purpose of being cross-examined as to his previous convictions, where such course was proper, but had been inadvertently omitted. The court had some doubts, but inadvertence is a fact of life, especially in a complicated case, and should not be allowed to prevent a fair trial, if it can be avoided.

8 *R v Sweet-Escott* (1971) 55 Cr App R 316.

It should, however, be noted that in one important case, relating to imputations on character, there is now a statutory restriction on cross-examination concerning credit. By s. 2(1) of the Sexual Offences (Amendment) Act 1976:

> If at a trial any person is for the time being charged with a rape offence to which he pleads not guilty, then, except with the leave of the judge, no evidence and no question in cross-examination shall be adduced or asked at the trial, by or on behalf of any defendant at the trial, about any sexual experience of a complainant with a person other than the defendant.

The section does not, of course, prevent questions about the sexual experience of the complainant with the defendant, which questions go to the issue of consent. S. 2(2) provides that the judge shall give leave only where, on application being made to him, he is 'satisfied that it would be unfair' to the defendant not to do so. This seems to require that the cross-examination must be such that the jury might well take a different view of the complainant's evidence from that which they might otherwise take, and not just an exercise in blackening her sexual character (9).

In cross-examination there is less restriction on the form of questions than in examination in chief, and in particular, leading questions may be employed freely. It has been said that the questions put should not be in the nature of comment on the facts (the proper place for which is in counsel's closing speech) or such as to provoke argument between counsel and the witness. Forms which offend against this rule are said to be: 'I suggest that . . . '; 'Are you asking the jury to believe that . . . ?' 'That's hardly consistent with . . . is it?' and the like (10). It is also undesirable that counsel should draw to the attention of the witness what has been said in evidence by other witnesses, and invite his comment on such other evidence, or invite the witness to agree or to disagree with it (11). It must be confessed, however, that the above forms are in regular use in practice and seem not to be restrained, unless obvious embarrassment is being caused, and of course it is not right that the flow of questioning should be interrupted for purely technical errors to be corrected.

The conduct of cross-examination is the subject of rules of professional conduct drawn up by the Bar Council, originally published in November 1950 and since modified. The detail of these rules is outside the scope of this work, but they are set out in Archbold (12) and should be studied in depth by every intending advocate. The essence of the rules may perhaps be expressed by saying that they impose upon counsel the duty fearlessly to represent his client, and to put in cross-examination every matter necessary for the proper presentation of the case (13). At the same time, counsel must use his judgment and discretion to avoid making unnecessary allegations, particularly against absent third parties and in a public trial. The more grave the allegation to be put, the more it should

9   *R* v *Mills* (1978) 68 Cr App R 327, a decision of the Court of Appeal, approving the earlier pronouncement of May J to the same effect in *R* v *Lawrence* [1977] Crim LR 492.
10   See the observations of Lord Hewart CJ in *R* v *Baldwin* (CCA) (1925) 18 Cr App R 175. Particular care must be taken when dealing with potentially sensitive matters affecting credit.
11   *North Australian Territory Co. Ltd* v *Goldsborough Mort & Co. Ltd* (CA) [1893] 2 Ch 381. However, there can normally be no objection to asking one expert witness for his comments on other expert evidence.
12   40th ed., para. 527. The rules are not binding on the court. If a judge seeks to persuade counsel to fail to comply with them, counsel must either withdraw, or comply under protest and look for redress elsewhere: see *R* v *McFadden and Others* (CA) (1975) 62 Cr App R 187. But counsel cannot be criticised in terms of professional conduct if he observes the rules.
13   The vexed question of what counsel may properly do when representing a defendant who does not give evidence, seems at long last to be settled, in favour of the view that he must fully present his case in cross-examination, as in any other case. The decision whether to give evidence is that of the defendant, not counsel, and

be scrutinised in relation to its necessity to the case. These observations apply most strongly to allegations directed to credit only, and counsel should seek verification of such allegations from his instructing solicitor, or personally ascertain that there are reasonable grounds for believing such allegations to be true, so far as he is reasonably able to do so. Cross-examination should be as short as is consistent with a proper presentation of the case, and should in no case be conducted with a view to harassing, intimidating or browbeating the witness.

14.5 Application of the rules of evidence to cross-examination

The normal rules of evidence apply to matters elicited in cross-examination, as they do to matters elicited in chief. There is no licence to elicit evidence which is inadmissible, merely because it arises in the course of cross-examination. Thus, in *R* v *Thomson* (14) where the defendant was charged with using an instrument on a woman (who had died) with intent to procure her miscarriage, the defendant's counsel was held to have been rightly prevented from asking a prosecution witness in cross-examination whether the deceased woman had not told her that she intended to procure her own miscarriage, and later, that she had in fact done so. The evidence was hearsay at any stage of the examination of the witness, and must be excluded. Similarly, where the judge has excluded an out-of-court statement, made by a defendant, as being inadmissible in law, it may not be referred to subsequently for any purpose, including that of cross-examination on behalf of a defendant (15).

But it should be noted that the course taken in cross-examination may, of itself, render admissible evidence which would have been inadmissible from the witness in chief, and then the witness may deal with the evidence in cross-examination and in re-examination. The point is that cross-examination may legitimately raise further issues, and therefore render admissible evidence which could not previously have been given. We saw in the last chapter that, where a witness is cross-examined upon the contents of a document from which he has refreshed his memory, if the cross-examination strays beyond those parts of the document actually used for that purpose, then the document becomes evidence where it certainly was not before, and may be referred to and asked about accordingly. Much the same will occur where a document is admitted in chief for the purpose, say, of identifying handwriting contained in it, and in cross-examination its contents are referred to. The contents are then made evidence by reason of the cross-examination. And where a witness is asked for the first time in cross-examination about acts done by him, or words spoken between him and a party to the proceedings, such acts and words thereupon become evidence, and may be dealt with accordingly. In the case of the words spoken the witness would be permitted, in cross-examination or re-examination, to state the whole of the conversation put to him.

We must now turn to look in detail at three important evidential matters which arise in

may be made at the very last possible moment. Of course, the failure of the defendant to give evidence, where grave allegations have been made on his behalf may properly be made the subject of strong comment in the summing-up. Any other rule would subject counsel to intolerable and embarrassing decisions about whether he should present his case fully, or hold back in case the defendant elects not to give evidence subsequently. See *R* v *Brigden* (CA) [1973] Crim LR 579. The view that it is wrong for counsel to make grave allegations in cross-examination and then not call the defendant was voiced by Lord Goddard CJ in *R* v *O'Neill; R* v *Ackers* (CCA) (1950) 34 Cr App R 108, but may now be regarded as abrogated. The view expressed in support of it by Waller LJ in *R* v *Callaghan* (CA) (1979) 69 Cr App R 88 was withdrawn by the learned Lord Justice in a statement reported in *The Times*, 19 February 1980, after representations from the Bar.

---

14 (CCA) [1912] 3 KB 19.   15   *R* v *Treacy* (CCA) [1944] 2 All ER 229.

the course of cross-examination. These are (a) cross-examination using previous inconsistent statements; (b) the rule that answers given on collateral matters are final; and (c) the consequences of cross-examination on documents.

14.6   Previous inconsistent statements

We saw in Chapter 13 that in the treatment of a hostile witness, the use of previous statements made by the witness on other occasions, inconsistent with his evidence, is a crucial weapon available for the purpose of directly discrediting the witness. The same weapon is no less potent in the case of witnesses called for the other side, who are expected and taken to be hostile. At common law, it was open to a cross-examiner to put to a witness his previous inconsistent statements, but the rule was circumscribed by the requirements (16) that, if the statement put was in writing, the witness must be shown the document before he could be asked whether he had said something different on another occasion (which removed the element of surprise); and that if the statement was proved, having been denied by the witness, it must be made evidence as part of the cross-examiner's case (which inhibited the use of statements in many cases). While the first of these requirements was relaxed to some extent by s. 5 of the Criminal Procedure Act 1865 the second, by a curious quirk of fate, has in effect received statutory force for civil cases by virtue of s. 3(1)(*a*) of the Civil Evidence Act 1968 (17).

The use of previous inconsistent statements in cross-examination is now governed by s. 4 and s. 5 of the Criminal Procedure Act 1865, which complement the provisions of s. 3 dealing with the use of such statements against a party's own hostile witnesses (18). S. 4 provides:

> If a witness upon cross-examination as to a former statement made by him relative to the subject-matter of the indictment or proceeding, and inconsistent with his present testimony, does not distinctly admit that he has made such statement, proof may be given that he did in fact make it; but before such proof can be given the circumstances of the supposed statement, sufficient to designate the particular occasion, must be mentioned to the witness, and he must be asked whether or not he has made such statement.

The section is not expressed to apply exclusively to oral or written statements, but it must be read in conjunction with s. 5 which does apply to statements made in or reduced into writing, and it is generally assumed that s. 4 is intended to refer primarily to previous oral statements. It is implicit in the section that the cross-examiner is entitled to ask the witness about the former statement, and the draftsman evidently considered that he was building upon that rule of common law. The right to prove any statement which is not 'distinctly admitted' not only deals with the possibility of ambivalent or evasive answers, when the witness is asked about the previous statement, but also precludes the objection that the proof of the previous statement, if denied, might offend against the rule of

---

16   Said to derive from *Queen Caroline's Case* (1820) 2 B & B 287, which itself is hardly compelling authority, but may well have reflected the contemporary position at common law.

17   Regardless of whose case it may form part of, the use of previous statements in civil proceedings now involves the risk of the judge accepting the statement as evidence of facts stated in it. This may be desired in the case of one's own hostile witnesses, but in the case of the other side's, may involve a searching assessment of how much of the statement may be favourable to the other side, inconsistencies notwithstanding: cf *R* v *Ford and Others* (1851) (CCR) 5 Cox CC 184.

18   Like s. 3, s. 4 and s. 5 apply to civil and criminal proceedings alike, and succeed provisions of the Common Law Procedure Act 1854.

common law that answers in cross-examination which go only to collateral matters must be accepted as final (19).

This section applies alike to statements made previously on oath, for example, a deposition made in committal proceedings, and those made previously unsworn in any circumstances, for example on being interviewed by the police (20). The question whether such statement is 'relative to the subject-matter of the indictment or proceeding' appears to be one within the competence and discretion of the judge, and not one solely for the judgment of the cross-examiner, or the opinion of the witness (21).

The words following the semi-colon correspond to those in s. 3, and require a fair and proper foundation to be laid before the statement may be proved.

S. 5 of the Act provides:

A witness may be cross-examined as to previous statements made by him in writing, or reduced into writing, relative to the subject-matter of the indictment or proceeding, without such writing being shown to him; but if it is intended to contradict such witness by the writing, his attention must, before such contradictory proof can be given, be called to those parts of the writing which are to be used for the purpose of so contradicting him: Provided always, that it shall be competent for the judge, at any time during the trial, to require the production of the writing for his inspection, and he may thereupon make such use of it for the purposes of the trial as he may think fit.

The section envisages two stages in the use of previous inconsistent statements made in, or reduced into writing. The first part of the section permits the cross-examiner rather more scope for surprise than did the common law rule, as applied in *Queen Caroline's Case* (22), and indeed was intended to abrogate the requirement of showing the witness the document before any questions were asked. The cross-examiner may show the document to the witness and ask questions while it is in the hands of the witness. But the use made of the statement must, in order to remain within the first part of the section, fall short of 'contradiction' of the witness. This seems to mean that the cross-examiner may ask the witness, first whether he has ever made a statement on another occasion inconsistent with his evidence, and second (showing him the document) whether, on seeing the statement, he wishes to adhere to the evidence he has given. If the answer is that the witness is prepared to alter his evidence materially, the damage to his credit is done. If he sticks to his evidence, the cross-examiner must choose whether to accept that answer, or whether to enter the second stage. If he chooses the latter course, he will proceed to contradict the witness by the document, in other words put to him that the relevant part of the document (identifying it to him) is a true account, and not the witness's evidence. At this point, but not before – another significant departure from the common law rule – the document may be proved to contradict the witness, and must then be put in evidence, having of course been made relevant by the second stage of cross-examination.

It may be useful to illustrate the working of the section by an example. Let us assume that in evidence in chief, Mrs Blackstone gives evidence that Margaret made a complaint

---

19 See 14.7, post.
20 *R v Hart* (CCA) (1957) 42 Cr App R 47: *R v O'Neill* (CA) [1969] Crim LR 260. In the latter, a defendant who gave evidence exculpating a co-defendant, was rightly cross-examined on his oral statement to the police, in which he had said the opposite of his evidence.
21 *R v Bashir; R v Manzur* [1969] 1 WLR 1303, per Veale J at 1306.
22 (1820) 2 B & B 287.

to her of being raped by Henry Coke, such evidence being admissible as a recent complaint. In the course of narrating this complaint, Mrs Blackstone states that Margaret told her that Coke had threatened her with a knife, in order to force her to have sexual intercourse with him. No reference to such a thing occurs in her deposition, and of course counsel for Coke will wish to test her accuracy and reliability as a witness. One way of doing so is to make use of the deposition, as permitted by s. 5. The cross-examination might proceed:

Q: Did you say your daughter told you that Coke had threatened her with a knife?
A: Yes.
Q: Is your evidence today the first time you have ever made any mention of a knife?
A: What do you mean?
Q: Did you make a statement, a written statement, to the police in connection with this matter, on the 12th of July 1979?
A: I did make a statement, yes.
Q: Did you make any mention in that statement of a knife?
A: I'm not sure now. Can I see it?
Judge: Do your best to answer counsel's question first.
A: I really can't remember.
Judge: Very well, look at the statement.
(Witness reads statement to herself.)
Q: Is that your statement, bearing your signature?
A: Yes.
Q: Did you read it carefully before signing it, including the declaration at the top of the consequences of its being false?
A: Yes.
Q: Having read that statement today, do you still say that there was talk of a knife?

Counsel has now reached the end of stage 1. If Mrs Blackstone is prepared to change her evidence, then the object has been achieved. If not, counsel must decide whether to go on, which would involve the jury seeing the whole of Mrs Blackstone's statement (perhaps edited in fairness to Littleton to exclude mention of his identification) or whether to stop, in which case he must accept her answer (23). The statement adds little to her evidence, and the discrepancy is fairly significant. Counsel may well take the risk, and go on to stage 2.

Q: You still say there was talk of a knife?
A: Yes.
Q: That statement was made just four days after this alleged offence occurred?
A: Yes, on the 12th.
Q: Do you think your memory was better on the 12th of July, just four days after the conversation with your daughter, than it is today?
A: I suppose it would be.
Q: If Margaret had said something about a knife, that would have been something fairly dramatic, which would have impressed itself upon you, wouldn't it?
A: I would think so.

23   *R v Riley* (1866) 4 F & F 964.

Q: Yet there is not one mention of it in your statement, is there? Can you explain why not? Just look at the third paragraph, would you.?

A: I must have forgotten about it. I was very upset by what happened.

Q: The truth is that there never was any mention of a knife, isn't it? The whole complaint was as you stated on the 12th of July, just four days after the conversation took place.

So at the expense of the jury seeing the whole statement, including the consistent passages, counsel has made a serious inroad on the credit of Mrs Blackstone as a witness, particularly if Margaret's evidence did not refer to a knife. The illustration is, of course, exaggerated to make the point, but it does show where stage 1 ends, and the factors which the cross-examiner must have in mind, if he has to consider going on to stage 2.

The provision in s. 5 that the judge may require production of the document, and may make use of it for the purposes of the trial, means that the cross-examiner must have the document available in court, even if it is never shown to the witness (24). The proviso does not, however, allow the judge to treat the previous statement as evidence of the truth of the facts stated in it, in a criminal trial. The evidential value of a statement proved under s. 4 or s. 5 is, at common law, the same as one put to a hostile witness under s. 3, i.e. it goes to the consistency of the witness and, therefore, to the credit of the witness, but no further. In particular, the statement cannot be substituted for the evidence of the witness (25). The contrary suggestion accordingly cannot be one of the 'purposes of the trial', for which the judge may make use of the statement.

In civil cases, as we have seen (26), statute has altered the position, as it has in respect of hostile witnesses. We may now set out s. 3(1)(*a*) of the Civil Evidence Act 1968 in its entirety:

Where in any civil proceedings—

(*a*) a previous inconsistent or contradictory statement made by a person called as a witness in those proceedings is proved by virtue of section 3, 4 or 5 of the Criminal Procedure Act 1865; . . .

that statement shall by virtue of this subsection be admissible as evidence of any fact stated therein of which direct oral evidence by him would be admissible.

It is clear that special care is needed with regard to the use of previous statements in civil cases. Whereas in the case of a hostile witness it may be desirable, from the point of view of the party calling the witness, that the judge be persuaded to accept the previous statement as evidence of the facts stated in it, and so to substitute the statement for the witness's evidence, the same is far less likely to be true in the case of a witness called for the other side, to whom a statement is to be put under s. 4 or s. 5 of the 1865 Act. Indeed, even if there is some discrepancy, the overall impression of the statement may be favourable to the party calling the witness. In any event, the judge might give leave to admit the witness's previous statement under s. 2 of the 1968 Act, and we have seen that it is now quite proper for this to be done, merely for the purpose of supplementing the

24 *R* v *Anderson* (CCA) (1929) 21 Cr App R 178.
25 See 13.4.2, ante.
26 Note 17, ante.

witness's memory. Thus, cross-examination along these lines must be far more restrained, and is likely to be far less effective in civil cases than in criminal.

14.7   Finality of answers on collateral issues

Because cross-examination may be directed to matters going solely to the credit or the character of the witness, and because cross-examination may elicit evidence which was not elicited in chief, and even evidence that would not have been admissible in chief, it is apparent that the course of cross-examination may result in some proliferation of the issues aired before the court. If this were wholly unrestrained, the time and attention of the court might be devoted, in a measure disproportionate to their importance, to a series of facts not directly relevant to the issues between the parties in the proceedings. There is, therefore, a sensible rule, designed to avoid undue proliferation of side issues, that a cross-examiner must accept as final answers given in response to questions dealing with 'collateral' matters. Acceptance as final means that the cross-examiner cannot seek to contradict the answer by further evidence, and not that he himself cannot continue to challenge it in cross-examination, or is obliged to admit its truth.

The test of what is collateral is not always simple, but turns upon whether the content of the answer is of direct relevance to some issue which must be decided in order to resolve the proceedings in favour of one party or the other. If the matter is of such direct relevance, it is not collateral. Perhaps the most helpful statement of the rule was that made by Pollock CB in *Attorney-General* v *Hitchcock* (27), which was to the effect that if the answer given is a matter which would have been admissible in chief, as a piece of evidence called for the cross-examiner, because of its relevance to or connection with the issues in the case, then the matter is not collateral, and may be rebutted. It would follow that cross-examination going solely to credit will lead to collateral answers. Thus, in *R* v *Burke* (28), an Irish witness, giving evidence through an interpreter, asserted that he was unable to speak English. He denied in cross-examination having spoken English to two persons in court. It was not permissible to call evidence in rebuttal to the effect that the witness had spoken in English. But the position would be quite different if the witness's command of the language had been relevant, e.g. to his alleged authorship of some material document, or his ability to make an alleged confession or adverse admission and so had gone to an issue in the case. The effect is that the tribunal of fact must form a view of the witness's answer from their observation of the witness and the other evidence in the case.

A useful illustration of the rule can be seen in rape cases. If, on behalf of Coke, it were to be suggested to Margaret Blackstone that she had had previous sexual experience with Coke, or had in some way deliberately provoked Coke to sexual activity with her, such questions would go to the root of the defence, in that they are clearly relevant to the issue of consent. Conversely, if, with leave of the judge (29), it were to be suggested that Margaret had previously had sexual relations with Coke's mate, Kevin, that matter would be one going to credit only and would be final, as being collateral (30).

There are cases in which the exploration of collateral issues cannot be avoided if a fair

27   (1847) 1 Exch 91.
28   (1858) 8 Cox CC 44. See also *Harris* v *Tippett* (NP) (1811) 2 Camp 637 (suggestion to witness that he had tried to prevent cross-examiner's witness from attending court: denial held to be a collateral answer).
29   Required because of s. 2 of the Sexual Offences (Amendment) Act 1976; see 14.4, ante.
30   See *R* v *Riley* (CCR) (1887) 18 QBD 481; *R* v *Holmes* (CCR) (1871) LR 1 CCR 334; *aliter*, where sexual relations with others is directly relevant, e.g. in affiliation proceedings.

trial is to be secured, and in such cases an answer may be the subject of further evidence even if collateral. In this connection, we shall look at the statutory exception permitting the proof of previous convictions which have been denied, and the common law exceptions of bias or partiality, reputation for untruthfulness and medical evidence affecting reliability.

14.7.1 Previous convictions
By s. 6 of the Criminal Procedure Act 1865:

> A witness may be questioned as to whether he has been convicted of any misdemeanour, and upon being so questioned, if he either denies or does not admit the fact, or refuses to answer, it shall be lawful for the cross-examining party to prove such conviction; . . . [(31).]

This provision must, of course, be read subject to those of s. 1 (*e*) and (*f*) of the Criminal Evidence Act 1898, which govern and restrict the circumstances in which the defendant in a criminal case may be asked about his previous convictions (see 4.9 et seq, ante); and to those of the Rehabilitation of Offenders Act 1974 and of s. 16(2) of the Children and Young Persons Act 1963, governing and restricting the use of certain previous convictions to which those provisions refer (see 4.17, ante). In other words, s. 6 must be taken as meaning that, in cases where such questions may properly be put to a witness, the previous convictions may be proved, unless admitted. Of course, unlike more general allegations affecting credit, character and other collateral matters, previous convictions may be proved easily and with precision, the more so as the keeping of records becomes increasingly systematic, and permits increasing ease of access. Previous convictions may be proved, pursuant to the section, by a certificate of the court of conviction, purporting to be properly signed by the appropriate officer and dealing with the substance and effect of the charge and the conviction recorded, coupled with evidence of the identity of the witness with the person so convicted (32).

14.7.2 Bias or partiality
Any fact tending to suggest bias or partiality on the part of a witness may be cross-examined to, and may be proved in rebuttal, if denied. Although in a sense collateral, the matter is a vital one to be considered by any tribunal of fact. In *R* v *Mendy* (33) it was said that the rule of finality is not absolute, and that it is wrong to keep matters from the jury, which may suggest some attempt to interfere with the course of the trial in order to favour some bias or partiality. In that case the defendant's husband, who was to be called as a witness on her behalf, was waiting outside court (according to the usual practice in criminal cases) until his turn to give evidence. He denied later, in cross-examination, that while outside court he had spoken to a man who had been seen in the public gallery taking notes of other evidence. The implication was that the witness was prepared to inform himself illicitly of what was going on in court, prior to his being called, for the

---

31   The original wording referred to 'any felony or misdemeanour'; but by s. 1 of the Criminal Law Act 1967 the distinction was abolished, and the practice in all cases assimilated to that relating to misdemeanours. *Quaere*, whether the section applies to purely summary offences, whose status at common law was unclear.
32   See the remaining provisions of the section, and s. 18 of the Prevention of Crimes Act 1871. The evidence of identity need only be such that the court can properly draw the inference that it has been established, and need not be conclusive: *Martin* v *White* [1910] 1 KB 665.
33   (CA) (1976) 64 Cr App R 4. And see *Attorney-General* v *Hitchcock* (1847) 1 Exch 91, per Pollock CB at 100.

purpose of tailoring his evidence to the advantage of his wife. The prosecution were allowed to rebut the denial.

There are many ways in which bias or partiality may be manifested. In *R* v *Shaw* (34) a prosecution witness, who denied in cross-examination that he had quarrelled with the defendant and had threatened to take revenge on him, was allowed to be contradicted. In *R* v *Phillips* (35) the defendant was charged with incest with his daughter. His defence was that the daughter, and another daughter called to give evidence for the prosecution, has been 'schooled' in their evidence by their mother, and that the charge was a fabrication. In addition to this, it was suggested that the daughters had given similarly schooled evidence at a previous summary trial, at which the defendant had been bound over in respect of an alleged indecent assault on the same daughter. The girls denied in cross-examination that they were giving false evidence, and further denied having made admissions that their evidence at the summary trial had been schooled. It was held that the trial judge had erred in refusing to permit the defendant to call rebutting evidence from persons to whom the admissions were said to have been made. The Court of Criminal Appeal held that such evidence went 'to the very foundation of the appellant's answer to the charge', and not just to a question of credit (36).

Bias or partiality may, in some circumstances, arise from the relationship between a witness and the party on whose behalf he is called, although there must be something over and above the relationship itself, suggestive of such quality, on the facts of the case. In *Thomas* v *David* (37) in an action on a promissory note, a witness called for the plaintiff denied a suggestion made to her in cross-examination that she was the mistress of the plaintiff, her employer. The defendant's case was that he was not the maker of the note: in effect that it was a forgery. Coleridge J held that the relationship was relevant to the facts, and that the witness might be contradicted. After further evidence, a verdict was entered for the defendant. Coleridge J said (38):

Is it not material to the issue whether the principal witness who comes to support the plaintiff's case is his kept mistress? If the question had been whether the witness had walked the streets as a common prostitute, I think that that would have been collateral to the issue, and that, had the witness denied such a charge, she could not have been contradicted; but here, the question is, whether the witness had contracted such a relationship with the plaintiff, as might induce her the more readily to conspire with him to support a forgery.

A party may exhibit 'partiality' in relation to his own case, where he behaves in such a way as to suggest that his claim is false or exaggerated. For example, the plaintiff may have been heard to admit that he suffered injuries in a manner inconsistent with his cause of action against the defendant in respect of those injuries (39); or there may be evidence that the plaintiff has suborned false witnesses (40). These matters go beyond the

34   (1888) 16 Cox CC 503.   35   (1936) 26 Cr App R 17.
36   The phrasing of the judgment is not, with respect, entirely happy. The foundation of the defence was that the charge was untrue, not that the girls were not to be believed because they had admitted fabricating evidence before. Nor is the court's view that the rebutting evidence could be treated as evidence of the truth of the facts stated, free from difficulty. However, the decision is clearly right on the facts, as an example of partiality being suggested and denied.
37   (NP) (1836) 7 C & P 350. The decision has not escaped criticism: see, e.g., *R* v *Cargill* (CCA) [1913] 2 KB 271.
38   Ibid at 351.
39   Cf *Moriarty and Another* v *London, Chatham & Dover Railway Co.* (1870) LR 5 QB 314.
40   Cf *Melhuish* v *Collier* (1850) 15 QB 878.

question of credit, and are receivable in evidence as an admission adverse to the case of the party affected. If, therefore, such matters are put to a party called as a witness and are denied, they may be proved in rebuttal as relevant to the issues.

But the exception seems to apply only where there is alleged in cross-examination actual bias or partiality. The mere fact that a witness is alleged to have admitted some fact consistent with bias or partiality, for example that he has been offered a bribe in connection with his evidence in the case, will not suffice to defeat the finality rule, unless it is suggested that he was in fact offered, or accepted a bribe, i.e., that he is actually biased or partial (41). The fact that a witness has spoken of being offered or receiving a bribe may drastically affect his credit, but is nonetheless collateral to the issues in the case; a suggestion that he has in fact been offered or has accepted a bribe points to some actual defect in his evidence, which is directly relevant to the outcome of the case. In *Phillips*, the suggestion that the girls had admitted having given schooled evidence on a previous occasion, was secondary to the principal suggestion made to them, namely that their evidence at the instant trial was false and schooled, and it was to this point that the cross-examination was ultimately directed.

In *Attorney-General* v *Hitchcock* the defendant, a maltster, was charged with using a cistern in breach of certain statutory requirements. His counsel asked a prosecution witness in cross-examination whether he had not previously said that he had been offered £20 by officers of the Crown, if he would state in evidence that the cistern had been so used. The witness denied the allegation. The question was whether the defence were entitled to call a witness of their own to state that the prosecution witness had said this. It was held that they could not. Pollock CB said (42) that the reason was:

> . . . that it is totally irrelevant to the matter in issue, that some person should have thought fit to offer a bribe to the witness to give an untrue account of a transaction, and it is of no importance whatever, if that bribe was not accepted. It is no disparage-ment to a man that a bribe is offered to him: it may be a disparagement to the person who makes the offer. If, therefore, the witness is asked the fact, and denies it, or if he is asked whether he said so and so, and denies it, he cannot be contradicted as to what he has said. *Lord Stafford's* case was totally different. There the witness himself had been implicated in offering a bribe to some other person. That immediately affected him, as proving that he had acted the part of a suborner for the purpose of perverting the truth.

14.7.3 Reputation for untruthfulness

A witness may be called to state his opinion that a witness called on the other side should not be believed, in that he is unworthy of belief on his oath. This form of evidence is little used, and almost devoid of modern authority, but did arise for consideration in *R v Richardson; R v Longman* (43) in which the Court of Appeal took the opportunity of restating the extent of this exception to the rule of finality. It said that a witness may be asked whether he has knowledge of the reputation of the impugned witness on his oath. In the case under appeal the trial judge permitted evidence to be given thus far, but refused to allow a further question to be put in the form: 'From your personal knowledge of Mrs C, would you believe her on her oath?' It was held that this question should have

---

41   *Attorney-General* v *Hitchcock* (1847) 1 Exch 91.
42   Ibid at 101.
43   [1969] 1 QB 299.

been allowed also, and that the witness may state his own opinion in addition to his evidence of general reputation, provided always that his evidence is based upon his own personal knowledge. However, the Court of Appeal emphasised that a witness called for this purpose cannot, in chief, give his reasons for his opinion of the credibility on oath of the impugned witness. The inadmissibility of reasons in evidence in chief is an old rule, which at one time applied strictly to any evidence of opinion. It has almost certainly ceased to have effect, so far as expert-opinion evidence is concerned, and has been doubted increasingly in modern practice. But it is submitted that in the present context, it is of considerable value in preventing a multiplicity of side issues from arising, which the court could not hope to investigate satisfactorily. There is no power to prevent the witness being asked for his reasons in cross-examination, although the course would ordinarily be a perilous one, and the answers would have to be accepted as final.

14.7.4   Medical evidence affecting reliability

Medical evidence may be called to show that a witness suffers from some disease or defect or abnormality of the mind, such as to affect the reliability of his evidence. The rule is akin to, but more specialised than that just discussed concerning reputation and opinion. The modern rule is to be gleaned from *Toohey v Commissioner of Police of the Metropolis* (44). Toohey and two others were charged with assault with intent to rob. Their defence was that the alleged victim had been drinking and was behaving very strangely, and that while they were taking him home, he had become hysterical and had imagined that he was going to be robbed. A police surgeon gave evidence for the defence and said that when he examined the alleged victim there were no signs of injury on him, that he smelt of alcohol, and that throughout the examination he was weeping and hysterical. The appeal turned on the question whether the trial judge was correct in refusing to allow the doctor to be asked his opinion of the part played by alcohol in the victim's hysteria, and whether he was more prone to hysteria than a normal person. The House of Lords held that the further questions should have been permitted, firstly because they sought to elicit matters of direct relevance to the defence, and secondly, because the evidence was admissible for the purpose of impeaching the victim's credit as a witness. The second of these reasons involved overruling the decision of the Court of Criminal Appeal in *R v Gunewardene* (45), in which it had been held that the most that could be asked of a medical witness was whether, from his knowledge, he would believe the impugned witness on his oath; and that no reasons might be given in chief. This would have equated a doctor with a witness called to deal with general reputation, or to give a lay opinion based upon personal knowledge. Lord Pearce reviewed the older authorties, concluding that 'the older cases are concerned with lying as an aspect of bad character, and are of little help in establishing any principle that will deal with modern scientific knowledge of mental disease and its effect on the reliability of a witness'. Later in his speech, with which the other members of the House concurred, Lord Pearce observed (46):

Human evidence shares the frailties of those who give it. It is subject to many cross-currents such as partiality, prejudice, self-interest and above all, imagination and inaccuracy. Those are matters with which the jury, helped by cross-examination and common sense, must do their best. But when a witness through physical (in which

44   [1965] AC 595.
45   [1951] 2 KB 600.   46   [1965] AC at 608.

I include mental) disease or abnormality is not capable of giving a true or reliable account to the jury, it must surely be allowed for medical science to reveal this vital hidden fact to them.

Lord Pearce concluded (47):

> *Gunewardene's* case was, in my opinion, wrongly decided. Medical evidence is admissible to show that a witness suffers from some disease or defect or abnormality of mind that affects the reliability of his evidence. Such evidence is not confined to a general opinion of the unreliability of the witness but may give all the matters necessary to show, not only the foundation of and reasons for the diagnosis, but also the extent to which the credibility of the witness is affected.

There is a clear distinction between medical evidence and lay opinion of credibility, which justifies the admission of a full and detailed assessment of the impugned witness by a doctor as a piece of expert-opinion evidence. This naturally involves giving reasons in chief, but where expert evidence is concerned the objections to the admission of reasons, which weigh heavily in the case of lay witnesses, are entirely absent; indeed, the evidence would be likely to prove unhelpful, if not meaningless, if reasons were not given.

14.8 Cross-examination on documents

We have already dealt with, and need not repeat, the rules relating to the use of previous written statements inconsistent with the present testimony of a witness, and cross-examination on documents used to refresh the memory (see 13.2.2, 13.4.2 and 14.6, ante). We saw that if a document is put in evidence as a result of cross-examination in these circumstances then its evidential effect is limited in criminal cases following the rules of the common law, but that, by virtue of s. 3 of the Civil Evidence Act 1968, it may in a civil case be treated as evidence of any fact stated in it of which direct oral evidence would be admissible. We must now look at the use in cross-examination of documents which do not fall into those categories, and which stand or fall in their own right as pieces of evidence, according to the normal rules of admissibility. Such documents are obviously of an almost infinitely various nature, and may be either in the possession of the cross-examiner or of the opponent of the cross-examiner.

A document in the possession of the cross-examiner is either admissible in itself, in which case it may be put in evidence and cross-examined in its own right, or inadmissible (usually on the ground of hearsay) in itself. We have seen that evidence cannot be made admissible just because it is used in cross-examination if it was inadmissible in chief, as in *R v Treacy* (48), where it was held improper to cross-examine upon the contents of a document which had been held to be inadmissible (49). The most that can be done with an inadmissible document, therefore, is to ask the witness to look at the document and, without describing the nature or contents of the document to the court, to invite him to consider whether he wishes to give any further or different evidence (50). If a witness, on

---

47 Ibid at 609.
48 (CCA) [1944] 2 All ER 229.
49 Of course, the contents of an inadmissible document may be extremely useful in providing information from which questions in cross-examination may be framed. It is perfectly proper to make use of the contents for the purpose of framing the most effective questions, provided that the existence and contents of the document are not revealed to the court: *R v Rice and Others* (CCA) [1963] 1 QB 857.
50 See *R v Yousry* (CCA) (1914) 11 Cr App R 13.

being shown a document, asserts or admits that its contents are true, then those contents which he so adopts become part of his evidence. But the contents of an inadmissible document cannot be made evidence unless they are so adopted. In *R* v *Gillespie and Simpson* (51) the defendants were charged with offences of dishonesty in accounting to their employers for sums of money less than those which, according to the documentation prepared by salesgirls, had been received from customers. The conviction was quashed, on the ground that the defendants had been asked in cross-examination to read aloud the documents prepared by the salesgirls, who had not been called. What the prosecution had done was to purport to make admissible the contents of documents which were inadmissible hearsay, merely by putting them to the defendants, when the defendants did not in any way adopt or acknowledge the truth of those contents.

Documents in the possession of the opponent of the cross-examiner are subject to a special rule. At common law, if the cross-examiner calls for and inspects in court, a document in the possession of his opponent or his opponent's witness, then the cross-examiner is bound to put the document in evidence as part of the cross-examiner's case. Thus, in *Stroud* v *Stroud* (52), in the course of a defended suit for divorce, counsel for the husband cross-examined a doctor called on behalf of the wife, and called for and inspected in court certain medical reports prepared by other doctors concerning the wife, which the witness had with him. It was held that counsel for the wife was entitled to insist upon the reports being put in as part of the husband's case; and counsel for the husband having elected to put in some of them, counsel for the wife was entitled to have the remainder put in also. The rule is a curious one, and it is to be noted that it comes into operation even if cross-examination has not been concerned with the contents of the documents. The rule developed in the absence of a general process of discovery at common law, and it was argued before Wrangham J in *Stroud* v *Stroud* that the modern principle of disclosure of all relevant, non-privileged documents, had rendered the rule obsolete. The learned judge accepted that in the case of documents which had not, but ought to have been, disclosed on discovery, the cross-examiner would be entitled to inspect them in court, as he would have been before the start of the trial, under the Rules of Court. But although the importance of the rule has undoubtedly diminished since the advent of a general principle of disclosure, Wrangham J pointed out that the rule may still be of significance in cases where there is no discovery, particularly in criminal cases; and indeed, it would seem still to apply to such cases.

One argument worthy of attention, which was not available at the time of *Stroud* v *Stroud* is that the position must have been altered, at least to some extent, by s. 1(1) of the Civil Evidence Act 1968 which provides that:

> In any civil proceedings a statement other than one made by a person while giving oral evidence in those proceedings shall be admissible as evidence of any fact stated therein to the extent that it is so admissible by virtue of any provision of this Part of this Act or by virtue of any other statutory provision or by agreement of the parties, but not otherwise.

This section may affect the rule in civil cases because of the clear limitation of the words 'but not otherwise', but only on the assumption that documents so put in evidence are admitted as evidence of the truth of the facts stated therein. Whether this is so

---

51   (CA) (1967) 51 Cr App R 172.
52   [1963] 1 WLR 1080. Contrast carefully the rule applying to documents used to refresh the memory, which is quite distinct: *Senat* v *Senat* [1965] P 172; see 13.2, ante.

appears never to have been decided in England (53), but it is difficult to see any other basis, which would apply equally to all cases, on which documents could be admitted if called for and inspected. It is strange that the point has never been decided in a criminal case, where s. 1 could not interfere with the admission of such documents. It may be that the courts would hesitate long before admitting hearsay in such circumstances, and would opt for some lesser evidential purpose according to the nature of the document in any given case. This would inevitably involve some difficulty, because no obvious evidential purpose presents itself (for example, consistency) which could be applied uniformly to all documents admitted under the rule. If the rule is to survive, some statutory clarification would not be unwelcome.

B: BEYOND CROSS-EXAMINATION

14.9 Re-examination

Very little need be said about re-examination. It is the process whereby a party calling a witness may seek to explain or clarify any points that arose in cross-examination and appear to be unfavourable to his case. Re-examination is, therefore, possible only where there has been cross-examination: it is not an opportunity to adduce further evidence in chief. Thus, in *Prince* v *Samo* (54) where cross-examination took place of a witness for the plaintiff about part of a hearsay statement, which would have been wholly inadmissible in chief, the plaintiff was entitled to re-examine on any matter arising from the portion of the statement referred to in cross-examination, but was not entitled to elicit any other portion.

But a witness is entitled to explain any apparent contradiction or ambiguity in his evidence or damage to his credit arising from cross-examination, and this may involve reference to facts which have not previously been given in evidence, if they are properly relevant in order to deal with the points put in cross-examination. Where, therefore, a witness was asked in cross-examination why his evidence was that the defendant was one of a number of persons who attacked a deceased, when he had made a statement in which he did not refer to the defendant at all, he was allowed to be asked in re-examination whether he had made an earlier statement, in which he had referred to the defendant (55). In this case, the re-examination was directed to re-establishing the credit of the witness but the principle is the same where it is sought to clear up some question of fact. And evidence admitted in re-examination can, therefore, be powerful and dangerous. The effect of cross-examination in letting in further evidence must be carefully considered before it is embarked upon. If, for example, it is suggested in cross-examination of a police officer that the officer followed the defendant because of a determination to be vindictive against him, the officer may be re-examined to elicit his true reasons for following him. The resulting evidence, which would have been wholly inadmissible in chief, is potentially devastating.

Leading questions are not permitted in re-examination, for the same reason as in the case of examination in chief.

---

53 The position appears to have been recognised as being so in Australia: see the authorities set out by Professor Cross, *Evidence*, 5th ed., p.262.
54 (1838) 7 A & E 627.
55 *R* v *Coll* (CCR, Ireland) (1889) 24 IR 522.

14.10   Evidence in rebuttal

The general rule of practice, in both criminal and civil cases, is that every party must call all the evidence on which he proposes to rely during the presentation of his case, and before closing his case. This involves the proposition that the parties should foresee, during their preparations for trial, what the issues will be, and what evidence is available and necessary in order to deal with those issues. The definition of the issues in a civil case by exchange of pleadings, and in a criminal case (to a far more limited extent) by service of the prosecution statements and the settling of an indictment (56), is designed to enable this to be done wherever possible.

It must, however, be recognised that in some cases, it will not be possible to foresee every piece of evidence which may be required, because proceedings have a habit of taking courses which occasion surprise and sometimes embarrassment to one or more of the parties. It has long been the rule that the judge may permit evidence to be called by a party who has been taken by surprise by some development at the trial, in order to 'rebut' evidence given against him by the other side, after that party's case has been formally closed (57). The circumstances in which this discretion will be exercised have not always been so clear.

It is certain that the power will not be exercised in order to aid a careless or inadvertent party, who has simply failed to take the trouble to prepare his case adequately. And it would be carelessness or inadvertence to fail to foresee that the other side will bring evidence designed to contradict and disprove one's case. The test was originally that laid down by Tindal CJ in *R v Frost* (58), in fairly restrictive terms:

> the crown...cannot afterwards support their case by calling fresh witnesses, because they are met by certain evidence that contradicts it. They stand or fall by the evidence they have given...but if any matter arises *ex improviso* which no human ingenuity can foresee...there seems to me no reason why the matter which so arose *ex improviso* may not be answered by contrary evidence on the part of the Crown.

In more modern times, it has been felt that the test propounded by Tindal CJ is unduly narrow, and ought to be restated to allow the trial judge more discretion to further the interests of justice (59), and it is pertinent to note that the competence of the defendant as a witness since 1898, coupled with his right in most cases (60) to withhold his defence until trial, has made the task of the prosecution more difficult. It may be, although *R v Frost* has not been overruled, that the test is now one of reasonable foreseeability, and that if the course of the trial takes a party into uncharted waters, which could not have been anticipated before trial on a sensible and alert view of the case, further evidence ought to be permitted to deal with the matters which have occasioned surprise (61).

56   The defence are not obliged to reveal the nature of the defence before trial, except where they are required to serve notice of alibi, and even then the judge has a discretion to permit evidence of alibi to be given, notwithstanding that no notice has been served: Criminal Justice Act 1967, s. 11.

57   But in a case tried with a jury, no evidence may be given after the retirement of the jury. In a criminal case, any breach of this rule will lead to the conviction being quashed: *R v Owen* (CCA) [1952] 2 QB 362; even where the evidence is apparently irrelevant: *R v Wilson* (CCA) (1957) 41 Cr App R 226; and even where the defence consent: *R v Corless* (CA) (1972) 56 Cr App R 341. Though the Court of Criminal Appeal has approved the admission of evidence for the defence, where a witness arrived at court during the summing-up (and so was not being recalled) and the judge summed up his evidence subsequently: *R v Sanderson* [1953] 1 WLR 392. As to the position in Magistrates' Courts, see *Webb v Leadbetter* (DC) [1966] 1 WLR 245.

58   (1840) 9 C & P 129 as reported in 4 St Tr NS 85 at 386.

59   See, e.g., *R v Crippen* (CCA) [1911] 1 KB 149

60   See note 56, ante.

61   Cf *R v Owen* (CCA) [1952] 2 QB 362, per Lord Goddard CJ at 366; *R v Milliken* (CA) (1969) 53 Cr App R 330 at 333.

Certainly, it would seem wrong for the court to be deprived of material evidence in such circumstances, which might be the case on the basis of an unbending interpretation of the words, 'which no human ingenuity can foresee'.

But on either test, the rule will not cover evidence which was clearly reasonably foreseeable, and ought to have been adduced as a proper and necessary part of the prosecution case. In *R* v *Day* (62) a conviction was quashed where the prosecution were permitted to call a handwriting expert, not only after the close of their own case, but after the defendant had given evidence, and where it was obvious from the outset that the evidence might well be required.

In civil cases, evidence in rebuttal has been permitted in cases where evidence has been given, or issues raised, which could not have been foreseen on the pleadings and which have accordingly taken a party by surprise; or where a party has been misled about the true nature of the claim or defence. But in a civil action, the judge may equally decline to entertain any unpleaded issue, and will usually do so if the departure from the pleaded issues is a serious one, going to the very nature of the claim or defence. This consideration indeed reflects the true objection to evidence in rebuttal, which is that the contrary case will already have been presented, to an end and in a way which does not correspond with the actuality, and the prejudice which can arise if a party is allowed to alter his case, after the case against him has been presented, is obvious.

Evidence in rebuttal is not permissible of collateral matters except in certain cases (63) or where it would simply be confirmatory of the party's case as already put (64).

14.11 Evidence admissible under s. 7 of the Civil Evidence Act 1968

The major objection to the admission of hearsay evidence is that it cannot effectively be cross-examined to, and in particular, it may be observed that it is difficult, if it is possible at all, to impugn effectively the credibility of the maker of a hearsay statement, who is not called as a witness. Nonetheless, in civil cases, certain hearsay statements are now admissible, as evidence of the facts stated in them, whether or not the maker is called to give evidence in those proceedings (65). Part 1 of the Civil Evidence Act 1968, which provides for the general admissibility of such statements, seeks to offer at least some compensation for the inability of an opponent to cross-examine the maker of a statement who is not called as a witness. S. 7 provides:

(1) ... where in any civil proceedings a statement made by a person who is not called as a witness in those proceedings is given in evidence by virtue of s. 2 of this Act—

(a) any evidence which, if that person had been so called, would be admissible for the purpose of destroying or supporting his credibility as a witness shall be admissible for that purpose in those proceedings; and
(b) evidence tending to prove that, whether before or after he made that statement, that person made (whether orally or in a document or otherwise) another statement inconsistent therewith shall be admissible for the purpose of showing that that person has contradicted himself: ...

The section, therefore, simulates the cross-examiner's weapons of cross-examination

62 (CCA) [1940] 1 All ER 402.
63 See 14.7, ante.　64 *Jacobs* v *Tarleton* (1848) 11 QB 421.
65 See 8.4 et seq, ante, in which the detailed working of part 1 of the Act is dealt with.

concerning credit, and the use of previous inconsistent statements. Although in the absence of the maker, the weapons provided by s. 7 are obviously less potent than in a case where cross-examination is possible, there are disadvantages also for the party putting in the evidence, who may be unable to restore the credit of the maker, or to explain any apparent ambiguity or inconsistency in his statements.

The same limits on the exploration of collateral matters are prescribed as would be the case in cross-examination. The proviso to s. 7(1) reads:

> Provided that nothing in this subsection shall enable evidence to be given of any matter of which, if the person in question had been called as a witness and had denied that matter in cross-examination, evidence could not have been adduced by the cross-examining party.

The section also equates the evidential effect of previous inconsistent statements proved by virtue of s. 7(1)(b) with that of such statements put to a witness under s. 4 or s. 5 of the Criminal Procedure Act 1865. Although the primary purpose of such statements, reflected in s. 7(1)(b) itself, is to show the inconsistency of the maker, in a civil case the statements put may also be used as evidence of the admissible facts stated in them, by virtue of s. 3(1)(a) of the Act. Accordingly, by s. 7(3), the provisions of s. 3(1)(a) are expressly applied to statements admitted under s. 7(1)(b), so that these statements also may be treated as evidence of any fact stated in them, of which direct oral evidence by their maker would be admissible.

S. 7(2) extends the operation of s. 7(1) to persons who originally supply information from which a record, admissible by virtue of s. 4, is compiled, and such a person may, therefore, be treated in all respects as if he were the maker of a hearsay statement admissible by virtue of s. 2.

14.12   Judge's power to call witnesses

Ordinarily, the working of the adversarial system in litigation requires that the judge should not interfere with the decision of the parties to call or not to call certain evidence. In a civil case, where the judge has the duty of finding the facts, as well as that of presiding over the conduct of the trial, he is entitled to draw any proper inferences about the strength or weakness of a party's case from failure to call what appears to be relevant and available evidence. In a criminal trial, however, somewhat different considerations apply, because of the incidence of the burden and standard or proof, and because of the judge's particular duty to ensure a fair trial of the issue of guilt or innocence.

It has long been recognised that the judge has power, in a criminal trial, to call of his own motion any witness who has not been called either for the prosecution or the defence, if in his opinion it is necessary to do so in the interests of justice (66). The power must be exercised with great care, bearing in mind both that it is the duty of the prosecution to call all the witnesses on the back of the indictment, unless they appear to be incapable of belief, even where they may give evidence inconsistent with the prosecution case. If the prosecution fail to call a witness who on the face of it ought to be called, it is open to the judge to invite the prosecution to call him (67). If neither side call a witness, the judge should assume that there is a good reason for such a course,

---

66   R v Chapman (1838) 8 C & P 558.
67   R v Oliva (CCA) [1965] 1 WLR 1028.

especially where neither side make any application to him in the matter. It has often been said that the judge's power to call a witness should be exercised rarely and sparingly (68). Like any other evidence, the witness must be called before the retirement of the jury, and there is no doubt that it must be even rarer than suggested above, that he should be called after the defence case has been closed.

In *R v Cleghorn* (69) a conviction was quashed where, on a charge of rape, the trial judge called a witness who had not been called by either side. The witness was called after the defence case had been closed, and the case thereafter assumed a different aspect. Although no rule applicable to all cases can be laid down, it has been helpfully suggested (70) that the calling of witnesses by the judge should generally be confined to cases where, analogous to the case of *R v Frost* (71), a matter has arisen '*ex improviso*, which no human ingenuity can foresee'. One proper use of the power is a case where the judge concludes that the prosecution are wrongly declining to call a witness, who ought to be called in the interests of a fair trial. It is not always an answer to say that the defence can call the witness, because they should be in a position to cross-examine and not be obliged to call him as their witness in chief (72). It may also be proper for the judge to call a witness who seems hostile to both sides, but whose evidence may nonetheless be material.

A witness called by the judge may be cross-examined by either side only with leave (73), although if his evidence affects adversely the case for either side, it is inconceivable that leave should be refused.

14.13 Questions for counsel

1 May counsel for Coke cross-examine Margaret Blackstone as to:
  (a) The fact that she consented to have sexual intercourse with Coke on 8 July 1979?
  (b) The fact that she had led him to believe on other occasions that she was prepared to have sexual intercourse with him?
  (c) The fact that Margaret is promiscuous?
  (d) The fact that Margaret has had sexual intercourse with Coke's mate, Kevin?
  (e) The fact that Margaret threatened to accuse Kevin of raping her?
  (f) The fact that Margaret has previous convictions for theft?
2 In relation to any of these matters on which cross-examination is possible, would the defence be entitled to call evidence in rebuttal if Margaret denies them in cross--examination?
3 If Margaret's evidence in chief varies materially from the contents of her statement to the police, what steps may Coke's counsel take? What results will any such course have, and what must counsel bear in mind before embarking on it?
4 If Margaret has a known history of lying, what evidence might be called on behalf of Coke to deal with this?

68 See, e.g., *R v Edwards and Others* (1848) 3 Cox CC 82; *R v Cleghorn* [1967] 2 QB 584.
69 [1967] 2 QB 584.
70 In *R v Harris* (CCA) [1927] 2 KB 587.
71 (1840) 9 C & P 129 as reported in 4 St Tr NS 85 at 386. See 14.10, *ante*.
72 Cf *R v Tregear* (CA) [1967] 2 QB 574. The prosecution's duty must be exercised so as to further the cause of justice, which must involve consideration of the consequences of the defence calling a witness in chief. But if the evidence of a witness would form a natural part of the defence case then the prosecution are not obliged to call him, particularly if doing so would merely confuse the jury: *R v Nugent* [1977] 1 WLR 789.
73 *Coulson v Disborough* (CA) [1894] 2 QB 316.

15 Corroboration

15.1 Meaning of corroboration

The word 'corroboration' connotes support or confirmation, and indicates, in relation to the law of evidence, that certain evidence (the evidence to be corroborated) is confirmed in its tenor and effect by other admissible and independent evidence (the corroborating evidence). In any case where one piece of evidence confirms and supports another, corroboration therefore takes place if both pieces of evidence are accepted by the tribunal of fact (1). Although, as an obvious truism, any case is stronger if evidence in its support is corroborated than it would otherwise be, this elementary proposition of weight is not what most concerns us in the law of evidence. The law must perceive and resolve the fundamental question of whether the court should ever be permitted to act, for the purpose of giving judgment in favour of a party, upon the uncorroborated evidence of a single witness or document, tendered alone and unsupported in proof of that party's case; or whether, conversely, there is any need to insist upon corroboration of evidence, so that the unsupported evidence of a single witness or document will always be sufficient, if accepted by the court; or whether, to take a middle view, there are certain cases (and if so, what cases) in which corroboration of the evidence of a single witness or document should be required before a case can be found to be proved.

Both extreme views present problems. A complete disregard for the desirability of corroboration may indicate a lack of sensitivity to the inherent unreliability of certain types of evidence, and may render some decisions unsafe. On the other hand, a rigid insistence upon corroboration may unnecessarily damn many a perfectly sound case which has the misfortune to have been witnessed by only one person.

15.2 The rule at common law

In contrast to systems of law based on Roman law, in which there is a general require- ment of corroboration, the common law holds that in the absence of some specific rule to the contrary, the court may for any purpose act upon the uncorroborated evidence of a single witness or document (2). The rule applies both to civil and criminal cases (3) and regardless of whether the evidence in support of the case is agreed or disputed. It need

---

1   There is nothing technical in the idea of corroboration. When in the ordinary affairs of life one is doubtful whether or not to believe a particular statement one naturally looks to see whether it fits in with other statements or circumstances relating to the particular matter; the better it fits in, the more one is inclined to believe it.' *DPP* v *Kilbourne* [1973] AC 729 per Lord Reid at 750.
2   Despite the apparent divergence, the rules of Roman and common law probably produce little significant difference in practice, there being a wide measure of agreement about the kinds of evidence which are reliable and those that are prone to be unreliable. The difference is that in one system, the result is arrived at by applying 'the general rule' and in the other by applying 'an exception to the general rule', according to the circumstances.
3   Corroboration is of greatest importance in relation to criminal cases, the critical authorities being concerned

hardly be emphasised that, quite apart from any question of requirement, any party is at liberty to adduce whatever evidence he sees fit by way of corroboration of other evidence in his favour, subject to the rules of admissibility.

The common-law rule has been modified by two groups of exceptions in which a requirement of corroboration has been recognised, either by statute or by the practice of the common law itself. The two groups differ considerably in nature and operation, and must be kept entirely distinct. Nonetheless, they share a common *raison d'être*, namely a cogent justification for not acting on the uncorroborated evidence of a single witness. In some cases, the justification is to be found in the gravity of the subject-matter of the case itself, but more frequently it lies in the inherent danger of unreliability of certain classes of evidence. Such danger may arise from the personal characteristics of a witness, for example age, from some personal interest in the outcome of a case or in the acceptance of his evidence, from some personal motive for giving evidence against a party, or simply from the nature of the evidence itself. The groups of exceptions comprise:

(a)   Cases where corroboration is required as a matter of law. In these cases, certain kinds of evidence are required as a matter of law to be corroborated, before any conviction or judgment may be based upon them. The requirement is provided for by statute and is mandatory, so that if there is no evidence capable of amounting to corroboration, the judge must withdraw the case from the jury, or dismiss the claim, as the case may be. A conviction or judgment obtained in breach of the requirement will be set aside on appeal.

(b)   Cases where corroboration is to be looked for as a matter of practice. In these cases, the common law has recognised the undesirability of a tribunal of fact acting on certain kinds of uncorroborated evidence, without warning itself of the danger of so doing. What is mandatory in these cases is an appropriate warning, usually conveyed by judge to jury in the course of summing-up, of the danger involved. The absence of such warning will be ground of appeal, and despite the use of the term, 'a matter of practice', the requirement of a warning is in effect a rule of law and is mandatory (4). The important difference between these cases and the cases in which corroboration is a statutory requirement is that here, provided the jury are properly warned, they may if they wish act on the uncorroborated evidence in question, for the purpose of convicting, and if they do so, no appeal will lie for that reason (5).

These two groups of exception must shortly be examined in detail, but it will first be useful to consider the respective roles of judge and jury in the treatment of corroboration, and the legal qualities which evidence must possess, in order to be held capable of corroborating other evidence. These considerations underlie the rules applicable to the exceptional cases.

with directions by judge to jury on the subject. Appellate courts are frequently apt to quash convictions on appeal for misdirection. In civil cases, appellate courts are slow to intervene unless it is shown that the trial judge simply did not advert to the question, and express references are not usually essential in the judgment, provided that the judge was alive to the dangers, if any, inherent in the evidence. It cannot be assumed so safely that juries will appreciate the problem.

---

4   *R* v *Baskerville* (CCA) [1916] 2 KB 658; *Davies* v *DPP* (HL) [1954] AC 378.
5   *R* v *Baskerville* (CCA) [1916] 2 KB 658.

15.3 Functions of judge and jury

The assessment of corroboration falls into two parts, which are respectively a question of law and a question of fact. Whether evidence is capable in law of constituting corroboration is a question of law for the judge. In deciding the question, the judge must consider whether the evidence said to be capable of corroboration fulfils the requirements dealt with in 15.4 below. In the light of his conclusions, the judge must then either withdraw the case from the jury, if corroboration is required as a matter of law and none is available, or give the jury the necessary warning, if the jury are required to look for corroboration as a matter of practice. The direction must, of course, include appropriate guidance on what parts of the available evidence the jury are entitled to regard as corroborative, or, if it be the case, that there is no such evidence (6). There is a real possibility that a jury may be confused by a direction couched in technical legal terms, and the judge should state the requirements using everyday language. It is unnecessary to use the word 'corroboration' itself, and indeed, it may be preferable to avoid it and employ some synonym such as 'support' or 'confirmation' (7). However, the question whether evidence capable of corroborating other evidence does in fact do so is one of fact for the jury, like any other question of the acceptance, rejection or weight of evidence (8).

15.4 Necessary qualities of corroborative evidence

In order to be capable in law of constituting corroboration, evidence must be (a) admissible in itself; (b) from a source independent of the evidence requiring to be corroborated; and (c) such as to tend to show, by confirmation of some material particular, not only that the offence charged was committed, but also that it was committed by the defendant. In *R* v *Baskerville* (9) Lord Reading CJ expressed the requirements in the following terms:

> ... evidence in corroboration must be independent testimony which affects the accused by connecting or tending to connect him with the crime. In other words, it must be evidence which implicates him, that is, which confirms in some material particular not only the evidence that the crime has been committed, but also that the prisoner committed it. The test applicable to determine the nature and extent of the corroboration is thus the same whether the case falls within the rule of practice at common law or within that class of offences for which corroboration is required by statute. [(10).]

15.4.1 Admissible
This means, of course, that the evidence must conform in itself with the general rules of

6   *R* v *Charles and Others* (CA) (1976) 68 Cr App R 334n.
7   *DPP* v *Kilbourne* (HL) [1973] AC 729 per Lord Hailsham of St Marylebone at 740; *DPP* v *Hester* (HL) [1973] AC 296 per Lord Diplock at 327.
8   The jury of course will not act for any purpose on evidence which they reject. See *DPP* v *Hester* (HL) [1973] AC 296 per Lord Morris of Borth-y-Gest at 315; *DPP* v *Kilbourne* (HL) [1973] AC 729 per Lord Hailsham of St Marylebone at 746.
9   (CCA) [1916] 2 KB 658 at 667. See also *DPP* v *Kilbourne* [1973] AC 729 per Lord Hailsham of St Marylebone at 741.
10   The same principles appear to apply to civil cases in which corroboration is to be looked for: *Alli* v *Alli* (DC) [1965] 3 All ER 480.

admissibility and so be capable of being received for the purpose of proving guilt as charged.

15.4.2   Independent

It is obvious that confirmation of the evidence of a witness is worthless coming from the witness himself, or for that matter, from one with whom the witness has been in collusion (11). In *R v Whitehead* (12), where the defendant was charged with unlawful sexual intercourse with a girl under sixteen, it was suggested that the girl's recent complaint made to her mother was capable of constituting the necessary corroboration of her evidence. Lord Hewart CJ pointed out that if this were the case, '... it is only necessary for her to repeat her story some twenty-five times in order to get twenty-five corroborations of it.' Thus, even where at common law, a previous statement made by the witness is admissible, as in the case of a recent complaint, it cannot amount to corroboration of the witness's evidence (13). At common law, such statements, previous inconsistent statements put in cross-examination, or documents used to refresh the memory admitted as a result of cross-examination, are admissible only exceptionally and even then are not evidence of the truth of their contents; so that in addition to their lack of independence, they fail the test of admissibility for the required purpose of proof of guilt (14). In civil cases, however, previous statements made by a witness are now, by statute, not only admissible but admissible as evidence of the truth of their contents, subject to the provisions of s. 2, 3 and 4 of the Civil Evidence Act 1968 (see Chapter 8, ante). It was accordingly thought necessary to deal expressly with the status of such statements for the purposes of corroboration, and the Act confirms that the lack of independence precludes their use for this purpose. S. 6(4) of the Act provides:

For the purpose of any enactment or rule of law or practice requiring evidence to be corroborated or regulating the manner in which uncorroborated evidence is to be treated —

(a) a statement which is admissible in evidence by virtue of section 2 or 3 of this Act shall not be capable of corroborating evidence given by the maker of the statement; and

(b) a statement which is admissible in evidence by virtue of section 4 of this Act shall not be capable of corroborating evidence given by the person who originally supplied the information from which the record containing the statement was compiled.

It is clear, therefore, that whatever other corroboration may be available of the evidence of Margaret Blackstone of the alleged rape by Coke, corroboration may not be found in her complaint to her mother, even if the complaint is admissible. It makes no difference whether evidence of the complaint is given by Margaret, her mother or both, because it is the source of the statement which lacks independence. It is, however,

---

11   A rule which is not avoided even by the ingenious suggestion made through the mouth of Jack Point in Gilbert and Sullivan's *Yeomen of the Guard* that the evidence of one of his eyes was corroborated by that of the other!

12   (CCA) [1929] 1 KB 99. See also *R v Christie* (HL) [1914] AC 545.

13   It has, however, been held that independent evidence of the complainant's distress near to the time of the alleged offence may amount to corroboration of the complainant's evidence, although where such condition is no more than part and parcel of the recent complaint, it is difficult to see that this is acceptable: *R v Redpath* (CCA)' (1962) 46 Cr App R 319; *R v Wilson* (CA) (1973) 58 Cr App R 304.

14   See Chapter 13, ante; and *R v Virgo* (CA) (1978) 67 Cr App R 323.

possible that corroboration may be found in the evidence of Margaret's distressed condition given by her mother and Dr Vesey, subject to the caveat referred to in note 13.

15.4.3 *Confirmation of material particular tending to show not only commission of the offence but also its commission by the defendant*

This condition is the most restrictive and limiting of the legal requirements for corroboration. The extent to which evidence needs to be corroborated is a question almost as fundamental as that of whether it should be required at all. Little reflection is needed to see that it cannot be required that evidence should be corroborated in every point, because the demands of such a rule would be too onerous, and because the evidence requiring to be corroborated would then become almost superfluous. On the other hand, confirmation of some minor or peripheral detail in an item of evidence would not be enough to increase confidence in it to the desired degree. The rule, therefore, is that the corroborating evidence must confirm the evidence requiring corroboration in at least one particular which is directly relevant to the issues in the case, in that it tends to suggest not only that the offence charged has been committed, but also that it has been committed by the defendant. It does not matter that the evidence may be circumstantial rather than direct, as long as the jury would be entitled to draw from it an inference, which, if drawn, would have the effect of implicating the defendant in the offence charged, in accordance with the rule.

Cracknell v *Smith* (15) was an affiliation case, in which the evidence of the complainant required to be corroborated as a matter of law. The complainant gave evidence of having had sexual intercourse with the defendant at about the likely time of conception. It was suggested that the evidence of her mother to the effect that the defendant had visited her home to see the complainant at about the relevant period, and had met the complainant at the corner of the street on various occasions, might amount to corroboration. The argument was rejected on appeal by the Divisional Court. The evidence amounted to no more than evidence of opportunity, and did not either directly or by any permissible inference implicate the defendant in an act of sexual intercourse with the complainant. And in *James* v *R* (16), on a charge of rape, it was held that medical evidence showing that the complainant had had sexual intercourse at about a time consistent with her allegation, was incapable of affording corroboration of her evidence of the rape, because it did not confirm any more than an act of sexual intercourse and in particular did not offer any confirmation of the identity of the man involved or of the alleged lack of consent. This authority is of direct relevance to the case of Coke, in so far as the evidence of Dr Vesey and Dr Espinasse goes only to show sexual intercourse, which is not in dispute, and does not confirm Margaret's evidence of lack of consent. Had the medical evidence gone further, and demonstrated some injury consistent with forcible intercourse, the position would be very different, and such evidence would, no doubt, be capable of corroborating Margaret's evidence.

The above rules apply in every case where corroboration is required as a matter of law or looked for as a matter of practice, as Lord Reading CJ pointed out in *R* v *Baskerville*, though it might be strictly more accurate to say that they apply to every such case, subject to any express modification suggested by the wording of the statute in the former class of case. As we shall see, the wording of the sections within this class is not uniform, but in

15   [1960] 1 WLR 1239.
16   (PC, Jamaica) (1970) 55 Cr App R 299.

practice, the actual requirement seems to vary very little. We must now turn to examine the cases involved in the two categories of exceptions to the common-law rule.

15.5 Corroboration required as a matter of law

We have already noted that the exceptions within this category are statutory cases, and that the absence of evidence capable of amounting to the necessary corroboration will be fatal to the conviction or judgment. It must also follow that if the jury reject all the evidence capable of amounting to such corroboration, no conviction is possible, and the jury should be directed in those terms. The terms and extent of the corroboration required in each case are provided for by the statute itself, and except as so provided no further corroboration is necessary as a matter of law. It may, of course, happen that the evidence in a particular case may be such as to bring the case also within one of the practice exceptions, so that the corroboration necessary to such cases will have to be looked for, but this will be coincidental, and in general only the requirements of the statute need be observed.

The principal cases are as follows:

15.5.1 Treason
In a prosecution for High Treason by compassing the death or restraint of the sovereign or the heirs of the sovereign, it is provided by s. 1 of the Treason Act 1795 that there should not be conviction without 'the oaths of two lawful and credible witnesses'. The use of the word 'credible' must presumably be taken to import that the jury must accept the evidence of both or all such witnesses, and be prepared to act on the evidence of each taken individually.

15.5.2 Perjury
Perjury was the one exception known to the common law, in which the evidence of one witness was insufficient for a conviction. However, the position is now governed by s. 13 of the Perjury Act 1911, which provides that a person shall not be convicted of any offence against the Act, or of any other statutory offence of perjury or subornation of perjury, 'solely upon the evidence of one witness as to the falsity of any statement alleged to be false'. It will be observed that the statute prescribes the element of the offence for which corroboration is required, that is to say the falsity of the statement, and no requirement is imposed in respect of other elements of the offence. The corroborative evidence must, therefore, be directed to that issue.

15.5.3 Personation at elections
A person charged with personation at any general or municipal election shall not be convicted summarily or committed for trial for such offence 'except on the evidence of not less than two credible witnesses': Representation of the People Act 1949, s. 147(5).

15.5.4 Speeding
Under s. 78A(2) of the Road Traffic Regulation Act 1967 (added by s. 203 of the Road Traffic Act 1972) a person charged with an offence of exceeding the speed limit 'shall not be liable to be convicted solely on the evidence of one witness to the effect that in the opinion of the witness the person prosecuted was driving the vehicle at a speed exceeding a specified limit'. The purpose of this provision is to provide a safeguard against the

possible unreliability of such evidence of opinion, because of the likelihood of error in
relating an impression of the speed of a vehicle to a precise speed limit. The corroboration must go to the observation of the witness (17). However, the evidence of the
reading of a speedometer or other measuring device is evidence of fact, so that readings
of such instruments are not within the section, and indeed may themselves be corroborative of opinion evidence of observation (18).

15.5.5   Sexual Offences Act 1956, s. 2, 3, 4, 22 and 23

These specific offences, which deal with procuring the defilement of women and girls by
various means, and with procuring women and girls for the purpose of prostitution, are
subject to a proviso in these terms: 'A person shall not be convicted . . . on the evidence
of one witness only unless the witness is corroborated in some material particular by
evidence implicating the accused'. The extent of the corroboration required in these
cases is equated by the statute with that looked for at common law in the practice
exceptions, under the rule in *Baskerville*.

15.5.6   Affiliation cases

By s. 4(2) of the Affiliation Proceedings Act 1957, as amended, it is provided that: ' . . .
the court may adjudge the defendant to be the putative father of the child, but shall not
do so, in a case where evidence is given by the mother, unless her evidence is corroborated in some material particular by other evidence to the court's satisfaction'. There is
clearly some reason for caution in affiliation cases, where the complainant is not only, in
a sense, the complainant in a 'sexual case', but also has an obvious interest in the
acceptance of her evidence, and this is no doubt the reason for the requirement of
corroboration. What is less clear is the provision that the evidence of the complainant
must be corroborated 'to the court's satisfaction'. It is, of course, true that the magistrates are the judges both of the law and of the facts, and must address their minds both
to the evidence capable of amounting to corroboration, and to the weight which they are
prepared to give to the evidence available. Nonetheless, just as in the case of a jury, it is
always necessary that the evidence be accepted by the tribunal of fact before corroboration can occur, and it is doubtful whether the words in question actually add anything to
the requirement of the section.

15.5.7   Unsworn evidence of children

It has been observed in 12.8, ante, that in any criminal case, a child of tender years who
does not understand the nature of an oath, may give evidence unsworn 'if, in the opinion
of the court, he is possessed of sufficient intelligence to justify the reception of the
evidence, and understands the duty of speaking the truth:' Children and Young Persons
Act 1933, s. 38(1). Because of the obvious danger of such a course, which may be gauged
by the fact that the common law looks for corroboration as a matter of practice even
where the child is sworn, the section contains a proviso that: 'where evidence admitted
by virtue of this section is given on behalf of the prosecution the accused shall not be
liable to be convicted of the offence unless that evidence is corroborated by some other
material evidence in support thereof implicating him'.

   The position of unsworn evidence given by virtue of s. 38(1) in relation to corroboration was comprehensively examined by the House of Lords in *DPP v Hester* (19). The

17   *Brighty* v *Pearson* (DC) [1938] 4 All ER 127.
18   *Nicholas* v *Penny* (DC) [1950] 2 KB 466; *Swain* v *Gillett* (DC) [1974] RTR 446.
19   [1973] AC 296.

defendant was charged with indecent assault on a girl of twelve, who gave evidence about the alleged offence on oath. Her sister, aged nine, gave unsworn evidence for the prosecution under s. 38(1). The question which fell to be decided by the House was whether the unsworn evidence of the sister could, in law, be capable of corroborating the sworn evidence of the complainant (20). It was argued that the requirement of corroboration as a matter of law contained in s. 38(1) precluded the use of unsworn evidence for the purpose of corroborating other evidence. This argument derived from the earlier decision in *R v Manser* (21), in which it was held that the unsworn evidence of a child given under s. 38(1) 'was not to be accepted as evidence at all' unless it was corroborated. *Manser* is open to some doubt simply because the report fails to make clear whether or not the complainant gave evidence on oath or unsworn (22), but is open also to the far more fundamental criticism that the decision appears to have been based on a wrong interpretation of the proviso to s. 38(1), which requires, not that the unsworn evidence shall be corroborated for the purpose of being admissible, but that the unsworn evidence shall not be sufficient for a conviction unless it is corroborated. The House of Lords in *Hester* corrected this view, holding that unsworn evidence, being admissible, is capable of corroborating other evidence in the case against the defendant. The House also considered in some depth the converse question of how the unsworn evidence of the sister could be corroborated, and held that such corroboration might be found in the sworn evidence of the complainant. The result was that the two girls were capable in law of corroborating each other (mutual corroboration) where one was sworn and one unsworn, and that the requirement of the proviso to s. 38(1) was satisfied by such corroboration of the unsworn evidence by the sworn.

The House of Lords further held, however, that the unsworn evidence of a child given under s. 38(1) could not corroborate or be corroborated by other unsworn evidence given under s. 38(1). Although obiter on the facts of *Hester*, it is submitted that this view is demonstrably correct. It may be based soundly upon the very wording of s. 38(1), which calls for 'some other material evidence in support thereof', which is apt to refer to evidence other than evidence admitted under the section. The same view was also expressed, equally obiter, in *R v Campbell* (23) by Lord Goddard CJ, who regarded *Manser* as authority for the proposition and intended to approve it in the course of a general review of the principles relating to the evidence of children.

These rules will be of importance if Angela Blackstone is thought by the court to be a child of tender years, who falls within the ambit of s. 38(1) on the principles discussed in Chapter 12. Her unsworn evidence will require to be corroborated, before Littleton may be convicted of indecently assaulting her. Such corroboration may be supplied by the sworn evidence of Margaret, provided that she can implicate Littleton in the commission of the offence, as it seems she can. Angela's unsworn evidence, thus corroborated, may reciprocate by supplying corroboration of Margaret's evidence, which is to be looked for as a matter of practice because she is the complainant in a sexual case (15.6, post). Although it may be thought that corroborative evidence is not in short supply in the case of Coke and Littleton, the implications of *Hester* are frequently of considerable importance in practice. For example, it is obviously significantly better for the prosecution

20   The complainant's evidence fell into a category of case where corroboration was to be looked for as a matter of practice: see 15.6, post.
21   (CCA) (1934) 25 Cr App R 18.
22   The Lords in *Hester* took the view that she had probably been sworn. In *R v Campbell* (CCA) [1956] 2 QB 432, Lord Goddard CJ favoured the alternative construction of events.
23   [1956] 2 QB 432. The witnesses in *Campbell* were all sworn, but the court expressed its intention of reviewing the question of children's evidence generally, so as to offer some guidance over the field as a whole.

if at least one of a number of children is found to be capable of taking the oath. Even though the jury may not find the evidence of a child significantly more compelling just because he or she is sworn, the fact may very well prevent the prosecution case from being held to be technically defective at its close, because the proviso to s. 38(1) cannot be complied with.

15.6   Corroboration to be looked for as a matter of practice

We have already seen that the common law recognised certain cases in which, because of some inherent risk of unreliability, the judge must warn the jury of the dangers of acting on uncorroborated evidence of the sort in question; that the requirement for the warning is one of law, the omission of which will be a ground of appeal (24); and that if the warning is properly given, the jury may if they see fit convict on the uncorroborated evidence (25).

The rules of common law have identified quite specific cases in which the dangers have been held to justify the application of the exception, and these will be dealt with individually below. It cannot, however, be said that the categories of such cases are closed. The proposition has been canvassed judicially on a number of occasions that it is proper and desirable for a warning to be given in any case where a witness may appear to be partial or biased, or to have any personal interest in the outcome of the proceedings, or to have any personal motive for giving the evidence in question. Such a course was, for example, advocated in *R* v *Prater* (26) and approved by Lord Hailsham of St Marylebone in his speech in *DPP* v *Kilbourne* (27). It would be difficult and unprofitable to attempt any definitive statement of the kinds of interest which might suggest that a witness's evidence ought to be treated with caution. Certainly, a variety of financial interests might be included, and there is already a rule, dealt with below, affecting claimants to the property of deceased persons. But there must also be many cases where the danger will spring from the witness's relationship with, or animosity towards, a party to the proceedings (28). It would, no doubt, be a matter for the judge to assess in each case whether a warning would be desirable, taking into account the nature of the evidence, the position of the witness and the potential effect of both on the case as a whole. There is no compelling reason why the rule should be restricted to evidence given for the prosecution, as in a case where evidence is given by a witness called for one defendant which has the effect of implicating another, though there are sound reasons for exempting the evidence of a defendant himself from a requirement for corroboration (29). There is no reason why the rule should be limited to criminal cases. The subject merits further elucidation from the Bench.

15.6.1   *Sworn evidence of children*

Quite apart from the specific danger of unsworn evidence admitted under s. 38(1) of the Children and Young Persons Act 1933 (see 15.5, ante), the common law recognised in the sworn evidence of children of tender years both the risk of unreliability inherent in

24   The appeal will almost always be allowed, the application of the proviso rarely being thought justifiable. See generally *Davies* v *DPP* (HL) [1954] AC 378.
25   See *R* v *Henry and Manning* (CA) (1968) 53 Cr App R 150. In *R* v *Thorne and Others* (1977) 66 Cr App R 6, the Court of Appeal confirmed the point in vivid terms, holding that 'the evidence of villains . . . can be admitted and that convictions based on such evidence can stand'.
26   (CCA) [1960] 2 QB 464.   27   (HL) [1973] AC 729 at 740.
28   See, e.g., *R* v *Allen; R* v *Evans* (CCA) [1965] 2 QB 295 (wife of one defendant).
29   A defendant giving evidence in his defence is not an 'accomplice'. He should be free to present his defence without such comment from the Bench as would lead the jury to suspect his evidence automatically.

the age of a young witness, and the danger of childish imagination and collusion. There are obvious dangers in the uncorroborated evidence of one child, and, where there is a likelihood of collusion, of more than one child to the same effect. The rule, therefore, is that the judge must always warn the jury of the danger of acting on the uncorroborated evidence of children of tender years, and, if there is a realistic possibility of collusion, of that possibility (30).

It has been seen in Chapter 12 that there is no prescribed age at which a child must be regarded as being, or as having ceased to be, one of tender years. And for the same reason, there is no defined age at which a child ceases to be a proper subject of a corroboration warning. The matter is one for the discretion of the judge. In *R v Morgan* (31) the defendant was charged with indecent assault on a boy of eleven. The victim, his brother aged twelve and a youth who at the time of the incident, some twelve months before the trial, was aged sixteen, gave evidence on oath for the prosecution. The trial judge warned the jury about the evidence of the victim, but gave no warning about the evidence of the brother or the youth. The Court of Appeal held that that judge had erred in his omission in the case of the brother, but that on the facts of the case, no warning had been required in the case of the youth. Roskill LJ said (32):

We do not think it possible to state as a general proposition what the age is above which it becomes unnecessary for a judge to give a warning such as I have already mentioned. This is an example of a situation where the trial judge is much better placed to consider the matter than any appellate court can be. The judge will, in those circumstances, obviously apply his mind to the problem and ask himself the question whether, having seen this boy in the witness-box, he was of an age which made it desirable to give this warning.

It is clear from *Campbell* and *Hester* that sworn evidence of a child is capable of corroborating both other sworn evidence in the case, and the unsworn evidence of another child admitted under s. 38(1) of the Children and Young Persons Act 1933. It may, therefore, be said that the evidence of different children is capable of being mutually corroborative, except in the case where all the evidence is given unsworn under s. 38(1). In *DPP v Kilbourne* (33) a logical and important extension of the principle was recognised. The defendant was charged with offences of buggery, attempted buggery and indecent assault on two groups of boys. Counts 1 – 4 comprised offences committed in 1970 against group 1; and counts 5 – 7 related to offences committed in 1971 against group 2. Evidence of the offences in each group was admissible both directly to prove the offences in that group and, under the similar-fact principle, to prove those in the other group. The House of Lords upheld the direction given by the trial judge that the evidence of the children in either group concerning any particular offence was capable of being corroborated by that of children in the other group, being evidence of admissible, similar conduct by the defendant. The decision depends, of course, on the principle of

---

30 *R v Campbell* [1956] 2 QB 432; *R v Morgan* (CA) [1978] 1 WLR 735.
31 [1978] 1 WLR 735. The appeal was dismissed because the evidence was so overwhelming that no miscarriage of justice could have occurred. The court recognised also the necessity of drawing to the jury's attention the possibility of collusion, and held that on the facts this had been adequately done. The question of collusion is probably no more than one aspect of the truism that the jury will not act for any purpose, including that of corroboration, on evidence which they do not accept as truthful: see the observations of Lord Hailsham of St Marylebone in *DPP v Kilbourne* [1973] AC 729 at 746.
32 [1978] 1 WLR 735 at 739.
33 [1973] AC 729.

mutual admissibility under the similar-fact rule: if the evidence of children dealing with other offences is admissible to prove guilt as charged, then there is no reason why it should not be capable of affording corroboration, as implicating the defendant in the commission of the offence charged. But where different offences do not fall within the similar-fact principle, evidence given on one would not be admissible to prove another, and would therefore be incapable of affording corroboration of evidence relating to the other.

15.6.2   Evidence of accomplices

In common parlance, the term 'accomplice' describes one who has in some way been involved culpably in the wrongdoing in question. In criminal cases, such persons are sometimes called for the prosecution to give evidence against a defendant. Frequently, they are persons who were originally charged jointly with the defendant, and are therefore competent witnesses for the prosecution only because they have pleaded guilty or have had proceedings against them discontinued or for whatever reason have ceased to be defendants in the proceedings. Habitually, they agree to give evidence for the prosecution in return for not being prosecuted, or for having their plea of guilty to a lesser offence accepted by the prosecution, or in the hope of attracting leniency in sentence. In other cases, the evidence given discloses that a witness may be implicated in the offence charged, and so stand in peril of being prosecuted subsequently. In all such cases, the common law recognised an obvious danger, arising from the motive of avoiding or minimising the witness's own involvement in the offence charged, and of emphasising, or it may be, fabricating, that of the defendant. A warning must accordingly be given to the jury that the evidence of an accomplice is dangerous to act upon, in the absence of corroboration.

The question of what persons are to be regarded as accomplices for the purposes of the law relating to corroboration was settled in modern times by the House of Lords in *Davies* v *DPP* (34). Davies and one Lawson were members of a group of youths, who attacked and fought with another group. A member of the other group was stabbed, and died. Lawson was charged with his murder, and acquitted. Subsequently, the defendant was charged with the murder and Lawson gave evidence for the prosecution. There was no evidence that Lawson knew that the defendant was carrying a knife. The House of Lords upheld the trial judge's decision not to treat Lawson as an accomplice to murder. In the course of his speech, Lord Simonds LC declared that an accomplice is one who, when called to give evidence for the prosecution, falls into any one of the following three categories:

(a)   Participants in the offence charged, whether as principals or aiders and abettors. This class, often referred to as '*participes criminis*' was described by Lord Simonds as the 'natural and primary meaning of the term "accomplice" ' (35).

(b)   Participants in offences held to be admissible as probative of the offence charged, under the similar-fact principle. These are, as it were, *participes criminis* by extension.

---

34   [1954] AC 378.
35   The question whether a witness falls into this class is usually, but not always, a straightforward one. One example of difficulty is the case of affray, in which the various participants may have no contact with each other in the fight. In such a case, they will not be regarded as accomplices, although it has been said that the jury should be warned that if the witness was not acting in self-defence, then he was committing an offence identical to that charged: *R* v *Sidhu; R* v *Singh; R* v *Singh* (CA) (1976) 63 Cr App R 24.

(c) On a trial for theft, handlers receiving stolen goods from the thief are accomplices of the thief (36).

Lord Simonds added that these categories were settled law, and should not be varied judicially.

Only witnesses called for the prosecution are accomplices, for the purposes of the present rule. In particular, a defendant who gives evidence in his own defence is not an accomplice, and no warning should be given in such terms about his evidence, even though he may implicate another defendant in the offence charged (37). The same rule applies to witnesses called for the defence, although there may be cases where the judge must balance the interests of the defendants by drawing to the attention of the jury a relationship of the witness to one defendant, or a personal consideration affecting his evidence implicating another defendant.

A police officer and an informer or other agent acting as an entrapper or *agent provocateur* appear not to be accomplices for the purposes of the rule, even though they may, in a sense, participate in the offence, for the purpose of detection or obtaining evidence against the defendant. In *Sneddon* v *Stevenson* (38) a police officer drove his car in such a way as to attract the attention of a known prostitute, and when she approached, arrested her for soliciting. The argument that the officer was an accomplice was rejected, primarily on the basis that the rationale for the rule is absent in a case where the activity of the witness is carried on in the course of law enforcement. It may be, however, that the rule would be too widely expressed, if it were held in all cases to exclude an entrapper, investigator or *agent provocateur*. Certainly, there are cases where such a person acts for reward or out of some personal motive, in which case a warning ought to be given along the lines advocated in *Prater* (39). It is submitted that there may well be cases where the officer or agent deliberately or inadvertently becomes too involved in the commission or planning of an offence, and becomes to that extent an accomplice in the sense that he has some motive for concealing or minimising his involvement, possibly at the expense of the defendant.

Whether a witness is an accomplice is a question of fact for the jury, and the judge should direct the jury as to any witness who is in law capable of being so regarded. In most cases, the witness's status is hardly in doubt, because he will be one who has pleaded guilty to the offence charged or to a lesser offence arising from the same facts, or will admit his complicity in his evidence in chief. There are, however, some cases where a witness may deny complicity in the offence, suggested to him in cross-examination, in which event the jury must determine his status according to their view of the evidence. There must be evidence from which the jury could properly infer that a witness is an accomplice, and this may arise from cross-examination, or from any other evidence, but the mere fact that complicity is suggested to the witness in cross-examination does not make him an accomplice if he does not accept it.

The judge must exercise his discretion on giving or withholding a warning where a

36   At the time of the decision in *Davies*, the offence was of receiving, under the Larceny Act 1916. It appears to have been assumed that the rule carries over to the offence of dishonest handling under the Theft Act 1968: see e.g. Archbold, 40th ed., para. 1425. There may, however, be cases where a person who handles other than by receiving has no real connection with the thief. It is also curious that Lord Simonds did not postulate the converse proposition that the thief is an accomplice on the trial of the receiver. Interestingly, Professor Cross comments that there are cases where a lack of connection would prevent the relationship from arising (*Evidence*, 5th ed., p. 199) as may be the case in Lord Simonds's category. There is some authority that the rule should apply both ways: *R v Crane* (CCA) (1912) 7 Cr App R 113; *R v Vernon* (CCA) [1962] Crim LR 35.
37   *R v Barnes; R v Richards* (CCA) [1940] 2 All ER 229.   38   (DC) [1967] 1 WLR 1051.
39   (CCA) [1960] 2 QB 464.

witness who may be an accomplice gives evidence which is of no or of marginal relevance to the guilt of the defendant. In such a case, it would seem unnecessary and sometimes undesirable to give a warning which may suggest undue prominence to the jury in their consideration of the evidence, but the point has been left open by the Court of Appeal (40). More difficult is the case where the witness gives evidence relevant to the issue, but favourable to the defendant. In *R v Peach* (41) it was held that the judge, although not required to give a warning, might do so, even where the effect of the evidence was to exculpate the defendant, because the witness might have his own motives for giving such evidence. Nonetheless, it is submitted that the true rationale is missing where the evidence does not materially increase the chances of conviction, and the judge should not impeach a witness for the prosecution who does not come up to proof. It is submitted that a preferable approach is that suggested in *R v Royce-Bentley* (42), where a witness for the prosecution, who on his own admission was an accomplice by participation in the offence charged, gave evidence mainly favourable to the defendant, but in part supporting the case for the prosecution. The Court of Appeal held that the trial judge had acted correctly in consulting counsel on whether a direction should be given, and thereafter taking the course which appeared to him to be more favourable to the defence.

If Coke were to plead guilty to raping Margaret Blackstone, and thereafter give evidence for the prosecution against Littleton on the charge of indecently assaulting Angela, some question might arise of whether he should be regarded as an accomplice. On his own evidence, to the effect that he neither knew what Littleton was doing, nor played any part in that offence at any stage, he would not be so. If, however, the jury formed the view on the evidence before them that Coke played his part in luring both girls to his flat for indecent purposes, knowing Angela to be under the age at which she could legally consent, then they might well take such a view of him, and it would seem that the judge ought to give a warning. Conversely, if Littleton pleaded guilty and gave evidence against Coke, he could not be regarded as an accomplice merely because he may have co-operated with Coke in arranging the meeting with Margaret, but might well be so if he knew that Coke was prepared to use force in order to have sexual intercourse with her, if necessary. As we have observed, if Coke and Littleton are jointly tried, having pleaded not guilty, they will not be accomplices if they give evidence in their defence.

15.6.3   Evidence of complainants of sexual misconduct

15.6.3.1   In criminal cases   Quite apart from the specific statutory provisions of the sections of the Sexual Offences Act 1956 which require corroboration as a matter of law (see 15.5), the jury should as a matter of practice look for corroboration of the evidence of the complainant in any case of a sexual offence, and they must be given a warning accordingly. The complainant for present purposes is the victim of the offence. Although the terminology suggests hostile action by the defendant, this is not necessarily the case, and in certain sexual offences, for example incest or buggery, the 'victim' may be a willing participant in the act charged. In such a case, the 'victim's' evidence may well fall within the accomplice rule, in addition to that now under consideration (43). In any event, however, the rule respecting complainants is distinct from that concerning accomplices, and founded upon different considerations. The justification for the rule is

40   In *R v Meechan* (CA) [1977] Crim LR 350.   41   (CA) [1974] Crim LR 245.
42   (CA) [1974] 1 WLR 535.
43   Mere submission to a sexual act will not, it seems, render the complainant an accomplice in the absence of the necessary knowledge and intent: *R v Dimes* (CCA) (1911) 7 Cr App R 43.

the inherent danger arising from the fact that sexual allegations are simple and often tempting to make, but difficult to refute, and from the characteristic possibility of hysterical or malicious invention or simply the instinct for preservation of the complainant's reputation or material interests. Of course, particular care is needed where the complainant is also a child.

The rule applicable to complainants has developed with considerable force, and applies somewhat inflexibly to all sexual offences, regardless of the age or sex of the complainant and of the nature of the issues in the case. It applies, therefore, even where the evidence of the complainant has no or only marginal significance in implicating the defendant in the offence charged. Thus, in *R* v *Midwinter* (44) the omission of a corroboration warning in relation to the complainant's evidence was held to be fatal to the conviction, even though the complainant had not idendified the defendant, and the case turned solely upon an alleged confession by the defendant. And in *R* v *Marks* (45) the absence of a warning was similarly fatal to a conviction for unlawful sexual intercourse with a girl under sixteen, where the only issue was the date upon which the intercourse had occurred, and therefore the age of the complainant at the material time.

Curiously, however, it has been held that the evidence of the complainant of a sexual offence does not require corroboration if it is admitted under the similar-fact principle in a trial concerning another offence, even though corroboration is required of the complainant's evidence of the offence charged (46). It is submitted that this decision, which conflicts with the rule in the analogous cases of children and accomplices, is difficult to justify and should be reversed. The danger,in a case where similar-fact evidence consists of as yet unproved allegations, must surely be considerable. There is presumably no doubt that the two complainants are capable of corroborating each other in such a case.

In *R* v *Longstaff* (47) the question was left open by the Court of Appeal (the appeal being allowed for other reasons) whether a police officer, to whom indecent overtures were made in a public lavatory, was 'the complainant' on a resulting charge of attempted indecency. It seems probable, by analogy with the authority on police officers alleged to be accomplices (48) that the answer should be in the negative. Certainly, wherever the officer was acting in his professional capacity, the rationale of the rule would be absent.

It follows from what has been said above that Margaret and Angela Blackstone, each of whom is the complainant in relation to the alleged offence against her, must be the subject of a warning, quite apart, in Angela's case, from considerations of age. Nor does it matter that the issues in the two cases differ, that is to say that in Coke's case the issue is solely one of consent, whereas in Littleton's case, the defence will be a complete denial coupled with an alibi. There is, of course, no reason in law why the evidence of Margaret and Angela should not be mutually corroborative and it may be left to the jury on that basis to say whether it is in fact corroborative or not.

15.6.3.2 In matrimonial cases The question of corroboration in civil cases generally is, as has been indicated, of less significance than in criminal matters, because of the greater likelihood of a judge directing his mind correctly to the inherent dangers of certain kinds of evidence. In matrimonial cases, the new approach to such cases dating from the Divorce Reform Act 1969, by virtue of which contested cases are discouraged, has greatly diminished the importance of a number of evidential matters, of which

44 (CA) [1971] 55 Cr App R 523.   45 (CCA) [1963] Crim LR 370.
46 *R* v *Sanders* (CMAC) (1961) 46 Cr App R 60.
47 [1977] Crim LR 216.   48 Cf *Sneddon* v *Stevenson* (DC) [1967] 1 WLR 1051.

corroboration is one. In affiliation cases, where the incidence of contested cases remains high and the dangers of uncorroborated evidence substantial, corroboration is required as a matter of law. There remains, however, a residual rule, applicable alike to proceedings in the High Court and magistrates' courts in the matrimonial jurisdiction, and its extent was, for modern purposes, defined by the Divisional Court in *Alli* v *Alli* (49). The principles may be stated as follows:

(a) In considering any alleged matrimonial offence, the court should, as a matter of practice, look for corroboration of the evidence of the complainant, and should normally require it if available on the facts of the case. This applies, not only to allegations of sexual misconduct, but to matrimonial offences generally.

(b) Whereas an appellate court may always interfere with a finding, if it appears clearly that the court of trial has proceeded oblivious of the dangers of uncorroborated evidence, the court will intervene on appeal in cases where sexual misconduct is alleged, or where evidence of adultery is that of a willing participant, unless the court of trial has warned itself expressly. In any such case, it is of course open to the court of trial, after a proper warning, to act on the uncorroborated evidence of the complainant, and in *Alli* the decision of the justices to do so was upheld on the facts. There is, nonetheless, in the decision of the Divisional Court, an obvious equation of sexual allegations and evidence of willing participants, with the analogous cases of complainants and accomplices in criminal cases.

15.6.4   Claimants to the property of deceased persons

The court will look, as a matter of practice, for corroboration of the evidence of persons within this class. There is, however, no requirement as a matter of law (50).

15.7   A note on identification cases

Cases which turn wholly or substantially upon evidence of visual identification have, in recent times, given rise to considerable anxiety. In the leading case of *R* v *Turnbull* (51) Lord Widgery CJ, in the course of laying down guidelines of practice for dealing with such cases, held that where the quality of identifying evidence is poor, the trial judge should withdraw the case from the jury, and direct an acquittal, 'unless there is other evidence which goes to support the correctness of the identification.' Lord Widgery continued: 'This may be corroboration in the sense lawyers use that word; but it need not be so if its effect is to make the jury sure that there has been no mistaken identification.' The judge should point out to the jury evidence capable of supporting the identification, and also any evidence which the jury might mistakenly think to be so capable, for example the defendant's decision not to give evidence.

It is to be observed that the Lord Chief Justice was not seeking to define a new area of corroboration, and indeed, he emphasised that his judgment was laying down, not new rules of law, but changes in practice. It seems, however, that there is at least an indication that a quasi-corroborative rule has developed, which differs from the formal corroborative rules discussed above, in that (a) there is no technical limitation on the nature of the evidence suitable for this purpose, so that it may be found in any evidence

49   [1965] 3 All ER 480.
50   *Re Hodgson, Beckett* v *Ramsdale* (CA) (1885) 31 ChD 177; *Re Cummins, Cummins* v *Thompson* (CA) [1972] Ch 62.
51   (CA) [1977] QB 224. See also 13.3, ante.

admissible in the case, whether capable of amounting to corroboration or not; (b) the requirement arises only when the judge makes a value judgment of the quality of the evidence to be corroborated, so that there is no general rule applicable to evidence of visual identification as such; and (c) if, but only if, the evidence is poor in quality, the judge should withdraw the case from the jury if it is unsupported.

15.8 Mutual corroboration

By mutual corroboration is meant the use of the evidence of two or more witnesses, each of whom require as a matter of law or practice to be corroborated, for the purpose of affording corroboration *inter se* and so satisfying the requirement in each case, irrespective of any evidence from other sources capable of affording corroboration. The rule is that, except in two cases, mutual corroboration is always permissible and is in law sufficient to satisfy the requirement in respect of each witness. The two exceptions are:

(a) The unsworn evidence of two or more children (52)
(b) The evidence of two or more accomplices, being *participes criminis* in the offence charged. The restriction does not affect the evidence of accomplices within the other two categories laid down by Lord Simonds in *Davies* v *DPP* (53).

15.9 Corroboration afforded by the defendant himself

Corroboration is to be looked for primarily in independent parts of the prosecution case, which may include evidence of acts done or words spoken by the defendant, which have the effect of confirming other evidence tendered for the prosecution in some material particular, and of implicating the defendant in the offence charged. There is no doubt that such evidence may amount in law to corroboration. Typical of such a case is where the defendant, when questioned, gives the police a story, for example an alibi, which he subsequently admits to be false, or which is subsequently proved to be false. In *Credland* v *Knowler* (54) the defendant at first denied having left his home and having accompanied children to a spot where it was alleged he committed an indecent assault. Later, he acknowledged this account to be false and admitted that he had accompanied the children to the place in question, but maintained his denial that he had committed any offence. It was held that the defendant's admission was capable in law of corroborating the evidence of the children, in that it confirmed what they had said in a material particular, namely his presence at the scene at the relevant time. It must be added, however, that the jury should be warned against treating lies told out of court as corroboration, if they think that the lies may have been told out of fear or panic, or otherwise than by way of a guilty attempt to evade detection.

We have also seen that, where evidence of the defendant's behaviour on other occasions is admissible to prove his guilt as charged, under the similar-fact principle, his behaviour on such other occasions is capable in law of corroborating evidence given for the prosecution concerning the offence charged (55).

52 *DPP* v *Hester* (HL) [1973] AC 296. See 15.5, ante.
53 (HL) [1954] AC 378. See 15.6, ante.
54 (DC) (1951) 35 Cr App R 48. In cases where the defendant's silence in response to an allegation may be held against him, it seems that such silence may amount to corroboration. See *R* v *Cramp* (1880) 14 Cox CC 390 (the point was not considered on appeal); *R* v *Chandler* (CA) [1976] 1 WLR 585. Such cases are very limited: see 7.12, ante.
55 *DPP* v *Kilbourne* [1973] AC 729. See 15.6, ante. For examples, see *R* v *Hartley* (CCA) [1941] 1 KB 5; *R* v *Mitchell* (CCA) (1952) 36 Cr App R 79.

Different questions arise with regard to the defendant's evidence from the witness-box in his defence on the trial of the offence charged. Here, a distinction of some importance must be drawn between the substance of the defendant's evidence (i.e., the facts to which he testifies) in which corroboration may be sought, and the mere fact that the jury may choose to disbelieve the defendant's evidence, which cannot amount to corroboration. In *R v Chapman; R v Baldwin* (56) the Court of Appeal held that the judge had been in error in directing the jury that if they rejected the defendant's evidence, that rejection of itself might be regarded as corroborative of the evidence for the prosecution. Roskill LJ said: 'Mere rejection of evidence is not affirmative proof of the contrary of the evidence which has been rejected' (57). On the other hand, as Lord MacDermott said in *Tumahole Bereng v R* (58): 'Corroboration may well be found in the evidence of an accused person; but that is a different matter, for there confirmation comes, if at all, from what is said, and not from the falsity of what is said.' Thus, in *R v Dossi* (59), the defendant's admission in evidence that he had fondled a child was capable of amounting to corroboration of the child's evidence, since it confirmed what the child said in a material particular, even though the defendant maintained that his fondling had been platonic, whereas the child said that it was in circumstances amounting to an indecent assault. Presumably, the evidence of a defendant, which is evidence in the case generally, is capable of corroborating prosecution evidence against a co-defendant.

It seems that a party who does not bear the legal burden of proof may decline to give evidence without running the risk of that decision being regarded as corroboration. In particular, in a criminal case, the defendant's failure to give evidence is not capable of affording corroboration of evidence given for the prosecution (60).

15.10 Questions for counsel

1 What requirements of corroboration arise in relation to the evidence of (a) Margaret, and (b) Angela Blackstone?
2 What evidence is to be found in the papers which would be capable in law of corroborating the evidence of each girl?
3 If either Coke or Littleton pleads guilty and gives evidence for the prosecution against the other, what requirements of corroboration may arise? How would the position differ from that where each pleaded not guilty and gave evidence in his defence implicating the other?
4 What are the respective functions of the judge and jury in relation to the requirements of corroboration?

56 [1973] QB 774. Of course, if the jury disbelieve the defendant, they may be more inclined to convict on uncorroborated prosecution evidence, if that course is open to them. It has been suggested that *Chapman* would not apply in every case: see, e.g., *R v Boardman*, when in the Court of Appeal, [1975] AC 421 per Orr LJ at 428–9. But it is submitted that *Chapman* must be correct in the overwhelming majority of cases.
57 Ibid at 780. The distinction is described as 'clear' (at 783).
58 (PC, Basutoland) [1949] AC 253 at 270.
59 (CCA) (1918) 13 Cr App R 158. See also *Corfield v Hodgson* (DC) [1966] 1 WLR 590.
60 *R v Jackson* (CCA) (1953) 37 Cr App R 43. And see *Cracknell v Smith* (DC) [1960] 1 WLR 1239.

16 Documentary and Real Evidence

A: DOCUMENTARY EVIDENCE

16.1 Documentary evidence generally

Thus far, this part of this book has considered the mechanics of adducing evidence by calling witnesses to testify on oath, or by the equivalent means of affidavits or admissible hearsay statements. But evidence may also be given by the production of documents of which the contents are admissible in evidence. It has already been seen in Chapter 6 that facts of public interest may be proved by production of certain public documents and from Chapters 6 and 8 that the contents of many documents are rendered admissible by statute. This chapter is concerned with the vast bulk of documents which are classed as 'private documents', which are not served by any of the rules previously referred to. Private documents are all those which are not 'public', in the sense that they have been compiled by public officials, for the purpose of constituting a record of facts of public interest or notoriety, but are records or communications made by all other persons and for all other purposes falling outside the public domain. Private documents form, therefore, the vast majority of documents generally, both as to kind and contents, and it would be literally impossible to classify the various kinds of document which may exist.

It is worth observing at the outset that documentary evidence is subject to the rules of evidence generally. The admissibility of a private document is subject to the same rules, subject only to statutory modification, as is that of oral evidence. A document may, therefore, be objected to on the ground that its contents are, for any reason concerned with the general rules of evidence, inadmissible, for example that they are hearsay and do not fall within any recognised exception to the rule against hearsay (1). Documents used as evidence must also be distinguished carefully from documents used to refresh the memory of a witness while giving evidence orally. The latter are not evidence in themselves, unless they are made so by the conduct of cross-examination, and even then are only evidence of their contents by statute in civil cases (2).

The question of what exactly may constitute a 'document' is far from easy to answer, and appears not to be capable of being answered uniformly for all purposes. It is clear that the prime characteristic of a document is that it should contain and convey information. It seems also that the word implies writing or other inscription, though in modern times, the storing of information in diagrammatic form or computer coding, or the audio or video recording of information is probably equally acceptable for many purposes. The form of a document, and the materials of which it is composed, are

---

1 See, e.g., *Myers* v *DPP* (HL) [1965] AC 1001.
2 See *R* v *Virgo* (CA) (1978) 67 Cr App R 323; Civil Evidence Act 1968 s. 3(2); and generally 13.2.2, ante.

probably of limited contemporary importance. In *R* v *Daye* (3) Darling J pointed out that paper itself had been preceded by parchment, stone, marble, clay and metal. He went on to say that an object may be regarded as a document, whatever its material, 'provided it is writing or printing and capable of being evidence'. In more recent times, a tape-recording of a conversation has been held to be a document which, if referred to in a party's pleading, must be produced for inspection on notice, under RSC, Ord. 24, r. 10(1): *Grant and Another* v *Southwestern & County Properties Ltd and Another* (4). And the majority view of the Court of Appeal in *Senior* v *Holdsworth, ex parte Independent Television News Ltd* (5) may prove to have discredited the older view that film (and presumably videotape) were not to be regarded as documents.

The following statutory definitions, dealing with the use of the word 'document' in the statutes to which they relate, have in any case for important evidential purposes, considerably widened the more traditional definitions:

(a) The Criminal Evidence Act 1965 renders admissible many statements 'contained in a document' to prove facts of which direct oral evidence would be admissible in criminal proceedings. This is an important statutory exception to the rule against hearsay. S. 1(4) of the Act defines 'document' as including 'any device by means of which information is recorded or stored'.

(b) For the purpose of the now general admission of hearsay evidence in civil proceedings, by virtue of part 1 of the Civil Evidence Act 1968 the word 'document', as defined by s. 10(1) of the Act:

. . . includes, in addition to a document in writing—

(a) any map, plan, graph or drawing;
(b) any photograph;
(c) any disc, tape, sound track or other device in which sounds or other data (not being visual images) are embodied so as to be capable (with or without the aid of some other equipment) of being reproduced therefrom; and
(d) any film, negative, tape or other device in which one or more visual images are embodied so as to be capable (as aforesaid) of being reproduced therefrom.

Having observed that private documents are subject to the ordinary rules of admissibility, including any statutory modifications, it remains only to consider whether there are any special additional rules applicable to documents as such. In this connection, three matters arise:

(a) The proof of the contents of a document.
(b) The proof of due execution of documents, where required to be proved
(c) The admissibility of extrinsic evidence for the purpose of explaining, contradicting, or varying the contents of a document.

Of these three considerations, the third is of contemporary importance only in relation to contracts, in the form of the 'parol evidence rule'. This is a rule of specialised

3   (DC) [1908] 2 KB 333.
4   [1975] Ch 185.
5   [1976] QB 23. For the older view, see *Glyn* v *Western Feature Film Co.* (1915) 85 LJ Ch 261.

application, and is outside the scope of the present work (6). The first two considerations will now be examined.

16.2 Proof of contents

16.2.1 General rule

It is an ancient, albeit much neglected, rule of the common law that a party who wishes to rely, for evidential purposes, upon the contents of a private document, must adduce 'primary' (as opposed to 'secondary') evidence of the contents of the document. The meaning of these expressions is considered below, but it may be observed that the usual form of primary evidence is the production of the original document. Various reasons have been advanced for the rule. The true origin of the requirement is shrouded in antiquity, although it would be surprising if it were not connected with an anxiety to give effect to the terms of the document with as much accuracy and certainty as possible.

The rule in favour of primary evidence applies to cases where a party seeks to rely upon the contents of the document as direct evidence. Thus in *MacDonnell* v *Evans* (7) a question sought to be put to a witness for the plaintiff in cross-examination was disallowed because it sought to elicit his reaction to a letter written to him accusing him of forgery, the contents of which had not been proved by primary evidence, and were accordingly inadmissible. And in *Augustien* v *Challis* (8) the defence of a sheriff, to an action for negligently withdrawing a writ of fi. fa. in favour of the plaintiff, was that rent was due to the debtor's landlord in priority to the plaintiff. The landlord's evidence that the rent was due under a lease was held to be inadmissible because the lease was not produced and so proved by primary evidence.

Where, however, the contents of the document are not relied upon as evidence but are referred to for some other purpose only, the requirement of primary evidence will not apply. Thus, where the existence of the relationship of landlord and tenant was to be proved, but not the precise terms of the lease, the relationship could be proved otherwise than by primary evidence of the terms of the lease (9). And where it is sought only to prove the existence of, or to identify the document, no reliance being placed on its contents, primary evidence is not required (10). In *R* v *Elworthy* (11) a solicitor was prosecuted for perjury, it being alleged that he had wilfully and falsely denied having prepared a draft of a statutory declaration. It was held that the prosecution were entitled to adduce evidence, other than primary, to show that the draft existed and was in the possession of the defendant. But the conviction was set aside because the prosecution had wrongly been allowed to prove by such evidence that certain alterations had been made to the contents of the draft. They were then seeking to rely upon the contents as evidence.

Nor does the rule apply where the contents of the document are admissible as hearsay under Part 1 of the Civil Evidence Act 1968. In such cases the Act makes more liberal provision for proof of contents: see s. 6(1) and 8.8 ante.

16.2.2 Kinds of primary evidence

The following kinds of evidence of the contents of documents are primary, within the meaning of the rule discussed above.

6 See Cross, *Evidence*, 5th ed., p. 608; Phipson, *Evidence*, 12th ed., para. 1871 et seq.
7 (1852) 11 CB 930.
8 (1847) 1 Exch 279.
9 *R* v *Holy Trinity, Kingston-upon-Hull (Inhabitants)* (1827) 7 B & C 611.
10 *Boyle* v *Wiseman* (1855) 11 Exch 360.   11 (1867) LR 1 CCR 103.

16.2.2.1   The original.   This is of course the most obvious and most satisfactory kind of primary evidence. It is usually possible to identify the original document with certainty, but difficult cases do arise. If a deed is executed by various parties in a number of duplicates, each such duplicate is 'the original' and all must be produced (12). Similarly, counterparts of a lease, one signed by the lessor only and the other by the lessee only, are each 'the original', so far as the party signing is concerned (13).

These cases result, of course, from the fact that duplicates and counterparts of the kind mentioned are not in any sense copies, but together represent the deed executed by the parties. Copies, whether carbons or produced by a machine, are not originals, unless specifically made so by being signed or executed as such, with any formality which may be required.

16.2.2.2   Copies of enrolled documents.   Where the original private document is one which is, by law, required to be enrolled in a court or other public office, the copy officially issued by such court or office is treated as the original. Thus, the probate copy of a will is conclusive of the words of the will. However, the court is entitled to look at the original enrolled will when considering any question of construction of the will, for example to look at erasures apparent in the original but not in the probate copy (14).

16.2.2.3   Admissions of contents.   A party may adduce as primary evidence of the contents of a private document an admission made by his opponent with respect to such contents. The rule applies both to formal and informal admissions, and to oral as well as written admissions. In *Slatterie* v *Pooley* (15) the plaintiff sued on a covenant, which had the effect of creating an indemnity in respect of certain debts. The debts covered by the indemnity were contained in the schedule to a deed, which was inadmissible in evidence. The inclusion of the debt in the schedule was allowed to be proved by an oral admission to that effect, which the plaintiff was able to prove.

16.2.3   Secondary evidence

A party who wishes to rely upon the contents of a document must, as we have seen, adduce primary evidence of the contents. Only in the exceptional cases enumerated below will secondary (i.e., non-primary) evidence be admissible. However, if secondary evidence is admissible, it may be adduced in any form in which it may be available, whether by production of a copy, of a copy of a copy, by oral evidence of the contents or, in any other form. It is often said that 'there are no degrees of secondary evidence'. The secondary evidence must be strictly proved, so far as possible, so that a copy will not be admissible even in an exceptional case, unless it is proved that the alleged copy is in fact a true copy of the original (16).

Secondary evidence is admissible to prove the contents of a document in the following exceptional cases:

(a)   If a party fails, after notice, to provide an opponent with the original of a document required for the opponent's case.

(b)   If a stranger to proceedings refuses to provide the original of a document required by a party, and the stranger has a lawful excuse for refusal.

12   *Forbes* v *Samuel* [1913] 3 KB 706.   13   *Roe* d *West* v *Davis* (1806) 7 East 363.
14   *Re Battie-Wrightson, Cecil* v *Battie-Wrightson* [1920] 2 Ch 330.
15   (1840) 6 M & W 664.
16   *R* v *Collins* (CCA) (1960) 44 Cr App R 170.

(c)   If the original of a document is lost.

(d)   If it is impossible to produce the original of a document.

(e)   If the document is or forms part of a banker's book.

16.2.3.1   Failure to produce after notice.   It would not be right for a party to be able to prevent his opponent using a document in evidence by withholding the original. Accordingly, where a document is in the possession of one party, an opponent may serve notice to produce the document (17). The notice to produce does not compel the production of the original, but if the original is not produced, its contents may be proved by secondary evidence. This means that a notice to produce may be served even on the defendant in a criminal case, because it does not compel, whereas process compelling production, in the form of a *subpoena duces tecum*, would not be available. If the notice is not complied with, not only may the document be proved by secondary evidence, but the party failing to comply will not be allowed to rely upon the original, if it should be inconsistent with the secondary evidence (18).

In certain cases, service of notice is unnecessary. Most importantly, by RSC, Ord. 27, r. 4(3):

> A party to a cause or matter by whom a list of documents is served on any other party . . . shall be deemed to have been served by that other party with a notice requiring him to produce at the trial of the cause or matter such of the documents specified in the list as are in his possession, custody or power.

For this purpose, therefore, notice will not be necessary in respect of documents in the immediate control of the opponent which are, following the usual procedure, disclosed by list after close of pleadings. Notice need not be served if the document sought is itself a notice, for example a notice to produce or a notice to rely on previous convictions for the purpose of s. 27(3) of the Theft Act 1968. Notice is not required where production of a document is implied by the nature of the proceedings, for example a charge of theft of the document; or where the document is admitted to have been lost or destroyed.

16.2.3.2   Lawful refusal of stranger to produce.   If a document is in the possession or custody of a stranger to the proceedings, its contents may be proved by secondary evidence in any case where the stranger is lawfully entitled to refuse to produce it, for example because it is privileged in his hands, or he is beyond the jurisdiction of the court. If, however, the refusal is unlawful, secondary evidence will not be admissible, because production of the original may be compelled. Refusal to produce by the stranger in such a case may be punishable by proceedings for contempt or by making him liable in respect of any resulting loss (19).

16.2.3.3   Original lost.   Where the original document cannot be found or identified after due search, its contents may be proved by secondary evidence. It is for the party seeking rely on the document to show that all reasonable steps by way of search have been taken.

---

17   Such notice is habitually served together with notice to admit any documents in the possession of the server; these documents will then be taken to be admitted unless objected to in response to the notice.

18   *Doe* d *Thompson* v *Hodgson* (1840) 12 A & E 135.

19   *R* v *Llanfaethly (Inhabitants)* (1853) 2 E & B 940.

16.2.3.4   Production of original impossible.   Secondary evidence will be admissible where the actual production of the original is impossible, for example where the document takes the form of an inscription on a tombstone or a wall. In *Owner* v *Bee Hive Spinning Co. Ltd* (20) the same principle was applied to a notice giving particulars of mealtimes in a factory, which by statute was obliged to remain affixed to the wall of a particular place, and so was 'legally impossible' to produce.

It is interesting to compare, in this respect, the question of production of public documents. Although such documents would rarely, if ever, be impossible to produce, the production of the original would almost always be a matter of very great inconvenience and difficulty. Such a difficulty faced Alderson B in *Mortimer* v *M'Callan* (21), where it was suggested that the original books of the Bank of England ought to be produced for the purpose of proving their contents. It was held that the resulting inconvenience amounted to impossibility of production. The proof of most public documents is now governed by statute, and it may be noted that in many such cases, the production of a certified or sealed copy will suffice (22), and that in the absence of any specific provision, a public document produced from proper custody may be proved by a certified or examined copy (23).

16.2.3.5   Bankers' books.   Bankers' books are relevant to a considerable variety of cases. With the exception of the books of the Bank of England, they are private documents, and so in theory should be proved by primary evidence. Because of the obvious inconvenience of the rule to banks, whose records of customers' accounts are often required in litigation, special provisions were enacted by the Bankers' Books Evidence Act 1879. By s. 3 of the Act:

Subject to the provisions of this Act, a copy of an entry in a bankers' book shall in all legal proceedings be received as prima facie evidence of such entry, and of the matters, transactions, and accounts therein recorded.

The provision is subject to two conditions in subsequent sections:

4. A copy of an entry in a bankers' book shall not be received in evidence under this Act unless it be first proved that the book was at the time of the making of the entry one of the ordinary books of the bank, and that the entry was made in the usual and ordinary course of business, and that the book is in the custody or control of the bank. . . .
5. A copy of an entry in a bankers' book shall not be received in evidence under this Act unless it be further proved that the copy has been examined with the original entry and is correct. . . .

S. 6 provides that where the contents of a bankers' book may be proved under the Act, a banker or officer of the bank shall not be compellable to produce the original or to appear as a witness to prove the contents 'unless by order of a judge made for special cause'.

A most important provision for the conduct of many kinds of litigation, in particular prosecutions for offences of dishonesty, is contained in s. 7 of the Act, which provides:

20   [1914] 1 KB 105.
21   (1840) 6 M & W 58.
22   Evidence Act 1845, s. 1.   23   Evidence Act 1851, s. 14.

On the application of any party to a legal proceeding a court or judge may order that such party be at liberty to inspect and take copies of any entries in a bankers' book for any of the purposes of such proceedings. An order under this section may be made either with or without summoning the bank or any other party, and shall be served on the bank three clear days before the same is to be obeyed, unless the court or judge otherwise directs.

The provision is an extremely wide one, applying to civil and criminal proceedings alike and for a great variety of purposes. It has rightly been held that it is a substantial interference with liberty, which should be contenanced only after serious consideration, although if it is necessary, it is no answer to the making of the order that the result may be such as to incriminate the party against whom it is made (24).

For the purposes of the Act, microfilm records may be a 'bankers' book' (25) and no doubt any record which complies with the requirements of s. 4 may in modern law be proved under the Act.

16.3 Proof of due execution

In the case of public documents, the mere production of an admissible copy is generally sufficient to satisfy any requirement of proof of due execution of the document, in accordance with the maxim, *Omnia praesumuntur rite et solemniter esse acta*. The presumption is, of course, rebuttable, although not without difficulty. In the case of private documents, due execution must be proved by evidence, except where the document is more than twenty years old and comes from proper custody, in which case there arises a presumption of due execution and so of formal validity.

Due execution is proved by evidence of the signature of the person by whom the document purports to be signed and by evidence of attestation, if required for the document in question. Due execution may be admitted in criminal proceedings by virtue of s. 10 of the Criminal Justice Act 1967, and in civil proceedings when the admission is deemed to have been made for the purposes of the rules: RSC, Ord. 27, r. 1 and r. 2. Proof of due execution is dispensed with where an opponent refuses to produce a document after notice to do so (26).

The means of proof of due execution, where required, are (a) evidence of handwriting; (b) evidence of attestation; and (c) by an applicable presumption.

16.3.1 Evidence of handwriting
There is an obvious relevance in evidence which proves the authenticity of the handwriting of the person purporting to be the signer or executer of the document. Handwriting may be proved in any of the following ways.

16.3.1.1 Direct evidence.
The evidence of the signer himself or of a witness who perceived the execution of the document is admissible and sufficient evidence of due

---

24 *Williams and Others* v *Summerfield* (DC) [1972] 2 QB 513. An order may be made to inspect the account of a person who is not a party to the proceedings, so long as the information is required for the purposes of the proceedings. Thus, where a woman charged with the theft of money was alleged to have told the police that the money was in her husband's bank account, it was held proper to make an order under s. 7 to inspect his account, even though he was not a party: *R* v *Andover Justices, ex parte Rhodes, The Times* 14 June 1980. (It does not appear whether any question of privilege arose for consideration.)
25 *Barker* v *Wilson* (DC) [1980] 2 All ER 81.
26 *Cooke* v *Tanswell* (1818) 8 Taunt 450.

execution. The proof of signature by such means will suffice to identify the signer, as well as to establish the name signed, unless the evidence reveals circumstances which call for further investigation, for example where the signature is not distinctive and the name signed is a common one (27).

16.3.1.2   Opinion.   Witnesses who are familiar with the signature of the purported signer, or who have on other occasions received documents bearing the purported signature or made in the purported handwriting of the purported signer, may state their opinion that the document is signed by the person by whom it purports to be signed. The weight of such evidence may, of course, vary very considerably according to the circumstances of the case.

16.3.1.3   Comparison.   The comparison of disputed writings with known writings by scientific means is a well established subject of expert-opinion evidence. The basis for such evidence is contained in s. 8 of the Criminal Procedure Act 1865 which applied to criminal proceedings a provision which had been available in civil cases since the enactment of the Common Law Procedure Act 1854. The section provides that:

> Comparison of a disputed writing with any writing proved to the satisfaction of the judge to be genuine shall be permitted to be made by witnesses; and such writings, and the evidence of witnesses respecting the same, may be submitted to the court and jury as evidence of the genuineness or otherwise of the writing in dispute.

The phrase 'to the satisfaction of the judge' leaves unresolved the question of the standard to which the 'genuine' writing must be proved, if disputed. In *R* v *Angeli* (28) it was held that the proof of such genuine writing need be made only on the balance of probabilities, and not to the higher criminal standard of proof. In practice, the proof is commonly effected by submission of samples supplied voluntarily by the suspected writer, often to the specification of the handwriting expert, but in the absence of such specimens, any available examples of his handwriting must be proved to be genuine, before any evidence of comparison with disputed writings may be made by virtue of the section.

Possibly because the section pre-dates the general recognition of the scientific study and comparison of handwriting, it is not expressly provided that the comparison should be made by a witness qualified as an expert. Nonetheless, it is unlikely that the evidence would command real weight if made by a 'lay' witness, unless giving evidence of his opinion based on personal familiarity. Scientific comparison of samples of handwriting is a matter for experts. The jury may, and inevitably will where it is relevant to do so, compare the appearance of various documents produced to them, but they should not be invited to make a comparison of handwriting without the help of expert evidence. In *R* v *Tilley; R* v *Tilley* (29) the prosecution obtained in the course of cross-examination samples of the handwriting of the defendants, with a view to comparing the samples with handwriting on a receipt said to be in respect of a car which the defendants were charged with stealing. No expert was called concerning the handwriting, and the point was not pursued by the prosecution. However, the conviction was quashed on appeal because the jury were supplied with photographs and a magnifying glass, and were invited by the

27   *Jones* v *Jones* (!) (1841) 9 M & W 75.
28   (CA) [1979] 1 WLR 26.   29   (CCA) [1961] 1 WLR 1309.

comments of the judge in summing-up, to form their own unaided comparison of handwriting. It follows, therefore, that where the jury are not being invited to make any such comparison, but have in their possession documents which may lead them to seek to do so, they should be warned specifically against such a course. This done, the jury may of course make other proper use of the documents placed before them in evidence (30).

The ultimate question of whether the handwriting on the known specimen is also that on the disputed writing, or the document whose due execution is to be proved, is of course a question of fact for the jury or other tribunal of fact. It follows that the handwriting expert should, technically, limit his evidence to a statement of the comparison made by him, and his resulting opinion should technically be confined to relevant similarities or differences (31). Nonetheless, the modern practice is for the witness to be permitted to state his opinion about authorship, and in civil cases this would seem to follow from the provisions of s. 3(1) and (3) of the Civil Evidence Act 1972 (32).

16.3.2 Attestation

Due execution of documents which require attestation may be proved by the evidence of the attesting witnesses, or one of them. At one time, documents requiring attestation could be proved to have been duly executed only in this way, but it was provided by s. 3 of the Evidence Act 1938 that in both civil and criminal cases, it might be proved as if no attesting witness were alive. This means that either of the other methods of proof suggested in this section may be employed, although the most satisfactory way will be to prove the handwriting of an attesting witness, where possible.

The older rule still applies to wills, and these must be proved by evidence of attestation, unless it is shown that all the attesting witnesses are dead, insane, beyond the jurisdiction or unable to be traced. However, the practice is not to insist on the strict application of the rule where probate is granted in common form.

An attesting witness is called as the witness of the court. So he may be cross-examined by any party, including the party seeking to prove the document (33). If an attesting witness proves hostile or unreliable, then he may be contradicted by other evidence by any party (34). An attesting witness may not claim legal professional privilege (35).

16.3.3 Presumptions
It is presumed:

(a) That a document which is proved or purports to be more than twenty years old, and which is produced from proper custody, was duly executed. 'Proper custody' means only that the document is shown to have been kept in a place, or in the care of a person who might reasonably and naturally be expected to have possession of it, having regard to the nature of the document and the circumstances of the case.

(b) That a document was executed on the date which it bears.

(c) That in the case of a deed other than a will, any alterations thereto were made before execution, and in the case of wills, conversely, that any alterations were made after execution.

30   *R v O'Sullivan* [1969] 1 WLR 497.
31   *Wakeford v Bishop of Lincoln* (PC, Consistory Court of Lincoln) as reported in 90 LJ PC 174.
32   For the scope of expert opinion evidence generally, including the expression of opinions on ultimate issues, see Chapter 9, ante.
33   *Oakes v Uzzell* [1932] P 19.
34   *Bowman v Hodgson* (1867) LR 1 P & D 362.
35   *In the Estate of Fuld (No. 2), Hartley v Fuld* [1965] P 405.

B: REAL EVIDENCE

16.4   Nature of real evidence

Real evidence is the name usually given to quite diverse forms of evidence which have in common the characteristic that the tribunal of fact is invited to observe and draw conclusions from things, persons, places or circumstances; and so to act on its own perception for any necessary evidential purposes. Real evidence may, therefore, rank among the most cogent kinds of evidence, but also among the most difficult to assess in terms of weight, at least before the event. The forms of real evidence in common use are the following.

16.4.1   Material objects

The court may look at and draw any proper conclusions from its visual observation of any relevant material object produced before it. The material object may itself be the subject-matter of the case, as where the court looks at the fit of a suit of which the quality is disputed. It may be an object ancillary to the issue but nonetheless relevant to it, as for example where the court looks at an object alleged to be an offensive weapon, by reason of having been adapted for causing injury to the person. The tribunal of fact is entitled to act on the results of its own perception, even where this conflicts with other evidence given about the object, although in a case where the true nature or characteristics of the object cannot be assessed by mere visual observation, without the assistance of expert evidence, the jury must be warned not to rely upon unaided visual opinion. This would be the case in looking at objects bearing examples of handwriting, comparison of which should not be made without assistance (36) although the jury may obviously make use of their observation for any purpose short of comparison. And it has been held to be wrong to direct a jury to feel entirely free to form their own view about the presence and age of blood stains on an object, in the face of categoric scientific evidence on that subject (37). If expert evidence called on behalf of the parties differs in its conclusions about the object, and the tribunal of fact has, therefore, to choose what evidence to accept, it may, no doubt use its powers of observation in making such choice.

16.4.2   Appearance of persons or animals

The physical characteristics of a person or animal may be observed for any relevant purpose. Thus, the height or other personal features may be ascertained by observation, and the nature and extent of any injuries examined. The court may also take into account any characteristics apparent to it on observing the person or animal, even if not intended to be conveyed, such as a tendency to left-handedness, defects in hearing or vision, or the propensity of an animal to be ferocious.

16.4.3   Demeanour of witnesses

In considering the credit of a witness and the weight to be given to his evidence, the court may consider not only what is said, but the way in which it is said. This includes the attitude of the witness to the court, his general demeanour, his apparent frankness, evasiveness or other reaction to questioning (particularly hostile, in cross-examination) and his apparent power or lack of power of recollection.

36 See 16.3.1.3, ante.
37 *Anderson* v *R* (PC, Jamaica) [1972] AC 100. See generally Chapter 9, ante.

16.4.4 Views

A view is an inspection, out of court, of the *locus in quo*, or other place relevant to the case, or of some object, person or animal which cannot conveniently be brought to court. The view may involve any appropriate test or demonstration, as if made in court. A view can be a difficult event to control. It is important that all interested parties, their legal representatives and the tribunal of fact should, as far as can be arranged, have the same sight and opportunity to observe. They must also be protected against exposure to extraneous and irrelevant matters. With a jury, the problems are particularly acute, and it is essential that each member of the jury should attend and be enabled to form an individual impression. Where one member of the jury, who lived close to the *locus in quo*, was 'deputed' to view it and 'report back' to the others, who accordingly had no such opportunity, the conviction was quashed (38). It is equally essential, if the view is attended by witnesses, in order to explain relevant matters or to give some demonstration, that the witnesses should speak or demonstrate only at the direction of the judge, in the presence of all concerned, and for the purpose only of the necessary demonstration or explanation (39). In a matter tried by a judge alone, the same rules should be followed, although the dangers to be guarded against are less acute, and the extent of the view may be widened. In the Ocean Island case (40) Megarry V-C spent a considerable time on the island and drew numerous conclusions from his lengthy and detailed observation of its characteristics; though the litigation was, on any basis, exceptional.

16.4.5 Tapes, photographs, film etc.

Although in modern law visual and audio recordings may be regarded as documents, at least for some purposes (41), they have a further, important potential to supply matter of evidential value, because of the possibility of direct perception. A tape or film may yield detail and nuances over and above the mere text of the matters recorded therein. Some detail of the circumstances of the recording, some visible characteristic, some inflexion of the voice may put a different complexion on the recorded matter, as compared with a mere transcript of the words spoken or the things done. The sound, accent of a voice, the physical appearance of a thing or person may resolve some ambiguity or clothe with meaning some unexplained passage in the text. The recordings are, therefore, to that extent real evidence and often have an effect similar to a view or the production of a material object. To the extent that recordings are admissible as real evidence, it is no objection to admissibility that the evidence is meant to, and does in fact, convey information, because it is offered for direct observation by the court, and not as a species of hearsay. Thus, in *The Statue of Liberty* (42) Sir Jocelyn Simon P admitted in evidence a record made on cinematograph film of the radar echoes, recorded mechanically without human intervention, of the vessels involved in a collision. The recording was the equivalent of a photograph or series of photographs, from which the court could, by observation, gain information about the courses of the vessels at material times (43).

38   *R* v *Gurney* (CA) [1976] Crim LR 567. See also Juries Act 1974, s. 14.
39   *Karamat* v *R* (PC, British Guiana) [1956] AC 256. See also *R* v *Martin* (CCR) (1872) LR 1 CCR 378.
40   *Tito and Others* v *Waddell and Others (No. 2)* [1977] 2 WLR 496.
41   See 16.1, ante.   42   [1968] 1 WLR 739.
43   While, no doubt, sound in principle, the decision in this case is open to some question on the facts. The problem is that the evidence was sought to be admitted for the purpose of proving the truth of the courses of the vessels, as recorded by the radar echoes. Under the Evidence Act 1938 (the 1968 Act not then being in force) and at common law, it is difficult to see how this could be admissible even if related from some human record. It would now seem to be admissible under s. 5 of the 1968 Act, but not under s. 4 because of the absence of personal knowledge of the information supplied; and for the same reason, it would not be admissible under the Criminal Evidence Act 1965: see *R* v *Pettigrew* (CA) [1980] Crim LR 239. It may not be the only case where the

The court must, before admitting recordings as evidence, be satisfied that the evidence which may be yielded is relevant and that the recording produced is accurate and original (44). The requirement of proof of originality is met by evidence sufficient to raise a prima facie case, in that the provenance and history of the recording up to the moment of production in court, are properly accounted for (45). If there is any real possibility that the recording might have been interfered with, and is not original, it should be excluded (46). It may be that where a recording is of such poor quality that it would be wrong to expect the jury to form a fair assessment of the contents, it should be excluded (47).

16.5 Questions for counsel

1 By what evidence should the contents of the writing found in Coke's flat (exhibit GG1) be proved?
2 By what evidence should it be proved, if possible, that the writing on exhibit GG1 is that of Coke?
3 What direction, if any, should the jury be given about their use of exhibits GG1 and GG3?
4 What is the evidential significance of the tape-recording of the conversation between Littleton and his wife, made by D/I Glanvil?
5 What matters must be established before the tape-recording can be admitted in evidence, and what matters, if established by the defence, might prevent its admission?

obsolescence of the approach of the hearsay rule to modern technology has driven judges into an uncomfortable refuge of real evidence: compare the use of the airline ticket in *R v Rice and Others* (CCA) [1963] 1 QB 857. Real evidence is derived from perception by the court, not from the conveying of information, by man or machine, with a view to proving the truth of the information.

44   *R v Maqsud Ali; R v Ashiq Hussain* (CCA) [1966] 1 QB 688.
45   *R v Robson; R v Harris* [1972] 1 WLR 651.
46   *R v Stevenson; R v Hulse; R v Whitney* [1971] 1 WLR 1.
47   *R v Robson; R v Harris* [1972] 1 WLR 651.

Subject Index